P9-DNW-059

The Total Traveler Guide To Worldwide Cruising

By Ethel Blum

Travel Publications, Inc.

14TH EDITION

"The Encyclopedia of Vacations at Sea"

Dance like no one is watching...
Love like you'll never be hurt...
Sing like no one is listening...
Live like it's heaven on earth.

William Purkey

Art Director: Tom Sterling
Printed by BookMasters, Mansfield, Ohio

ISBN #0-9720748-0-5

dedication

To Ted Arison (1924-1999). Founding Father of the cruise experience as we know it today. Ted was an optimist with a vision and he had the fortitude and perseverance to take that vision to fruition. He was convinced that people who live in Middle America should have a chance to see the ocean, and he made it possible in affordable vacations at sea. Carnival Cruise Lines and the "Fun" ships were born and cruise ships almost overnight dropped their heady atmosphere and were no longer reserved for the privileged few.

Ted experienced ups and down along the way. Few financial experts gave the fledgling company and its concept much chance of survival, and none even considered the possibility that the company would climb from "bottom feeder" to the largest cruise company in the world. Success breeds success and today's cruise industry is a mainstream vacation option.

While cruise ships and business acumen made Ted the Horatio Alger of our times, he remained a very private person. Like Alger, he epitomized the great American dream and inspired ideals with his philanthropic contributions. Ted was a many faceted person, and, he was my friend. A friend who allowed me behind the scenes so I could understand all of the dynamics that make up this complex cruise industry.

At every inaugural of a new ship, I would ask Ted if this one was his "dream ship." His answer was always the same. "Wait until you see the next one."

I have seen the next one, and a parade of next ones. I know that somewhere in the Great Beyond, Ted is still working on his dream ship which may very well be the "next one."

I thank you Ted Arison for your friendship. The cruise industry thanks you for your dynamic input. And, the millions of passengers who cross gangplanks continue to thank you for making their vacation dreams a reality.

contents

acknowledgements

No one person can research and keep pace with the developments and expansion of the cruise industry, which has experienced phenomenal growth during the past 25 years. For help and in-put, I went to some the most experienced and respected cruise writers in the industry. Their opinions, ship reviews and comments have been incorporated in the book.

I thank them sincerely. Between us and the 20 travel agents who specialize in cruise ships, readers will find the answers they need to help them make the right selection for their cruise vacations.

More than a few special words of gratitude are in order for **SHIRLEY SLATER** and **HARRY BASCH** who contributed their opinions, comments and reviews for major sections of the book. They are a Los Angeles-based husband-and-wife writing team, authors of *Fieldings Worldwide Cruises, European Cruises, Alaska Cruises and Caribbean Cruises* 1996 thru 1998. Their column, *Cruise Views,* has appeared in the *Los Angeles Times* and other newspapers for 18 years. They are the recipients of numerous writing awards and are recognized internationally as knowledgeable and impartial cruise critics.

Other major contributors:

STEVEN FABER has logged more than 60 cruises and been writing about ships for 17 years. You can find his articles in magazines like *Cruise Travel*, and travel sections in U.S. and Canadian newspapers.

PETER KNEGO a well known ship historian who has traveled the world in search of "endangered" vessels. His articles and photographs appear regularly in national and international shipping magazines. He produced the five-volume video series, *The World's Passenger Fleet.*

MARCIE LEVIN, former travel editor of a metropolitan newspaper, her articles appear in newspapers and magazines across the country. She is also a contributor to AOL's Cruise Critic and the president of the Society of American Travel Writers.

TOBY SALZMAN award winning Toronto-based travel writer whose work appears regularly in the *Toronto Globe and Mail,* and other major U.S. and Canadian publications. She is cruise editor of *Conventions and Meetings Magazine.*

JAY CLARKE, Former travel editor and current columnist for the *Miami Herald,* whose articles appear in major newspapers and magazines. Jay has been reporting on cruise ships for more than 20 years.

And, the 20 travel agents whose contributions were extremely important in the ratings of ships. Their opinions are not personal, but represent their thousands of clients who have cruised many thousands of ships.

The first edition was published in 1975. In 225 pages it covered everything a passenger needed to know about ships at that point in the evolving history of cruising. As the industry grew, so did The *Total Traveler,* then published as *Total Traveler by Cruise Ship.* An estimated 60 million travelers have crossed gangplanks in North America during those 28 years. A new generation of ships was born during the 1970s followed by still another generation of contemporary vessels in the 1980s and again in the 1990s. Still coming is another generation for this century. The industry will have nearly doubled its capacity by the year 2003 as vessels are berthed to meet demands of travelers newly converted to the joys of cruising. This 14th edition, with a slight change of name, The *Total Traveler Guide to Worldwide Cruising* strives to tell the complete story. In almost 600 pages, it covers everything you need to know about ship travel--cruise, river boats, freighter, cargo liner, barge cruising, inland waterway small liners and ports of call around the world.

The *Total Traveler Guide to Worldwide Cruising* includes - Information and tips to make the most of your holiday at sea by selecting your ship, your cabin, and even your dining room table. Dining and drinking, tipping and entertainment, and gambling at sea are discussed. The genealogy of ships, bargain cruise opportunities (how to get the best deal), and special interest cruises (honeymoons at sea; facilities for handicapped travelers) are all highlighted in this book. Worldwide ports of call are part of the cruise experience and are included from the standpoint of the limited time allowed during a ship visit. The book covers - what to do, see, and buy in ports throughout the Bahamas, Caribbean, West Indies, Canada, Alaska, Northern Europe, Mediterranean, Greek Islands, North Cape, Baltic, China, and Australia, and other Pacific ports.

The *Total Traveler Guide to Worldwide Cruising* includes fleets of smaller vessels offering opportunities to cruise inland waterways and visit islands with harbors too small to accommodate ocean liners. The reader is informed about ports of embarkation, docking versus tendering, and how to find the real cost of a cruise as well as the right path through the maze of rates and air-sea packages. There are ratings of more than two hundred ships, price categories, with a higher number of anchors denoting exceptional facilities, fewer anchors pointing out limited facilities or those that could use improvement. Ships are compared within price categories and very important, comparative value. This book reveals the truth of what to expect from a cruise experience and what passengers get. The *Total Traveler Guide to Worldwide Cruising* separates perception from reality.

A Note to the Reader

Every effort has been made to verify accuracy of rates, itineraries, and ship specifics. World conditions affect rates, which change with fluctuations in costs, and most important, supply and demand. Because companies operate ships to show a profit, cruise prices, package rates, port charges and shore excursion charges are subject to change. Itineraries may change with little or no notice. Cost of alcoholic drinks may go up, and even flags on the mast are subject to change if the ship is sold or marketed differently.

In this highly competitive and volatile marketplace, it is impossible to avoid errors despite careful research. It also is impossible for the author to sail on every ship and inspect every galley and stateroom every month. True, she has help. But, she does look under bunks when she sails from port to port on dozens of ships each year. Close to 200 industry professionals send personal evaluations reporting on cruise experiences to Ethel Blum, and their overall evaluations are included in this book. During the past three years, Ethel has spent 550 days on board ships.

Readers who find the food or service better or worse than expected on board ships profiled in this book are encouraged to write to Ethel Blum, Travel Publications, 19500 Turnberry Way, Suite 25AB, Aventura, FL 33180 or to e-mail her at ebtravel@aol.com. Your comments will not be ignored. She'll pass your words along to steamship companies and alert them that future editions of *The Total Traveler Worldwide Guide to Cruising* may earn them a "Rusty Anchor."

A Word in Advance

The very mention of shipboard travel brings visions of romance to our happy daydreams. We anticipate champagne, caviar, and delightful shipmates bent on sharing romantic encounters on board floating luxury resorts. Romance has been implied and probably over-rated in cruise brochures. Adding to our fantasies, there's the landlubber's late night favorite, *The Love Boat*, now in rerun status, which continues to send romance-seekers up gangplanks. Another movie, *Out To Sea*, is a delightful comedy and spoof filled with romantic promises. However, after just one cruise experience, you'll know that Hollywood fiction bears a closer resemblance to life in a floating soap opera than to lifestyles aboard any of today's cruise ships.

Romantic fantasies, however, do surround life aboard these floating resorts. Cruise companies keep it alive by embellishing reality in descriptive brochures. Even back in the "good old days" of 1818, a 424-ton vessel with two decks and three masts, the *James Monroe*, advertised "extensive and commodious" accommodations. She was grandly decorated with Egyptian porphyry, carved arches, black cloth-covered chairs, and shiny mahogany tables. But her staterooms were described as "sleeping closets" by the passengers. They were seven square feet, though paneled in satinwood. Over the entrance to each cabin was an arch supported by pillars of pure white Carrara marble. Seven square feet wouldn't earn them even one anchor in this 2003 edition of *The Total Traveler*.

In those days passengers were regarded as cargo and assigned to quarters that should have been holding salt or cotton. The emigrant was thankful for passage and could be counted on to sweep the decks, cater to the crew, and of course, pay for passage. Because of severely overcrowded conditions caused by greedy owners eager to earn a fast dollar on each voyage, the U.S. Congress passed a law aimed at curing the situation, but it wasn't until eighteen years later, when a second statute was passed, that each passenger was guaranteed a minimum of fourteen feet of clear deck space.

As scheduled voyages increased, competition for passengers reached a heady level, and appointments and fittings on rival ships became as much a matter of one-upmanship as speed records. The *Liverpool* is an example of a famous ship of the last century that fell into this category. Her most touted feature was a bathing room where passengers could shower with saltwater hauled aboard by the crew. Fastidious passengers determined to bathe left their modesty on shore. Private tubs on ships were not even in the blueprint stage, and running water did not exist. On other ships, arrangements had to be made with a crewmember to haul a bucket of seawater aboard and douse the passenger in a semi-private area somewhere on the ship, but the *Liverpool* had a special room for this "luxury" and was a forerunner of sorts.

With competition on the upswing, passengers became more important to ship owners. Service improved and the privileged on three-class vessels began to dine gluttonously, sleep fitfully, and devise activities to break the boredom of long weeks at sea. Four times during every twenty-four hours, ladies and gentleman of quality sat down to a table of largess sufficient to nourish an emigrant for a week. They called it the "groaning board" for obvious reasons.

Many sea styles have carried over into 21st century cruising. For instance, there's a logical explanation of why passengers are not encouraged to socialize with crewmembers that are not officers. It all started long ago. As ships became vehicles of mass transport, moral fortitude sank. The number of young emigrant girls en route to America who embarked as virgins and disembarked as outcasts moved the priests of Galway to protest publicly against the lack of adequate shipboard chaperones. When the taxpayers of New York City got fed up with supporting illegitimate children born of transatlantic dalliances; they took their case to Congress. The result was an act providing that if any member of an American crew seduced a passenger "under promise of marriage, or by threats, or by the exercise of his authority, or by solicitation, or the making of gifts or presents," his choices were to marry the girl, pay a fine of $1,000, or spend a year in jail. It probably is written about in law books as the first law covering sexual harassment.

As they embarked on their journeys, those emigrant girls were filled with dreams of new lives. But it was different dreams that sent six million passengers up the gangplanks of U.S.-based ships last year. Those millions, and the additional couple of million or so who boarded ships beyond our shores, were likely induced to spend vacations at sea by promises of a lifestyle much different than that at home; a lifestyle more closely resembling perceptions of the good-old-days of semi luxury and service.

But romances that last do happen and there are tales of romances kindled at sea that developed into life-long commitments. I know several captains and other officers who married Americans who either worked on their ships or sailed frequently. I even know men and women who met on board cruise ships and returned to honeymoon on the same vessel. So, that elusive romance is possible, but I wouldn't count on it.

Most women who cruise in a cabin by themselves have few notions about meeting the man of their dreams on the voyage. What they want is a person to talk with; preferably one who will ask them to dance. Cruise lines are responding with special rates for single passengers and for "hosts" who are usually retired businessmen, Army and Navy officers, doctors, lawyers, and merchant chiefs. Each host's sole responsibility is to dance and mix with single female passengers. This is not a new idea. It started with gigolos who sailed the transatlantic liners to meet and fleece "rich widows." Today's "hosts" are definitely not in the gigolo class. They are governed by specific rules, and hanky-panky is not included. There have, however, been a few cases of serious involvement between passengers and hosts, but for the most part, one on-one relationships are rare.

Making "someday" plans and dreams come true is what this book is all about. The *Total Traveler Guide to Worldwide Cruising* is dedicated to travelers who include cruising or travel by sea in their "someday" wish lists. Every aspect of those dreams may not come true on board ships these days, but your experience will be a 21st century facsimile. If you know what to expect, know how to take advantage of all the alternatives, and select your ship carefully and wisely, dreams can come true. It's the nightmares that this book should help you avoid.

Cruising aboard a first-class ship to interesting ports can be one of the supreme pleasures of life. It is civilized, unhurried, and economical, especially when you consider services rendered and included in the basic cruise fare. Cruising also is a unique form of travel. Some people take to the seas for special purposes such as participation in bridge tournaments, finding romance, gourmandizing, exploring exotic parts of the world while sleeping in the same bed every night, being entertained, or just plain resting. Movement from port-to--port has been stripped of the urgency that goes along with merely being transported to a specific destination.

Romance? Romance at sea is listening to music, attending extravagant shows, and dressing up without worrying about an escort if you travel alone. For single women, the romance of cruising lies in eliminating the necessity of an escort, and more importantly, never having to eat alone. There's no chance of being seated at the most undesirable table in the dining room because you're traveling solo, and no reason to hesitate starting a conversation with a fellow passenger. Like they say, "We're all in the same boat."

On a North Sea cruise a few years ago, the passenger manifest was made up of people of many nationalities. When the Americans on board discovered I was a travel reporter, they bombarded me with their complaints as though I could wave a magic wand at the captain and compel him to come up with caviar and lobster. That cruise is a good example of the importance of selecting your ship wisely. That series of North Sea voyages was designed primarily for the lower middle-class European market, and each cruise was priced far below those of competing vessels. The comparatively inexpensive package was developed to introduce a rebuilt vessel into the marketplace, and the galley was not overly generous with food (not that anyone left the dining room hungry). But Americans who boarded with visions of grandeur at bargain prices complained constantly. Europeans ate everything served and were content with a bargain holiday. On the other hand, had the American travelers (or their travel agents) known what to expect, they could have enjoyed the voyage knowing they were saving money, or they may have opted for a higher priced vessel offering better quality food and more luxuries.

Somehow food seems to be the one shipboard delight which causes the most preoccupation and the most complaints. We should levy some of the blame for the emphasis on food on cruise companies that tend to overshadow quality with picture displays of quantity. Some ships have hired "name" chefs and are operating specialty restaurants with a surcharge, some don't charge anything. These restaurants are not to be missed if you like intimate dining that is not possible when cooking for a thousand people.

Another worry that tugs at confidence in sea travel is the question of solvency of cruise companies. With so many cruise lines with so many ships and with four companies closing up after September 11, how safe is the money passengers are required to pay in advance? It seems that Uncle Sam's enforcement folks have considered the risk, and there is a strict bonding system under which ships operate from U.S. ports. Even more stringent laws are being considered and will likely be passed. U.S. laws do not cover Americans boarding ships in foreign ports, but when purchased in the U.S. they do offer more consumer protection than is available to sea travelers in other parts of the world. The source of this protection is Section 3 of U.S. Public Law 89-777, enacted in 1966 to prevent cruise company failures that could cost the traveler money and leave him stranded.

The shipping industry has faced an amazing situation during the past 30 years. There has been tremendous expansion of cruise fleets consisting of new or reconditioned vessels. This, coupled with public acceptance and satisfaction, has accounted for more ships cruising to more places than at any time in the previous history of sea travel. A recent study indicates that the number of Americans boarding cruise ships increases annually at a steady rate averaging close to eight percent.

It is estimated that more than three hundred passenger--carrying ships operate around the world. About one hundred berth in, or regularly sail out of, North American ports. *The Total Traveler Guide to Worldwide Cruising* profiles in detail more than two hundred ships and covers about one hundred others with information useful to passengers. These ships sail the Caribbean, Atlantic, Canadian, Alaskan, Mediterranean, Greek Islands, South American, North Cape, Australian and Pacific routes. Rates fluctuate and 2003 may be one of those years the average passenger will spend seven days at sea and will pay less than he did two years ago. Per-day rates run from $85 on a low budget older ship or freighter to $900 on a super-deluxe liner, and the passenger will spend an additional $225 during the week for shore excursion costs, tips, and alcoholic beverages. Casino gambling is not included in that estimate. There will be a choice of more than three thousand departures.

An industry survey of last year's passengers indicates that 85 percent plan to vacation at sea again. A poll of Americans returning from Europe by air indicates that 70 percent have never cruised, and 50 percent are considering spending their next holiday at sea.

The Total Traveler Guide to Worldwide Cruising is dedicated to confessed cruise-a-holics like me and to the millions who will join our ranks in the coming years.

Research for the book took more than 30 years. I have traveled millions of air and sea miles to islands and foreign countries, inspected thousands of staterooms and kitchens, and interviewed dozens of cruise ship owners and thousands of passengers. This book covers everything a traveler should know about ships (cruise ships, transit vessels, and freighters) from the first inclination toward ship travel to planning the next holiday. The information is factual. It is intended as guidance in selecting and enjoying your cruise by presenting all the options.

Everyone has a favorite ship. I keep mine a secret. While reading *The Total Traveler*, you may find several clues as to which ship is "mine." In truth, I don't have a lasting favorite. It's always the last ship I sailed and the next one. And, it all depends on what I want out of a cruise. If it is destinations, the ship is secondary. If it is a vacation, the ship is very important. I must admit, however, I've never sailed a ship I didn't enjoy. It's true; enjoyment was more on some, less on others.

The Total Traveler Guide to Worldwide Cruising rates vessels only as a guide for readers to select ships within price categories (see Ship Ratings). All aspects of the cruise experience contribute to these ratings. My personal evaluations were fed into the computer along with the others. I waited a long time before publishing ratings because I am convinced there is a ship for every traveler, and every traveler has a ship waiting at a port with facilities almost tailor - made to meet demands. Making that match is what this book is all about.

Judging cruise ships is very much like judging a beauty contest. Broad beams narrow beams, tall or short--to each his own. As long as passengers know the important facts about the ship selected, such as costs, itineraries, service, and atmosphere, they are qualified to make choices.

Ships are rated to help readers select cruises within price categories (see Ship Ratings), not all against each other. Of course, a ship that charges $900 per day, per person, is going to have a lot more going for it than a vessel tagged around $125 a day. We considered each amenity, every facility, the hardware and the software, and then we rated them with anchors. The more the better within the same price range.

Ralph Waldo Emerson wrote, "Sea life is an acquired taste, like that for tomatoes and olives." I like to add "caviar." There are many reasons for ship travel. For me, the sea is enough.

Bon voyage!

Ethel Blum

Yesterday, Today, and Tomorrow

Each journey is an experience of the past
Robert Better

I like to think cruise passengers owe Cleopatra a vote of thanks for setting the mood and lifestyle on cruise ships. When she took that historic cruise up the Nile, her vessel was more than point-to-point transportation. It was the setting for a romantic escapade and it must have served its purpose—Cleopatra ended up with a couple of husbands and a lover. Current nostalgic trends may not extend quite that far back in time, but many a traveler has been converted to cruise addiction for similar reasons.

The late British author Somerset Maugham was a devoted cruiser who termed shipboard life an "experience above all else." Millions of Americans turning to cruise holidays are discovering that both Maugham and Cleopatra had the right idea when they decided on holidays at sea.

Cruising took the lead some 25 years ago as the fastest growing segment of the multibillion-dollar travel industry. It continued to maintain a healthy lead in the 1990s and promises to hold the position through the foreseeable future. While international events influence and dent occupancy from time to time, cruise ships continue to register increased numbers of passengers despite increased capacity on the sea-lanes. Taking a cruise in the first decade of the 21st century does not guarantee that passengers will be pampered in the style of Cleopatra or that experiences will live up to Somerset Maugham's fancy, but they are assured of a vacation at sea: a total experience stretching from sunup to sundown and beyond. Not to mention, visits to exciting and interesting ports of call.

Passenger shipping wasn't always the traveler's favorite. There have been periods of ups and downs, and too many downs turned glamorous ocean queens into rusty maidens waiting in dry dock for the fickle traveler to turn again in their direction. The cruise industry has learned from the past and was in position to respond immediately to the tragic events of September 11th. Faced with new ships nearing completion in shipyards and reluctant passengers, lines lowered rates and repositioned fleets out of areas considered unsafe. The immediate results found bargain shoppers filling vessels. Less than four months after 9/11, bookings turned solid and by the beginning of 2002, rates were moving upwards and getting closer to where they were prior to that terrible day.

Low fares have always brought more customers up gangplanks. In 1845, a German ship owner placed an ad in a Hamburg paper proposing to equip one of his large sailing vessels for a cruise around the world. "The fare for the whole voyage is so low that it only represents a very slight addition to ordinary living costs incurred on shore. In return, the passenger will have many opportunities of acquiring first-hand knowledge of the wonders of the world," he wrote.

The ship owner was ahead of his time. What he said 157 years ago still applies to cruising today. The same ad in any newspaper travel section today would fill a dozen sailing vessels. But in those days, passenger ships were for transportation between ports. They provided the only way for emigrants to move to new countries promising greater opportunity and the only way for merchants to hawk their wares in countries separated by oceans. Passenger use of ships on a round-trip basis offering sightseeing and service began to attract attention when 45 years later, another imaginative German suggested switching the *Augusta Victoria* from her Hamburg-New York run to a Mediterranean cruise.

But that was not the first "cruise." The steamship *Enterprise* sailed from London to Calcutta on a voyage that covered 11,000 miles and took 103 days. Although her engine was steam, she used sails for all but 64 days. In 1835, P&O (Peninsular and Oriental Steam Navigation Company) chartered the 206-ton *William Fawcett* to open the company's first regular service between London, Spain and Portugal. In 1837, P&O was, like Cunard, a British shipping company that began attracting attention. The company advertised a fleet of seven steamships. Ads read "new, powerful, large, and splendidly fitted up." Instead of heading west, P&O's ships traveled in the opposite direction with regular steamer service between England and India and routes across Egypt through the Suez Canal when it was opened in 1869. Before that, its vessels were sailing regularly to China, Australia and Japan. Additionally, P&O could easily be credited with virtually inventing exotic cruising as it offered round-trip passage to ports in Greece, Palestine, and Turkey. It featured "tramps to pleasure steamers," but never ventured westbound to compete with heavily traversed sea-lanes to America.

P&O deserves recognition for inaugurating what could well have been the first Mediterranean cruise in 1844. Noted author William Makepeace Thackeray sailed to ports in Greece, Egypt, Italy and Turkey. While on board, he wrote his chronicles, *Diary of a Voyage from Cornwall to Grand Cairo*, under the pseudonym of Michael Angelo Titmarsh. Although he complained bitterly about prices, bugs, seasickness and the lack of suitable companionship, at the end of the voyage, he wrote, "...it leaves such a store of pleasant recollections that I can't think but recommend all persons who have the time and means to make a similar journey."

It was a highly competitive era for ship owners and one after another ran into financial difficulty. Acceptance of steam engines was slow in coming and all early steamships were driven by paddles, which were frowned upon by their best customers—the navy in England and other countries.

By the beginning of the 1870s, Rotterdam was a very busy port without a promising future. Trade with the United States was expanding and the newly opened Suez Canal provided a steamer route to the East Indies; both factors favored introduction of larger ships. The size of vessels entering Rotterdam's harbor, however, was seriously limited by the Voorns Canal with its Hellevoetsluis locks, which could accommodate a maximum length of only about 270 feet. Larger ships, however, could pass at high water when the gates were opened. A more serious handicap was the draught limit of about 17 feet, making it necessary for larger ships to part-load or unload at other ports. So ship owners moved their ships and cargo to the rival port of Amsterdam.

At about that time, two young partners with sufficient capital to build only two ships—not four as originally hoped—founded the private firm of Plate, Reuchlin, and Company. Equally disappointing was the late delivery of the two ships, the first of which, the *Rotterdam*, did not sail on her maiden voyage to New York until October 15, 1872. During her trial voyage, the builder announced it was his firm's custom to interpret orders generously and the owners would find they had obtained a vessel somewhat longer than specified! When entering the lock at Hellevoetsluis, the ship's carpenter stood at the bow and the boatswain at the stern, hatchets in hand, ready to cut away ornamental scrollwork. But to the great relief of all on board, the lock gates barely closed with a fender at the bow and the center of the stern just touching the outer lock gate.

The *Rotterdam* was an iron ship of nearly 1,700 gross tons, brig-rigged, with a single screw driven by a 1,300-horsepower compound engine giving her a service speed of 10.5 knots. She carried 8 first-class passengers, 380 steerage-class passengers and 15,000 tons of cargo. She made the voyage to New York in about 15 days and with her sister ship, the *Maas* (later *Maasdam*), a monthly service was maintained.

Results of the first voyage were encouraging and expansion was decided upon. But with insufficient funds for the project, Plate, Reuchlin, and Company appointed the more-experienced W. Van der Hoeven as managing director. The firm was renamed the Nederlandsch-Amerikaansche Stoomvaart-Maatschappij

(Netherlands-American Steam Navigation Company), or NASM for short, in April 1873. In 1896, this famous company became Holland America Line.

Two new and larger ships, fittingly named after the two founders of the company, were ordered: the *P. Caland* and the *W. A. Scholten*. Over 2,500 gross tons, they could carry 50 cabin and 600 steerage passengers, as well as 2,400 tons of cargo. Barkentine-rigged, they were the only clipper-bowed ships built for the line. Unfortunately, the promising state of affairs was not destined to last. In the autumn of 1874, when the new ships were due to come into service, there was a severe depression in the United States. Freight rates and the number of steerage passengers fell alarmingly and, in 1875, very heavy weather crippled the *W.A. Scholten*.

In addition to carrying mail and immigrants, 19th-century ships were a great source of national pride. Speed was of utmost importance because ships linked the continents. One of the first transatlantic races was in 1847 between the newly commissioned U.S.-flagged carrier *Washington* and Cunard's *Britain*. Although the pride of the American fleet lost the race, she was feted on her arrival in England because she was the first ship to offer an alternative to first-class or steerage travel. She provided respectable second-class passage, thereby opening sea-lanes to another level of travelers. The Washington offered amenities passengers had come to expect as her salons were decorated in marble and gilt.

The *Washington* was part of a five-ship fleet owned by an American, Edward Collins. Two of his ships, the 2,856-ton *Atlantic* and *Pacific*, were larger than other vessels except Cunard's *Britain*. Both ships were launched in 1849 and introduced charismatic appeal previously lacking at sea. The *Atlantic* was rounded at the stern, which gave her a tub-like appearance, but Collins made up for her looks with steam heat, bathrooms and a barber shop, considered almost a miracle by ocean voyagers.

Collins was successful in luring passengers from Cunard. He broke speed records and his name and his ships made headlines, but his ledgers were written mostly in red ink. His extravagances in food and service were not open to compromise. Speed demanded extra coal and larger crews and Collins' menus made Cunard's look like boarding-school fare. But the outlay was crippling. Collins' captains were paid $6,000 a year and Cunard's, $2,500. Cunard survived the century; Collins did not.

During the same period of maritime history, another American was stirring up the sea-lanes. Cornelius Vanderbilt had worked almost all his life. Now, at 59, he wanted to take his first real vacation with family and friends. His family included 11 children, a wife, and a number of servants. This Horatio Alger of American financing was already pulling in a couple of million dollars a year. Vanderbilt planned his dream holiday—a grand tour of the capitals of Europe by sea and land. His plans and his voyage would influence shipping for the next 150 years. He arranged the first publicized pleasure cruise in luxurious accommodations and is probably the founding father of the multi-generational cruise trend so popular today.

Other people had yachts, but Vanderbilt would have nothing less than his own ocean liner. The result was the 2,500-ton *North Star*, which cost $500,000 and was ultimately launched in 1853. The rosewood furniture in the main salon was Louis XV updated with Victorian plush velvet upholstery. Family quarters consisted of 10 staterooms enameled in white, each with a plate-glass door, and berths fitted in silk. The crew was made up of young men from prominent families who simply wanted to be part of the entourage. The steward of New York's famed Racquet Club was enticed aboard to serve as purser, and the ship had her own clergyman and physician. Vanderbilt's welcome when the *North Star* arrived in London was somewhat lukewarm. The American merchant seaman's yacht was more splendid than the queen's.

Toward the end of the 19th century, ocean transport was showing a pattern and a temper. The passenger market was still made up mostly of people who traveled out of necessity, so speed was important. But a new breed of traveler was emerging: a traveler who thought a round-trip to Europe might be good for one's physical condition. A sea cure, some felt, was just the thing for damaged emotions. A young woman who had fallen in love with a ne'er-do-well or had been left waiting on the church steps was bundled off to Liverpool so she could avail herself of the one sure cure for lovesickness—an ocean voyage.

Probably the most notable ship at the end of the 19th century was the first *Oceanic*. She was the forerunner and archetype of six sister ships that flew the red swallow tailed burgee with the five-pointed star of the White Star Line. Her greatest innovation was not her size, but the placement of her grand ballroom. It was high and amidships, ending the tradition in force since the Middle Ages of confining privileged travelers to quarters in the rump of the stern. The lounge extended the full width of the ship, was lighted by huge chandeliers (candle-lit), and had fireplaces at both ends. Cabins were larger and there was a bell in each that commanded the instant attention of stewards. There were taps for water and steam heat.

Top of the luxury line at that time was the beautifully appointed *City of Rome*. She made her maiden voyage to New York in 1881 with a figurehead of the emperor Hadrian, three times larger than life, leaning out over the waves.

On her stern, embossed in gold, glittered the arms and crest of the Eternal City. Her hull was jet black, her superstructure, the color of cream. Her music room was paneled in ebony and gold. Luxury had been carried just about as far as human invention and imagination could take it; but, again, the financial burden of limited capacity and high operating costs was too much for her owners. The *City of Rome* ended up on the auction block.

Holland America also was adding tonnage during this decade and was expanding as quickly as Dutch and other European harbors were deepened to accommodate its ships. In April 1898, the base color of its funnels was changed from black to yellow to avoid confusion with funnels of an American company operating at that time. The Spanish American War had just broken out and a resemblance to American ships might have been risky.

Later that same year, the new *Statendam* was setting passenger-freight records and the company commissioned construction of three twin-screw 12,500-ton vessels—the *Potsdam, Ryndam* and *Noordam.*

American authorities were feeling the lack of suitable merchant ships during the Spanish American War, so the government began buying interests in foreign shipping companies under the title of International Mercantile Marine Company (IMM), a combine that embraced the Atlantic Transport, National, American, Red Star, Leyland, White Star and Dominion lines into a fleet totaling one million gross tons. Holland America Line was an unwilling participant in IMM.

Another type of ocean traveler was developing almost unnoticed while shipping companies were busy wooing the elite, real or pretended. Young Americans were going to sea. Of modest means, they simply wanted to see the Louvré and the Prado, sign their names in visitor's books in famous castles, shout toasts in Munich beer halls and meet the famous women of Paris. This astounded Europeans and made for excited parlor conversation about uninhibited American men and women traveling alone or in large groups with chaperones.

Thomas Cook, the man responsible for mass travel in the Western world, introduced a good part of this movement. In a period of less than four decades, the domestic trips that Cook first organized in the English Midlands had grown into grand tours. With fresh tourist money pouring in, what at first seemed like a boon to some areas soon turned into a nightmare as they were overrun with hordes of people. Cook, undaunted by the criticism and ignoring complaints of rudeness or lack of "refinement," continued to group 30 or 40 people who found it convenient and beneficial to travel on the same train or ship and to sojourn in the same city. Hence the birth of group tours, rates and packaging. When large numbers of genteel young people reported they had survived the rigors of steerage class and had seen Europe for less than the cost of first-class passage on one of the luxury liners, an endless army of students began to travel the Atlantic on their own.

Another milestone in ship travel came with the advent of the turbine engine, which brought a different dimension to transatlantic voyages. Sea-lanes, once considered romantic avenues of freedom, golden tracks of commerce, adventure and history, now became highways for hundreds of thousands of people who insisted on being pampered, beguiled, entertained day and night, and delivered precisely on schedule. The broad Atlantic had been narrowed and regulated. Instead of challenging the whims of the sea gods, the traveler merely tested the limits of his self- indulgence. Among a plethora of offerings, voyagers could pick and choose the most convenient time, the right ship, the best accommodations and even the type of companions most likely to prove congenial.

German ship interests in sea travel peaked at this point in time, but they were largely concerned with transporting endless streams of America-bound emigrants from Europe. Their ships were sound but hardly spectacular. The *Deutschland* docked in New York in 1847, part of a fleet belonging to Hamburg Amerikanische Packetfahrt Actien Gesellschaft (Hamburg-Amerika Lines, in later years). In 1856, the same company introduced the first German transatlantic steamship. Several other German companies competed for the emigrant traveler and they rode the Atlantic to the Teutonic merriment of lager beer, cheese and pretzels while the band played merrily for the seasick passengers.

In 1900, the rival Red Star Line of Antwerp put the 12,000-ton *Vaderland* into service, the first of a very successful series of four-masted, two-funneled ships. In 1904, Holland America Line ordered a larger and improved version with only one funnel. The 17,000-ton *Nieuw Amsterdam* was named after the first settlement in New York. She sailed on her maiden voyage in April 1906 and subsequently became one of the best-known ships in the world. At the time, she was the largest ship under the Dutch flag. Her graceful lines belied her huge capacity of 417 first-class, 391 second-class, and 2,300 third-class passengers and more than 14,000 tons of cargo. Although she was not fast, her comfort, cuisine and standards set levels still anticipated by passengers today. The *Nieuw Amsterdam* was the last of the company's ships to carry sails for emergency use, but they were never used.

The immediate success of the *Nieuw Amsterdam* led to ordering a much larger ship, the fourth *Rotterdam* (24,000 tons), which for many years was the largest vessel in the Dutch merchant marine and the seventh largest in the world at that time. Her two pole masts, two funnels and long superstructure made her typical of the liners of the Edwardian period. Completed in 1908, she was the first large Atlantic liner to be built with a glassed-in promenade deck. Carrying 520 first-class passengers, 555 second-class passengers and 2,500 emigrants, the *Rotterdam* was driven by two fine quadruple-expansion engines, each exceeding 7,000 horsepower, giving her a speed of 17 knots. In 1909, the Dutch government awarded the Rotterdam to New York mail contract to Holland America Line and, in the following year, a call at Plymouth, England, was included in the schedule.

Because the *Rotterdam, Nieuw Amsterdam, Potsdam, Ryndam, Noordam,* and *Statendam* were more than capable of maintaining weekly Rotterdam-New York service, the *Statendam* was sold to Allan Line and renamed the *Scotian*, which, as the Canadian Pacific, *Marglen*, was finally scrapped in 1927. Before being sold at the end of 1910, the *Statendam* sailed on the second Holland America cruise, which included a stop in the Holy Land. The *Rotterdam 2* made the company's first cruise to Copenhagen in June 1895.

One of the largest and most lavish ships of the time was operated by Hamburg-Amerika, the 24,000-horsepower *Kaiser Friedrich*. At the turn of the century, German sea power claimed Atlantic speed records and German vessels paraded their finery in the sea-lanes as though on military parade on Unter den Linden.

Albert Ballin was a name frequently heard in shipping circles at that time. He was chairman of Cunard's greatest competitor, Hamburg-Amerika Line. Ballin paid careful attention to every detail of passenger comfort and quickly developed an enthusiastic and loyal following for Hamburg-Amerika vessels. He was the first in the industry to employ interior decorators, chefs de cuisine and other specialists. He built large steamers in direct competition to North German Lloyd, Cunard's other major competitor. His *Columbia* and *Augusta Victoria* were considered among the finest of their day. By 1900, Hamburg-Amerika Line was a recognized leader in the industry. The 16,500-ton *Atlantic* set transatlantic speed records, but she was too expensive to operate, and Ballin decided to build large, very comfortable, passenger-oriented slower vessels. His *Imperator* was launched in 1912 and considered by some as a 52,226-ton monster; but passengers loved her, so the 56,000-ton *Vaterland* and *Bismarck* were inaugurated in 1914.

That year marked the start of World War I. By the time it was over, German passenger shipping companies were just about out of business. Ballin committed suicide in 1918 but his company regrouped and built new, smaller liners. The first, called the *Albert Ballin*, made her maiden Atlantic voyage in 1923. Other ships came on line soon thereafter and, by the end of the decade, Hamburg-Amerika was again one of the world's largest shipping companies. It eventually merged with North German Lloyd and is known today as Hapag-Lloyd.

North German Lloyd is another story. When Cunard introduced the *Mauritania*, North German Lloyd dominated the North Atlantic. Founded in 1857, the company was prosperous almost from its inception. By 1887, its ships were plying Caribbean and South American routes to Brazil and Argentina. But it wasn't always smooth sailing for North German Lloyd. In fact, the company came in for more than its share of disasters. The *Deutschland* ran aground in 1875 and was a total loss. A few years later the *Condor*, *Hansa* and *Mosel* were wrecked and before the end of the century, the *Eider* and *Elbe* were also lost. But the company's most disastrous day occurred in 1900 at a New York pier. Fire broke out and seriously damaged the *Bremen*, *Main* and *Saale*. The company's flagship, *Kaiser Wilhelm der Grosse*, was also dockside at the time but was towed clear of the raging fires.

New leadership at the beginning of the 20th century changed the direction of the company. More economically feasible medium-size vessels were ordered. The 24,000-ton *George Washington* was probably the most notable. But like other companies, North German Lloyd found itself virtually out of business at the end of World War I. It regrouped and reemerged as an industry leader with the introduction of the 32,500-ton *Columbus* on transatlantic service. She was followed by two super ships, the *Europa* and the *Bremen*. But, with the advent of World War II, NGL vessels were again in jeopardy. The *Bremen* was destroyed and at the end of the war the *Europa* was ceded to France and became the *Liberte* in 1945.

One change in cruise styles was tried again and again but was ultimately destined to fail—the introduction of meal options. The traveler could buy his steamer ticket with or without meals. If he chose the latter, he dined in a lavishly decorated room presided over by Escoffiér-trained chefs and waiters schooled at the Paris Ritz. There were no fixed meal hours and no prix fix, an arrangement that pleased the affluent traveler but displeased the average passenger, who preferred unlimited food and regular dining hours.

At the beginning of the century, sea traffic was a great source of revenue for the British, Germans, French, and Scandinavians. Americans were again eyeing the sea-lanes for profitable ventures. Men such as J. P. Morgan, already railroad-rich, decided to enter the field; but once more, Americans just couldn't make money at sea.

Cunard had meanwhile been named sponsor of a royal succession of liners and again emerged as a leader. The first vessels of its 20th-century fleet were the *Caronia* and the *Carmania,* big-funneled ships with black hulls and cluttered, high white superstructures. The ships were known as the "pretty sisters," but their real distinction was not in their looks but in their character, and ambience. They offered total British atmosphere—afghan throws, high tea and well-mannered service. Therein began a period when ships developed an affectionate following of contented passengers who would remain faithful for generations.

Costa Cruises was born in 1924 when the three Costa brothers opted to cut transportation costs for their olive oil empire by buying the 1,100-ton freighter *Ravenna.* Within a dozen years, seven more freighters had joined the Costa fleet and there was a natural transition to passenger service. In 1948, the company bought the *Anna C,* which carried passengers between Genoa and South America. She was Italy's first air-conditioned ship and, within a few years, three more vessels, *Andrea C, Giovanna C,* and *Franca C* , joined the growing fleet. Cabins and accommodations were spacious in first-class, smaller in second and crowded but profitable in steerage. Twentieth-century technology took over on the bridge of new vessels but brought with it unusual problems. Most notorious were the loudspeakers, telephones and public address systems.

Other illustrious vessels that contributed to today's cruise ship style were the Scottish *Lusitania* and the English *Mauritania.* They introduced elevators, marble statues, trees and such amenities as private bathrooms, genuine antique furniture and original decorative oil paintings. Ships became seagoing museums showing unrelated artworks from every period. It was at about this time that "hotelism" crept into shipping. The idea was to give passengers the feeling that they were not at sea but on solid ground.

Etiquette on board ships was clearly spelled out. A gentleman just didn't hop up on a barstool next to a lady and offer to buy her a drink. For one thing, a lady didn't sit at the bar and, for another, there was a "proper" route for introductions. A friend in common from back home or, better still, a tip to one of the pursers brought a "proper" introduction. It was "always done with diplomacy and tact," according to society wags of the time.

Already king of the ship, the captain, under English maritime law, was also a magistrate at sea. He could, if he wanted, perform marriages on board that were as binding as those performed on shore. He could require a woman of suspicious repute to sequester herself, and he could even put his company's president in irons, if he so desired. Listings in Who's Who determined priority for invitations to the captain's table.

The *Mauritania* rapidly gained the affection of her passengers because of her homey character. She wasn't a beauty, but she cut through the waters with grace and charm. She burned 1,000-tons of coal a day; a Black Squad of 324 fireman and trimmers attended her furnaces. The famous and the infamous sailed on her. Franklin Delano Roosevelt, in a letter describing his trip, wrote, "If there ever was a ship which possessed a thing called soul, the *Mauritania* does. Every ship has a soul, but the *Mauritania* had one you could talk to. At times she would be wayward and contrary as a thoroughbred. As the captain once said to me, 'She had the manners and deportment of a great lady and behaved herself as such."

Competition between liners of different countries in attracting passengers to sail the Atlantic knew no bounds. No other shipping route in the world spawned such extravagances and follies. Ships were fitted with Byzantine chapels and Pompeian swimming pools, dining rooms in the style of the Palace of Versailles, lounges decorated like Turkish baths and Eastern harem-rooms. A trio of liners ranging from 45,000 to 50,000 tons proved to be the ships that broke the economic back of sea travel. They were the *Olympic, Titanic* and *Britannic* (also called *Gigantic*), and the era of truly grand passenger liners was born. Later decades produced replicas of these super ships and many surpassed them in tonnage and opulence.

The French also were in the passenger-shipping business and loathed having national pride tarnished by imitations of their ships' amenities aboard British, German and American competitors' vessels. For years, the French had maintained a standard of comfort and modest luxury on their ships that appealed to the cultured, affluent traveler. But by 1912, they, too, entered the competition by building the first *France*, which promised to outdo the tapestries ambience, haute cuisine, and decor of any ship afloat. At 24,000 tons, the *France* was smaller than her rivals, but the design afforded more deck and lounge space. Her low funnels were placed far astern and her lounge was super-deluxe. There were royal suites of rooms large enough to accommodate six passengers. As to cuisine, the *France* was tops. Records indicate that provisions for every voyage included 18 barrels of paté de foie gras.

Ship travel was reaching new heights of popularity and the decade before 1914 was one of major expansion for shipping lines. In 1911, Holland America ordered construction of the 32,000-ton new *Statendam*. This ship would have put Holland America in league with the shipping giants of the time. But the war intervened and the great ship was destined to become a U-boat victim without ever flying the Dutch flag.

American-financed Harland and Wolff Shipbuilding designed and built two really superior liners for White Star Line. The *Olympic* inaugurated service in 1911 to press reviews calling her the "world's greatest liner." The *Titanic* followed her into service and the rest is history. On her maiden transatlantic voyage, the *Titanic* hit an iceberg off the Newfoundland Banks and sank with a loss of 1,500 lives. The date was April 15, 1912.

After the outbreak of war in 1914, the *Rotterdam, Nieuw Amsterdam, Potsdam, Noordam* and *Ryndam* continued to maintain New York service. With other vessels, they formed the principal link between neutral Europe and America. Passage on these ships was in enormous demand. In November 1914, the *Noordam* was mined in the North Sea, but reached port and was under repair for some months. As the war progressed, the demand for passage fell off and emigration ceased. In 1915, the *Potsdam* was sold to Swedish America Line and became the *Stockholm*. In the spring of 1916, the *Ryndam* was mined off the English coast. The *Rotterdam* was taken out of service and laid up. The *Noordam* was again mined and put out of action in August 1917. The *Ryndam* was chartered by the United States as a troopship, leaving only the *Nieuw Amsterdam* valiantly maintaining the run to New York. In the early days of the war, American passengers were so grateful for the service provided under very difficult conditions that they presented the captain of the *Nieuw Amsterdam* with a memorial tablet that was mounted in the ship.

This story would be incomplete without further description of the 32,000-ton *Statendam*, ordered in 1911 and never put in the company's service. Launched on July 9, 1914, she was taken over by the British government and departed from the docks in 1917 as the *Justicia*. Interesting features of this ship were the glassed-in promenade deck and the triple-screw machinery layout. Since she was to be a troopship on war service, her third-class accommodations were fitted out to carry 286 noncommissioned officers and 4,031 men. On July 19, 1918, she was hit by a torpedo off North Ireland and taken in tow by escorting ships. During the next 20 hours, she was hit by four more torpedoes and finally sank.

After World War I, travelers who had never been anywhere outside their home city joined sophisticated travelers who had been everywhere at least twice. This was the self-confident American, part of the "uncultured masses" who wanted to see more of the world. Author and columnist Irvin S. Cobb described this traveler as the one "who would swap an Old Master for one peep at a set of sanitary bath fixtures." He also advised that the best way to travel the Atlantic was to be on an English ship if the traveler was looking for "exclusability" and to come back on a German ship if he wanted "sociableness."

The last of the four-funneled ships, the *Aquitania*, introduced innovations that became traditional over the years. The crew was trained in a sort of father-to-son heritage of stewardship that marked whole families in Liverpool and Southampton. Service was on a par with British tact, grace, and professionalism, which positively dazzled American travelers, although some considered the attention excessive to the point of being downright rude.

At the end of World War I, the Allies shuffled the German merchant fleet into oblivion. Ships worn and weary were repaired and reconverted, refurbished, and sent out again, but business just wasn't there. The German and British ocean giants had been built the ships in time for them to be converted from floating pleasure palaces into barracks or hospitals. The *Nieuw Amsterdam* was still in passenger service in 1918 and the *Rotterdam* rejoined her in February 1919, the *Noordam* in March, and the *Ryndam* in the autumn of that year after her release from American troop service. Two new 15,000-ton turbine ships, the *Volendam* and the *Veendam*, were ordered from Harland and Wolff and completed in 1922 and 1923, respectively. When they came into service, the *Noordam* was chartered to Swedish-America Line as the *Kungsholm*.

When WWI hostilities ceased, other ships were once again converted. Their engines were changed from coal burners to oil guzzlers, and appointments were hauled out of storage. The *Olympic*, one of the first, had what was considered at the time an enormous passenger capacity, but she hit the sea-lanes just as the United States restricted liquor sales, as well as immigration. One by one, the ships started depending heavily on their liquor stores and a great advantage was handed to foreign-flagged carriers. American-flagged ships were "dry" by act of Congress, so Prohibition sent American travelers on board foreign-flagged ships and inaugurated the golden age of ocean travel. Ships became more and more like hotels and, because family travel was encouraged, daylong activities for children were organized and around-the-clock merriment was in order for the adults.

The waterways out of New York were soon jumping to the beat of Dixieland bands. Embarkation resembled class reunions as passengers in formal ties posed squinting for the inevitable sailing-day photograph. The person center front always had his head stuck through a life preserver on which the ship's name was printed.

A new *Statendam*, similar to her previous, but somewhat smaller than her namesake, was ordered. She was launched in 1924, but that was the year the United States began restricting immigration and the whole pattern of North Atlantic passenger services changed again. Work on the vessel was suspended until 1927 when the ship was towed to Holland for completion. She sailed on her maiden voyage in April 1929, reaching New York on the 300th anniversary of the arrival of the first Dutch ships carrying the founders of the settlement that had become New York City.

With the advent of Prohibition, economically hard-pressed steamship companies came up with a new marketing idea. Instead of letting their fleets gather rust in shipyards, why not send them on short voyages to Nassau, Palm Beach, Havana and Miami?

Thus the birth of the "booze cruise" emerged, the low-cost junket into society playgrounds—the weekend at sea where the secretary could rub elbows with her boss for $29.50. Bathing-suit-clad beauties were substituted for ships in advertising, and the swinging sets of the 1930s set sail.

No one can truly say which ship offered the first pleasure cruise for paying passengers. The only thing certain about cruises, as compared with ocean voyages, is that they did not happen until the rigors of sea travel had been modified to the point where passengers could not just endure, but enjoy the travel experience. Short cruises by big ships during Depression years were a sad and almost futile attempt to keep these liners alive. When business on the Atlantic picked up, the ocean traveler demanded new ships. By then, big ships gathering rust in shipyards had to be replaced by smaller vessels built to follow the sea-lanes of the Caribbean, Mediterranean and North Sea.

The unquestioned authority on what to wear on ships was Emily Post, who wrote it all down in 1925. "On deluxe ships," she said, "nearly everyone dresses for dinner; some actually in ball dresses, which is in the worst possible taste, and, like overdressing in public places, indicates that they have no other place to show their finery. People of position never put on formal evening dress on a steamer, not even in the á la carte restaurant. In the dining saloon, they wear afternoon dresses, without hats, for dinner. In the restaurant, they wear semi-dinner dresses. Some smart men on ordinary steamers put on a dark sack suit for dinner after country clothes all day, but in the deluxe restaurant, they wear tuxedo coats. No gentleman wears a tailcoat on shipboard under any circumstances whatsoever."

But ship travel was changing again and the art of mass travel, a phenomenon that began with a few 19th-century lovers of Old Masters, was moving into the mainstream of the vacation market. Anyone who could scrape together $80 or $90 for a round-trip ocean ticket and another $200 for a long summer in Europe could join the scene. This led to phenomenal success in third-class travel, then called tourist class, and to the inevitable abolishment of this level of travel. Eventually, the one-class liner, a floating symbol of democracy, took over the sea-lanes. It was as American as apple pie, and it changed the entire character of ocean travel.

Americans whose parents had stood at the steerage rail were taking to the ships. The big three in the late 1920s were the *Berengaria, Aquitania* and *Mauritania.* In popularity they were followed by the *Conte di Savoia*, with its Italian dash, and the *Ile de France.* The Germans, back in passenger shipping, had two new vessels, the *Bremen* and the *Europa.* The *Bremen*, a passenger ship with the cut and capabilities of a destroyer, was launched in 1929 to the strains of "Deutschland uber Alles." Her hull was constructed on an oval plan, and her lines gave her an air of graceful staunchness. The two massive funnels were stocky and short (and eventually were replaced by taller ones), and a streamlined profile emanated from her rounded bridge. She was 102 feet wide, which gave her the broadest beam on the Atlantic. Her interior was the first to be designed along "functional" lines, eliminating the grandeur that added weight and personnel. She set transatlantic speed records and traveled at an average of 28 knots.

In the annals of vanished Atlantic liners, the *Normandie* figures as a ship without equal. A number of new cruise ships continue to claim similarities in design to the *Normandie.* Some come close, but none duplicate this lively and beloved legend. She was launched early in 1935, a year before the *Queen Mary.* A compact, graceful 80,000 tons with a clipper-type bow, she was requisitioned during the war and converted into the troopship *U.S.S. LaFayette.*

The first of the great British ships was the *Queen Mary.* Her power was estimated to be equal to the muscle power of seven million galley slaves rowing in unison.

For the record, the largest passenger liner ever built until that time was the *Queen Elizabeth*, whose construction began in the summer of 1935. Much the same type of ship as her sister the *Mary*, the *Elizabeth* had one less funnel, a few more cabins and more decorative art. Where the *Normandie* had a full-size tennis court, the *Elizabeth* had a big, partially enclosed deck for the use of tourist-class passengers. With her fast elevators and increased deck space, she was finally ready to sail after five years of construction. But instead of having streamers fluttering from her decks, she found herself painted battleship gray and sitting in New York Harbor. One year after she was launched, the *Elizabeth* was carrying troops across the Atlantic. Another new silhouette appeared on the Great Circle, the *S.S. America*. The U.S. standard-bearer was launched in 1939 but during the war sailed as the *West Point* and chalked up 500,000 miles in military service.

Demand after World War II far exceeded supply and shipping companies moved rapidly convert liners that had served the Allies into oceangoing passenger vessels. Norwegian America Line's *Stavangerfjord* set a 12-year high in transatlantic traffic in August 1945. Other liners fresh from refitting quickly followed the same sea-lanes. Demand was heavy. Displaced persons, immigrants, the military and a new breed of American tourists quickly occupied available berths.

New passenger ships sailed side by side with older favorites such as the *Queen Elizabeth, Queen Mary, Liberte, Nieuw Amsterdam* and *Ile de France*. New and luxurious amenities were introduced. Cabins had private facilities, and the *Kungsholm* was the first vessel with all outside cabins. Outdoor swimming pools became design standards once American Export Line put them on the *Excalibur, Exeter,* and *Exochorda*.

Business was brisk on the Atlantic and new tonnage was ordered to accommodate the growing mass market. The industry was unprepared and overstocked in 1958 when a Pan American jet cut transatlantic travel time from six days to a little over six hours. Within a year, airlines were carrying 1.5 million people across the Atlantic, and ships were sailing with empty berths.

Maritime history comes up with a single grande dame in every decade. The *S.S. United States,* a mechanically and structurally advanced vessel, ruled the 1950s. The *United States* was built in secrecy in a special shipyard. Her defense features were those of full-scale warships, and her capacity was large enough to transport 14,000 troops. Of aluminum construction, 1.2 million rivets held her together. At 53,000 tons, she was only two-thirds as large as either of Cunard's *Queens,* yet she could carry as many passengers. With a length of 940 feet and a beam of 102 feet, she could still glide through the Panama Canal. The *United States* was the first big ship to be completely fireproof. She also was the first to be fully air-conditioned. The least decorated of all ships in her class, she was graceful and fast, and had the lines of a clipper.

During the 1950s, the *Liberté* and the *Flandré,* the first transatlantic vessels to come out of a French shipyard after World War II, joined the aging *Ile de France*. Holland America Line welcomed the *Nieuw Amsterdam* in New York in 1940 as she sought safe haven during the war. Used as a troopship for six years, she finally headed home for Holland on the seventh anniversary of her launching. A beautiful gray ship, she was an immediate favorite with sea travelers. She retained three classes, as well as old manners and comforts, and satisfied the postwar hunger of thousands of travelers who wanted something close to what they had once enjoyed. Her owners were responsible for a major change in the class system when they launched their sister ships, *Maasdam* and *Ryndam*. These ships each accommodated 800 tourist-class and 40 first-class passengers.

In a single stroke, travelers in first class became almost underprivileged. Their cabins were larger, certainly, but the first class restaurant was not much larger than that in a modest private house and deck space was limited to the size of a dog run. Their less affluent shipmates drank at 10 cents per drink, danced into the late hours and had the run of the rest of the ship. The reversal of privileges of first and tourist classes was so successful that almost every company followed suit. By the time the one-class *Statendam* was joined by the huge, new *Rotterdam*, tourist and first classes had melded into a one-class system.

The largest company sailing vessels in the Mediterranean in the '50s and '60s belonged to Italian Line. During the 1960s, it had six liners in regular service during high summer seasons. In July 1956, the Italian Line built an exotic replacement, the *Leonardo da Vinci*. Her New York welcome in 1960 was as close to a ticker-tape parade as any ship has ever come.

One bright morning in the 1960s, a jazzy ocean liner pulled out of her Manhattan berth and moved down the Hudson River. Termed the "Pearl of the American Merchant Marine," the *Independence* looked more like a painted billboard than a ship. She offered cut-rate "experimental" cruising, whereby passengers could cruise and pay for their meals in any one of four restaurants. This option was not popular. Cruise passengers wanted, and still want, a sea experience that includes more food than they can possibly consume.

While European countries were raking in money on passenger-shipping efforts, American vessels with outstanding qualities—the *United States, Constitution, Independence, Argentina, Brasil* and *Santa Rosa*—were in serious financial trouble.

The last great liner built in that era was the 66,000-ton *France*, the longest ocean liner ever constructed until recently. She promised to return ocean travel to the luxuries of old. Her handsome, proud design included two large funnels with swept-back wings. Inside, she was overly ornate, with gilt and glitter mixed with ironwork, carved gold-edged windows, and ceramic wall plates. A single error in construction planning made it impossible for her to transit the

Panama Canal: she is a couple of feet too wide. Her vastness, however, was enough to lure passengers, and she quickly became the most successful Atlantic carrier of the decade. Italy countered with her own glamour vessels, the *Leonardo da Vinci,* followed by the *Michelangelo* and the *Raffaello.*

The 1960s and 1970s witnessed construction of compact smaller ships, with only the *Queen Elizabeth 2* remaining as the last of the big liners built in these decades. With about two-thirds of the tonnage of the *Mary* and the old *Elizabeth,* her length is less than theirs, while her height is a little more. She was computerized with the precision of a Rolls Royce and designed and decorated in a mood of controlled elegance. She was conceived as more of a cruise ship than a transatlantic liner, because that's the way the dollar crumbles. Yet she still fills up on around-the-world voyages because there are passengers with money willing to pay for upper-priced cabins that sell first on what seemed destined until last year to become Cunard's last *Queen.* She still travels transatlantic with two classes of passengers, and she is probably the most beautifully and efficiently designed passenger ship of all time.

A few words are in order about the importance of passenger vessels in time of war. This was obvious in the Falklands/Malvinas dispute between Britain and Argentina. When Britain urgently needed to transport troops to a combat zone some 8,000 miles away, the government ordered the takeover of the *Queen Elizabeth 2, Canberra* and *Uganda* for military duty. All three ships are registered in the United Kingdom. Under the laws of the country (and other agreements), they were requisitioned and saw some battle.

This could happen in other countries and it did in both world wars. All it would take in the United States, for example, would be a presidential declaration of a national emergency. The Merchant Marine Act of 1936 authorizes the Maritime Administration to requisition or buy any ship owned by U.S. citizens or companies operating or under construction in U.S. shipyards. In actuality, there are no large U.S. flagged ships operating at this time but some of the oldies could be put back into service, but it would hardly be practical with the growing size of aircraft now used to ferry troops around the globe.

During the Gulf War, the *Cunard Countess* was chartered and used for R&R for troops stationed in the region. About 50,000 officers and enlisted men were treated to a glimpse of cruise life for two or three days. During Haiti's period of returning to democracy, the *Britanis* was leased from Chandris Cruises and provided housing for U.S. troops assigned to keep the peace. Both of those ships have left the fleets and Chandris Cruises is out of business.

The Good Old Days—Then and Now

> *The traveler must be born again*
> *In the road and — Earn a passport from the elements*
> Henry David Thoreau

Yesterday

Sea transportation and cruise ships continue to change flags, ownership, and routes. As they age, some ships are laid up in far-flung shipyards awaiting their fates. But the real change in sea travel is the evolution of new generations of cruise ships. Each generation is outdoing the last with contemporary resort-type ships built for the ever-growing number of contemporary passengers. It is interesting to note that the cruise industry contributes well over $4 billion annually to the U.S. economy in the direct purchase of goods and services.

As ships change, so do passengers. They grow younger every year. Nothing really comes close to the feeling that accompanies the blast of the ship's horn as the crew gets ready to pull up the lines. It's a feeling that comes with the popping of champagne corks when visitors have disembarked. The ship puts out to sea and there's hardly a dry eye onshore. On board? The party is just beginning. Old-timers like to talk about the good old days. Everything does seem to look better in retrospect, but when it comes to cruising, the good old days are now—and the future is very bright. Onboard conveniences are getting better and better and passengers have reached new heights in vacations at sea.

Take a look back to the early 1800s, for example. Accommodations on oceangoing vessels placed the passenger behind cargo in importance. In the old days, passenger cabins were in the least desirable locations. The motion of the ocean far forward or aft must have sent passengers in those pre-stabilizer and pre-private bathroom days to the rails in droves. But as competition increased, the pendulum started to swing in favor of the passenger. By the latter half of the 1800s, iced drinks, private bathrooms and good food were no longer considered outlandish requirements.

And a new word was added to the vocabulary: POSH. It began as P.O.S.H., stamped on tickets of Indian Ocean travelers, and it indicated cabin location—"Port Out; Starboard Home," the most desirable on each leg of the voyage. But "posh" took on another meaning on board ships as amenities increased and lines competed for paying passengers.

The media reporting on these trends toward opulence was hard-pressed to find words to express the lengths to which ship owners were going to impress passengers. No expense was spared as ships competed in decor, amenities, and entertainment. What resulted was the ultimate in social scenes. It became a matter of one-upmanship as jewels and ball gowns, tuxedos and white ties became the "normal" way to dress on transatlantic crossings. One journalist's description of a Captain's Dinner caught my attention. He wrote: "Hundreds of multi-colored fairy lamps shed their soft gradients on forms of beautiful women gloriously gowned and handsome men in immaculate evening dress who danced the hours away to music provided by jolly orchestras."

Life aboard those liners was a kaleidoscope with little relationship to life on shore. Like today's ships, romance and adventure were foremost in the minds of passengers boarding liners at the close of the century and into the 1900s. Talk to an old-timer who experienced those days and you will hear of the glamour, the heel-clicking service, ten-course dinners, and breakfast menus that some-times included as many as a half dozen different kinds of bacon. You'll hear of flowing champagne, abundance of caviar and elegantly paneled smoking rooms. There were live flowers, enclosed promenades and celebrity-filled manifests.

And the clothes! Grace Kelly sailed to her fairy-tale wedding in Monaco on the *Constitution*. There were servants, dogs in kennels, touring cars and lots of luggage. When the Duke and Duchess of Windsor crossed the Atlantic on the *Queen Elizabeth,* they took 95 pieces of baggage with them for the five days. In that kind of setting, pity the poor captain who had to select the crème de la crème of the passenger manifest to share his prestigious table during the voy-age. With a veritable Who's Who in royalty, politics, arts and letters, a seat at the captain's table was an important, sought-after honor. No wonder ship mas-ters have abandoned the practice of sharing their tables with a select few for the entire voyage. On most vessels, VIP dinner guests are invited to the captain's table for one meal only.

The staff on ships of those times faced a mammoth task just keeping up with this social whirl and passenger efforts to outshine each other. There seemed to be a total disregard for money and transatlantic crossings generated definite snob appeal. As life aboard ship became more glamorous, it became more popular. The middle class wanted a piece of the life seemingly reserved for the upper crust with lots of money. Some saved for years for a single experience, and life in the first-class section became a high point of the American Dream.

Demand by the growing American middle class influenced changes aboard ships, and by the mid-1920s, a new look in shipboard life was developing. New vessels were built to accommodate more passengers, but interiors were just as opulent in appeal to tinsel-seeking crowds. Social barriers were bending as ships divided passengers by the price of their tickets into first class and tourist class. Steerage became third class and was used by immigrants and students, for the most part. The good life was in first class, and the fun times in tourist class. It was permissible for first-class passengers to mix and participate in tourist-class activities, but the doors opened only on the first-class side. It took a steward to unlock them on the tourist-class side. It is said many a first-class steward retired with money reaped from gratuities required to open that door.

At about this time, shipboard life was showing the first signs of shedding some of the fictional Hollywood image, but passengers continued to board for the same reasons. They came for those special experiences, the camaraderie of loosened inhibitions, and, of course, the promise (implied or real) of a romantic interlude.

The Oldies

Where Are They Now

Old ships, like great generals, never die. They just change names and sail on to different waters with new owners, flags, crews, and passengers. It's like a game of musical names on the bows of some vessels. Old names stubbornly cling and refuse to be completely obliterated; it is sometimes possible to see traces of former names beneath freshly painted bows.

Topping the list of previous lives is a vessel best known for the years she sailed as the *Emerald Seas*. Originally built in Kearney, New Jersey as a troop transport, in 1944, she had a name change from *General R.M. Blatchford* to *General W.P. Richardson* before she was launched in 1946. She was chartered by American Export Lines in 1949 and renamed *LaGuardia*. She was returned to U.S. Maritime Commission In 1951 and promptly returned to troop service in Korea. Between lay-ups for various reasons, she went through countless refurbishments and refits and name changes. She was *Leilani*, the *President Roosevelt*, the *Atlantis*, but had the longest run as Admiral Cruises' *Emerald Seas* with short voyages out of Miami. In 1992, when the company folded, she was purchased by Festival Cruises and renamed *Sapphire Seas*, then became the *Ocean Explorer 1* to serve as one of three Hotel ships for Expo98. Unfortunately, her fate was sealed when she went to World Cruises, a Canadian based company that offered continuous world circumnavigations at prices so low the company folded.

Intra-island cruising in the Greece-Turkey neighborhood is a good place to find old favorites that continue to sail, albeit with different names. First built in 1931, as the *Ellinis*, she sailed under various names until 2000 when she sank under tow 50 miles west of Cape Town. Name on the hull was *Belofin-1*, but Americans and Greeks knew her best as the *Britanis*, owned by Chandris Cruises. Between construction and demise, the vessel carried passengers as the *President Hoover, Panama, James Parker, Regina; Regina Prima* and *Luriline* where she was intended as a floating hotel and museum. Her last change of ownership came in 1998 when she was purchased by a Lichtenstein company for scrapping in India or Pakistan as the *Belofin-1*.

The once-beautiful 1940-vintage *S.S. America* became the *Australis* and sailed as the *Italis*, but never regained her status. The *Victoria* was built in 1936 for Union Castle Line as the *Dunnotar Castle*, while the *Amerikanis* was built in 1952 for the same line as the *Kenya Castle*. The *Victoria* now sails for Louis Lines as the *Princessa Victoria*, but the others could not be traced and have most likely been scraped.

The *Bremerhaven*, commissioned in glory in 1960, sailed for some time as Sun Line's *Stella Maris*. Sun Line, now part of Royal Olympic Cruise Lines, also owned the former *Santa Paula*. Built in 1958, she sailed as the *Stella Polaris*. The second *Kungsholm*, built in 1953, became the *Europa*. She sailed the North Atlantic for Hapag-Lloyd until the new *Europa* was built. She sailed for some years under the Costa banner as the *Columbus* and plied the waters between Europe and South America.

Norwegian Caribbean Line's first, *Sunward*, was purchased by an American-operated company as a floating Holiday Inn in Saudi Arabia. She joins Zim Israel Navigation Company's (Zim Line) former *Bilu*, which had the Hebrew writing scraped off and flies the Saudi flag as the *Saudi Moon*, transporting pilgrims to Mecca. Italian Line's *Raffaello* and *Michelangelo* were turned into floating hotels at the Iranian port of Banda Abbas before they were scrapped.

A survivor ribbon goes to *OceanBreeze*. Christened by Queen Elizabeth II in 1954 as the *Southern Cross*, at press time she was offering two night cruises out of Fort Lauderdale as the *OceanBreeze*. Her maiden voyage was an around the world cruise and she was considered a daring and innovative ship, being the first major ship to have engines in the aft of the vessel, and set the trend for ships that followed her. Her interior as well as her bow have undergone several refits and rebuilds when she sailed as the *Calypso, Calypso I* and *Azure Seas* before her current life.

If you happen to be in the Mediterranean, you may spot some freshly painted ships built by Zim Line when the Israelis thought passenger cruising would bring hard currency to their fledgling country. Ulysses Line's *Ithaca* (rebuilt in 1973) was the *Lion*, built in Germany in 1956. She sailed from 1966 until 1972 as the *Amelia de Mello*, but the Hebrew writing is still visible on the ironwork. Later, she sailed for a number of years as the *Dolphin* from Miami. The *Veracruz*, now laid up, was the *Theodor Herzl*, built as part of the Zim fleet in 1957. At one time in her history she was also known as the *Carnivale* and as the Freeport.

Zim Line's flagship *Shalom* became the *Regent Sun* in 1988. This is one ship that truly has a soul. Built for the Israelis in Germany, *Shalom* was sold to Hapag-Lloyd when Zim Line decided to leave the passenger side of shipping. She sailed briefly as the *Hanseatic* and was then sold to Home Lines, where she enjoyed successful years as the *Doric* before she became the *Royal Odyssey*. She was sold again to Regency Cruises and became the *Regent Sun*. She was a delightful ship that carried a single reminder of what she once was— a magnificent Agam sculpture designed especially for the vessel. Most of the original Chagall paintings were removed along the way. Sad to say that when Regency went under; so did the *Shalom* and all its history along with the famed Agam sculpture. She sank on the way to the breakers and none of the artwork was recovered.

Ship-a-holics remain ever faithful to their favorite vessels. The *Rotterdam V* is a good example. Launched in 1958 and christened by Queen Juliana, the *Rotterdam V* was the last great Dutch "ship of state." She was designed for both transatlantic and cruise travel and survived the jumbo jet era very well by switching to full time cruising. Her annual world cruise was legend to the loyal cadre that returned annually. So loyal, they formed the Steamship Rotterdam Foundation (www.ssrotterdam.org) in hopes of keeping the ship afloat as a museum if not an ocean going vessel. In 1997, *Rotterdam V* was sold to Premier Cruises and Holland America replaced her with a new *Rotterdam*. Premier did nothing to change the ship's charm or décor, but did convert her somewhat into another Big Red Boat. She was renamed *Rembrandt* but her life was shortened when the company went out of business in 2000. Still laid up in Freeport, Bahamas, and, with no suitors waiting, her future looks bleak.

The fourth *Statendam* also found a new home that didn't last very long. Built for Holland America, she was a standout favorite. For a brief time she was the *Volendam*, then sailed again as the *Statendam* before being sold to Paquet Cruises, where she sailed as the *Rhapsody*. When Paquet left the North

American market in 1986, the vessel was sold to now-defunct Regency Cruises. After an engine replacement and other major work, she sailed as the *Regent Star* out of Montego Bay, Jamaica, to Panama.

Carnival's *Mardi Gras* was built in 1961 as the *Empress of Canada*. After Carnival sold her, she had a brief life as *The Pride of Texas*, but she's now abandoned in a "graveyard" for old ships off the coast of Piraeus hoping for a new suitor. The *Carnivale* was built in 1956 for Canadian Pacific as *Empress of Britain* and sailed as Greek Line's *Queen Anna Maria*. She is now sailing for Royal Olympic as the *Olympic*.

When a ship makes headlines, good or bad, ship followers ask questions. Take the *Achille Lauro*, for example. She was a hard-luck ship from the beginning. Built as the *Willem Rhys* in 1939, she wasn't launched until 1946. She changed ownership a few times until she was sold to Flotta Lauro in 1965 and rebuilt as the *Achille Lauro*. A fire delayed the work and she never made a voyage under her new name until 1972, only to collide with a livestock carrier. In 1982, she was impounded because of unpaid bills and was laid up in Tenerife, in the Canary Islands, until 1984, when she returned to service. She made worldwide headlines when terrorists attacked her, but she recovered for a time and sailed as the *Star Lauro* until she was totally destroyed by fire in 1994 off the coast of Africa.

The *Independence*, also known as the *Oceanic Independence*, sailed her 100th Hawaiian cruise under the American Classic Voyages banner and received the "Ship of the Year Award" from the Steamship Historical Society of America in 2000. But those events had little bearing on her future. In 2001, American Classic Voyages filed for bankruptcy protection and the ship ceased operations.

Defunct Commodore Cruise Lines' venerable *Boheme* is now owned by the Church of Scientology and sails as the *Freeport*. The *Constitution* has been retired. Sitmar's *Fairwind* sailed for a few years as the *Dawn Princess*, was then leased to a German operator, and is currently sailing as the *Albatross*.

Costa Cruises, under Carnival Corporation ownership, has divested itself of some of the oldies. The *Enrico Costa* is sailing as the *Aegean Spirit* while the *Eugenio Costa* is out of service, sailing as the *Edinburgh Castle* on charter to a new company, Direct Holidays that is spending $10 million on refurbishment. The *Fair Princess*, a Sitmar favorite as the *Fairsea*, is lying in wait at the pier in Mazatlan, Mexico, since the demise of Regency Cruises. Royal Caribbean's *Nordic Prince* was sold to Airtours Sun Cruises and sails as the *Carousel*, while the *Ocean Islander* is currently sailing for Star Line Cruises in Africa with *Royal Star* painted on the hull.

The *Ocean Princess* was not as fortunate. After serious damage to her hull, she was declared a total loss. Yet a second life awaited her. She was purchased by a Greek company, rebuilt and named the *Sea Prince*, and now sails for a Cyprus company with still another new name, *Princesa Oceanica*. Another vessel with a lot of names gained attention with unique itineraries: the *Ocean Pearl*, ex-*Pearl of Scandinavia,* a former North Sea ferry. She is owned by Costa Crociere of Genoa and sailed from Jamaica to Havana, Cuba.

The *Sagafjord* , after being retired from the Cunard fleet, was sold to Saga Holidays and sails as the *Saga Rose*. The *Sea Princess* sailed for a while as the *Victoria* for P&O until she was replaced with a new *Victoria*. Norwegian Cruise Line's *Southward* is sailing as Airtours Sun Cruises' *Seawing*, while the *Starward* is now the *Bolero* and flies a Greek flag. The old *Victoria* is the *Princesa Victoria* for Cyprus Line, and the *World Renaissance* is sailing somewhere in Indonesia. The *Regal Empress* is the old *Caribe* (ex-*Olympic*), and Carnival's *Festivale*, former *Empress of Britain, Queen Anna Maria*, sailed as *Fiesta Marina*, then as the *Island Breeze* until the demise of Premier Cruises. She is now cruising for Thomson Holidays as the *SS Topaz.*

The magnificent *Queen Elizabeth* was retired in 1968 and sold to a Hong Kong shipping magnate. She was renamed *Seawise University,* only to be destroyed by fire in the Hong Kong harbor in 1972. Her sister, the *Queen Mary,* is a hotel and sightseeing attraction in Long Beach, California. Holland America's *Nieuw Amsterdam* was scrapped in 1974, and the *Homeric* (built as the *Mariposa* in 1931) was destroyed in 1974. The *Oranje,* launched in 1939 for world service, sailed as the *Angelina Lauro* for 15 years before she was destroyed by fire dockside at St. Thomas.

We can't talk about oldies without talking about the most talked about sea disaster, the *Titanic,* a British ship that struck an iceberg and sank in the North Atlantic in 1912. The story has been told in dozens of books and in the Oscar winning movie epic. *Titanic* carried enough lifeboats to accommodate about half of the 2,200 passengers and crew. A total of 1,517 people died in the disaster. The largest and most luxurious ocean liner of its time, the ship was touted as unsinkable because its hull was divided into 16 watertight compartments. Even if two of those compartments flooded, the ship could still float. As a result of the collision with the iceberg, six compartments initially flooded.

In 1985, a team of French and American scientists led by Robert D. Ballard of the United States and Jean-Louis Michel of France found the wreckage of the *Titanic*. The ship lay in two sections about 400 miles (650 kilometers) southeast of Newfoundland at a depth of about 12,500 feet. Until this discovery, people thought that the *Titanic* sank because the iceberg cut a huge gash in its hull. But the wreck showed no sign of a gash. A study of steel samples from the ship concluded that the hull was made of steel that became brittle in the frigid North Atlantic waters and fractured easily during the collision. Inquiries have also shown that the *Titanic* was traveling too fast in an area where there was danger of icebergs. The ship was traveling at about 21 knots (nautical miles per hour), nearly its top speed, when lookouts sighted the iceberg.

The tragedy had a great impact on International laws governing passenger vessels and safety measures required by SOLAS (Safety Of Life At Sea) the organization that enforces regulations, has stringent rules that are updated regularly

At last count, about 30 ships built before 1950 were still in service, albeit under different names and different flags. Most of the ships mentioned have been updated, some beyond recognition. Engines have been changed, profiles have been extended, furnishings have been replaced and interiors have even been completely gutted and rebuilt (see "Ship Profiles" chapter). Others retain the same outward appearance with internal face-lifts as the only evidence of the passage of time. Other less fortunate glamorous ladies of the sea have ended up as rusty wrecks or as somebody's Toyota. Still others are serving as hotels.

It's like a game of musical names in Davey Jones Locker. When "for sale" signs get rusty and no buyers show up, ships have been known to sail, or try to sail, to Alang, India (near Bhangvar) or Aliaga, Turkey (near Izmir). After beaching, equipment, fittings, and interiors are systematically removed and sold off or disposed of before the cutting process begins. The steel is then melted down and recycled into new cars, building girders, and yes, even razor blades. Within weeks or months of arrival, the only trace left of a wonderful old ship is an oil-stained embankment. But some manage to come back to life.

Premier Cruise Line's *Seabreeze I*, ex *Federico C* built in 1958 became Premier Cruise Lines first "Big Red Boat" in 1989 and was promptly renamed *"Starship Royale*. While enroute to Freeport for maintenance work, she developed a leak in her engine room during a storm off Cape Charles and sank in December 2000.

The former *Gripsolm*, another twin funneled veteran, keeled over and sank in 12,000 feet of water 83 miles off Cape Recife, South Africa, enroute to the Indian breakers, in July 2001. She began her career as Swedish American Line's ultra-deluxe *Gripsholm* in 1957, carrying the elite (including Greta Garbo) on transatlantic and long worldwide voyages until 1975, when the owners ceased operations. Her next career was as the Greek-owned *Navarino*, and following a grounding, fire, and dry dock accident, managed to serve a relatively long final career as Regency Cruise Line's *Regent Sea* between 1985 and 1995. When Regency abruptly filed for bankruptcy, the *Regent Sea* was laid up in the Bahamas where the humidity and a lack of upkeep took its toll. When she was released from her liens in 1997, she was sadly dilapidated, but things got even worse when new owners began the process of rebuilding her for gambling service. After two of her decks were stripped to bare steel, they ran out of funds and the ship, by now renamed *Sea*, was left to rot. By 2001, her fate was sealed and the once pristine pride of the Swedish merchant marine undertook the long, slow voyage to India. On route, she was pillaged by West African "pirates" who boarded the slow-bound tow and stole furniture and equipment just weeks before she met her watery end.

A good example of a ship that refused to die is *Freewinds* which sails out of Curacao under the Majestic Cruise Line banner. Originally built in 1976 as the *Italia*, a sleek, deluxe 12,219 ton, 525 passenger ship, frequently described as a miniature *Oceanic*. She was chartered to Costa Line for three Mediterranean cruises before being sub chartered to Princess Cruises when she became *Princess Italia*. In 1983, Ocean Cruise Lines rebuilt her into their *Ocean Princess*. Ten years later, she was sinking upright in shallow water in the Amazon. Although all aboard were rescued, the ship was declared a Constructive Total Loss, which means the insurance company paid, not that the ship would become an underwater reef. Instead, she was refloated, towed to Greece, rebuilt and sold to Louis Cruise Lines which renamed here the *Sapphire*. With more lives than a cat, she went to Thomson Cruises for a further refit and since 1999, has been sailing for Louis Cruises on short cruises out of Malta

Most readers may not recognize the delivery name of *Mirto* on the rust-streaked 6,390-ton, 1964-built hull beached at Alang in April 2001. This modest vessel was the one-time Israeli ferry, then cruise ship *Bilu*. Her claim to fame was her charter in the mid 1960's by Ted Arison for Miami-based winter cruise service. Arison went on to phenomenal success (Carnival Corporation) and the *Bilu* went on to anonymity under the names *Saudi Moon, Golden Sky, Vergina,* and *Mir*.

Possibly the saddest of all recent scrapings because of her pristine condition, was Costa Cruises' dowager *Costa Riviera* which arrived at Alang under the delivery name of *Liberty* in March 2002. The 701-foot liner was the second of two Cantieri Riuniti Del'Adriatico-built sisters. Following the *Galaleo-Galilei* (which burned and sank in Indonesia in 1999 as the *Sun Vista*), the *Guglielmo Marconi*, after several refits, was transformed into *Costa Riviera*. In 1993, she received a $25 million refit that would turn her into American

Family Cruises' *American Adventure,* a misadventure that lasted less than a year before she was again restored and returned to the Costa fleet.

Several vessels are nearing the end of their ropes. Among them are the last large US ocean-going passenger ships in service. Following the October, 2001 collapse of American Hawaii Cruises' parent company, American Classic Voyages, the *Independence* was laid up at the Suisuin Bay Reserve Fleet. Built in 1951 for American Export Line's, she and her sister *Constitution* (which sank 700 miles northwest of Honolulu in November of 1997 while under tow to India for scrapping) garnered headlines for their celebrity-filled passenger lists and occasional film and television roles.

Among the luckier liners, some have new lives as floating hotels, museums and restaurants. The legendary 1927-built 5,209 gross ton *MV Scandinavia* still sports the name *Stella Polaris* on her clipper-like bow. Her new Japanese owners renamed her *Scandinavia* and sailed her from Lisbon to her present moorings at Mitohama, Japan. The deluxe accommodations were meant to be used as hotel rooms and public rooms as a restaurant in the quaint fishing village some two hours by train or car south of Tokyo. Unfortunately, the concept didn't work, but the restaurant is open and tours are offered.

Builders of the old *Ryndam* in 1951 could not have foreseen her future. She was an instant hit on the Rotterdam - New York run. With newer and larger ships replacing her, in 1968, she became the *Waterman* and was used as a floating university, She returned to service as the *Ryndam* and sailed until 1971. After that, it was a name changing game. From Epirotiki's *Atlas,* to *Pride of the Mississippi* for gambling cruises, to the *Pride of Galveston* for similar cruises and finally to her present name *Copa Casino* positioned in Gulfport, Louisiana where she bears little resemblance to her original self.

Wanna buy a ship? The *Augustus* (an almost identical twin to the *Andrea Doria*) has had a rather sedate, if mysteriously silent existence since her sale in 1976 to Hong Kong interests who refitted and renamed her several times over the years. In mid 1998, she left her moorings for a refit at Subic Bay, this time for use as a hotel ship in Manila. Her owners, Philippine President Lines, renamed her *MS Philippines* for use as a floating restaurant and hotel at a pier near the Manila Hotel. But, the concept didn't work and efforts are still underway to bring her back to her old home port of Genoa for preservation. Meanwhile, the "For Sale" sign is till up.

As for the *United States,* the greatest maritime achievement of 1952, the asking price is $30 million, but you should know she has been completely gutted so there's no memorabilia to sell. Another former great vessel built in 1956 as the *Carinthia* is also available. She had a stunning career during when she sailed for Sitmar Cruises as the *Fairsea* in Australia and then the *Fair Princess* for Princess Cruises after it purchased Sitmar Cruises. The attempt to convert her to a gambling vessel failed, so she's available.

The *Dolphin IV's* fate was sealed when Kosmos Cruises tried to sail her as a gambling vessel and it didn't work. She sailed briefly as the *Amelia de Mello* in West Africa, but was the *Ithaca* in the Mediterranean. Most of us knew her as a fixture on three and four day Bahamas cruises from Miami with *Ithaca* painted on the hull. She's laid up in Freeport, Bahamas, awaiting a suitor or the ax, whichever comes first.

Another casualty in the demise of Regency Cruises is the 24,413 ton *Sea Harmony* (ex *Regent Star*) . She was purchased by Perosa Shipping and her fate is still to be announced.

Also looking for new owners are the *Enchanted Isles* (ex *Argentina, Veendam, Brasil, Monarch Star, Bermuda Star, Enchanted Isle*) which last sailed on weekly Caribbean cruises from New Orleans in December, 2000, when Commodore Cruise Lines ceased operations. She's laid up in New Orleans, her last port of call.

Also for sale is another casualty of the Premier Cruises bankruptcy -the *Seawind Crown* (ex *Infante Dom Henrique, Vasco da Gama, Seawind*). She is docked in Barcelona and her future is uncertain.

Grave yards for ships are all over the globe. *Big Red Boat II* (ex *Eugeneo Costa, Edinburgh Castle*) is dockside in Freeport, Empress Cruises' *Empress* (ex *Sunward*) lies in wait in Singapore, and a number of Russian ships built during the 70's and 80's have similar "for sale" signs.

Ships of Today

The cruise industry has changed dramatically during the past 40 years. It's hard to come up with the ship that offered the first pleasure cruise for paying passengers. The only thing certain is that cruising developed when ships began offering amenities that competed with land based resorts. In actuality, those short cruises during the Depression years were a sad and almost futile attempt to keep liners alive. When the economy turned around and business on the Atlantic picked up, the ocean traveler demanded new ships. By then, big ships gathering rust in shipyards had to be replaced by smaller vessels built to follow the sunny sea-lanes of the Caribbean and Mediterranean.

There are differences of opinion on when the current "cruise revolution" began. Most cruise historians agree that sometime during the 1960s the concept of the ship as a destination started to take hold in the form of pleasure cruising. It came at a time when the old class system still existed on board ships, although winds of change were visible. Some credit the introduction of all-inclusive air-sea packages with the "cruise revolution" Others say it was a backlash from the era of speed. I contend that two factors turned cruising into the fastest growing segment of the vacation industry: (1) The Love Boat television series; and (2) the all-inclusive air-sea package, which brought millions of passengers from inland U.S. homes for a view of the ocean at affordable prices.

In the early 1960s, trends began to develop and aggressive investors, some with shipping backgrounds, others optimistic about sea travel, ventured into the fledgling marketplace. At the beginning of the decade, there were barely 30 passenger-carrying vessels in operation. By the end of the 1960s, there were new companies and new optimism in the industry. In 1961, Charalambos Keusseouglou formed Sun Lines to carry emigrants, and a year later, the longest 1,033-foot liner in the world, *S.S. France,* inaugurated transatlantic service.

Dodge Island, now known as the Port of Miami, with more demand than the small port could accommodate, began dredging the harbor to handle larger vessels and expansion plans were put in place. While in the early 1970s Miami was growing as a Caribbean embarkation port, passenger tonnage inventoried in the millions was gathering rust, abandoned in shipyards around the world. The *United States* was laid up following a strike, and the U.S. Government lost interest in subsidizing the vessel.

Glamour queens of the sea had been deserted by fickle jet-setters who have a way of setting travel trends and perhaps dictating where we go and how we get there. They opted for wide-bodied jets to transport them across oceans and to romantic islands at speed rivaling that of sound.

But trends are cyclical and longing for the good old days of relaxation and slower paces began emerging. The dawn of the '70s signaled the dawn of a new age in cruising. It took on a contemporary air. The class system was abandoned in favor of single-class cruising at affordable rates. Travelers in all economic and social strata were becoming less obsessed with speed. They yearned for a measure of service and luxury not generally available to them on a daily basis. They wanted, and continue to want, experiences that do not remind them of home. They started looking for comfort and some degree of luxury as they visited strange-sounding places with names they could hardly pronounce. They began finding a combination of those amenities in cruise vacations. The groundswell breathed new life into the cruise industry, an industry that for a while looked as if it were fading away and becoming obsolete.

Cruise companies began building ships specifically for cruising purposes in the early 1970s. While ship owners kept a careful eye on profitable ventures, they expended huge amounts of money to improve amenities. In the process, cruising was democratized and first class was eliminated so there was no need to duplicate public space for two classes. Swimming pools became larger, while theaters, lounges, supper clubs and ballrooms were built to accommodate at least half of the ship's capacity. Ships were scaled down and ranged in size from 17,000 to 25,000 tons. Staterooms became compact and standardized; and cargo was eliminated as public rooms took over with atmosphere rivaling shore side resorts.

In 1970, a triumvirate of Norwegian companies founded Royal Viking Line with each contributing one ship and a new era of luxury cruising was born. In the mid-1970s, the industry experienced an unprecedented rebirth and demand far outstripped supply. Ship owners realized they had under-built the size of their fleets. They searched shipyards for overlooked tonnage and some oldies came back to the sea-lanes. Other owners planned new tonnage, which would take three or four years to complete, and still others decided to simply expand capacity by stretching fairly new ships.

But it was events in 1965 that had the greatest impact on modern-day cruising. Sitmar Cruises began operating cruises on the *Fairstar* out of Australia and Seattle entrepreneur Stanley McDonald founded Princess Cruises. In 1966, Knut Kloster, a Norwegian shipping magnate, teamed up with Israeli-born Ted Arison and formed Klosters Reederei, a partnership which provided that Arison Shipping Company would be responsible for sales, marketing and management for the Miami-based company and Kloster would furnish the vessels. Also in 1966, Commodore Cruise Line was founded with a single-ship fleet, the *Boheme*.

The Kloster-Arison union prospered and brought four new ships into the one-week Caribbean cruise market out of Miami. The partnership lasted until 1972, when Arison formed Carnival Cruise Lines after a much-publicized split with Kloster. Carnival's growth is legend. The company that started with one ship, *Mardi Gras* (former *Empress of Canada*), is now one of the three largest cruise conglomerates in the world. Ted Arison deserves the credit for growing the industry. His vision and his courage were responsible for the industry's growth as companies vied to keep up with his innovations at sea. Kloster, on the other hand, became Norwegian Cruise Line but didn't add new vessels to the four-ship fleet until the 1980s.

In the interim, Royal Caribbean Cruise Line was founded in 1969 by a group of Norwegian shipping companies. Miami became the marketing headquarters and, by the end of its first year, the company ordered two new ships for delivery in 1970 and 1971.

While companies like Sitmar, which entered the United States in 1972 with two luxury vessels, *Fairwind* and *Fairsea*, continued moderate growth, Carnival, Royal Caribbean, and Princess became the dominant forces in the industry. Realizing that local markets could not fill additional vessels, the air-sea program was born. Almost every company claims credit for the very successful concept that put middle-American travelers almost literally at sea the minute they entered their local airport. It doesn't really matter who was first because within days, it seems, every cruise line was offering air-sea packages and the industry took off.

Demand for berths and airline space soared, and new vessels were ordered as quickly as yards could build them. Smaller ships were stretched; Royal Caribbean's *Song of Norway* was the first to be cut in two and to have a new identically matched midsection installed. The expansion was so successful the company immediately had the same operation performed on the *Nordic Prince*. Royal Viking Line had all three of its ships stretched by the same method, and it's hard to find the seams binding new and old sections.

Ships were pulling in their lines with hardly an empty berth on board until 1980. Ship owners were riding high and without hesitation committed themselves to additional tonnage. They backed up bullish outlooks with investments of more than a billion dollars for construction of new ships.

In January 1982, the first of this new generation of ships inaugurated service. Carnival Cruise Lines' *Tropicale* had a cost estimated in the neighborhood of $110 million. Home Line's 33,800- ton *Atlantic* was completed the same year for about the same cost. In December 1982, Royal Caribbean Cruise Line introduced its new *Song of America*, a $140-million, 37,584-ton ship that holds 1,414 passengers. Holland America Line's *Nieuw Amsterdam* began service in mid-1983 and her almost identical sister ship, the *Noordam*, was completed a year later. Each 33,930-ton ship accommodates 1,214 passengers and costs around $150 million.

In April 1984, Sea Goddess Cruises introduced the first of its luxury 4,000-ton ships, the *Sea Goddess I*. Sitmar Cruises also introduced the *Fairsky*, the only newly built passenger ship with turbo engines. The 46,314-ton

Fairsky was the largest ship built up to that point in time exclusively for cruising, but records don't hold up very long in the cruise industry. The year was topped off with style in late November when Princess Cruises christened the new Love Boat, *Royal Princess*, and inaugurated sailings. The 45,000-ton vessel cost nearly $200 million to build and accommodates 1,200 passengers, all in outside cabins. And with about 25% of the cabins boasting private verandas, another new trend was born.

During the following two years, Carnival Cruise Lines built and inaugurated sailings on two additional super liners, *Jubilee* and *Celebration*, and nearly a dozen additional ships were either contracted for or making their way to drawing boards.

Ships launched in the 1970s and 1980s differ greatly from ships planned for the next century and those built before the 1960s. Ships constructed in the 1990s and those planned for the next century are configured with totally different designs. Economies of scale have had a great influence on projects. Inflation, currency values, and rising operational and sales costs have influenced construction and reconstruction plans. With the price of building new ships soaring above the $300 million and up to the $500 million mark, smaller companies are going out of business and entrepreneurs newly turned on to the shipping business are treading carefully before investing millions.

As new tonnage comes on line, some companies are selling off older vessels. Interesting to note: what is considered replaceable tonnage in some fleets is being snatched up by companies operating outside U.S. shores. In some cases, a complete refurbishing job is done. In others, merely cosmetic work. In either case, flags on the mast are changed. A new name goes on the bow, and the ship is sold to another segment of the cruising public. The vessel takes on a new personality, although it is hard to erase every aspect of her past.

During the 1980s and '90s, new companies emerged, and some old companies ceased operations or were taken over by more successful operators. Cruising took on a globalized look as the Japanese reentered the passenger-shipping marketplace. Nippon Yusen Kaisha (NYK) Lines bought Salen Lindblad Cruising and introduced the *Asuka*, the first vessel designed specifically for Japanese passengers. In 1990, Crystal Cruises, owned by NYK, introduced its first vessel, *Crystal Harmony*, built for North American passengers.

Carnival Cruise Lines acquired Holland America, which owned Windstar Sail Cruises in 1989, then bought a stake and later purchased all of Seabourn Cruise Lines in 1998. In 1990 Carnival bought Costa Cruises and Cunard Line. In 1996, *Carnival Destiny* was the first ship to exceed

100,000 gross tons. She did not remain the largest ship afloat for very long. Later that year Royal Caribbean's *Voyager of the Seas* and the *Grand Princess* broke size records.

New builds introduced in the latter half of 1990s made the *Queen Elizabeth 2* look like a mid-size ship. Tonnage went from the 70,000-ton super liners of the earlier part of the decade to over 100,000 tons of floating resort luxury. But business has not been booming for all companies. Admiral Cruises ceased operations and *Azure Seas* and *Emerald Seas* were sold to Dolphin Cruise Line and then to the now-defunct SunFest Cruises. American Family Cruises, which operated one of the Costa ships, had a short life, and Kloster Cruise Ltd. closed its Royal Cruise Line and Royal Viking Line divisions in 1996.

In the wake of September 11th, Renaissance Cruises, Commodore Cruises and American Hawaii Cruises filed for bankruptcy and ceased operations. Some of their ships have been sold at auction; others have "For Sale" signs hanging from masts and are being sold off at auction. Two of the Renaissance ships were purchased by Princess Cruises and will be operated out of French Polynesia.

Earlier in this book I said, "Companies operate ships to show a profit." It has not taken major companies long to discover that the cost of operating a larger ship with more passengers is a lot less on a per passenger basis. For example, compare a 25,000-ton ship that carries 700 passengers with a 70,000-ton ship with 2,000 passengers. The difference in actual cost per passenger is in an additional onboard service staff and in the cost of food. Fuel, number of officers, and entertainment costs remain relatively stable. Hence, most ships built in the 1990s and beyond were bound to get bigger and bigger and bigger.

Capacity in 2003 is scheduled to grow by 16.8 percent with 10 new ships entering service. That will add almost 100,000 beds to the industry this year. Creating demand and filling those new berths as well as existing capacity is a dynamic challenge facing the industry.

A quick look at what's sailing today shows Carnival Cruise Lines' super liners (*Holiday, Jubilee, Celebration*) of the 1980s in the 46,000-GRT range, its mega liners of the 1990s in the 70,000-GRT range, and *Destiny* and her sister vessels of the new millennium, *Triumph* and *Victory*, over 100,000 tons each. Royal Caribbean's *Sovereign of the Seas* and her sister vessels, *Monarch of the Seas* and *Majesty of the Seas,* as well as the six Vision-class ships, *Legend of the Seas, Grandeur of the Seas, Splendour of the Seas, Rhapsody of the Seas, Enchantment of the Seas,* and *Vision of the Seas,* are in the over-70,000-GRT class. However, in

2000 Royal Caribbean International (as it is now known) introduce 141,000-GRT vessels with amenities that broke the mold – rock climbing, ice skating rink and shows, miniature golf courses, and inside cabins with a view of Promenades. Princess Cruises' *Star Princess, Crown Princess*, and *Regal Princess*, all vessels of the 1990s, look very small alongside the 110,000-GRT *Grand Princess* that debuted in Europe in mid-1998. She was followed by sister-ships *Golden Princess* and *Star Princess*. A fourth sister, *Crown Princess* is due to join the fleet in Spring 2004. The cost for each of these vessels is running close to $500 million.

Mergers, acquisitions, sales, takeovers, and public offerings have drawn interest in the cruise industry from financial managers around the world. Publicly listed companies like Carnival Corp., Royal Caribbean International, P&O (London Exchange), and others contemplating public offerings of stock have attracted investors. It is interesting to note that investment publications list these companies under "leisure," not under "transportation," as was done for many years.

While the big companies continue to take delivery of even larger ships, on the other side of the size picture are new vessels catering to the moneyed few who can afford the luxury of small, deluxe vessels. All of the new ships, and many of the older refurbished vessels, have the same basic amenities considered luxuries not too many years ago. Stabilizers, air-conditioning, private facilities, swimming pools, exercise rooms and huge spas are standard on almost every ship. Onboard sanitation systems and garbage compactors, satellite navigation and televisions in cabins are common on the latest generation of ships.

Fuel prices and shortages during the latter half of the 1970s became an important consideration and influenced the size and shape of ships built in the decade of the '80s. Except for Sitmar Cruises' *Fairsky*, ships built during the '70s and '80s were (and some continue to be) fitted with diesel engines instead of steam turbines for propulsion. Marine engineers are quick to point out advantages and some disadvantages in both types of engines, but there is total agreement that diesel-powered engines use a lot less fuel than steam turbines. New technology and engineering designs have cushioned engines so vibration on new ships is minimal. A number of new vessels are powered by gas turbines and the computer age has reached bridges on new ships. Safety is thereby max-imized and the bridge on every new ship looks more like a computer center than a place to steer the vessel.

The number of ships in the world fleet doubled during the past decade and the number of berths will nearly double again in the next five years. Not only are the ships new, they are trendsetters designed for new generations of passengers with broader, more varied interests. Ships run from under 100 passengers to behemoth mega liners built to please more than 3,500 pleasure-seeking passengers. As shore side lifestyles become more active, new liners are adding options that cover the gambit—sports, recreation, entertainment and culture. No longer is a cruise a sedentary experience. Albeit, it is safe to predict quiet corners will always exist, even on futuristic vessels geared to constantly changing environments.

Mega liners have mega features—multilevel hotel-style atrium lobbies, bubble-glass elevators, significant artworks, glitzy casinos, theater-lounges for Broadway- and Las Vegas-style musicals, shopping arcades, state-of-the art fitness centers, hot tubs and observation lounges that offer wide-angle views of the sea. Picture windows are replacing portholes. There are more private verandas and space planners are designing comfortable cabins with good closet space. High-tech innovations are also going to sea: direct-dial telephones, satellite television, and VCRs in cabins and Internet Cafes and direct connections to the Internet from cabins and suites.

Posh small vessels accommodating up to 500 passengers are becoming exclusive country clubs at sea. These are all-suites, scaled-down versions of new mega liners catering to the luxury-minded, more adventurous passenger.

Then there is the *World of ResidenSea*, a floating condominium resort for the super-affluent. A group of investors with a background in shipping came up with the idea that there is a small cadre of very rich people who would like to take their home with them as they sail worldwide. Most of the industry never thought this project would come to fruition. But it has and it is sailing. Early brochures indicated that the vessel would be 85,000 square feet with a beam of 105 feet. She would have 15 decks and carry only about 700 passengers. Accommodations would be from one bedroom to three with square footage from 1,105 to 2,834. Purchase prices are running from $1.1 million to over $5 million. Annual maintenance fees are estimated from $61,000 to about $240,000. To sweeten the deals, all apartments will be fully furnished. Meals, however, are not included. Not to worry, there will be seven restaurants on board and lots of entertainment.

The ship was downsized and emerged as a 43,000-ton luxury cruise ship capable of accommodating 975 guests in 110 ownership apartments and 88 cruise passenger suites. It's a pricey country club gone to sea. Apartments go for upwards of $2 million. The *World of ResidenSea* bills itself as the first resort community at sea.

Ships of the Future

The number of cruise passengers has increased more than fivefold since 1969. At the Port of Miami alone, the number increased from 569,000 in 1969, to 1,466,581 in 1980, to 3.2 million in 1992 and up again to close to 4 million in 2000. Capacity is scheduled to grow by 16.8 percent with 10 new ships entering service in 2002. That will add almost 100,000 beds to the industry this year. Creating demand and filling those new berths as well as existing capacity is a dynamic challenge facing the industry.

Another challenge is finding names for new vessels and names are being recycled which may be confusing in the marketplace. Some names keep reappearing in different forms. At last count, there were three ships with the word "Legend" in the name. Some companies continue to recycle names of former ships in the fleet. Holland America is a good example. My father came to New York as a youngster on the first *Statendam* before the turn of the century. It bore no resemblance to the fifth *Statendam* currently cruising the world. So, ships reviewed in this book are all 21st century versions of what started over 100 years ago.

While travelers remain somewhat cautious at this point in time, cruise lines remain "cautiously optimistic" that the effect of September 11 will take time to wear off and the value offered by a cruise vacation will turn caution to action and ships will fill.

To take advantage of travelers' reluctance to fly, cruise lines have been juggling homeports and developing drive-to markets. The theory is that travelers may prefer a drive of five or six hours that eliminates the need to fly and the cost of fights. Another important benefit is reduction of cost for families who take the kids along on vacation. Most companies have redeployed vessels from Eastern Mediterranean ports bringing them back to Caribbean, Mexico and Alaska sailings. Others have rescheduled or increased Northern Europe sailings. According to Carnival Corp.'s enthusiastic chairman and chief executive officer Micky Arison, the cruise industry is in its infancy and has a bright and exciting future. His company and others are investing billions of dollars in support of this growing industry. Ships of the future will deliver every phase of the good life and a lot more. If this is the infancy stage of cruising, passengers are in for adolescent years that will be not only exciting but far beyond their wildest fantasies.

Bold new concepts are shattering traditional ship designs. Architects, engineers, and designers are capitalizing on basic amenities associated with cruising and minimizing inherent drawbacks. Some designs that represent what ship-yards would like to build may never come to pass in our lifetime. Others are more realistic and some have already taken to the sea-lanes.

It's hard to beat rock climbing walls and ice-skating rinks, but new ships are countering with new amenities. Look for everything you can find in a shore side resort and then some. Will there be condominiums at sea? Will there be time-share vessels? Skeptics doubted that people would call a ship home on an annual basis, but it's happening, albeit it's happening among the select few who have multiple dwellings – a home in Aspen, one in the South of France, maybe one in London or New York and one on a ship that will take them to exotic ports of call in the comfort of an environment which they create for themselves.

But most of us will depend on cruise companies to come up with what we really want in a ship. In a column I wrote for a magazine, I talked about what I would build if I were a ship owner. Interesting to note that my wishes didn't focus on the hardware – the physical ship, but more on elimination of lines, leisurely service, choices and non-regimentation. And, that's the direction in which the industry is going.

There will undoubtedly be purpose-built ships. The trend is already beginning. Canyon Ranch is building a spa ship where fitness and health will be the mind set. It is slated for completion in 2004. Within the next 10 years, I will go out on that dangerous limb and predict other purpose built vessels that will appeal to specific market segments: maybe Weight Watchers?

I'm not the only dreamer. There are others who have even grander dreams for ships. Some of the designs by dreaming architects could easily have originated in a science fiction movie. But, then again – who knows? In my wildest dreams or imagination, I never thought I would be in the middle of the ocean watching a live performance that was a reasonable facsimile of the Ice Capades.

One designer at a recent convention showed plans for a 1,000-capacity-passenger vessel with 13 decks stacked in a wedge with a huge observation lounge encircling the funnel and the forward mast. Of course, the ship would have an exotic indoor Japanese gardens and a restaurant.

Another design termed MACS3000, which stands for Multi-Activity Cruise Ship. She is designed to carry 3,000 passengers in 1,500 cabins. The deck plan calls for cabins built in a U-shape around an eight-story open-air atrium. The sun deck would have four full tennis courts, in addition to traditional shuffle-board courts, tanning areas and two jogging tracks. Instead of selecting inside or outside cabins, passengers would opt between sea-view and atrium-view rooms. Shore excursions would be by way of launches docked between twin hulls or by way of a helicopter taking off from a heliport.

European designers are thinking along similar science fiction lines but are turning out contemporary vessels while imaginations run rampant. The Bremer Vulcan shipyard in Germany has unveiled a square-rigged sailing cruise ship for 140 passengers. Similar to the French-built *Wind Star* and *Wind Song*, the German design incorporates computer-controlled sails but in a non-conventional form.

In Singapore, there's a ship that's more like a hotel. Havila Offshore is building a 200-room floating hotel to be placed over Australia's Great Barrier Reef as a mecca for divers. The *Coastel* will be entirely self-contained, with restaurants, bars, conference rooms, and a disco.

At a recent conference, I heard about super size vessels. One proposal included a "mother ship" with four auxiliary vessels that could be detached and sent ashore for supplies or detached for Panama Canal passage as separate boats.

Most major companies bent on increasing the size of their fleets are not planning projects even remotely resembling ResidenSea's World. They are, however, making financial commitments for construction of new ships in keeping with realistic and optimistic views of the economic future of the cruise industry. These new vessels will come in two sizes for the most part. The mega-companies will build in the 80,000-ton range, boutique operators will build in the 25,000- to 50,000-ton range. The ships will be broad-beamed, but unlike the over-100,000 GRT ships, not too broad to transit the Panama Canal. All will have fuel-conserving devices like bulbous bows and will be extremely maneuverable, thereby requiring fewer tugs in ports. And, they will be fast enough to reach more ports of call and/or to spend more time in ports. Cabins, for the most part, will be larger than on the ships of the 20th century, but the greatest difference will be in public facilities. Newer designs and construction concepts allow for what might seem like oversize public space even by today's standards and enough space to eliminate regimentation and allow for more choices in food and entertainment.

This trend offers great advantages for cruise lines and even greater advantages for passengers. In many respects, ships of the early 21st century will bear a marked resemblance to ships of the past. Engines will be piston-operated instead of steam-driven and will be engineered to cut down on vibration and noise generally associated with piston-driven engines. Ships are switching to gas turbine engines that are more environmentally friendly.

Ship watchers will be first to note the change in external appearance. With only a hint of the sleek lines of yesteryear, bows will be stubbier and transoms squared off, giving these mega liners the look of condominiums that have gone to sea. As far as passengers go, it will make little difference. It will be the inside that counts.

Should Cuba ever open as a cruise port, another trend is likely to develop. Look for converted North Sea ferries sailing from South Florida to Cuba. These ferries are hardly the type on which passengers book deck space for short transfers between nearby ports. Some are as big as apartment houses, to which their designs also bear a striking resemblance.

Always an innovator, Carnival Cruise Lines has the first and only non-smoking vessel afloat. *Carnival Paradise* began sailing in the fall of 1998, but none of the other companies have copied this concept. It takes courage and competitors continue to watch, and it's likely there will be another ship that caters to non-smokers only.

The ship destined to make headlines even before she left the drafting tables is Cunard Line's *Queen Mary 2*. She will be the first new liner designed for transatlantic service in about 35 years. From futuristic ships to classic ocean liners, the next few years will set new trends and paces for the cruise industry and those of us who sail the vessels. After all, when the 20th century dawned, we didn't have television, air travel or the Internet, and cruising was simply point-to-point transportation. There are a lot of surprises ahead in this technical century.

We have enough people who tell it like it can be
Now we could use a few who tell it like it is...

Robert Orben

What you should know before you cruise

INSIDER TIP

This chapter is designed to answer your questions about cruise vacations. It highlights important features that should help select the right ship that meets your expectations, or comes very close. The chapter covers questions you may have about security, insurance, what to look for and everything you should, or might want to know before you book your cruise. It's all about packaging ships, itineraries and prices, then coming up with one, two or three ships that will fit smoothly into your vacation plans. To help you select your ship, our panel of experts has come up with their choices of "The Best of the Best" by price and on board lifestyles. We explore itineraries in more detail in another section of the book. This chapter deals with identifying who you are, what you want and zeros in on ships that fit your vacation dreams.

Security

In this post 9/11 era, security and safety are top priorities on every traveler's mind. We'll cover that topic first, then go on to cruise vacations and choices.

As the U.S. government struggles to get a handle on making airports and other forms of travel, including cruise ships, safer through baggage screening, the cruise industry has taken steps on its own to ensure the safety of its guests and crew. There is no industry-wide policy or standard, but all lines with vessels sailing from U.S. ports require passengers to put carry-on bags through airport-like metal detector machines. Checked luggage, for the most part, goes through x-ray machines. Cruise lines are required to submit passenger manifests to Immigration and Customs authorities in advance of embarkation and debarkation. There's no way passengers can show up at the pier and buy a last minute bargain. That's a trend of the past.

On board security has been enhanced and a laudable safety measure is the photo ID card which is issued on embarkation. It also serves as your on board credit card and unlocks your cabin door. This card must be shown at debarkation and in ports of call for re-entry to the ship. As an added safety precaution, no visitors are allowed on board in ports of call. Cruise lines have spent millions on this new technology which requires that passengers be photographed on embarkation. When the card is swiped through the machine, the photo is compared with the person boarding or leaving the ship. Some ships require two photo ID's in ports of call and while a valid driver's license is usually accepted, the best ID is a valid passport.

What are the Choices?

It's a maze out there. So many ships, so many options and so many choices. Choosing your cruise is the most important vacation decision you'll make and it can be confusing. After all, they all float. But that's where the sameness ends. Ships present a case of different strokes for different folks. There are big ships, small ships, sailing vessels, river boats and in-between everything boats and ships. Selecting the right ship that measures up to your vacation requirements most often makes the difference between a dream boat, a nightmare or just a so-so vacation. If time is the determining factor, it makes decisions a lot easier. On the other hand, if you have time on your hands, where the ship goes becomes less important and the price becomes the prime consideration.

There are a few facts you should know about cruising in general, before becoming more specific and matching your vacation requirements with a ship, or ships that meet them.

Most cruise ships have scuttled highbrow reputations in favor of casual conviviality, which makes ocean voyages relaxing, economical or plush and an enjoyable vacation for travelers of all ages. Small wonder travelers' fickle fancies have again turned to the sea lanes for relaxing holidays. They are discovering that cruising aboard a first-class ship to exotic ports is one of the supreme pleasures in life. It is civilized, unhurried, and often likened to vacationing on a fabulous estate, complete with swimming pools, gourmet cuisine, and a staff anxious to please, entertain, and look after every whim and wish.

A cruise can be defined in many ways. A cruise is an escape from reality into the glitzy, world without clocks. It's a world of casinos, nightclubs, and discos. A cruise is a fabulous resort that floats to exotic ports of call with ever-changing scenery. It is like a trip to Las Vegas but with lower stakes. Perhaps the greatest appeal of a cruise vacation is the fact that all of one's worldly cares are suspended for the length of the voyage. Driving is left to the captain, cooking to the chefs. Serving and cleaning is for waiters and busboys; bed making is in the hands of stewards, who magically appear twice a day with fresh linens and towels.

A cruise is an expedition to Antarctica or the Sea of Cortez, with new sights, sounds, and smells over every crest. A cruise is China, Singapore, Bangkok, and Bombay; Norway's fjords and Alaska's glaciers; the Suez and Panama canals; the Bahamas, Caribbean islands and Mexico. It's a geography and history lesson taught with 21st-century political overtones. A cruise is a family reunion, where no one gets stuck with the dishes. It's a summer camp for the whole family, where everything is done for you. A cruise is a honeymoon, an anniversary, or a romantic interlude and it's even the place for an exquisite wedding. It is stargazing, beachcombing, shopping, dancing under the stars, and a sunrise stroll. It's a card player's fix where the addicts can meet, and maybe beat, new opponents every day. A cruise is a photographer's playground where new images fill the lens in a passing kaleidoscope. On some ships, a cruise is a chance to challenge your computer knowledge, to try out new software. Maybe even learn to use the Internet. A cruise is hippie heaven, a polka party, The Grand Ole Opry gone to sea. It's a sports fan's dream with a chance to meet players off the field.

A cruise is anything you want to make it. As cruising sails through the new decade with new ships, new shipboard amenities and facilities, new types of cruises, and new ports of call, it doesn't matter whether you select the top of the line or a budget priced weekend at sea, the cruise will be an excellent travel value when chosen wisely.

As for boredom and confinement, where else can one enjoy the outdoors all day, dance until dawn, participate in all kinds of sports—jogging, tennis, golf, skeet shooting, sunbathing, swimming, and relaxing in a sauna—and be stimulated with seminars on bridge, golf, investments, or just curl up in a quiet nook with that book you have been trying to read for months. On a recent cruise, I learned to tango, found out I should be investing in tax-free municipal bonds, had time to read a best-seller, watched the sun rise, brushed up on duplicate bridge, danced to two different full-size orchestras, and visited five Caribbean islands in ten days. And I didn't participate in half of what was offered on board ship!

Another misconception should be put to rest. Cruise directors are not camp counselors. They encourage participation because passengers who participate have more fun, but they respect the right of free choice. The cruise ship experience is not a regimented experience. It's up to the passenger to set the pace, participate or not, party or just chill out.

Most ships have given up on masquerade parties, but they all seem to cling to passenger talent events. I have never worn a costume to a masquerade party or gone on stage during the talent competition on any of my 350 or so cruises, but I never miss either of those happenings. The most austere passenger at embarkation invariably turns up wearing the silliest costume and crooning Sinatra melodies.

After hundreds of cruises, there's little doubt in my mind that a more pleasant way to spend a vacation has yet to be invented. But I would be less than honest if I didn't confess that no two cruise experiences are identical, no two ships the same. Not every voyage surpasses expectations and not every voyage comes close to a perfect 10 on the enjoyment scale. In all fairness, however, I can honestly say I have enjoyed every cruise experience, albeit in different ways. Travelers should understand that a cruise is a vacation experience; wherein amenities and environment influence who sails that particular ship. Those qualities make a vast difference in passenger manifests and fellow travelers. While there are no exact clones when it comes to ships, they do have more in common than just floating around. They transport, feed, and entertain passengers in a holiday spirit in as painless an environment as tomorrow's technology allows. It's the obvious and sometimes-subtle differences that influence every cruise experience from start to finish.

All ships develop loyal followings, and there's little chance you'll find a devotee sailing on any vessel other than the one to which he or she has become faithful. On a Holland America cruise, I met a woman on her 100th voyage on the same ship, the old *Rotterdam*. In her mind no ship afloat compared with her "home at sea." On the old *Mardi Gras* I met a gentleman who had sailed the ship every month for five years. The line named a suite in his honor. The *QE 2* has a couple of widows who call the ship home year around.

Not even twin ships cut from the same mold are identical, and only the truly experienced observer detects differences, which do not show up on deck plans. Often, cruise lines learn from the first ship in a series and later ships may have the same vital statistics, but changes – which are usually improvements – do occur. Despite similar menus, cuisine differs. The human element involved in service also varies, even on ships operated by the same company.

The experienced cruise passenger has learned to discriminate in selection of ships. The land lover newly turned on to sea travel places more emphasis on where the ship is going. The experienced cruise passenger is more likely to scrutinize amenities offered before selecting a vessel.

Cruise line concerns about filling their ships have resulted in innovative expansion of itineraries, amenities, and facilities. Cruise companies are constantly researching and planning new itineraries, a delicate and complex process that often involves financial risks. The Computer Age may have produced completely automated ships, but to discover new itineraries, cruise areas, or ports that satisfy passengers' sightseeing and shopping requirements is an art. With more megaships on the sea-lanes, new challenges are developing. There are a limited number of islands and ports of call with infrastructures capable of handling thousands of tourists within a six-hour period. In the competitive marketplace, cruise lines must continue to deliver more and different itinerary offerings to an ever-increasing, diverse segment of the travel market.

The future of the cruise industry depends on attracting first-time passengers. Ship owners believe, and have been proved correct, that once a traveler has tasted the salt of the sea, he comes back again and again. Cruising is even more addictive than sand in their shoes, for they have discovered that no land package can equal the value received at sea.

Offerings are diversified, and a quick glance at what's available is likely to convince even the most skeptical traveler that cruising is for everyone, providing they board a ship with personalities that closely match their own vacation preferences.

In an effort to be all things to all vacationers, ships are lining up special interest, theme cruises often staffed with celebrities who perform, lecture, or just sign autographs. During the past year, there were "cruises to lose" (weight), gourmet voyages for those interested in learning to cook or those who merely enjoy eating, others for those trying to kick the smoking habit, and one for shopping addicts that is usually repeated every year before Christmas. There are cruises for singles, bird-watchers, jazz fiends, science-fiction fans, those with green thumbs, and individuals interested in lectures on high finance on the high seas. There are cruises on which bridge addicts can earn master points and tennis buffs can improve their game. Cruise ships have served as lecture halls and concert halls. On a Royal Viking cruise to China some years ago, the San Francisco Opera Company was on board for several performances. There's something special about hearing "Madam Butterfly" as you cruise the China Sea.

There are schools at sea and cruises with musical festivals at sea. Shakespeare and concerts were featured on several voyages. Showboats and name entertainers are used as bait for passengers. Country-music fans dominate special entertainment cruises. I have never selected a cruise because of a special interest on board, but if something in particular turns you on, by all means let that influence your choice of ship. It costs no more, and you're bound to meet other people who share your passion for onions or tomatoes, jazz or classical music.

Itineraries

First questions by most travelers newly turned on to cruising concern itineraries and price. Taking itineraries first, choices cover most of the world. Routes vary, depending on the length of the cruise. The Caribbean cruise is the most difficult to classify because it attracts a greater cross section of Americans. But there is no such difficulty in making up a profile of three-month around-the-world cruise passengers. Cruise rates alone determine who they are. High-priced cruises also mean older passengers with time on their hands and money to spare. There is greater informality on short cruises than on long cruises catering to the well-to-do.

Take it from world travelers, just as there is a ship for everyone, there's a port for everyone. There are three primary port types. (1) Sun and fun ports that focus on beaches and water sports; (2) Shopping ports and destinations that offer bargains in a variety of merchandise and these ports attract passengers who spend their time ashore hunting for bargains. They border on being known as shop-a-holics, determined to win a Black Belt in Shopping, and (3) Sightseeing ports that offer cultural, historic, and scientific land excursions. While all ports fit into at least one, and sometimes all three of these categories, cruisers should do their homework and book the ship that meets their level of vacation expectations.

While the itinerary may generate the initial interest in a particular cruise, often it's the ship and its attractions that ultimately clinch the decision. The vacationer who wants to party all night is seldom the same one who wants to explore a jungle river in an inflatable raft. Selecting the right ship the first time around is vital to enjoying the experience. I say first time because seasoned cruisers often go up the ladder. They start with a mid-level contemporary Caribbean cruises, up the scale to Europe, Alaska and eventually to everyone's dream, the World Cruise.

Price

The next question is price. As surprising as it may be to first time cruisers, there's a cruise that will not break budgets, from economy to first class. A cruise in every instance and in every price category is a better value than a land based resort even if half the facilities were offered on board ships. Ask anyone, even the 10 percent who try cruising and find that it doesn't quite do it for them, and they'll tell you that a cruise vacation offers the best value.

Rates as low as $249 for a three night cruise out of Miami are advertised in my local travel section as I write this book. True, $249 will not buy you a suite, but it will buy a bed in a double-berth room with private bath, your meals, entertainment and transportation to the Bahamas. You couldn't take a similar trip at that price and fly round trip from Miami, as an example, stay in a hotel in Nassau, be offered all you can at breakfast, lunch and dinner, not to mention snacks throughout the day and night, entertainment and round the clock fun and games.

INSIDER TIP

In these anything but "normal" times, almost every cruise line is making special price offers. It is safe to say that ships have all gone down a notch or more in price. When figuring price, consider the category above what you would normally be willing to pay for the cruise. For example, I just received a postcard touting a $$$ (moderate price) ship at a $$ (Budget) price. A one week cruise that listed for $899 was being sold for $499! A luxury ship was offering "second person in the cabin sails free." That amounted to a 50 percent discount and put that $$$$$ (luxury) category ship in the $$$ (moderate) price category.

Cruising Comes with a Guarantee

If you have never cruised, try it. You'll like it. Carnival Cruise Lines even guarantees that you will like it. To back that up, the company promises to refund your money on a per diem basis and fly you back to the port city if you find before reaching the first port of call that cruising is not for you. The company reports that fewer than one tenth of one percent of the more than two million passengers carried annually have taken advantage of the guarantee

First time cruisers are in for an experience they will never forget. Remember the first time you did almost anything? The first time stands out in your memory as the best and will linger forever. Select your first cruise carefully. I have heard passengers talk about their favorite ship and their favorite cruise. Almost always, it is their first cruise. Usually, that first ship doesn't measure up anymore to the ship they are currently sailing, but memories are bright and beautiful, and it was their first exposure to cruising. I'm confident if they returned for a second cruise after gaining some experience, that first ship would look a bit shabby. Unless, that is, they were very selective and sailed the right ship first.

I remember returning to a house I had lived in as a child. My memories were of a huge place, and my disappointment was great. The house wasn't nearly as nice as my present home and close to half its size.

INSIDER TIP

If you select the ship and the cabin solely because the price was too good to be true, write yourself a big note and paste it on the bathroom mirror. It should read: "I am in this cabin because it was a bargain. Think of all the money I saved!" Then, relax and enjoy your holiday.

Ambience

That's the unknown quality that decides the personality of a ship. Cruise ships sometimes like to identify with an ethnic group as to food and service. If you are an Anglophile, look for a ship that is British in flavor. If Italian food is your weakness, look for a ship proud of her Italian chefs and staff. You may even want to combine your ancestry with the type of ship you select. Many passengers do. Ambience also means atmosphere aboard the ship. If you like to dress for dinner and consider a cruise a good time to air the finery, select a ship that boasts about "formal" nights. If you're the slacks or jeans and no-tie type, look for a ship proud of its "informal, casual atmosphere."

Ambience is not confined to ships but is equally applicable to hotels, resorts, restaurants, shops, and bars. Its effect is simple: It makes you feel very comfortable. It is ambience aboard a ship that results in fierce passenger loyalties, even if the ship is not luxurious. In part, ambience explains the often-puzzling passenger attachment to a certain vessel over its more opulent sister. Sometimes attachments or loyalty extend to an entire steamship line and partially explain heavily patronized cruises sailing side by side with others that have a hard time filling staterooms. Selecting a cruise ship involves an emotional element not required when booking an airplane seat.

Old vs. New

There are new ships and old ships, big ones and little ones, and like people, each has a unique personality. Even ships that look alike can be quite different, depending on the character and nationality of the service staff and officers.

Let's take the age of a ship. If the lady is an old and famous luxury liner that has been refurbished, air-conditioned, and brought up to today's standards, passengers generally have nothing to worry about. A ship that was patronized by millionaires a couple of decades ago, when she was in world service, is likely to have remained exceptional. For some, the newest luxury hotel will never come close to the Waldorf Astoria.

But not all old ships measure up. If it's a refurbished ship no one has ever heard of, watch out—especially if the vessel originally operated in European waters and the ship happens to measure less than 10,000 tons. These ships were built for the European market more than a decade or two ago; a market looking for economy, bargain holidays, and passengers not inclined to lodge a single complaint if the mattress was hard and lumpy.

Passengers need not be leery of any ship, large or small, that was built or torn down and completely rebuilt during the past 15 years. Ships in this category were designed for the American-style cruise trade, and they all produce a good measure of what passengers have come to expect.

Another difference between older and newer ships is in accommodations. On older ships, cabins range from very small to comfortably large, and sometimes no two staterooms are alike. There will be inside cabins and outside cabins, singles, doubles, twins, studios, and double-decker bunk rooms, some accommodating as many as four passengers. A few still have cabins without private facilities (bathrooms). Ships built before the 1970s were two- and three-class vessels, and the differences in classes are still evident. If you get a tourist-class cabin on the *Queen Elizabeth 2*, for example, it will be very small, while an old first-class cabin will be spacious.

New ships, particularly those built specifically for cruise service, are constructed so that nearly all rooms are identical except for a few suites or deluxe cabins. Unlike traditional vessels, they were planned for so-called one-class service. Ships built during the past three years boast larger staterooms and a greater number with private verandahs. Except for higher categories staterooms, they usually have small bathrooms with showers and no bathtubs, but they are functionally designed to make the most of available space. The number of staterooms with ocean views is increasing on new ships, and some offer all outside staterooms and more are being built where every accommodation has a verandah. Cruise rates are based on a combination of the ship's equipment, cabin sizes, services offered, and other real and imagined factors considered desirable.

Amenities such as stall showers, hair dryers, personal safes, and refrigerators in cabins are built-in features on all ships built during the past five years. Until a recent renovation, the *Queen Elizabeth 2* did not have most of them, even in the luxury-priced cabins. Carnival's newest mega liners may be short on bathtubs and refrigerators in lower-priced cabins, but other amenities (safes, etc.) are in every cabin.

Size Does Make a Difference

A big difference, which doesn't mean a big ship, is always better than a small ship, or vice versa. While there may be a difference in riding qualities between a big ship (over 50,000 tons) and a smaller one, the degree of difference may not be large enough to notice, except on vessels under 20,000 tons. A small, newer ship may have modern engineering features to make her sail more smoothly than a large, older vessel. Most ships of any size can give you a pretty good bouncing around in rough weather, but since cruises are usually planned for calm waters, rough sailings are not a common problem. As a captain friend said, "It's not the roll of the ship, but the motion of the ocean."

One important difference between small and large ships is that the big ones may not be able to tie up at piers in all ports of call. This necessitates going ashore by tender, which means descending steps (gangplank) and boarding a smaller boat for a short ride to the dock.

On the plus side, larger ships have more space for more amenities like multiple dining and entertainment venues, more deck space and more choices in every area. On the other hand, smaller ships with shallow drafts can venture into ports the big ones cannot enter.

Classification of big and small has changed with mega ships over 100,000 tons making headlines. *Here's how we define size:*

BOUTIQUE: Ships range in size from under 5,000 tons up to 20,000 tons. The smaller the ship, the more likely the intimate environment is conducive to passengers getting to know each other without waiting for introductions. Most of the very small ships are known for their gracious service, single seating dining, and exotic itineraries. Boutique comes in two forms – Boutique Luxury and Boutique Adventure.

MID-SIZE: Ships are up to the 50,000 ton range. At one time they were considered BIG, but all that has changed. These are comfortable contemporary resort-type vessels that take the waters smoothly; offer high energy entertainment, family-type environment, traditional ports of call and some have recently added multiple dining choices. These are excellent ships for first time cruisers and multi-generation cruise vacations.

RESORT XL (EXTRA LARGE): Ships in the 70,000 ton range. They offer everything Mid-Size ships offer but they do it on a grander scale. They carry more passengers, but they have more public rooms. Entertainment is high energy and there's something to do around the clock, if that's what passengers want in a vacation experience. These ships ride well and were built in the 1990s for the most part.

RESORT XXL (EXTRA EXTRA LARGE): are the really big ships in the 85,000 to over 100-000-ton range. They are mega cruisers that sometimes are too wide to transit the Panama Canal. They offer choices in every phase of the cruise vacation – dining, spas, sports, entertainment, staterooms, public space, smoking rooms, dance clubs and the list goes on and on. Some carry over 3,500 passengers when the ships are full. Some are Las Vegas transported out to sea. Royal Caribbean's Voyager-class ships have rock climbing walls, ice skating rink and miniature golf. Carnival's Destiny-class ships have the best professional entertainment, the largest and most lavish spas and children's facilities at sea.

Here's how we identify pricing:

BUDGET $$: Under $125 per person, per day

MODERATE $$$: between $125 and $225 per day per person

PREMIUM $$$$: Priced from $250 to $375 per day, per person

LUXURY $$$$$: Priced over $400 per day, per person

Smooth Sailing

All ships built during the last two decades have stabilizers and most ships built before that have installed stabilizers. There are several types but they all help make for a smoother cruise. The most highly developed of the active stabilizers is the fin type, usually shaped like a balanced rudder. They are retractable in housings within the vessel. The fins are arranged to tilt through an angle of about 20 degrees. With the ship rolling to port, the port fin is inclined downward from the leading edge and the starboard fin upward. Each fin thus contributes a stabilizing movement. On a roll to starboard, the slope of the fin is reversed. In practice, fins are normally designed to give a roll reduction of about 90 percent, which means that if the ship is equipped with stabilizers, the seas won't seem quite as rough when the fins are in use. Stabilizers don't help when the ship hits seas that cause pitching from bow to stern. That's the motion of the ocean, and technology has not come up with a solution to what seamen call pitching.

Sanitation at Sea

U.S. Public Health inspections have made a few headlines and alerted passengers to cleanliness of galleys and ships. Some passengers have been more concerned with kitchen cleanliness than with ship facilities, amenities, and itineraries. Even veteran cruise buffs are asking questions, and the U.S. Public Health Services in Miami and Atlanta, which issue monthly reports on cruise ship inspections, are receiving almost 50 inquiries a day. These reports cover some aspects of the ship sanitation story, and overall, ships are meeting stringent requirements regarding galley cleanliness.

In fact, most ships pass inspections with flying colors. Of the ships based in U.S. ports on year-round service, more than 90 percent routinely pass Public Health inspections with no problems. True, publicity and inspections may have shined up a few galley sinks, but 30 of the 34 ships listed on a recent list rated between 85 and 100 on their inspections as this book was completed.

But a passenger is entitled to ask, "Can cruising be hazardous to my health?" Sanitation inspectors all answered with a resounding "no." They say that ships meeting Public Health's stringent requirements are cleaner than most shoreside restaurants.

The modern vessel-sanitation program began in 1970 after an outbreak of typhoid on a ship. The program was revised in July 1975, when a severe dysentery outbreak on board a passenger vessel required a helicopter to bring toilet paper and medicine to the ship which was a couple of days from land. An investigation followed, and authorities decided the inspections program at the time was not doing an adequate job of reporting ship cleanliness. The program was updated and revised, and when it was instituted, not a single ship met U.S. Public Health Service standards. It took three months before the first vessel scored 98 percent. In order to rate a passing grade, ships had to change food-handling procedures and had to install water-disinfecting equipment. Some had to rebuild food-storage facilities completely; others had to purchase new refrigeration units.

Contrary to what negative publicity may imply, cruise lines welcome Public Health inspectors, and most major companies employ sanitation consultants who sail the ships on a full-time basis. Their sole job is to maintain Public Health Service standards at all times. On the other hand, inspectors are not out to get the ships. When a deficiency is noted, ships are no longer allowed to make a correction while the inspector is still on board, thereby avoiding a low mark. If the inspection mark is below passing, an unannounced recheck of the vessel is made within a short time. Follow-up inspections are conducted within two weeks, when possible, on ships with serious deficiencies.

The old adages about cleanliness don't seem to hold true when it comes to ships that pass or do not pass stringent sanitation inspections. A careful check of the number of gastrointestinal infections requiring medical attention on board ships gave no clues as to the ships' sanitation ratings. One ship earned a perfect score on a Saturday inspection following a cruise on which 67 passengers needed medical treatment for diarrhea. Another ship came off with a 98-point inspection on the day the ship returned to Miami with 55 diarrhea cases on board. Interesting to note, that almost all of the sick passengers had eaten at a Mexican restaurant on shore.

According to ship medical logs, gluttonous indulgence is responsible for almost all gastrointestinal upsets on board ships these days. However, the U.S. Public Health program of unannounced regular inspections has helped reduce incidences of mass outbreaks of diarrhea.

Public Health inspectors pay careful attention to water supply and food. The inspection system is stricter, but not very different from shoreside restaurant sanitation inspections, where high priority is assigned to specific areas termed "disqualifying." Fresh and potable water, the method of disinfections, and connections between the two systems are of great concern to inspectors. Public Health requires certain devices to protect the water supply so there is no back siphoning, for example, between the water you drink and the water used for scrubbing the decks. Also checked are engine-room waterlines to make sure there is no contamination from bilge fluid.

An ongoing check of inspection reports gives no hint as to whether older ships or newer vessels have a better record of passing inspections. Neither do the flags flying from the mast have much influence on the outcome of inspections. Public Health inspectors also take a good look at swimming pools. If you've wondered why the water is drained from pools when your ship is in a U.S mainland, Hawaii, Alaska, or U.S. Virgin Island ports, it's because the vessel is complying with requirements. This means using a filtration system with chlorination, and that's hard to accomplish for vessels alongside for just a few hours.

Public Health Service recommends against using swimming pools and open-air Jacuzzis when the vessel is in a foreign port or harbor because of possible contamination. Many ports around the world are polluted, and when the pool is filled with that kind of water, there's a possibility of waterborne illness. Public Health officials say most ships are immaculate and live up to shipshape traditions. They say the most frequent health problem posed on board cruise ships is the common cold that spreads among passengers.

If you want to check the rating of a particular ship with individual reports on most recent inspections, write to Vessel Inspection Division, Public Health Service, 1015 North America Way, Room 111, Miami, Florida 33132, or access the Internet at FTP.CDC.GOV//PUB/SHIP_INSPECTIONS/SHIP-SCORE.TXT, or telephone (404) 332-4565, which is a fax-back service, and ask for document 510051. Monthly reports listing passing and failing inspection grades are available from the same sources.

Tonnage

Tonnage was first measured in 1422, when the British stipulated that vessels carrying coal had to be measured and marked. No clear system was organized as to how this was to be carried out. Some say the term "tonnage" came into use when fees charged were based on the number of casks of wine a vessel carried. The "tun" at that time was a legal standard measurement, so a tun of wine measured no less than 252 gallons. Over the years, various commissions were appointed, that formulated rules for determining tonnage. The Moorsom System, developed in 1854, is the basis for all current tonnage laws and regulations of most maritime nations.

Tonnage laws provide for gross and net, under tonnage and over tonnage (the sea line), and to the layman it has come to mean the size of the ship. Actually, gross tonnage is the under-deck tonnage, together with the between-deck spaces and all enclosed spaces above deck, including access of hatchways. To judge the size of a passenger ship, consider the tonnage, but look closely at the length, the beam, and the number of decks.

INSIDER TIPS

Tonnage is a confusing aspect of measuring the size of a ship. Ships are not put on a scale and weighed to determine tonnage. According to the Passenger Services Act, tonnage is a measurement of space, not weight. GRT (Gross Registered Tonnage) measures the enclosed space within the confines of the hull and superstructure and there's no uniform way of measuring. Then there is "displacement tonnage." That is the amount of water the ship pushes aside and represents the weight of engines, steel, wood, aluminum and the rest of the vessel. Interesting to note that naval ships are measured by displacement tonnage, while passenger ships are measured by gross tonnage. Also interesting to note that comparing "tonnage", the length and width of new ships is often less than that of some of the great liners of old, but the tonnage is much higher. This is probably due to the height of the new vessels which soar like floating skyscrapers.

Ship Registry

Where the ship is registered or which flag waves in the breeze from the mast has little influence on the type of vessel you will be sailing. Most ships are registered in countries that offer the most "conveniences." Translated into layman's language, this literally means tax and other financial savings. Hence, a "flag of convenience" is defined as registration in a country offering the best savings for an owner who is not necessarily a native of that country. Savings may be in taxes, licensing fees, and wages. This practice has become widespread over the years, as ship-operating conditions have changed. One thing, however, is certain. Growth of large international companies and the pressure of trade unions have combined to make flag havens welcome ports of refuge for a large number of ships.

Many rusty old tubs found it convenient after World War II to trade under the PANLIBHONCO (Panama, Liberia, Honduras, and Costa Rica) flag, and conditions aboard these vessels varied. To the outsider, it appeared that these countries were building substantial fleets, when, in fact, almost all the ships were foreign owned.

In response to the many inquiries by passengers, I have checked further into ship registry and have come up with some rather startling statistics. A recent report of the United Kingdom Chamber of Shipping indicates how the flags are flying these days. Back in 1939, Britain had 16,892 ships flying the royal colors; Liberia had none; Japan had 5,427; and Panama had 722. By the end of the last decade, the figures had changed dramatically. Britain had 21,782; Liberia had 18,404; Japan had 11,902; and Panama had 4,255. In 1973 (the latest figures available at press time), Liberia had 49,824; Japan had 35,031; Panama had 9,414; and British flags remained constant at around 20,000.

The numbers of ships mentioned include tankers, freighters, and cargo liners, and only a small percentage may carry passengers. Also, some countries have built fleets of merchant and fishing vessels, and it is not easy to determine under which flag the ships of multinational companies should sail.

So, you ask, what happened to all those ships flying the Stars and Stripes? Tied up, for the most part, or sold off to foreign owners after the waiting period imposed by Congress. But there's more to it. The real answer was presented on the Senate floor several years ago during a debate designed to channel more oil-tanker trade to U.S.-flag vessels. The gist of the verbal combat indicated it costs an American shipper considerably less to operate under the Liberian flag than to use a vessel registered in the United States.

Foreign registration offers hard-to-match advantages to shippers. Charges can range as low as $1.20 per 100 feet of cargo space, plus a yearly tax of 10 cents per registered ton of capacity. By contrast, American corporate taxes for a ship operating under the U.S. flag could run up to 50 percent of the revenue produced by the vessel.

In addition, U.S. crews cost more. U.S. seaman is paid at least $20,000 a year, or about twice what his foreign counterpart earns. U.S.-flag ships must deal with U.S. unions and pay costs of work benefits, while Bahamian registry, for example, is much more lenient and does not require a minimum-size crew. Don't be surprised to find that the ship's flag has little influence on the personnel working on board ship. Most vessels turn out to be a tossed salad of nationalities. The engine-room crew may be recruited from one country, the catering and housekeeping from another, while the flag on the mast is that of a third. During the past two years, several companies traditionally flagged by home countries have changed registry and flags.

The *Queen Elizabeth 2* caused quite a stir when the flag on the mast was almost replaced by a Bahamian flag a few years ago. The Union Jack stayed, but the crew became international instead of loyally British. Norwegian Caribbean Line gave up the Norwegian flag also in favor of the Bahamas, and Royal Caribbean International threatened, but never did give up the Norwegian flag. It is not unusual to find a ship registered in Panama, for example, and flying that country's flag, but owned by Norwegians and Americans, operated by a U.S. company with a German, Spanish, and Italian deck crew and longer claims an all-English service and deck staff, and is in fact owned by an service by European, Caribbean, Filipino, and Korean staffs.

Even lines traditionally identified with one country are usually hybrids. The *Queen Elizabeth 2* is now part of an American company, but the Union Jack still flies from the mast. British-owned Princess Cruises flies a variety of flags on its vessels and has a staff made up of British, Italian, Indonesian and Portuguese personnel. Carnival Cruise Lines' ships fly Panamanian, Bahamian and Liberian flags and are staffed by Italian deck crews, with service crews from the Caribbean, Europe, and the Orient, and an all-American information and purser's office.

Safety at Sea

The flag flying from the mast has little effect on the safety of passengers and crew because every ship calling at a U.S. port and boarding paying passengers must operate under the rules and regulations of the SOLAS (Safety of Life at Sea) Law.

The U.S. Coast Guard inspects all passenger ships (American and foreign registry) when they board passengers at U.S. ports to make sure they comply with SOLAS. The criteria applied are very close to U.S. safety standards, covering such things as emergency equipment, fire safety regulations, drills for the crew, and safety of the hull and ship's machinery. These standards are agreed to by all major seafaring countries (about 90 nations, including the United States) and have been in effect since 1966. Even ships from countries not covered by the 1960 SOLAS convention are also inspected and must meet present U.S. standards for safety at sea, which are even more stringent. The only ships not inspected by U.S. Coast Guard are those that board passengers in foreign ports and never enter a U.S. port for embarkation of passengers. Coast Guard inspections are always held during a ship's first call at a U.S. port. A thorough check of safety equipment is made at that time, and the vessel is certified to embark passengers in the United States. After that, inspections are held at least once every three months, when the cruise ship comes dockside at a U.S. port. The Coast Guard has about 900 inspectors assigned to check for ship safety.

What happens if a ship doesn't measure up? The Coast Guard can either detain the vessel until the problem is corrected or prohibit her from boarding passengers in U.S. ports until the ship meets requirements.

Shipping companies welcome these Coast Guard inspections and cooperate. I am reminded of a Panamanian-flag ship that entered the cruise market a few years ago. She was touted and advertised, but on inaugural sailing day, Coast Guard inspectors were not satisfied with the way her electrical system was put together. She didn't receive sailing papers, and passengers who had already boarded for this first cruise were disembarked and sent home while the cruise line imported electricians, completely rewired the vessel, and delayed her entry into the U.S. market for about three weeks until she met the tough Coast Guard standards.

Since 1965, cruise ships have tightened safety standards at sea by adding automatic fire doors, smoke detectors, and sprinkler systems. They have eliminated most combustibles used in ship construction. All cruise ships are required to have watertight compartments with watertight doors that can be closed from the bridge to prevent the ship from sinking, even if several compartments are flooded. By the end of 1997, ships were required to install low-level lighting in public areas, additional fire doors and sprinklers, and smoke alarms. Some companies decided not to invest the many hundreds of thousands of dollars required to bring vessels up to these standards, and many older vessels were retired or sold to companies planning to sail them in waters exempt from SOLAS.

There is a catch-22. Vessels operating within maritime waters of the flag on the mast are exempt from some of the requirements. Hence, many of the ships sailing between Greek island ports, for example, or on the Nile do not meet the 1997 SOLAS safety rules.

International convention requires that all passengers participate in lifeboat drills on cruise ships. If there is an emergency at sea, passengers will be told via a public address system what to do. Ship personnel are assigned responsibility for specific passengers. It is wise not to disregard the drill just because it is a nuisance to don the lifejacket and report to a muster station. Although accidents at sea are rare, passengers should be familiar with boat stations and emergency procedures.

As far as ship construction is concerned, modern cruise ships are considered fireproof, which doesn't mean there can't be a fire on board. It means that should a fire break out, it will be contained quickly with fire proof doors that close automatically. All countries abiding by the present international convention are required to conduct at least yearly inspections of every ship's hull, machinery, and safety equipment, regardless of the age of the vessel. These inspections are in addition to U.S. Coast Guard drills.

According to an officer in charge of the U.S. Coast Guard's inspection-compliance unit, passengers can feel safe on a cruise ship. He says, "You will be safer on a modern cruise ship than in some of the new high-rise buildings; both are designed to be basically fireproof, but on a complying ship there is less danger."

The only time you should check as to whether the ship meets SOLAS requirements is when the ship boards passengers outside the United States and offers air-sea packages. In this type of situation—for instance, when passengers board the ship in Barbados or Martinique or a romantic Greek port—the ship is not inspected by the U.S. Coast Guard, and it's up to travelers to ask whether the ship meets SOLAS requirements.

Itineraries

Cruise lines are globalizing and sending ships to roam the waters of the world visiting exotic ports of call. Ships that traditionally cruise the Caribbean are venturing into European waters. Ships that sailed to Mexico's west coast have come east. Some Florida vessels have moved to California, others have moved their homeport to San Juan to allow for cruising to the lower Caribbean. The number of cruises to South America has increased with everything from 10 to 50 day itineraries offered. In the comfort of a cruise liner, passengers can cruise through the Panama Canal, the Straits of Magellan, and around Cape

Horn via Punta Arenas, Tierra del Fuego, and Beagle Channel.

The Caribbean has long been a popular cruise destination, but there are still islands that are seldom visited. New additions to itineraries include Dominica, Grenada, Virgin Gorda, Tobago Cays in The Grenadines, and the Abacos in the Bahamian Out Islands chain. Australia, New Zealand, Tahiti, Fiji, and other regions of the South Pacific are listed in itineraries. Most navigable waterways anywhere in the world welcome one or more of the hundreds of cruise ships. Voyages last from two to more than 100 days, and they carry a new breed of passenger.

Cruise the Mediterranean and your fellow passengers are most likely lovers of history and antiquity. Shore excursions allow for stops at ancient walled cities, homes of great artists, and museums housing treasures we learned about in school. In selecting a Mediterranean cruise, one needs only to focus on a favorite period in history and select an itinerary that covers that region.

Archaeology buffs are delighted with Eastern Mediterranean cruises to Egypt, Israel, Greece, and Turkey, world conditions permitting. It's a chance to see monuments of the ancient world blended into modern societies. A typical itinerary could include a couple of Greek islands, Haifa for a day in Jerusalem, and Alexandria for a tour to the pyramids. Closer to home are cruises to the Western Caribbean and a chance to visit Mayan ruins on the Yucatán Peninsula.

For a close-up of American life along the Mississippi, there are steamboat cruises; and for a glimpse of Asia's carefully guarded past, there are voyages through China and Japan, Hong Kong and Singapore, India and Sri Lanka, and down through the South Pacific and New Zealand.

Sun and fun attract passengers to ships that cruise the Caribbean, the Atlantic, and the Mexican waters; and adventure seekers are taking to ships cruising the Amazon and uncharted seas. There are companies devoted to sending their vessels to those hard-to-reach places of the world, and one company (Salen Lindblad Cruises) even retraces three Northwest Passages from Newfoundland across the northern ice cap to Yokohama, Japan.

Time in Port

Tell me and I will forget – Show me and I will remember
Involve me and I will understand
Confucius

The length of time a ship stays in each port should be a major consideration if visiting that island or that city influences your selection of the ship. Less than six hours in any port is almost a waste of time. To find actual time in port, add at least an hour to the scheduled arrival time, because it takes that long to clear formalities in each country; then subtract an hour from the sailing time. What you're left with is the time you'll have on shore. And if that leaves you with a feeling of having rushed around on a hot and sticky island, don't cruise the ship because of that specific port, look for other reasons. Should you sail anyway, figure the visit was a teaser for your return at another time. Subtract an additional hour if the ship tenders. It takes at least that long for the roundtrip tender ride from ship to shore and back again to the mother ship.

Remember, cruising is a unique form of travel in which transportation is incidental, and the urgency of arriving at a specific destination has been deleted as a requirement. The sojourn aboard ship is the major consideration. Ports of call are a bonus, an added attraction.

Read the fine print on your passage contract (cruise ticket), and you'll find the captain has the right to change the itinerary at his discretion, and he does, when certain conditions prevail. There is no voting on his decisions. His vote (and the ship owners') is the only one that counts. Be assured, however, changes are made only when necessitated by safety concerns, tides or mechanical malfunctions, and decisions are not made frivolously. Passenger safety and convenience are a top priority.

INSIDER TIP

In times of International crises, such as 9/11, ships will change courses almost over night in order to cruise in safe waters. Cruise lines reserve the right to change itineraries without prior notice. When international conditions swing to that kind of situation, there's a good chance you may not reach the farthest point on a short cruise. It won't help threatening to sue, and it won't help if fellow passengers take up the cry and pass a petition demanding a refund. The "conditions" of your cruise purchase define responsibility. Cruise lines making itinerary changes usually notify travel agents and passengers already booked, so they have the option of canceling prior to sailing time. When changes are made for mechanical reasons, there are no options open to passengers. Select your cruise for the ship and the cruising area of the world. If you happen to miss an island or two, you'll disembark having had more time at sea, and that's not all bad.

Long or Short Itineraries

Life is already too short to waste on speed
Edward Abbey

The shorter the cruise, the younger the passengers on the manifest. Cruises lasting more than two weeks attract people with time and money, both qualities are found more often in the over-60-year-old community. The greatest cross section is found on one-week cruises.

There's a wide gulf between a weekend cruise from Miami to Nassau and a North Cape cruise as well as between a one-week Caribbean trip and a world cruise. Obviously, in each case passengers and their interests are different. The weekend trip to Nassau attracts those who want to be entertained aboard ship, to sun themselves on beaches, and to gamble in the Nassau casinos. The short cruise out of Los Angeles (San Pedro) attracts a similar crowd anxious to escape the California city tumult. The contrasting North Cape passenger is generally the type of tourist who prefers the wonders of sea travel over fast indoor entertainment. He or she is a traveler more at home in the ozone-filled air of a quiet fjord than in the noise of a smoke-filled nightclub.

Cruises range from an overnight or a day trip to nowhere to around-the-world voyages lasting more than 100 days. Quick to capitalize on a growing trend toward short vacations and easy-to-book quickie getaways, several ships are now positioned as year-round "weekenders." They sail on Monday to Friday and Thursday to Sunday on three night schedules. Four night sailings are the other option. The Friday afternoon sailing that returns early Monday morning and attracts the younger working crowd anxious to leave it all behind for three nights. Carnival Cruise Lines, Norwegian Caribbean, and Royal Caribbean International depart from ports in Florida, and Disney Cruise Line as well as Carnival and Royal Caribbean offer short cruises out of Cape Canaveral. Some include stops at "private" islands in the Bahamas as well as at Nassau. Monday sailings also include a visit to either Key West (Florida) or Freeport (in the Bahamas) in addition to Nassau. Some are venturing as far as Cozumel, Mexico. Similar short cruises sail from San Pedro, outside Los Angeles, to Catalina Island and Ensenada and add San Diego on four-night cruises.

Wherever you find yourself in your travels, if there's an ocean nearby, there are bound to be short cruises. Inland New England waters are being navigated by American Cruise Lines, and there are riverboats on the Ohio River and

Mississippi River. KD German Rhine Line offers two- and three-day cruises up the Mosel and Rhine rivers. There are dozens of short cruises from Piraeus to the Greek islands, and there's even a 23-hour cruise out of Portland, Maine.

For years, short cruises were considered the domain of aging vessels, but that has changed along with travelers' habits. which are moving toward more frequent, shorter vacations. Cruise lines have a tendency to keep up with trends and are committing new and larger vessels to this short cruise market, which appeals to families, fitness buffs, reunion groups, and younger passengers who cannot afford the time or money for a week at sea. Short cruises also appeal to travelers as a "safe way" to test the waters. It is possible to take a two-to-five-day cruise, not only from Miami, Fort Lauderdale, and Cape Canaveral but also from Alaska, Bermuda, Africa, and in the Far East. Voyages in some areas are seasonal, but even world cruises sometimes offer segments of as few as five days.

The best opportunity to test the waters on super liners, which normally sail longer voyages, is when companies reposition a ship's homeport and the ship finds itself with a day or two or three between voyages. This is called a "repositioning voyage." Rather than leave the ship sitting idle at the dock or crossing the Atlantic without passengers, the company runs a "sale" either to fill the ship or to introduce it to potential customers.

Few people are aware, for example, that they can book the *Queen Elizabeth 2* for a short cruise. Last year, the ship had a couple of cruises to nowhere out of New York between transatlantic crossings. The consensus of opinion on board was that going nowhere is a marvelous experience. There are no ports of call, but there are lots of activities, entertainment, and superb food and service. Itineraries are more important when the cruise lasts longer than one week. If you're a sailor at heart and are cruising for the love of the sea, don't select a ship that calls at a different port every day. You'll be happier on board a vessel that spends more time at sea, especially if you're looking to cultivate new friends. On the other hand, if the pulse of a ship renders you lethargic, sail a vessel that puts into port at least every other day.

By far the most popular cruise length is the one-week voyage. During a seven-night period, the ship visits three to five foreign ports of call aboard contemporary and usually almost brand- new cruise vessels offering every price range. They sail from San Juan and U.S. East and West Coast ports. During summer months, almost a dozen very good ships sail from Vancouver, in British Columbia, to Alaskan waters, and others sail from the Greek islands and in the Mediterranean. Next in popularity are 10- to-14-day voyages from these same ports and from more exotic embarkation points such as Hong Kong, Singapore, and Kobe, Japan.

Around the World

If you're like me, spending over 100 days circling the globe on a cruise ship is first on your "someday" dream list. We have several options in the coming years. For a while, these lengthy voyages were decreasing in number and popularity due to world events and aging vessels. In 2003 and 2004, six ships will be offering voyages of between 75 and 105 days, and additional vessels have announced long voyages that can be combined into as many as 80 days at sea.

U.S.-based vessels on world cruises normally tend to make lengthy voyages in the Pacific Basin, around South America, or circling the Indian Ocean. Although cruise lines prefer to sell complete voyages, economic reality dictates that lengthy cruises also be sold in segments. On the theory that part of a world cruise is better than none, most lines are offering free (or low-cost) air arrangements so passengers who cannot afford the time or money for the entire journey may join the vessel for as few as 10 or 12 days or more in some exotic area of the world.

Crystal Cruises, Cunard Line, Holland America Line, Silversea, Radisson Seven Seas Cruises, Silversea Cruises, P&O and Princess Cruises have vessels are scheduled for lengthy voyages in the next few years, but not all are circumnavigations. Some voyages focus on the Pacific, others on South America and Antarctica, but the most popular world cruise itinerary remains a complete circumnavigation.

The largest ship making a true world cruise is still the venerable 70,000-ton *Queen Elizabeth 2*. The smallest vessel on a world voyage is the *Deutschland*, which incidentally makes the longest sailing from Las Palmas, Canary Islands, to Yemen. Official language on board is German, so that should be an indication of the passenger manifest.

The *QE2* sails for 106 days round trip from New York, but passengers may embark in Ft. Lauderdale, Los Angeles and Honolulu, as well as a various ports around the world for shorter segments. Holland America's *Amsterdam* sails round trip from Ft. Lauderdale on the company's 38th world cruise. The cruise will visit 38 ports including Antarctica, China, South Korea and Japan. *Crystal Symphony's* 104-day odyssey from Fort Lauderdale will terminate in Los Angeles. The voyage also includes Cape Horn and Antarctica. Radisson's *Seven Seas Mariner's* 108-night voyage begins in Los Angeles and ends in Fort Lauderdale.

P&O has two vessels on world cruises and are very well priced. Both voyages sail round trip from Southampton. The *Oriana* makes a 92-day voyage heading west while the *Aurora's* 91-day voyage heads east toward the Caribbean, through the Panama Canal to San Francisco, then through the Pacific for a true circumnavigation. Rates are extremely attractive and minimums start at less than $100 a day, per person.

Rates vary greatly on world cruises. On *QE2*, for example, they go from a minimum of about $25,000 to $250,000. On Holland America, rates are as low as $27,000. Rates quoted include early booking, special incentives, past passenger discounts and a myriad of other opportunities to save some money. All of the voyages are available in segments, some as short as one week, some almost as long as the complete voyage.

INSIDER TIP

About 25 years ago, after my 10th cruise, my travel dreams changed. Everyone has a "someday" cruise and mine was to circumnavigate the world on the venerable *Queen Elizabeth 2*. My dream cruise came true in 2000 and it was repeated in 2001. How lucky can I get? Here's what I learned about some-day cruising. Don't put it off! Do it when you are physically able, mentally free of family and work responsibilities and reserve your space a year or two before you retire! Do it when you become an empty nester. The least expensive cabin on any ship is the experience of a lifetime. A brief summary and tips follow. For a detailed diary, from preparing for the voyage to debarkation, read my weekly diary on the Internet: www.cruisecritic.com. Keyword: **worldcruise**

World Cruises

> *The future belongs to those*
> *Who believe in their dreams*
> Eleanor Roosevelt

Here's an excerpt from Ethel's World Cruise Diary:

"There are 380 of us in the same boat. Of the 1200 passengers on board, we're committed to sailing the entire 104-day *Queen Elizabeth 2* Millennium World Cruise. Each of us has a story; each has a reason that brought him or her on board. There's the lotto winner from Ohio, the former model from New York who spends her afternoons taking dance lessons and her evenings dancing with social hosts. There are a couple of young dot-com millionaires from Silicone Valley who sold out before the E Market crashed.

But there are others like Bill Pensley from Middlesex (U.K.) who lives alone in the house he was born in 69 years ago, worked the same job for 40 years, walked the same route between his house and office daily and week end visits to the local pub was recreation. His routine never varied and his curiosity never even took him to London. But all that changed one windy December day when he took notice of a travel bureau window display beckoning vacationers with palm trees and oceans and offering the world on the *QE2*. He says the picture kept flashing though his mind all morning as he sat at his drafting table. Instead of lunch, he headed for that travel bureau, booked the minimum priced inside cabin on the world cruise leaving the following week. He never went back to the office. Bill books every year in the same minimum-priced cabin and continues to see the world, but he still hasn't taken the train to London.

At the other end of the economic spectrum is the couple from the Isle of Man sailing their eighth world voyage. They occupy the two top priced duplex suites and consider *QE2* their "winter home." The ship is also the winter home of a St. Louis retired doctor and his wife who were sailing their 27th world cruise on this ship. They leave their cruise clothes and family pictures on board and when they arrive the following year, their cabin is set up with their personal items.

The repeat world cruise contingent is made up of about 150 passengers who comprise the "inner circle", or what I call *QE2* Groupies. It's a tale of fidelity for passengers who come back in a mode similar to coming home. They have developed a fierce loyalty to the ship and wouldn't consider a different vessel. Itinerary is unimportant. It's the ship and the familiar camaraderie that bring them back year after year. They have seen it all; done it all and don't bother with shore excursions or adventurous explorations on shore.

This is my second world cruise and I have learned a lot about people who take cruises that last 100 days. They are not a different breed of traveler. For the most part, they are the same passengers I have met on seven and 10 day cruises during the past 30 years. They are just at different stages of their lives and are living their "someday" travel dreams. Most of us sign up for shore excursions, attend lectures that enhance the experience and understanding of ports of call and we never leave our cabins without a camera. We are easy to distinguish from the groupies who never carry cameras, shop familiar flea markets around the world, seldom take an organized tour and dress for dinner nightly.

In this regard, the *QE2* is no different from Holland America ships, Seabourn, Silversea, Crystal, Princess or the P&O ships that offer long cruises and world circumnavigations. Each has developed a cult following that cruises annually and books on board to guarantee the same cabin for the following year.

QE2 is best compared to a small city, divided in suburbs. The groupies are the permanent residents who study the newcomers before accepting them as neighbors. Seasonal visitors are passengers who opt for segments, board for as few as three days and as many as 60 or 70 days. In all, I would guestimate that some 8,000 passengers have been on board, embarking and debarking, during this 104-day voyage.

Our neighborhood changes in every port. On this voyage, we are carrying passports from 42 countries. The demographics also change with each segment. At one point, Americans made up less than one-third of the manifest. Brits and Australians divided the remaining two thirds almost equally, but there also were passengers from Japan, Germany, India and South Africa.

Picking up on my own diary, I discovered early on that full world passengers have a few perks that are not offered to segment travelers. It sort of follows the neighborhood plan, although all economic tiers are included. Let's call it the World Cruise Country Club, which has exclusive access to the Boardroom for newspapers, late coffee and sweets, light sandwiches, tea and whatever.

When it comes to housing and dining, people who live in the most expensive neighborhood, eat in the 231-seat super elegant Queen's Grill. Not quite so posh, but still qualified as deluxe are accommodations booked by passengers assigned to Princess and Britannia Grills. Then comes the mid-category Caronia, a really beautiful restaurant accommodating 554 passengers. It was completely gutted and rebuilt during the late 1999 refit and a few Grill category passengers are opting for Caronia dining. Lowest cabin category passengers are assigned to the Mauritania Restaurant, the only one that uses two sittings to accommodate about half of the passenger manifest.

Interesting to note that menus are practically the same in all dining rooms, but number of choices decreases restaurant-to-restaurant, as does the opportunity for off-the-menu special orders, service ratio, ambiance and attention to detail which make the difference. While *QE2* is a one-class ship when it comes to public rooms and entertainment venues, dining room and stateroom categories run true to the adage, you get what you pay for. That's not the case on other ships that follow world routes. Everyone eats in the same dining room and enjoys the same facilities but suite passengers do enjoy extra perks on all of the world cruise ships.

Big differences are in size and location of cabins. Rates for the entire world cruise can range from a low of about $20,000 per person to a high of about $250,000 per person, based on discounts for early booking, early payment, past passenger perks and a few more possibilities.

The voyage has been a memorable experience, but it wasn't all fun and games from day one. There were moments when I wasn't sure a world cruise was the best decision I had ever made. I missed my bed, my friends, my family and my e-mail connections. After our casual at-home dress code, it took some getting accustomed to dressing up every night.

And, when the reality of being away for over three months and living in one room hit me, a heavy down feeling took over my usual disposition. Adjustments were required. I had a hard time sharing a bathroom even with my husband and I was emotionally uncomfortable in a strange environment that would control my life for 104 days.

On one of my early down days, I met Jane and Bill Gilbert from Denver in the Boardroom. On their 19th world cruise, Jane noted my feelings and said, "It takes a month to become part of the community." She was right on! Sometime during the third week, I found what I was looking for in my cabin in less than 10 minutes. That was the moment I started to feel at home and in the mood to socialize with fellow passengers and reacquaint myself with the vessel.

I also learned that romance at sea is alive and well. A gentleman from Oxford who worked on the ship four years ago as a social host is on board as a passenger with his new Australian wife who also happened to be a passenger four years ago. A couple who met last year at a dance class on board is honeymooning on a repeat voyage. Then there's a young computer whiz who fell in love with his Japanese tablemate three years ago on a similar world voyage. They were married on board in San Francisco during this cruise.

There also are same-time-next year romances. Jane is a retired judge from Illinois. Frank is from the U.K. No one is talking about his or her personal marital status but they have been meeting on board for the world cruise since that first encounter 10 years ago. We shared a taxi with them in Cape Town and they readily admit that they don't see each other during the rest of the year and only communicate when it gets close to the next world voyage.

It's easy to spot other budding and rekindled romances. Three months together in the same boat is longer than most courtships these days. We see passengers who embarked single, debarking as couples. We see couples who were grumpy and distant from each other at embarkation dancing cheek to cheek after the first few weeks.

By mid-cruise, our pace slows to match the balmy Southern Hemisphere weather. We're into the rhythm of the ship. Something seems to happen to the psyche on a lengthy voyage. Days and weeks run into each other and the reality of life on shore gives way to the reality of day-to-day life at sea where you have no control over where you are going or when you will arrive. What's more you really don't care. The most frequently asked question is "What day is this?" Never mind the date. That becomes unimportant. The day is measured in importance because it denotes the evening dress code and the number of sea days before the next port of call. Without our Daily Program, we would be lost at sea.

While one of the great luxuries of living on a ship is avoiding decisions, there are a few we are forced to make. I counted 10 pre-lunch choices ranging from dance classes to financial lectures and 12 more options during the afternoon.

Evenings are just as laced with choices. Tonight, there's a classical concert by a cellist in the Theatre, two shows featuring Britain's top society jazz band and The Gold and Silver Ball in the Queen's Room. There's also dancing in the Yacht Club, socializing in the sophisticated Chart Room with a harpist providing background music, the larger Crystal Bar and the less formal Golden Lion Pub, which is an all-day watering hole. The Yacht Club's Caribbean Island music attracts the late night disco crowd while most of the ship heads for the Lido and more food to tide them over until morning.

During the first few weeks, we tried to do everything, attend every lecture, and move from event to event. By the fourth week, we settled down, slept a little later and did some picking and choosing. The Dance Class remained on the schedule, as did the most knowledgeable speakers who could keep our eyes from drooping. We dropped afternoon tea because it was too close to the time we finished lunch and those were calories we could eliminate without too much salivating, except for the scones. Our after dinner activities remained fairly constant. We chose dancing in the Queen's Room and usually the late show if the entertainer was in the not-to-be-missed category. We were particularly interested in Australian and South African entertainers considered "name stars" back home, but rarely, if ever, heard of in the U.S.

We have traveled more than 55,000 miles, visited five continents, 40 ports of call, learned to dance a great tango, were introduced to varied cultures and people, topography and languages. We met authors, historians, politicians and "name" stars of stage, television and screen that came on board to entertain us every evening. We sailed the Atlantic, Pacific and Indian Oceans as well as the Coral, Celebis, Tasman, and China Seas and crossed the equator four times and changed our watches 14 times, going and coming. It's more than most people will ever experience in a lifetime, yet it feels like we have just scratched the world's surface.

World cruising should come with a warning. It really is addictive. More than 200 passengers rushed to book the newly announced *Queen Mary 2* which is not scheduled to be completed and launched until January 2004. Surprisingly, very few of the groupies are showing much enthusiasm. Most of the *QM* bookings came from world cruisers like us and passengers opting for segments of this voyage. We figure by 2004, we'll be able to afford the time and money."

INSIDER TIPS

Total Traveler Cruise Critics choices for "The Best" are indicated after most areas of the cruise experience. A complete listing is in "The Best of the Best" Index. The "Best Ships" are not listed in the order of "Best', but as a choice in ships that will appeal to travelers who are looking for specific features in vacation choices. Ships were rated on a scale of one to 10 in all phases of the cruise product. In some instances, three ships or companies make the top list; in others it is one or two ships or companies. In all instances, ships were rated against other ships in the same price and size category. For specific details, see the chapter, Cruise Companies and Their Ships", which profiles all of the major vessels.

TT CRITICS CHOICE FOR THE BEST WORLD CRUISES:

$$ to $$$$$ – *Queen Elizabeth 2*
(Traditional ship very popular with repeat passengers; some take the three month voyage annually. Itinerary calls for a complete circumnavigation)

$$$$$ – *Seven Seas Mariner*
(A mid-size all-suite, all-veranda new ship with new amenities. Three month itinerary begins in Los Angles and finishes in Fort Lauderdale).

$$$$$ – *Crystal Symphony*
(Very popular cruise itinerary that includes South America's east and west coast ports, as well as Easter Island)

$$$$ – Holland America's *Amsterdam*
(Veteran world cruise passengers sail the company's annual voyage. It's an extremely comfortable itinerary that goes around South America. Round trip from Fort Lauderdale)

$$ – P&O *Aurora*
(Budget-priced, it is an excellent value for a circumnavigation from Southampton)

Fellow Passengers

A good holiday is one spent among people
Whose notions of time – Are vaguer than yours
John Boyton Priestly

It may come as a surprise to the uninitiated, but cruise ships are no longer floating repositories of the archaeological remains of Geriatrica. The contemporary cruise passenger is a cross section of America on the upbeat side. Passengers are couples and singles, families and friends, secretaries, company presidents, blue-collar workers, shop owners, housewives, movie stars, dowagers and doctors, lawyers and merchant chiefs.

There is such a wide cross-section of cruise passengers these days that it is hard to define the mix on any passenger manifest. But there are a few general personal preferences that carry over from life ashore to life at sea. Short cruises tend to attract younger passengers because of time and money. Large ships on one week cruises have passengers from every walk of life – the plumber, the baker, the merchant and the professional – with the family in many cases. On honeymoons, first, second, or who's counting, and even passengers who spend winters on world cruises and those who take off for one week here and there.

Seasonally, the passenger mix changes. During school holidays, contemporary ships carry lots of kids and multigenerational groups. The rule of thumb that experienced travelers follow is simple. The longer the cruise, the older the crowd. The more expensive the cruise, the less chance of meeting your house cleaner on board. It's more likely your fellow passengers will be in the upper economic strata. On theme, or special interest cruises, you will find at least half of the passengers share similar interests.

INSIDER TIP

So who sails which ships? Single women travelers are found in large numbers on ships with onboard gentlemen hosts. Single men are discovering that ships with onboard hosts have more single women who like to dance. That's the over-50-year-old traveling crowd. Under-40- year-olds usually opt for a ship with discos and/or smaller vessels. Professional types want more boutique-size ships with less entertainment and more ports of call. Over-70-year-old passengers who have been there, done that are on board ships that require less air travel. (See "Ship Profiles" chapter for details.)

Romance at Sea

I would love you all the day – Every night, we would kiss and play,
If with me you'd fondly stray, – Over the hill and far away.

John Gray

Ships and romance have been synonymous in song and prose since Cleopatra sailed the Nile. Closer to our time period, who can forget Cary Grant and Deborah Kerr when they found love during a transatlantic voyage in the classic movie, *An Affair to Remember*? The film's theme song conjures up visions of elegant cabins and dinners for two. Or, the Fred Astaire-Ginger Rogers courtship in *Shall We Dance*? In verse and in song, in fiction and in fact, society has come to suspect that love declared under the stars is never quite the same unless there is a deck beneath our feet.

Every ship offers romance, from the 100-passenger to the 3500 – hundred passenger vessels. There's just something about sea air that puts passengers into a romantic mood. The most grumpy couple married more than 25 years and sniping at each other at embarkation are holding hands before the end of the voyage.

Maybe it's the isolation from day-to-day chores. Could be leaving the kids with grandma and having a chance to rekindle those romantic candles. Whatever it is that puts cruise travelers into romantic moods, it works. Sex does happen on ships. Many a child has been conceived on a cruise, including my own two youngest grandchildren. One carries the name of the ship for life. His middle name is Paul and the parents will recall the voyage forever.

TT CRITICS CHOICE OF THE MOST ROMANTIC SHIPS AT SEA:

Boutique $$$$
> *Paul Gauguin* (The Tahiti itinerary adds to the romance of the intimate and plus vessel. Quiet corners on board, and romantic settings on shore)

Wind Spirit/Song/Star/Surf
> (Nothing beats the romance of evenings on deck with the huge sails flapping in the breeze)

Silver Wind/Cloud
> (Intimate vessels with superb staterooms and lots of tables for two in the dining room)

Resort $$$ XL-XXL
Carnival Spirit/Pride/Legend
(Mix, if you like, or settle into a quiet spot. Dine in the supper club, dance until the sun rises)
Dawn/Sea/Sun/Ocean Princesses
(Sophisticated vessels with lots of cozy corners)
Millennium, Summit, Infinity
(Celebrity Cruises – Private small rooms, a chatty Martini Bars, tables for two)

Getting Married at Sea

Nothing beats the dream experience of holding hands with your significant other, strolling a teak deck on a moonlit night and the lulling sounds of rippling waters as a backdrop. It's a scene repeated frequently in late night movies and it usually culminates with the ship's Captain legalizing the union in a romantic wedding ceremony. But that was just a dream until a few years ago. As one of my favorite captains, Ferrucio Rocconi used to say, "Marriages performed at sea were valid only for the duration of the voyage."

Working within the legal system, cruise lines are making those romantic realities legal. Wedding ceremonies and receptions are held on ships, but those ships had to be in port when the binding ceremony was performed with a properly licensed notary or clergyman officiating. The Captain's role was reduced to a guest or witness, until recently when Princess Cruises found a way to make dreams come true and the company added another stripe to it's Love Boat tag. When Princess ships were reflagged, the company registered its Grand-class vessels in Bermuda and that paved the way for legal weddings to be performed on the high seas in accordance with Bermuda laws. Weddings at sea were in the planning stages when the vessel was built and the 36-seat "Hearts and Mind Wedding Chapel" was included in construction plans.

Weddings at sea have become so popular, Princess, Carnival and Royal Caribbean and other cruise lines building new ships include chapels designed specifically to accommodate the growing number of requests for weddings. Cruise lines have shoreside personnel well versed in the details required prior to seaboard nuptials. Except for the *Grand Princess* and her newer sisters, *Golden Princess* and *Ocean Princess*, marriage ceremonies still take place on board ship when it is docked in a U.S. port or on shore in ports of call.

Withstanding the amenities offered in wedding packages by all ships, there's no better (and no less expensive) place to celebrate vows than on a ship. It's also an economical honeymoon and is available in all price ranges from budget to super deluxe. A large percentage of couples who married or honeymooned at sea return to the same ship to celebrate anniversaries and other special occasions. Ships must be doing something right for newlyweds. Some even return for another honeymoon, sometimes with the same man or woman.

Caribbean cruises are the most popular for floating weddings. The Port of Miami leads the pack, but there have been weddings on secluded beaches along the route, on private islands, on a glacier during an Alaska voyage and even an undersea ceremony for a couple of committed divers.

Weddings at sea are win-win situations. The happy couple experiences that late night movie moment, albeit usually during daylight hours, and they do it without breaking the budget. Compared to formal wedding in swanky hotels, weddings at sea are relatively inexpensive and combine the cost with a romantic honeymoon.

The basic requirement enforced by all cruise lines is that wedding arrangements include the honeymoon. With numbers of shipboard weddings increasing dramatically, companies that specialize in sea-related weddings have been formed and cruise lines recommend dealing with them, or with someone in the company's "Wedding Department." All cruise lines have departments that handle weddings.

The happy couple is required to book a honeymoon cruise and it's not unusual for family and friends who attend the wedding to come along on the honeymoon. This is particularly true when the wedding is held in an offshore port like St. Thomas, for example, or when it is held on board in port prior to departure.

I was invited to the first wedding held on *Grand Princess* during the inaugural voyage. Members of both families and a few friends were on board for the big event. Thirty guests paid their own way on a 10-day cruise so they could attend the wedding. My own second wedding was on board Carnival's *Ecstasy* at noon on a port day in Miami. We had 150 guests and 20 of the out of towners stayed on board for the one-week cruise. We jumped ship at the first port and headed to Europe to catch another ship for an extended honeymoon cruise. I have yet to sail a ship without a bride and groom who were either married on board prior to sailing or who tie the knot in one of the ports of call.

HERE'S A BRIEF RUN DOWN ON CRUISE LINE POLICIES COVERING WEDDINGS AT SEA:

Princess Cruises remains the only company that offers wedding ceremonies with the Captain officiating while the ship is sailing. The *Grand Princess* has hosted more than 1,000 weddings since the program started about four years ago. The company has expanded the program to the *Ocean* and *Golden Princesses* and they feature the first Wedding Chapel Cams, which allow couples to invite stay-at-home family and friends to their wedding via cyberspace. A special link on the Princess web site allows direct access to the wedding as it happens.

Carnival Cruise Lines hosts over 2,000 weddings annually on board its ships. The company limits the number in each port but weddings are hosted on all of the company's ships. Carnival's new Spirit class ships (*Spirit, Pride* and *Legend*) have wedding chapels.

Celebrity Cruises reports that its homeport of Fort Lauderdale is its most popular wedding site, but passengers have been married in Alaska, Bermuda, San Juan and Jamaica. Norwegian Cruise Line has hosted more than 5,000 weddings since its program began about four years ago with as many as two to five ceremonies performed on most cruises, with ceremonies taking place in Miami or on an island port of call.

Disney Cruises arranges weddings on its private Bahamian Island with a Bahamian minister officiating. Royal Caribbean's *Voyager* and *Explorer of the Seas* each have Skylight chapels, which seat 40 for in-port ceremonies.

Holland America typically has one wedding per sailing, mostly in Fort Lauderdale, but the line has added ceremonies in Hawaii and on a glacier in Alaska where the bride and groom wear traditional formal garb and booties over their shoes.

Cunard's *Queen Elizabeth 2* is the only ship with a synagogue, which appeals to couples of the Jewish faith. Ceremonies are usually held in port and, like all weddings at sea, arrangements must be made in advance.

Here's a partial list of wedding planners specializing in weddings at sea. Additional information is available from cruise lines.
A Wedding for You – (800-929-4198)
A Story Book Wedding (800-962-3568)
Royal Romance (888-475-5511)

Almost all ships offer not-so-newlyweds the opportunity to renew their wedding vows and at least a dozen couple "remarry" after 25, 35 and even 50 years of wedded bliss.

Honeymoons at Sea

Honeymoons, romance, and cruises have a lot in common—excitement, moonlit nights, sunny days, warm beaches, intimacy, and adventure all wrapped into a single package suitable for storage in memory banks. It's small wonder honeymooners, attracted by descriptive brochures offering tempting amenities, are taking to the seas in droves. Almost all cruise lines offer afford-able all-inclusive honeymoon packages complete with movie-like settings of champagne breakfasts served in bed.

The couple usually finds champagne, a wedding cake, and flowers awaiting them in their cabin. But if it's intimacy they yearn for, they should carefully check sleeping arrangements and tables for two. Not all ships can provide dou-ble or queen-size beds, and tables for two are usually limited. When they are available, romantics should reserve them early as they are not usually obtain-able for last-minute bookings. Cruise lines, however, make every effort to seat honeymooners together at large tables when smaller tables are not available.

Food and Dining

One of the highlights of a cruise vacation is the ever-seductive menu. Visions of caviar from the Black Sea or chilled papaya soup, roast pheasant with chestnut dressing, or sautéed Halibut Amandine and iced fruit parfait are like-ly to appear. And for good reason. Today's cruise passengers find themselves faced with the delicious dilemma of up to nine meals a day. The fact that the cost of all these meals is included in cruise prices encourages passengers to engage in their wildest culinary fantasies and to sample dishes they never before dreamed of trying.

Let's face it. Dining is an important part of the cruise experience, but it is a lot more than simply eating a meal. It is the time for trying new dishes, for socializing with traveling companions, and for enjoying the kind of service we could easily become accustomed to. Cruise lines try hard to outdo each other in the food they serve, and passengers often judge a ship by its cuisine. The chefs like to show off creative talents at the grand buffets, and passengers delight in photographing mountains of food enhanced by museum-quality ice carvings. When it comes to quantity of food, no other holiday package comes anywhere close to a cruise, except of course, if you're visiting your grandmother. You can eat almost every hour on the hour, and some passengers do.

Feasting starts with morning coffee and tea for early birds, followed by breakfast in either the dining-room, the informal indoor/outdoor area frequently called The Lido, or in your bed, if you prefer. Mid-morning bouillon, afternoon tea, and midnight snacks are traditions, and some ships have two midnight buffets, one at midnight and the other for swingers at 1:30 a.m. Of course, there's lunch and dinner, ice cream and pizza parlors, and cabin service, should passengers feel the slightest hunger pang.

If the thought of all that food and the addition of two inches to your waistline is keeping you off the sea-lanes, take heart. Ten years ago, advertising featured "gourmet" and ship cuisine was geared to the overeater. In a picture under the headline, a waiter offered a menu and the copy went on and on about food. Today, food ads are about as rare as "G"-rated movies. Cruise companies are doing everything to lure contemporary passengers on board by keeping ahead of food trends. Whether featuring "nouvelle" or "California" or "low-calorie," almost every ship is catering to passengers' requests for lighter, more slimming fare. They are addressing your hesitation with low-fat, low-calorie menu options. During the past year, I didn't find a single vessel without low-calorie items highlighted on menus.

Cruise companies also cater to special dietary requirements, such as salt-free or vegetarian diets. Many ships have kosher meals, too. But not all ships are equipped to cater to all kinds of special requests, which, incidentally, should be made at the time of booking your space. If a specific diet is required or preferred, check with your travel agent (and in some cases with the company) before you hand over your deposit. It's a good idea to request confirmation of your dining preferences to avoid problems once on board. While some ships can handle last-minute special requests, others cannot when the request is not considered normal. Vegetarian, salt-free, low cholesterol, and diabetic entrées are considered routine by most ships.

Despite trends toward healthier menus on ships, the "groaning board" tradition has not been abandoned, and passengers bent on ordering everything on the menu are encouraged by waiters to do so. On a recent cruise, one of my tablemates rated each of her half-dozen annual cruises by the weight she gained. A one-week cruise, according to her, was a "four pound" voyage.

If you have a fondness for certain foods, you might want to keep in mind the "nationality" of the ship or its crew, because ship cuisine frequently reflects the cruise line's ownership and staff. If the ship boasts an all-Italian crew or an Italian captain and officers, the dining-room specialties are bound to be pasta-based. For the most part, however, ship brochures describe food as "international," which translates into an ample choice of meats, fish, and poultry, laced with mouthwatering and calorie-enhanced desserts.

Variety and quality are key factors, although everyone's taste buds are different. One person's caviar is another's fish eggs so judging food is subjective. In compiling the votes for "Best Food and Dining," we found that every ship received votes by members of the Critics Choice panel. So, we decided not to select "The Best" in this category. We do comment on food and presentation in individual ship profiles and include pertinent comments by members of the panel based on presentation, quality and variety,

INSIDER TIP

Not all ships are equipped to handle kosher food requests. Company policy on kosher foods, how they are served, and availability are detailed in The Shipping Companies and Their Ships Chapter. If your agent says, "Not to worry" when you ask about kosher foods, or any other special dietary request -- start worrying.

TT Critics Choice for Cruise Companies with the Best Kosher Food:

$$$ – Holland America
$$$$$ – Radisson Seven Seas
$$$$$ – Crystal Cruises
$$ to $$$$ – Cunard Line

Alternative Dining Options

Passengers have become more sophisticated and dining at a fine restaurant, recognizing premium wines and exotic fare is the lifestyle of choice these days in spite of world wide events. The cruise industry has been keeping a watchful eye on these changes and has moved elegant dining experiences to sea. Beautifully designed intimate restaurants offer the option of a quiet romantic evening for two, a chance to dine with new and/old friends or just to escape a specific dress code in the formal dining rooms.

Optional restaurants usually come with a surcharge and reservations are required. Early attempts at supper clubs with surcharges on *Royal Viking Sun* and by Norwegian Cruise Lines were doomed within a year, probably because it was a feature clearly ahead of its time and the surcharge of $35 was considered high in the 1980s. But the concept remained viable and remained on the back burner until Crystal Cruises introduced two ethnic restaurants on its *Crystal Harmony* in 1989.

Today choices range from fast food at Johnny Rockets on Royal Caribbean's Voyager-class vessels to elegant restaurants operating under the guidance of celebrity chefs to high in the sky supper clubs on Carnival Spirit-class ships. Additional charges range from none, a recommended six dollars for gratuities, to $35 and few passengers complain. These intimate restaurants have limited seating and reservations are usually hard to come by unless booked early in the cruise.

I make it a point to dine at least once during every cruise in the optional restaurant regardless of the charge. I have found them all to be an excellent "night out" experience even on a short cruise. I have also found that some are more excellent than others, but then "excellent" is a subjective word. Service, on the other hand, and ambience is always memorable.

TT CRITICS CHOICE FOR THE BEST OPTIONAL RESTAURANTS AT SEA:

$$$ – Carnival *Spirit/Pride/Legend*
  (Topside and built into the funnel, these restaurants are posh supper clubs with music and dancing high in the sky. Menu is geared to steaks and chops, but the specialty is Joe's Stone Crabs)

$$$$ – Celebrity *Millenium/Summit/Infinity*
  (Restaurants are products of renowned chef Michel Roux. Food is superb and setting imitate what it was like on famous old liners)

$$$ – Disney's *Wonder/Magic*
  (Unlike the rest of the ship, no one under 18 is admitted to the intimate restaurants serving excellent Italian-themed food)

INSIDER TIP

Optional restaurants with surcharges of from $6 to $30 per person have been opened on almost every new ship. Cruise lines are employing "celebrity chefs" to create new menus and discarding regimentation in assigned dining times and places. Dining policies and optional restaurants with and without surcharges are detailed in individual ship profiles.

ShipShape at Sea

Spas at sea, in one form or another, are not new. Even in the golden years of transatlantic sea travel, passengers were encouraged to work off gargantuan meals by walking the deck and participating in sports such as shuffleboard or table tennis. As cruising replaced transoceanic travel, the concept took on a different complexion. In order to compete with shoreside resorts, lifestyles at sea became more contemporary. Ships added fitness rooms in addition to traditional massage, hairdressing, and facial salons. Aerobic classes became part of the daily activity plan.

Although much has been made of the trend toward health facilities on cruise ships, the concept is now approaching its full potential. All ships constructed during the last 10 or 12 years have devoted major public space to spas, and some offer larger and better-equipped facilities than can be found in a high-priced spas or fitness centers on shore. Older vessels have spent millions to redesign and bring spa and fitness facilities up to standards developed by newer vessels.

A spa vacation combined with a cruise offers the best of two worlds, and passengers are responding in large numbers. Celebrity Cruises remains the only line that allows passengers to pre-book spa packages. Treatments offered run the gamut and are detailed in Ship Profiles

Other ships also have extensive spa programs, and almost all ships offer massage and facial treatments,

Most of the spas are operated by Steiner Transocean Ltd. Of London but prices vary somewhat between ships. So does the service. It's like going to a beauty shop in a strange country and the hairdresser doesn't know whether you will ever make another appointment. Spa employees come from all over the world – South Africa, Australia, France, Sweden, Germany and the U.K. Most of the spa and hairdressing salon employees are young and are on board for the travel experience. Exceptions seem to be the managers who have been at sea with the company for a long time.

INSIDER TIP

When you make your appointment, discuss your hair style with the manager and ask for someone who is experienced in long, or short, wavy or straight, whatever your case may be. That way you stand a better chance to get a more experienced stylist. No guarantees, however. Staff has been trained, but you must be specific about what type of massage, for example, you prefer – light, sports, pressure point, etc. If you're trying a new exotic-type treatment, go with the flow. Some are really sensuous.

Gymnasiums boast the latest in work out equipment and every ship offers classes. A recent trend on some ships come with a small surcharge for Pilates, Yoga and other classes that work best with small numbers of participants. Some ships are charging for special classes. At one time, hairdressing and spa treatments were priced lower than they are in home town spas. That is no longer the case. Prices run about 10 percent above shoreside and vary from ship-to-ship. On average, a 55-minute massage runs close to $90, sometimes including gratuity.

TT CRITICS CHOICE FOR THE BEST SPAS AT SEA:

$$$ XXL – *Carnival Triumph/Carnival Spirit*
NauticaSpas are multi-level and are among the largest afloat. Ten treatment rooms. Fresh fruit juice bar, Nautica fare is on evening dinner menus.

$$$ XXL – Norwegian Sky
Body Waves Spa is an Asian-inspired featuring ancient Japanese hands-on healing. Guests in suites may request in-cabin massages.

$$$ XXL – Royal Caribbean Voyager - Class
Ships have 14 treatments rooms and a solarium with a retractable roof for relaxation before or after treatments.

$$$$ Luxury – *Prinsendam*
Spa du Soleil has a full menu of treatments in a Mediterranean inspired spa. Rasul room is where couple may privately apply detoxifying mud mixture. It also has a Dry Float room where guest lie on a waterbed-like table and are covered with seaweed and other detoxification substances.

$$$$$ Luxury – *Seven Seas Mariner*
Judith Jackson Spa is different from others at sea. Treatments are from the best International spas. Private areas and quiet relaxation area for use before or after treatments.

Cruising with Kids

Ships seem to be made for children, who are the first to find their peers and adjust to new surroundings. There's nothing confining about 10 decks of open space. Kids are quickly involved in planned activities, between-meal snacks, parties, bingo, and shipboard-style horseracing. They are the first to learn the Italian words that bring the fastest response in the dining-room or the Jamaican dialect that turns a grouchy waiter into a smiling friend, and they become positively cosmopolitan as they make friends with fellow travelers from all parts of the world. They acclimate quickly to Baked Alaska, Eggs Benedict, and the service. The major adjustment comes when it's time to disembark and the realities of daily living hit home.

Working parents who rarely spend much time with family find cruising an ideal way to get to know each other again. It's togetherness free of the strains of day-to-day living. Families swim together, go to movies together, share shore experiences, dine together, and come away closer. Cruising is a guilt-free holiday without the anxiety that follows parents when they leave the kids at home or the worries that come with taking teenagers to a landlocked resort. Ship captains tell me they have never lost a child at sea, and that's a comforting thought.

Even Robert Benchley who advocated that "children should be seen, and not heard," would approve of programs designed to keep pint-size and teenage travelers almost out of sight. There's baby-sitting available to take over where the counselors leave off. On most ships, sitters are reserved through room stewards for four to eight dollars an hour. Clever programming keeps children at arm's length from adults in public rooms. Deck games are scheduled while most adults are indoors or on tours. Kids get their turn at the movies, disco, and pizza grill about an hour before those activities show up on the grown-up schedule. Imagine the thrill of a pizza grill, ice cream parlor, or disco where there are no cash registers. It's all on the house—enough to delight passengers of any age!

All things considered, it's easy to understand why cruising is becoming a family affair. I'm reminded of a friend who finds the first week back home the most difficult for the whole family. He tells about his two daughters, aged eight and 10, who have a hard time adjusting to cold cereal at the family breakfast table after a week at sea. Seems they prefer their eggs on toast, topped with cheese and bacon. And Eggs Benedict can easily become a habit.

Ships offer active vacations for every segment of the family market, including single parents, grandparents, and extended family reunion groups; reunions are, incidentally, growing in popularity.

To learn firsthand what a family cruise is about, we invited our then-seven-year-old grandson, Michael, to sail with us on *Disney Magic*. We found everything promised in the brochure and a few surprises. He became an instant cruise addict. By age 12, Michael had sailed a half dozen ships and had become quite an authority on ships and children's programs. On a New Year's cruise last year, we hardly saw him. He ate almost all his meals with new friends, and since the cruise, they have kept in touch via the Internet. One lives in London, another in Germany, the rest spread around the United States. They are trying to get parents, or grandparents, to book the same ship so they can cruise together again next year.

One way to describe children's programs is to say that kids get the same amount of attention as adults do and maybe a little more. For starters, they mingle with their favorite characters and do their own thing with their peers. Kids have their own menus in the dining rooms, their own daily bulletin and activities, and their own swimming pool and entertainment, but they share the ice cream parlor.

Ships are also coming into their own for family reunions. It is not unusual for extended families numbering into the hundreds and aged from a few months old to the mid-90s to meet on board ship. There are reunion plans that allow family groups of 10 or more sharing three or more cabins a 10 percent discount for everyone in the group. Special rates for singles traveling with children under 18 allow the parent to pay the normal fare while paying a substantially reduced rate for the children.

Shirley and Harry comment and offer a bit of advice:

How well a child does on a cruise also depends in large part on the parents. You can't just let your youngster run free all over the ship without supervision, any more than you would on a busy city street. The ship should not become a playground for an unsupervised child. Kids do not belong in bars or casinos, adult swimming pools, or running up and down on decks or in hallways.

Generally the older and more independent and outgoing the child, the more pleasurable the cruise experience can be. Mature 10- to 12-year-olds and teenagers usually take to cruising instantly, heading off on their own to explore the vessel from top to bottom, learning their way around quickly and striking up friendships with other passengers their own age.

A larger ship works better for children than a smaller vessel, because there are more scheduled activities and more space. Many big modern ships offer all-day TV programming in cabins with education series from public television and programs about upcoming ports, good ways to keep kids occupied during quiet time.

An itinerary with frequent or daily ports of call is more desirable for restless, active children than one that spends two or three days in a row at sea.

The omnipresent food service pleases even the fussiest of young eaters. Most cruise lines offer special children's menus; unfortunately, most of them run to rich, fatty, fried foods of the fast-foods type, which kids will happily devour but which are not very healthy for them. On some ships at Norwegian Cruise Lines, children have their own buffet area in one corner of the Lido restaurant with special foods and scaled-down tables and chairs. And on P & O ships, there is a special children's tea or supper served at 5:15 in the afternoon in a dining room or the Lido restaurant and supervised by youth counselors.

Some lines are simply inappropriate for kids – small deluxe ships and expedition vessels such as American Yacht Safari and American Cruise Lines that simply don't have space for a dedicated playroom; vessels like Orient Lines' Crown Odyssey and Marco Polo or the little ships from American Canadian Caribbean Line that attract older passengers who may not want to share space with active, often noisy children.

Family reunion cruises with kids, especially celebrating Christmas or seasonal holidays, take advantage of a hassle-free vacation. Think of it: no getting up at dawn to stuff a turkey, no staying up late at night to trim a tree, no endless clean-up and December 26 depression. Instead, you can look forward to another day with the family on a sunny day at sea, being pampered in the spa while the kids are participating in a planned shipboard program instead of watching them get bored with the expensive new toys.

With kids traveling at a minimum rate when they occupy third and fourth berths in the stateroom and the possibility, if your family group is large enough, of a group rate discount (check with your travel agent), a cruise is not as expensive a prospect as it sounds at first.

Shirley and Harry's Checklist for Cruising with Kids:

Always book a ship that is likely to have other children aboard. Whether a kid is six or 16, he's always happy if he can find someone his own age. Otherwise, he can get bored and fidgety.

Don't expect free 24-hour babysitting. The youth counselors are there to enrich your child's vacation, not take him off your hands. A few lines offer babysitting in the youth center in the evenings, usually with a surcharge; others may provide babysitting in your cabin for a fee. Be sure, however, to determine before booking that such babysitting will be available on the ship you're considering. On one ship, we met a young couple who failed to do that, and were spending their entire cruise with the child. He dined at the first sitting, and Mommy on second because they were unable to get evening child care.

Don't take the kids on a cruise line that doesn't tout a children's program in the brochure. and offers fare discounts for sharing a cabin with parents. If none of these are available, it's a tip -off that the line and its regular passengers would be happier without your child on board but they're afraid to say so in print in the brochure.

Cruising with Infants:

If your child is under two years of age or if he is not toilet-trained, check with the cruise line to see if the children's playroom will allow him inside. All cruise lines have minimum ages for children aboard; others do not permit children in diapers to stay in the play group unless one parent is with the child at all times.

It's a good idea, if you can afford it to have a nanny, grandma or mother's helper along to share the cabin with the child so the parents can have some time alone. Take an inside minimum cabin to save money. Take a connecting cabin when available. It will cost a little more, but it's worth it.

If you plan to cruise with an infant, remind your self that while babies adjust easily to the gentle rocking motion of a ship at sea, their internal clocks stay on home time, so you may have to adjust care and feeding times.

Tender skin can be easily sunburned in tropical climates, so carry a sun block safe for babies and don't let them be exposed to the full sun. And, by all means, notify the line know well in advance if you'll be cruising with a baby. Here is a minimum age for babies on board and it is usually three or four months. Also, ask whether cribs and strollers will be available or if you'll need to bring your own. Determine what foods and liquids are stocked for infants and whether disposable diapers can be supplied by the ship.

INSIDER TIP

Carnival Cruise Lines is the only cruise line that has a minimum age of two for toddlers in the Camp Carnival Program. The other lines have put the minimum age at three. And, if you're concerned about medical care on board, inquire in advance whether the ship's doctor has experience in pediatrics. One doctor we know on a small ship sailing in remote regions prayed daily that an infant on board would not get sick "because I haven't worked in pediatrics for 30 years. "

TT **CRITICS CHOICE FOR THE BEST CRUISE LINES FOR FAMILIES:**

(Based on facilities, supervision, programming for multi-generational families)

$$$ – Carnival Cruise Lines

(Programs and facilities for kids from ages two to teens. Group baby sitting evenings so parents, grandparents and adults can enjoy multiple entertainment venues)

$$$ – Disney Cruise Line

(Ships were built for kids and facilities take up most of the public space, but kids must be at least three and potty trained. Limited nursery facilities. Children love it, but parents who prefer night life – casinos, etc – should probably look at other ships)

$$$ – Princess Cruises

(Excellent programs and facilities, but no kids under three. Baby sitting evenings and at other times so parents and grandparents can participate in activities.)

$$$ – Royal Caribbean – *Adventure/Explorer/Voyager of the Seas*

(Excellent program for kids and there's plenty to do for adults)

$$$$ – Holland America Line

(Ships with good facilities and programs include *Amsterdam*, *Rotterdam*, *Maasdam* and a HAL program for ages five and up. Just for kids shore excursions in Alaska and Caribbean)

Cruising for Seniors

Shirley and Harry Comment and offer Tips:

For many seniors and retirees, a cruise is the ideal vacation. You can do as much or as little as you like each day, have the comfort and convenience of familiar surroundings to come back to after an exotic excursion ashore and be secure in the knowledge that there will be no last-minute surprises in this mostly all-inclusive package to destroy your carefully planned budget.

There will be staff personnel who will quickly learn your needs and preferences for cabin and table service, and a medical facility with doctor, hospital and pharmacy to cope with basic care.

With many cruise lines, your purchase of an air/sea package also means escorted travel and assistance with baggage, customs and transportation in foreign ports. But even with all these inducements, your ultimate guarantee of a pleasurable and healthy cruise can only come through your own care and common sense.

A leisurely cruise aboard a luxury ship or expedition vessel usually provides a satisfying and comfortable vacation for older travelers with all the basic expenses included in one overall price. And most cruise ships have a caring and attentive service staff that makes a special point of looking out for and assisting older travelers, especially when crew members come from countries where older people are always treated with dignity.

Cruises are easier than land motor coach tours, because passengers need to pack and unpack only once during the trip rather than every time the tour changes hotels. An air/sea package with transfers usually includes cruise line representatives who meet arriving planes and supervise transportation from the airport to the ship or an interim hotel.

Consider the ports of call on an itinerary. Shore hospital facilities may be both rare and rudimentary in primitive or sparsely settled areas, and air service in or out may be infrequent in case of a medical emergency.

Check the deck plans (with a magnifying glass if necessary) to ensure that toilet facilities are available near the major public rooms and from the decks. See if there's one continuous promenade deck all the way around the ship, so you won't have to negotiate up and down stairs on a deck stroll.

Savvy seniors who lead an early-to-bed, early-to-rise pattern at home head for early bird coffee and breakfast lightly off the fruit, juice or cereals provided there. They request first-sitting dinner and frequently opt to lunch on a salad or sandwich.

Pick and choose. Enjoy the six or eight meals a day and the busy activities schedule by sampling a little bit at a time – skipping dinner to enjoy afternoon tea or late-night buffet, choosing between a team trivia quiz and a grandmother's bragging party instead of trying to do both. Don't feel you have to do everything all day long just because you paid for it.

Wear loose-fitting and airy clothes that breathe, sensible walking shoes and a sun hat when going ashore. Save your fancy dresses, stockings and high heeled shoes, your white shirts, jackets and ties for gala dinners on the ship, where it's air conditioned.

One veteran travel agent from Arizona's retirement communities of Sun City says he advises clients who have recently lost a spouse to consider taking a cruise to get themselves into different surroundings among different people. A cruise can provide an important psychological boost in a trying emotional period without being difficult for a person traveling alone for the first time.

We've also met many retirees who split up on their trips. One Ohio lady we've traveled with several times always heads off on an expedition cruise while her husband goes on more strenuous overland adventures. Each has a special vacation, and they can compare notes when they get back home.

Make certain, too, that the cabin category you're considering provides two lower beds rather than an upper and lower berth, as is often the case on older ships in the lowest-price category.

While studying the itinerary, note where the ship will dock as opposed to where it will anchor offshore and take passengers in by tender (small boat). Going up and down a steep gangway on the side of the ship and transferring to a bobbing launch calls for steady footing. You're better off with a ship that docks at most or all of its ports.

If you're concerned about the possibility of a medical emergency during the cruise, remember that a ship's size and itinerary directly affect how quickly sophisticated medical care can be obtained in an emergency. Large ships usually have more medical staff and facilities aboard, and a few, the *QE2*, for example, even have a landing pad for helicopters in case of an emergency medical evacuation.

Only a few of the large ships and a couple of mid-sized vessels, Royal Olympic's new *Olympia Voyager* and *Olympia Explorer* among them, have well-stocked pharmacies aboard, so passengers must always be sure to carry an adequate supply of prescription medications. Never pack medicine in your checked luggage; always carry it in your hand baggage.

Both the *QE2* and Holland America's *Zaandam* carry dentists on board, primarily for the crew, but their services are available to passengers as well.

It's a good idea to ask your doctor at home to write details on any ongoing medical condition, as well as prescriptions for regular drugs or serious allergies, on a sheet of paper that you can give to the ship's doctor after you board.

Smoke-free areas are emphasized in many ships now. Even European-based lines that carry many more Italians and French than Americans have banned smoking in the restaurants and sometimes in the show lounges. One cruise line, Carnival, even has a totally smoke-free ship, the *Paradise*. No one aboard, from the captain to the passengers to the waiters, cabin stewards and deckhands, is permitted to light up a cigarette anywhere, indoors or out. Not only that, but shipyard workers, too, were forbidden to smoke inside the *Paradise* while it was under construction.

TT CRITICS CHOICE FOR THE BEST SHIPS FOR SENIORS:

$$ – World Explorer Cruises
(Inexpensive way to see the world on a budget without obsessing
in airports)

$$$ XL – *Carnival Paradise*
(This is the only large ship that prohibits smoking by passengers and
crew. The pristine air and the lively atmosphere is very popular with
senior travelers)

$$$$ – *Amsterdam/Rotterdam/Prinsendam*
(Seniors love Holland America and its special attention to
older passengers.*

$$$$ – *Caronia*
(Traditional, the way cruising used to be. Very few steps and
excellent cuisine)

$$$$$ – *Seabourn Pride/Spirit/Legend*
(Top of the line, small vessels. Careful attention to
special dietary requests.)

$$$$$ – *Crystal Harmony/Symphony*
(The majority of guests are over 50. High end cruise experiences
in mid-size ships. Easy to get around, seniors opt for the
luxury of butler service on 10 deck)

Traveling Solo

No pessimist ever discovered the secrets of the stars,
Sailed to an uncharted land,
Or opened up a new heaven for the human spirit.
Helen Keller

Nothing gripes a single passenger more than rate quotes of "per person,
double occupancy," when all he or she wants is "single occupancy." There are
ways of traveling solo and still taking advantage of the per person, double rate.
Most cruise companies will go to great lengths to pair single travelers (of the
same sex), but it is easier to find a roommate if you're a woman. Two women
rather than two men occupy most shared cabins. For some reason, men are
reluctant to share. Some ships are offering less desirable or smaller cabins to sin-

gles at little or no price increase over the per person, double occupancy rate.

Singles who want to avoid the surcharge that most cruise lines add for one person occupying the space of two should look for ships, mostly older vessels, with designated single cabins. These lines include American Cruise Lines, Costa Cruise Lines, Cunard Line, Fred. Olsen Lines, Norwegian Cruise Lines, Orient Lines, Princess Cruises and Regal Cruises.

Lower than-usual single supplements – and sometimes none at all off-season – are available on Norwegian Coastal Voyage, which also offers a seniors discount of from $95 to $220 for passengers 67 and over on most sailings. Crystal Cruises has one of the lowest single supplements, but capacity is controlled. Singles who book early sail for only 20 percent more than the per person, double rate and have the cabin for themselves.

A singles' share program, which provides a roommate of the same sex and general age range is offered by lines such as Carnival, Celebrity, Cunard, Delta Queen, First European Cruises, Holland America, Norwegian Cruise Line, Orient Lines, Princess Cruises, Regal Cruises and Royal Olympic.

TT CRITICS CHOICE FOR THE BEST SHIPS FOR SINGLES:

(Single rates, activities, and overall ambience determined the choices)

$$$ – Carnival Cruise Lines.
   All ships (Company probably carries more singles than anyone else. It's the "Fun Ships" and the line offers "guaranteed" single rates. It's easy to meet other singles.)

$$$$$ – *Crystal Harmony/Crystal Symphony*
   (Single rates are as low as 20 percent over per person, double rates and there are gentlemen hosts on board to make sure there are no wall flowers left waiting for a dance.)

$$$$$ – *Silver Cloud/Silver Wind*
   (Single supplement on selected sailing is as low as 10 percent over the per person, double rate. These ships and the supplement attract older women who want to dance with the gentlemen hosts)

$$$$$ – *Radisson Seven Seas Mariner/Navigator*
   (Low single supplement on all ships. Gentlemen hosts on most sailings)

GENTLEMEN HOSTS:

Since the largest number of singles on cruise ship is female, cruise lines have implemented Gentlemen's Host programs. It's encourages single women to come aboard and assures them they will not feel like the wallflower at the school dance. Gentleman hosts, also referred to as escorts, are being added to staffs on ships catering to single women travelers. Hosts are not synonymous with gigolos.

While hosts are not really a new addition to shipboard manifests, the concept was not an important aspect of single cruising until late 1982. Cunard and other companies employed dashing middle-aged gentlemen during world cruises in the glory days of lengthy voyages. In the contemporary cruise world, Royal Cruise Lines (now out of business) took the lead 2015 years ago and set the rules for hosts and the standards for host programs that have evolved into today's version of shipboard "gentlemen callers" of the 2000s.

Crystal Cruises, Holland America Line, Cunard Line, Holland America Line, Seabourn Cruise Line, Radisson Seven Seas and Silversea Cruises are among companies that have s host programs in place on long cruises. Some have them on every cruise, the number depending on the number of single women booked. To set the record straight and dispel any misconceptions, Hosts are nothing like Walter Matthau in the movie, *Out to Sea*. Hosts are considered part of the cruise staff and are governed by a strict set of rules, which varies little from line to line. No hanky-panky, no teaming up with one passenger for the duration of the cruise, and no conduct unbecoming a gentleman. Hosts must be single, and many come from the ranks of retired military officers, professionals, and businessmen in the 50-plus age range. Most are in their 60s, and I have met a few in their late-70s. On a recent cruise, a schoolteacher in his 40s was hosting during summer vacation. Hosts are not paid and serve as dancing, dining, and card-playing partners for women traveling without male companions.

They also accompany groups on shore excursions, attend cocktail parties, and participate in other shipboard social activities. They are expected to mingle without showing favoritism to any one passenger or group. Hosts must have socially assertive charm that encourages people to mingle and to get them into a partying mood, and they must know how to dance. They are required to attend the ship's dance lessons every day

Romantic relationships are strictly prohibited, but there's no way to put a lock on romance and there has been talk of a few deviations. No one mentions names, but there are stories circulating on every ship. Like the one about the host who fell so hard for a passenger he jumped ship in a Mediterranean port a few years ago. The passenger must have been similarly struck, because she gave up the rest of her cruise and disembarked with him. And, there are several stories about hosts who later married women they met on board.

Rules or no rules, based on feedback from single passengers, the host program has widened, if not opened, cruise travel for a wide segment of women traveling alone.

Hosts are seldom engaged for a single cruise and usually stay for a month or longer. With no pay, why do hosts take to the seas, and who are these twinkle-toed gentlemen? A typical example is Seth Deutsch, a retired psychotherapist from Palm Springs, California. I met him on a Royal Viking cruise some years ago and marveled at the way he had the most reticent over-70-year-old giggling like a schoolgirl on the dance floor. He said his role was to pull people out of their shells so they would enjoy the cruise. His professional background is useful.

As one of my widowed friends puts it, "We're on board because we love to cruise. We sail to wonderful places, meet interesting people, are as busy as we like during the day, and we know we'll dance at least once each evening with each host at the party."

Cruising for the Disabled Traveler

The most recent U.S. Department of Transportation survey indicates there are approximately 54 million persons with disabilities in the United States. That number makes it the nation's largest minority group. With an aging population, DOT concludes that "we can expect that number to increase dramatically."

While most new DOT regulations concern accessibility in air and land transportation, a recent court ruling turns the focus to accessibility on cruise ships. This ruling puts cruise lines under legal notice to improve services for disabled travelers.

Persons with disabilities are finding cruising and excellent easy way to travel. Recent developments that encourage the disabled to sail on cruise vacation and cruise lines are improving facilities. Holland America has installed America's first wheelchair-accessible tender transfer system on board its ships. A ramp on the tenders allows the chair to be wheeled directly onboard and locked into place atop another lift. Once dockside, a hydraulic system on the tender allows the wheelchair to be rolled off the tender directly on to the dock.

Royal Caribbean has installed pool lifts on most of its ships, so passengers with disabilities can enjoy the swimming pools. Princess Cruises and other lines have posted signs in Braille. Carnival has increased the number of wheelchair accessible cabins. Most of the major lines have text phones and flashing phone ringers for the hearing impaired. Disney Cruise Line has special wheelchairs designed to make navigating sandy beaches a lot easier.

Four of the *Rotterdam's* 23 wheelchair accessible staterooms have connecting doors to adjoining non-handicapped staterooms to accommodate non-challenged passengers who are traveling together. Crystal Cruises arranges for lifts on tour buses to accommodate wheel chairs and challenged passengers. Accessibility for major destinations in Alaska is provided by Princess Cruises through lift equipped coaches, vans and ADA approved hotel rooms. The lower level of the Midnight Sun Express offers complete access.

Princess, which claims the highest number of wheelchair accessible staterooms in the industry, has special wheelchair-transportation gangway mechanisms on most of their ships to simplify embarkation/debarkation in dozens of ports worldwide. This allows passengers to disembark in their own power chair in ports of call. Speaking of power and oversized chairs which will probably not fit through some of the widest entryways,

Carnival and others are advising passengers with battery operated chairs to leave the chair outside the cabin door. A call to housekeeping will bring a porter to pick up the chair and recharge it. The chair is delivered back to the room when the passenger phones in the morning.

Gone are the days when wheelchair accessible cabins were limited to inside, lower deck space. Costa is a good example of that change. The *Costa Victoria* built in 1996 had six accessible cabins. All insides measuring a mere 175 square feet and there were no public accessible restrooms. That was remedied on *Costa Atlantica* built in 2000 which has four inside and four outside cabins on higher decks as well as several accessible public restrooms.

The *Grand Princess* has 28 accessible cabins in various categories ranging in size from 233 to 312 square feet which represents a big increase from the four accessible cabins on the *Royal Princess* built in 1984. Royal Caribbean's accessible cabins on its new vessels probably have the widest doors and most complete facilities which include Braille numbers on cabin doors, Braille lettering outside accessible public restrooms and in elevators.

Cruise lines have set up "Special Needs Desks" staffed by persons with answers to all possible questions. Many lines have published Special Needs brochures and others are in the process of developing similar brochures.

In researching facilities for the physically challenged, it became obvious that older vessels have fewer accessible staterooms and those designated as "wheelchair accessible" are usually not fitted with many of the ADA recommended features. Vessels built during the past five years are more likely to have purpose built staterooms, usually in more than one category – inside outside and suites-amidships and conveniently located for easy access to elevators. Most adhere closely to ADA (Americans with Disabilities Administration) requirements and some even go several steps beyond. Others are retrofitting staterooms to conform.

An exception to the new-is-better is Norwegian Cruise Line's *Norway*. Built and rebuilt, refitted and retrofitted, the 1960's vessel has 10 accessible cabins, both inside and outside. Assistance, however, may be needed as there are no grab bars and the company requires a companion in most cases. The cabins, however, are spacious, elevator doors are wide and all decks, with the exception of topside are accessible. NCL also requires that passengers bring their own wheelchairs.

Upscale cruise lines take upscale care of passengers with special needs. Seabourn Cruises has four suites on each of its three ships designated for physically challenged. *Seabourn Pride*, *Spirit* and *Legend* are totally accessible, but the line requires a letter from a doctor in order to reserve a handicapped suite. *Silver Shadow* and *Silver Whisper* each have two oversized suites with verandahs located near the atrium and elevator. *Radisson Diamond* has two accessible cabins and *Seven Seas Navigator* has four which cannot accommodate electric wheelchairs. Access or scooters and notes that access to some outside decks and to verandahs "may be difficult due to raised doorway sills." The *Seven Seas Mariner*, newest and largest in the fleet, has six suites with verandahs in prime locations around the atrium area. Radisson is another company that adheres to the requirement of a doctor's letter before assigning a handicapped cabin or suite.

INSIDER TIP

Not all ships are recommended for passengers with disabilities. Wind Star's three smaller ships are good examples. There are no elevators and getting between decks is limited to a narrow stairway. The same holds true for other sailing vessels and applied to *Wind Surf* until its recent retrofit which allows for embarkation at a low level and eliminates climbing 42 steps at embarkation. The vessel has an elevator that will accommodate a narrow wheelchair. Some ships are more disabled-friendly than others although brochures indicate "wheelchair accessible" staterooms.

Watch out for ships with limited numbers of accessible cabins which list "partially accessible" cabins as well. These accommodations do not conform completely to ADA standards which call for doors wide enough to accommodate wheel chairs, turn around space in cabins for wheel chairs, lower sills, grab bars strategically placed, glide in bathrooms and showers with a bench among with a lengthy list of other features. "Partially accessible" cabins have some of the amenities, but not all. Space for wheel chair turn around is usually tight or impossible. Service dogs are permitted on all ships with required documentation but may not be allowed to disembark at all ports. The number of service dogs allowed per sailing is usually limited.

Word has gotten around the cruise community that "handicapped" cabins are more spacious and requests outnumber availability. To separate the needy from the greedy, some cruise lines are requiring letters from doctors before confirming cabins. Most cruise lines have alert kit for guests with hearing impairments which can be fitted to any cabin. These TTY kits include visual notification of the door knocker and smoke alarm; also a vibrating alarm, door knocker, bed shaker and phone amplifier.

TT CRITICS CHOICE FOR THE BEST SHIPS FOR DISABLED TRAVELERS:

$$$ XXL – *Carnival Spirit, Pride, Legend*
(Accessible cabins have wide doors and elevators with tactile controls and accessible gym equipment)

$$$ XXL – Royal Caribbean Voyager-class vessels
(Company has installed pool lifts at swimming pools)

$$$ XXL – *Grand-Princess, Ocean Princess*
(Large cabins for disabled travelers and easy access to swimming pools, embarkation and debarkation)

$$$$ – *Rotterdam*
(This ship has 23 wheelchair accessible cabins. Holland America on all of its ships has reengineered embarkation and debarkation to make it easier and disabled guests)

Gay and Lesbian Cruising

There are dozens of choices if you're gay or lesbian with a same-sex traveling companion. There are additional choices if you are traveling alone. These range from small groups on small ships, small groups on large ships, large groups on all ship sizes and charters. Most ships are gay and lesbian friendly and your most important choice is whether to book on your own, join a group, or opt for full-ship charters by companies that special in travel for this segment of the population. Gay and lesbian travelers I have spoken with tell told me they prefer a full-ship charter because ports of call are gay-friendly and activities scheduled on board are geared to their interests which are as varied as homosexual passengers. They also said that full ship charters allows for more freedom.

Gay and lesbian passengers blend into the cruise scene on every ship and are welcomed by every cruise company. Booking with travel agents who specialize in gay and lesbian travel is a good idea if you have any concerns. Here are three of the top travel companies specializing in gay and lesbian cruises. They are among the oldest companies and have been operating full ship charters for almost a decade. RSVP charters vessels, furnishes the entertainment and activities and adjust itineraries so ship port visits are limited to places that are gay-friendly. About 10 percent are men, the remainder women. Good information: www.rsvpvacations.com, www.rsvpvacations.com, www.oceancruiseconsultants.com and www.piedpipervacations.com.

Conventions, Meetings and Fund Raisers at Sea

Cruise companies are building convention and meeting facilities on every new ship and converting some areas on older ships to accommodate business meetings. A developing area is charity fund raising cruises. Affinity charity groups run from 30 to 300 and are extremely popular. From personal experience, I have been involved with 20 cruises for two of my favorite charities. Here's how it works. A small committee (not more than three) selects approximate dates, itineraries and price range. The committee gives the information to three travel agencies in the community and asks them to come up with "bids." The lowest bidder doesn't always get the group. It's the one who offers a good package which includes transfers, insurance, a shore excursion, and social events on board. The amount of money raised on the cruise is secondary to the loyalty to the charitable cause that is developed through camaraderie.

Toby Salzman Comments:

"In the corporate world where nothing is too good for that valuable client or a top-performing employee, cruising has the ultimate "wow factor." Better than a cash bonus or expensive watch, rewarding a client or employee with a cruise to great adventure in exotic ports nurtures memorable experiences that motivate them toward greater productivity. Meanwhile, as the corporate CEOs and top management mingle aboard the cruise ship with the recipients, opportunities abound for interacting, breeding loyalty and learning how the other side thinks. This strengthens corporate bonds and cultivates new ideas.

Corporate planners and company decision makers should choose a cruise ship that fits the corporate culture, or charter an entire vessel, brand it with the corporate logo on flags and signs and recreate the corporate culture on board. Aside from its sybaritic image, offering a cruise provides purposeful, positive returns on the investment. For executive retreats, cruise ships offer intimate meeting spaces, chances to socialize or brainstorm over dinner, beside the pool, in the cigar club. Cruising provides myriad opportunities for teambuilding o the basketball or tennis court, at island beach Olympic games and, in far flung ports, during rounds of golf, car rallies or nature hikes, to mention a few. With all the cruise options for meals and snacks, built-in entertainment, organized activities and port excursions, planners can rest assured the guests are looked after without tendering the proposals necessary at land resorts.

With security and exclusivity, cruise ships provide outstanding venues for corporations to launch new policies and introduce innovative research or new technology to employees or clients far from the eyes of prying competitors. When it comes to staging conferences and lectures aboard ship, delegates are a captive audience. Contrary to misconceptions that cruising will capsize the budget, planners often find that, when comparing the costs of cruising versus land-based resorts, prices generally balance out, but returns are greater in memorable experiences."

TT CRITICS CHOICE FOR THE BEST SHIPS FOR
CONVENTIONS AND MEETINGS:

(Toby Salzman, cruise editor of Meetings and Conventions Magazine made the selections)

$$$$$ – Radisson Seven Seas Mariner

(Dedicated convention and meeting space. Areas have breakout space and the ship is small. so companies can charter the whole ship with out being part of a group on a larger ship. Technical facilities for staging in the tiered theatre are state of the art)

$$$$$ – *Crystal Symphony*

Ship is small enough that it can be chartered. Staging is excellent.

$$$$$ – *Silver Whisper/Silver Shadow*

There's a small dining/board room, good for private meetings on corporate retreats. The conference center connects to the card room and dining/board room so there can be breakout space following conferences

$$$$ – *Radisson Diamond*

Good for small ship charters when corporations can only spend 5 days in the Caribbean -Ship can be "branded" with corporate logo, flag, etc. meeting space good enough, open seating - good for gala dinner dances, awards ceremonies.

$$$$$ – *Seabourn Pride, Spirit*

Small enough for elite corporate charters, ship can be branded with company logo, etc. Also, they will customize ports and itineraries for charters.

$$$ – *Adventure of the Seas*

Facilities on the stage on Studio B for events, awards ceremonies, product launches; the latest in lighting and audio-visual techniques. Excellent meeting facilities with breakout space.. Good for large corporate event charters

$$$$ – *Celebrity Millenium/Summit*

Facilities for sensational events, awards ceremonies, product launches requiring the latest in lighting and audio-visual techniques. Also excellent meeting facilities with technical and audio-visual facilities as well as plenty of breakout space. Good for large corporate event charters

$$$ $ – Holland America's *Maasdam*

Ship can be chartered, not too big, and can be branded with corporate logo, etc. Staging is good, plenty of meeting and conference space dedicated for that purpose.

Active Vacations at Sea

Sports at sea aren't exactly news, either. Everyone expects the table tennis and bridge tournaments and the shuffleboard playoff, but today's ships offer a lot more. While most ships can't build a Par 3 on the sports deck, the really big ones have a golf pro in residence and a place to practice the shots. They organize visits to championship courses on shore, and returning cruise passengers talk about golf experiences in the Philippines and Singapore as highlights of the trip. Tennis players can also sharpen their skills on many ships, and when it comes to diving, lessons are given in the ship's swimming pool in anticipation of diving expeditions in warm-water ports of call.

Some ships are catering to sports addicts by bringing sports celebrities on board to talk to and mingle with passengers. Royal Caribbean International has such a program in place, and Norwegian Cruise Line has an agreement with the NFL, so passengers rub elbows with well known name players. Almost all of the new large ships have installed sports bars with direct live CNN and ESPN broadcasts on huge screens. Carnival's new ships and some of the Holland America vessels also have sports bars adjacent to casinos.

Cruise lines are lining up active and adventurous shore excursions in exotic places. Sure, the traditional bus tour is still on the menu, but there are other options in excursions that offer active participation – horse back riding on the beach, a jeep safari in desserts, rafting on raging rivers and participation in local events.

BEST SHIPS FOR ADVENTURE SEEKING TRAVELERS:

$$$$ – *Clipper Odyssey/Clipper Adventurer*
    (Both are small enough to get into exotic ports. The Antarctica and Greenland cruises as well as the China, Bali and Indonesia voyages are extremely popular.)
$$$$$ – *Seabourn Spirit/Legend/Pride*
    (Ships offers luxury as guests explore places like Sri Lanka, Singapore, Mumbei and Bangkok)
$$$ – *Orient Line's Marco Polo*
    (This traditional vessel is named for the explorer and offers some really exotic voyages – Antarctica, Africa and Australia)

Other adventure opportunities are available on ships with exotic itineraries. For example, *Amsterdam, Crystal Harmony* and *Queen Elizabeth 2* world cruises and segments include visits to places like Namibia, Wallis Bay, Antarctica and a full menu of exotic ports with exploration-type excursions.

Theme and Special Interest Cruises

Special interests are not confined to ports of call or itineraries but have become integral segments of onboard entertainment programs. Music lovers have marvelous choices at sea. Classical, jazz, big band, chamber, and disco sounds ring through theaters and lounges. There are music festivals at sea with outstanding solo performances by musicians, ballerinas, and lecturers.

The sound of music is everywhere on cruise ships. It rings through the hallways, in public lounges, and on stage. Some cruise lines offer special cruises featuring areas of the wonderful world of music. There are cruises for jazz buffs, opera lovers, classical-music enthusiasts, big- band collectors, country-music fans, and symphonic impresarios, with onboard concerts by celebrated classical and contemporary performers. Some itineraries are planned to coincide with major music events at ports of call.

Some music cruises are sold with a surcharge to cover special entertainment costs; others, at rack rates. It's interesting to note that few, if any, ever sell at a discount. Concertgoers are accustomed to paying high prices for tickets to events and book quickly on cruises catering to their special tastes in music.
Slated to repeat popular appearances on the *QE2* are jazz pianist Dave Brubeck on the Floating Jazz Festival; Frank McCourt and Mary Higgins to discuss their work during the ship's "Literary Festival." In all, *Queen Elizabeth 2* has scheduled 21 theme voyages that include mystery, exploration, a fine arts festival, great authors, comedy, opera and dance.

Astronaut Buzz Aldrin is a frequent guest on Silversea and Seabourn, although I met him a couple of years ago on a *Norwegian Sky* eclipse voyage. Crystal Cruises has scheduled 29 theme cruises in its worldwide 2003 itineraries. They range from fine feats of culinary masters during the Wine & Food Festival, Health and Fitness, Jazz and Big Band and an Enrichment Series featuring speakers from a broad range of disciplines – politics, academia, science and the arts.

Costa Cruises goes the Italian theme route with entertainers the likes of Don Cornell, Julius La Rosa and Al Martino performing on the *CostaAtlantica*, CostaRomantica and CostaVictoria throughout the Caribbean season.

Holland America Line has scheduled a couple of dozen theme cruises for 2003 ranging from Oktoberfest to Grand Bingo. Country and Big Band Music is scheduled to highlight seven day voyages. Crystal Cruises' has expanded its very successful Computer University at Sea.

Sports continue to dominate and live remote telecasts of major events have become routine on most ships. Some, however, are attracting sports fans with focus on specific sports with "name" players hosting on board lectures and events.

On Orient Lines's Antarctica voyages, expeditions are under the direction of naturalist Nigel Sitwell and field zoologist Dr. Peter Carey and feature Sir Edmund Hillary on the Grand Antarctic Circumnavigation voyage.

Princess Cruises features on board lectures geared to destinations. They are conducted by renowned naturalists during Alaska cruises, art and architectural historian during select Europe cruises, and regional historians and political scientists on Asia and Pacific sailings. Holland America and Royal Caribbean Cruise Line also have lecturers on board Hawaii, Alaska and Europe cruises. Topics covered include history, culture, politics, travel photography and art history.

Windstar Cruises offers a series of 2003 voyages that include world famous chefs and unique personalities. Among those scheduled to appear are CNN style editor Elsa Klensch, glass artist Dale Chihuly and Gourmet magazine wine editor Gerald Asher.

A good example of unusual theme programs is Crystal's Biking and Walking Cruises. Guests can choose to bike through Italy's Venetto region, or stroll the byways of the Costswold or Mallorca, as well as the pristine landscapes of Alaska and New Zealand. Each activity is part of a new series of pre- and post-cruise land packages developed for Crystal by Butterfield & Robinson, the leading operator of worldwide luxury biking and walking trips.

Musical headliners frequently appear as guests on cruise ships. Singer and songwriter Jack Jones was the special entertainer on one of Princess Cruises' inaugurals. It was most appropriate since his the voice on the television Love Boat theme song.

Culinary cruises, food and wine are passenger favorites. On a cruise Down Under, we attended wine seminars presented by Australian vintners. On Celebrity sailings when Master Chef Michel Roux is on board, his special meals are a special treat. Holland America has what it calls a University at Sea with medical experts talking about tops that include family medicine, dermatology, and internal medicine.

Fitness themes and yoga classes are well attended and high profile sports names draw fans who want to improve their swing with the likes of Jack

Nickolas. My favorites are on the *QE2* transatlantic crossings featuring the Tommy Dorsey orchestra or Ragtime and the Roaring 20's.

Playing the Odds – Casinos at Sea

There are very few exceptions to the rule that if you are cruising, you'll have a hard time avoiding the casino on any ship, except Disney Cruise Line. Gaming rooms are in prominent locations and are what I call walk-through rooms. You are almost forced to walk through the casino as you go from bow to stern on some decks. Casinos are reasonable facsimiles of what you would find in Las Vegas or Atlantic City, depending on the size and age of the vessel. They are always the glitziest rooms on board with flashing neon and contagious tumult. Usual games of chance are rows of slot machines in denominations of a quarter to five dollars, blackjack tables, a roulette table or two, sometimes craps and Caribbean Poker. If you are an experienced player, you'll opt for the large ships with big casinos. You'll find odds at some games are not always what you expect in Las Vegas. Novices should pick up brochures and play for the fun of it. All ships offer gaming lessons as an inducement to sampling casino action. Cruise lines say, "Casinos are part of the entertainment offered passengers."

A sign of the times is the increase in minimum bets at various games. Long gone are the two dollar Black Jack tables. Minimum bet on most ships is $10, with maybe one $5 table with a three-deep crowd waiting for seats. On smaller luxury vessels (Radisson Seven Seas, Silversea, Seabourn), casinos are more subdued and are more like small European-style casinos. Some of the large cruise lines are forming gaming "clubs" for more serious gamblers.

Entertainment

I think I have mentioned the word a dozen times in this chapter, so entertainment must be an important component in the cruise vacation package. Daily activities, piano lounges, Martini Bars, discos, bands, orchestras, specialty entertainers, "name" stars or wan-a-bees, and huge Las Vegas production-style shows make up entertainment at sea. We could also include sports activities, shoreside special events and the daily routine that leaves little to the imagination.

Judging entertainment is like judging food. In order to judge entertainment, our panel of cruise writers left their personal preferences on shore and judged entertainment solely on the basis of audience reaction. For example: I may have thought the production show was amateurish, but the audience gave it a standing ovation.

The opposite has also happened, so we polled our panel and used opinions of the travel agency community to come up with the best entertainment offered at sea.

TT CRITICS CHOICE FOR THE CRUISE LINES
WITH THE BEST ENTERTAINMENT AT SEA:

$$$ – Carnival Cruise Lines

(The company continues to walk off with all of the top awards for entertainment, particularly for the spectacular production shows on every vessel. Shows are professionally produced, fast paces with dazzling costume changes and original music and choreography. There are two, and some times three, production shows on every cruise, depending on the length of the voyage. Every show brings audiences to their feet clamoring for more! Other entertainment features one night stands by a series of individual performers who are rotated from ship-to-ship, so the same artist does not appear more than once during a cruise)

$$$ – Princess Cruises

(On larger and new ships, there are two major shows almost nightly. Well produced by professional entertainers. Grand Class ships have two show lounges and timing is set so guests can take in two shows almost every night)

$$$ – *Norwegian Star/Sun*

(The newest ships in the fleet take Freestyle Cruising" another step up with rotating shows that allow the dine-where-and-whenever, with show times that offer variety and a lot of spice.)

Medical Facilities at Sea

Things happen even to healthy people on land and on cruise vacations, so it's comforting to know that someone is available on a 24-hour emergency basis to take care of the unexpected. All ships carrying 50 or more passengers have at least one doctor, one nurse and some kind of a hospital facility, even if it is just an examining room. The larger ship, the larger the hospital and medical facilities. Some, like the *QE2* which spends long periods at sea have a fully equipped hospital with two doctors, three or four nurses and a couple of orderlies. Cruise ships that sail closer to shore and stop at a port almost every day usually carry one or two doctors and one or two nurses.

The ICCL (International Council of Cruise Lines) has come up with guidelines for medical treatment standards at sea and almost all of the companies are exceeding those suggestions. Most ships that cater to North American passengers tend to carry doctors licensed in the United States, Canada or Britain, but others have doctors who come from a variety of countries. Some medical organizations, such as the American College of Emergency Physicians, have created a special department for cruise ship medicine. There is no industry standard or requirements. Most ship doctors are general practitioners, but some are specialists who are on a short term contract. Some have emergency room training and there are ships with virtual floating well equipped hospitals.

Major cruise lines have facilities to take care of emergency treatment and have examination rooms, an isolation area or bed, external pacemaker, oxygen, x-ray machine, cardiac monitor, hematology analyzer, and facilities to care for cuts and bruises.

Here's what you can expect the cruise ship medical center to provide: an ICU room, minimum number of inpatient beds of one bed per 1000 passengers and crew; isolation room; portable medical equipment, cardiac monitors, defibrillators, respiratory support, and a supply of the most common medications.

If you have a medical condition that requires special attention, you should contact the cruise line directly and you must notify them of any disabilities when you make your initial reservation, Cruise lines have the right to refuse passage if the disability is one the medical staff on board is not able to handle.

You should also remember that the medical facilities on any ship are not hospitals. The doctor in charge is qualified to minimize and stabilize patients and at his discretion to disembark them at the next port of call for admission to a hospital when the condition is serious. Ships do not, as a rule, have pharmacies. Bring your own medications and a copy of your prescriptions.

Expect to pay for any and all medical services rendered. Rates vary from ship-to-ship but can add up quickly. Standard fees are charged for treatment, including seasickness shots and any medication required. Add this to the list of good reasons to purchase travel insurance which will reimburse you for charges and pay for evacuation, if that becomes necessary.

I always suggest a dental check-up before leaving on an extended voyage. Only the *QE2* and a couple of Holland America ships have dentists on board.

INSIDER TIP

I broke a tooth over lunch in port one day and was delighted to find the Dental Office on board the *Zaandam*. The dentist was a retiree from Seattle and the temporary fix lasted for longer than the duration of the voyage. In all my years of travel, I had only one medical incident that required treatment. I must have eaten something in one of the exotic ports during my world cruise that resulted in food poisoning. After suffering for several hours in my cabin, we called for help. The doctor hospitalized me immediately, set up intravenous with medication. Within 12 hours, I was back in my cabin. The treatment was professional, timely and the cost was minimal, compared to what it would have been back home. In retrospect, I was treated better on the ship than I would have been at my local E.R. I probably would still be waiting to see the doctor.

Service at Sea

Service is another priority in selecting a ship. It is ironic that many American passengers, who may never have had the services of a maid in their homes, become quite emotional on the subject, especially if it involves foreigners. I have heard complaints about the most trivial shortcomings in service that somehow become magnified on board ships. The same passenger may endure the rudeness of a New York waiter, but once he boards a cruise ship, he expects the kind of service promised in brochures.

THE KEY TO SHIP RATINGS AND CLASSIFICATIONS:

To simplify the cruise marketplace, TT Cruise Critics Panel classifies and rates ships by categories based on brochure rates, amenities offered, and overall cruise experiences.

Budget – $$
> The low-price end of the scale. Usually older ships converted
> to cater to groups and low-budget-minded passengers.

Resort Mid-Size – $$$
> Moderately priced

Resort XL and Resort XXL – $$$
> Big (XL) and Bigger (XXL) ships carrying up to 3,800 passengers

Premium – $$$$

Vessels that may not carry fewer passengers, but offer more space per passenger, are somewhere between Moderate and Luxury in amenities, service, and ambience.

Luxury – $$$$$

High-end vessels that charge high-end prices and offer amenities, spaciousness, service, food qualities, and ambience above and beyond what is available in the Premium category ships.

Boutique Luxury – $$$ to $$$$$

Vessels that carry fewer than 500 passengers and have special dining facilities, offer unique products, and charge luxury or higher rates.

Boutique Adventure – $$ to $$$$$

This category can be broken down further to separate – adventure, resort, itinerary-driven, sailing ships, and exploration vessels. Rates vary as do itineraries, but it is an expanding segment of the cruise experience.

(For details on specific ships and categories in which they fall, see "Cruise Companies and Their Ships)

INSIDER TIP

Now that you know what to look for, turn the page and learn how to get the best deal and the best accommodations on the ship of your choice. Smooth Sailing and Happy Memories! Bon Voyage !

We'd all like a reputation for generosity,
And we'd all like to buy it cheap."

Mignon McLaughlin

Getting the Deal

To help you book your cruise and head you in the right direction, check TT (Total Traveler) Critics Choices and the Ship Profile Chapter before you limit your ship selection to one, two or three ships in your price category and one or two in the price category above. One never knows where the bargains are and it pays to think big. Cruise lines run sales and it is not unusual to end up sailing booking a higher priced ship for your budgeted price.

Armed with the time of year, length of vacation, destinations that intrigues you, activities or interests you enjoy perusing, your travel mates, and the amount of money you are willing to spend, it really is time to do more than dream about cruising. Take the next step – Book your cruise.

Here are a few tips:

When to Book

The time line on booking varies. If you had booked almost any cruise within a week or two after 9/11 you could have been sailing at a discount of more than 75 percent from brochure rates. Right after Thanksgiving the prices started climbing and by the end of January 2002, they were almost at pre 9/11 levels. As it stands at press time, prices are about the same as they were at the same time last year. Barring unforeseen domestic and international events, prices will probably close the gap before 2003 and "normal" rates will prevail. That is not intended to mean that you will be paying brochure rates, which have been proven to be fictional. Every cruise line has standard "special pricing" for early bookings, repeat passengers, early payments and a few other reasons.

Early bookers catch the best prices if they book cruise lines that offer "price guarantees." This guarantees them the lowest advertised price as the sailing date approaches. For example, at some point, the cruise line may find itself with an unacceptable number of empty cabins. It could be the result of cancellation of a large group or just that the cruise didn't sell well. Cruise lines usually face facts at the point when booked passengers must come up with final payment or they cancel the booking to avoid penalties. For example, you paid $1200 per person for your cruise and the line is advertising the same cabin on the same sailing for $900. A guarantee means that you will receive a refund check of $300 prior to embarking on the cruise. That's another place where a reputable and reliable travel agent will make the difference. It's up to the agent to monitor price reductions for clients and make sure the cruise line acknowledges and reduces the client's fare.

Another advantage to early booking, aside from price guarantees, is the opportunity to select the preferred cabin. The best cabins sell first and, with a price guarantee, you know you'll be sailing in the cabin of your choice at the lowest price.

Booking late has become a bargain hunter's dream. I met a couple on a recent cruise who say they keep their cruise clothes packed. They have a travel agent alerted that they will sail at the right price on practically a moments' notice. With current safety requirements in place, last minute has become one week before the sailing. This couple spends more time at sea than at home and are having the time of their lives. They have senior airline coupons that cut airline costs and admit they are long on time and short on cash. Cabins and itineraries do not matter. Their life is based on spending as much time as possible on ships. During the preceding twelve months, they managed to cruise monthly, albeit in cabins that ranged from minimum insides to a suite on one cruise.

But last minute booking is not for most of us who like to plan at least three or four months ahead so we not stressed taking care of details that need attention when we are away from home. Last minute booking isn't booking at the pier any more; not since 9/11 and changes in security at ports and on ships. The passenger manifest and pertinent information must be in the hands of U.S. Immigration and/or Customs officials several days before sailings. Last minute pricing usually shows up about 30 to 60 days before departure.

You might want to start your hunt for the best deal in your Sunday Travel Section but you should pay careful attention to the fine print. The lead price advertised is usually for an inside, upper and lower berth cabin and the not included list is probably a hidden factor. But, the ad itself indicates there is space waiting to be sold on that particular ship on that specific date. Check to see if the price includes port charges that can be considerable and there may even be a service charge imposed by the travel agency paying for the ad. But, it is a good lead and frequently also leads to an enterprising travel agent who knows the ropes to good prices.

Booking the Cruise

Travel agents, the Internet or the Cruise Line

Booking a cruise is not like booking a seat on an airline flight. There are a number of decisions to make. Cabins, itineraries, price and the ship itself are the major required pre-cruise choices. Who to book with is another one. Just put "cruises" in "Keyword" on the Internet and thousands of opportunities come up. I have checked dozens of them for price, service and choices. Some run the gamut and compare favorably to what is offered by reputable travel agencies. Internet cruise bookings lack that personal touch required by cruise vacationers. The little details that can make or break a cruise are lacking. Internet booking may be best for researching the facts and the price.

The Internet lacks the human element that explains, for example, that if you are traveling with a couple of kids, it may cost about the same, or just a little more to put the two kids in an inside cabin across the hallway from your outside cabin instead of having all four of you share one room with one bathroom. In that option, which is well worth the small additional cost, there would be two bathrooms, plus more elbow room and you can still keep an eye on the kids. Another advantage is a chance for private togetherness with your spouse or significant other.

As an experienced traveler, let me assure you that a knowledgeable travel agent is your best bet. While the Internet is a great source for information, it doesn't have all of the answers. At a recent conference, I polled Internet travel agency owners and the majority agreed that 85 percent of the time, the actual booking is completed by telephone. On board a ship recently, one of my tablemates was employed in the customer relations department of a major credit card company. She said 90 percent of the complaints lodged about cruises were by travelers who had booked on the Internet.

If you have never used a travel agent before, selecting your agent should come before final selection of the cruise ship. Look for the ASTA (American Society of Travel Agents) and CLIA (Cruise Line International Association) shields in the window or in advertising. ASTA membership is an indication that the company has been recognized by the professional organization and that the company has pledged to uphold industry standards. This does not mean the travel agent is an expert in every field. CLIA certification as a "Master Cruise Counselor" (MCC) or an "Accredited Cruise Counselor" (ACC) indicates the agent has been through training courses and has inspected and usually sailed, a good number of ships.

You'll know within 10 minutes whether the agent is patient, understanding, and willing to spend time to help you. Although airlines have reduced commissions to zero on domestic tickets, cruise lines still pay agents anywhere from 10 percent up, depending on the amount of business they do with a particular company. You pay no fee for the advice, information and cruise reservations. As the name implies, the travel agent works for the ship operator and is paid a predetermined commission by the cruise company. It's very much like the relationship you have with a real estate broker when buying a house. He gets paid by the seller but he works to find the right property for you.

The Internet, as I said, is an excellent information source. Every cruise line has a web site and they are easy to navigate. You can find everything you need to know, about a particular ship, including the going rate for specific cabins. Armed with that information, you might want to check the rate for the identical cabin and cruise with a couple of Internet travel agencies, then head to a reputable travel agency if a face to face encounter to put your mind at ease. In most cases, travel agents will match, or beat, Internet rates.

INSIDER TIP

Be wary if the agent tells you "XYZ ship is the only one for you." Some cruise lines pay higher commissions and overrides, and this can influence the agent's recommendations. Good travel agents will offer several suggestions and will take time to explain differences between ships after they understand the kind of vacation that suits your lifestyle.

To take advantage of the valuable assistance the agent can provide in your final cruise selection, you should offer some help. Be honest about how much money you want to spend, how much time you have, whether you want an informal atmosphere or dress-up parties, and whether there are specific ports you want to visit. Most importantly, if you have been shopping around, tell the agent what you have found and ask for his/her opinion and whether the agency can match or do better. Be sure to tell the travel agent what you don't want in a cruise vacation. Everyone's wish list is long and no single ship can fill every desire, but it's the travel agents job to come as close as possible to filling that list.

Chances are the agent will start loading you up with brochures, all colorful, glowingly descriptive, and somewhat misleading. There's always a handsome gray-haired fellow dancing with a youngish blond; he in a white dinner jacket and she in a ball gown dripping with jewels. There are always bikini-clad girls playing shuffleboard and buffet tables laden with caviar and lobster. Disregard the photos of people. The good-looking man is a professional model, and his partner's jewels would be out of place on most cruise ships these days. And what about the food? It was a setup for the photo session.

A good relationship with a travel agent could be the difference between a dream cruise and a nightmare. There are travel agents who only sell cruises. This does not mean they are more knowledgeable or less knowledgeable. Check bonding. There have been cases in the last few years where agents were under-bonded and went out of business. Agents who sell cruises are all members of CLIA (Cruise Lines International Association), and a $10,000 bond comes with membership. But that's not enough to cover a major default. Some states require sellers of travel to be licensed and to carry additional bonds. When dealing with a travel agent for the first time, ask questions.

When you take a travel agent's advice and the cruise turns out to be less than you expected, give the agent a factual report when you return. The vessel may have changed since the agent's last inspection. Conversely, when the cruise turned out to be more than you expected, be sure to tell the travel agent, so future passengers will share your discovery also.

INSIDER TIP

Where do you go when your Internet booked cruise is a lot less than you expected? A cruise is not merchandise you can pack up and return for a refund. As far as I can tell, your only choice is to go directly to the cruise line. When you take a travel agent's advice and you have a problem, there's no doubt that travel agents have more clout than individual passengers.

Readers ask whether "cruise only" agencies are in a position to offer a better deal. The answer is "no." Deals are not totally price related. Travel agents are paid commission based on production. It is more important to work with an agent who can handle your entire trip from start to finish then to be shuffled off to someone else to handle the air, and pre- or post-cruise hotel stays.

So what about going directly to the source and booking directly with the cruise line? To the best of my knowledge, no cruise line turns down a direct booking, but cruise lines do not have the personnel to respond to all your questions, and, like airlines, they may not quote the low rate you can get by shopping with travel agents. In many cases, the reservation agent will refer you to a travel agent in your community. I know of one line that accepted a group booking, and then turned it over to a travel agent expert who handles large groups. The reservations manager told me they could not handle the number of telephone calls involved with booking 100 people. Besides, dealing with an agent who is savvy about group travel could lower cost substantially.

Reading a Cruise Brochure

All brochures are beautiful, multicolored, and enthusiastically descriptive. Many brochures picture life aboard a cruise ship Love Boat-style, but not all ships are equipped to live up to their brochures.

Selecting the right ship with the right itinerary at the right price is almost a game of elimination. If you long for a relaxed, informal lifestyle and book on a ship with brochures showing black-tie-clad men, your dream cruise could turn out to be a nightmare. If you require a special diet and the ship's kitchen is not equipped to handle your needs, you could turn out to be the one passenger in a million who disembarks hungry. If you travel with young children and the ship doesn't have a playroom or planned children's programs, you and the rest of the family could be climbing the mast by the time the cruise is over. Conversely, if you want to get away from the kids and you happen to find yourself on a ship catering to families, you might be tempted to jump ship at the first port.

There are a few basics that should tell you what you need to know about any ship. Study brochures. True, most look alike, and except for logos and names, it may be hard to tell one ship from another based solely on brochures. But a quick read will show which amenities the cruise line is emphasizing. Cruise lines tend to devote more brochure pages to features they want to brag about. If there are brilliant pictures of group activities, you can count on a busy program. If there are photos of grand buffets and varied dining opportunities, the line is proud of its food. If most of the brochure is dedicated to ports of call, the vessel is itinerary oriented. And if there isn't a single photo of children on board, this is not the ship for a family cruising with youngsters not yet in their teens.

Check the ship layout, particularly with large ships. If you are bothered by steps and there are few elevators, you may be considering the wrong ship. Study cabin configurations and dining-room locations. If all photos show tuxedo-clad passengers in the restaurant, the ship may be more formal than you prefer. Then again, if male passengers are in short-sleeved shirts, the vessel may be a lot more casual than you imagined for your "dream" voyage.

I like to recommend a careful reading of the "Not included" and "Terms and Conditions" portions of brochures, usually placed on the last few pages in smaller type. It is important to know the penalties involved with cancellations. And try to read between the lines.

INSIDER TIP

Seasoned travelers have learned to translate some of the key words this way:

- Δ Informal or casual atmosphere: Not necessary to wear jackets in the dining room or elsewhere.
- Δ Children's special rates: Lots of kids, counselors, and planned activities, especially during school holidays.
- Δ Elegant dining: More than two out of seven dress-up "formal" nights.
- Δ European crew: Sometimes more expensive. Usually higher tips are recommended.
- Δ Compact cabins: Small staterooms. Very small staterooms.
- Δ Dietary arrangements: Special menus possible.
- Δ Standard stateroom: On the small side. There are larger cabins, but not necessarily smaller ones.
- Δ Gala evenings: Captain hosts a cocktail party for the entire ship at which the special menu at dinner usually includes lobster and sometimes caviar. Always one of the best meals of the cruise.
- Δ Casual night: Men, leave your jackets and ties in the stateroom. Ladies, follow your inclinations, but usually "no jeans."
- Δ Dressy casual: Resort wear of the "designer" type.
- Δ Casual atmosphere: Leave your best clothes at home.
- Δ Night owls: Late-night hangout for swingers and insomniacs.
- Δ Ultimate: See "deluxe."
- Δ Intimate: Low-key on ships with less than 300 passengers; small. Small lounges away from the disco crowd on the big ships.
- Δ Deluxe: The most overused and meaningless brochure adjective. What's deluxe to a budget traveler is not deluxe to a luxury traveler. My interpretation: It doesn't remind passengers of home.

INSIDER TIP

If you don't relish the thought of going into a small boat in order to get ashore, check brochures carefully and ask your travel agent: "Does the ship tender or dock in every port?" If the answer is "tenders, in some," expect to go down some steps, although many of the newer ships have tender platforms that make tendering a lot easier for passengers. Don't be timid about tendering, and don't let it put you off the ship of your choice. It requires care, but there is no danger. Sailors are where they should be to assist you. Sometimes tendering in a port (such as St. Maarten) puts you in the middle of town and has an advantage. You arrive mid-city and don't have to take a taxi to explore. (For more tender information, refer to the "Ship Profiles" chapter for the ship you are considering.) In all fairness, I should say that tenders on newer ships are very comfortable, some are air-conditioned and have toilets. Ships have also built landing platforms which connect the big ship to the small boats and boarding and getting off tenders has become a lot easier.

Big or Small?

Depending on preferences, there are advantages and disadvantages to both. Besides the smooth ride, big ships have many public rooms, and you'll probably have your choice of nightclubs, quiet and busy lounges, showrooms, more dining options, and possibly more than one swimming pool. Because of size, there's more varied entertainment and generally a wider choice of cabin accommodations. With more minimum-and maximum-priced cabins, there is a better chance to get the lowest priced staterooms.

But there are disadvantages. The larger the ship, the more likely it is that it will not be able to pull up dockside at many of the small islands and tendering will be required. And, when it returns to homeport at the end of the voyage, disembarkation and customs formalities may take longer. Also, there may be lines for various services, although computerization has eliminated many of the inconveniences.

While small ships offer intimacy, large ships offer the opportunity to meet more of your fellow passengers and there are usually intimate lounges hidden away for special "encounters" and quiet moods. It doesn't necessarily follow that passengers have more elbowroom and feel less crowded on larger ships, but it usually turns out that way. If you long for quiet corners, would rather walk a mile than stand in line, and would rather switch than fight, passenger space ratio should be considered before selecting a ship. Ship management has crowd handling down to a science on most vessels, but I like to blend activities with solitude on board ships; my own space is important to me.

So, a big ship or a small ship? More important than ship size is the space ratio that is a good indicator of elbow room. The higher the number, the more space per passenger is offered on the ship. To find the number, tonnage is divided by the number of passengers. For example, a 70,000-ton ship that carries 2,000 passengers has a space ratio of 35. With the industry average closer to 30, there's a lot of space to move around on this giant liner and there's less chance of lengthy lines for services.

However, a small ship does not necessarily mean a crowded ship. The 9.975-ton *Seabourn Pride* and *Spirit* each carry 200 passengers, making a whopping space ratio of close to 48.50. By comparison, the plush *Song of Flower* at 8,282-tons and 198 passengers offers a ratio of 42 (for space ratios on individual ships, see "Ship Profiles" chapter).

The number of lounges and ballrooms also contributes to real passenger space. If the ship carries 1,000 passengers and has one nightclub and one ballroom for entertainment, count on lots of togetherness. On the other hand, if the ship carries 1,000 and has eight lounges, three nightclubs, two ballrooms, and six bars, you'll have plenty of opportunity to find intimate corners, despite the number of passengers. In fact, when complete decks are devoted to public space; chances are you will never be totally aware of the number of passengers on board.

Ratio of Service Crew to Passenger

It stands to reason that if a ship has 500 crew members and 500 passengers, passengers will be pampered. Should the ship have 1,000 passengers and the same crew of 500, you're going to share that attention with another passenger, which still means a lot of personal attention. Should the ship have 1,000 passengers and a crew of 300, it will cut the service level a couple of notches.

Cabins a.k.a. Staterooms

The words are interchangeable and some lines think "stateroom" sounds better. Both words refer to the room in which you will live for the duration of the cruise. Selection of your cabin is one of the most important decisions, after selection of the ship. Bear in mind that every penny spent over the advertised minimum rate is spent on the size, location, and decor of your cabin. All cruise ships (except the *QE2*) are one class, which means that everyone eats the same food, sees the same entertainment, and travels to the same ports of call. Only the cabin is different.

The size of your cabin is much more important on long cruises for obvious reasons: more time is spent in staterooms. Cabin size becomes less important on short cruises and on a ship with an especially lively schedule of activities and entertainment. Cruise lines with small cabins claim passengers spend most of their time outside the cabin, but that's not true. The cabin is your personal space. It's your hotel room for the duration of the voyage, and there's little to no chance of making a change once the ship has left port.

Photographers shooting pictures for brochures have a way of using wide-angle lenses to make all cabins look huge in brochures. This is misleading. Most new ships built specifically for cruising are like motels, built for compact efficiency. The more cabins a ship can hold, the greater the passenger capacity and the greater the possibility of financial success. Cabins are larger on older vessels and on some new super ships. In determining the size of a cabin from a brochure, compare it on the diagram with the size of the largest suite. An average cabin is usually less than half the size of the largest suite.

You will do yourself a favor if, before you decide on your cabin category, you ask yourself a few questions. How much is size worth to me? And, how big IS that cabin? Those seem like easy-to-answer questions, but the information is not always readily available on most ships. Deck plans in brochures are color-coded by price and category, but I have never found a minimum-priced cabin larger than higher-priced accommodations.

Most passengers sailing newer ships are disappointed when they board and are ushered into their cabins for the first time. They find cabins small, smaller, and smallest. But take heart-even the smallest cabin has space to stow your gear, and as one travel writer put it: "Cabins somehow get larger toward the end of the cruise."

There are all kinds of ways to figure cabin size, but I rely on what I know. Based on experience, any cabin measuring under 150 square feet is small, very small. For minimum comfort, I would need 175 square feet or better. Another ship "expert" recommends a formula as a guide to cabin size. He says most shipboard berths (beds) measure three-by-six feet 18 square feet. Estimate the number of additional berths the cabin can accommodate. He cites an example: If the diagram shows the cabin has enough room for two more berths in addition to the berths already in the cabin, multiply 18 square feet by 2, giving you 36 square feet. Add to that the two berths in the cabin (an additional 36 square feet), and you come up with 72 square feet. Measure the space off in your own bedroom and decide whether you can live in it, or whether it's a sure route to claustrophobia.

Too confusing? Square footage of cabins is usually available and, if space is a consideration, ask your travel agent for the numbers. Average cabin square footage is usually listed in ship brochures when the company is proud of the size.

It may help to know that cabin sizes range from 140 to 200-square feet on new moderate priced and upscale vessels. Suites, of course, go to over 300 square feet, some reaching one-bedroom-apartment size, or even larger. Square footage usually includes closets and bathrooms, and the measurement is likely to include the outside wall.

There are two sides to the big-versus-small cabin issue. Some cruise lines will do everything short of getting physical to get passengers out of their cabins. They design activities around the clock to encourage participation in scheduled, planned and unplanned activities in lounges, in dining rooms, and on deck. On some vessels, cabins are so small that passengers are only too happy to comply. On others, cruise lines realize that passengers do more than sleep and change clothes in their cabins, and design staterooms with comfortable chairs and sofas. Almost every cabin has television these days, but in some, viewing is possible only in a horizontal position.

As for how much is a higher than a minimum priced cabin worth, the answer is really up to the traveler. The new breed of cruise ships offers a lot of options in cabin selection. Cabins and suites are preconstructed and installed on ships after the superstructure is in place. On all new ships, every inside cabin is the same. Every outside standard cabin is the same. Every deluxe cabin and in most cases every suite is the same, except for those named "owners suites." Cabins may be the same, but you pay for location, location, location. The higher up and the more centrally located, the higher the price.

If you are price sensitive, inside cabins go for the lowest rates and are on the lowest decks. These cabins are usually about 20 percent smaller than minimum outside cabins. They are comfortable, hold two or more berths, and have sufficient closet space for a short cruise. Bathroom facilities are about the same as in outside standard cabins.

Unless you are claustrophobic, the inside may have just as much to offer as the outside for the budget-minded traveler. Admittedly, it is the best buy on the ship. The bad news is that there are very few. Sometimes less than three percent of the total number of accommodations is classified as "minimum," and they sell quickly. First to sell are minimums and top suites, which leaves average-priced cabins in the "usually available" category.

Another choice has become very desirable. Once you've sailed in one of these cabins, you're not likely to cruise in any other stateroom category. More than half of the cabins on new ships come with private verandahs. Cabins are the same size as standards, but verandahs add another dimension to the cruise experience. Instead of just a view of the ocean, the cruise experience is expanded and includes your own private space seemingly right on the ocean. Rates are higher, but price differences are not outrageous. On some ships, private verandah accommodations run an additional $100 per person for a one-week cruise for a similar cabin without a verandah. But they come with a warning. Once you have breakfasted on your private terrace, communed with the ocean, relaxed with a drink alone or with a significant other, and experienced the "private yacht" feeling, it's hard to go back to verandah-less cabins.

Then there are suites, which really do offer the sweet life at sea. Suites come in all shapes and sizes and differ on every ship. They sell for as much as three or four times minimum rates and, as they say, you get what you pay for. Amenities are multifaceted: robes, champagne, hors d'oeuvres, butlers to attend to your every whim, and even dining opportunities not available to other passengers. (See "Ship Profiles"). Suites are for travelers who want more than the comforts of home and are willing to pay for them. It's interesting to note that suites are often the first to sell out on popular sailings.

Another price consideration is how far up or down you are willing to sleep. A tradition of the sea is "the higher the price, the higher the deck." Before air-conditioning and modern, quiet engines (diesel ships may still vibrate a bit more but are faster than turbine), upper-deck cabins were coolest, quietest, and sunniest. They still may be sunniest and more prestigious, but disadvantages make them a poor money value. Because they are farther from the ship's center of gravity, there is more motion. On some ships, topside may be a long way to public rooms and the dining room, which are usually close to the waterline. Lower-deck cabins often provide a more comfortable ride.

Some people buy the highest-priced cabins and suites for the intangibles they offer (such as dressing room, bidet, and sitting area), not to mention an almost guaranteed invitation to the captain's private VIP party. Some passengers prefer lower-priced cabins because of the value they represent. Most of us find comfort, convenience, and happiness in average-priced cabins, inside or outside, as long as they are on a middle deck. If the motion of the ocean bothers you, select a cabin as close to midship as you can get.

If you are thinking of sailing high, you should know that the late, late bars are generally topside, and party goers have been known to be noisy until dawn.

Other sources of noise and activity are the nursery and teen rooms. I was once berthed in a cabin directly below a teenage discotheque, and the rock-and-roll beat like a steel hammer over my head into the wee hours. Other questions you should ask include: Do I want to be close to the dining room, bar, nightclub, swimming pool, and elevators? Will early-morning joggers pass my windows as I settle into a deep sleep? Cabins close to engine rooms and air-conditioning units may vibrate more than others, and, if your cabin is near the galley, remember that chefs start working when the rest of the ship is asleep.

Vertical cutaways of the deck plan show how close a cabin is to various public rooms, so look closely at whether your cabin is on or off a main passageway (the latter cabins are a lot quieter).

Cabin location is really important. On a recent cruise, our cabin was second from the bow of the ship. We were almost directly over the bow thrusters, so whenever the vessel got into position to pull into a port, even our teeth were rattling. On another cruise, our cabin was far aft on a low deck. That placed us almost directly over the anchor and engine. Vibrations, particularly at slow speeds, were more than merely a nuisance.

Where's the best location? Divide the ship diagram in half, both vertically and horizontally. The closer you can come to dead center, the smoother the ride and, also, the most convenient to other parts of the ship. Avoid far forward or far aft, but you should know you will pay for a better location on almost every ship.

If you need elevators to get around the ship, opt for a cabin near elevator lobbies. Cabins and suites for disabled passengers are much larger than average cabins and are well located. Unfortunately, there never seem to be enough to go around and nonphysically challenged passengers are requesting these cabins. Most ships now require a doctor's letter verifying your needs. The "Ship Profiles" chapter lists the number of these cabins available on every ship.

For the cabin of your choice on the ship of your choice, book as far in advance as possible. In checking with all of the major lines, I learned that minimum cabins are booked sometimes one year in advance, but this does not mean minimums are not available as sailing time draws near. There are usually cancellations in every price category, and cruise lines have been known to realign cabin categories when space is available. There's a good chance of getting what you want on a last-minute basis, provided you are under deposit so the line knows you have serious intentions.

Some cruise lines accept TBA (to be assigned) reservations when a category is sold out. TBA guarantees that you will sail on a specific cruise in a cabin at least as good as the price you paid. Your tickets may be issued TBA with no cabin number showing. At check-in time, or within a few weeks prior to sailing, you will be assigned a cabin number, and chances are it will be better than what you paid for. At the very least, you will be in a cabin priced at what you paid. Ask your travel agent if a TBA is possible on the ship of your choice.

INSIDER TIP

If cabin space is what you're looking for, check the deck plan for the number of closets in the stateroom. A cabin with four or five closets is bound to be larger than one with two closets. Also, unless you don't mind climbing the ladder into an upper berth, be sure the cabin you select shows two larger beds in the diagram. The term generally used is "twin-bedded stateroom," and that could mean one bed on top of the other. Be sure the brochure reads "two lower beds." Another guide to judging cabin size is to check the number of chairs in the cabin. These are indicated on the plan. Some cabins are so small there's no space for even a single chair.

Traveling Solo

Nothing gripes a single passenger more than having to pay for the empty bed in the cabin. There are three ways to go, other than paying double. You can opt for a "guaranteed single" rate which means that the cruise company will try to find a roommate of the same sex and smoking preference. It's easier to find a roommate if you're a woman. Two women rather than two men occupy most shared cabins. For some reason, men are reluctant to share. If the cruise line fails to come up with a roommate, the cabin is all yours. Or, you can look for a ship that lists "single cabins." You should know that they are less desirable or smaller cabins, but you won't have to share the facilities.

The third possibility is the one I recommend. When booking, tell your travel agent that you are traveling alone and that you will pay for single occupancy, but you don't want to pay full price for the unoccupied bed. Normal single occupancy rates run from 20 to 100 percent over per person, double prices. Quite a price for solitude!

However, cruise ships are not always completely filled, and some companies are marketing aggressively to single travelers by offering "guarantees" for single occupancy at the per person, double rate 30 days before sailing. That means you will be assigned an unsold cabin close to the sailing date. (Information is detailed in the "Ship Profiles" chapter.) The best single occupancy rate at press time was on Crystal Cruises, where singles pay only 15 to 20 percent more for having the stateroom to themselves.

Radisson Seven Seas and other companies offer a limited number of cabins for 40 percent over the per person, double rate.

INSIDER TIP

You pay for one category cabin and your travel agent "promises" an upgrade to a better cabin. Unless that upgrade is confirmed at the time of booking and in writing as a "guarantee" or with a cabin number, forget about it! The travel agent has no authority to upgrade you. It all depends on how heavily booked the ship is on a specific voyage. Upgrades are sometimes offered as price incentives, and, in those cases, your written confirmation will reflect the higher category. When a ship is heavily booked in a specific category, the cruise line will sometimes upgrade passengers based on the earliest bookings being offered upgrades first. I have seen lines of passengers at pursers' desks complaining that their travel agents "had promised an upgrade after they boarded the ship." It doesn't happen. If it is not in writing, don't count on an upgrade. If there is space in a better category, the purser will offer it at the brochure difference between your cabin and the available category. And no, a gratuity to him or the hotel manager will not get you an upgrade. It may have been possible in the old days, but computers have changed the upgrade scene.

Price or Value

Whatever the price tag is for your cruise, you have still purchased the best vacation value in the travel marketplace. Your basic cruise ticket includes transportation to exotic or interesting ports of call, your cabin, meals (as much as you can eat and as often as eight times a day and more), shipboard activities, entertainment, and use of ship facilities such as swimming pools and fitness centers. Your ship is a floating hotel complex. When you purchase a cruise, you buy a vacation package.

Not usually included in quoted rates are tipping, personal onboard expenses, sightseeing on shore, spa/salon charges and the cost of reaching the port of embarkation (air, train, car or bus). Port charges and taxes may be included or listed separately. A passenger on a tight budget can figure almost to the penny what his expenses will be for a given number of days on a given ship. There are no cover charges in the nightclubs, no minimums assessed for drinks. Everything in the brochure is included, except for soft drinks, alcoholic beverages, gratuities, shore excursions, and gambling. On some European and Greek ships, there are charges for coffee at the bar. Some American-based ships charge for designer ice cream at kiosks and dinner in specialty restaurants. Some upscale lines include certain items (such as tipping or beverages) as part of the fare. Again, read the fine print.

INSIDER TIP

To protect yourself against default by travel agencies and/or cruise lines, pay by credit card. If the travel agent says, "Cruise lines require checks," book with a different agency. All cruise lines accept American Express, VISA, MasterCard, and others, and credit card payments do not cost the agent anything. Cruise lines cover whatever the card company assesses. Besides, if your credit-card gives air mileage, you will be that much ahead.

Cancellation and Penalties

Insurance

There is no penalty if you cancel up to 60 days before sailing, but some companies charge an "administrative fee" of about $100 per person unless you rebook for a later date. At the discretion of and in accordance with company policy, you may be charged 25 percent of your cruise fare as a penalty if you cancel within 45 to 60 days of sailing. There could be a 50 percent penalty if you notify the company of your changed plans up to 15 days of sailing, and if you do not show when the ship pulls up the lines, you may be charged full fare. You may also forfeit the price of the cruise if you simply miss the ship. Even if you or a member of your family becomes too sick to sail, you probably will not receive a refund unless you are covered by insurance.

It's easy to understand a company's position. An empty cabin at sailing time is revenue that can never be recouped. Your travel agent should suggest cancellation and interruption insurance. This is strongly recommended although it does add to the cost of the cruise. To insure against emergency cancellation and interruption of your cruise, plan on spending approximately five to six percent of the cruise price for this coverage. It is available through travel agencies, directly from the cruise line, or through your own insurance company or insurance companies specializing in travel insurance.

INSIDER TIP
Travelers who purchased cancellation and interruption insurance directly from Renaissance Cruises and American Classic Voyages were out of luck when the companies went into bankruptcy. If you are dealing with a company with an iffy reputation, purchase insurance with a reputable company and make sure the insurance covers "default." Passengers who purchased insurance with a default clause did not lose money when the companies went out of business.

If your cruise is taking you halfway around the world or even just out of your familiar neighborhood, travel insurance is almost a requirement unless you are one of those people who doesn't insure anything and believes nothing could ever happen to him or her. Companies also offer trip-interruption insurance to cover emergency situations requiring air transport to hospitals or back home. This insurance also covers missing the ship because of a late plane arrival, baggage loss, and limited medical bills. There are a number of companies offering this kind of coverage, and every traveler is urged to consider buying this insurance. There are catch-22s, so read the policy carefully.

Some cruise lines offer Cancellation Waivers for a lot less money, but you must pay for this coverage at the time of deposit, and it is not refundable even if you cancel more than 60 days prior to sailing. Waivers are not insurance and only cover penalties that will be imposed should you cancel within 60 days for any reason whatsoever, including just changing your mind. If something happens the day before the cruise, it does not cover your refund. You can purchase insurance that covers interruption and cancellation with the same terms and conditions through cruise lines at a smaller fee. But it comes with a caveat. If the cruise line goes into bankruptcy (highly unlikely with the big players), you will not be covered.

A recent case came to my attention when there was a "caution alert" for Boston and passengers scheduled to sail out of that port were concerned and cancelled about a week before sailing. Passengers who had purchased the cruise lines' Cancellation Waivers were covered, but the uninsured and those who purchased individual insurance were not covered. The latter just takes care of cancellations for health reasons, not for changing your mind or fear of a terrorist problem. For the $60 cruise lines charge for Cancellation Waivers, I am recommending both types of insurance, particularly on expensive trips. It's worth the peace of mind.

Be sure to ask your travel agent about coverage against cancellation penalties before making final arrangements for your cruise. Also, watch out for "preexisting conditions" clauses. This states that if you have a chronic illness or are being treated for an illness that causes you to cancel, the insurance company may not reimburse you for the cancellation if you have been treated for the same illness or chronic condition within 30 to 60 days prior to purchase of the insurance.

Trip cancellation and interruption insurance is a good option for most travelers. Insurance usually covers not just the purchaser but also family members, traveling companions, and sometimes business partners. So if a severe illness or death of a close kin causes cancellation or interruption, travelers are covered. But two persons traveling in the same cabin (spouses, friends, etc.) must each buy insurance in order for coverage to be complete.

Post 9/11 bankruptcies impacted the way we travel and travel insurers were quick to cover their backs. Most policies used to cover bankruptcy by cruise lines or tour operators. Some policies will not cover cancellation or interruption caused by strikes or, natural disasters (like hurricanes), or terrorist actions, nor are you covered if you travel to places the U.S. State Department has advised travelers not to go. Jury duty is usually covered. For travel to underdeveloped countries, emergency evacuation insurance is recommended, as is emergency medical and dental coverage.

When shopping for travel insurance, be sure to be specific about the coverage. Even after you get the verbal replies, read the fine print in the policy. You should know that throughout the travel industry, "acts of war" that cause trip interruption, cancellation or delay are not covered in travel insurance policies. Most companies have also eliminated default coverage and no company covers "I changed my mind and don't want to go."

It's a good idea to remember that Medicare and most other medical insurance does not cover travelers outside the United States, so check your personal insurance to avoid buying more than is necessary. Additionally, when travelers are denied payment for purchased insurance because of preexisting conditions, some cruise lines will make up the difference with travel vouchers. Crystal Cruises is one company that has announced that policy.

A lot of travelers are breathing a sigh of relief, particularly the 50-plus age group, which until recent changes in travel insurance coverage were not able to buy trip cancellation and interruption coverage if they had preexisting health conditions that could possibly cause trip cancellation. Some of that has changed, but with caveats.

Until now, people with conditions like high blood pressure, kidney or heart problems, for example, would not be covered if cancellation of a trip occurred within penalty periods because of these conditions. Insurance companies have been known to refuse payment even when next of kin had a preexisting condition that caused cancellation or even death of a family member.

Travel policies still have exclusions for preexisting conditions, but most will waive the exclusions if you buy cancellation or medical insurance to cover the full cost of your trip within five to seven days of making the initial deposit. However, there are still two sides to the coin.

On the plus side, if a traveler has a preexisting condition and is forced to cancel the trip within, let's say, 60 days of departure, the insurance company will refund the total cost of the trip but not the insurance fee. On the other hand, if the traveler canceled 90 days before departure, the insurance company would refund the entire cost of the trip including the cost of the insurance.

Unfortunately, we cannot have it both ways, and travelers with preexisting conditions who follow the rules are secure in knowing that they are covered to some extent. Not all companies offer a preexisting waiver. Some require that preexisting conditions be stabilized and no medication changed within specific periods of time prior to purchasing the insurance. Also, some companies add an additional fee to policies that offer a preexisting waiver.

Among companies selling insurance with preexisting waivers directly and through travel agents are: Access America, (800) -284-8300; Berkley Care, used by many cruise lines, (800) -343- 3553; CSA, (800) -348-9505; Travel Guard, (800) -228-9792; and Travelers, (800) -243-3174.

INSIDER TIP

When you purchase travel insurance, remember that the premium is non-refundable. What you are insuring is the cost of the trip, or evacuation as the case may be. Once the premium is paid, and your claim is made within the penalty period, don't expect a refund on the cost of the insurance. When I get these complaints, I always ask whether they have car insurance premiums refunded if they never put in a claim. That seems to take care of that question.

Dining

Another decision you should make at booking is whether you prefer eating at first or second sitting, which means about 6:30 or 8:30 p.m. Depending on the ship, you may not have to make that decision and you will be able to eat whenever in any of the restaurants on board. Breakfast and lunch is usually "open sitting" which means available between certain hours. Some ships have self-service restaurants open 24 hours, so if you get hungry at 3 a.m., there's a choice of room service or even a full dinner available somewhere. Each of the dining policies is detailed in Ship Profiles.

On ships where passengers have the choice of assigned sitting or freestyle choices, I recommend assigned sitting. You can always change once you get on board and it's easier to change from assigned to open, then the other way around because all of the best tables are usually gone on pre-assignment.

Finding the Deal

Everyone loves a bargain, but how many of us take the time to make sure that bargain is a real value, one where we get at least our money's worth, at best a little more than we expected for our money. Most cruise passengers want value and do not want to pay more than their next-door - cabin-neighbor.

Brochure rates, in most cases, are fictional. Those printed numbers are generally unreasonable inflations of what the cruise will ultimately sell for. They represent the price the cruise line hopes to get for the berth, what it thinks the berth is worth. What the berth actually sells for is anywhere from 10 to 55 percent less, depending on ships and sailing dates.

There are exceptions, of course. Brochure rates are usually reality on holiday cruises, on special theme cruises with outstanding performers, some river cruises, and special events cruises. The New Year's cruise ushering in the year 2000 was sold out and under deposit on most ships before companies announced itineraries or rates. Other than those sailings, every cruise line offers some incentive that reduces the rate from what is printed in the brochure.

Ship Quality

While price is important, before you decide on a "bargain," compare rates on vessels of comparable quality. You'll find they do not vary more than 10 percent. If one ship is charging $100 a day, and another $350 a day, there will be a difference; and they may each be a bargain based on what is offered on board. When a luxury ship on a specific sailing includes air as an added value when it normally offers cruise-only rates, it may be a better value to buy the higher priced vessel. When a luxury vessel comes out with a two-for-one, take a good hard look and compare prices. That luxury ship may end up costing just about the same amount as a contemporary resort-style vessel. Even if it costs a little more, a little luxury may be worth the price. When price differentials are small on similar quality vessels, let itineraries and shipboard lifestyle and other amenities influence your choice.

Value

Exceeding your expectations makes the price a good value. "Discount" is not a dirty word in the cruise industry. Every company has a policy that allows passengers to take advantage of prices lower than the brochure rate. The standard discounts for every company are listed in "The Cruise Lines and Their Ships" chapter. Here are some basic discounts that are available from almost every line.

Early Booking Discounts

Cruise lines are anxious to sell space early and to prevent last-minute discounts and costly advertising. They encourage passengers to book and deposit early by offering hefty discounts. Almost every line has an early-booking discount program. Some companies offer additional discounts from five to 15 percent to passengers who pay in full for cruises at least six months in advance of sailing dates. This is common on world cruises and other lengthy voyages. Interesting to note that cancellation and refund options remain the same even with early-booking discounts, but some lines are charging a $100 cancellation fee.

To discourage last-minute bookings, companies are protecting rates. Should a last-minute bargain be announced, passengers with deposits or those who are fully paid for the cruise at the time rates decrease will receive a refund in the amount of the rate differential.

Group Rates

Cruise lines have special rates for groups, and each company determines how many passengers qualify as a group and how much of a discount it will allow. Participants need not even know each other. The most common group is one organized by a travel agent and sold to clients. Depending on the ship and time of year, group rates can reflect discounts of as much as 50 to 60 percent. But group travelers may not be assigned cabin numbers until a couple of weeks before departure.

There are two types of groups. Affinity groups are usually clubs, organizations, churches, or family reunions that offer the lowest rate to members and friends of the organizing group. The other type is non-affinity, where any traveler may book into the group that is being organized by a travel agency. Some large agencies block space on a number of departures; others always seem to have group space because of the volume they generate for specific lines. On this type of a group, you may never meet others in the group unless a community leader or a representative of the agency escorts it.

Travelers with flexible schedules should always ask whether the travel agency has group departures or group rates.

Past-Passenger Discounts

To encourage loyalty to their ships, most of the luxury lines offer past-passenger discounts. This could often amount to as much as 10 percent. Other amenities are also offered to passengers who cruise again and again with the same company. Upgrades, special onboard parties, and even hosted group sailings at reduced rates are available to past passengers.

INSIDER TIP

Most cruise lines have past-passenger clubs that keep in touch with passengers. Clubs encourage and promote loyalty to their ships. Passengers are either automatically enrolled as members after sailing once on a company vessel or are solicited for membership by mail on completion of the cruise. Join! You will receive newsletters and brochures, and you'll be the first to hear about "special club" cruises, sometimes at lower rates. Should you sail with the company again, you'll be invited to a past-passenger party hosted by the captain. On board, you'll receive something like a commemorative glass in the hopes you'll sail on one of the ships in its fleet enough times to complete a service for 12.

Last-Minute Bookings

Gone are the days when you could go to the pier on sailing day and play Let's Make a Deal. Due to security restrictions, no one is permitted to book and board a ship at embarkation. Last minute now means 30 to 60 days before departure. Companies sometimes find themselves with empty berths as it comes close to sailing dates and rates are reduced. There are special offers that are advertised publicly, but some are circulated to travel agencies and Internet sources that have a track record for sales with a particular company. For example, it could be a special rate available only from a specific Midwestern city. Or, lines may run a short national campaign to fill empty berths. When that happens, early bookers are usually protected and last-minute bookers get the leftover cabins. It's not a bad deal for either the early or late booker, but it is not recommended for passengers who have preferred locations or decks on ships. It's a matter of leftovers, but the discounts are substantial. Some of the distressed merchandise has been known to make its way to E-bay and savvy buyers have sailed for a fraction of the price. The price paid on the auction site has no affect on what booked passengers pay. The "guarantee" only covers advertised rates.

Repositioning Cruises

Seasonally, some ships change home ports and itineraries. The voyage between Port "A" and Port "B" is a repositioning cruise. It's a seasonal sailing and per diems are almost always below usual rates. Most popular repositioning cruises are between Florida and Vancouver or California in the spring, when ships head for Alaska itineraries, and again in the fall, when they return to Caribbean cruises. Other popular repositioning cruises are transatlantic, when ships head across for European sailings. In 2002, rates reflected 50 percent and greater discounts on ships that included the option of taking the first cruise out of the seasonal home port. In some cases, savings on the two voyages were close to 65 percent and included air.

Back-to-Back

When there's unsold space, cruise lines nudge passengers to stay on board for more than one cruise, and they do it by offering discounts of up to 50 percent, and sometimes more, when two or more cruises are combined. Travelers with time should check this out. It is possible to combine, for example, a 12-day Mediterranean cruise with a 14-day repositioning cruise that heads up to the capitals of Europe, then tack on a transatlantic crossing and save about 50 percent on the entire trip. This kind of deal is for travelers who are flexible and are ready to wash and wear, instead of repacking when the deal is too good to pass up. Retirees are discovering this kind of deal and are saving a lot of money.

Low Season Sailings

Bargain hunters know that the only real bargains are available during off-season periods. There are no bargains during holiday periods, but sail the week before Christmas (or the week after the New Year dawns), and you'll cruise for at least 25 percent less than holiday travelers pay. Good bargain months begin after Easter and go through mid-June, then start up again after Labor Day and extend through to the week before Christmas.

Rates in 2002 reached levels that matched 1980 rates during these off-season periods, and there's no reason to think 2003 and 2004 will be any different.

Credit Card Incentives

To encourage use of their credit cards, card companies are working with cruise lines and offering major incentives for charging your cruise purchase on their cards. These offers change periodically, but are worthwhile when applicable. MasterCard and VISA offer two category upgrades on some lines. American Express offers upgrades and, with its Platinum Card, allows $300 per cabin shipboard credits on most luxury lines.

INSIDER TIP

The travel industry has attracted a number of bucket-shop operators who contact potential cruise passengers with offers too good to refuse. Most are for island vacations and come with requirements that you spend time to inspect, and, hopefully, buy, a time -share. Several states are cracking down on this type of solicitation, and some cruise lines tell me these operators have no authority to sell their products. People have lost money. The best advice I can offer is to check the seller carefully before you hand over any money. A good place to start is the Better Business Bureau in the city where the company is located. It is worth the long-distance call. When in doubt, call the cruise line and ask whether the travel agency is authorized to do business with them.

The Real Deal

Air and Sea

Forget the days of "free air." Free air was the hook, but like everything else in life, there was no free lunch. Cost of air had to come from profits when it was subsidized, or from on board revenue, or from somewhere. Someone had to pay, and eventually, it was the passenger in every case. Cruise companies are still offering packages with subsidized air but the price may be higher than you can get if you unbundled the package and buy the cruise and air separately. On the other hand, cruise line air fares are sometimes lower than advertised fares but lines report there has been a sharp decrease in the number of passengers who buy total packages. It pays to check it out.

However, there are some packages out there that include air and transfers between the airport and pier. These packages are usually offered for cruises in Europe, Asia, and Africa, for segments of World Cruises and for the entire voyage. Air allowances are usually a lot less than what the ticket would cost even if you use frequent flyer mileage. In 2002, ships sailing in Europe were reducing cruise rates and as sailing time approached, added "free air" from U.S. gateways.

Every cruise line breaks prices into what is known as a "cruise only rate," and offers an "air allowance" when the passenger makes his own arrangements for travel from home to the pier and then back home again at his own expense. In those cases, the passenger purchases only the cruise from embarkation to debarkation. In brochures with all-inclusive rates and free air, all companies allow for a reduction in price when air is not involved, and this amount is listed in brochures as an air allowance.

The reasoning is understandable. The packages are being unwrapped, and all the components—cruise, air, transfers, and pre-and post-land stays—are available with choices like a Chinese menu. Passengers have the option of one from "A" and two from "B" or something like that.

To find the real cost of your cruise, deduct the air allowance, then add on the components you need to make your trip easy and enjoyable at the lowest possible price. If you are traveling across the country or to an international port of embarkation, it pays to check the cruise line's package. The price may be almost the same, but it is easier to be met at the airport and transported to the pier.

INSIDER TIP
It is now possible to purchase transfers between airports and piers from cruise lines without buying the air. For example, I am flying to London on frequent flyer mileage, spending four days in London on my own, and then buying the Carnival Cruise Line transfer from London to Harwich which is about a two hour drive and would cost me close to $200 for a private car. Carnival is charging $35 and we were given a meeting point at a mid-London hotel and a departure time.

To combat increasing airfares and remain competitive, some lines are using charters for long hauls to Europe, San Juan, Aruba and Costa Rico. There are a number of packages to Mediterranean and European ports that use charters from New York. In some cases, you pay your own fare to and from New York, or the cruise line offers an add-on fare lower than the lowest economy ticket to get you to the charter flight.

Different rules cover charters used in air-sea packages. If your package is on a charter flight, you are obligated to return with the same group on a predetermined date. You will not be permitted (at the package rate) to arrive earlier or stay longer. You will, however, be met when the charter arrives and transferred; and your baggage will be delivered to the ship. At the end of the cruise, you will be transported to the airport for your return flight home.

On scheduled air, you may sometimes remain in the port area for up to 30 days, stop over in another city on your way home (sometimes for a small additional charge), and arrange to arrive in the embarkation city in advance of the sailing date. Every package includes transfers to and from the airport, security charges, and baggage handling, except when you deviate from the cruise line's air arrangements. A variable is port taxes, which only recently are being included in advertised cruise rates. Rules on deviating from the cruise line's air arrangements vary from cruise line to cruise line. Some lines have "Air Deviation Desks" and here's another area where a travel agent could turn out to be your new best friend. There is usually a $25 or $35 charge for changes from the "normal" itinerary or to use your favorite airline instead of the one selected by the cruise line.

INSIDER TIP

If your flight is delayed and you miss your ship, if you purchased the cruise line's air-sea package, the cruise line will take care of you and arrange for you to catch up with the vessel at the next port. If the same situation arises when you have made your own air arrangements, you are responsible for getting to the next port on your own. Don't expect the cruise line or the airline to come up with any compensation for the days missed on board or for the cost of the flight to reach the next port of call. Tip: I always fly into a foreign destination at least one day before the ship sails. Gives me a chance to catch up on jet lag and I never worry about missing the ship.

Cruise-only rate: This rate does not include air transportation or transfers between the airport and the pier. It is the basic price to which air transportation is added when the passenger wants the total cruise vacation packaged for him or her.

To find the per day cost of just the cruise, on a seven-day cruise, for example, take the cruise only rate and divide the number by seven. That will be the per day, per person cost.

Gateways

If your city is not listed as one from which the cruise line includes round-trip air as part of the cruise package or charges a nominal add-on fare for the flight to the port of embarkation, you are responsible for getting yourself to one of the cities listed in the package or for arranging your own air to the port. In the latter case, you'll pay the cruise-only rate. Air-sea cities are not the same for all cruise companies. Most companies list from 35 to 120 cities from which air-sea packages originate.

Shop Around

Cruise lines aren't the only innovative ship marketers. One travel agency offered a transatlantic cruise, combined with a Mediterranean cruise. Included in the package were land stays in Nice and a five-night Italy package. Price of the package was about $2,000 below the brochure rate offered by the cruise line. Travel agents in other cities are making similar attractive offers in newspaper, radio, and television advertising. In these cases, the agent either has made a special deal with the cruise line or is using part of his commission to sweeten the package and sell more cruises. It's called rebating, but not in cash.

Catch-22 on most fly-and-cruise programs is the cold fact that minimum and close-to-minimum priced cabins are usually not available. I can't say that cruise line computers block them out and use them for cruise-only sales or that there is no availability due to the limited number of these loss- leader advertised rates. I do know, however, that very few air-sea passengers go aboard having paid minimum rates. There are bargain fly-and-cruise combinations on ships sailing everywhere, including the Mediterranean, Pacific, Greek islands, and around the world.

INSIDER TIP
Scheduled airline tickets issued on air-sea programs are usually marked "nonre-fundable," or "Refund to Agency Only" which means you cannot get any money back for unused portions. These tickets are almost always "non endorsable," which means you can use the ticket toward another flight only as long as it is on the same airline. You also can pay additional amounts (except in rare cases) to extend the time period. In some cases, the air part of the air-sea package is as good as cash as long as you spend it on air travel on the same airline.

Port Charges/Taxes

Until late 1997, port charges and taxes were never included in advertising. But some states now require that port charges and taxes be included in adver-tised rates either in the price of the cruise or prominently listed as an addition-al charge that will be added to the cost of the cruise.

It is difficult to figure how a cruise line arrives at the amount it charges for port charges and taxes. Every port has a different method of charging ships that use its facilities. In Boston, for instance, the charge is for wharfage for coming and going. In New York, port taxes are based on whether the passenger is first class or tourist class and on the length of the cruise. But like taxes on airline tickets, port charges will not go away and passengers must figure on somewhere around $100 charged for port "taxes" on a seven-night Caribbean and Mediterranean cruises. Surprisingly, port charges in the Pacific are lower, and on a 110-day world cruise, the port charge is about $500.

When port charges are added to the price of the cruise, the cost usually appears in brochures on the same page with cruise rates, but since these charges are subject to change, cruise lines do not guarantee them. Arguing about port charges is like fighting city hall. Whatever amount is quoted, it probably will break down to what is being charged for port taxes, wharfage, and administra-tive fees for handling the port charges.

Paying for Your Cruise

Deposits and cancellation penalties vary from ship to ship, but the usual procedure requires up to a 25 percent deposit with your travel agent or cruise line at the time the reservation is confirmed. The balance is due 60 to 70 days before departure. Payment may be by check, cash, or credit-card, but take my advice and pay by credit card. Based on Murphy's Law that if something can go wrong, it will, it's nice to know that your credit card company will back you to the hilt. It's also nice to know that credit card companies picked up charges made to Renaissance Cruises when the company went out of business. Passengers who charged their vacations received full credit for the charges.

Several cruise lines have cruise now, pay later plans. Depending on your credit status, you can charge your cruise and pay it back monthly after the fact to your credit card company at the usual rate of interest. Each line has a variation of the plan and it should be checked out carefully.

INSIDER TIP

Most ports charge half the normal tax for children; some ports do not charge anything for children under 12. These taxes vary depending on whether the ship is delivering cargo and passengers to the port. Very few cruise lines reduce port charges for children. Most cruise lines that cater to families offer special rates for kids sleeping in the same cabin with two adults. Also, most cruise lines have special reduced rates for third and fourth persons (adults or teenagers) in the cabins with two full fare passengers. Not bad for four friends who don't mind sharing a bathroom. Just remember, you may have boarded as friends and disembarking as former friends.

Let's Count the Extras

The price quoted to you either on the Internet or by a travel agent is not usually an "all-inclusive" price. There are some luxury lines (Seabourn, Silversea, Radisson Seven Seas) that include literally everything –air, gratuities, alcoholic and non-alcoholic beverages, most shore excursions and special events. But, even on those ships, there are extras but it's not a nickel and dime situation.

On most ships, the extras pile up in the spa to pamper yourself a little ($80 to $100), shore excursions which run about $45 for a half day, and then there's the bar. Beer runs from $3.00 to $4.50; soft drinks are $1.50; bottle of wine with dinner anywhere from $35, and a glass of wine usually goes for about $3.50. I didn't mention the casino which has no limits and cash advances on your credit cards are readily available.

But if you are on a tight budget and take advantage of every possible discount routinely offered by cruise lines, you can reduce the cruise price by a substantial amount. On my second world cruise, after taking every possible discount, we were able to cut the price by 50 percent!

If you are total teetotaler and will never frequent a bar even for a soft drink and you will explore ports walking on your own, you do not need transportation to the embarkation city, and you do not buy insurance, your cost is limited to the cruise and gratuities which run an average of $12 a day.

However, for most passengers, there are additional costs. But if you are driving to the embarkation port or using frequent flyer mileage, vow to stay out of the casino and the shops both on shore and on board, walk around every port of call and never sip a soft drink, it can be done. On my world cruise, two senior-age British ladies were settling up their bill at the Purser's office. After almost four months on board, they had total bills of under $100 each. Gratuities were included for full world cruise passengers, but I still do not know how they managed not to order a soft drink. Just shows that it can be done if you watch your pennies.

Here's a more normal estimate of costs: I would add at least 10 percent to allow for those temptations that will pop up during the week and are likely to increase your cruise cost, see the next chapter - From Embarkation to Debarkation.

Cruise per person	$1500
Insurance	$82.50
Transfers	$50.00
Gratuities	$87.50
Bar, incidentals	$100.00
Shore excursions	$100.00
Photographs	$25.00
Total	**$1,945.00**

INSIDER TIP
Recent security regulations at ports of embarkation make it difficult to visit a ship, even if you live in or near the port of embarkation (port from which a ship sails). However, in some cases, travel agents can sometimes arrange for a visitor's pass. Arrangements should be made about two weeks in advance. If you are not using a travel agent, call the cruise line, but I wouldn't count on success. Visitors are required to deposit valuable identification papers (driver's license, etc.) with a cruise line pier representative before they are issued visitor passes.

Ports of Embarkation

Cruising habits are changing, and new ports of embarkation are emerging as favorites. They are conveniently located for easy outlet to the ocean and easily reached by car, train, or plane. There are guarded parking lots for storing your car while you cruise, and limousines, taxis, and buses to transport you quickly to hotels and airports (see the "Ports of Embarkation" chapter).

Be absolutely determined to enjoy what your do,
Every day Every hour, every minute.
For every day is the first day
Of the rest of your life

Unknown

Before You Embark

You've chosen the ship, put down your deposit or final payment and now it's time to get ready for the vacation experience. Here are some steps helpful tips that should help make a seamless transition from land to sea. They are simple, but important. Some concern specifics; others attitude. Nothing is perfect, but your cruise vacation is more likely to exceed your expectations if you are prepared and those expectations are realistic.

Documentation: Passports should be at the top of your preparation list. If you don't have one, get one as soon as, or when you start thinking about foreign travel. Current security regulations required government photo identification and nothing is better I.D. than a passport from your country of citizenship. Prior to 9/11 United States and Canadian citizens traveling by ship to most Caribbean islands, Canada, Bermuda, or Mexico needed proof of citizenship but in many cases a birth certificate or certified copy, voter's registration card showing your signature, or a U.S. naturalization certificate was enough. It may still be accepted under some circumstances, but it is a hassle and can easily be avoided.

All U.S. citizens, including children, are required to obtain passports in their own names for identification while traveling abroad and for re-entry into the United States. Unless specifically authorized by a passport issuing office, no person may have more than one valid U.S. passport of the same type at any one time. Following is a summary of the passport application process that was compiled from information provided by the U.S. State Department, which maintains a web site at http://travel.state.gov/passport_services.html.

First-Time Passport Applications: If you are applying for your first U.S. Passport, you must apply in person at one of over 3,500 Clerks of Court or Post Offices which accept passport applications or at one of the regional Passport

Agencies listed in local telephone books. If you can't find a Passport Agency, call your county courthouse or the largest regional post office in your area or look under the U.S. Government in your phone book. You will need to provide the following documents: Proof of United States citizenship or nationality such as: a certified copy of a birth certificate (one issued from a government office, not a hospital) for all applicants born in the US, a Certificate of Naturalization or Citizenship, or an expired US passport. You will also have to provide proof that you are the same person and a driver's license or any valid government or military identification card. You will need two identical passport photographs taken within the last six months. The photographs must be 2x2 inches with an image size between 1 and 1 3/8 inches. Photographs must be a front view, full face, taken in normal street attire without a hat or dark glasses and with a plain white background. You must present a completed passport application form DSP-11 which contains all the required information except your signature. This form must be signed in the presence of an authorized executing official.

Passport Renewals: Applicants who have had a previous U.S. passport issued within the past 12 years, and who were 16 or older when the passport was issued, may be eligible to apply for a new passport by mail providing they can submit their passport and their name has not changed. They may also apply in person. Documents required for passport renewals include: the Passport; two passport photos; a completed passport application form DSP-82 which contains all the requested information and is signed and dated. You can order an application form by calling the passport agency nearest you. Mail the completed application and attachments to: National Passport Center, P.O. Box 371971, Pittsburgh, PA 15250-7971

If you are sending your renewal by overnight delivery other than the U.S. Postal Service, send it to Mellon Bank, Attn: Passport Supervisor, 371971, 3 Mellon Bank Center, Rm 153-2723, Pittsburgh, PA 15259-0001. Your previous passport will be returned to you with your new passport.

Passport Fees: Passport fees for an initial ten-year passport are $60 if you are 16 years of age or over;, and $40 for a five-year passport if under 16. The fee may be paid by check or money order made payable to Passport Services for $45 & $15 to the county clerk's office, so you may need to bring two checks. Passport renewal fee is $40. Some local governments are charging additional processing fees.

When to Apply: Passport application processing time varies with passport agencies workloads. It is best to apply in the fall when workload volume is at its lowest. Processing time is normally about 3-4 weeks, but you should apply at least 4-6 weeks prior to any scheduled international travel. The spring and summer months are the busiest so the application process may take longer during these months.

In A Hurry? If you are leaving on an emergency trip within five working days, apply in person at the nearest passport agency and present your tickets or travel itinerary from an airline, as well as the other required items. Or, mail your application overnight express mail and enclose a self-addressed, prepaid envelope for the overnight return of the passport, along with a check made out to Passport Services and a request for its return by overnight express mail. Be sure to include dates of departure and travel plans on your application. Applications are processed according to the departure date indicated on the application form. If you give no departure date, the passport agency will assume you have no immediate travel plans. If you are leaving the country in less than 15 work days, enclose a $35 expediting fee (in addition to the overnight mail fee) and clearly mark the envelope "EXPEDITE."

Passport Security: When traveling abroad, carry your passport with you at all times in a safe place. It is a good idea to take a photo copy of your passport with you and keep it in a separate safe place along with copies of your credit cards, traveler's checks and plane tickets. If your passport is lost or stolen, U.S. embassies will usually accept the copy as proof that you're a U.S. citizen and can issue a temporary passport. It's also a good idea to leave a copy of your passport with someone at home in case of emergency.

Obtaining Additional Visa Pages: If you require additional visa pages before your passport expires, submit your passport with a signed request for extra pages to one of the passport agencies listed below. If you travel abroad frequently, you may request a 48-page passport at the time of application.

Changing Your Name: The name on your passport must be the same name on your airline ticket and on your cruise passage ticket. If your name has been changed, you may have your current, valid passport amended with this new name. To do so, mail your passport with your Court Order, Adoption Decree or Marriage Certificate showing your name change, and a completed passport application form DSP-19 to the Passport Agency nearest you. You must complete the application and sign it in your new name.

Passport Agencies: There are agencies that will handle passports and visas for a fee.

All have limited 24-hour recordings which include basic information about the passport agency location, hours of operation and information regarding emergency passport services during non-working hours. For additional information try the U. S Department of State's Passport Information web site: http://travel.state.gov/passport_services. You can also listen to automated recordings or talk to a live person by calling the new privately run passport information service at 900-225-5674. Callers will be charged 35 cents per minute for automated service which will explain what's in this document and $1.05 per minute to speak to a real person who answers your questions immediately.

Most countries require that passports be valid for six months after the conclusion of the trip.

Inoculations and Immigration: Depending on your ship's itinerary, you will need a passport, visa, and/or other proof of citizenship. Non-U.S. citizens who have been admitted to the United States for permanent residence should bring their alien registration receipt card, form I-151 or I-155l. In addition, some non-U.S. citizen residents may be required to have sailing permits and should check with the local immigration offices. Other non-U.S. citizens must have valid passports and necessary visas for the countries visited during their cruise. They must also have a visa that allows reentry into the United States if it is a round-trip cruise.

No documentation is required of U.S. citizens for cruises to Alaska. In some ports - Russia, for example - the visa requirement is waived for one-day visitors, or the ship is given a "group visa" that covers all passengers eligible to go ashore. Mediterranean and North Sea cruises require passports, although most have dropped visa requirements for cruise passengers.

For ports in South America, Mexico, the Mediterranean, and Asia, some cruise lines still suggest an international smallpox vaccination certificate, although the World Health Organization no longer lists it as a requirement. Check with your local or state health department or the U.S. Centers for Disease Control Baggage in Atlanta, Georgia. Information is also available on the Internet.

When visas are required for entry, your travel agent should assist you with the necessary applications and should forward them to a visa company for processing. Photos and payment will be required.

Security at Sea: Everything changed after 9/11 and one of the first concerns that should be put to rest is about security on the high seas. Cruise lines are operating at what is called Level III security mode. Expect heightened security measures in your embarkation port and ports of call. Increased security is very obvious at check-in. You will see uniformed persons at every entrance and exit, checking identification and ship boarding tickets. There also is a Coast Guard presence and escorts by Coast Guard and local law enforcement boats cruising the harbor as the cruise ship enters and leaves ports.

Every cruise line is enforcing extremely strict security programs and most are so subtle passengers, and would-be trouble makers, are not aware of the new measures.

Almost overnight a no visitor policy was enacted on every ship. Identification of every person embarking is carefully checked and proper identification (passports preferred) is required to board the ship even with a fully paid ticket. All hand-carried items of both crew and passengers are hand searched in every port and all luggage is being scanned. All packages and provisions brought onboard are scanned with hand-held detection equipment.

Security personnel are stationed at all points of entry to the ship. .In addition, every ship has professionally trained on-board security officers as well as many other measures in place to ensure safety. Vehicles entering ports of embarkation may be searched and checked luggage is x-rayed by most lines.

Interesting to note that while airports are still training security personnel, the cruise lines went to the ranks of former navy and marine personnel who have maritime experience. With tightened security, passengers should expect some delays, both during the initial boarding process and when coming and going in ports of call. Vehicles may be searched before entry into the port area and luggage will be scrutinized, either by hand or x-ray. Be prepared to carry a photo identification along with your boarding pass at all times.

In ports of call, passengers are not permitted back on board without the identification issued to them at embarkation. Some ships require two forms of photo identification. With new identification systems, it's hard to forget your I.D. card because you must swipe it through a machine to disembark, then again when you return. When the card is swiped through the machine, your photo appears and when questions arise, the security officer in charge is usually right there to handle the situation.

He who would travel happily,
Must travel light.

Antoine de Saint Exupery

Packing

Before you think of clothes, remember to pack your medications, favorite cosmetics and whatever it is that you never leave home without. If you have an existing medical condition, bring a copy of your medical records, just in case. I also recommend: a sewing kit, tape for emergency use if a hem comes loose, spot remover, and normal toiletry items. You can replace almost everything in the ship store, except medications and if you think they are expensive at your neighborhood pharmacy, wait until the ship's doctor bills you.

Best advice I can offer comes from lessons I have learned in the 30 some years of traveling the world. Clothes that I consider "old" are "new" to my fellow travelers. I never buy a new wardrobe for a trip! I may discard the clothes when I get back and go on a shopping spree to fill my closet, but that comes after I get home and these new items rarely see the inside of a suitcase for a couple of years. That keeps travel costs within acceptable limits.

The number of suitcases you take on a cruise is not really limited. Most ships do not have luggage storage rooms or space to stack your luggage during the voyage, so you will be living with suitcases in your cabin unless they are soft-sided bags and will fit under the bed. You should block-print your name and cabin number on baggage tags and firmly attach them to your luggage before arriving at the port of embarkation. If you have more luggage than you can hide in your room or under your bed, ask your room steward to store it for you. It is surprising how many corners he can find that you never saw.

Gone are the days when taking a cruise meant buying a gown or tuxedo. Cruise ships reflect clothing trends of the decade, and life aboard ships is casual, informal, and easy. Shipboard rules are flexible. People take a cruise to have fun, and if wearing a tuxedo is going to ruin the cruise, leave it at home. On the other hand, if the tux has been hanging in the closet and could use an airing, by all means take it along., If the urge to wear a tuxedo overcomes you, not to worry, They rent them on board and surprisingly, the shop is able to fit short and tall, portly and slim.

Cruise travel is a delight for heavy packers. When in doubt about whether to take something on a cruise, don't hesitate—take it along! Part of the fun is dressing up for a special night, and those nights can come as frequently or as infrequently as you like. Conversely, if you dress up for work daily and the thought of wearing a jacket and tie on vacation turns you off, there's no problem. Alternative dining options where casual dress is always appropriate are there for you to use even when the rest of the passengers are in formal garb.

When you receive your cruise tickets, there is usually a pamphlet outlining details of the cruise and recommended dress included in the packet. Use that as your guide. Daytime dress is similar to what you would wear in a resort and depends on climate in the region you will be sailing. Recommended dress code also is specified in the ship's daily newspaper, and there is a code used on all ships. On nights designated as "formal," a dark business suit or a tuxedo with a white, dark, or fancy jacket is appropriate. Women wear anything from dressy pants suits to an evening gown (depending on the ship) or long or short cocktail clothes. "Informal"indicates jackets and ties for men, and women feel comfortable in cocktail dresses, pants outfits, long skirts, or whatever they would wear in the evenings in a resort hotel. "Casual" is the night the men leave jackets and ties in cabins, and the women show up at dinner in slacks and patio clothes. But, no shorts, swimsuits, or jeans in the dining room for dinner, please.

Most of the contemporary ships list suggested dress as "resort casual". What it really means is that anything but jeans and shorts is acceptable.

On seven-night and shorter cruises, there will be one or two "formal" nights with the rest listed as "resort casual." This is quite a change from the old suggestion of two formal-, two informal-, and three casual-dress nights in effect not too long ago. Many seasoned cruisers find they are overdressed on short cruises these days.

While cruise lines rarely restrict the number of bags a passenger may board, most passengers are fly to ports of embarkation and are subject to airline luggage restrictions of a limit of two bags per passenger and one carry-on. Weight of each bag may not exceed 70 pounds.

INSIDER TIP

The weight restriction of 70 pounds does not apply to intra-Europe or intra-anywhere other than the U.S. Weight restriction is still 40 pounds outside of the U.S. and, take it from me, there's no point in arguing. If you are flying from Venice, for example, through to the U.S. with a connection in Paris, U.S. baggage rules apply. However, if you decide to spend a few days in Paris, then continue your trip to the U.S., your baggage will be checked from Venice to Paris and you will be charged for the overweight. I write from experience. It happened to me last year and I paid $125 for "excess baggage:"

The question of cruise clothing for kids shouldn't worry parents. Requirements vary from ship to ship, and parents are surprised to find their jeans-clad kids don't resist wearing a jacket a couple of nights during the week. Daytime dress is comparable to what they would wear ashore for any sports activity.

I always pack one or two just-in-case outfits. Just in case the ship is dressier or less dressy than expected. Just in case, I don't feel like dressing on a formal night and just in case my husband refuses to wear a jacket on a night when one is required in a specific restaurant.

BE SURE TO PACK THESE ITEMS IN YOUR HAND LUGGAGE:
- Δ *Medications*
- Δ *Normal first aid items like band aids*
- Δ *Cruise documents*
- Δ *Passports*

INSIDER TIP

I take pre-addressed labels with addresses of family and friends to whom I plan to send a postcard along the way. I also take a summary of the research information I have gathered on the ports I will be visiting. The guide books are usually too big and too heavy, so I photocopy pertinent information.

Between Airports and Ships

If you have purchased an air-sea package, look for a greeter in the baggage collection area on arrival. The greeter will be holding a sign with the name of the ship or cruise line. The greeter will direct you to collect your luggage and put it with other guarded luggage that is slated for delivery to your ship. You will be escorted to a bus, but you should know that you may be sitting on that bus for an hour or so while they wait for passengers arriving on other flights. Cruise lines try to synchronize arrivals, but it doesn't always work. My worst experience was in Fort Worth where the airport is about an hour away from the pier. We waited for two hours, then left our luggage on the bus and headed for a taxi. The greeter apologized no end and paid for the cab which was about $90.

If you are buying your own airline tickets, you can still purchase transfers from the cruise line through your booking agent or you can pick up your luggage and hop a cab. I recommend the taxi if there are two of you. It's quicker and there are always taxis available. You'll also beat the check-in of a bus load of passengers which usually results in lines at embarkation. However, in foreign ports, particularly in London, the taxi ride from Heathrow or Gatwick to Southampton or Harwich can cost more than $100. I suggest you buy the transfer from the cruise line. If you arrive several days before the cruise, the fare from London to any of the ports will still cost about the same. In that case, call or have your travel agent call the cruise line and find our which hotel is the departure point from the city to the port and purchase the transfer from that point. The same holds true for the reverse.

The Ports of Embarkation Chapter details approximate costs and distances between airports and piers in major embarkation ports. Most ships sell transfers to airports as the cruise draws to a close. These transfers are convenient, but usually cost about the same as a taxi for two, except in foreign countries.

Embarkation (Boarding Your Ship)

Embarkation begins three or four hours before sailing, so if you are handling your own arrangements, plan your port arrival accordingly. Stevedores will take the luggage out of the vehicle and stack it with other baggage to be loaded on the ship. The next time you see the luggage will be in your cabin. Stevedores or porters on the dock handling the luggage expect to be tipped, although signs usually say tipping is not necessary.

Depending on the port from which you are sailing and the number of bags you have, your tip should vary from 75 cents to $1 per bag. Secured parking for your car is available at all ports of embarkation.

When transfers are included in air-sea packages, no luggage handling at the pier is required, but dockhands have a habit of asking passengers getting off buses to identify luggage. If you saw your luggage when it was put on the bus, there is little chance it was dropped off during the nonstop ride from the airport to the pier. But if you did not identify your luggage, the stevedores would not have the opportunity to suggest a tip. This tip is not necessary when baggage handling is included in your air-sea package, but I learned long ago not to fight that establishment. To avoid harassment, pay the tip.

INSIDER TIP

No baggage-claim checks are issued when you hand the porter your baggage at the pier, but few bags (if any) ever go astray between the pier and your cabin. However, I am told most cruise lines assume responsibility for your baggage once it is turned over to their representative on the dock. Dockhands have a passenger manifest, and when they take your luggage, they are supposed to check your name on the list and note the number of bags you have given to them. Make sure baggage tags with your name and cabin number are firmly affixed to the baggage.

Embarkation Procedure

You should have received an embarkation form (sometimes called an immigration form) in the same envelope with your cruise tickets. This must be completed prior to embarkation. The information is required for the ship's manifest and for immigration purposes. To avoid delays and unhappy glares from other passengers, complete this form before you get to the check-in counter. Some of the questions on the immigration form are personal. If you do not feel like telling your age, leave it blank. The required information is name, address, place of birth, marital status, sex, occupation, passport or alien registration number (where required for entry), and your signature. Social Security number is also requested.

When you arrive at the check-in counter, a clerk will take your documents and cruise-passage tickets. Check-in procedure is very much like checking in for a flight. At the ship's entrance (sometimes up a flight of stairs or by elevator or escalator), there's that photo op which is hard to avoid. You know the picture with the ship's logo and date of sailing. It's a nice memento that will cost you $6.95.

Once on board, stewards or members of the cruise staff will direct or escort you to your stateroom. Your room steward or stewardess, as the case may be, usually introduces himself shortly after you arrive, and there is nothing more to do until your baggage is delivered to your cabin except to join partying passengers. It could take several hours before the luggage is delivered and when it does, it's time to unpack and settle down in your "home away from home."

Bon Voyage Party

Blame it on 9/11, but without visitors on board who are you going to invite to a Bon Voyage Party? The tradition is fun but unless you are sailing with friends, a group, or your family, Bon Voyage parties have been another victim of the times. Ships usually have giant sail-away parties in lounges or on decks and it's a good time to mix and mingle with fellow passengers. But, even if it's just the two of you and a Bon Voyage party is part of your dream cruise, you should make arrangements through your travel agent, or booking person, before sailing day. To the best of my knowledge, no company allows you to bring your own booze, so you will be charged for whatever you order, except the ice and glasses. A tray of hors d'oeuvres could run up to $35 on some ships, so you may decide to join your fellow passenger at the ship's party. Your room steward will help with your party if it is held in your stateroom. You do not have to tip him for these efforts, but he should be remembered at the end of the voyage for "service beyond the call of duty." If your party is large and a public room on board ship is used, you will be charged per drink and for snacks as ordered and you will be expected to tip waiters serving your party.

Settling In

Before your luggage arrives and before you head for the buffet lunch or the afternoon snack that is available on all ships at embarkation, check your dining room reservations. I hope you have followed suggestions made in the last chapter about making dining-room table and sitting arrangements at the time you booked your cruise. In most cases, your embarkation card which also serves as your cabin key has the sitting, dining room and table number on the card. I suggest you head down to the restaurant listed on your card and check to see that the table can accommodate the number of people you expect. This is very important if you requested a table for two. If there is an error, head for wherever the dining room manager is taking reservations and try to correct the situation immediately.

Some companies pre-reserve by early or late sitting only and require that passengers check with the dining-room for specific table assignments. Others reserve specific tables at early or late sittings, and the information is waiting for passengers in their cabins or at embarkation. If there is any doubt, check with the dining room when you embark.

If you are traveling with friends, make sure you list their names and they list yours as requested tablemates when you book your cruise. I have seen families separated because of confused requests. Even if you have made specific dining-room requests, if your table-assignment card is not waiting in your cabin when you embark, check immediately with the dining-room. There is many a slip between requests and sailing day. If a problem develops, the ship will not be able to blame your travel agent if you have copies of the correspondence. Don't be timid. You'll have a strong leg to stand on if your cruise confirmation also confirms all your shipboard special requests, including dining-room sitting.

The way I see it, if you want to sea the rainbow
You gotta put up with the rain.
Dolly Parton

Disappointments

You walk into your cabin and stop short. It's a lot smaller than you expected and there's no way you are going to manage to live there for a full week, or maybe longer. Take a deep breath and talk to yourself. If you selected the cabin because of price, write yourself a big note and paste it on the bathroom mirror. It should read: "I am in this cabin because it was a bargain. Think of all the money I saved!" Then, relax and enjoy your cruise.

There's no doubt that cruising in a deluxe suite with a private balcony (also known as a verandah) adds a greater dimension to the experience. But unless the price of the cruise means little to you, be sure you understand that every dollar paid for the cabin (stateroom) above the "loss leader" minimum price is for the room in which you sleep. The price of the cabin determines the price of your cruise. Everyone eats the same food in the same or similar dining-rooms, sees the same shows, and visits the same ports. The only difference is the cabin. Unless you can afford the duplex suite on the *Queen Elizabeth 2*, all other cabins are a lot smaller than you would expect, and a lot smaller than a hotel room. Once you have boarded the ship, settle down and smell the ambience. As you unpack, you'll be surprised at how much space there is for your clothes. There may not be enough cabinet space in the bathroom, but take it from this old salt, by the end of the cruise you won't remember the size of the cabin. Somehow passengers grow into cabins and even suites.

The second most common disappointment concerns the ship not meeting high expectations. There is a tendency to expect perfection and realistically, no vacation is perfect. No product is perfect. Travel agents and Internet descriptions draw images of total luxury in every detail. It's not going to happen even on the most expensive ship afloat, or the most expensive hotel in the world. In all fairness, cruise lines come very close to what they list in brochures. The hardware (meaning the ship design and décor) will be exactly as described, but food, entertainment and service are subjective features, as is perfection and satisfaction.

Most important is to ask yourself – Am I getting my money's worth? If the answer is yes, you should not be disappointed in the cruise vacation. If it was cabins that disappointed, try to upgrade next time around.

The time to voice displeasure with service features is during the cruise. That gives the Hotel Manager a chance to correct the problem and improve your pleasures during your time on board. If you don't tell anyone and wait until you get home to write a letter, you have waited too long to do yourself any good. If your heart is set on being pampered in the spa and a massage is part of that plan, make your appointments even before you head for the lunch buffet. It will avoid disappointments.

INSIDER TIP

Many well-planned pre-sailing arrangements made by travel agents have turned into disappointments the minute honeymooners are shown to their cabins and discover stationary single beds. Worse still when they discover upper and lower bunks. Travel agents are not infallible, and if a double, queen, or king-size bed is important to the enjoyment of your cruise, check on it again and again. The type of bed in each cabin is described in the brochure. If you are not sure, telephone the cruise line and confirm your reservations to make sure your receipt for payment shows the type of sleeping arrangements you have been promised. Whatever you do, do not count on rearranging the furniture to accommodate your sleeping habits once you leave port. Many a romance at sea has stalled at the rail because of bed arrangements. I read some place that 75 percent of the world's married couples sleep in the same bed at home. If altering your sleeping habits will ruin your cruise, look for a different ship. Moving mattresses to the floor can become quite a hassle and can be embarrassing if you don't put them back on the beds before the room steward arrives in the morning. (See"Ship Profiles" for ships with double-bedded cabins.) Conversely, if you are two single persons who do not intend to share a bed, make sure you have two single beds in your cabin. If you are assigned a cabin with a stationary queen-size bed, head straight for the Purser who will try to arrange an exchange with a couple longing for the larger bed.

When the luggage arrives, unpack immediately and settle in. Some passengers never unpack and when I peak into cabins, I am amazed. They are the ones who complain throughout the cruise. The sooner you unpack, the faster you will get into the rhythm of the ship. If you need additional pillows, more hangers or towels now is the time to ask for them. If you want your beds pushed together or separated, tell your room steward and you'll be ready to start your vacation without wasting any time.

Getting to Know the Ship

Passengers are awe struck on boarding some of the really big ships. While the reaction is somewhat less overwhelming on smaller vessels, it still requires adjustment to surroundings and learning the most direct route between two points which is usually between the cabin and the restaurant. Most ships have easy to use diagrams and there are deck plans, or what I like to call "you are here" signs at all elevator lobbies. Take the tour offered by the ship, or with deck plan in hand, spend the first hour (after lunch or snacks, of course) to walk the ship from stem to stern. It will pay off in an at-home feeling that comes when you know where to find the room hosting the activities that interest you. Most ships are designed for easy access to public rooms which take up all or most of two or three decks, depending on the size of the ships. Suites are usually mid-ship or on higher decks, with most of the decks devoted to cabins, inside and out.

In the Swing of Things

Daily broadcasts on the ship's radio, television, and loudspeaker system, plus a printed daily program, keep passengers advised of port arrival times, entertainment, scheduled meal hours, and limited news of the outside world. Without the what's happening on board information, you will be totally lost at sea. I suggest an extra copy in your pocket, so you can refer to it during the day. Some ships insert smaller versions of the activities schedules for that purpose. There is also a four page headline type of newspaper, but it's enough to highlight important news and sports events going on in the real world. Almost all ships are picking up CNN by satellite, and keeping up with world events is as close as the remote for the television set in your cabin. A strange feeling of detachment is likely to take over after the second day. The daily news broadcast that you never miss back home becomes less important than when dinner is served or when the production show is scheduled to start. The news is "out there" and somehow you are temporarily disconnected from the real world. That's one of the reasons many of us cruise again and again.

Safety on Board

Cruise lines take safety of their passengers very seriously. They follow "the be prepared" theory. 24 hours of sailing that is required by law. Every passenger is required to don a life jacket and go to a muster station. The number is posted on the back of your cabin door and there are members of the staff in hallways to direct you to the right muster station. Attendance is taken on most ships and passengers who don't show up receive a "demerit" in the form of a notice and sometimes a visit by a ship officer who explains emergency procedures. Passengers who need assistance and have reported their condition prior to embarkation will be escorted to muster stations, usually by their room steward who has been notified of their needs.

Cruise ships have a remarkable safety record but just-in-case, it's comforting to know that everyone on board and everyone connected with the ship is taking every precaution to make

If you always do what interests you
At least one person is pleased.
Katherine Hepburn

Making the most of your cruise

Here's where you really have choices. The daily program lists activities scheduled at 15 minute intervals and frequently, at the same time. From napkin folding to cooking demonstrations, from games on deck to bingo indoors, from wine tasting to a relaxation session. There's hardly an activity or interest that isn't covered in any one week cruise. There is no way anyone can do everything offered.

So how do you plan your day? Or maybe you don't want to plan anything, Take your choice. You'll notice that more than one activity is scheduled for the same time and there is no way you will be able to participate in every activity or attend every function. It's a Chinese Menu. Pick and choose. Whatever you do, don't stay in your cabin and just emerge for meals. Cruising is fun and you can watch television at home. Get out and mingle. Take in the sun. Plan on attending the production shows. Play bingo if that's what you call fun.

Entertainment is a day and night feature of cruising. The emphasis is on choice. Cruise lines are constantly improving diversity in choices of cerebral and active daytime pursuits, destination oriented lectures and high-tech cinemas as well interactive Internet access.

Music and dancing play an important part in almost every line's entertainment. By day, live music is used as a backdrop to a number of daytime activities. Lazy days or busy days, it's your choice.

Cruise Care

The ship's Sick Bay. You hope you won't need it but it's comforting to know that every ship has a sick bay and, depending on the ship, there's always a doctor and/or nurse on 24 hour duty. Just remember that a ship's hospital is not an emergency room. It is not equipped for major surgery and should the unexpected happen, you'll probably be evacuated to the nearest hospital.

Seasickness

Feeling squeamish? Could be Mal de Mer: Most people do not get seasick. Modern cruise ships are equipped with stabilizers activated when the seas kick up. Stabilizers are used at the captain's discretion to make for a smoother ride and to keep the ship from rolling with the waves. But stabilizers are not very effective against forward and backward motion (called pitching), so if you experience a light-headed feeling, a queasy tummy, or a slight headache, don't despair. Motion-sickness tablets usually correct the symptoms within an hour or so.

Nothing compares with seasickness as a factor in discouraging sea travel. Boredom, scurvy, claustrophobia, hijacking, sunstroke, malaria, shipwrecks, ice, or fog do not compare with the dread of suffering from mal de mer. Anyone who has ever been seasick—I mean really seasick, not just feeling squeamish—knows it is the ultimate kind of illness, albeit temporary. Early sea travelers tried everything: Mothersill's Seasick Remedy, morphine with atropine, pork fried with garlic, seawater, arrowroot and wine, tomato sauce, mustard leaf, cocaine, a belladonna plaster on the stomach, and Sodium Phenobarbital. Like Mothersill's, these remedies worked only for those who thought they did.

The true remedy for seasickness (apart from the contributions made by engineering and construction of ships) came abruptly and quite by accident. The cure was discovered at the allergy clinic of Johns Hopkins University Hospital in Baltimore. A couple of doctors were researching the use of several drugs for the relief of allergic conditions. One of the drugs used was a synthetic antihistamine called "dimenhydrinate" (later known as Dramamine). They were giving it to pregnant patients afflicted with allergies. Their patients soon began reporting that the drug also was soothing for car sickness and nausea.

The discovery of Dramamine made other remedies for the prevention, cure, and endurance of mal de mer obsolete. There have been improvements in the original Dramamine formula, and a number of drug companies offer nonprescription and prescription motion-sickness medicines. Should you board the ship without them, your room steward, the purser's office, or the ship's hospital will dispense them usually without cost. If you want to bring your own, there are the likes of Bonamine, Dramamine, or Marezine in the nonprescription section of most drugstores. In severe cases, the ship's doctor will administer an injection, which I have seen cure motion sickness in time for the passenger to enjoy his next meal.

Another product appeared in the marketplace a few years ago and it is reportedly effective. It's an elasticized wristband with a small plastic disk called Sea Band. It is similar to an acupuncture procedure that puts pressure on the inside of the wrist, but it does not pierce the skin. Affectionately called a cruise bracelet by passengers, who report excellent results, the Sea Band is available through mail order, at drugstore sundry counters and at most sporting-goods stores that sell fishing gear.

There are other techniques to cure motion sickness that do not involve medication. Mixed with common sense, they may work. Try inhaling lots of fresh air, deep breathing, and no overindulging in tempting food or drink. Motion sickness makes you feel as though your clothing is too tight. When the seas swell, you may have a tendency to expand in the same direction. If you're inclined toward motion sickness, wear your loosest garments and munch dry crackers. I know an old salt who says the best cure is a good shot of brandy to go along with the crackers.

Solo Cruising

Traveling alone on board ship is not the same as traveling alone on shore. There's one great difference. You may not know anyone when you board, but if you disembark in the same condition, it's because you preferred it that way. Ships have a way of blending strangers. Without even trying, you will know your fellow tablemates in the dining-room and the passengers who sit near you at entertainment events, out on deck, in game rooms, and at activities. If you want to meet other singles, there are parties for the unattached where cruise staff members handle introductions. One ship has even designated a smaller bar-lounge as a gathering place for "Singles' Happy Hours" on a daily basis.

Women traveling alone who are uncomfortable about frequenting a bar without male companionship have nothing to feel uncomfortable about on board ship. Fellow single travelers are in the same boat. Singles who don't want to meet other people don't vacation on ships. My best advice is to pre-request dining-room sitting at the largest possible table. When traveling alone, I always request a table for eight. That way, I'm fairly certain to find at least four compatible folks with whom to share my meals. When pre-selection is not possible, as soon as you board, run, don't walk, to the dining-room manager or maitre d'. With your best smile showing (and a gratuity), ask for a table for eight with other singles. If you are female, make sure you will not be dining with seven other women. It is sometimes safer to request a "mixed table," meaning a few singles and a married couple or two.

If you are male, don't worry. You have a good chance of being outnumbered by the opposite sex. You need only worry about the age of your tablemates. Single travelers usually prefer late sittings. There's more time to linger longer in the lounges before dinner.

Dining at Sea

Itineraries and ports of call often influence menus. Ships sailing in Hawaiian waters, for example, feature exotic local specialties such as cream of fresh coconut soup, baked bananas, and a luau of island pork baked in taro leaves. On Mississippi River boats it is not surprising to find Creole and southern food highlights, such as Shrimp Remoulade and Shrimp Creole. Royal Olympic vessels have Greek crews, so expect baklava and souvlakia. Vessels sailing Alaskan waters always feature freshly caught salmon, and those in the North Sea are bound to serve German bratwurst and kraut, Swedish pancakes, Norwegian salmon, and Russian borscht as they sail into harbors in those countries.

Incidentally, if visions of caviar and lobster nightly influenced your decision to cruise, you may be disappointed. Except for luxury vessels, some ships serve lobster one or two nights during the cruise, others not at all. I wouldn't count on caviar. Some have caviar at a price in champagne bars but those fish eggs are scarce in dining rooms, except on luxury vessels.

Dining at sea is a movable feast because that's the single ship activity in which everyone on board participates. Some passengers eat more, others less. You may not want to reorder every dish served at every meal, but passengers who disembark hungry at the end of a cruise are few and far between.

Rest assured, cruise lines keep up with contemporary trends in food services, as well as throughout vessels. Some companies employ famous chefs as consultants to spark up menus and recipes; others are offering optional dining in smaller specialty restaurants so passengers do not tire of the same table with the same tablemates for the entire journey.

You can eat around the clock on most ships, but that's not "dining". If you are assigned to a specific restaurant at a specific time with the same waiter and you and your tablemates are not compatible, change tables. See the Dining room manager and explain your dilemma. The longer you wait, the harder it is to change tables.

As for food choices and special dietary requests, ask to speak with one of the managers and make sure your food is prepared in accordance with what you specified at the time of booking. Waiters and all of the dining room staff will do everything possible to please guests. After all, their gratuities depend on it. Some ships offer bonuses to staff who receive high ratings from guests.

Many of the ships have optional restaurants that charge anywhere from six dollars to $35 for an evening in a small and very elegant restaurant and a meal that would easily cost twice as much in a comparable restaurant on shore. By all means, go for it, but make your reservations early to avoid disappointment. These restaurants fill quickly.

If there is nothing on the menu that tempts you, ask for alternative options. The dining room manager will usually come up with something. Try new dishes. Experiment with wines. You may find the taste buds developed at sea carrying over to your shore side lifestyle. Maybe not with escargot nightly and probably not with the ice carvings and the napkins folded into elegant forms.

Going Ashore in Foreign Ports

If your ship is heading in directions other than the Caribbean or Mexico, it's always a good idea to have a small quantity of local currency with you in case of emergency. You will probably get the best rate of exchange in a local bank, but they are not always conveniently located and hours of operation may not coincide with the ship's arrival time. Ships will usually have an exchange desk open on board shortly after the ship arrives and again an hour or so before departure. I recommend changing $10 or $20 and reconverting whatever you have left back to U.S. dollars. Just remember to spend your coins. Most exchange places do not accept coins. I usually keep a few as souvenirs and donate the rest to kids who hang around the ship. Taxis do not usually take dollars in most countries, but many accept credit cards.

It's also a good idea to keep some small U.S. bills with you when you're traveling overseas. I take a stack of one dollar bills which come in handy for tipping, soft drinks and souvenirs. You can always exchange traveler's checks for local currency and ATM machines are everywhere. Incidentally, ATM's frequently offer the best exchange rates because you are dealing directly with a bank. The bad news is that some limit the amount you are permitted to withdraw and others do not honor all bank cards.

The only way you are going to know if you are getting the best exchange rate, is if you are aware of what the current rate is and that changes so fast, it's almost impossible to keep current. The difference between the best and not quite the best is so small; I don't waste precious time in port shopping for the best rate after I have spent thousands on the trip. Use your ATM or credit cards and you'll do well in the exchange business. On a recent trip, we used a credit card to pay for a pricey sculpture in Murano, outside of Venice. When the bill arrived, it was about $200 less than what we thought we had paid. Seems the Italian lire had taken a drop and we benefited from the exchange.

Credit card companies add fees for transactions made in foreign currencies but it shouldn't deter you from using them. It beats carrying a lot of cash or travelers checks.

INSIDER TIP

The worst rates are usually in change bureaus in touristy areas. There's a tendency in those areas to post the sell rate for $US instead of the buy rate which is what you want when you are exchanging US dollars for local currency. Money changers also are known to list a super rate, but that only applies if you are changing $100 bills. With the Euro being used in many countries, the exchange rate per Euro is based on the country's currency and fluctuates although the currency is the same.

Shore Excursions

You may feel like you are landlocked at a resort, but the realization that you are sailing to foreign places sets in when you must decide what you will do in every port. Your choices are really easy. Follow your interests. If you have been to St, Thomas a dozen times, shopped Main Street from one end to the other and would rather play golf, opt for the golf tour offered by the ship.

Shore excursions in every port have been expanded beyond belief. You can horseback ride on the beach, swim with the stingrays, climb mountains, drive your own jeep to ancient ruins, visit Ephesus or Petra, or just chill out on a beach. No matter what you choose to do, the ship probably offers a tour. Prices run about $45- $50 for half day tours; more for golf at a local club; and about $100 for a full day, which usually includes lunch at a local eatery. (See Ports of Call for more tips on shore excursions, shopping and sightseeing)

In English speaking countries, it is sometimes less expensive for four people to hire a taxi with a driver who acts as a guide. If you're lucky, he'll talk you through a couple of hours, but it's more likely that unless you have a planned itinerary for the half or full day, you'll end up in his "cousin's" shop for most of the day.

Shipboard Facilities

Although facilities and conveniences vary from ship to ship, most offer similar, if not identical, services, but degree and quality of these services differ. Every attempt has been made to detail the services and differences in the "Ship Profiles" chapter, but here's what you can expect on most ships.

Banking: The U.S. dollar is the official currency used on all ships sailing from U.S. ports or marketing in the United States or Canada. On ships sailing from Mediterranean, British, or other ports, and marketed to residents of countries other than the United States or Canada, official currency used on board is based on the ship's registry, ownership, and/or nationality of the majority of the passengers. The purser's office maintains a bank for cashing traveler's checks, but his supply of cash is often limited on non-American-based ships. Caribbean cruising vessels always have enough greenbacks on hand to take care of demand.

Just about every ship has converted to a computerized cashless society. It is a credit-card system wherein you give the ship an imprint of your MasterCard, VISA, American Express, Diners, or Discovery card and receive a ship identification card, which permits you to sign for your drinks, shore excursions, and usually purchases in shops on board. A final printout of your charges is placed under your door during the last night on board so you can verify the amount that will be charged to your credit-card and will ultimately show up on your next credit-card statement.

It's an excellent system. I have found errors, however, but they were quickly corrected before I left the ship. The system eliminates the need for carrying cash, except in the casino, and most casinos are happy either to charge up to a certain limit to your ship's account or to charge chips to your credit card. There are limits, of course.

If you are one of the minority who does not carry a credit card, you will be asked to deposit an amount of money that you think will cover your expenses during the voyage. When the balance runs out, you'll have to come up with more cash. Personal checks are not accepted but Travelers Checks are as good as cash.

INSIDER TIP

Should you run short of cash, use your credit cards in ports of call for allowable cash. VISA and MasterCard and others allow you $250 with your card. Carte Blanche and American Express allow up to $500. Gold cards and Platinum cards allow more. Shipboard casinos will give you cash or chips up to your credit-card allowance, but most charge a 3 percent fee for this service. Other will give you chips or cash and charge limited amounts to your ship account. Also, where currency other than U.S. dollars is used on board ship, you can expect about a 10 percent differential in favor of the ship on the exchange, compared with the official rate. The purser calls this breakage, but it's more like extra revenue for the ship. If you learn the ship will be using English pounds, for instance, you might want to exchange your money at a bank en route to the ship or at your first port of call. You'll be pence and pounds ahead, and there's no problem converting back if you have extra. When you decide on how much to convert, remember that tipping is in whatever currency is "official" on board, but dollars are always accepted. Many ships bring local bank representatives on board when the ship arrives in port. This is a great convenience to passengers, and the exchange is at bank rates. The bank representative usually stays on board until an hour or so before the ship sails so passengers can convert leftover local currency back into dollars. When this system is used, passengers are advised in advance and the exchange rate is listed in the daily bulletin. .

Money changing is getting easier in Europe with the Euro, Once you convert into Euros, you can use them in most countries. The exception is the U.K

Personal Safes and Safety Deposit Boxes

Most of the ships built in the late 1980s and 1990s have eliminated the need for safety deposit boxes at the Purser's Office by installing personal safes in all cabins. Almost all ships a limited number of safety deposit boxes at the purser's office, which works like a vault in your neighborhood bank. They are available to passengers from the purser in charge of the ship's bank. I keep everything in the cabin safe, but if you're traveling with the family jewels, it may be advisable for passengers to deposit valuables and large sums of money in safety deposit boxes. Some ships have 24-hour access to the vaults; others, 12-hour access. Older ships still use a master safe for all passengers' valuables. In those cases, you are given an envelope, which you seal. A portion of the envelope is used as your receipt. I don't particularly like that system, but it has worked for many years. I much prefer the newer system of small safes in state-rooms. (See "Ship Profiles" chapter.)

Bars and Lounges

Opening and closing times of bars are announced daily and vary when the ship is at sea or in port. Bar prices are listed, and alcoholic mixed drinks cost close to what you pay in a shoreside bar: $3.75 to $4.50 per drink, depending on the ship. The highest price I have come across was $6.75 for a premium brand. Gone are the days of cheap booze cruises. Almost all ships have happy hours and daily specials when these same drinks sell for half the price. The good old days when a Scotch and soda cost 35 cents have disappeared. It's hard to find a ship charging less than $3.75 per drink, and, sorry to say, it's getting easy to find ships where drinks are going for more than $5.

The sale of alcoholic beverages may be restricted by U.S. Customs while the ship is in port and in territorial waters, or the price may be higher during U.S. port times because of taxes.

INSIDER TIP

Which bars are for you? Based on about 30 years of cruising, I find that certain passengers seem to congregate at "favorite" bars and lounges. For example, singles who want to mingle can be found in piano bars and intimate rooms. Couples like quiet bars and lounges, and the "crowd" seeks the noisiest bar with the loudest music. It is always the same bar on every ship. The place for singles to meet on Carnival ships is the midship bar on Promenade Deck. On Royal Caribbean, it's always the Schooner Bar. On Princess, it's the piano lounges, and on Silversea, it's The Bar. If you're wondering which bar is the singles' choice, ask any bartender or the cruise director.

Casinos

There are very few exceptions to the rule that if you are cruising, you'll have a hard time avoiding the casino on any ship, except on *Disney Wonder* or *Disney Magic*. Gaming rooms are in prominent locations and are what I call walk-through rooms. You are almost forced to walk through the casino as you go from bow to stern on some decks. Casinos are reasonable facsimiles of what you would find in Las Vegas or Atlantic City, depending on the size and age of the vessel. They are always the glitziest room on board with flashing neon and contagious tumult. Usual games of chance are rows of slot machines in denominations of a quarter to five dollars, blackjack tables, a roulette table or two, sometimes craps and Caribbean Poker. If you are an experienced player, you'll opt for the large ships with big casinos. You'll find odds at some games are not quite the same as in Las Vegas. Novices should pick up brochures and play for the fun of it. All ships offer gaming lessons as an inducement to sampling casino action. Cruise lines say, "Casinos are part of the entertainment offered passengers."

American riverboats that carry overnight passengers do not have casinos. Neither do riverboats in Europe. Casinos are closed in most ports and within certain territorial waters. At sea, they stay open until the predawn hours.

Keeping in Touch

Letters, parcels, and telegrams will be delivered to your cabin shortly after they are received on board. Your packet of travel documents should have names and addresses of the shipping company's port agents who receive the ship mail and deliver it to the vessel when it arrives in port.

If your packet does not include these addresses and telex numbers, ask your travel agent to get the list for you or contact the cruise line if you want to receive letters from home while you are cruising. Leave this information with family, friends, or the office and include the ship's radio call letters for emergency purposes.

Just because you're out at sea doesn't mean you must be out of touch with family, friends, or your business, unless you want to be. All ships are equipped with radio and telegraph facilities, and depending on sophistication of the equipment, it is possible to telephone anywhere in the world from the radio room. On most ships, direct dialing is available from your stateroom telephone and it is possible to charge the call to your calling card or credit-card. If there's a problem, the ship's radio operator will assist you with rates and placing calls. On some of the new ships, passengers have the option of placing telephone calls through the marine operator or through satellite communications networks. Prices vary. On one ship, it cost me only $6.50 per minute to telephone Miami from somewhere off the coast of China. On another, it was $30 to call Miami from somewhere off the coast of Colombia. Satellite communications have reduced ship-to-shore telephone costs, and on a recent cruise, a three-minute call "special" was being promoted for a total cost of $4.95.

Due to international law, the radio room is closed and telephone calls from the ship cannot be made while the vessel is in port. The ship information office will assist you in locating communications facilities on shore. Almost all ships have intra-vessel telephone service so you can telephone ship offices and other passengers in their cabins.

Almost every cruise ship has some kind of Internet connection. Some have large supervised Internet Cafes open 24 hours for checking personal mailboxes, or surfing the Net. They all offer easy access to the Net, but on some you must use the ship's e-mail address to receive messages. (See Ship Profiles) Cost is nominal and ranges from 75 cents to one dollar per minute. Access is fast and some ships offer access from staterooms and suites as well as from the Café.

Electricity on Board

Ships of the 1980s and 1990s have 110/115 and 220/240 volt AC outlets in staterooms and special outlets in bathrooms for electric shavers. Your hair dryer will sometimes not operate from this outlet. Current and cycles vary from ship to ship, and plugging in without checking could destroy your appliance. If electricity does not match that of your appliance, ask the room steward for the loan of a converter to step the 220 volts down to 110, or ask him where you can safely use your curler or dryer. I travel with voltage convertible appliances and only need adapters in order to use whatever current is available. Adapters are available in the ship's stores or from room stewards. All ships built after the mid-1990s have both 110 and 220 in cabins, and you usually do not need adapters.

Beauty Shops

All ships have hairdressing salons for men and women. The beauty shop gets mighty busy halfway through a cruise, and early appointments are suggested. Expect to pay about $35 for a shampoo and set or blow-dry, plus a $5 tip. Same for men. Operators range from rushed to surprisingly good. Don't expect Vidal Sassoon. I might hesitate when it comes to coloring or cutting my hair, but a shampoo and set or blow-dry has never been a real problem. A British-based company, Steiner Leisure, runs most of the salons, but some ships are moving toward boutique operators.

INSIDER TIP
Hairdressers and masseurs or masseuses get a nice commission on products they sell to passengers. On some ships, the sales pitch is subtle, on others, very direct. The products may be wonderful, and you may be very pleased with the purchase. On the other hand, wear your strongest sales-resistant armor if you do not intend to purchase any of the high-priced products.

Laundry

Every ship offers valet laundry service. Price lists and laundry bags are available from your room steward. Ships designed for cruises longer than one week usually have self-service laundry rooms with electric washers and dryers for the use of passengers at no charge. Some ships even furnish the soap. There is also an iron and ironing board available for passengers' use in laundry rooms, and room stewards will arrange to have your clothes pressed, as needed, by professionals for a little more than a reasonable fee. Some machines require a token, obtainable at the purser's office for about 50 cents. Laundry and dry-cleaning services do not cost much more than on shore and I find the Chinese laundrymen do an excellent job on tuxedo shirts. To play safe, I always bring my own stain remover.

Libraries

Ships' libraries range from fair to excellent, but most ships have adequate reading material at no cost. Some require a deposit, others just a signature that is crossed off when the book is returned. Some ask for $5 deposits. If you are an avid reader, best advice is to bring your own reading materials with you. Libraries also lend videos when cabins have recorders in cabins. Most have an excellent inventory of new and old films. On some ships, 24-hour use of a video is offered without charge.

Medical Services

All cruise ships have medical facilities, but they are not prepared to provide more than emergency care, which is usually no problem on Caribbean, Mexican, and Alaskan cruises because the next port of call is never more than 24 hours away. There is always a doctor on board, sometimes two, and at least one nurse, three or four on larger vessels. Some ships are equipped with small hospitals.

There is no charge for treatment of seasickness, but doctors do charge for treatment of conditions unrelated to shipboard travel. The fee is generally $35 to $45 for treatment in the ship hospital and $40 to $60 if the doctor makes a stateroom visit. Limited amounts of prescription medicines are available aboard ship, so passengers are advised to bring an adequate supply with them. Medicare does not reimburse these charges, but cruise insurance usually includes some medical coverage. Be sure to ask for a paid receipt itemizing treatment and diagnosis.

If you suffer from a chronic ailment that may require special care during your cruise, be sure to bring a brief medical history to aid the ship's doctor. This also is true if you are allergic to specific foods or medicines. In extreme emergencies, the ship's doctor will telephone your doctor on shore, and complete records can be faxed or E-mailed to the ship. Remember, the ship is equipped to handle first-aid care on an emergency basis. More serious conditions may require hospitalization, in which case the ship's doctor has the authority to arrange for hospitalization in the next port of call, or the ship will arrange for your transportation back home. This will be at the passenger's expense, and there is no refund due for the unused portion of the cruise. However, cost of evacuation for medical emergency reasons is included in recommended trip cancellation and interruption insurance.

Newer and larger ships have mini-hospitals on board and can even accommodate overnight patients. They are equipped with X rays and life-saving drugs and machinery, which will hold patients until the next port of call for transport to a full-facility hospital. (See "Ship Profiles" for exceptions to medical facilities on riverboats.)

INSIDER TIP

Be sure your teeth are in good condition if you're off on a long cruise. Just two ships have dentists on board, and a ship's doctor can do little for a toothache. Although cruise ships do not have fully staffed hospitals, there have been unexpected babies born on board. I know of one named "Holiday." Most lines will not knowingly board passengers who are in the last trimester of a pregnancy.

Religious Services

Most ships have a minister, priest, or rabbi who officiates at all denominational services. Announcements are made daily on board ship.

Ship Shops

Every ship has shops. Not surprisingly, the ships stock items passengers are bound to forget, such as toothbrushes, toothpaste, hairspray, and the like, but more interesting are the luxury items carried in ship stores. These shops are duty-free, which means the shopkeeper did not pay duty on the items being sold, and purchases not manufactured in the United States must be declared on customs forms. Perfume, crystal, cameras, and jewelry are sometimes cheaper on board ship than on shore, and it pays to check them out. Some shops are lavish; others stock little more than essentials.

Cabin Service

This is a variable. Some ships serve no food in staterooms; others pride themselves on 24-hour cabin service. As a general rule, breakfast service may be restricted to a Continental breakfast (uncooked items such as juice, coffee, and rolls. Completed forms left on the outside of cabin doors will handle breakfast orders for delivery at selected times. Other ships have room-service menus in cabins, and sandwiches, coffee, snacks, and other items are a telephone call away. On some ships like the *Crystal Harmony* or *Crystal Symphony*, cabin service is so complete even pizza and frozen yogurt is available. On the Silversea and Seabourn ships, all accommodations are in suites in which a butler serves an elegant dinner course by course.

Weight Control

"Cruise" is synonymous with "food," and many travelers resist the lure of the seas because they fear eating too much and gaining weight. Experts say you can feast on gourmet foods, satisfy your most discriminating taste buds, enjoy the service and atmosphere, and disembark at the end of the voyage without damage to your waistline. If you cruise infrequently, forget about the waistline and enjoy the voyage. If you're a frequent cruiser, try to eat the way you would at home - with a few exceptions, of course.

Another alternative is to skip one of the meals. If you sleep late, skip breakfast and enjoy a protein-laden brunch. If noontime catches you topside at the pool deck, pass on the six-course luncheon served in the dining-room and settle for a hamburger (without the bun) and a cold drink out in the balmy breezes. If weight problems are keeping you on land, cut out the midnight buffet. In fact, don't even look at the tantalizing display of food if there's one chance in a million your resistance is vulnerable.

Desserts, of course, are every dieter's downfall. While your tablemates are eating Baked Alaska, instruct the waiter to serve you fruit or opt for the sugar-free choices, which include ice cream and usually cake or pie. Also, order only one entree. One portion, no matter how good it tastes, is enough.

Food authorities offer other suggestions: Budget your calorie intake. If you anticipate all the goodies bound to be served at the captain's dinner, limit yourself to a salad for lunch or omit the main course the next day. Increase your physical activity. Exercise, run, walk, swim, or dance, especially before meals. Doctors say it tends to diminish the appetite.

I am not an authority on dieting, but I have found my own system for leaving the ship in the same shape I boarded. I have juice and coffee served in my cabin in the morning by the room steward; I always order a salad for lunch; then I enjoy my dinner. I don't nibble peanuts or snacks with alcoholic beverages, which eliminates a few calories, and I stick to dry wine with my dinner. Desserts? At my first encounter with my waiter, I lay it on the line. If he expects a tip at the end of the voyage, absolutely no desserts, other than fruit, can be served to me no matter how much I beg. You would be surprised at how well that works!

Drinking at Sea

Drinking water is generally safe, and ships inform passengers when tap water is not potable, but I prefer bottled distilled water and I order it through my room steward. Carafes of water are placed in cabins along with ice. Soft drinks and alcoholic beverages are available at bars and through cabin service. Prices are generally between $2 and $4.75. Ships have daily specials, and drink prices sometimes drop to $1.50. For some reason, be it the state of relaxation or the ready availability, passengers seem to drink more on cruise ships than they do on land. You'll get to know bartenders, but you should also get to know the sommelier in the dining-room. He's the one who wears the large key and tasting cup around his neck and asks nightly whether you would care for wine with your dinner. He's the wine steward, and he has a wine cellar guaranteed to liven up the party. Wines are impressive extras for that special meal at sea. The price of wines is not included in cruise rates, but good wines cost as little as $30 to $40 a bottle. Tips to wine stewards are usually included in the service when 15 percent is automatically added to your tab, but most passengers who order wine regularly give the sommelier an additional gratuity at the end of the voyage.

INSIDER TIP
Watch out for the water on foreign-flagged ships sailing in foreign waters. It is usually not potable. On the Nile, for example, don't drink the water! Same is true on some Greek island cruising vessels. Trust only bottled, capped, or distilled water.

Lounges

There is usually more than one lounge, and on board ship a lounge is a bar that serves alcoholic beverages. Lounges are also great meeting centers for passengers. Singles should have no hesitancy about sitting at the bar alone. No one considers a single woman a pickup at a ship's bar.

Art Auctions

Art is in the eyes if the beholder and if Art Auctions at Sea are an indication, there are lots of beholders on every ship. Cruise lines invest millions of dollars in art collections displayed on board ships. Now passengers have the opportunity to take an inside look into the art world and learn the difference between a lithograph and an etching, a silk screen and a serigraph, a watercolor and an oil painting.

Passengers are invited to participate in art auctions and to bid or purchase some prestigious works at less than prestigious prices. Art auctions have become a regularly scheduled event, and a company called Park West has signed exclusive arrangements with noted artists and is hosting art auctions at sea. It's a fun and rewarding activity even if you have never been to an auction before or know nothing about collecting art. One of the most popular contemporary artists is Tarkay, recognized as a leader in neoclassical works. His pieces sell for about $1,000 in galleries, but bids on board ships were starting at around $200 and selling for about $300. Miro signed-in-stone lithographs went for about the same price.

Art purchases may be charged to shipboard accounts, and the auctioneer will arrange for delivery of the piece, framed or unframed, to your home, for a small additional charge. I have found these works to be great cruise souvenirs, and they enter the United States duty-free.

INSIDER TIP

Prices are lowest on the first day of the auction before the word spreads around the ship. Attend an auction and stay through the whole event and you'll receive a free print. They are great souvenirs and you'll find a few in my home.

Parties, etc.

There is no minimum beverage charge, nor is any beverage purchase required in nightclubs or lounges. Passengers can dance without drinking, laugh at the comedian without sipping, and sit on a barstool drinking coffee. Seats are on a first-come basis for shows, and movies are shown at announced times. Everyone is entitled to participate in all the entertainment offered.

If you have sailed on the ship before, you will be invited to at least one special party, but if you enjoy extra attention, have your travel agent inform the cruise line of your qualifications for VIP status. Some companies have eliminated VIP parties and invite all passengers to a cocktail party hosted by the captain. Others continue the tradition with very small gatherings in the captain's quarters. Most ships invite the entire passenger list to a welcome party, but some have eliminated the Farewell party.

INSIDER TIP

So you want to sit at the captain's table in the dining room? Impossible on some ships, limited possibility on others. One company says, "Every passenger is a VIP, and no one is ever invited to dine with the captain." Another company seats VIPs with the captain for the entire trip, and since this limits the number of VIPs to no more than four, six, or eight, chances for this honor are slim. On some lines, VIP passengers are invited on a rotating basis. Passengers who sail the cruise company's vessels most frequently are among the first considered for coveted invitations. Residents of top suites are always invited to dine with the captain. Best chance is to have your travel agent impress the cruise line with your importance at the time of booking.

Sports at Sea

When taking a cruise, pack athletic gear. Sports fans get together in Sports Bars and compete in shipboard events. Responding to the steadily growing interest in maintaining physical fitness while on vacation, cruise lines have modernized old facilities and built new ones, added sports programs on board and ashore, even expanded restaurant menus to offer health-conscious cooking. One company has an Olympic program for passengers. It is in this area of physical fitness that cruise ships have made the most dramatic changes in recent years.

Many ships, particularly the new vessels, have installed the latest exercise equipment and weight-training devices and have hired trained staffs to supervise their use. Jogging is encouraged, and many vessels have decks dedicated to this purpose.

Cruise lines have developed exercise programs, dancercise classes, aerobics, and training schedules for vacationers who want to continue their home program or start a new one. Ships have personnel on board who will help plan individual exercise programs in cooperation with shipboard nutritionists and medical staff.

In addition, land activities are available to cruise vacationers. Increasing numbers of passengers are including golf clubs in cruise baggage. Not only can they practice putting and driving on board ship, but they can sample some of the finest golf courses in the world while in port. One cruise line has organized golf tournaments in which passengers on 14-day cruises in Europe and the Orient compete on several of Asia's best-known courses.

Tennis players, too, are finding that a cruise need not mean putting away the racket. Ships spend part or all of many days in resort-oriented ports or major cities, and tennis buffs play on courts in the Caribbean, Mexico, Europe, Asia, and the United States.

What to Wear When and Where

Check with your travel agent for the number of formal, informal, and casual nights, and pack accordingly. The more expensive the cruise and the longer the voyage, the more formal the atmosphere. On *Queen Elizabeth 2* Caribbean cruises, the daily activities bulletin suggests formal dress nearly every night, but fewer than half the passengers wear black tie except on special formal nights and holiday sailings.

A cruise ship is a floating resort. Wear whatever you would wear at a nice resort in your cruising area. Swimsuits for sunning are a must, but wear a robe for cover-up en route to the swimming pool. Evenings at sea can be breezy, and it is recommended that stoles, sweaters, or wraps be included even on Caribbean cruises. Ships are air-conditioned, and the wrap may feel good in some corners of the theater. Leave your furs at home; they are cumbersome and not generally worn at sea. However, if you are heading toward Alaska or the North Cape, take a windbreaker or even a coat. It might make the difference between comfort and a chill.

Women have more questions than men do about what to wear on board ship. "Casual" to the female traveler could mean a slacks suit; "informal" could stretch from slacks to a long or short cocktail-type dress. "Formal' ranges from dressy pants to beaded evening gowns (and you'll see a few of those on some of the around-the-world cruises).

Toward the Journey's End

No matter how much you want to postpone it, the end of the cruise is bound to come. At the final captain's party, the captain usually makes his farewell speech, inviting passengers to cruise the vessel again. Invariably, the cruise director stands up and says he has a special message for the passengers: "The captain wants me to announce that you have been so nice we are turning around and repeating the cruise." At this point, everyone stands up and cheers. But as with all good things, the end of the cruise means showing how much you appreciated the service extended, and this is called a gratuity.

Tipping

How much, when, and whom should I tip are the most frequently asked questions about cruising. Tipping is a personal matter, but cruise lines make it less personal by recommending how much, when, and to whom at a briefing session toward the end of the cruise. In the "Ship Profiles" chapter, recommended amounts are indicated for every ship.

The list of how much and to whom has grown over the years, and contemporary one-class cruising has changed the way we tip. The couple sailing in a top suite for $3,500 a week eat in the same dining-room, enjoy the same entertainment, and visit the same ports as the couple paying under $2,000 for an inside cabin with upper and lower berths. Yet recommended tipping for both couples is the same. No longer does the total tip represent a percentage of the cruise fare.

Tipping rules of the sea vary little from ship to ship. Basically, all recommendations are per passenger per day of the voyage, which really means per night. Even if you boarded at midnight and disembarked at 8 a.m. a week later, count the nights, not the days in calculating gratuities. With very few exceptions, cruise lines and ship personnel expect passengers to tip, but no passenger has ever been thrown in the brig for defying tipping codes. Cruise directors admit that non-tipping passengers must be very good at avoiding the room steward, who miraculously appears even though you may not have seen him for days, and dining-room service is exemplary on the last night of the voyage.

Few Americans object to tipping for services rendered. On board ship, however, recommended tips have little to do with degree and quality of service. In fact, cruise directors point out that recommended amounts are "basic" and outstanding service should be recognized with additional tips.

It is also interesting to note that recommended tipping does not correspond to price category of the ship except for ships at the top of the price scale. Tipping policies, however, depend greatly on nationality of the service crew. Surprisingly, higher priced ships frequently recommend less tipping than budget and moderately priced vessels. Italian union crews, for example, command high salaries, so tips are not as major a factor in employment agreements. Caribbean and Indonesian crews depend almost entirely on tips and very little on salaries.

Your waiter and his assistant expect to be tipped. Most ships recommend giving between $3 and $3.50 per person per day, to each of them. When the waiter is assisted by a busboy, he receives half of what you give the waiter. When there are two waiters serving your table, they each get the same $3 or $3.50 per person per day tip. The tips do not depend on how many times you ate at the table. Even if you showed up only for dinners, the tip is the same because your waiter probably worked in the optional dining areas, and somehow, it evens out. Some ships recommend $4 per person per day, for the waiter, and he takes care of his assistant.

Holland America Line says, "Tipping is not required and is included in the cost of your cruise." However, when HAL first introduced the no-tipping policy, it was "no tipping permitted." They have bowed to pressure by the American traveler who insists on showing his gratitude personally and with cash. HAL found there was no way to overcome the American tipping syndrome, and passengers continue to tip, but not as much as they would ordinarily. On Cunard, Seabourn, Silversea and Radisson ships, all gratuities are included in the cruise price and tipping is not permitted.

On other ships, if the dining-room captain in your section has cooked up special dishes, tossed a Caesar salad, and extended himself, you might want to tip him about one dollar a day, per person. If the maitre d' has been super and the service has been far beyond the call of duty, half of what you tip the captain would be fair. Some companies suggest giving as much as $2 a day to each of these supervisors, but unless they have really gone overboard for you, it seems excessive.

Bar and wine stewards who have not been tipped with each order will expect 15 to 20 percent of what you have spent with them. Most ships automatically add 10 or 15 percent to every bar bill, so read the check before you sign for your drinks or wine. Not much reason to over tip or tip twice for the same service.

Depending on the ship and the service, room stewards expect anywhere from $3 to $4 per person per day, more if you are in a suite and have been entertaining throughout the cruise. The room steward takes care of his assistants.

A good rule of thumb based on per night on board per person, is to count on about $8 for tips on budget-priced ships; at least $10 on higher-priced vessels, and $20 on luxury ships. It is recommended that you distribute all gratuities on the last night of a 3-, 4-, 7- or 14-night cruise. On longer cruises, it's appropriate to tip at the end of each week and at the end of the cruise.

Waiters say they sleep better if they are tipped the night before the ship reaches home port. Very few passengers skip the last breakfast and skip passing a few bucks to the waiter who served them during the cruise.

Vessels sailing worldwide follow similar guidelines. However, Mediterranean and Greek island ships (except for the few in the luxury category) recommend between $10 and $20 as the total tip required in the dining-room and cabin, per person, per day. Some Greek-flagged ships follow an old island custom and pool tips. Passengers are requested to place gratuities in an envelope, and the money is divided among service and behind-the-scenes personnel such as cooks and dishwashers. Americans find this procedure impersonal, so they continue to tip according to their own experience. Europeans follow suggestions and like the idea of pooling. They say it takes the "commercialism" out of tipping.

Ships have come with a very convenient tipping system. An amount is calculated using the guidelines mentioned and the total is automatically charged to your ship account. A notice is sent to staterooms, and if passengers prefer to tip at their own discretion, the amount is not added to their bill. Most passengers prefer the new system. The ship delivers vouchers to staterooms and passengers give them to waiters, busboys, stewards and anyone else covered instead of cash.

INSIDER TIP

Contemporary cruise trends have changed service customs on board and added another person who may not have his hand out, nonetheless expects to be tipped: Cabin service in one form or another is offered by almost every ship, but it is not like it was in the old days when your room steward answered your call for breakfast in bed. Few of the new ships even have call buttons. Instead, passengers telephone Room Service and a bellboy delivers breakfast, drinks, or sandwiches. He is not included in the "regular" list to be tipped, but he expects a gratuity every time he delivers. One dollar per person served seems adequate. These little niceties that are touted in brochures as "all included" cost a little more these days, but most passengers consider them well worth the few extra dollars.

If cabin service is provided by your own room steward, do not tip each time he does something for you, including food service in your cabin. Tip him at the end of the voyage, remembering the special services provided.

As for the longshoremen, when the sign at Port Everglades, for instance, reads "Tipping Not Required," I remember the high wages being paid these porters, and I never tip more than $1 per bag. They carry the bags less than 30 feet to a loading machine. I understand the situation is different in big-city ports such as New York, where I have heard reports from passengers who undertipped and found their baggage on the wrong ship headed for a different part of the world. So even in New York, I'm told that one dollar per bag satisfies greed. Over tipping is a no-no. The gesture seems to take on a life of its own and becomes contagious.

Passenger Comment Cards

Have you ever wondered what happens to passenger comment cards after they are carted off the ship or mailed in? Cruise lines value your opinions and pay close attention to how you rate your cruise experience. Comment cards are kept in locked boxes until they are taken off the ship shortly after docking. A special staff member transfers the comments to computers, and within hours, the company has an overall passenger rating of the cruise. Before the ship departs for the next cruise, comments are reviewed with the captain and division heads, who take immediate corrective action whenever possible. Bonuses frequently depend on your comments. Service personnel who practically beg for "excellent" ratings should not influence passengers. Rate the way you see it, and take the time to write your praise or complaints. Company execs read the comments and you'll probably receive a phone call, or at least a letter, to discuss a really important complaint.

Past Passenger Clubs and Booking on Board

Almost every company has a club with a membership roster made up of past passengers. Procedures differ from company to company. Some automatically enroll passengers in the club after their first cruise on one of its ships. Others request that passengers complete an enrollment form with detailed information about their vacation habits. Do take advantage of these past-passenger clubs. On a periodic basis, you will receive a slick magazine with news about the company and changes in itineraries. The cruise line will also keep you informed of special sailings at special rates before they are announced to the public. Most lines offer discounts of at least 10 percent to past passengers. It's their way of keeping a loyal following.

Debarkation

No matter what the brochure lists as the arrival time in home port, if your ship has visited foreign ports, it will take a minimum of two hours for baggage to be unloaded and for customs and immigration officials to clear the ship for passenger debarkation (also referred to as disembarkation). If you are making a plane connection, plan accordingly. Allow four to six hours from scheduled arrival time for airplane connections.

You will be asked to place your packed luggage outside your stateroom door at a specific time on the last night at sea. Save a small bag to pack your nightclothes and toilet articles. On the morning of arrival, eat breakfast at leisure and wait until the purser announces that the ship has been cleared before you vacate your cabin. Don't congregate in public areas or near the gangplank. It's the surest way to ruin a pleasant cruise.

Clearance takes longer than it did before 9/11 and few passengers complain. In most cases, every passenger must report to the Immigration officials who board the ship when it arrives in a U.S. port.(This is now happening in foreign ports as well) It is usually called for an ungodly hour of the morning, but with passports in hand, it goes quickly. Non U.S. citizens report to a different area which decreases the length of lines.

Customs clearance is also done on board the ship.(See Shopping and Customs Chapter" for details of what you should buy where and how much enters duty free and what charges you can expect)   If you owe any money because you exceeded customs limitations, you will be asked to pay a cashier either on board or in the baggage area.

Most ships have designed efficient systems for getting passengers off quickly. It is done by the letter of your last name, by color-coded cards, or by your cabin deck. You disembark when they call your group. Then you find your luggage by color, or by the first letter of your last name, or by deck, assemble it, and face the customs inspector if you have not been pre-cleared on board.

Most people who have trouble with customs inspectors bring it on themselves, either through disregard or ignorance of customs laws. Customs is a serious business, and it's not the right time to joke around. Customs inspectors are stricter on citizens of their own country than they are on foreigners. The "Customs—U.S. and Canadian" chapter details duty-free allowances ($400 per person, including one quart of alcoholic beverages, except from the U.S. Virgin Islands). This includes everything you bought on board ship or received as a gift. It will help if you have your receipts with you when you go through customs. It will also help if all your purchases are in one suitcase and you can produce them quickly, should the inspector ask to see them. (See U.S. Customs declaration form.)

Once you have collected your luggage, porters in the baggage area will carry your luggage to your transportation. Don't pack your wallet just yet. They expect tips equivalent to what you would tip an airline porter.

INSIDER TIP
With shipboard customs clearance becoming more common in U.S. ports, passenger declarations are on the honor system. If you are caught underestimating purchases, you stand the risk of losing the merchandise and facing a big fine. Honesty does pay!

The Ship's Family, or Who's Who on Board

If you think of your captain as Captain Steubing of Love Boat fame, forget it! The captain of your cruise ship didn't get his master's papers in a school for actors or through a mail-order mill. He and the rest of his officers are professionals. While it is fun and games for passengers, tending to your safety and catering to your requirements are serious business for the crew. Although titles, duties, and services vary from ship to ship, the basic responsibilities of care and feeding of passengers remain the same.

Cruise ship deck officers have usually been trained in their own countries and received their education and seamen's papers from an internationally recognized maritime school. While it may sound glamorous and perhaps inviting, there's practically no way a dishwasher can ever climb the ladder to captaincy without fulfilling educational and legal requirements. Not to say that many a shipmaster didn't go to sea at a tender age, but you can bet your passport there were many years in between during which he completed lengthy study and training requirements.

Most ships are organized into three main departments: deck, engine room, and purser's office. Since cruise ships have become floating resorts, they have added hotel departments headed by a hotel manager. Here's a rundown on the ship's family and what you can expect from each.

You should know that you may be seeing fewer uniforms on some ships. Royal Caribbean International has changed to a total hotel system. The only uniforms will be deck and engine officers. The hotel staff is dressing like staffs in hotels; jackets and ties for top management, casual for service personnel.

Captain: He is absolute king on board. His responsibility is the safety and welfare of his passengers as well as their pleasure, although he relegates the latter to subordinate departments and is involved only in emergency situations. He is judge, jury, sheriff, and king, and he is usually the most genial and outgoing member of the ship's family. You won't make points if you call him Skipper. Sir or Captain are more acceptable forms. While the crew calls him The Old Man behind his back, passengers are not afforded the same privilege.

Staff Captain: He is second in command and deals with all matters relating to the crew. He is sometimes called Chief Officer on Norwegian and English ships. When you meet him at dinner or on deck, his proper title is Captain.

Chief Engineer: He reigns supreme in the engine room and holds the same maritime rank as the captain. His department is responsible for moving the ship through the waters comfortably and for keeping arrivals and departures as close to scheduled times as possible. His department is also responsible for almost all other machinery on board, and he has engineering officers and an engine-room crew to help him keep the propellers turning.

Staff Engineer: He is second man in the engine department.

Chief Purser: He's the head of the department that handles the ship's finances and on some ships, all the hotel operations. His office and staff serve as the general information center and clearinghouse for immigration and customs formalities in all ports. He and his staff of assistant pursers supervise entertainment, accommodations, meal services, printed material distributed on board, and special requests.

Hotel Manager: His is a fairly new position at sea, and his duties vary greatly from ship to ship and overlap with those of the chief purser. He usually wears a uniform only on formal nights and dresses the way a hotel manager would the rest of the time. He does what the chief purser does on most vessels (supervises bed, board, and entertainment).

Doctor: He and his staff (usually a nurse) are available on a 24-hour basis, as needed.

Chief Radio Officer: He supervises your link to the outside world. His staff monitors the ship's radio and arranges for cablegrams and telephone calls between ship and shore. They also receive cablegrams and deliver them to passengers and crew.

INSIDER TIP

In this Era of the Woman, I apologize for using the masculine in referring to ship officers. More women are joining higher ship-management ranks. Royal Caribbean International has female staff captains, and women on several ships serve as chief pursers, hotel managers, dining-room managers and in other important positions held exclusively by men in years past.

Non uniformed Members of the Family: The cruise director and his staff are key to onboard entertainment, shore excursions, activities, and fun and games on board. They don't wear seamen's uniforms, but are easily identified because they dress in company-approved classic seagoing sports attire. They are genial and outgoing, and will engage you in conversation from embarkation throughout the voyage.

The food and beverage manager is becoming a familiar face on board many ships, which are finding it practical to divide ship operations into maritime and passenger services. He supervises everything concerning food, although the hotel manager is ultimately responsible for all guest services, including food. The food and beverage manager may or may not wear a uniform; he may appear in black-tie garb in the dining room, in sports clothes on deck.

INSIDER TIP

Uniform insignia varies by country. For instance, Italian officers' uniforms have gold stripes on a red background for the engineers' and pursers' departments and green for the communications department. Norwegian and British insignia are gold braid on black epaulets. The colored braid between the stripes tells you the department; the number and width of the stripes tell the rank. There is no color used for deck officers; gold braid is used on blue sleeves, epaulets on white shirts.

Don't hesitate to talk with officers on board ship. They are interesting people who know a lot about the vessel and the ports you will be visiting. They know the best restaurants and beaches on shore, and they'll be happy to share information.

We have listed the most popular ports of embarkation. For information on embarkation ports that are not listed, contact the cruise line or www.portsofembarkation.com

Acapulco (Mexico)

Cruise passengers usually arrive in Acapulco by air and then take a private taxi or a bus provided by the cruise line to the pier. There are a couple of large ship terminals but, on busy days, there are not enough piers to accommodate all of the ships. Some vessels anchor out in the bay and tender passengers and their baggage between ships and shore. Photographers love the picture post-card harbor. When the ship anchors, it is practically surrounded by the peaks and valleys of Acapulco. The tender ride takes less than 15 minutes to deliver passengers close to the center of town. Mexican airports are famous for their chaotic atmosphere. Luggage pickup and transfers are sometimes a hassle. Look for your official ship representative who will assist you with your luggage and getting you on the right bus. Transfers between the airport and piers take about 30 minutes. Taxi fare is more or less $15, depending on your bargaining skills, and cabbies expect a tip. There's a public bus that makes the run and charges $5.50, but I don't recommend it because makes a number of stops and schedules are not reliable.

Anchorage (Alaska)

Ships naming Anchorage as a port of call actually use three terminals—Anchorage, Seward and Whittier. Check which terminal your vessel is using. The Port of Anchorage is 10 miles from the airport and two miles from downtown. Cab fare runs $15 to $18. The City of Whittier has a sizable airport and is located 50 miles from the Port of Anchorage. It is a two and a half hour train ride to Anchorage or a 35-minute train/bus ride between Whittier and Portage, followed by a taxi ride to Anchorage. Seward has its own pier and the ride from Anchorage airport is a couple of hours. It is strongly suggested that passengers use transportation arranged by cruise lines when flights arrive or depart from Whittier or Seward unless the ship docks in the Port of Whittier.

Athens/Piraeus (Greece)

There are two airports and if you arrive on an intra-Europe flight, you may land at the domestic terminal. All trans-Atlantic flights arrive at Athinai (Athens) International Airport, which is located between Athens and Piraeus. A taxi from the airport will cost about $30 to a midtown Athens hotel and will take about 40 minutes. A taxi from the airport to the pier in Piraeus, from which all ships depart (and arrive), should cost about $35. Fare is about $45 from a mid-Athens hotel to the pier. Both rides should take approximately 30 to 40 minutes in normal traffic, but allow more time because Athens traffic is rarely "normal."

Auckland (New Zealand)

The airport, located about eight miles from the pier and the center of the city is modern and easy to maneuver. Taxi fare should be about $15. The port area is named "The City of Sails." Piers are practically alongside the downtown area of the city.

Baltimore (Maryland)

Dundalk Marine Terminal is off the Broening Highway in east Baltimore and vehicles are directed to the Passenger Services Building for unloading and parking. The secured parking compound adjacent to the building charges five dollars per day. Visitor parking is free. The 25-minute taxi ride from the terminal to the International Airport runs about $25. The terminal is closer to downtown hotels and taxi fare is around $20.

Barcelona (Spain)

Barcelona has developed into the home port hub of choice for Western Mediterranean cruises and for voyages to London and beyond. Its proximity to exotic destinations, the natural deep harbor and the port facilities built during the Exposition have made it a central port of embarkation. The very modern airport is about 15 miles from the pier and a taxi costs about $25.U.S. The pier is across the inlet from the center of Barcelona but it is a long walk. Taxis are plentiful and relatively inexpensive. The port area is congested and seems to be a development in progress. Construction in the port area slows traffic considerably.

Bridgetown (Barbados)

Grantly Adams Airport is about 15 miles from Bridgetown Harbour; allow about 30 minutes to get there from the pier. Don't expect a totally modern or air-conditioned airport. It's easier to arrive in this airport then leave. Baggage pick-up and check-in are in non-air-conditioned areas. All cruise lines meet air-sea passengers, but those who want a car or who have missed the bus because of late air arrival on individually arranged air should plan on paying about $25 for the ride between the airport and pier.

Boston (Massachusetts)

Commonwealth Pier 5 is in South Boston. By car, it is easily reached from Central Artery via High Street exit or Northern Avenue-Atlantic Avenue ramp. The pier is 15 minutes by taxi from the airport and the taxi rate is approximately $25. Indoor secured parking is available to cruise passengers for six dollars per day, payable in advance. An outside guarded lot opposite the terminal is available for $3.50 per day. Visitor parking is free.

Cancún (Mexico)

Cancún International Airport is 54 miles south of the city and is best reached by boat. Taxis are available but expect to pay more than $50 for the ride that will take you over causeways and through picturesque terrain. Cancún's hotel zone is on an island connected by a natural causeway to the mainland.

Civitavechia (Rome, Italy)

This is the only port for the city of Rome and it is a good two hour ride from the city's outskirts. Time depends on traffic. The new highway has shortened the time somewhat but don't count on it. There are buses and trains that run regularly between Civitavechia and the City, but they are difficult to use with luggage and are recommended only for backpackers. A taxi from Rome to the pier could cost as much as $80, so my suggestion is to use the ship's transfer even if you are not using the pre or post-cruise hotel package.

Charleston (South Carolina)

The passenger terminal is located on Concord Street at the foot of Market Street. It's in the heart of the historic district and well worth a visit. The Charleston International Airport is about a 25-minute, $30 taxi ride. Shared limousines charge $10 per passenger. Secured long-term outdoor parking for cruise passengers is available for four dollars per day with shuttle service provided. Visitor parking is free.

Copenhagen (Denmark)

Depending on traffic, the pier is about 20 minutes from Kastrup Airport and very close to the center of Copenhagen. Airport luggage handlers expect higher tips than in the U.S., so use carts which you can pay for with a credit card if don't have local currency. Carts are plentiful and readily available to wheel your luggage to the transport area where you will meet the ship representative who will escort you to a bus for transport to the pier. If you are on your own, taxis to the pier or to hotels charge about $40.

Cozumel (Mexico)

Cozumel Airport is less than two miles from the city center and about four miles from the major piers. There is not enough dockage for the number of ships visiting Cozumel on a regular basis, so more than half anchor out in the bay. Taxis are inexpensive and should cost about $10 to the dockside pier, less than that to the tender pier.

Fort Lauderdale/Port Everglades (Florida)

Port Everglades is north of Hollywood at the southern tip of Fort Lauderdale between Highway U.S. 1 and the Atlantic Ocean. The main entrance is at the intersection of Route 84 and U.S. 1 (Federal Highway). There is easy access from I-95, Route 7 (U.S. 441), or the Florida Turnpike. The port is only five miles from Fort Lauderdale/Hollywood International Airport and taxis charge less than $18 for the ride. The port is 25 miles from the Miami International Airport, and taxi rides cost as much as $50. Red Top Limousine Service is available for $10 per person. Garage long-term parking is available at piers for eight dollars per day (payable in advance).

Genoa (Italy)

The pier is about three miles from the principal airport and a taxi should not cost more than $10. Stazione Marittima (Passenger Terminal) is practically in the middle of the city of Genoa.

Hong Kong (China)

The International Airport is about 40 minutes from the pier that is in the heart of Tsimshatsui district, within walking distance of the main shopping district. Harbour City is almost adjacent to the Star Ferry Pier and arriving passengers can arrange to have hotel cars or limousines waiting for them at the airport. The cost runs between $50 and $75 depending on the type of vehicle you select. Cost may be charged to your hotel room or prepaid by credit card. A private car or taxi between the pier and airport runs around $40 to $50 depending on the size and make of the vehicle. It's not unusual to be picked up in a Rolls Royce or Bentley. Even some of the taxis are Mercedes.

Honolulu (Hawaii)

The airport is about 45 minutes from the pier and a taxi could run $50, but the ride is worth it. You'll see some of the most beautiful scenery in the world. The airport is modern and easy to maneuver. Ships meet passengers and, again, you can purchase transfers if you are going directly from the airport to the ship. It is highly recommended that you arrive a few days early and spend them in Honolulu. Every cruise line offers pre-and post-cruise cruise packages. Or, book your own hotel. A taxi from mid-town to the pier will cost about seven dollars.

Houston (Texas)

The new Houston International Airport is beautiful but confusing. There are so many different terminals that unless you know exactly which terminal your aircraft will use, it is difficult to make prearrangements for pickup. Allow approximately 90 minutes to get between the airport and pier that is at least a 50-minute drive from the airport. Best advice is to rely on cruise line transportation because the terminal is still fairly new and many taxi drivers do not know where it is or how to get there. Count on about $50 per ride, each way, between Houston International Airport and the pier. Hobby Airport is a lot more convenient and cuts the time to the pier as well as the taxi cost by about half. The Houston pier is temporary, but even when a new one is built, it will be in the same general vicinity. The pier is also a good hour away from downtown Houston.

Lang Chabang (Bangkok, Thailand)

It's Bangkok's connection to the sea and it's a good hour and a half ride even on the new highway that connects the pier to the city. It takes just as long to get between the new airport and the pier or the city. Traffic is unbelievable, so allow plenty of time. I have spent four hours, admittedly during rush hour, to get from Bangkok to the airport. Private cars are available and cost about $45 (after some bargaining) from the airport to the pier or to mid-Bangkok. Pre or post hotel stays are recommended, as are the ships' transfer buses.

Los Angeles/San Pedro (California)

The San Pedro and Wilmington terminals are named "The World Cruise Center." Located 25 miles south of downtown Los Angeles and 15 miles south of the Los Angeles Airport, it is not difficult to find. If you are coming by car, for Berth 95, exit the Harbor Freeway at C Street; go east to Avalon and south to the pier. For Carnival Cruise Lines, Princess Cruises, Royal Caribbean International, and the Queen Elizabeth 2, take Harbor Freeway to Harbor Boulevard and exit to Berth 95. There is no long-term parking at the indoor terminals. Secured outside parking is available by prearrangement through Five Star International, (310) 548-4537. Contact them directly for rates. Parking is also available through Central Garage, 127 West B Street, Wilmington, CA, (213) 834-3123, or Seventh Street Garage, 777 S. Center Street, San Pedro, CA. Public transportation from the Los Angeles airport is not dependable. It's 45-minute taxi ride and it will cost about $55. Cruise ship transfers are available.

Miami (Florida)

Port of Miami passenger terminals are on an island in Biscayne Bay, connected to downtown Miami by a new bridge spanning Biscayne Bay. The bridge replaced a drawbridge, which slowed traffic. By car, it is easily reached from Biscayne Boulevard at NE 5th Street. Complete directions to piers are available at port entrance. There are separate air-conditioned lounges for each of 12 passenger terminals. Saturdays and Sundays are the busiest days of the week. There is secured parking opposite each terminal. Long-term parking is available for $10 per day and visitor parking is charged the one day rate.

Bus and privately owned Super Shuttle service on a half-hour schedule is available between the airport and pier for $7.50 per person. A taxi for the 20-minute ride from the airport costs about $20.

Montego Bay (Jamaica)

The cruise facility is located at Montego, a free-port area, eight miles from the International Airport and four miles from the city center. Taxi fare runs about $18 between the airport and pier. A duty-free shopping area is available near the pier. A representative of the Jamaican Tourist Board attends all cruise ship arrivals and departures and will assist passengers with transportation and information. The Tourist Office at the airport also provides assistance and information.

Montreal (Canada)

Montreal International Airport is about 18 miles from the pier and downtown Montreal. A taxi will take about 20 minutes and cost about $25 U.S. The Ibervill Passenger Terminal is located at the foot of McGill Street and within easy walking distance of old Montreal.

Nassau (Bahamas)

The Nassau International Airport is about 15 miles from the pier and takes about 20 minutes to reach. Taxi costs vary greatly but should run about $20. Prince George Wharf is centrally located just off Bay Street and the main downtown section. Water taxis and ferries, as well as buses and taxis, will take you to Paradise Island for nominal per person charges.

New Orleans (Louisiana)

The New Orleans International Airport is 16 miles from the pier and downtown area. It takes about 40 minutes and a taxi ride will cost between $20 and $30. The New Orleans Julia Street Passenger Cruise Terminal is located on the Mississippi River almost alongside the Riverwalk Marketplace between Thalia and Julia streets. It is within walking distance of the French Quarter, historic sites and clubs. Indoor parking facilities are available at the World Trade Center, opposite the Hilton Hotel, at the Erato Street Wharf. The rate is $6 per day. Weekly rate is also available. Visitor parking is free.

New York City (New York)

Port facilities are on the Hudson River alongside the West Side Highway between 48th and 55th streets. Cars and taxis reach them from exits on the West Side Highway by an easy-to-miss automobile ramp at 55th Street and 12th Avenue. The ramp is always congested when more than two ships are embarking passengers, so bring your patience with you as the taxi meter keeps clicking away. There is a couple of golf carts that will help disabled travelers get to the right pier. Open rooftop parking for 1,000 visitor cars is available on sailing and arrival days for a minimum of eight dollars. Long-term covered parking next to Passenger Ship Terminal at Pier 94 is also available. For parking reservations, write Roosevelt Parking, c/o New York City Passenger Ship Terminal, 711 12th Avenue, New York City, NY 10019. From La Guardia Airport, a taxi should cost about $30; from Kennedy, about $45. Metered taxis from midtown hotels are about $10. Limousine service is available from both airports.

Norfolk (Virginia)

Norfolk International Terminals are on the Chesapeake Bay, adjacent to downtown Norfolk. Hampton and Terminal boulevards are the road arteries leading to the terminals. Free round-trip transfers are provided between the airport and the cruise terminal for individually arriving passengers and for air-sea travelers. A taxi ride would cost about $10. Insured valet parking is available at the pier for five dollars a day (payable in advance), with no charge for visitor parking. A shuttle bus runs between airport and pier at no charge for individual and group cruise passengers. Five Norfolk hotels also offer free shuttles to the pier.

Philadelphia (Pennsylvania)

The pier at Penn's Landing is about 20 minutes by taxi from Philadelphia International Airport. The fare runs around $25 and secured parking is available for $50 per week.

Port Canaveral (Florida)

Port Canaveral is located on the U.S. East Coast within easy cruising distance of the island of Bermuda, the Bahamas, and the Caribbean. Port Canaveral serves all of Central Florida from its coastal location in Brevard County. It is the closest deep water port to the nearby Orlando-area attractions and neighboring Cape Canaveral Air Force Station, Patrick Air Force Base, Kennedy Space Center and Cocoa Beach.

The pier is about an hour's drive from the Orlando International Airport and about 40 miles from Melbourne International Airport. It will take 90 minutes to or from Disney World on a super highway. Drive straight across Beeline Highway and you can't miss the pier. The growth of passenger facilities at these terminals is so rapid that the complex now covers 3,300 acres and has 10 modern terminals and piers. Secured outdoor parking is available without advance reservations for six dollars a day. A taxi from the airport runs about $40. Cruise lines operate free bus service between the airport and piers.

San Francisco (California)

Piers are adjacent to downtown San Francisco and Fisherman's Wharf along the Embarcadero. They are easily reached by car from the Bay Bridge (Main Street exit to Mission Street) and the Golden Gate Bridge. Most ships leave from Pier 35 at the foot of Bay Street. Cars and taxis are allowed in the pier area only to discharge passengers. Parking is available at nearby Pier 39 for six dollars per day. Long-term parking arrangements are possible through Savoy Corporation, (415) 673-2424. A taxi from the St. Francis Hotel (midtown) is about $15; from the airport, about $30. The ride takes about 45 minutes from the airport.

San Juan (Puerto Rico)

The passenger terminals are located in the Old San Juan waterfront district, within walking distance of the Old City center. Piers are about a 45-minute taxi ride from the airport, and fares run around $25. It is difficult to get long-term parking. Rates at the piers are by the hour. Most passengers arrive on air-sea packages and are transferred by air-conditioned bus from the airport. Taxis are readily available at the ship terminal with dispatchers supervising loading and unloading. They are generally the best way to get around San Juan quickly and easily - as long as you and the driver agree on rates and routes beforehand. A word of caution: in the past, some taxi drivers have been accused of overcharging passengers, especially tourists. The Public Service Commission has begun a program to improve service. Rates are set and taxis should use meters. Taxis will charge for waiting time and 50 cents for each piece of luggage.

Seattle (Washington)

Cruise ship facilities are at Pier 48 and Pier 66, almost across the street from Pike Place Market and the downtown district. The airport is about 20 miles from piers and it takes about 30 minutes to travel between them. Taxi fares are about $35. Short-term parking is available at Pier 48. Long-term parking is available across the street at Pier 66.

Singapore

The city's geographic location has been responsible for growth of pier and port facilities at this regional hub. The new Singapore Cruise Center has extensive passenger terminals with modern facilities including duty-free shops, banks and telecommunication offices. The Singapore International Airport is an example of what efficiency should be. Everything is swift, clean and correct. The airport is about 35 minutes from the seaport. Taxi fares are listed at the airport and run around $30. The Cruise Center is adjacent to a mall and tourism officials are present to assist passengers. When the piers are filled, which is often, ships dock at the freighter terminal and some taxi drivers do not know how to get there. Be sure to check at the airport, or hotel, for directions to the correct pier. The airport information kiosks should be able to furnish the information.

London (England)

All cruise ports in England are a long way from airports and London. Southampton is about 75 miles; Tilbury, about 40 miles; Harwich about 50 miles and Dover, about 35 miles. It is best to let cruise lines arrange for your transfers between airports or hotels and piers. Transportation could run as much as $100 when arranged on an individual basis. However, there are trains, as well as buses, that take at least 90 minutes to any of the ports but lugging luggage is no way to start or end a journey.

Sydney (Australia)

Sydney Harbour is the principal port in the Australian/New Zealand/Pacific region for cruise liners. The airport is about 45 minutes from the harbor and a taxi will cost about $40. It is an excellent harbor and photographers should be on deck when the ship comes into port.

St. Thomas (U.S. Virgin Islands)

St. Thomas has two cruise ship facilities—the West Indian Company Cruise Ship Dock and the Crown Bay Cruise Ship Pier, but even two are not enough to accommodate all the vessels calling at the island during winter months. The Crown Bay facility is only about two miles from the airport and taxi fare is about five dollars. The West Indian docks are on the other side of town and heavy traffic may delay you for at least 40 minutes although the distance is short. Rate will be between $15 and $20, depending on traffic. Taxis like to charge per person, but negotiate for the entire cab and luggage. Ships that anchor in the harbor tender passengers directly into the center of St. Thomas.

Tampa/St. Petersburg (Florida)

The Port of Tampa is adjacent to downtown Tampa and is 20 minutes from Tampa International Airport, which also serves St. Petersburg. Easy to reach by car, there is secured parking available for $6 per day. Taxis should cost about $20.

Vancouver (British Columbia, Canada)

Most ships sailing on one-week cruises to Alaska use Vancouver as home-port during the sailing season. The Port of Vancouver operates two cruise facilities, Canada Place and Ballantyne Pier. Both are about a 30-minute ride from the airport and about 10 minutes from downtown Vancouver. Taxi fare to the airport and piers is approximately $20 U.S. Long-term parking is available through parking concessions that provide complimentary shuttles to and from piers. Call Citipark, (604) 684-2251, or Select Valet Parking, (604) 669-7708, to reserve space. The cost is about $5 U.S. per day. There is a tendency by U.S. travelers to forget that Canadian and U.S. dollars are not at par. Taxis will quote fares in Canadian currency which is wroth about 65 U.S. cents. If you don't have Canadian dollars, ask for the rate in U.S. Everyone in Canada accepts U.S. dollars.

Meeting the Customs Inspector
(U.S. and Canadian)

Ships offer the inveterate shopper a myriad of enticements. There are few travelers who can resist "bargains" that seemingly appear at every corner once a traveler leaves our continental shores. Travel souvenirs come in all sizes, price ranges, and levels of appeal, and it's much easier to bring bulky purchases home by sea than it is by air.

U.S. import laws are of special interest and offer benefits to the shopper who opts for the sea-lanes. Travel by ship eliminates size and weight limitations still enforced by airlines and makes it easier to succumb to the temptation of lugging home that four-foot porcelain vase from China. Lawmakers in the United States considered inflation trends when they liberalized duty-free exemptions, but economists are keeping an eye on the changes and continue to worry about increased deficits on our balance-of-payment ledgers.

As a comparison shopper of some repute, my advice is not to worry about dollar balance of payments. Concern yourself more with how far the dollar stretches. Ours is a cyclical greenback. One day it buys more pesos and the next day fewer pence. As the strength of the dollar fluctuates, so go the joys of shopping. But through it all, exciting finds are almost unlimited and there are still bargains to be found. It is possible to buy china and perfume at savings of more than 30 percent in Caribbean and West Indies ports of call. It is also possible to buy jewelry in Hong Kong for about 20 percent off U.S. prices and silk ready-made dresses in Bangkok for a fraction of U.S. prices. True, the days of really cheap booze in St Thomas are probably gone forever, but there are new outlet stores opening throughout the islands that make shopping fun. Smart travelers should know what similar items cost when they are on sale in neighborhood malls before they leave home. It's the differential that classifies a purchase as either a bargain or a souvenir.

A common sight these days is to find cruise passengers, with lists in hand, comparing hometown prices with bargains offered in faraway ports. Most memorable purchases are native-made goods, which in most cases are not subject to U.S. import taxes. Some of the "Best Buys" are detailed in the "Ports of Call" section of this book.

Customs laws separate "insular possessions" from the rest of the world. Insular possessions are the U.S. Virgin Islands (St. Thomas, St. Croix, and St. John), American Samoa, and Guam, but since few vessels call at Samoa and Guam, we concern ourselves mostly with the U.S. Virgin Islands.

Although imported inventories are similar on shop shelves throughout the Caribbean, prices are far from identical. Signs offering "duty-free" and "tax-free" merchandise lure shoppers and those two inducements also vary from island to island. The terms "duty-free" and "tax-free" refer to the shopkeeper's purchase price and the laws of the land or country. For instance, Jamaica assesses no duty or tax on merchandise brought onto the island for resale to visitors who are taking the merchandise off the island. In most countries, true duty-free merchandise cannot be sold over the counter and must, by law, be delivered to the purchaser at his or her departure point (airport or ship). Duty-free and tax-free have no bearing on what U.S. or Canadian customs services will assess the traveler on return to home shores.

Cruise ship passengers are wise to avoid mailing bulky items whenever possible. Not only are shipping costs high but, even with liberalized laws (covered later in this chapter), delayed shipments, inspections, and dual documentation can be frustrating, to say the least.

Almost every shoreside merchant will deliver bulky packages to the ship and they always seem to arrive before sailing time. Shopping in flea markets and buying from vendors, is a pay and take purchase. Since there is no limit on size of your purchases, On most vessels, parcels (small and oversize) will share your cabin for the remainder of the voyage. On others, room stewards will arrange for safe storage until the night before you disembark. With proper prearrangements, ship personnel will help get the loot to the customs area. But from there on, you're on your own for arrangements with airlines if your sea travel is a flight away from home.

Cruise passengers in the market for big-ticket items such as cameras, porcelain, silver, crystal, and quality Swiss watches, would do well to educate themselves on how to differentiate between the real thing and reasonable facsimiles, which are readily available in many ports of call. If you're planning to buy china, for example, you should check whether the particular pattern is available in your hometown. If replacing a broken plate requires ordering by mail from an overseas address, you may want to reconsider your purchase. Gold jewelry should be bought only from reliable merchants; street-merchant offers sounding too good to be true should be avoided. The same holds true for cut semiprecious stones.

On a trip to Rio, I succumbed to the brilliance of the stones and the sales talk of a handsome street vendor. He ushered me behind a building for a semi-discreet display of faceted "tourmalines, emeralds, aquamarines, and topaz." I now own the most extensive collection of faceted colored glass this side of Rio.

The moral of the story: For big ticket items, shop only at reputable and long-established stores. In some ports, look for the approval stamp or logo of the tourism association. In Hong Kong, for instance, should you find that your "diamond" is faux when you show it to your jeweler back home, there is recourse. If the shop is a member of the Hong Kong Tourist Association, that organization's consumer force will take action and represent you in the dispute. When in doubt, pass it up. If you shop at street stalls and hawkers, it's a case of buyer beware. The authentic copies are just that – copies. Some turn out to be very good copies and the fun you had buying them is worth whatever you ended up paying after an hour of haggling.

On the other hand, a bargain really depends upon personal likes and dislikes. Show me a cruise passenger, and I'll show you someone who cannot resist the booze in the Virgin Islands, the perfume in Martinique, or the handicrafts in Mexico, or the handbags sold by street vendors in Venice and Naples. Those are just a few of the worthwhile items available on some of the more popular routes.

I should add that if you find a locally made or even an imported item you really want, buy it when you see it. You may never find it again. If you pass it up, you'll think about your "shoulda" purchase for years to come. There's a sculpture in Bermuda I passed up because I thought it was too expensive. When I returned a few years later, the artist had been discovered and similar sculptures were selling for five and six times the original amount. And there is a pair of porcelain horses in Shanghai that I really wanted, but I didn't speak Chinese and I couldn't have carried them home. Next time, I'll bring a translator with me, but I doubt those horses are still waiting for me.

(For TTT best buys in specific ports, see Ports of Call Chapter)

Meeting the U.S. Customs Inspector

You're just back from a foreign country, where you bought souvenirs, a couple of tee-shirts, a pack of cigarettes, maybe stowed a local beer mug. For entertainment, you brought along your personal cassette player. Are you going to be detained by customs while they count your cigarettes and demand a receipt for the cassette player? It could happen, but it's not likely.

Getting in line at customs can be among the most intimidating events in your travels; figuring out just what the heck "duty free" means is most confusing. Just tell the truth and if you know the rules and applicable fees, you will not have any trouble bringing those souvenirs and high-end purchases home. U.S. Customs rules and regulations apply to returning U.S. citizens, permanent residents and nonresidents alike. If you have shopped local markets and loaded up an extra bag or two with souvenirs and handicrafts, or even if you splurged on a piece of jewelry, you must deal with customs.

What Must You Declare

The simple answer: everything that you didn't have with you when you left the country. I quote: "Articles acquired abroad and brought into the United States are subject to applicable duty and Internal Revenue Tax." That means gifts for others, gifts given to you, things you found, clothes you purchased and wore during the cruise -- you name it.

Note that the law is very broad with respect to "acquisitions;" you must even declare "Repairs or alterations to any items you took abroad and then brought back, even if the repairs/alterations were performed free of charge."

You are expected to have proof for foreign-made items purchased at home and to register them with the Customs office nearest you. In our experience, Customs is generally lax in this regard and we're not seeing Walkmans confiscated for lack of a receipt. However, if you are traveling with something unusual, you'll want to follow the letter of the law.

Additionally, you must declare all food items in the event that the items might carry pests or disease

Determining Value of Items

If you bought it out of the country, you must declare the price you paid for it. So, if you bought some socks at the beginning of the trip and all but wore them out, you can't depreciate them; they're worth what you paid for them new.

Exemptions

Your exemption from duties may total $400, $600 or $1200, depending on how you reenter the country. The standard exemption is $400 per person. However, you are eligible for a $600 exemption if you are returning from any of the 24 Caribbean Basin Economic Recovery Act countries and a $1200 exemption if you are returning directly or indirectly from a U.S. insular possession - American Samoa, Guam, or the U.S. Virgin Islands

Time Limitations

As a general rule, you qualify for your exemption only when returning from a stay abroad of at least 48 hours and you have not used any part of your exemption in the preceding 30 day period. If you do not meet the 48-hour or 30-day restrictions, you are eligible for only a $200 exemption.

Be careful of itineraries that take you out of the US and bring you back to the US only briefly before leaving yet again (for example: California-Australia-Hawaii-Japan). You can lose your exemptions very quickly in these cases; the Customs Dept. is flexible, however, and you may retain your exemptions if you meet certain requirements. See a Customs officer if you encounter this situation.

Cigars and Alcohol

The laws are very explicit: If you are bringing back more than one liter (33.8 fl. oz.) of alcoholic beverages, 200 cigarettes (one carton), or 100 cigars, you must declare them. If you don't meet the 48-hour or 30-day restrictions, you may include any of the following: 50 cigarettes, 10 cigars, 150 milliliters (4 fl. oz.) of alcoholic beverages, or 150 milliliters (4 fl. oz.) of perfume containing alcohol.

Laws have changed regarding Cuban cigars: Only persons returning from Cuba after a licensed visit there are permitted to bring Cuban cigars into the United States, provided the value of such cigars does not exceed $100 US dollars and the cigars are for that individual's personal use and not for resale. All other importations of Cuban cigars are illegal.

INSIDER TIPS

A number of islands are selling Cuban cigars, some real and some facsimiles. Beware of the make-believes. If you buy the real thing, you would be wise to smoke them before you disembark. Customs can literally smell them. Or, the dogs used at entry points will sniff them out.

Mailing Items from Overseas

Your exemption applies only to those things you have on your person when you return to the United States; if you mail anything back, you're responsible for paying the duties and taxes on those items separately.

Gifts

Gifts mailed from overseas valued at less than $100 are duty-free; non-gift purchases mailed to the US valued at less than $200 pass duty-free. You can send multiple gifts to the same recipient; however, they cannot receive more than one gift per day (a "day" counts as the day it arrives at customs for processing, not the day it is sent or arrives at the recipient's address). Travelers cannot send a "gift" parcel to themselves, nor can persons traveling together send "gifts" to each other.

The outer wrapping must be marked with: the fair retail value of the contents; the contents' identity (e.g., shirts, belts, watch, figurines, etc.); and whether the package is a gift ($100 exemption) or for personal use ($200 exemption).

INSIDER TIPS

When mailing gifts from your cruise or trip, be sure to (1) mark the package "Unsolicited Gift"; (2) state the nature of the gift; and (3) give its fair retail value. This will facilitate clearance of the package. When sending back oversize packages, like artworks, rugs, furniture, or china, remember that the parcel will probably arrive by ship or air and all incoming shipments must be cleared through U.S. Customs. Customs employees cannot, by law, perform entry tasks for the public, but they will advise and give information about customs requirements. There may be handling charges by freight forwarders or other delivery charges even though your sales slip reads "door-to-door" delivery. You may need the services of a customs broker. They are not U.S. Customs' employees and they charge fees for clearing your items. The fee may seem excessive because of how little you paid for that "sculpture," so the most cost-effective thing to do is take your purchases with you, if at all possible. If you can't handle the size, expect additional costs to send it to your home.

Agricultural and Food Items

All agricultural and food items must be declared, but this gets tricky. Bakery items and all cured cheeses are admissible; most fruits and vegetables are either restricted or prohibited. Make no assumptions: a piece of fruit bought in a foreign airport that you didn't eat must be declared.

Currency

You can take out of the U.S. or bring into the country unlimited "monetary instruments," as the Customs folks call cash, money orders, traveler's checks, and the like, but if you are carrying more than $10,000 worth of monetary instruments, you must file a report with US Customs. As defined by the Customs Service: "Money" means monetary instruments and includes U.S. or foreign coins currently in circulation, currency, traveler's checks in any form, money orders, and negotiable instruments or investment securities in bearer form.

If you get very lucky in the casino and didn't spend it on something outrageous and still have more than $10,000 when you meet the Customs Inspector, you are supposed to declare your loot.

Medications and Drugs

The transport of medications and drugs is not something to take for granted, under any circumstances. Carry only over the counter drugs in their original packets and carry prescription drugs in containers issued by the pharmacist and make sure it shows the date of purchase and the doctor's name. It's also a good idea to have a copy of prescriptions with you. Drugs are a problem everywhere and border agents are getting very fussy about unmarked drugs.

What About Leaving the US?

If you will be traveling for a considerable length of time, and will be crossing borders around the world, it would be a good idea to check with individual countries as to what is not allowed to enter. Some limit alcohol and cigarettes; others require registration of electronic equipment. You can get the information on the Internet by using the name of the country as your key word. All of the countries have embassies in the U.S. and they will be able to furnish the information. If you are using a visa service, it will be a good source of a lot of useful information.

What is Duty-Free?

Duty-free is a confusing term; it means only that the price you pay at the duty-free store, or on the airplane or ship, does not include the additional cost of duty and taxes. Thus, you must declare these items when you arrive at your destination. Additionally, for items bought at a US duty-free shop, if brought back into the US, you must pay the duty and taxes, and cannot include them in your exemption.

Articles purchased in duty-free shops in foreign countries are subject to U.S. Customs and restrictions. Articles purchased in U.S. duty-free shops (airport transit lounges) are subject to duty when reentered into the United States. Articles purchased on board ship also must be declared and are subject to the same restrictions and customs duty when your allowance is exceeded.

Alcohol may be included in exemptions if the quantity does not exceed one liter (33.8 fluid ounces) and, if you are 21 years of age or older, if it is for your own use or for use as a gift, and if it is not in violation of the laws of the state in which you arrive. Information on state restrictions and taxes should be obtained from state governments, as laws vary from state to state. Alcoholic beverages in excess of the one-quart limitation are subject to duty and Internal Revenue tax. U.S. postal laws prohibit shipping alcoholic beverages by mail. Exceptions to alcohol limits apply to purchases in the U.S. Virgin Islands. Providing you are over 21 years of age, you may include in your declaration five liters of alcohol, which must have been purchased in the U.S. Virgin Islands.

Customs officers cooperate with state officials, so California residents arriving by ship or air in California ports may find their liquor confiscated or taxes collected on the spot. The same applies to Texas. However, Californians landing at Florida ports, for example, will not be taxed or subject to laws other than those enforceable in Florida. Then again, Floridians landing in California are subject to the same laws as returning California residents; but customs officers are allowing in-transit passengers to land their liquor quotas if they present airline tickets for a connecting flight. This is a touchy subject, and neither state nor U.S. officials will commit themselves on an "official" policy, but few travelers encounter difficulties. What if Californians arrive at domestic air terminals within your state with five bottles of booze landed in a Florida port? Unless you are spot-checked, let your conscience be your guide.

You may import articles in excess of your customs exemptions unless they are prohibited from entering the United States. Items not entitled to free entry will be subject to customs duty calculated by the customs inspector. Duty assessed will be based on "fair retail value in the country of origin." Payment of duty must be made in U.S. currency and may be made by a personal check drawn on a national or state bank or trust company of the United States and made payable to the "U.S. Customs Service," or by money order, major credit card or traveler's check. Cash is the only means of payment that will not require personal identification such as a passport or social security card.

Customs Declarations

In clearing U.S. Customs, a traveler is considered either a returning resident of the United States or a nonresident. You are a returning resident if you leave the United States for purposes of travel, work, or study abroad and return to resume residency in the United States. Nonresident regulations are covered in the section "Canadian Customs Regulations."

You may make an oral declaration if your purchases do not exceed $1,400. You are required to itemize your purchases and gifts if you exceed that amount. You must also declare items shipped (other than $50 gifts) from the U.S. Virgin Islands. The wearing or use of an article acquired abroad does not exempt it from duty and it must be declared at the price you paid for it.

The customs officer will make an appropriate reduction in value for wear and use. An opened bottle of liquor, even partially consumed, must also be declared. The customs officer will approximate the number of ounces and include it in the total of your alcoholic imports. Your declaration also must include items you have been asked to bring home by another person, any article you intend to sell or use in your business, alterations and repairs made to articles taken abroad, and gifts presented to you while abroad.

Customs declaration forms are distributed on vessels and planes and should be prepared in advance of arrival for presentation to the immigration and customs inspectors, who may request a written list even if you have not exceeded the duty-free allowance.

Family Declaration

The head of a family may make a joint declaration for all members residing in the same household and returning together to the United States. For example, a family of four may bring in free- of duty articles valued up to $1,600 ($4,800 from the Virgin Islands) on one declaration, even if the articles acquired by one member of the family exceed the personal exemption allowed. Infants and children are entitled to the same exemption as adults except for alcoholic beverages.

Avoiding Customs Penalties

It's hard to fool Uncle Sam's customs officers. Not even nice little old ladies escape the scrutiny of customs agents assigned to some 300 points of entry along about 96,000 miles of U.S. borders and at posts in Canada and the Bahamas. After years of people watching and baggage inspections, agents say there is no "profile" of a typical smuggler. Very few, if any, cruise ship passengers are professional smugglers, and most give themselves away by nervousness, by being too helpful or talkative, or by simply doing "stupid things," according to experts in the customs service. French-made gowns, for instance, are easy to spot. They say zippers are a dead giveaway.

The best way to avoid penalties is to declare everything! If you understate the value of an article or if you otherwise misrepresent an article in your declaration, you may have to pay a penalty in addition to payment of duty, to say nothing of the possibility that the article will be seized and forfeited if the penalty is not paid. If you fail to declare an article, not only is it subject to seizure and forfeiture, but you will also be liable for a personal penalty in an amount equal to the value of the article in the United States. You may also face criminal prosecution. Smuggling is not worth the embarrassment and possible problems. Besides, duties have been simplified and tax decreased. If an article is worth purchasing overseas, it's worth paying assessed duties.

INSIDER TIPS

Another bit of advice: Don't rely on know-it-all persons outside the customs service. Merchants abroad (and some shopping "experts" on cruise ships) are more interested in selling than they are in repeat business, so they frequently come up with bad advice leading to violations of customs laws and costly penalties. Some merchants offer travelers invoices or bills of sale showing false or understated values. This can be another costly route. Customs inspectors know the fair retail value of all popular items and are aware of the reliability and practices of shopkeepers throughout the Caribbean, and probably most of the shopping capitals of the world. If in doubt about whether an article should be declared, declare it, and then ask the customs inspector for advice in establishing the value. Customs inspectors handle tourist items day in, day out and are acquainted with normal foreign prices. Another good source of up-to-the-minute information is a cruise director.

INSIDER TIPS

Items purchased on board ship must be included in your customs declaration. Some ship shops are supplying U.S. Customs with computer printouts of purchases, along with passengers' names and amount of purchases. Ships that allow you to charge purchases to your cabin with a single ship account are more likely to be sharing the information with Customs. I was recently involved in a minor dispute when I did not include a purchase made on board and was confronted with the amount and date of purchase by the customs officer. In my case, the item was manufactured in the United States and I was convinced that anything purchased outside the States but manufactured in the States enters the country duty-free. It wasn't worth the dispute, so I added the amount to my declaration and the Inspector said it was free of duty, but had to be included in my declaration.

Customs Exemptions

If you take foreign-made articles (such as watches and cameras) out of the United States, these items are supposed to be registered with U.S. Customs before departure because they are dutiable each time they are brought into the country unless you have proof of prior possession. To obtain a certificate of registration, take the article to the Customs Office nearest you (they are at all international airports and major ports of embarkation). If you have not registered these items before boarding your ship, check with the purser. I usually take an appraisal or an invoice from my local jeweler and produce them if the item is questioned. There is usually a customs officer on board ship until sailing time, and he has the necessary forms for registration. He will want to see the items and check the serial numbers of cameras. The certificate will expedite free entry of these items when you return to the United States. Only items with registration numbers will be preregistered by customs. Jewelry can no longer be registered. If you are concerned, take a copy of an insurance policy or have your jeweler give you a written appraisal. Customs Officers are equipped with an inner sense. They have an instinct that ferrets out new jewelry and never questions the old pieces.

Restricted items

No, you cannot take a doggie bag off the ship. Fruits, vegetables, plants, cuttings, seeds, unprocessed plant products, and certain endangered plant species either are prohibited from entering the country or require an import permit. Pirated copies of copyrighted books (those produced without authorization of the copyright owner) are prohibited. These include photo-offset copies of American best sellers and expensive textbooks produced and sold in the Far East for a fraction of what their cost would be if they were produced in the United States.

INSIDER TIPS

Customs inspectors are on the lookout for clones of personal computers manufactured and sold in the Far East. Prices are about 75 percent less there, and the PCs are marketed under names that are a tip-off on compatibility. If it's an Orange, you know which machine has been ripped off. Inspectors are authorized to confiscate the machines. Inspectors also are on the lookout for copies of genuine imitation Rolex watches sold on the streets of Bali for $10, $15 in Hong Kong and Bangkok.

Exemptions

Art Objects

All original art is exempt from duty, but the purchaser must have a certificate attesting to exactly what the art is. Art purchased on board at art auctions enters the United States without any duty. Antiques (over 100 years old) and original art purchased worldwide must have a Certificate of Authenticity, which you should be ready to present to the customs officer. If it is being sent, do not agree to have the certificate sent along with the work of art. Insist on a certificate at the time of purchase. It will assist you in clearing formalities when the article arrives and you have to claim it at the local Customs Office.

GSP (Generalized System of Preferences) is a system that is boon for shoppers. The law went into effect in 1976 and is reviewed annually. It is a boon for the shopper and is a little-known law that permits duty-free entry of certain articles brought into the United States from some 100 developing countries and 40 dependent territories. It is intended to help developing nations improve their economies through export trade. It allows duty-free importation of a wide range of products otherwise subject to customs duty.

At press time, about 2,700 items have been designated as eligible for duty-free treatment. Many items, such as footwear, textile articles (including clothing), watches, some electronic products, and certain glass and steel products, are excluded from duty-free entry. This exemption list is determined by the effect importation has on U.S. manufacturers in specific industries.

To take advantage of GSP, you must have acquired the eligible article in the beneficiary country where it was grown, manufactured, or produced. Articles may accompany you or may be shipped from the developing country directly to the United States: the same duty-free GSP status applies.

To play it safe, request that the merchant complete a Certificate of Origin or reasonable facsimile. Be aware that most items purchased in duty-free shops are not eligible for GSP treatment unless the merchandise was produced in the country in which the duty-free shop is located. You can't purchase a Brazilian gem in Jamaica, for instance, and claim a GSP exemption. You can purchase the same gem in Brazil and receive the exemption.

GSP items are not exempt from Internal Revenue taxes. If you bring back Barbados rum, for example, there won't be any duty, but there will be IRS tax due. Duty-free items brought back from the designated countries will not affect your normal $400 duty-free allowance ($800 from the Virgin Islands). But you must list all items brought into the United States, no matter whether they are subject to duty or come under GSP. If articles fall into the GSP category, note country of purchase and origin on your declaration.

Visitors and nonresidents are entitled to bring in articles that are duty-free under GSP, in addition to their basic customs exemption.

INSIDER TIPS

If you shop in flea markets and buy from street vendors, you will not get receipts. Best advice is lump all of those purchases together with a total amount and list it as "miscellaneous" on your Form. It works because you have included everything, even tee shirts you wear during the trip, and placed a value on the lot.

Here is a partial list of countries included in the exemption and visited by cruise ships. A complete list is available from any U.S. Customs Office: Antigua, Argentina, Bahamas, Barbados, Bolivia, Brazil, Bermuda, Cayman Islands, China, Colombia, Costa Rica, Dominica, Dominican Republic, Egypt, Fiji, Grenada, Haiti, Hong Kong, India, Indonesia, Israel, Jamaica, Kenya, Republic of Korea, Mexico, Morocco, Netherlands Antilles, Panama, Paraguay, Peru, Philippines, Portugal, St. Vincent and the Grenadines, Singapore, Syria, Thailand, Trinidad and Tobago, Tunisia, Turkey, Uruguay, Venezuela, and Yugoslavia.

Here's a partial list of items that qualify if purchased in a country that qualifies for GSP: Cameras, Chinaware, Earthenware, furniture, games, golf balls and equipment, jewelry of precious stones, or of precious metal set with semi-precious stones vale at not over $18 per dozen, precious and semi-precious unset stones, pearls that are not strung with a clasp, printed matter, silver, toys and wood carvings.

If you ship the merchandise, it must be accompanied by the merchant's invoice in order to take advantage of GSP exemption.

INSIDER TIPS

Do you have recourse if you think you have been charged Customs taxes when the item should have been duty free? Yes, you do. It happened to me. The line behind me was long and I was disputing the assessment being made on a strand of South Sea pearls that were temporary strung and had no clasp. People in the line were becoming more and more agitated, so I paid the charge although I was confident I was right. After settling in, I gathered my purchase receipt and my Customs receipt, got a letter from a local jeweler who was stringing the pearls for me and wrote a letter to the Director of the Regional U.S. Customs Office. It took about three months, and two follow-up letters before the mailman delivered a letter apologizing for the error and a check refunding the full amount of the Customs tax. It pays to know the rules!

Canadian Customs

Canadians planning a trip outside Canada should take a close look at the amount of exemptions allowed and the restrictions imposed on them when they return home to Canada. Registration of such valuable items as cameras, jewelry, and electronics with Canadian customs at departure points is strongly recommended. This will facilitate reentry of these items.

Exemptions

Any resident of Canada returning from abroad may qualify for personal exemption and bring into Canada goods up to a specific value free of duty and taxes. There are no age limitations, and even an infant can qualify.
The personal exemption, however, has limitations on the frequency of its use, on the length of stay abroad, and, concerning alcoholic beverages and tobacco products, on the age of the individual.

Goods brought in under a personal exemption must be souvenirs, for personal or household use, or gifts for friends or relatives. The exemption is a very personal thing for which an individual qualifies at a given time. It cannot be pooled with or transferred to other individuals. You cannot, for example, combine your quarterly and yearly exemptions and claim the total as a special exemption. Nor can you use half of your yearly exemption and save the remainder for another trip six months later.

After 48 hours or more of absence for an unlimited number of times during a year, you may bring in goods valued up to $10, and only an oral declaration is required. Once in every calendar quarter you may bring in goods valued up to $50, and a written declaration may be required. After seven days' absence or longer, once every calendar year you may bring in goods valued up to $150, and a written declaration will be required. You can claim a yearly ($150) and a quarterly ($50) exemption in one calendar quarter provided these are claimed for separate trips.

Tobacco and Alcoholic Beverages

You may bring in alcoholic beverages and tobacco products free of duty and taxes if you are eligible for the quarterly ($50) or yearly ($150) exemption. The dollar value of these items will be part of your personal exemption. Any person 16 years of age or older may bring in 200 cigarettes, 50 cigars, and two pounds of tobacco. Additional quantities may be brought in, but are subject to duty and taxes on the excess amount.

If you meet the age requirements set by the province or territory through which you reenter Canada, you may bring in 40 ounces of wine or liquor or 24, 12-ounce cans or bottles of beer or ale (288 fluid ounces). All provinces except Prince Edward Island and the Northwest Territories allow you to exceed the normal allowance by up to two extra gallons, but the cost is high and a special permit is required. All tobacco products and alcoholic beverages must accompany you in order to qualify for exemptions.

Gifts: You may send gifts from abroad to friends or relatives in Canada as long as these parcels are not valued at more than 15 Canadian dollars and do not contain alcoholic beverages, tobacco products, or advertising matter. Duty and taxes will be assessed on gifts valued over that amount. Make sure a gift card is enclosed to avoid misunderstanding. Gifts mailed from abroad are not declared on reentering Canada and are not counted in your exemption.

Canadian Declarations

When you reenter Canada, you must declare to Canadian Customs everything acquired abroad: purchases as well as gifts. You must also declare all goods you bought before you left at Canadian duty-free stores and are still carrying with you. Goods should be easily accessible for inspection, and it is a good idea to have receipts available.

Goods brought in under any of the exemptions must accompany you in hand or checked luggage, no matter what countries you have visited. It is advisable to declare all "goods to follow," meaning you should declare purchases being mailed to you in Canada. When you are notified that your parcel has arrived, you have 30 days to clear it through Customs. You must present your copy of the declaration form.

Exceeding the Exemption

There is no law that prevents you from bringing back any quantity of goods provided you are willing to pay the full rate of duty and taxes. On the first $150 worth, there is a special rate of 25 percent if you have been away from Canada for 48 hours or more. On quantities over that, regular duty and taxes will be assessed.

INSIDER TIPS

If you are bringing in far less than your allowable personal exemption, the customs officer will advise you if it would be to your advantage to clear the goods under the 25 percent special rate and save your personal exemption for another trip.

Duty and Taxes

Customs assessments depend on what you buy and where you buy it. Canada's trade agreements list "British preferential" and the "most favored nations." The "British preferential" tariff rate applies to goods purchased in Britain and in most Commonwealth countries. The United States is listed as one of the "most favored nation" group.

The following items are free of duty and all taxes: coin and stamp collections, signed original paintings valued at more than $20, and original sculptures valued at more than $75.

A 12 percent sales tax is imposed on the following, regardless of whether the items are included in your exemption: camera accessories, electric razors, and some musical instruments. Most audiovisual equipment (radios, televisions, and so on) is taxed, and duty is assessed at an average of 15 percent; sporting goods can cost returning Canadians as much as 20 percent, and jewelry up to 25 percent.

INSIDER TIPS

Although uniforms have a tendency to intimidate, travelers should be aware that "customs phobia" is a highly overrated condition. Misconceptions aside, customs inspectors are not ogres. They are simply interested in getting their job done without harassment of innocent travelers. Their job is simple: to prevent the smuggling of narcotics and other contraband, and to provide the federal government with the import revenues to which it is entitled.

Nevertheless, customs inspectors do not like smart alecks and, being human will sometimes be tougher with the occasional traveler who tries to outsmart them. Unless you like to play games and are trying to bring in a barrel of diamonds, it makes little sense to try to avoid paying duty.

Facing any customs inspector is a lot easier if you keep your sales slips, invoices, and other evidence of purchases available, because the inspector may ask for verification. Pack your baggage so that inspection of purchases is easy. Try to pack separately the articles you acquired abroad. When the customs officer asks you to open your luggage, don't hesitate or try to talk him out of it.

If you know before you go and follow the rules, clearing customs anywhere is a breeze.

Preclearance

Cruise lines and the U.S. Customs department are cooperating to speed passenger clearance and quick debarkation. Passengers arriving by ship in Florida and other U.S. ports are cleared by Customs before disembarkation begins. The procedure is simple. Customs and immigrations officers board vessels as they enter the harbor. Passengers are asked to complete forms, and one member of each family meets with an inspector to declare the goods. If there is a tax to be paid, the amount is determined by the inspector and paid by the traveler on debarkation. Once you have been cleared on board ship, you need only collect your luggage on shore and be on your way.

A word of caution is in order. Don't try to cheat U.S. Customs and make a false declaration on board ship. Taxes are very low on items exceeding duty-free quotas, but the embarrassment and fines can be very expensive.

Also, be sure you have your customs form completed before you get into a line for clearance. This holds true on board ship or in airports. Nothing is sharper than the edge created when a traveler holds up a line while he completes a simple form.

INSIDER TIPS

If there is a little larceny in your soul, you should know that a preclearance is a matter of honor, but inspectors in the customs area make spot checks. If you are caught and have cheated on your declaration, penalties and seizure can be imposed. Preclearance speeds debarkation and helps passengers and cruise ships. It also avoids mob scenes in small customs areas. More ships are using preclearance systems, and you will be told at the debarkation briefing whether your vessel uses onboard preclearance or whether you will have to show and tell your luggage and purchases.

rating the ships

Rating the ships is the most difficult part of writing *The Total Traveler Guide to Worldwide Cruising*. It would be a lot easier if ships were all the same size and charged the same per day price for cruising. But that's not the reality of the marketplace. With some charging $100 a day, per person and others with rates going up over $900 a day, per person quality, service, and amenities vary greatly. There are new ships, old ships, big ships, small ships, mega ships, and sailing vessels. Ships for all seasons. Ships for all people.

In the first edition of this book (*The Total Traveler by Cruise Ship*), published in 1975, choices for vacations at sea were limited. We profiled 40 ships and filled pages with pictures. The current edition covers more than 400 ships.

Arriving at unbiased reports and evaluations is an ongoing process. I am convinced that no one person's opinion or preference should influence total ship ratings, so *The Total Traveler Guide to Worldwide Cruising* is a critical composite analysis of what experienced travelers have found on every vessel profiled. Expert and unbiased cruise writers and critics contributed to the ratings and many of their comments are included to help travelers select the right ship for their cruise vacation. A cross section of 20 travel agents also contributed to the ratings. The total consensus and ratings were reached by a panel whose members have experienced more than 3,000 cruises. We call the group –The Total Traveler Critics Circle. Their ratings determined "The Best of The Best."

The book in its entirety is based on the assumption that travelers should get what they pay for. A ship charging $500 a day should deliver five times as much and should be five times better than a ship charging $100 a day. It would be unfair to lump all ships into a single category for comparison purposes without regard to prices charged for days at sea. In fairness to lower - and medium-priced vessels and to allow for a better comparison of ships charging comparable rates, eight categories were developed.

CATEGORIES

Ships were categorized by average daily rates (ADR) printed in brochures. ADR was used because of varying cruise lengths. Air-sea packages and discounts were not considered in categorizing ships since the published rate is what the cruise line has decided the cabin should be selling for when demand catches up with supply and world conditions permit a return to normalcy which in itself is a condition hard to define. When that happens, the brochure price will be the price passengers pay for the cruise, but price differences between ships will likely remain the same.

Discount policies are listed in every company profile. These include early booking, past guest, groups and off-season special prices. These rates do not include special regional discounts, last-minute off-season drastic fare cuts, non-affinity groups arranged by travel agencies, or affinity groups offered through organizations, churches, etc. Rates quoted should be used as a guide and an aid in selecting ships in the price range that fits the traveler's vacation budget. Rates quoted are per person, based on two persons occupying the same cabin. Wherever available, single rates and third and fourth passengers (any age) occupying a cabin with two full fare-passengers are included in "Company Policies." All discounts are subject to prior sale and are capacity controlled. This means that early bookers may have claimed all the lowest prices or that the line has set aside a limited number of cabins at the very low rate. When they are sold, rates climb.

TIPPING POLICY

The cruise company's tipping policy is covered in the cruise line profile. The amount quoted is the amount recommended by the cruise line. Passengers should tip based on quality and quantity of services. Small gratuities should also be given to deck stewards, tearoom waiters, and the like, if they have extended themselves. When the recommended tip suggests an amount for the cabin steward or the dining-room waiter, it is not necessary to tip their assistants. They are included in the single tip. Bar tips are based on shore side recommendations of 15 to 20 percent and tips are given when service is rendered. Most lines add 15 percent automatically to the bill and it goes on your running tab set up as a charge system by the ship. Ship officers are never tipped. All tips are per person, per day (more accurately per night), unless otherwise noted.

Reading the Ratings

CATEGORIES

Ships were divided into the following categories based on size, number of guests carried, lifestyle and brochure rates. There is some overlap between categories because some ships bridge the narrowing gaps between classifications either in lifestyle or price, or both. Categories are used to assist travelers in narrowing their vessel choices to those that match their interests and vacation budget.

Budget $$:

Vessels offering cruises at extremely low rates. Usually older vessels priced at $125 and under per day.

Traditional $$ to $$$$$:

Usually vessels built prior to 1980 offering classic shipboard lifestyles. Rates and amenities could run from Budget to Luxury.

Resort Mid-Size $$ to $$$:

Ships built during the past 10 to 15 years with amenities focusing on a casual lifestyle. Ships usually measure out at less than 50,000 tons and are priced from $150 to $250 per day.

Resort XL $$$ or Resort XXL $$$:

This category covers many of the ships sailing out of North America and is often referred to as "mass market." or "contemporary." I thought that XL (extra large) and XXL (extra, extra large) would best describe the size of the ship. Resort XL ships are big and include ships that measure out between 50,000 and 80,000 tons and carry upwards of 1800 guests with rates from $175 up. Resort XXL applies to the giant or megasize vessels that range upwards from 85,000 tons to over 100,000 tons. They usually have the capacity to carry more than 3,000 guests.

Premium $$$$:

Ships that combine amenities of both traditional and contemporary vessels in a more sophisticated environment. In order to be considered Premium, they can't be XXL. Rates run from $225 to $400 per day.

Luxury $$$$$:

Ships of all sizes that combine all the amenities offered on traditional, contemporary, and premium vessels with higher levels of food, service, and ambience. They are spacious vessels priced at over $400 per day. The term "luxury" puts most of the ships into a smaller size range.

Boutique Exclusive $$$$$:

Smaller vessels with fewer than 500 guests providing a unique experience at prices of over $400 per day.

Boutique-Adventure $$ to $$$$$:

Destination-driven vessels that emphasize ports of call over ship amenities. Rates can range from Budget to Luxury.

Rates:

Since rates fluctuate seasonally and for various other reasons, dollar signs ($) indicate the approximate rate you can reasonably expect to pay. All rates are per person in double occupancy cabins. The more $'s, the higher the rate.

INSIDER TIP

Rates overlap and it is not unusual to find an offer on a $$$$$ or $$$$ class vessel at $$$ rates. In 2002, discounts at the $$$$$ (luxury) level brought some of the cruise rates down to the $$$ (mid-price) level. Savvy travelers were quick to take advantage of these offers.

Average Daily Rate: Rate was determined by adding the prices of an average inside and outside cabin to minimum and maximum rates, excluding suites, unless the ship has a large number of these superior accommodations. Total was divided by number of price categories and then by cruising days. Seasonal increases were considered, as were published high-season rates; discounts normally offered by the cruise line were not included in ADRs. Airfare allowance was deducted from the published rate when air is listed as "free." ADRs do not include air. Unless otherwise indicated, ADRs are cruise-only rates.

Ratings: Evaluations were tallied on a scale of 1 to 10 (see "Reading the Ratings" below), averaged and final ratings were reached. Different values were assigned to each participant depending on experience and the number of vessels cruised during the past five years. In reading the ratings, remember that ships were evaluated and compared with other ships in the same price category. Everything on board was evaluated and rated. Evaluations were fed into the computer and translated into anchors, from ⚓⚓ to ⚓⚓⚓⚓⚓++ for each important feature that influences ship selection.

INSIDER TIP

Be aware that a ship in the Resort XL or XXL categories may have five plus anchors ⚓⚓⚓⚓⚓+ in Spa and Fitness, but three anchors ⚓⚓⚓ for overall cabin facilities. Conversely, a Luxury vessel may have been awarded five plus anchors ⚓⚓⚓⚓⚓+ for dining but three ⚓⚓⚓ for entertainment. Also, a ship rated ⚓⚓⚓⚓ in the Budget category does not offer the same product as a ship rated ⚓⚓⚓⚓ in higher priced categories.

Other Evaluations

Value Award: It's not the price, but the value of the vacation product that is most important. Using the same scale of 1 to 10, the panel rated shipping companies on (1) money's worth; (2) accuracy of brochures; (3) consistency of product; and (4) guest satisfaction. Eighty-five percent of the companies rated above 8.5 in all four areas. Highest ratings went to Carnival Cruise Lines,

Princess Cruises, Holland America Lines, Crystal Cruises and Silversea Cruises. They were rated above 8, which means the lines are delivering superb products and guests are satisfied that they are getting their money's worth.

The *Money's Worth Top* award goes to Carnival Cruise Lines for the sixth consecutive edition. Carnival Cruise Lines rated a solid "10" in the money's worth category.

Key to Reading Ship Profiles

Specifics: Includes vital statistics such as tonnage, medical services, elevators and other physical features.

Space Ratio: Computed by dividing the gross tonnage by the maximum guest capacity (usually based on two guests per room). Space ratio is a good indication of whether public areas will be crowded. For example, if a ship weighs 20,000 tons and carries 500 guests, the space ratio is 40. Take another 20,000-ton ship carrying 1,500 guests and the space ratio is 13.3. The higher the space ratio of guests to facilities, the more spacious the vessel will be.

Crew to Guest Ratio: Indicates of the type of service passengers can expect. To find the Crew to Guest Ratio, divide the number of guests by the number of crew members. For example, if a ship carries 200 crew members and 1,000 guests, the Crew-to-Passenger Ratio would be one to five. If the ship has 500 crew members and 1,000 guests, the ratio would be one to two. The lower the second number, the better the service. A ship with 1,000 crewmembers and 1,000 guests would have one crew member for each guest and service would be exceptional.

Cabins and Suites: Size, decor, configuration, storage space and amenities are covered. All ships, unless otherwise noted, have private bathrooms with a toilet, shower and/or tub, and washbasin. Ships with limited or no private facilities have been noted as such. All ships are air-conditioned and have temperature controls in cabins, unless otherwise noted.

Public Space: Showrooms, bars, lounges and open decks.

Food and Dining: Type and variety of menus, dining rooms and optional dining facilities, quality and presentation of food. Also covered: special dietary requests—spa, vegetarian, kosher, etc.

Dress Code: Type of dress suggested for wear during and after dinner hours.

Spa and Fitness: Size, type of equipment, programs and unusual features.

Junior Cruisers: Facilities, program, ages and supervision.

Itineraries: Ports of call or the region in which the ship is scheduled to sail.

Overall: General impressions, what to look for and what to expect.
Rates: All rates quoted are per person, based on two persons occupying the same cabin (double occupancy), except where otherwise noted. Rates are subject to change and often fluctuate. All third- and fourth-passenger rates, as well as children's rates, are based on sharing the same cabin with two full-fare adult passengers. Rates do not include airfares, transfers to ports of embarkation, or port charges in most cases.

INSIDER TIP

All the major cruise ships have a charge system. Guests present their credit cards (American Express, VISA or MasterCard), and they are issued a card, which in some cases is also the cabin key and in all cases, it is the identification needed to re-board the ship in ports. The card also permits them to sign for bar bills, spa services, and purchases made anywhere on the ship. Cash is also accepted, of course, but some cruise lines balk at accepting personal checks to settle final bills. There are ATM machines on all the major vessels.

Reading the Ratings

⚓⚓⚓⚓⚓++	*Even better than Excellent. As good as it gets.*
⚓⚓⚓⚓⚓	*Excellent*
⚓⚓⚓⚓	*Very Good*
⚓⚓⚓	*Good*
⚓⚓	*Fair: Limited Appeal*
NR	*Not Rated*

(Ships are either too new to rate or have changed ownership and cruising style)

INSIDER TIP

Ship owners don't just pick letters to be put before a ship's name. Letters in front of the name of a ship indicate the type of engine used to run the vessel. In recent years, cruise lines have taken to eliminating the letters, so the Total Traveler follows that trend. If the cruise line uses the initials in front of the ship's name, so do we. If they don't, we don't. Here's a rundown:

MS	Motor Ship (uses diesel oil)
MTS	Motor Turbine Screw
MV	Motor Vessel (has piston engine)
RMS	Royal Mail Ship (sometimes referred to as Royal Majesty Ship)
SS	Steamship
TS	Turbo Ship (similar to TSS)
TSS	Turbo Steamship (turbo engines; uses heavy fuel oil)
TTS	Twin Turbine Screw

All cruise lines boarding passengers in U.S. ports and selling passage in the United States are bonded for default and must abide by state laws covering consumer rights. But travelers should know more about these companies, their financial stability, history and track record in the industry.

For those reasons and others (such as a natural curiosity about the people behind the companies), the *Total Traveler Guide to Worldwide Cruising* includes background and historical information about the owners and operators of cruise ships. In the research process, I learned that many are being operated by second and third generation shipping families; others have the financial and business backing of European companies with decades of experience in passenger and cargo vessels. In recent years some cruise lines have consolidated and some large conglomerates operate other familiar brands.

Some well-known names have disappeared. Among them is Commodore Cruise Lines, one of the oldest sailing out of the Port of Miami. Others include Premier Cruises, and Renaissance Cruises that folded shortly after September 11th. American Classic Voyages also went under, but there's new hope for its Delta Queen division, which has been sold to new owners who promise a resurrection. It has been a game of musical chairs for some companies, while others remain solid and continue growth. Carnival Cruise Lines, Royal Caribbean International, Princess Cruises and Norwegian Cruise Line make up the Big Four and their growth continues.

Public ownership of privately held companies has increased. Shares in cruise lines are traded on the New York Stock Exchange, in London, Norway, Hong Kong and other stock exchanges.

This book is all about the companies and their ships and what differentiates one from another and makes each a different experience. In other words, this book points out differences likely to influence your choice of ships.

In this chapter, we have included small companies with small ships all the way up to the largest cruise lines and their megaships. Ships primarily marketed or headquartered in North America are included in this chapter. They range from boutique adventure vessels that carry less than 20 guests to mega liners that can accommodate more than 3,000 guests. Keep in mind; ratings are within price and size categories. Luxury vessels, for example, are never rated against budget priced ships.

American Canadian Caribbean Line

461 Water Street, Warren, RI 02885
(401) 247-0955 – www.accl-smallships.com

The company is a reflection of its owner, Captain Luther Blount, who built his first vessel in 1964 for Hudson River crossings. He is a hands-on owner/manager who believes in building his own small ships in his own ship-yard in Rhode Island. In business for more than 30 years, American Canadian Line continues to do something larger companies envy – turning a profit.

Known as "The Small Ship Cruise Line," Blount says his vessels must be built with a shallow draft of not more than six feet and must be able to go through the Erie Canal. His vessels are easy to recognize. Bow-landing ramps allow passengers to go ashore in places without piers and glass bottoms make viewing below ocean, river and lake surfaces part of the cruise experience.

Vessels come closer to country inns than cruise ships in passenger experiences and on board ambience. All are equipped with lifeboats, serve meals family-style and offer few frills. The company enjoys a loyal following of passengers who want easy adventures at a slow pace in a family-type atmosphere.

Who Sails American Canadian Caribbean Line? A few singles, but 85 percent of the guests are couples over 55 years of age. They are not generally over-active types of travelers. Most have cruised the big ships and have settled down to a slower pace. No children under 14 are accepted for passage, so that's a good indicator of on board ambience.

Lifestyle: Casual, yacht-style cruising in quiet waters. Everything is done at a slower pace as though guests and crew have slowed the clock. It is adventure and leisurely cruising at near budget prices and the repeat rate is among the highest at sea. There's little pomp and no pampering. The company offers small ship experiences without a lot of frills. It is so hands-on, it doesn't use computers on board or on shore.

Dress Code: Very casual although there is a captain's party and some of the guests do change clothes for the event.

Dining Rooms: Service is family-picnic-style with paper plates, etc., but the food is good American-style cooking and there's plenty of it. Single sittings on all vessels. Special dietary requests are possible but requests must be made at time of booking.

Service: Casual and informal. Small service staff is friendly and personal and definitely family style which is exactly what the owners are touting.

Tipping Policy: $10 to $12 per day per person. Tips are pooled and divided among the entire crew. The normal 15 percent is expected for bar service.

Itineraries: With a maximum of 100 guests, ACCL vessels cruise along the New England coastline and Canadian inland waterways from late May through October. Other months, they are based in the Bahamas, Caribbean Islands, Belize and Guatemala. They also cruise U.S. inland waterways from Palm Beach to Hobe Sound.

Discount Policy: Frequent cruiser plan where, after nine cruises, the tenth is free. Otherwise, discounts are limited. Back-to-back cruises are discounted 10 percent and a similar discount is offered on repositioning cruises and sometimes in the Caribbean. Third cabin passenger gets a 15 percent discount.

HIGH MARKS

△ Ramps that come out at the bow to allow vessels to pull right up to shore. The ramp is lowered and guests walk ashore without getting their feet wet.

△ Itineraries are not molded in stone and may change with the wind, literally. That's a plus for most people; guests don't usually mind unless they selected the cruise for a specific itinerary.

△ The unusually casual attitude of the company and crew. It is totally laid back and contagious.

△ The low cost of shore excursions. ACCL offers them on a complimentary basis and, in some cases, charges guests exactly what it costs the company.

WEAKEST LINKS

• No doctor on board
• No swimming pool or Jacuzzi
• No children under 14
• No liquor is sold on board. If you bring your own, bartenders will tag your bottle with name and cabin number and serve it to you on request.
• No casino

INSIDER TIP

The three ships are not identical but very similar in size, décor and amenities. These are no-frill vessels at no frills rates. What you pay for is what you get. Inside cabins are not for claustrophobics. My suggestion is to book the best cabin your budget allows. You'll be glad you did.

The Fleet

GRANDE CARIBE
Built 1997

GRAND MARINER
Built 1998

NIAGARA PRINCE
Built 1994

Category: Boutique-Adventure
Rates: $$
Overall Rating: ⚓⚓
Country of Registry: United States
Former Names: none
Nationality of Crew: American
Cruising Area: United States, Canada and Caribbean
Length of Voyages: 7, 11, 14 and 15 nights

Ship Specifics

Tonnage	89-95	Elevators	0
Length*	182 feet	Decks	3
Beam	38-40 feet	Children's Facilities	no
Stabilizers	no	Fitness Center	no
Passengers	90-100	Spa	no
Crew	18	Verandahs	no
Space Ratio	n/a	Casino	no
Crew/Passenger Ratio	1-6	Wheelchair Access	no

*Length: Niagara Prince 165 feet

Cabins: ⚓⚓ Small. Really small. There are no complaints as guests are light packers since dressing up is not part of an ACCL experience. There's little hanging space and cabin doors do not lock. Leave your valuables at home. There's a choice on all three vessels of inside and outside cabins and sleeping arrangements of single or double beds. Cabin size averages about 108-square feet. Largest are on upper decks and sell quickly. Lower deck cabins do not have windows. Bathrooms on *Grand Caribe* and *Grand Mariner* have curtains sepa-

219

rating the sink and toilet from hand held shower. A trap door lets the water out of the shower and the toilet has a fill and flush system similar to what you may find on some private yachts but the vessels resemble a yacht with teak trim. There are a limited number of no-smoking cabins on each vessel.

Public Space: ⚓⚓ There is a single lounge/bar on each vessel. It is a multi-purpose room and is used for all of the entertainment and for various activities. Each vessel also has a small library

Spa and Fitness: ⚓ None. Aerobics classes are scheduled.

Entertainment ⚓⚓ While local entertainers are sometimes brought on board for evening shows, entertainment is really shipboard activities on these vessels. There are lectures covering cultures of the cruising areas, but there also is bingo, horse racing on deck and snorkeling instruction.

Food and Dining: ⚓⚓ American family-style service. Special diets are possible when arranged in advance of sailing. One full meal is served at dinner only with one choice of dinner entrée. Lunch is light and may be soup and sandwiches or soup and salads. Breakfast is buffet. Self-serve fruit, tea, coffee and snacks are available on a 24-hour basis.

Junior Cruisers: ⚓ None

Itineraries ⚓⚓⚓ *Grand Caribe* and *Mayan Prince* sail through the eastern inland and coastal waterways of the United States and Canada and along the eastern seaboard around Florida and Central America. *Niagara Prince* sails on five to 15-day cruises and includes the Great Lakes.

Overall ⚓⚓ Tonnage on these ships is confusing. They are low and are registered at less than 100-tons, but that does not mean they are crowded. Ships are informal. Meal service is American family style. Not much entertainment and there's no need to dress up. No liquor is sold on U.S. inland cruises, so a bottle in the room is suggested. Great feature is the ramp that goes down when ships pull up at a beach. It allows guests to walk down the slight incline to get ashore.

HIGH MARKS

Δ Mixes and nonalcoholic drinks are free at the bar.

Δ Board a day before your cruise in some Caribbean ports and use the ship as your hotel for $50 per night, per person.

Δ Excellent shore excursions.

WEAKEST LINKS:

• No beach towels. Brochure suggests you bring your own.

• No cabin service

American West Steamboat Company

2101 Fourth Avenue, #1150, Seattle, WA 98121
(206) 292-9606 – www.columbiarivercruise.com

With the purchase at auction of the *Columbia Queen* from the Delta Queen fleet, American West Steamboat Company becomes a major player in steamboat vacations on American rivers. The company is credited with bringing stern-wheeler cruising back to America's most historic and scenic rivers aboard the authentic paddlewheel *Queen of the West*, currently America's newest and largest and what some call, the most elegant small cruise ship.

Since 1995, the company has operated the 163-passenger *Queen of the West* on the Columbia, Willamette and Snake Rivers along the Lewis & Clark discovery route, Oregon Trail and Columbia River Gorge. Like the *Queen of the West*, *Columbia Queen* will provide guests a cruise into history featuring the scenery, culture and geology of the region.

In addition to acquisition of the *Columbia Queen*, the company is building a third luxury sternwheeler, the 236-passenger Empress of the North, scheduled to begin service in Alaska in June 2003. *Empress of the North* will operate in Alaska between May and September and then join the *Columbia Queen* and *Queen of the West* on the Columbia River for the remainder of the year.

Who Sails American West Steamboat Company: Travelers who want to follow the history of the west and want to be immersed in the culture and scenery of the Pacific Northwest. They want to do it in comfort and style. More than half of the guests are over 55 year old couples. There are few singles and very few families with young children. Most are from the United States. Most have sailed the big cruise ships and are opting for the advantages of small vessels.

Lifestyle: Casual, yet refined. Within a few days, all of the guests and crew know each other.

Dress: Casual and comfortable. Guests dress for the weather since most of the days are spent in port sightseeing. Jackets and ties are never suggested or required.

Dining: All meals are open sitting and are served family-style. There are good choices of American-style specialties; home cooking, fresh breads and pastries.

Entertainment: There is nightly showboat variety entertainment in showrooms with different performers and musical themes each night of the cruise. Just like the vessels are a step back in time, so is the entertainment – Riverboat Jazz, Golden Oldies, Big Band and Country Western.

Discount Policy: Reserve and deposit four to six months before sailing and save up to $400 per couple. Early booking rates are guaranteed which means if rates do down closer to sailing, early bookers get the lowest advertised rate. Special occasion group rates come with 15 percent discount. Special occasions are interpreted as birthdays, anniversaries, family reunion and holiday sailings but there must be six or more sailing for the group celebration. The company offers air/sea, air/rail packages from most U.S. cities.

Itineraries: Vessels follow the Lewis & Clark Route, the Oregon Trail, the Columbia River Gorge National Scenic Area and sail in the wake of the historic Great Sternwheeler Era. Seasonal Alaska itineraries.

Length of Voyages: 4, 7 and 10-nights nights

EMPRESS OF THE NORTH
Built: May 2003

Category: Boutique-Adventure
Rates: $$$
Country of Registry: United States
Former Names: None
Nationality of Crew: American
Cruising Area: Alaska and Columbia, Snake and Willamette Rivers
Length of Voyages: 7 and 10-nights

Ship Specifics:

Tonnage	n/a	Elevators	2
Length	360 feet	Decks	4
Beam	58 feet	Children's Facilities	no
Stabilizers	no	Fitness Center	no
Passengers	236	Spa	no
Crew	84	Verandahs	yes
Space Ratio	n/a	Casino	no
Crew/Passenger Ratio	1-4	Wheelchair Access	yes

Cabins: Of the 112 cabins and suites, 105 have private verandahs, a first for any steamboat vessel. Cabins all have sitting areas, writing desk, picture windows,

TV with DVD and minibars. Two cabins will be equipped for disabled travelers with ramp access and wide doors.

Empress of the North is an authentic sternwheeler-driven small cruise ship with all modern amenities. The dining room has the capacity to seat all of the guests in a single sitting. The ship has a formal show lounge, three bars and windows throughout for guest viewing. In total, 228 windows or one for each guest if you do the math.

Entertainment will be similar to *Queen of the West* with music of early Americana, Golden Oldies, Broadway and Dixieland Jazz.

Following company policy, shore excursions, which are included in rates, will be by private motor coaches with historians and guest speakers. Shipboard décor will feature paintings, photographs and rare artifacts depicting the history of the inhabitants and explorers along the cruise routes.

COLUMBIA QUEEN
Built: 2000   Refurbished: 2003

Category: Boutique-Adventure
Rates: $$$
Overall: New ownership. Not rated
Country of Registry: United States
Former Names: none
Nationality of Crew; United Sates
Cruising Area: Columbia, Snake and Willamette Rivers
Length of Voyages: 4 to 7-nights

Ship Specifics:

Tonnage	n/a	Elevators	1
Length	218 feet	Decks	4
Beam	60 feet	Children's Facilities	no
Stabilizers	no	Fitness Center	no
Passengers	161	Spa	no
Crew	57	Verandahs	no
Space Ratio	n/a	Casino	no
Crew/Passenger Ratio	1-3.2	Wheelchair Access	yes

Cabins and Suites: More than half are outside cabins. The largest are 220 square feet; smallest is a cabin designated as a "single" at 91 square feet. While there are no real verandahs, there are some with French balconies and others that open out to the Promenade. Most expensive accommodations open out to semi-private verandahs. Accommodations are riverboat décor and it is carried out in accessories. Cabins also have ironing boards and hair dryers.

Public Space: There's a Lewis & Clark Lounge where passengers gather for pre-dinner drinks and hors d'oeuvres. Explorer Bar has a grand piano and lots of wood paneling in the tradition of steamboats. The room has huge windows for scenic viewing. The Purser's Lobby area is a meeting place and there is a gift shop. The Back Porch is a cozy place for breakfast, coffee and a small bar. French doors enclose the deck in inclement weather but it's an open deck at other times.

Entertainment: Follows the company policy

Food and Dining: Similar to *Queen of the West*

Junior Cruisers: Very few youngsters sail these vessels

Overall: American West Steamboat has announced that the ship will undergo "some refurbishment and aesthetic upgrades such as new artwork throughout the ship to include historical paintings and photographs of the region and a new exterior paint scheme to match the other vessels in the fleet."

QUEEN OF THE WEST
Built: 1995

Category: Boutique-Adventure

Rates: $$$

Overall Rating: ⚓⚓⚓

Country of Registry: United States

Former Names: None

Nationality of Crew; United Sates

Cruising Area: From Portland to Columbia, Snake and Willamette Rivers

Length of Voyages: Seven nights

Ship Specifics:

Tonnage	n/a	Elevators	1
Length	230 feet	Decks	4
Beam	69 feet	Children's Facilities	no
Stabilizers	no	Fitness Center	no
Passengers	163	Spa	no
Crew	47	Verandahs	no
Space Ratio	n/a	Casino	no
Crew/Passenger Ratio	1-3.5	Wheelchair Access	yes

Cabins: ⚓⚓⚓ *Suites:* ⚓⚓⚓⚓ Cabin size ranges from an average of 144-square feet to some nice suites at 272-square feet. About one-third are outside and have verandahs. The décor is Victorian throughout the boat with dark woods. Cabins have television, private bathrooms with showers and are comparable to some of the small cruise ships.

Public Space: ⚓⚓⚓⚓ There's a formal show lounge, three bars and lots of memorabilia that decorates the vessel to resemble an authentic steamboat of the 1800s. Original pieces from those vessels make an interesting background. The steam whistle and the wheel used to steer came from a Seattle fireboat that operated at the turn of the century. All of the artwork is designed in the spirit of those days. Historic photographs and painting from the Pacific Northwest's riverboat past and the area's pioneer heritage add to the ambiance.

Entertainment: ⚓⚓⚓ Showboat variety entertainment performed in two Showrooms with a different entertainers and musical themes each night of the cruise, such as Riverboat Jazz, Golden Oldies, Big Band and Country Western. The resident pianist becomes an entertainment favorite on every cruise.

Food and Dining: ⚓⚓⚓ Open seating for all meals family-style. American cuisine with choices. Guests give rave reviews to the home baked breads and desserts. Menu includes regional favorites.

Junior Cruisers: ⚓ Few guests bring young children. Teenagers enjoy the open bridge policy and the interesting history of the area.

Itineraries: ⚓⚓⚓⚓ There are no major cities on the schedule, other than Portland where the boat calls home. Boat sails the Columbia, Snake and Willamette Rivers.

Overall: ⚓⚓⚓ The vessel is very much like the river boats of the 1800s when it comes to décor, but the amenities are definitely contemporary.

It's comfortable and there's no other way to follow the Lewis & Clark routes that opened commerce to the west. The vessel is intimate, friendly and comfortable.

HIGH MARKS:
- △ All shore excursions are included in the cruise price and are escorted by historians.
- △ The staff is motivated, cheerful and loves the rivers
- △ Ease of disembarkation. No customs; no long waits in lounges.

WEAKEST LINKS:
- • Acoustics in the Lewis & Clark and paddlewheel lounges need improvement.

Cruise West

2401 Fourth Ave, Suite 700, Seattle, WA 98121
(206) 441-88687 – www.cruisewest.com

Founded in 1946 as an Alaska sightseeing company, it was sold as Westours to Holland America Line in 1973. Owner Charles "Chuck" West then founded Alaska Sightseeing, now known as Cruise West, offering cruises along the Inside Passage. In 1990, he added the 58-guest *Spirit of Glacier Bay* for overnight cruising. The following year, he began U.S. flagship sailings between Seattle and Alaska, a route neglected since 1954.

Most of the vessels are less than 100 tons, which allows unrestricted access to Glacier Bay. Sailing season runs from early April through October. The company offers other exploration voyages, such as cruises in Baja Mexico's Sea of Cortes, British Columbia, California Wine Country and Columbia & Snake Rivers.

INSIDER TIP

A single feature distinguishes the fleet: Each vessel has a bow-landing capability or a front gangway so passengers can disembark directly onto shore. Most were built in U.S. shipyards and carry mostly American crews.

Who Sails Cruise West? About 80 percent of the guests are American and Canadian couples with half of them between 35 and 55, the rest over 55 years of age. Very few singles or children come aboard these vessels. Guests, for the most part, are active explorer-types who want to experience the smaller ports big ships cannot enter. Itinerary and outdoor activities are more important than the luxuries of a cruise ship. Guests who are in tune with the ecology and natural surroundings are more apt to sail one of the Alaska Sightseeing vessels. Many return year after year to sample different itineraries.

On Board Lifestyle: Very relaxed. An open bridge policy encourages conversations with the captain, other officers and the crew. Everything is geared to nature and the wonders of the areas visited.

Shirley and Harry comment:
"Cruise West ships look outward toward shoreside experiences and scenery rather than inward toward shipboard life. Don't expect luxurious surroundings and gourmet meals, but the friendly young American crew will make your feel welcome."

Dress Code: Very casual. Leave tuxedos and sequins at home. Anything that goes with jeans is acceptable.

Dining: What the boats lack in amenities, they make up for in food. There is a lot of emphasis on dining and wines. There are set menus at each meal with three choices for main courses. The chef announces the dinner menu for the following evening and guests turn in their selections. Lunch is usually soup, salad and sandwiches. Hor d'oeuvres are served in the lounge before dinner and breakfast is self-service with the usual eggs, cereal and bacon. Special dietary requests (vegetarian, low salt, low fat, kosher) are possible, but must be made at time of booking.

Service: Consistent throughout the fleet. The staff is young and enthusiastic, coming mainly from the Pacific Northwest and Alaska. The same person who waits your table usually wears many hats and also cleans cabins or helps with shore excursions. Staffs are friendly and willing to assist guests. There is no cabin service but tea and coffee are always available in lounges.

Tipping Policy: $10 per person, per day added to your ship account. Tips are divided among staff, including bar service.

Past Passengers Perks: Quyana Club encourages repeat passengers with discounts on specific voyages and added value, which could be shore excursions or special events

Discount Policy: Except for small discounts for early booking and full payments, this company has been an exception to discounting practices. But it seems to be changing. In 2002, the company offered special summer rates for children and free round trip air from over 70 U.S. and Canadian cities on Sea of Cortes cruises. It also offered free air or 50 percent off for the second person on Costa Rica and Panama voyages. Vessels are small and fill early seasonally, so discounts are not part of the marketing plan. But, with more ships in the fleet, there's no reason to think that some price incentives will not be available in 2003.

HIGH MARKS

△ Boats sail into harbors big ships cannot enter.

△ Close-up encounters with an eagle in a tree on a rocky islet or hump backs close enough to see the barnacles on a fin.

△ Opportunities to kayak off a wilderness island in Mexico or walk through jungles in Costa Rica.

WEAKEST LINKS:

- No doctors or nurses.
- No elevators.
- No entertainment, other than regional lecturers.
- No well-stocked library.
- No cabin meal service, except in the Owner's Suites.

The Fleet
MV SPIRIT OF '98

Built: 1993   Refurbished: 1998

Category: Boutique-Adventure
Rates: $$ to $$$
Overall Rating: ⚓⚓
Country of Registry: United States
Former Names: *Victorian Empress, Colonial Explorer, and Pilgrim Belle*
Nationality of Crew: American
Cruising Area: Alaska
Length of Voyages: 7 to 10 nights

Ship Specifics:

Tonnage	96	Elevators	1
Length	192 feet	Decks	4
Beam	40 feet	Children's Facilities	no
Stabilizers	no	Fitness Center	limited
Passengers	98	Spa	no
Crew	12	Verandahs	no
Space Ratio	n/a	Casino	no
Crew/Passenger Ratio	1-4	Wheelchair Access	no

Cabins: ⚓ ***Suites:*** ⚓⚓⚓ All air-conditioned outside rooms with private facilities (showers only, except in the Owner's Suite). Limited storage space but some have minibars, large picture windows and a writing desk. No private safes. Deluxe cabins have queen-sized beds. Minimums (five cabins) have upper and lower berths. Size ranges from 110 to 120-square feet. Cabins on top two decks open onto the promenade. The Owner's Suite is almost four times the size of average cabins and probably more when compared with minimums. It is 552-square feet and sits by itself topside on the Sun Deck. It even has a stocked wet bar with complimentary beverages and a dining table. It also has a separate bedroom with a king-sized bed, marble bath and lots of storage space.

Public Space: ⚓⚓ Open promenades bring guests closer to a yacht-like experience and the forward area is great for spotting bald eagles. There are two lounges on board. The Grand Salon is a crowded multi-purpose room. Continental breakfast and hot hors d'oeuvres are served here. It is also the room used for card playing, reading, writing and visiting with other guests. Soapy's Parlour is an intimate room aft of the dining room.

Spa and Fitness: ⚓ No organized fitness or spa programs are offered. There is a single Stairmaster, exercise bike and rowing machine. No space is really set aside for these activities.

Entertainment: ⚓⚓⚓ Bird watching, wildlife watching and lecturers knowledgeable about Alaska and its wildlife population. The crew stages some shows and there is sometimes a pianist or other light evening entertainment. Guests consider the itinerary as a major entertainment factor.

Food and Dining: ⚓⚓⚓ Guests dine in the Klondike Dining Room in one open sitting. Table sizes vary and guests may change tables nightly, sit wherever they like and select their own tablemates Cuisine is surprisingly good and could be called Pacific Northwest-style. Fresh seafood, local products and wines and microbrews of the region are menu favorites.

Junior Cruisers: ⚓ There are no facilities or programs for children and very few families sail the vessel.

Itineraries: ⚓⚓⚓ Home ported in Seattle and Juneau on alternating seven-night itineraries. *Spirit of '98* calls at Haines, Ketchikan, Skagway and Sitka and cruises for two days along the British Columbia coastline.
No swimming pool or Jacuzzi

PACIFIC EXPLORER
Built: 1995   Remodeled: 1998

Category: Boutique-Adventure
Rates: $$$
Overall Rating: ⚓⚓⚓
Country of Registry: Panama
Former Names: Temptress Explorer
Nationality of Crew: Costa Rican
Cruising Area: Costa Rica and Panama
Length of Voyages: 7 nights

Ship Specifics:

Tonnage	437	Elevators	1
Length	185 feet	Decks	4
Beam	40 feet	Children's Facilities	no
Stabilizers	yes	Fitness Center	limited
Passengers	00	Spa	no
Crew	12	Verandahs	no
Space Ratio	n/a	Casino	no
Crew/Passenger Ratio	1-4	Wheelchair Access	no

Cabins: ⚓⚓ *Suites:* ⚓⚓⚓ Rooms are extremely small, but adequate for these adventure-style voyages. The total capacity is 100 guests. Average cabin size is 121-square feet. Deluxe cabins (also known as "suites") are slightly larger at 147-square feet that is a far cry from cruise ship size, even on budget-priced vessels. A positive feature is the large window in every cabin that makes them seem larger and all cabins have private facilities (sink, shower and toilet).

Public Space: ⚓⚓⚓ Ship is air-conditioned. There is an observation room and a lecture room as well as two lounges, a library and a bar on Sun Deck, which is where guests gather at sunset.

Spa and Fitness: ⚓⚓ Water sports of all sorts are offered.

Entertainment: ⚓⚓ Lecturers, movies and a limited selection in the library.

Food and Dining: ⚓⚓⚓ This and itinerary are the strong points. Cuisine is laced with Central American specialties prepared daily. Fresh fruits, vegetables, meats and fish are brought aboard in most ports. All breads and deserts are made fresh daily by the pastry chef.

Junior Cruisers: ⚓ No specific program, but during summer months, when families bring teenagers, special activities are planned.

Itineraries: ⚓⚓⚓ This is what attracts passengers. The vessel offers travel through Central America in comfort, which is not the norm. Vessel explores remote regions of Costa Rica.

Overall: ⚓⚓⚓ The *Pacific Explorer* is used mainly for charters and groups and it is not unusual to find a college alumni or an exploration group on board. Travelers who want to explore in total luxury will probably not enjoy the atmosphere. On the other side of the coin, if exploration is more important than the size of the cabin, this one's for you.

HIGH MARKS

Δ Passengers with similar interests who want an up–close look at the mysteries of Costa Rica and the Panama Canal.

Δ As "un-cruise-like" as it gets.

WEAKEST LINK:

• No one dresses up, but that's good as long as you know in advance.

MV SPIRIT OF ALASKA
MV SPIRIT OF COLUMBIA
Built: 1980   Refurbished: 1991 & 1995

Category: Boutique Adventure
Rates: $$$- $$$$
Overall Rating: ⚓⚓
Country of Registry: United States
Former Names: *Pacific Norwest Explorer* and *New Shoreham II*
Nationality of Crew: American officers and service staff
Cruising Area: Alaska
Length of Voyages: 7 to 10 nights

Ship Specifics:

Tonnage	97	Elevators	0
Length	147 feet	Decks	3
Beam	28 feet	Children's Facilities	no
Stabilizers	no	Fitness Center	very limited
Passengers	82	Spa	no
Crew	21	Verandahs	no
Space Ratio	n/a	Casino	no
Crew/Passenger Ratio	1-4	Wheelchair Access	no

Cabins: ⚓ *Suites:* ⚓⚓⚓ Both ships are nearly identical in layout. Cabins range from tiny (73-square feet) to fair sized (176-square feet). *Spirit of Columbia* has 11 suites and deluxe cabins with small sitting areas. Six suites on Bridge Deck have oversized double beds and windows on two sides and can accommodate a third person. The new Owner's Suite stretches the width of the vessel. Some average cabins have sinks in the cabin instead of the mini-sized bathroom, which measures a mere 9 x 11 feet. Minimum priced cabins have portholes high on the bulkhead and can almost be called 'insides' because a view of the ocean is possible only if you stand on a chair.

Public Space: ⚓ There is a single lounge on each ship where guests gather for all activities. On the *Spirit of Columbia*, it's the Glacier View; on *Spirit of Alaska*, it's Riverview Lounge. *Spirit of Alaska's* western-inspired interiors and décor emulates colors and design found in national-park lodges. Lounges are forward with comfortable sitting designed for viewing surrounding wildlife and unspoiled terrain. There are unobstructed decks for jogging and walking but it will take 12 laps to complete one mile.

Spa and Fitness: ⚓ No organized fitness or spa programs are offered. There is a single Stairmaster, an exercise bike and a rowing machine.

Entertainment: ⚓ Ranges from none-to extremely-limited. A ranger sometimes boards to talk about the local environment, but otherwise guests are pretty much left to their own devices. Bridge games, reading, conversation and itineraries are highlights.

Food: and Dining: ⚓⚓⚓ Single dining rooms with single sittings, although breakfast and lunch are usually buffet style. Cuisine is American-style and makes good use of local products such as fresh fish and vegetables. The Grand Pacific Dining Room on the *Spirit of Alaska* has replaced family-style large tables with smaller round and square tables.

Junior Cruisers: ⚓ There are no facilities or programs for children and very few families sail the vessels.

Itineraries: ⚓⚓⚓ *Spirit of Alaska* sails from June through August on weekly cruises between Seattle and Juneau. In late September, she moves to weekly cruises from Sausalito, California, up the Sacramento River Delta to Stockton and the wine country. She is home ported in Seattle and Sausalito. *Spirit of Columbia* is home ported in Portland, Oregon, and sails from early spring until late November weekly from Portland to Clarkston in Washington and Lewiston in Idaho. The seven-day trip has five days for shore excursions.

Overall: ⚓⚓ Décor on the *Spirit of Alaska* is likely to remind passengers of a small hotel in the northwest. The shallow draft allows the vessel to come almost totally aground in remote areas allowing passengers to walk directly ashore on bow ramp stairs. The *Spirit of Columbia* has a raised wheelhouse offering 360 degree viewing from the bridge deck. Her bow is hinged and forms a ramp when lowered giving guests direct access to the shore from the forward lounge. Both vessels are well maintained and have a riverboat atmosphere.

MV SPIRIT OF DISCOVERY
Built: 1976 Refurbished: 1992

Category: Boutique Adventure
Rates: $$ to $$$$

Overall Rating: ⚓⚓
Country of Registry: United States
Former Names: Columbia, Independence
Nationality of Crew: American officers and service staff
Cruising Area: Alaska
Length of Voyages: 3,4, 7 to 10 days

Ship Specifics:

Tonnage	94	Elevators	0
Length	166 feet	Decks	3
Beam	37 feet	Children's Facilities	no
Stabilizers	no	Fitness Center	very limited
Passengers	82	Spa	no
Crew	21	Verandahs	no
Space Ratio	n/a	Casino	no
Crew/Passenger Ratio	1-4	Wheelchair Access	no

Cabins: ⚓ All 43 cabins are outside. Most are on the compact side and have minimal storage space. Two cabins are sold for single occupancy. Four deluxe cabins are largest on board with queen-size beds, mini-bars and refrigerators. Minimum priced cabins are a mere 64-square feet. Largest cabins are 127-square feet. Two cabins have upper and lower berths.

Public Space: ⚓ Social gatherings and limited activities are held in the forward lounge. It is comfortably furnished, has a bar and a mirrored ceiling that adds a feeling of space. It's the best place to see glaciers and whales from both sides of the passing landscapes that are the reason most guests are on board. Tall windows on both sides and direct access to one of the two deck areas. In good weather, activities are moved outside to deck areas.

Spa and Fitness: ⚓ No organized fitness or spa programs are offered. There are three pieces of equipment on board – a Stairmaster, exercise bike and rowing machine.

Entertainment: ⚓ Similar to what is offered on other vessels in the fleet. Ranges from none to extremely limited. A ranger sometimes boards to talk about the local environment but otherwise guests are pretty much left to their own devices. Bridge games, reading, conversation and itineraries are highlights.

Food and Dining: ⚓⚓⚓ Single dining rooms with single sittings, although breakfast and lunch are usually buffet-style Cuisine is American-style and makes good use of local products such as fresh fish and vegetables

Junior Cruisers: ⚓ There are no facilities or programs for children and very few families sail the vessel.

Itineraries: ⚓⚓⚓ During summer months, *Spirit of Discovery* sails one-week cruises between Seattle and Juneau. September and October find her making weekly round-trip cruises from Seattle into the Inside Passage. Other months, the vessel sail around the San Juan Islands. Homeport is Seattle.

Overall: ⚓⚓ *Spirit of Discovery* is the most yacht-like of the fleet, but her raked bow gives the vessel a mini-cruise ship-appearance. A pleasant vessel for people who want to see Alaska close-up. It appeals to those who are not claustrophobic about sleeping arrangements and who do not spend any time in their cabins. For some reason or other, this vessel is priced higher than others in the fleet.

MV SPIRIT OF ENDEAVOR
Built: 1983   Refurbished: 1996

Category: Boutique –Adventure
Rates: $$ to $$$
Overall Rating: ⚓⚓
Country of Registry: United States
Former Names: *Sea Spirit* and *Newport Clipper*
Nationality of Crew: American
Cruising Area: Alaska
Length of Voyages: Seven nights

Ship Specifics:

Tonnage	100	Elevators	0
Length	206 feet	Decks	4
Beam	37 feet	Children's Facilities	no
Stabilizers	no	Fitness Center	limited
Passengers	107	Spa	no
Crew	30	Verandahs	no
Space Ratio	n/a	Casino	no
Crew/Passenger Ratio	1-3	Wheelchair Access	no

Cabins: ⚓⚓+ All are outside and some open onto the deck rather than into a narrow hallway. They have the largest picture windows in the fleet but accommodations are small, but surprisingly comfortable. Some have connecting doors and all bathrooms are tiled and have showers. There are refrigerators in the larger cabins and televisions in all of them.

Public Space: ⚓⚓⚓ The lounge topside is larger than expected and is really very well designed and furnished. Large windows are good for viewing and the lounge is where most of the activities take place. There's more outdoor space than on sister-vessels and guests enjoy an outdoor bar and the really nice teak decks. Wide hallways and good décor give vessel a more updated look than some of the others in the fleet.

Spa and Fitness: ⚓⚓ Three machines for the indoor type of guests. The deck is unobstructed and 12 laps equal one-mile for walkers and joggers.

Entertainment: ⚓⚓ Similar to what is offered on other ships in the fleet.

Food and Dining: ⚓⚓+ The dining room is on a lower deck and serves all guests in a single sitting for dinner. Breakfast and lunch is usually buffet-style. A lot of emphasis is placed on food that is probably best described as American-style.

Junior Cruisers: ⚓ No facilities for children. Few families sail Cruise West except when special family programs are announced during school holiday periods.

Itineraries: ⚓⚓⚓ From April through September, she sails from Seattle to the Inside Passage, then moves to warmer waters for the rest of the year and sails along the California coast, the Panama Canal, Central America and the lower Caribbean.

Overall: ⚓⚓ The *Spirit of Endeavor* is the largest in the Cruise West/Alaska Sightseeing fleet. Originally built for Clipper Cruise Line, she bears a striking resemblance to the *Spirit of Discovery* in design. She's the only Alaska ship with a full-size bridge and is one of the longest vessels cruising these waters.

HIGH MARKS
Δ Telephones in every cabin
Δ A quiet ride because of shrouded propellers.

MV SPIRIT OF GLACIER BAY
Built: 1971   Refurbished: 1990

Category: Boutique –Adventure
Rates: $$$ Overall Rating: ⚓
Country of Registry: United States
Former Names: *New Shoreham I* and *Glacier Bay Explorer*
Nationality of Crew: American
Cruising Area: Alaska and California
Length of Voyages: Three and four nights

Ship Specifics:

Tonnage	97	Elevators	0
Length	125 feet	Decks	3
Beam	28 feet	Children's Facilities	no
Stabilizers	no	Fitness Center	no
Passengers	58	Spa	no
Crew	14	Verandahs	no
Space Ratio	n/a	Casino	no
Crew/Passenger Ratio	1-5	Wheelchair Access	no

Cabins: ⚓ All accommodations are very small and measure from 63-square feet for minimum insides to 90'square feet for better outside cabins. All have private facilities and furnishings are as minimal as space permits. Outside cabins have picture windows that helps prevent claustrophobia. All have twin beds except for two cabins that have double beds. Facilities include a very unusual combination unit of toilet, shower and sink.

Public Space: ⚓ There seems to be less public space than on other vessels in the fleet. The forward lounge has port and starboard picture windows with upholstered banquettes that run the length of the room. Chairs are placed in intimate conversation groupings and the room houses a television set and a small bar. Upper deck is unobstructed for walkers and joggers.

Spa and Fitness: ⚓ None

Entertainment: ⚓ Limited on board but the vessel spends more time in the ports it visits than many of the large ships.

Food and Dining: ⚓⚓ Grand Pacific Dining Room is amidships and serves all of the guests in a single open sitting. Food is American-style and surprisingly tasty.

Junior Cruisers: ⚓ There's nothing on board for families or youngsters.

Itineraries: ⚓⚓⚓ The vessel sails on seven- to 10-night cruises between Seattle and Juneau and includes Glacier Bay. Three and four-night cruises from Juneau sail through Glacier Park. In October, the *Spirit of Glacier Bay* sails from San Francisco to California's wine country.

Overall: ⚓ The *Spirit of Glacier Bay* is not only the smallest in the fleet, but the oldest. She's also the slowest. Guests who want hands-on Alaska experiences see her size as an advantage as the vessel practically goes ashore in remote places where even her sisters in the fleet do not dare to venture.

American Hawaii Cruises
(Ceased operations in October 2001)

Carnival Cruise Lines

3655 NW 87th Avenue, Miami, FL 33178

(305) 599-2600 – www.carnival.com

Carnival Cruise Lines is the largest and the most financially successful cruise company in the world. But it wasn't always that way. The line got off to a bumpy start in early 1972 when its first vessel, the *Mardi Gras*, on her maiden voyage ran aground—harmlessly, but it was embarrassing. The good news was that the company made headlines around the world.

From a single-vessel company, Carnival Cruise Lines has grown to the largest cruise line in the world with a fleet that numbered13 ships by the end of 1997, 15 by the end of 1998, 16 before the year 2000 and 19 by the end of 2002. Carnival is credited with turning cruising topsy-turvy, making the shipboard experience so much fun that cruising between ports turned into a recreational rather than just a relaxing mode of travel. It was the beginning of the "Fun Ship" concept, which has become the hallmark of Carnival's success.

Carnival Cruise Lines made headlines in 1987 with one of the largest public stock offerings. It sold 20 percent of the company to the public and received close to $400 million in return. The founding Arison family also retained management and ownership of the remaining 80 percent. Some of that ownership has been sold off in additional offerings.

The company was formed in 1972 specifically to operate the *TSS Mardi Gras*. Owner Ted Arison had just separated business interests from Norwegian Caribbean Lines when he acquired the *Empress of Canada* and, within a short time, transformed the vessel from a two-class transatlantic vessel to a one-class cruise ship geared to Caribbean vacations at sea on a year-round basis.

Carnival's intention has always been to bring cruising to middle America; to the cross section of Americans who had never seen the ocean and never thought of sailing an ocean liner. From those marketing dreams evolved the "Fun Ship" concept of cruising. By 1975, the *Mardi Gras* was carrying more guests than competing vessels and Carnival purchased her almost identical sister ship, the *TSS Carnivale*, formerly the *Empress of Britain*. Demand was so great, the ships set occupancy records in 1976.

In 1977, the company purchased the *SA Vaal*, rebuilt and refurbished her in a Japanese shipyard at a cost of more than $20 million and expanded the fleet to three one-week ships sailing from the Port of Miami. The vessel was renamed the *Festivale*. One year later, at a time when oil prices were dramatically increasing and cruise lines were concerned about operational costs, CCL began construction of a new larger liner, the *MS Tropicale*. She inaugurated service in January 1982 and launched a new generation of ships.

Expansion and growth of the Miami-based company was just getting started. Three even larger ships (*Holiday, Jubilee, Celebration*) were built for almost a half billion dollars and joined the fleet in 1985, 1986 and 1987. All three ships are 48,000-tons. The 70,000-ton *Fantasy* entered service in late 1989 and was joined by her sister ship, the *Ecstasy*, a year later. Then came the *Sensation* in November 1993, *Fascination* in 1994, *Imagination* in 1995, the *Inspiration* in 1996, *Elation* in 1998 and the innovative *Paradise* in November of the same year. Vessels carried price tags of over $300 million each.

Carnival Cruise Lines surprised the industry with announcement of still another generation of new ships. In late 1996, the company introduced the *Carnival Destiny* which at 101,000-tons was the largest cruise ship ever built prior to her inauguration. She was an overnight success and Carnival immediately announced construction of the *Triumph*, which came on line in 1999, the *Victory* in 2000. . The company currently has six new "Fun Ships" under construction: three 88,500-ton "Spirit Class" and three 110,000-ton "Conquest Class" vessels, at an estimated total cost of $2.6 billion, scheduled for delivery over the next three years.

Carnival ships operate voyages of three to 17 days in length to the Bahamas, Caribbean, Mexico, Alaska, Hawaii, the Panama Canal, New England and the Canadian Maritimes

The company that started as Carnival Cruise Lines is now part of the family of companies under the parent company, Carnival Corporation, Inc., which includes ownership of Costa Cruise Line, Cunard Line, Holland America Line, Windstar, and Seabourn Cruises. Each company, however, operates as a totally separate entity in marketing and sales, as well as in on board services. Carnival Cruise Lines continues to redefine contemporary cruising with "Today's Carnival," a term coined by the line to describe its commitment to enhancing all aspects of the "Fun Ship" vacation experience. From upgraded cuisine and new and expanded facilities to a greater variety of onboard activities and shore excursions, a 'Fun Ship' cruise is significantly different from just a few years ago. "Today's Carnival" reflects a contemporary product that continues to evolve in tune with contemporary lifestyles.

Shirley and Harry Comment:

Carnival was probably the first line that took the attitude that cruising is not brain surgery and so came up with the lighthearted slogan "Fun Ships." While no ships can be all things to all people, Carnival comes close. Innovative designs by Joe Farcus. Love it or hate it, you can't ignore it."

Who Sails Carnival Cruise Line ships? Contrary to past perceptions, Carnival's guests are predominantly over 25 years of age. Guests are a cross section of all age groups and, according to the company, more over-55-year-olds sail Carnival than sail on its sister company, Holland America. Carnival guests are on board to have a good time and a pleasurable vacation, no matter what their age is. Carnival carries more families and more children than any other line. Entertainment, food and the environment are geared to all ages.

Carnival places great emphasis on families. The fleet anticipates hosting more than 800,000 guests over the age of 55 during the next year. Carnival believes that fun isn't limited to the very young and President Bob Dickinson says, "The huge range of choices in a casual and entertaining environment is one that virtually everyone enjoys." Which is the reason the company attracts "so many multi-generational family groups."Also on board are guests who want their money's worth and a lot more. Carnival was the first company to restrict bookings of single guests under the age of 25 unless they are married and traveling as a couple, or are accompanied by an over 25-year old in the same cabin. This, of course, does not apply to families. No alcohol, including wine or beer, is sold to guests under the age of 21. Carnival is very strict about those rules. Ships' photo identification cards block purchase by under 21 year olds when the card is swiped through computers. This rule has effectively eliminated high school graduation groups and college-age groups, both of which tend to over drink and annoy other guests.

Carnival also is the first and remains the only major company to offer a completely smoke-free vessel, the *Paradise* that began service toward the end of 1997.

INSIDER TIP

I know first hand that Carnival passes up a lot of business in order to maintain their image of fun without rowdiness. My grandson's Emory University fraternity planned a summer cruise and Carnival was the first choice. Imagine their surprise when Carnival said, "Thanks, but no thanks" and recommended another cruise line that was happy to get the business.

Lifestyle: Like the commercials say, "fun," which translates into having a great vacation with a choice of activities and experiences that enhance the voyage. Carnival ships allow guests to shed their inhibitions when they come up the gangway and to be and do whatever they please, within social limitations. On board lifestyle has been evolving in keeping with guests who sail Carnival. There are no beer drinking contests around the swimming pool and no wet tee-shirt contests, but discos go until dawn.

As hardware on ships became more sophisticated, so did activities and entertainment. There are quiet corners and there are places that are magnets for the party crowd. There are congenial piano bars and dance clubs. In short, Carnival ships have something for every age group and something for every economic level. Carnival doesn't promise luxury or deluxe cruising but delivers a lot more than what guests expect and a lot more than brochures promise.

Dress Code: On seven-night cruises, the daily program lists two "formal" nights and five "resort casual" nights. Although black-tie is not required, a surprising number of young guests rent tuxedos on board or bring them along. Other nights, no jeans in the dining room, but if guests return late from shore tours or just don't feel like dressing, casual dining is offered in Lido areas.

Dining: Considered the highlight of any "Fun Ship" vacation, "Today's Carnival" offers a diversity of new dining options and enhancements. Carnival's Total Choice Dining is one of the cruise industry's most flexible dining programs offering a wide variety of formal and casual options at sea. There are two sittings and two restaurants on some of the larger ships in the fleet. Guests have a choice of dining at four different time periods at assigned tables, in casual self-service Lido areas which are opened 24/7 or in cabins which offer service around the clock. Newest ships offer elegant dining in optional restaurants.

Food style and menus on all vessels have also changed with the times and are now among the best in the mid-price Resort Category. The dining experience competes head-on with Premium Category ships and in many cases surpasses higher priced vessels. There are five choices of main courses, five courses in addition to separate vegetarian and low-fat menus. Presentation is picture-pretty and food is plentiful. Lido areas are self-service and have excellent salad bars and 24-hour pizzerias.

In addition, the company has introduced a new casual dining option called "Seaview Bistros" on all of the ships. The bistros are set up each evening from 6 to 9:30 p.m. in the casual Lido restaurants. The new cafes have a distinctive bistro-like feel with personal touches like tablecloths, pre-set silverware and floral arrangements. Full menu choices are available.

Special Dietary Requests: They should be made with the initial booking. Vegetarian and light cuisine dishes are on the menu. Carnival has no set menu for kosher foods. Guests who want kosher food should contact Carnival's Guest Services Department. Once they embark, they should also contact the maitre d', He will make the necessary arrangements, which may not meet strict orthodox requirements.

Internet Availability: Internet Cafes have been installed on all ships in the fleet. Cost is 75 cents per minute with very fast access to your personal e-mail account.

Tipping Policy: Carnival recommends $9.75 per person, per day, and automatically adds the gratuity to a guest's shipboard account. Guests have the option of bowing out of that arrangement by contacting the purser's office. The $9.75 is divided into $3.50 per person, per day, to the waiter, $2 to the assistant waiter; $3.50 per person per day to the room steward, and 75 cents per person per day for "alternative dining service" in the Lido. A 15 percent gratuity is automatically added to all bar services. In checking with the Purser's office, only about 10 percent of the guests opt out of the tipping program.

Discount Policy: A SuperSaver program is in place for early bookings. In "normal" times, as ships fill closer to sailing dates, particularly in high season, rates start climbing. Carnival offers seasonal and regional specials on all of the ships. In fall 2002, Sunday travel sections carried ads quoting rates from $599 for inside cabins on one-week cruises on some of the ships. That's the "loss leader" price and I'll bet my passport there is limited capacity and the cabin has upper and lower berths. A more realistic minimum would be $799 for a one-week cruise.

Carnival offers a cruise-now, pay later option called the "Fun Finance Plan." The plan is available starting at $28 per month (based on a 24-month payment term at the lowest annual percentage rate available). Actual monthly payment and terms may vary according to the applicant's credit qualifications. This plan is valid for U.S. individual bookings only. Certain other restrictions apply.

Still Growing: Ships under construction include *Carnival Glory* scheduled to inaugurate service in mid-2003, *Carnival Miracle* in early 2004 and *Carnival Valor* in late 2004. Cost of each ship is estimated to be in the $500 million range. *Carnival Glory* will be home ported in Port Canaveral for one week alternating eastern and western Caribbean cruises.

HIGH MARKS
Δ In-cabin amenity baskets.

Δ Terrycloth robes in all outside cabins and suites

INSIDER TIP
Carnival is so confident its product will be everything promised in brochures, it "guarantees" the cruise, the only such program in the industry. Designed to eliminate fears, particularly by first-time cruisers, guests who are disappointed in the cruise need to notify the purser prior to the first port of call that they would like to leave the ship. They will be reimbursed the cost of coach air transportation back to the port of embarkation and will receive a pro-rated refund of their cruise fare, depending on the number of days left at the point the guest disembarks. The program has certain restrictions and the company says that less than one tenth of one percent of the guests have taken advantage of the guarantee.

The Fleet
CONQUEST CLASS

CARNIVAL CONQUEST
Built: December 2002

Category: Resort XXL

Rates: $$$

Overall Rating: n/a

Country of Registry: Panama

Former Names: none

Nationality of Crew: Italian officers; International service staff

Cruising Area: Caribbean from New Orleans

Length of Voyages: 7 nights

Ship Specifics:

Tonnage	110,000	Elevators		14
Length	925 feet	Decks		13
Beam	116 feet	Children's Facilities		yes
Stabilizers	yes	Fitness Center		yes
Passengers	2,974	Spa		yes
Crew	1,160	Verandahs		yes
Space Ratio	37	Casino		yes
Crew/Passenger Ratio	1-3	Wheelchair Access		yes

Carnival Conquest, the first in a new class of vessels, entering service in December 1, 2002, is missing our publication deadline for a rating. Here's a preview based on pre-inaugural information:

Carnival Conquest features 22 bars and lounges with dramatic interiors inspired by the world's most famous Impressionist painters, appropriate for a ship based in New Orleans, a city possessing a rich European heritage.

The ship also features 13 guest decks housing four swimming pools–one with a 214-foot-long water slide; a 15,000-square-foot health and fitness facility, an Internet café, four restaurants and a "boulevard" of shops and boutiques. Expanded "family-friendly" facilities, including "Action Alley," a recreation center housing a video arcade, teen coffee bar and dance club, along with a 3,300-square-foot children's play area -- the largest in the "Fun Ship" fleet will be featured as well.

Other features aboard the *Carnival Conquest* include a conference center, an expansive sports deck with basketball and volleyball courts, a jogging track and a full gambling casino. Additionally, approximately 60 percent of the vessel's 1,488 staterooms will offer ocean views with 60 percent of those featuring private balconies.

As part of Carnival's Total Choice Dining, *Carnival Conquest* continues the line's tradition of offering guests a wide variety of formal and casual options at sea. Dining choices will include twin two-deck-high formal restaurants and an expansive two-level poolside eatery offering casual alternatives for breakfast, lunch and dinner, a 24-hour pizzeria and a variety of specialty areas. A reservations-only supper club, a patisserie, a sushi bar and complimentary 24-hour room service will also be available.

Carnival Conquest sails from the Port of New Orleans every Sunday on week long voyages to Ocho Rios, Jamaica, and George Town, Grand Cayman. *Carnival Conquest* is the largest vessel sailing year-round from New Orleans. The company expects to carry more than 167,000 guests per year aboard the *Carnival Conquest*.

That, combined with an estimated 118,000 guests annually who will sail from Tampa on the *Inspiration* and visit New Orleans on Fridays as part of that vessel's itinerary, represents a nearly 600 percent increase in Carnival's New Orleans volume from the company's first full year of operation there in 1995.

Late News: Carnival Cruise Lines has confirmed an order for an additional Conquest-class vessel with the Italian shipyard. The as-yet-unnamed 2,974-passenger, 110,000-ton ship is scheduled for delivery in late fall 2005. Cost is estimated at $500,000 million.

DESTINY CLASS

CARNIVAL DESTINY
Built: 1996
CARNIVAL TRIUMPH
Built: 1999
CARNIVAL VICTORY
Built: late 1999

Category: Resort XXL
Rates: $$$
Overall Rating: ⚓⚓⚓⚓
Country of Registry: Bahamas
Nationality of Crew: Italian officers; International service staff
Cruising Area: Caribbean
Length of Voyages: 7 days

Ship Specifics:

Tonnage	110,000	Elevators	14
Length	892 feet	Decks	12
Beam	116 feet	Children's Facilities	yes
Stabilizers	yes	Fitness Center	yes
Passengers	2,642	Spa	yes
Crew	1,050	Verandahs	yes
Space Ratio	38	Casino	yes
Crew/Passenger Ratio	1-2.5	Wheelchair Access	yes

Cabins: ⚓⚓⚓⚓ *Suites:* ⚓⚓⚓⚓ Standard cabins are probably the largest at sea and certainly the largest in this price range. Standard outside cabins measure 220 to 260 square feet. Colors are warm wood tones accented with pastel shades and all outsides have separate sitting areas. If space is more important than a private balcony, opt for a cabin with a window wall instead of a verandah. They are the largest standard cabins. Single beds convert to queen-size and storage space is more than ample for one or two week cruising, even for heavy packers. Inside cabins are slightly smaller. Adjoining cabins for families are especially popular and are located on Sun Deck 10.

The eight luxurious penthouse suites measure 430–square feet, while the remaining four suites are a very comfortable 340–square feet. Each has every amenity guests should expect in premium accommodations. Separate dressing, sleeping and sitting areas as well as VCRs, a bar and refrigerator, adjustable height coffee tables for room service as well as private balconies with solid side panels for privacy. Rich furnishings included leather-upholstered sofas, burled wood furniture, granite tabletops, copper trim and dimmer controlled lighting. Bathrooms have handmade Murano glass tiled walls and combination shower/whirlpool baths.

Carnival Triumph is the second in this series of vessels and is slightly different from her sister ships. *Triumph* has an additional deck that adds a few verandah cabins and a couple of suites. The additional deck also added outside open deck space and improved configuration of the pool area.

Facilities for Disabled Travelers: ⚓⚓⚓⚓ Each of the three Destiny-Class ships has 19 cabins designated as accessible staterooms. There are both insides and outsides and measure 196-square feet. Cabin doors are 33.5" wide and have no sills. Bathroom doors are 35 inches wide and have roll-in showers with fold down seats, hand held showers and the required grab bars. Cabins with verandahs have a 33.5 inches balcony door with a four-inch step for which the steward can provide a ramp. The balconies are too small for wheelchair turn arounds. All decks except Sun and Sky are accessible. There are public accessible restrooms on two decks.

Public Space: ⚓⚓⚓⚓ All three ships offer multiple options and choices. Something for every palate. On *Carnival Destiny*, walk Destiny's Way and your options are wide-ranging. Extending from the Rotunda, Destiny's Way provides access to many of the public room on Promenade Deck and functions as more than a thoroughfare. It takes on a life of its own. There are two showrooms and discos, a wine bar, coffee house, multiple lounges, bars, a well-stocked library, card rooms, meeting rooms, uncrowned sun decks, two swimming pools, eight Jacuzzis, a shopping arcade with a tuxedo rental and flower shop, and Virtual World, a video game and virtual reality emporium. Destiny's Way incorporates the Destiny Bar, Café on the Way and Cheers.

Carnival Triumph has a soaring seven-deck atrium called The Capital. The ship has a global theme that focuses on the world's greatest cities. The New Orleans-themed piano bar is a guest favorite for mixing and meeting new and old friends. Along World's Way on Promenade Deck, the Vienna Café draws a crowd. It's probably the aroma of freshly brewed coffee and freshly baked goodies that attracts people. The underground Tokyo Video Arcade was intended for teenagers, but adult guests are outnumbering the kids.

Carnival Victory has Neptune's Way. The promenade is the main access route for the ship but it could well be considered an entertainment complex in itself. The walkway is lined with ocean-view street-side sitting areas with refreshment and entertainment venues tucked along the inboard side. Colorful glass panels created by Italian artist Luciano Vistosi add charm in highly stylized, brightly colored sea life. The ceiling, which starts with the glass atrium dome, extends the length of the promenade.

Spa and Fitness: ⚓⚓⚓⚓ The 15,000–square foot spas & fitness centers rival the best on shore. State-of-the-art equipment faces seaward and the environment makes exercise a pleasant pastime. Two spacious 12-person-size whirlpools set in a base of marble are separated from the gyms by a curved clear glass wall. Large, carpeted aerobics rooms are up one deck via a curved staircase that connects the two levels. Juice Bars and relaxation chairs complete the facilities. For joggers and walking enthusiasts, the Nautica Jogging Tracks are located on the aft part of Sun Deck 11, positioned over the Sun & Sea Pools.

Entertainment: ⚓⚓⚓⚓+ The Palladium on *Destiny*, the Rome Lounge on *Carnival Triumph* and the Caribbean Lounge on *Carnival Victory* are stunning three-deck high chandeliered showrooms with excellent sight lines. From the lowest level in the orchestra pits to the highest levels in the overhead scenery staging areas, the main showrooms actually span five decks in height in order to allow for the required scenery and lighting in order to present the most elaborate and sophisticated entertainment at sea.

Shows are professionally produced with an international cast of 16 to 20 dancers and singers, accompanied by 11-piece orchestras. I have yet to see a Carnival production show that doesn't end with the audience on its feet applauding for more. Two different shows are featured on each ship. They are fast-paced, high-spirited Las Vegas-style revues offering toe-tapping tunes, mind boggling scenery, awesome costuming, intricate dance numbers and elaborate, exhilarating pyrotechnic, video and lighting effects.

On other nights, there are specialty acts that appear just once during a cruise and are rotated between CCL vessels at different ports. There's always an "R" rated late night show in the second lounge, deck parties, music and dancing in all of the lounges. Daytime menus of activities are extensive, but some of the more zealous activities (like beer drinking contests) have been eliminated on all Carnival ships.

Food and Dining: ⚓⚓⚓⚓ Restaurants are identical in decor, but the Galaxy is smaller than the Universe and seats fewer guests on the *Destiny*. Each restaurant features a large central covered ceiling. Deep blue anodized aluminum panels trimmed with clear automated chaser lights create a chandelier effect as they surround a painting of a romantic sky at sunset. Extra-large windows are trimmed with gold-colored moldings while wood veneer in a brown and black chevron pattern form arches around the windows. Decorative glass lighting units covering automated fiber optic starlight complete the arch motif.

Restaurants on the other two ships follow the same mode except for décor that differs from ship-to-ship.

Innovative seating arrangements have been incorporated into the design of the restaurants. They feature a greater number of smaller tables for two or four guests. Larger tables for six and eight are also available. Almost every table enjoys unobstructed sea views. A glass balustrade with a brass rail surrounds the balconies and helps create a spacious, airy atmosphere. Bandstands are the venue for dinner music and other entertainment with meals. A nice touch is the cleverly concealed service areas that upgrades the restaurants and keeps noise levels at a minimum.

Food and menus are similar on all Carnival ships and are described in detail in the company profile.

Service: ⚓⚓⚓⚓ Somehow service personnel respond to environment and with ships like the *Destiny, Triumph* and *Victory*, the staff goes a step beyond. There's 24-hour cabin service with full breakfasts and menu choices during other hours. In the Lido, self-service is assisted by waiters who refill coffee and otherwise assist guests. With a service staff of almost one to two, guests can't take too many steps before someone is there to offer something. Staff is friendly but not overly familiar.

Junior Cruisers: ⚓⚓⚓⚓ Children's facilities are outstanding. Destiny-Class ships boast two-deck-high, 1300-square-foot indoor/outdoor children's play centers, complete with their own pools and state-of-the-art jungle gyms and fun zones, both indoors and outdoors. The playrooms are home to video walls, which enhance the kids' version of Karaoke, pajama and video parties. For 13 to 17 year olds, there's a teen version of Camp Carnival, featuring a teen casino night, coketail parties, makeover and fashion tips from the salon and photography workshops have been added to enhance the teen program.

A large staff of counselors supervises activities. Carnival, is offering complimentary baby-sitting to parents who wish to go ashore or participate in shore excursions. Centrally located near family sized and connecting staterooms on Spa Deck 10, Camp Carnival has its own bathrooms and internal staircase to a deck area and wading pool just for kids.

Designed to appeal to children's senses, the Children's Club is decorated in brightly colored durable materials with a fanciful touch. Green and white alligator skin vinyl zed fabric covers furniture while walls feature back, yellow, orange, red and blue dinosaur carpeting adorns the floor. Movable desks and pint-sized chairs offer areas for coloring and a large projection television with a motorized screen can be lowered for movie watching.

Itineraries: ⚓⚓⚓⚓ *Carnival Destiny* sails weekly round-trips from San Juan to the Southern Caribbean. *Carnival Triumph* is home ported year around in Miami sailing alternating eastern and western Caribbean cruises. *Carnival Victory* sails weekly, alternating eastern and western Caribbean cruises from Miami during winter months, then moves to New York for four and five day Canada cruises and seven day cruises from New York to New England and Canada.

Overall: ⚓⚓⚓⚓ Destiny Class vessels are big, bold and beautiful. What's more, these over 101,000-ton vessels are considered the prototype of a new generation of cruise ships. There's no doubt they have dramatically impacted and changed cruise styles and influenced ship designs into the next century. Destiny Class ships are complete resort cities with rudders that happen to take guests to interesting ports of call. They sail without vibration and, at times, guests are reassured that ships are really sailing when they look out at the sea. But, it's what's inside that makes these Destiny Class ships so special. Utilizing traditional and modern architecture, Carnival design architect Joe Farcus says he aimed to create "the ideal resort cities at sea. An urban environment with a sense of community where people can relate to each other in a way different from normal life at home. A varied environment where all their needs are taken care of, where there is no uniformity and a lot of diversity."

Two of my favorite rooms on *Carnival Victory* are down one deck from the promenade. The Ionian Room is connected to the disco by a winding stairway. I found it to be a quiet room for reading during the day and a place to meet and have a conversation away from the disco area. Soft piano music adds atmosphere for afternoon tea and pre-dinner cocktails. The Ionian Room also houses the Internet Café, which has 12 individual stations, with access to e-mail and the Internet, for 75 cents per minute.

My other favorite is the almost mid-ship Indian Library. Liberal use of wood and rich colors lend a British Colonial feel to the décor. This intimate room is designed for quiet relaxation and features flexible sitting for 17 readers or small group events.

On *Carnival Triumph*, it's the décor that makes me feel like I have traveled the world without jet lag. Using the world as a palette to design the *Triumph* gave architect Joe Farcus a lot of latitude. Each room is themed to a major city with history or romance as its hallmark. The names fit the functions of the rooms and designs emphasize features associated with each.

HIGH MARKS

- △ Spectacular laser and pyrotechnic effects that top off the production show finales.
- △ Spaciousness, without losing intimate areas
- △ Small public rooms are no larger than on ships half her size.
- △ Special places: Destiny Bar, the popular meeting spot; Café on the Way is "the" place for cappuccino and pastry; if you're ever hungry after 24-hours of eating opportunities.
- △ Self-service laundries on every stateroom deck. ($2 per wash; dryers $1)
- △ Soda machines on every stateroom deck. ($1 per can)

WEAKEST LINK:

- • None

SPIRIT CLASS

CARNIVAL LEGEND
August 2002
CARNIVAL PRIDE
January 2002
CARNIVAL SPIRIT
Built: 2001

Category: Resort XXL
Rates: $$$
Overall Rating: ⚓⚓⚓⚓
Country of Registry: Panama
Nationality of Crew: Italian officers; International Service staff
Cruising Area: Caribbean/Canada/ New England
Length of Voyages: 7 nights

Ship Specifics:

Tonnage	88,500	Elevators	15
Length	960 feet	Decks	12
Beam	105.7 feet	Children's Facilities	yes
Stabilizers	yes	Fitness Center	yes
Passengers	2,124	Spa	yes
Crew	930	Verandahs	yes
Space Ratio	40	Casino	yes
Crew/Passenger Ratio	1-2.2	Wheelchair Access	yes

Cabins: ⚓⚓⚓⚓ *Suites:* ⚓⚓⚓⚓ Eighty percent of the cabins are outside and 80 percent of those rooms have private balconies. Interesting to note that inside cabins measure the same 185-square feet as the outsides without verandahs. Staterooms with verandahs increase in size to 225-square feet. There are 58 suites in three types starting at 360-feet and going up to 465 square feet, including wrap around terraces. All staterooms and suites are tastefully furnished with twin beds that convert to queen-size, large closets, plenty of drawer space, televisions and refrigerators, plus the usual amenities found on new vessels (telephones, private safes, tubs and showers or showers only, depending on type of accommodation)

Suites (Categories 11 and 12) include separate dressing and sitting areas, refrigerators, double sinks and bathtubs, as well as showers, and large balconies. Good design and soft lighting add to a feeling of spaciousness in Category 4 interior staterooms. Category 5 staterooms are outside and have French doors that open but views are partially obstructed.

Facilities for Disabled Travelers: ⚓⚓⚓⚓ There are 16 accessible cabins in a variety of categories. Several have private verandahs. Others are inside and outside cabins. Smallest is 185-square feet, All have 35 inches entry doors and a 32 inches bathroom door. There are no sills. Bathrooms have roll-in showers with hand-held showerhead, grab bars and fold down seats. There are accessible public restrooms. The only areas of the ships that are not accessible are the dance club, children's wading pool, whirlpools, laundry room and Deck 11. TTY kits are available at the purser's desk for the hearing impaired and include doorknockers, bed shakers, smoke alarms and phone amplifiers.

Public Space: ⚓⚓⚓⚓ There are 17 public rooms on each of the ships, including lounges, bars and dining venues. The large interior has been subdivided into smaller rooms that offer the best of both worlds. Intimate and quiet spaces and a variety of options only possible on jumbo-size vessels. Guests quickly find favorites. The Sunset Garden and Butterflies Lounge on *Carnival Pride* are special, but finding both is a discovery challenge. Entrance to the Sunset Garden is alongside the Taj Mahal. It lines the bulkhead and is favored as a quiet, relaxing area decorated in gold, umber and burnt red with murals of Old Sol painted on interior walls.

Butterflies Lounge, directly below the lowest level of the Taj Mahal, is an inside room with an outside feeling. It has faux windows decorated with colorful transparent fabrics that resemble butterfly wings. These disappear under special lights that illuminate flocks of butterflies. The Ivory Bar is a masterpiece in ivory décor and is a favorite after-dinner sing-a-long area. There are a dozen other public rooms, all offering a full menu of activities and all themed to beauty.

Other major rooms on all three ships include piano bars, chapels, which host about four weddings on almost every cruise, elegant card rooms, Internet Cafes and libraries. Passageways are treated as public lounges and on Promenade Deck are divided into intimate groupings by two sided replicas of old masterpiece paintings that add to the museum quality of the vessel. Other public spaces include five self-service launderettes (a wash is $1, a dry is $1; soap and softener is 50 cents each)

Food and Dining: ⚓⚓⚓⚓ When it comes to food and dining, "Today's Carnival" is really paying attention to changing lifestyles. Lunch and dinner menus, as well as wine choices, have been upgraded and expanded. It's near impossible to disembark hungry. In fact, it's hard to avoid food service at any hour and in almost any room. Lido areas offer full self-serve breakfast and lunch buffets that include meat carving and pasta stations, expansive salad bars, and a 24-hour pizzeria, as well as a deli. Casual dinners are also available nightly. Dining room options are lengthy and include five course menus with a choice of four or five main courses a low calorie specialty daily as well as vegetarian choices. Presentation is picture perfect and service rates "excellent."

Optional Restaurants: ⚓⚓⚓⚓+ + Dinner in the reservations-only optional David's Supper Club on *Carnival Pride*, Nouveau Supper Club on *Carnival Spirit* and the Golden Fleece Supper Club on *Carnival Legend* comes with a $25 surcharge. Dinner in any of them is worth twice that amount. Service is on Versace china and elegant flatware while a trio plays soft dance-able music and tuxedo-clad waiters attend to every detail. But, it doesn't stop there. While steaks and chops are specialty items and dessert is hard to pass up, it's Joe's Stone Crabs that top the menu choices. For the first time at sea, stone crabs from Joe's, the internationally famed South Beach landmark, are an exclusive item on the *Pride*, *Legend* and *Spirit*.

INSIDER TIP

David's (and the counterpart restaurants on *Legend* and *Spirit*) rate as the best and the most exceptional supper clubs at sea, but it is *Carnival Pride's* full size exact replica of the famous Michelangelo sculpture, "David" on the second level of the room, that is the most talked about on the ship. He commands the view fully exposed and there is talk about placing a leaf over a strategic body part. David presented other problems even before he came on board. The statue had to be hoisted into place by a giant crane while the ship was under construction.

Entertainment: ⚓⚓⚓⚓+ When it comes to entertainment, Spirit-Class vessels exceed expectations that run high on all CCL ships. There are lounges and activities to fit every mood. Three-level-high show rooms are as close to any in Las Vegas when it comes to performances, acoustics, lighting and sound. Décor, colors and themes differ from ship-to-ship. But the dra-matic scale of passenger pleasing production shows continue to highlight entertainment. Some 18 dancers and singers backed by a ten-piece orchestra bring the rooms alive with two high-energy shows each cruise.

Costuming is breathtaking with more than 20 quick changes per show. Elaborate scenery and unbelievable special effects dazzled even critical New York audiences. Professionally executed and choreographed, the audience is transformed to Broadway and Las Vegas. On other nights, guest entertainers are flown in for specialty acts.

INSIDER TIP
Carnival vessels have been walking away with top national award for entertainment at sea. Production shows rival Broadway and Las Vegas events that come with price tags in excess of $50 per ticket. Whatever your pleasure may be, don't miss these shows.

Spa and Fitness: ⚓⚓⚓⚓ Spas are two-level 13,700–square feet that turn exercising into fun. From aerobics and kick boxing classes to relaxing facials and body treatments, as well as the latest work out equipment, the multi-level spas rival the best of the best facilities found shore-side. Gymnasiums are fully equipped including stationary bicycles, resistance machines, treadmills and a lot more. Instructor-led classes are scheduled throughout the day. Also offered: sauna, steam, beauty salon, one whirlpool (within the spa; there are four others aboard each ship) 10 treatment rooms for European-style therapies including Aroma and Stone (using heated, scented oils and warm basalt stones). There are jogging tracks (15 times around equals a mile) and four swimming pools, one of which is covered by a retractable dome used in inclement weather.

Junior Cruisers: ⚓⚓⚓⚓ Carnival expects 350,000 kids to sail its ships in 2003 and the Spirit-Class vessels are ready with some of the largest and most complete children's facilities at sea. On each ship, Camp Carnival is centered on 2,400-square foot enclosed play areas on Upper Deck, away from adult activities. The Fun House is headquarters. Divided by age groups, the supervised programs have activities for children ages 2 to 15. Themed to the bottom of the sea, three areas are connected by tunnels: one area for crafts, a second one for computer games and a third for games and a video wall for movies and cartoons. Outdoor play areas offers mini-basketball, jungle gyms and other playground equipment. Children's wading pools and corkscrew water slides are among opportunities for kids to make a splash.

On one of my recent cruises, during an afternoon in Cozumel, the counselor gathered about 20 kids on the aft pool deck and fascinated them with her Mayan Indian tales and stories about Mexico. Teenagers had overnight slumber parties among their menu of activities. Carnival offers a Fountain Fun card, good for unlimited soft drinks during a one-week voyage for $19.95. Babysitting is available from 10 p.m. to 3 a.m. at the Fun House ($5 for the first child and $3 for each additional child in the same family).

INSIDER TIP

Carnival is the only cruise line that accepts toddlers from age two in the Camp Carnival program. Recent enhancements include play areas featuring computer labs and indoor climbing mazes, as well as updated children's menus and a new turn-down service providing kids with freshly baked cookies on the first and last night of their voyage. Carnival is also the only company that has strollers available for rental.

Itineraries: ⚓⚓⚓⚓ *Carnival Pride* moves from one week sailings from Port Canaveral to Long Beach, California, for seven night Mexican Riviera cruises in September 2003. *Carnival Legend* is sailing on eight-night alternating eastern and western Caribbean voyages out of Miami during winter months, then moves to New York for May to September eight-night eastern Caribbean cruises. *Carnival Spirit* sails on one-week voyages between Seward and Vancouver from May through mid-mid-September, seasonally transiting the Panama Canal. She makes four 12-day Hawaii cruises, then returns to Miami to resume the winter schedule of Caribbean sailings.

Overall: ⚓⚓⚓⚓ Although *Carnival Pride*, *Spirit* and *Legend* are virtual triplets on the outside, they bear little resemblance on the inside. The central interior design theme on *Carnival Pride* is "Icons of Beauty", which really describes the ship. Beauty is interpreted in many ways from the physical to the spiritual to the experimental on *Carnival Pride*. Focus is on the 15th and 16th century Renaissance period that emphasized beauty in every lifestyle phase – art, music, the human body, extravagance and indulgence. On the *Pride*, beauty doesn't mean flashing lights and neon signs. Moving from one room to another is an experience best likened to a museum tour that goes from replicas of paintings and murals by acclaimed masters with familiar names – Raphael, Bramante, Michelangelo da Vinci and Botticelli, for example, to art deco and contemporary artworks.

Carnival Legend, the newest in the triplet series, merges heroes of antiquity with tributes to 20th century jazz masters and great athletes. Legendary people and places inspired the interior design of the *Carnival Legend*, which inaugurated sailings in Harwich, England, in August 2002. The overall design theme of "legends" is realized in many different ways, both literally and figuratively. Ancient Greece and the legendary, classical city of Rhodes provided inspiration for the ship's atrium.

The Medusa's Lair dance club offers a playful twist on the mythological legend of the mysterious gorgon Medusa. The poignant Russian folktale of a talented seamstress from a small village who is turned into a bird by an evil sorcerer is the inspiration for the Firebird Lounge. Follies, the main show lounge, recalls the magnificent movie palaces of the 1920s. Satchmo's Club, named after legendary trumpeter Louis Armstrong, is decorated to resemble an old New Orleans bar, while the Dream Team Bar is a paean to sports greats from the past, some obscure, some instantly recognizable. Named for the aromatic delicacy treasured by chefs and gourmands alike, Truffles Restaurant is the main dining room on *Carnival Legend*.

Spirit Class vessels are class acts that typify what guests and the industry expects of "Today's Carnival." *Carnival Spirit* was first in the series of 85,000-ton newbuilds and set the style for sister vessels that followed. These ships incorporate the best features of Destiny and Fantasy-class vessels with the company's 30 years of experience of operating vessels designed to meet vacation dreams. Spirit -Class ships are not clones of previous ships. They introduce new features. Guests who have become accustomed to standardized Carnival deck plans may need a few minutes to familiarize themselves with the new look of "Today's Carnival."

On Spirit Class ships, the lowest three decks are devoted to public space. The middle of the ship is filled with cabins and suites until you reach Deck 9 and above where space is again devoted to public areas. The new configuration allows for smooth guest movement, more lounges and recreational areas, additional entertainment venues, more spa amenities and space, and allows for large spaces subdivided into intimate lounges and bars. Another plus for guests is that no cabin has a disco-type activity pounding on its ceiling from the deck above which makes for a much quieter ship.

Missing from Spirit Class ships are the miles of neon and flashing lights, which have been replaced by resplendent crystal chandeliers and softer colors. A quick count showed 19 different design themes in as many rooms. Carnival seems to follow the theory that if one fun environment is good, 19 are a lot better!

Several innovative features and the overall design put Spirit-Class ships several rungs closer to vessels charging premium rates. Topping the list of features new to Carnival are the supper clubs, located at the top of the soaring atriums.

Second on the list are chapels, a first for Carnival. Chapels are decorated in elegant Gothic style and are available for wedding or other ceremonies. Other new features include expanded meeting and convention facilities, and good-sized Internet Cafés.

In addition to software, Carnival also is setting the pace in hardware with a list of engineering firsts that include two separate engine rooms, each capable of providing its own sources of propulsion and power. Spirit Class ships also have the largest enclosed bridges of any cruise ship and are among the first in the industry to feature "black box" technology similar to that used by the airline industry. These boxes, which have the ability to record voice commands, radar images and outside noise, allow the company to track pertinent information in the event of an emergency and to store and review data for training purposes. Other high tech features include four anti-collision detectors, two autopilots, a Global Positioning System that continually transmits Spirit Class vessels' positions via satellite, enabling officers to pinpoint the vessel's location to within 10 feet.

HIGH MARKS
△ David's Restaurant on *Carnival Pride*, Golden Fleet Supper Club on *Carnival Legend*, and the Nouveau Supper Club on *Carnival Spirit* are not to be missed.
△ A full tour of a floating art gallery in every nook and cranny on all three ships.

WEAKEST LINK:
• Nothing to complain about.

HOLIDAY CLASS

MS CELEBRATION
Built: 1987
MS HOLIDAY
Built 1985
MS JUBILEE
Built: 1966

Category: Resort Mid-Size
Rates: $$ to $$$
Overall Rating: ⚓⚓⚓
Country of Registry: Panama
Former Names: none

Nationality of Crew: Italian officers, International service staff
Cruising Area: Caribbean & Mexico
Length of Voyages: 7 nights

Ship Specifics – Holiday

Tonnage	47,262	Elevators	8
Length	733 feet	Decks	10
Beam	92 feet	Children's Facilities	yes
Stabilizers	yes	Fitness Center	yes
Passengers*	1,452	Spa	yes
Crew	670	Verandahs	10
Space Ratio	32	Casino	yes
Crew/Passenger Ratio	1-2	Wheelchair Access	yes

__Celebration & Jubilee__ – Passengers: 1,486

Cabins: ⚓⚓⚓ ***Suites:*** ⚓⚓⚓ Inside and outside cabins are nearly identical throughout the ships. At an average of 185-square feet, they are among the largest at sea although the "L" shape configuration is awkward when twins are pushed together to make a double bed. Furnishings are being updated to match newer vessels in the fleet suites are high up, spacious and beautiful with small verandahs. They are probably the best buys on the ships, but some are partially obstructed by lifeboats. All cabins and suites have telephones, televisions, radios and plenty of storage space. Showers only in all cabins. Suites have showers and whirlpool tubs.

Facilities for Disabled Travelers: ⚓⚓⚓ Each ship has 14 accessible cabins, inside and outsides, on Main Deck. Accommodations measure 185-square feet and, surprisingly, the inside cabins are slightly more accessible. Doorways on inside are 30 inches wide with no sills and the hallway width is 33 inches. Outside cabins have the same size door opening, but there are 3 inches sills. Bathroom doors are 30 inches wide with a ramped 6 inches sill. There are 3 inches sills at the showers that can also be ramped. There are hand-held showerheads, shower stools are available and grab bars at toilets. Sinks are 31 inches high. Except for Sun Deck, the Espresso Café, the Gazebo and balconies in the show lounge, the rest of the ship is accessible. There are no totally accessible public restrooms.

Public Space: ⚓⚓⚓⚓ Like the rest of the fleet, the ships are floating resorts with virtually every possible amenity: two indoor-outdoor swimming pool areas, enclosed promenade decks, whirlpools, super-sized casinos, discos, hospital, boutiques, seven lounges and bars. Lido Decks have wide-open spaces and swimming pools with spiral water slides that were so popular they became a standard feature on all CCL ships.

Spa and Fitness: ⚓⚓⚓ Nautica Spas have become a Carnival trademark. The gym is smaller than on CCL's newer ships, but still larger than on other vessels built during the 1980s. There are saunas for men and women and a spa treatment center.

Entertainment: ⚓⚓⚓⚓ Take your choice. Party around the clock or head for the quiet libraries. Daily programs list activities at 15 to 30 minute intervals and evenings are filled with lavish Vegas-style production shows and individual entertainers who are not seen more than once during a one-week cruise. Casinos are large and very active and still have two-dollar blackjack tables. Discos go until dawn. There's always the amidships bar for mixing and mingling and the late night adults-only show.

Food and Dining: ⚓⚓⚓⚓ Two dining rooms serve guests three meals daily in two sittings with a choice of four dining times. Menus throughout the fleet have been standardized and offer wide selections. Lido areas are particularly popular since they become bistros for very casual dining between 6:30 and 9:30 p.m. Another popular feature in the Lido is the ice cream and frozen yogurt available throughout the day. In addition, there are lavish midnight buffets and 24-hour cabin service.

Service: ⚓⚓⚓ Non-intimidating and very friendly. Staff is anxious to please

Junior Cruisers: ⚓⚓⚓ The year around Camp Carnival program was originated on these vessels, but only the *Holiday* has the virtual reality entertainment complex that is as popular with adults as it is with kids. The program is supervised and divided into age groups with different activities.

Itineraries: ⚓⚓⚓⚓ *Celebration* sails on four and five-day western Caribbean cruises from Galveston, Texas. *Holiday* sails on four and five-day cruises from New Orleans and *Jubilee* now sailing on four and five-day cruises changes to one week southern Caribbean cruises from San Juan beginning in late September 2003.

Peter Knego Comments:

(The Holiday) "Ship is spotless and, while the oldest in the fleet, is now considered intimate. Décor is over the top but with tongue in cheek humor. I had a much better time on Holiday than I did on a competitor's higher priced vessel." He adds, "Food on Carnival has improved significantly and in some ways is better than on higher priced competition."

Overall: ⚓⚓⚓⚓ While the ships were built from the same plans and are generally sisters, interior décor and design gives each vessel its own personality. They are glitz and glamour with neon, brass, glass and marble. The *Celebration* is New Orleans-themed, complete with Bourbon Street, a streetcar named Desire, Dixieland music and an outdoor café. The *Jubilee* is more or less themed to England with the Park Lane Promenade, Victorian gazebo, the Trafalgar Square meeting point and a beautiful library, Churchill's. The theme on *Holiday*, oldest of the three sister ships, is hard to define. One lounge is in the style of an underground grotto, the piano bar is old-time Casablanca and an authentic double-decker London bus is a snack bar strategically placed on the promenade.

HIGH MARKS
Δ Rick's American Café on the *Holiday*.
Δ Picture windows in all of the dining rooms.
Δ Helen Weber artworks and tapestries on the *Jubilee*.
Δ Miles of polished teak decks encircling outside decks.
Δ Multi-deck open atriums on all three ships

WEAKEST LINK:
• Time to participate in half of the activities offered.

FANTASY CLASS

MS ECSTASY
Built 1991

MS FANTASY
Built: 1990

MS FASCINATION
Built: 1994

MS IMAGINATION
Built: 1995
MS INSPIRATION
Built: 1996
MS SENSATION
Built: 1993
MS ELATION
Built: 1998
MS PARADISE
Built: 1998

Category: Resort XL
Rates: $$$
Overall Rating: ⚓⚓⚓⚓
Country of Registry: Liberia
Former Names: none
Nationality of Crew: Italian officers, International service staff
Cruising Areas: Caribbean, Mexico, and Panama Canal
Length of Voyages: 3, 4, 7 nights

Ship Specifics

Tonnage	70,367	Elevators	14
Length	855 feet	Decks	10
Beam	104 feet	Children's Facilities	yes
Stabilizers	yes	Fitness Center	yes
Passengers	2,044	Spa	yes
Crew	920	Verandahs	10
Space Ratio	34	Casino	yes
Crew/Passenger Ratio	1-2.2	Wheelchair Access	yes

Cabins: ⚓⚓⚓⚓ *Suites:* ⚓⚓⚓⚓ Cabins are Carnival-size which means close to 190-square feet for outsides and a little less inside. All outside cabins are identical. All inside cabins are identical. It's location and deck that determines the price. There are large windows in all outside cabins which have been refurbished in Destiny-class upscale fabrics and carpeting in pastel prints. There is ample closet space, personal safes, television, telephones, writing desks and a lot more in all cabins. There are a few cabins in minimum categories that have upper and lower berths; these are not recommended, except for kids. The price differential is only about $35 between these minimum insides and inside cabins with two beds. Well worth the difference.

Suites come in two sizes: Demi-Suite and Full Suite. The Demi Suites are up on Verandah Deck and have small balconies and real queen-size beds and small sitting areas. They are in the quietest location on the ship. The real suites are on Upper Deck and are really very comfortable and spacious. A divider separates the living room from bedroom. There's a bar, VCR, hair dryer, refrigerator, whirlpool tub, marble-topped bathroom counters and a nice size private verandahs. Beds in all cabins, except Demi-Suites, convert to king-size. The 432 cabins with private verandahs are about 20 percent larger and suites range from 340 square feet to about 430-square feet, also including private verandahs.

Facilities for Disabled Travelers: ⚓⚓⚓⚓ Each of the ships has 20 accessible cabins (10 inside and 10 outside). Average size is 185-square feet. Doors are 30 inches wide with no sill. Bathroom doors are 31.5 inches wide, also without sills, showers have a 7.5 inches sill. Sinks are 32 inches high. All of the public areas are accessible, except the top sports deck, the Observation area, the children's pool and laundry rooms. There are no totally accessible public restrooms.

Public Space: ⚓⚓⚓⚓⚓ In a word-awesome. Showrooms, bars, lounges, discos, indoor-outdoor areas are spacious.

Spa and Fitness: ⚓⚓⚓⚓ Nautica Spas take up 12,000-square feet and fitness areas cover the width of the ships with equipment facing the ocean. Spas are complete and offer every possible stateside service. Aerobics and other exercise classes are held several times a day even when ships are in port.

Entertainment: ⚓⚓⚓⚓⚓ In line with the rest of the fleet, Fantasy-class ships put great emphasis on entertainment and spend millions on award-winning production shows and individual entertainers. There are at least two major productions on each voyage complete with mind-boggling laser, extravagant lighting, brilliant costuming and original music. Professionally produced, dancers and singers are auditioned in London, Las Vegas, New York and elsewhere for these shows. Daytime activities run the gamut from discos to dance classes, bingo to bridge, art auctions to art classes, and casino action to casual lounging. There's something for everyone.

INSIDER TIP:

Carnival Cruise Lines doesn't usually have Theme Cruises but when it does they are unusual. Last year, there were themed NASCAR cruises hosted by racing champion Rusty Wallace on the *Imagination* and on *Triumph*. Partnered with the American Lung Association of Connecticut, Carnival's smoke-free *Paradise* schedules "Quit Smoking" Caribbean Cruises The onboard atmosphere that prohibits smoking by guests and crew is the encouragement many need to quit. It has been a very successful program and continues in 2003. Check with Carnival for sailing dates and particulars.

Food and Dining: ⚓⚓⚓⚓ It's hard to miss a place to eat. In fact, with new Bistros and 24-hour Pizzerias, 'round the clock cabin service, breakfast and lunch buffets, a Carnival cruise could be an overeater's delight. Or a nightmare. Dining room menus are extensive and throughout the fleet offer vegetarian and spa cuisine on a daily basis with no pre-orders required. Food is high quality, well prepared and beautifully presented. Two dining rooms with balconies and huge picture windows accommodate all guests in two sittings. There's space between tables to prevent eavesdropping, but very few tables for two. Most seat six or eight.

Service: ⚓⚓⚓⚓ Throughout the fleet, service is excellent with a ratio of about two guests to each crewmember.

Junior Cruisers: ⚓⚓⚓ Camp Carnival operates on all ships year-round with more counselors on board during summer months and holiday periods. Kids are divided into four age groups with activities suited for that age level. Teenagers have their own space and video game rooms.

Itineraries: ⚓⚓⚓⚓ *Ecstasy* sails on three and four night cruises from Los Angeles (San Pedro) to Baja Mexico. *Elation* also is home ported in Los Angeles but sails on one week Mexican Riviera cruises and moves to Galveston, Texas, in late September 2003 for one-week western Caribbean voyages. *Inspiration* sails from Tampa on weekly western Caribbean cruises, while *Sensation*, also home ported in Tampa does the shorter four and five night cruises. *Imagination* also does four-and five-night sailings from Miami and the *Fasination* sails on three-and four-night cruises from the same port. *Fantasy* sails on three and four night cruises to the Bahamas from Port Canaveral. *Paradise* cruises weekly on alternating eastern and western Caribbean voyages from Miami.

Steven Faber Comments:

"On the Paradise, the feeling of breathing clean air in the casino is so unusual as to be virtually eerie. The Paradise will never be confused with an elegant private club at sea but the non-smoking policy somehow does seem to filter out rowdier elements."

Overall: ⚓⚓⚓⚓ There's nothing traditional about Fantasy class vessels, although configuration still keeps cabins on separate decks from public rooms and lifestyle aboard is Carnival fun-related. The *Fantasy*, first in the generation, was so successful, the company ordered more and then still more in the same size and shape. Sister ships are so alike, even the decks have the same names. Each, however, develops its own personality based on themed décor and seemingly influenced by names. Computerized lighting goes from bright to light and designs are revolutionary, except for dining rooms and cabins. Guests may not want their homes decorated like the ships, but the color, flash and the glitz is fun, and that's what Carnival is all about. The glitziest is the *Fantasy*, first of the series, but they have settled down and the newest, the *Elation*, is almost subdued in comparison.

As for themes and décor, *Ecstasy* is styled after a city at sea with décor reminiscent of Manhattan. The *Elation* is the first in this series of ships to feature a multi-purpose conference room. The *Paradise* is the first and only vessel in any fleet to be entirely smoke-free. Even the crew is not permitted to smoke on board or out on open decks.

HIGH MARKS:

Δ The *Paradise* no smoking policy with absolutely no exceptions, crew or guest.

Δ The 24-hour pizzeria on all ships.

Δ The *Sensation's* 20-foot kinetic sculpture made up of geometric design rotating on cylinders.

Δ The vintage Rolls Royce on the *Ecstasy's* "City Lights Boulevard."

Δ The Touch of Class Lounge on the *Sensation* where even the seats are in the shape of hands.

Δ The life-size figures of Hollywood star of bygone days – Marilyn Monroe, Bette Davis, John Barrymore, Vivien Leigh and Clark Gable on the *Fascination* present once in a lifetime photo opportunities, albeit with deceased personalities who never seem to fade away.

Δ The Jeykll and Hyde Dance Club, with its eight-foot-tall sculptures, faces split to convey both benevolence and menace, on the *Elation*.

Celebrity Cruises

1050 Caribbean Way, Miami, FL 33132

(305) 539-6000 – www.celebritycruises.com

Celebrity Cruises, once the upscale division of Chandris Lines established in 1990, was purchased by Royal Caribbean Ltd, parent company of Royal Caribbean International, and integrated into the growing company. Celebrity operates as an independent subsidiary company, but many of the operational aspects have been combined. Celebrity, however, maintains its own personality, its own brand of service, food, entertainment and ambience. Under RCL ownership, Celebrity Cruises has grown and has increased the number of ships in the fleet to nine and is still growing. Chandris Cruises has ceased to exist.

First vessel in the Celebrity fleet was the *Galileo* rebuilt into the 1,106-passenger *Meridian*, which unfortunately is now resting in Davey Jones Locker.   This was followed by the newly built *Horizon* in 1990 and her sister-ship, *Zenith*, in late 1991. These were mid-size ships and Celebrity embarked on construction of a series of 70,000-ton vessels built at the same German shipyard. This enabled the company to expand itineraries to Alaska and Bermuda. The *Century* was completed in 1995, *Galaxy* in 1996 and the *Mercury* was delivered in November 1997. As part of the upscale product's intent to deliver fine cuisine, the company engaged Britain's best-known French chef, Michel Roux, to consult and supervise menus and cuisine on all five ships. His involvement continues, but as a consultant.

(See "Royal Caribbean International" for details on the parent company.)

The former owner, Chandris Cruises, was a diversified, worldwide company with an important presence in international tourism. The company's leisure group operated the fifth-largest cruise-vessel fleet in the world with seven ships in the Americas and Europe. The group continues to operate five hotels in leading Greek travel destinations.

I would be remiss if I didn't give credit and spend a few paragraphs in an epitaph to Chandris Cruises. John D. Chandris purchased his first vessel, the sailing ship *Simitrios* in 1915, an event that marked the founding of Chandris Cruises. He followed that with purchase of steamers and entered the cruise industry in 1922 with the *Chimara*. Serious entry into this side of shipping came with purchase in 1936 of the 1,705-ton *Corte II* from the French. Some of the well-known ships operated by Chandris include *Lurline, Ellinis, Regina Prima, Queen Frederica, America* (renamed *Australis*, then *Italis*), *Amerikanis, Aurelia, Romanza, President Roosevelt, Atlantic, Britanis,* and the *Victoria.*

Who Sails Celebrity Cruises? Couples make up about 80 percent of the manifest on most voyages and they are closely divided between the 35 to 55 age group and the over 55 folks. Demographics indicate few singles, although there is a singles program on every voyage. The first-time cruiser is more likely to be a traveler whose first car was a Pontiac or Buick, not a Honda. Experienced cruisers select Celebrity for the food, service and laid-back ambiance.

Dress Code: On one-week sailings, there are two "formal", three "casual" and two "informal" nights. Jackets and ties are requested for men on informal evenings; dark suits or tuxedo on formal nights and resort wear on other evenings. Daytime is strictly casual – jeans, shorts, tee shirts, etc. Dress code, however, is being relaxed and on my last 10-night cruise, there were only two "formal' nights. The rest were "resort casual" which makes men happier because they can dine tie-less.

Dining: Celebrity prides itself on food preparation and presentation. Based on its many awards, the company has succeeded. Much of the credit goes to Michel Roux, a three-star Michelin chef and one of the most famous French chefs in Britain. He created the ships' excellent menus, developed wine lists and assisted with training of the executive restaurant staff. His involvement continues with the new ownership. Menus are varied but include specialties of his Waterside Inn at Bray in Berkshire, England. In addition to gourmet dishes, the menu includes vegetarian and low calorie choices. Choices have been expanded and include gourmet pizza for stateroom delivery. In addition to dining rooms and Lido self-service for breakfast and lunch, there are lavish midnight buffets and 24-hour room service.

Special Dietary Requests: should be made at least 15 days prior to sailing. Celebrity retains an assigned table, two sittings for dinners and open sittings for breakfast and lunch. Vegetarian, low salt, low cholesterol, low fat are always available and vegetarian dishes and low calorie items are on every dinner menu.

Kosher food requests must be submitted in writing to Celebrity's Special Services Department no later than 21 days prior to sailing; 60 days for cruises in Europe and South America. Celebrity's kosher meals are prepared by Weberman Catering and brought on board either partially or wholly cooked. Kosher foods are available only at dinner with several choices. Dinner is served on plates, unless otherwise requested.

Service: Unusually attentive and professional are words that best describe staff attitude throughout the fleet. It's also friendly and from a deck hand to the captain, staff members never miss an opportunity to greet a guest. On board attitude and training seminars stress "every guest is a celebrity."

Tipping Policy: Recommendations cover more service people than on other lines. Per person, per day to waiter $3,50; the same to room steward/ess The busboy gets $1.50; and the suite butler $3, if you have one. Also recommended on a per person basis is $5 each to the Maitre d' and $3.50 to the Chief Housekeeper.

Past Passenger Perks: Captain's Club is offered after the first Celebrity sailing. It's the only past passenger club that charges a fee ($35 per family). Benefits include promotional packages, special fares on specified sailings, cabin upgrades in some cases and in general follows the rule - the more you sail with Celebrity, the more perks. Members receive priority embarkation, pre-sailing optional restaurant reservations, and an invitation to a private party. Other perks: sail five or more cruises and you earn an upgrade; sail six or more times and you also receive priority status for on board reservations.

Discount Policy: Called "Five Star Rates" are early booking discounts representing as much as 50 percent off published fares. These rates are seasonal and capacity controlled. Children travel at a reduced rate and single supplements range from 150 to 200 percent. A quick Internet rate check showed savings of from 25 to 50 percent. An outside standard cabin for a one-week Bermuda cruise listed at over $2,000 was offered for $1229 with similar savings for verandah cabins. Overall, up to 50 percent discounts are offered with early booking, past guest special sailings, senior savers and back-to-back cruises.

INSIDER TIP

Celebrity built its reputation on the catch phrase – "Exceeding Expectations" but few travelers have the same expectations when it comes to vacations. No one ship or company can fill every expectation. That phrase should flash a warning with a bit of advice. Expect "very good" in every area of the ship you sail and be pleasantly surprised when something, or hopefully everything, exceeds those expectations. Pre-booked spa packages are possible. For as low as $195, you can choose several great treatments and be assured of appointments. For $695 you get the works spread out over the length of your cruise. Spa packages must be booked through travel agents prior to embarkation.

LATE NEWS

Celebrity is launching what is being called "Celebrity Escape Cruises." There are four of these sailings scheduled for 2003. Sailing are for guests 21 and over and offer special amenities unique to the sailings, such as complimentary Bloody Marys or Mimosas at certain breakfasts, complimentary house wine at select dinners and extended hours in the AquaSpa and pool areas.

The Fleet
HORIZON
Built: 1990   Refurbished: 1996
ZENITH
Built: 1992

Category: Resort Mid-Size
Rates: $$$
Overall Rating: ⚓⚓⚓⚓
Country of Registry: Liberia
Former Names: none
Nationality of Crew: Greek officers; International Service Staff
Cruising Area: Bermuda, Caribbean, Panama Canal
Length of Voyages: 7, 10, 11, 15-nights

Ship Specifics

Tonnage*	46,811	Elevators	7
Length	682 feet	Decks	9
Beam	95 feet	Children's Facilities	yes
Stabilizers	yes	Fitness Center	yes
Passengers	1,354	Spa	yes
Crew	642	Verandahs	no
Space Ratio	35	Casino	yes
Crew/Passenger Ratio	1-2.2	Wheelchair Access	yes

Zenith - Tonnage: 47,255 – Passengers: 1,374

Cabins: ⚓⚓⚓ *Suites:* ⚓⚓⚓ Staterooms range from 172-square feet in an inside to 340-square feet in the Presidential Suite on the *Horizon* and 500-square feet for the Royal Suite on the *Zenith*. Average cabins are closer to the minimum size, but are comfortable and have interactive television, radios, telephones, individual safes, minimal bathroom amenities and hair dryers. Suites have a range of extras that almost make the price difference worthwhile. Amenities that include butler service, express luggage delivery to cabins, priority check-in and debarkation, fresh fruit in cabins, a bottle of welcome champagne, terrycloth robes, oversized bath towels, full meal service en suite, dining room sitting preference, hors d'oeuvres daily, fresh flowers, complimentary espresso and cappuccino, afternoon tea service, laundry valet service, assistance with packing and unpacking, shoeshine service and a stocked mini-bar. Some cabins have double beds; others have single beds that convert to queen-size. Lengthening of the top three decks on the *Zenith* allowed for 10 additional deluxe cabins and suites.

Facilities for Disabled Guests: ⚓⚓ Four cabins are wheelchair accessible with doorways wide enough to allow average sized chairs. Bathroom doorways are 39.5 inches wide. Showers are wheelchair accessible, public elevators are 35.5 inches wide and there is one wheelchair accessible public toilet on Galaxy Deck on each ship. Some public areas may present difficulties for wheelchair bound passengers.

Public Space: ⚓⚓⚓⚓ Largest public room is the Palladium Show Lounge that seats 870. Other rooms are more intimate; all are beautifully decorated in classic minimalistic designs. Eight lounges and bars, card room, library, three swimming pools, large sunning area and quiet corners and places to play and meet fellow guests. Layout of the ships makes it easy to find your way around quickly.

Spa: ⚓⚓ *Fitness:* ⚓⚓⚓ Facility includes good equipment and plenty of space for workouts. The spa and beauty salon are not as well planned as on other ships.

INSIDER TIP

The Celebrity Spa Package is available on both *Horizon* and *Zenith*, but facilities are not as generous as on the larger vessels in the fleet. In order to shower or dress after a massage in some of the rooms, you must go through the spa reception area wrapped in a towel.

Entertainment: ⚓⚓⚓ Traditional cruise ship style with production shows passengers tend to ignore. Daytime activities are plentiful with poolside fun, contests, bingo, horse racing, etc. In addition to shows, there are individual performers. There's also dancing in show lounges prior to formal entertainment and in several lounges scattered throughout the ships.

Food and Dining: ⚓⚓⚓ One dining room on each ship serves guests in two sittings. Rooms have large picture windows and a raised area so almost every table has an ocean view. Menus offer wide selections. Center area of dining rooms tends to be noisy with tables within eavesdropping distance.

Junior Cruisers: ⚓⚓⚓ Like other Celebrity ships, *Horizon* and *Zenith* offer Family Cruising Programs during summer months. Designed to keep children from three to 17 busy and happy, youth counselors are on board to supervise a full activities program. A popular event encourages young thespians to participate in "Celebrity Summer Stock." They produce, direct and perform in a theatrical show, complete with dance, costumes and an audience.

Itineraries: ⚓⚓⚓ *Horizon* sails seasonally from New York to Bermuda on one-week cruises, then follows the sun south and sails from Fort Lauderdale on seven and 10-day Caribbean cruises. The *Zenith* cruises on 10- and 15-day cruises between Fort Lauderdale and Acapulco and Acapulco and San Juan during winter months. During summer months, the *Zenith* sails on one-week cruises from New York to Bermuda.

Overall: ⚓⚓⚓ Both ships combine traditional with contemporary cruising and offer excellent value for vacation products that border on premium quality. While entertainment doesn't quite measure up to the quality of the ships, food and service make up for whatever entertainment lacks. Both ships are beautifully styled and easy to live on for longer than a week.

HIGH MARKS:

Δ The Black Forest cake and jumbo chocolate chip cookies served on all ships.

Δ The America's Bar on the *Horizon* and the Fleet Bar on the *Zenith*, both virtually surrounded by window walls.

Δ Celebrity Blue – the deep blue used as an anchor color, in most major rooms and even on the ships' lines.

Δ The sleek profiles of both ships.

WEAKEST LINK:

• The noise level in restaurants.

• Production shows that are dated with costumes on the shabby chic side.

INSIDER TIP

With addition of the larger and newer *Century*, *Galaxy* and *Mercury*, the *Horizon* and *Zenith* have become even more attractive for guests who want a premium-type product at moderate prices and who don't want to share their shipboard space with a lot of people. If there was a theme for the vessels, it would probably be classic-modern with a touch of art deco, subtle colors and rounded edges.

CENTURY
Built: 1995
GALAXY
Built: 1999
MERCURY
Built: 1997

Category: Resort XL
Rates; $$$ to $$$$
Overall Rating: ⚓⚓⚓⚓⚓
Country of Registry: Liberia
Former Names: none
Nationality of Crew: Greek officers; International service crew
Cruising Areas: Alaska, Caribbean, Mexico, and Panama Canal
Length of Voyages: 7 days

Ship Specifics

Tonnage*	70,606	Elevators*	9
Length*	815 feet	Decks	10
Beam	105 feet	Children's Facilities	yes
Stabilizers	yes	Fitness Center	yes
Passengers*	1,750	Spa	yes
Crew*	843	Verandahs	yes
Space Ratio	41	Casino	yes
Crew/Passenger Ratio	1-2.2	Wheelchair Access	yes

Galaxy & Mercury – *Tonnage: 73,000, 77,713 • Length: 852 feet*
Passengers: 1870 • Crew: 909 • Elevators: 10

Cabins: ⚓⚓⚓⚓ ***Suites:*** ⚓⚓⚓⚓⚓ Although cabins are about the same square footage as on the *Horizon/Zenith* (175-square feet), the two indoor walls have been contoured which makes them seem more spacious. The narrower side accommodates a tower that houses a 21-inch interactive television set, safe (*Mercury*) and mini-bar. On the other side, the dressing table/desk is faced with mirror with a personal safe behind it on the two older ships. All cabins and suites have minibars and video players. Penthouse Decks offer butler service in mini-suites, full suites and those big super suites, *Galaxy* and *Mercury* have 220 cabins and suites with private verandahs; 54 on the *Century*.

Facilities for Disabled Travelers: ⚓⚓⚓⚓ One inside and seven centrally located ocean view oversized staterooms measuring 259-square feet are among the best disabled facilities at sea. Doors are wide enough to accommodate average size wheelchairs. Bathroom doors are 35 inches wide and showers are large enough for wheelchair turn arounds. Elevator doors are 39 inches wide. All public rooms are wheelchair accessible and it is no problem for physically challenged guests to attend all functions.

Public Space: ⚓⚓⚓⚓ There are large pool areas, theaters which double as conference rooms, libraries, medical centers, card rooms, two outdoor swimming pools, one indoor-outdoor pool with a retractable roof, a children's pool and four outdoor whirlpools on each ship. Each also has nine lounges, bars and nightclubs. There's plenty of space for everything. Each ship has an observation room topside surrounded by windows for daytime relaxation and nighttime dancing and partying.

Spa: ⚓⚓⚓⚓ ***Fitness:*** ⚓⚓⚓⚓ While not the largest at sea, AquaSpas are some of the most extensive. The 10,050-square foot facilities have some unusual features. There are tranquil retreat areas in which guests can unwind and de-stress and treatment rooms with windows for views of the ocean while being pampered. The fitness rooms are fully equipped with what looks like next generation machines.

Entertainment: ⚓⚓⚓ As the vessels grew in size, so did the quantity of entertainment, but professionalism stayed the same. It is almost non-stop with fun and games during daylight hours and three different production-type shows during a one-week cruise. They are lively, fast paced but not up to the other standards of the ships. Not the most spectacular at sea, but enjoyable. Individual performers on other nights range from poor to good.

Food and Dining: ⚓⚓⚓⚓ Each ship has a double-tiered dining room feeding guests in two sittings. Rooms are restaurant-style and are sort of the style of the old *Normandie* with grand staircases leading into the lower level.

Menus offer a number of selections and the Lido area is open for casual dining. There are very few tables for two. Most seat four to eight people. The noise level on the balcony is higher than on the main floor.

Shirley and Harry Comment:

"With its rapid fleet expansion and further incorporation into the Royal Caribbean parent company, Celebrity at this writing is losing some of the critical edge that distinguished the line at its inception. Without constant vigilance, the carefully laid menu plans and service details set forth by Michel Roux can get shunted aside by the demands of the moment."

Junior Cruisers: ⚓⚓⚓⚓ Not only are there activities for every age group, there are "club houses" especially designed for each group so they remain interested and occupied. Ship Mates (under 10) are divided into two groups and have the Fun Factory, specifically designed to be explored with hands and imagination. For the Arcade Generation, there's Cyberspace, an action-packed room filled with the latest video games. Teens also have their own room just off the starboard entrance to the Stratosphere Lounge. Telephone system allows for monitoring of cabins from any phone on board.

Itineraries: ⚓⚓⚓⚓ *Century* sails on one week cruises from Fort Lauderdale on alternating Eastern and Western Caribbean itineraries visiting either San Juan, St. Thomas, St. Maarten and Nassau or Ocho Rios, Grand Cayman, Cozumel and Key West. The *Galaxy* sails on one week round trip cruises from Vancouver to the inside Passage, Juneau, Skagway, Haines, Hubbard Glacier and Ketchikan from May through August, then transits the Panama Canal to San Juan for one week cruises to Barbados, Martinique, Antigua and St. Thomas. The *Mercury* sails on one-week cruises from Fort Lauderdale to the western Caribbean with stops at Key West, Calica, Cozumel and Grand Cayman. Other months, she moves through the Canal for one week cruises between Vancouver and Seward and round trips from Vancouver on an itinerary similar to the *Galaxy's*.

Overall: ⚓⚓⚓⚓ Celebrity's leap into technology is most evident in staterooms. Through the television remote control, passengers are privy to an innovative, in-cabin entertainment and information center providing comprehensive information about shipboard life and ports of call. At the touch of a button on the remote, guests can purchase tickets, check the dining room menu, order cabin service, book a spa appointment, select a pay-per-view "R" rated movies (which can be blocked out), play casino games (charged to cabin account); respond to comment surveys, review shipboard account summaries and it's all offered in English, French, German, Italian and Spanish.

While the ships are virtual triplets, they are not identical on the inside. Each newbuild has added features that appeal to some guests. Décor is different on each and it's hard to say which is the more beautiful. If you're the suite-type of guest, there's a better chance of getting one on the *Mercury* because there are more of them.

HIGH MARKS:

Δ   The 115,000-gallon Thalassotherapy pool with jet massage stations.

Δ   There's a $10 charge for the use of the facility, but no charge if used in conjunctions with other treatments. Well worth the low cost. There's nothing quite like it at sea.

Δ   The Rasul Treatment that should be taken by two people who are connected in a very personal way. Each rubs the other with therapeutic mud; then both go into a steam room that becomes a rain shower. It's the best buy on the ships and a lot of fun. Cost: $35 for one; $60 for two.

Δ   Cigar smokers love Michael's Club, a haven for stogie addicts. Non-smokers might want to stop by just to watch the little old cigar maker role a special brand.

WEAKEST LINKS:

•   The spa menu looks good but watch out for high fat and sugar content that pushes the calories upward.

•   Tired and dated production shows.

•   The cigar aroma from Michael's Club that lures smokers into the room and sends non-smokers as far away as possible.

MILLENNIUM CLASS

CONSTELLATION
Built: mid-2002

INFINITY
Built: 2001

MILLENNIUM
Built: 2000

SUMMIT
Built: 2001

Category: Premium
Rates: $$$ to $$$$
Overall Rating: ⚓⚓⚓⚓
Country of Registry: Liberia
Nationality of Crew: Greek Officers; International service staff
Cruising Area: Alaska, Caribbean, Mediterranean, and Northern Europe
Length of voyages: 7 to 12 nights
Crew Nationality: Greek Officers; International Service Staff

Ship Specifics

Tonnage	91,000	Elevators	10
Length	965 feet	Decks	11
Beam	105 feet	Children's Facilities	yes
Stabilizers	yes	Fitness Center	yes
Passengers	1,950	Spa	yes
Crew	999	Verandahs	yes
Space Ratio	47	Casino	yes
Crew/Passenger Ratio	1-2.2	Wheelchair Access	yes

Cabins: ⚓⚓⚓⚓ *Suites:* ⚓⚓⚓⚓ There are nine categories of staterooms and suites for a total of 975 rooms. Of these, only 195 are inside accommodations and the smallest is 170 square feet, the same as average outside staterooms. The largest category is made up of 292 deluxe ocean view rooms with verandahs and they size up at a very comfortable 208-square feet. Penthouse suites are suite-sized at 2,530 square feet with their own Jacuzzis and verandahs large enough to host 100 guests. My favorite affordable luxury accommodations are the 26 Sky Suites with verandahs which are more than comfortable at 308-square feet and a better "buy" than deluxe cabins and less pricey than the larger suites.

Sky Suites have floor-to-ceiling glass doors, sitting areas with sofa beds and lounge chairs, entertainment centers with mini-bars, walk-in closets, and bathrooms with whirlpool tubs. All suites have verandahs s and butler service.

All accommodations have sitting areas, refrigerators, interactive television, hair dryers, minibars, private safes and robes. Suites come with lots of other perks like the separate shower with bench and multiple jet spray and powder room with shower in the two Penthouse Suites, eight Royal Suites and eight

Celebrity Suites. Designer-type amenities are available only in suites. Limited amenities are offered in staterooms and terrycloth robes are only in deluxe rooms and suites..

Staterooms are designed with a feeling of "home away from home" a retreat and place to call one's own for the duration of the voyage. Centerpiece of each is the media tower that blends with the rest of the room.

Facilities for Disabled Travelers: ⚓⚓⚓⚓ Wheelchair accessible accommodations are available in almost every category from six Sky Suites to five inside staterooms for a total of 26 overall. All of the staterooms are conveniently located. The entrance door is 36 inches wide and there is no sill. The bathroom door is the same size and has a roll-in shower with fold down bench, the required grab bars and hand held showerheads. There is knee clearance under the sink and the mirror is adjustable. All decks are accessible via elevator that has audio floor indicators and Braille numbers. There are a number of accessible public restrooms.

Public Space: ⚓⚓⚓⚓ In spite of size, guests find it easy to find their way around the ships. All of the ships are nearly identical in layout, but rooms have different names, in some cases. If you have sailed one, you'll feel right at home on the others. Embarkation is on the lowest of the three decks spanning the impressive atrium, the main reference point that leads to public rooms. Ships are light and bright. Millennium Class ships cut large spaces into small and intimate rooms. Each develops its own following depending on guest interests.

In addition to traditional lounges and bars, there are a few **INSIDER TIPS** worth mentioning. For example, Words, a richly paneled two-level library with comfortable chairs and a good selection of books in several languages. Its counterpart, Notes, a digital music library is stocked with thousands of recordings. Music choices range from jazz to opera. Revelations, the topside observation lounge is lined on three sides with 10 foot windows and comfortable sitting for ocean viewing. A skylight over the dance floor expands the room's height and enhances lighting when the shades are drawn. The room changes atmosphere when the sun sets and becomes a lively disco on an illuminated glass floor. Rendez-Vous Lounge is another popular venue. Located amidships, it is a dance room, second showroom and a lead-in for guests heading to the restaurant.

Cova Café de Milano is where you'll find me late mornings, late afternoons and before heading for bed. Named for the renowned Italian café in Milan, it has been a favorite stop off point since it was first opened on the *Century*. The

Milan café was built in 1756 near La Scala Opera House and remains a meeting place for fashionable Milanese society and serves as the model for Celebrity's shipboard version. Afternoon and early music entertains café goers with high-end music and makes the area more than just a replica of a traditional classical café. Charges are nominal for excellent coffees and teas. Pastries and other goodies are complimentary. It is an open space decorated with eyebrow raising artworks that don't seem to have any connection with an Italian-style café.

Spa and Fitness: ⚓⚓⚓⚓ The AquaSpas are nearly twice the size of spas on Century-class vessels and among the most extensive at sea. Under a fan-shaped, double vaulted glass roof, the hydro pool forms the focus of the glass-covered Aqua Dome, or solarium. The pool is raised on a large teak deck. Each of the four corners provides a different type of massage by under water jets and air emanating from beneath the water. This allows bathers to literally float on air. But that's just part of the experience. Open to all guests at no additional charge, the hydro pool also has a counter current against which bathers can gently push.

Super comfortable lounge chairs provide a relaxation area where the health and fitness conscious can also enjoy food service to complete the holistic approach to personal well-being. There are natural juice cocktails and a diet menu combining seafood and light meats with salads and fruits.

But that's just the beginning of what the spa offers. Fitness Centers are equipped with the newest types of machines and actually makes walking treadmills a pleasure as you ocean watch. Bordering on a holistic-type of spa that caters to the senses, 14 treatment rooms each have a private shower and treatments run the gamut from a massage for one to Rasul for two or three. It takes little to imagine a Cleopatra Bath, hot rock massages, mud-steam sequences, thermal baths, rain forests and the like in an atmosphere of Citrus topiary and sculptured trees combined with fragrances that open all the senses.

The AquaSpas may well be the sexiest spas at sea and some packages can be booked before the cruise embarks. There are additional charges for some of the classes (Yoga, Pilates and training sessions).

Entertainment: ⚓⚓⚓ The major entertainment venue is the Celebrity Theater that has a prominent aft position on Entertainment Deck. There are two or three production shows during a cruise, depending on the length of the voyage. The shows are pleasant with dancers, some high tech equipment, laser and smoke and guests seem to enjoy them. Other nights feature solo performers, fun and games. Daytime activities are the usual, with lots of bingo.

Food and Dining: ⚓⚓⚓ Similar to other main dining rooms on the larger Celebrity ships, the restaurants have two entry levels that bring guests into the multi-level restaurant. On port and starboard sides on both entry levels, formal foyers announce the restaurant and serve as an elegant and comfortable transition. Foyers are identical, except for the counterpoint sculptures located in the niches framing the entries. The restaurants are beautifully decorated and waiter stations are unobtrusive which helps keep noise levels down. Sitting is at a limited number of tables for two, with most tables for six or eight. Menus are extensive with five entrée choices and specialty recommendations featured almost daily. In addition to regular menus offered for all meals, spa cuisine is highlighted. Reasonable dietary requests are honored, particularly if the ship has been informed prior to sailing. Spa suggestions list calorie and other contents on the back of the menu, but calories are high and there are no "fat free" items offered. Sugar free, however, is available in desserts.

The Waterfall Grill falls somewhere between the old-style Lido and new casual dining options that start at breakfast, go through lunch, snacks, themed midnight buffets and informal dinners. These are actually three facilities that merge into one and is also the casual food option adjacent to the swimming pool. The primary facility is a self-service buffet with four separate lines. Ample seating is arranged within eight cantilevered bow windows on a raised level. Aft is the outdoor grill and bar. There's a pizza oven, pasta bar and the grill. Décor throughout this area is based on a Mediterranean outdoor café with hand painted ceramic tiles, synthetic stones and wood patterned laminates.

Optional Restaurants: ⚓⚓⚓⚓ Tucked away from other activities are the jewels in the dining crown. On *Millennium*, it's the Olympic with original Edwardian wood-carved paneling from the *Olympic*, sister ship of the *Titanic*. On *Infinity*, it's the venerable *SS United States* and on *Summit*, the restaurant honors the French liner *Normandie* while on *Constellation*, it's Ocean Liners recalling the best of classic transatlantic travel with artifacts from some of those famous liners. Restaurants seat 130 and according to Michel Roux, who designed and created them, they are restaurants "that look forward to the past and reflect the globalization of food preferences of the present and the future."

Even if you decide not to enjoy a superb three-hour meal in one of these restaurants, you must go by and see the authentic artifacts. Original artwork has been installed and works that once graced famous vessels are part of the décor. Reservations are required and the meal at $25 is a bargain for an evening of excellent dining, service and music. Our evening for two on a recent Summit cruise, including one martini, sparking water and a good grade bottle of wine cost us $100, including an additional gratuity which was not required. It was an evening impossible to duplicate in any major city in the world for anywhere near the price.

Junior Cruisers: ⚓⚓⚓⚓ Celebrity is reaching out to families in a big way. The teen center has been enlarged and the entire kid's program expanded. There are so many activities for kids from three years up; guests are likely to forget they brought the kids along. The Tower is the teen club and disco and is an environment that encourages "just hanging out." Activities are divided by age groups: three to six, seven to nine, 10 to 12 and 13 to 17. From building a cruise ship to building an undersea habitat, there's enough to keep them busy throughout the day. Area also includes a children's library.

There's a sign-in/sign-out system and each child wears a wristband for identification. There are slumber parties in the playroom nightly from 10 p.m. to 1 a.m. ($6 per child per hour). Limited babysitting is available for $8 per hour

Itineraries: ⚓⚓⚓⚓ The *Constellation* spent her inaugural season in the Mediterranean before moving to the Caribbean for cruises from Port Everglades (Ft. Lauderdale, Florida). She will move back to Europe in late spring 2003, then return to Florida in October. The *Infinity* sails on one week southern Caribbean cruises from San Juan. *Millennium* sails on 10 and 11-night Caribbean cruises from Port Everglades and the *Summit* spends winter months in Fort Lauderdale on 10 and 11-night itineraries that differ from the *Millennium*. She cruises in Alaska in summer months. *Summit* does a few Hawaii sailing, spends warm weather season in Alaska and then return to warm weather Caribbean cruising.

Overall: ⚓⚓⚓⚓ *Constellation*, *Infinity*, *Millennium* and *Summit* continue Celebrity traditions. The vessels are an interesting maritime bridge to the past and integrate glass and steel, power and grace. They combine features of a bygone era in ocean travel. It is most noticeable in the ships' specialty restaurants. First in the series, the *Millennium* introduced the industry's first smokeless gas turbine propulsion. It is the same technology used in aircraft and military vessels. Considered to be quieter, cleaner and more reliable than diesel, there's another big advantage in the small space required for engines. This allows for significantly more guest and crew accommodations.

INSIDER TIP

In reviewing cruise ships, I find three areas that are subjective when it comes to commenting on them – food, entertainment and art. I learned early on that one person's caviar is another's fish eggs. I can't tell you that all of the guests rave about the food. I can say, however, that there is a lot of choice in dishes, quality is good, presentation can be improved and that no one disembarks hungry.

Art is another subject. There's a lot of it on board these ships and I assume it cost a lot of money. Some of it was pure whimsy, like the reclining overweight lady in the spa area on *Summit*. The artist, Fernando Botero is known for his rotund, voluminous shapes and dimension. There are some spectacular pieces, however, and one I should have recognized. It's the bronze statue that greets guests in the *Summit* Restaurant. In her most recent past life, she was a swimming pool area decoration at the Fontainebleau Hotel in Miami Beach. I must have passed her by a hundred times and never realized who she was in her first life. She is the real thing and was created for the original *Normandie*.

HIGH MARKS:

Δ The conservatories on all four ships. Designed by Paris-based award-winning floral designer Emilio Robba, the areas are unique and tranquil. Silk and fresh flowers fill the towering spaces. On *Summit*, it's named Secret Garden and houses a collection of botanical flower arrangements, fragrant candles and decorative objects. If you like an arrangement, it's for sale and will be duplicated and shipped to you. Silk flowers are so real, they have simulated dew on them.

Δ The Internet Cafés are set up with views of the ocean and a couple of dozen computers. Access is quick and personal mailboxes are accessible. Priced at 95 cents per minute or a flat $99 for unlimited use throughout the cruise, the area was never crowded since it was open on a 24-hour basis. Internet is also available in every cabin and suite for guests who bring their own laptops. Fee depends on length of the voyage.

INSIDER TIP

My husband and I have different likes and preferences, which may cause minor problems in a marriage, but helps me in writing ship reviews. I get to see what other guests prefer. His absolutely favorite rooms on these ships are the Martini Bars which develop an almost cult following by the second night of the sailing. It is three deep standing room around the bar starting about an hour before dinner is announced. The area itself is pleasant, but it was the Summit bartender Suni's personality, and his super sized martinis, which influenced the camaraderie in the area. A native of Bali, he had worked the bar at Four Seasons Hotel on the island. Celebrity might do well to name the Martini Bar "Suni's" on the next ship.

WEAKEST LINKS:
- Food presentation could use some tweaking. It tasted better than it looked.
- The same goes for entertainment. I have yet to see a Celebrity audience rush to its feet for standing ovations. That tells the story.
- It's a case of find it if you can. It takes guests at least a couple of days to figure out how to get to the lowest level of the showrooms. Access to the main level is on deck four, but the stage is on three, so guests are obliged to take the stairs or elevator down to get to stage level. Wheelchair access to the lowest level is limited. Access to front seats is on three, but there are no entrances, only emergency exits on that level. Balcony access is on deck five. Go figure that design. I couldn't!
- Word has a great 24-hour open policy, but I never could catch the limited times scheduled to withdraw a book. Everything is under lock and key, except during about two or three hours on sea days; less on port days.

Clipper Cruise Line

7711 Bonhomme Avenue, St. Louis, MO 63105

(314) 727-2929 – www.clippercruise.com

Headquartered in St. Louis, Clipper Cruise Line was founded and operated by Barney Ebsworth. In 1996, the company was acquired by its sister company, Intrav, a highly successful wholesale tour operator. In 1999, Swiss-based Kuoni Travel Holding, Ltd. acquired both Clipper Cruise Line and Intrav. It's good to know that Ebsworth's intentions when he founded Clipper 1982 are being followed and expanded. He founded the company with a single purpose – to build and operate small vessels to cruise America's inland waterways and exotic destinations.

The first of three 100 to 110-guest vessels, the *Newport Clipper*, went into service in 1983 and was followed by the *Nantucket Clipper* in late 1984. The *Charleston Clipper* began service in 1986. The *Newport Clipper* was replaced with the *World Discoverer* in 1991. The company currently operates four vessels – *Clipper Odyssey*, *Clipper Adventure*, *Nantucket Clipper* and *Yorktown Clipper*.

Vessels are well run with American and International crews. They operate seasonally from Florida to the Bay of Fundy, through the Caribbean to Costa Rica and Mexico's Sea of Cortez, Antarctica, Alaska. With new and larger vessels, itineraries have been expanded to Asia.

Yacht-like in personality and size, they are not for travelers looking for casinos and round-the-clock entertainment. Nor are they for the budget-priced traveler. They are for travelers who enjoy a quiet, relaxed atmosphere in compact staterooms cruising through almost still waters. Since vessels are in a different port almost every day and evening, entertainment is based on shore-side lecturers, and what is available in each port.

Who Sails Clipper Cruise Line? The sailing crowd with about 90 percent of them couples over 55. Very few families or singles are on board. Guests are in upper income brackets, well educated and worldly more interested in learning experiences than production shows or casinos. They are experienced travelers who do not shop for bottom prices and will book a bed-and-breakfast rather than a huge hotel

Lifestyle: Casual and relaxed with emphasis on destinations instead of organized shipboard activities or nightlife. Guests mingle and an informal atmosphere prevails.

Facilities for Disabled Travelers: Clipper Cruise Line ships may not be the best choice for disabled travelers. Most ships do not have elevators and no cabins meet wheelchair-bound traveler needs.

Dress Code: Very casual. It's not necessary for men to bring more than one jacket.

Dining: Single restaurant on each ship with open sitting for all meals affords an opportunity to interact with fellow guests. You sit where you like. Food is American-style and regional cuisine. Four course dinners, buffet breakfasts and lunches, freshly baked goods at tea time. Some cruises include hotel overnights and land-based restaurants for evening meals.

Clipper has established an ongoing relationship with some of the most prestigious American culinary institutes, where many of the chefs have trained. Another Clipper specialty is its excellent cuisine using the freshest of ingredients possible — seafood, fruits, and vegetables — prepared each meal from scratch. Healthy American and regionally influenced cuisine and a variety of choices are offered at each meal. Included are "light" selections and half portions.

Entertainment: At many ports, local musicians or artisans will come aboard to add regional flavor in music and folklore. An important part of the entertainment program is educational in content — naturalists, historians, and other experts often accompany cruises to enhance enjoyment and understanding of the places visited, spot and identify wildlife, explain natural phenomena and bring history to life.

Service: Attentive and personal by the young staff fresh out of college, for the most part, and just as inquisitive and anxious to learn about port of call as the guests.

Medical Facilities: When the *Nantucket Clipper* and *Yorktown Clipper* sail within reach of American, Canadian, or British medical facilities, a physician will not be on board the vessel. However, a certified physician will be on board when the ships sail more than a day away from ports and shoreside medical facilities. There is always a certified physician on board the *Clipper Adventurer* and the *Clipper Odyssey*. Tipping Policy: About $10 to $15 per person, per day, paid at the end of the cruise. Tips are pooled and divided among entire crew.

Discount Policy: Reduced rates are rarely offered but there special promotions from time-to-time. Air-sea packages and pre- and post-hotel stays are offered on most cruises, particularly at locales where conditions do not lend themselves to independent exploration.

HIGH MARKS

Δ The a total lack of regimentation and flexibility.

WEAKEST LINKS:

- No casinos
- No entertainers
- No bingo, which some of think should go into the High Marks

INSIDER TIP

Food, entertainment and overall experience are the same on all vessels in the Clipper fleet, so we are not detailing overall food, dining and entertainment except where there are differences. We are pointing out differences in accommodations, ship size and amenities to assist readers in making choices that should be based on itineraries when it comes to Clipper Cruise Line.

The Fleet
CLIPPER ADVENTURER
Built: 1976   Rebuilt: 1998

Category: Boutique Adventure
Rates: $$$$$
Overall Rating: ⚓⚓⚓
Country of Registry: Bahamas
Former Name: *Alla Tarasov*
Nationality of Crew: International
Cruising Area: Mostly South America, Antarctica
Length of Voyages: 14 days and longer

Ship Specifics

Tonnage	4,364	Elevators	0
Length	330 feet	Decks	5
Beam	38-40 feet	Children's Facilities	no
Stabilizers	no	Fitness Center	no
Passengers	122	Spa	no
Crew	84	Verandahs	no
Space Ratio	43	Casino	no
Crew/Passenger Ratio	1-1.5	Wheelchair Access	no

Cabins: ⚓⚓⚓ *Adventurer* has 61 new outside cabins and three suites with sitting areas. Cabins are 130-square feet with large windows. Accommodations are not luxurious by any means, but they are comfortable. *Adventurer* is air-conditioned and heated throughout. Each stateroom has individual controls to meet personal requirements. Power on board the vessel is 220-volt, with recessed outlets of the round, 2-pronged European type. If you plan to bring U.S.-standard 110-volt equipment with a flat-pronged plug, you will need to bring a converter and a round, 2-pronged European adapter plug. Each stateroom is provided with a 220-volt hair dryer for your convenience

Public Space: ⚓⚓⚓ There are two lounges — the Main Lounge & Bar on Promenade Deck seats 130 and the Clipper Club, also on Promenade Deck, seats 45. There's a library/card room, a small workout room, a gift shop, and a hair salon. Unique to the *Clipper Adventurer* is a spacious, covered promenade with a beautiful wooden deck (varnished Oregon pine) where guests can view the seascapes. There's also plenty of open deck space on Boat and Sun Decks. The observation platform forward below the Bridge is ideal for wildlife viewing

Spa and Fitness: ⚓ There is a small gym on the Main Deck with weights and stationary bicycles for individual use

Entertainment: ⚓⚓⚓ Onboard activities often parallel destinations and excursions. Rather than entertainers, the ship travels with selected "enlighteners" — naturalists, historians and other experts — who, in fact, do entertain as they offer informal lectures, lead expeditions ashore and invite questions. Depending on the part of the world, options might include, for example, swimming, snorkeling and a hike in an island's wildlife preserves, or a museum visit, Native folk dances and a discussion of totem-pole storytelling.

Clipper's veteran travelers particularly appreciate the unregimented approach to activities and excursions.

Food and Dining: ⚓⚓⚓⚓ The window-lined dining room seats all guests at leisurely single sittings, where superb American and Continental cuisine is served by Clipper's friendly staff. Special dietary foods can be provided but the company must be notified in writing four weeks before sailing. The galley is not equipped to prepare or serve kosher cuisine. Other special requests such as food allergies, lactose intolerance, etc., can be accommodated.

Junior Cruisers: ⚓ No programs or facilities

Itineraries: ⚓⚓⚓⚓ Seven to 14-day cruises in Asia, Australia and New Zealand.

Overall: ⚓⚓⚓ The *Clipper Adventurer* is a handsome expedition vessel reminiscent of the days of the great ocean liners, with lots of varnished wood and brass. She sails on a wide variety of voyages — in Europe, the Canadian Arctic, the U.S., South America and Antarctica.

Clipper Adventurer underwent a $13-million conversion in 1998 in Scandinavia. The Clipper Adventurer is an ocean going vessel equipped with an ice-strengthened hull (A-1 ice class) ideally suited for cruising in remote environments such as Antarctica, but supremely comfortable anywhere she sails. A fleet of Zodiac landing craft provides access to areas where no infrastructure exists. The vessel is equipped with state-of-the-art satellite navigation and communication equipment including telephone, fax, and e-mail.

The Captain and his officers maintain an open bridge to give guests an opportunity to observe and ask questions. An experienced cruise staff, physician, and onboard lecturers accompany all voyages to enhance guest enjoyment of the places visited.

CLIPPER ODYSSEY
Built: 1989 Refurbished: 1998

Category: Boutique Adventure
Rates; $$$$
Overall Rating: ⚓⚓⚓
Country of Registry: Bahamas
Former Names: *Oceanic Odyssey, Oceanic Grace*
Nationality of Crew: International
Cruising Area: 14-day cruises Australia, Asia and New Zealand

Ship Specifics

Tonnage	5,218	Elevators	1
Length	340 feet	Decks	5
Beam	50.5 feet	Children's Facilities	no
Stabilizers	yes	Fitness Center	limited
Passengers	128	Spa	no
Crew	52	Verandahs	no
Space Ratio	43	Casino	no
Crew/Passenger Ratio	1-2.1	Wheelchair Access	limited

Cabins: ↧↧↧↧ *Suites:* ↧↧↧↧ Staterooms are all outside and average a generous 186-square feet in size. They are furnished with either twin or queen-size beds and a sitting area with a sofa. Each cabin features a spacious bathroom with tub bath and shower, individually controlled air-conditioning, in-room music system, ample wardrobe space, three-sided mirrors, personal safe, minibar/refrigerator and television. The *Clipper Odyssey* is air-conditioned and heated throughout. There are three suites that are good size; there is one cabin designed to accommodate disabled travelers.

Public Space: ↧↧↧ There are several lounges and bars, but the guest favorite is the main lounge and bar on main deck. There's a well-stocked library and observation room and more outdoor space than one would expect on this size vessel. The no-smoking-inside policy adds to the pristine décor that is Oriental, a mix of Japanese and Indonesian. Most guests find it soothing.

Entertainment: ↧↧↧↧ People who sail these ships are more interested in local culture, exploration and a quiet atmosphere. The piano bar satisfies most. Expert lecturers are on board to reward inquiring minds. The cruise director takes care of planned shore excursions and individual requests.

Food and Dining: ↧↧↧↧ This is a high point in a Clipper experience. Like all Clipper ships, menus tend to relate to itineraries.

Overall: ↧↧↧↧ This is a really beautiful yacht-like exploration vessel. It was designed in the style of Sea Goddess ships and originally intended to entice luxury Japanese clients on board. The ship is beautifully furnished and has expansive deck space. Ambience is warm. *Clipper Odyssey* offers luxury adventure cruising at its best! Worth the price and then some.

HIGH MARKS:

Δ A decompression chamber for divers.

Δ Half-portions are available in the dining room for any entrée.

Δ Freshly baked chocolate chip cookies instead of high tea.

Δ There is a doctor on board.

NANTUCKET CLIPPER
Built: 1983
YORKTOWN CLIPPER
Built: 1988

Category: Boutique Adventure
ADR: $$$
Overall Rating: ⚓⚓⚓
Country of Registry: United States
Former Names: none
Nationality of Crew: American
Cruising Area: Caribbean and Inland U.S. rivers.
Length of Voyages: 7 to 28 nights

Ship Specifics: Nantucket Clipper & Yorktown Clipper

Tonnage	100	Elevators	0
Length*	207 feet	Decks	3
Beam	37 feet	Children's Facilities	no
Stabilizers	no	Fitness Center	no
Passengers*	128	Spa	no
Crew*	28	Verandahs	no
Space Ratio	10	Casino	no
Crew/Passenger Ratio	1-2.1	Wheelchair Access	no

__Yorktown Clipper__ – Length: 257 feet • Passengers: 138 • Crew: 32

Cabins: ⚓⚓ As expected in this type of vessel, cabins are small, but they are all outside. They hold a lot for their size: two beds, a dresser, desk, bathroom, and a closet. Top deck cabins are a little larger and are nicely furnished with blond woods and printed fabrics. Most cabins have large windows; others have portholes. Topside cabins open on to the promenade. Cabins have radios. There are no facilities for handicapped travelers.

Public Space: ⚓⚓ Each ship has a forward observation lounge and bar and a cozy social or entertainment center with a bar and library. There's an obstructed deck for walkers and joggers.

Entertainment: ⚓⚓⚓ Guest lecturers come aboard to discuss local history, culture and nature. Nightly entertainment is provided in local ports but reading and socializing are the most popular activities. Clipper pioneered golf cruises and it arranges for guests to play in almost every port with a golf course.

Food and Dining: ⚓⚓⚓⚓ One dining room with open sitting on each ship. Food is prepared by graduates of the prestigious Culinary Institute of America and is surprisingly good. Menus are limited but there's plenty to eat.

Junior Cruisers: ⚓ Very few children ever sail Clipper Cruise Lines.

Itineraries: ⚓⚓⚓⚓ Both vessels sail throughout the Americas on seven to 22-day itineraries that change frequently. They travel in spring through fall from Canada and New England, along the Eastern Seaboard to the Caribbean, south and Central America, the Panama Canal, the Pacific coast and some rivers of the Northwest and Alaska.

The U.S.-flag *Nantucket Clipper* sails various itineraries along the Canadian and U.S. Atlantic Coast from Prince Edward Island to Jacksonville, Florida, as well as along the St. Lawrence River and Seaway, into the Great Lakes, and, in the winter, the Caribbean.

Overall: ⚓⚓⚓ The *Nantucket Clipper* has a draft of eight feet, making it ideally suited for cruising shallow waterways. The spacious Observation Lounge serves as the main gathering place for informal briefings and social gatherings. The window-lined dining room accommodates all guests in leisurely single open sittings. Healthy regionally influenced American food is served, with every dish individually prepared to order. Outside, you'll find ample deck space and a promenade for viewing the passing scenery. An onboard a naturalist and historian will explain and recap each day's events in informal talks. The *Nantucket Clipper* has an all-American crew.

The *Yorktown Clipper* offers voyages along the U.S. and Canadian Pacific Coast, from Alaska's Inside Passage to the Pacific Northwest to San Francisco Bay; plus the Sea of Cortez; Costa Rica and Panama; the Lower Caribbean and Orinoco River; and the Grenadines and the Windward & Leeward Islands.

Ships are well appointed and designed for shallow water cruising. Shallow draft allows entry into ports not visited by large cruise ships and guests may go ashore even in the shallowest waters by inflatable rafts.

HIGH MARKS:

- Δ A chance to photograph rare birds on shore.
- Δ Clipper Chippers – freshly baked chocolate chip cookies served with tea.
- Δ No activity to remind you of a cruise ship.
- Δ A doctor on board each vessel.

WEAKEST LINKS:

- • No amenities in your cabin.
- • No beauty shop.
- • No swimming pool.

Costa Cruises

South Park Road, Suite 200 , Hollywood, FL 33021
(954) 266-5600 – www.costacruises.com

Costa Cruises has come a long way since patriarch Giacomo Costa started a modest olive oil import-export business back in 1860. After he died in 1916, his sons and heirs, Federico, Eugenio and Enrico, bought a freighter to transport their oil themselves and, by 1935, they owned eight freighters. After World War II, the Costas went into the cruising business with the *Anna "C"* – the family initial that still decorates the company's yellow and blue stacks – followed by three more in just four years.

It was 1958 before Costa constructed its first newbuild, the 20,400-ton *Federico "C,"* and soon the five-ship line was making Caribbean cruises from Miami. Another newbuild, *Eugenio "C,"* arrived in 1966; that same year brother Enrico had the *Enrico "C,"* the former French liner *Provence*, named for him. In the 1970s, Costa had eight of its own ships and six charters sailing in a fleet that cruised the Mediterranean, Caribbean and South America.

Some of Costa's old fleet is still sailing for other lines, including the *World Renaissance* for Royal Olympic and *Enrico "C"* for MSC Italian Cruises as the *Symphony*.

Beginning in 1985, the line was aggressively marketed in the U.S. by a series of entrepreneurs determined to give a new look to the family-owned company. The C's in the ship names were changed to spell out Costa and were run together into a single name, i.e., *CostaRiviera* (the former *Marconi*). The whiz kids in marketing departments created the theme "Cruising Italian Style," a sure-fire winner with Americans, but mystifying to Italians who love to cruise Costa. They issued bed sheet togas for guests to don for dinner on the last night of the cruise and they still do. One Costa cruise director went so far as to warn his guests not to ignore the toga dress code with the memorable phrase, "No sheet, no eat!

The family opened up to outside investment in 1989 and soon a pair of sleekly designed renovations of existing hulls by Italian architect Guide Canali debuted as *CostaMarina* and *CostaAllegra*. The *CostaClassica*, the first new-build for the company in 26 years, appeared in 1992, followed by the *CostaRomantica* in 1993.

Each new ship added to the fleet made its own emphatic design statement, but it was not always something American guests wanted to hear. A new team of marketing geniuses dropped the successful "Cruising Italian Style" theme for the *CostaClassica* to tout the ship as "EuroLuxe." While the new ship was indisputably dramatic and dazzling with its bare marble floors and white plaster statuary, guests expected more lush carpeting and cushy surroundings. With the change of several key American executives, "Cruising Italian Style" returned by the debut of the *CostaRomantica*. The *CostaVictoria* built in 1996 again pushed the envelope by increasing capacity to 2,000, continuing the clean, contemporary architecture while ignoring the biggest design change in the cruise industry, private verandahs.

By the mid 1990s, the company caught the eye of cruise giant Carnival Corporation, which had already attempted several mergers to get a foothold in the European market. After acquiring a 29.54 percent interest in 1996 in Airtours, the second largest tour operator in the United Kingdom, Carnival and Airtours together purchased Costa in 1997. In 2000, Carnival bought out Airtours' share and now owns 100 per cent of Costa.

The Costa fleet was further expanded in 2000 with the introduction of the *CostaAtlantica*, decorated by Carnival's resident designer, Joe Farcus. Instead of being a sister ship to the *CostaVictoria*, the new vessel was actually the first ship in the series that would continue with the *Carnival Spirit*. With its bright, bold, bigger-than-life design, the *CostaAtlantica* knocked the socks off European and American guests alike.

To keep up with the new demand for cruises by Europeans, Costa has most recently acquired the *CostaTropicale*, Carnival's former *Tropicale*, and the *CostaEuropa*, the former Holland America *Westerdam*. Three more new-builds are due to join the fleet soon, the *CostaMediterranea*, a sister to the *CostaAtlantica*, in the summer of 2003 and the two even larger vessels at an estimated 105,000 tons each, the *CostaFortuna* in 2003 and the *Costa Magica* in 2004.

The entire fleet cruises Europe in summer from Eastern and Western Mediterranean itineraries to the Baltics, Russia, the North Cape and the Canary Islands. In winter, the *CostaVictoria* and *CostaAtlantica* sail the Caribbean, while the rest of the fleet sails in South America, the Canary Islands and Eastern Mediterranean except for the *CostaMarina*, which has been relocated to operate exclusively for the German market.

Who Sails Costa Cruises? As the biggest cruise company in Europe, Costa counts Italians, French, Spanish, British, Swiss and other Europeans as its main guests, as well as some North and South Americans. Only about 20 per cent of the guest complement on Europe sailings is from the United States, and many of them are Italian-Americans from the northeast who never say "Basta!" to pasta ("Enough!"). Winter sailings, especially in the Caribbean, attract older guests, while summer cruises in Europe draw younger travelers, many of them families with children. Europeans like a family vacation where they can take grandparents and children along.

Lifestyle: "Cruising Italian Style" is a concept tailored for the American cruise market. In Europe, the ships use the euro as the official currency and soft-pedal the Roman Bacchanal toga nights in favor of Carnival in Venice masquerade parties. You can play bocce ball on board, learn the tarantella, make a Venetian mask for masquerade night and enter a pizza-dough tossing contest. Shipboard life follows the traditional cruise pattern, although Europeans pay less attention to things like dress codes and no-smoking areas than Americans do. On summer sailings, when shipboard announcements are usually made in five languages, an American hostess is on board to assist as a special liaison and hostess when there are more than a dozen English-speaking guests on board.. She also sometimes hosts a cocktail party so the English-speakers can meet each other.

Dining: The food aboard stretches from good to excellent, especially when guests pay attention to the menu and look to the waiter, dining captain or maitre d'hotel for guidance. Nothing flatters an Italian waiter more than asking his opinion on certain items from the menu – not "What's that?" but rather, "Which dressing do you recommend for the salad?" or "Could I have the pasta this way instead of that?" Meal hours are earlier in the Caribbean to accommodate American guests, usually 6:15 and 8:45, while in Europe, dining begin at 7 and 9. Breakfast and lunch are usually served on an open sitting basis, which means simply that the waiters rush you to the next two empty seats at a large table. Most of the Italian guests prefer room service breakfast and buffet lunches to allow more time at the swimming pool in the sunshine.

Service: Instead of all-male Italian stewards the line used to provide, service personnel aboard these days is Italian, both male and female, in the upper echelons of the hotel staff, with Filipino and Eastern European backups. Cabin stewards are usually very efficient making up the rooms but we've found bar service aboard sometimes very lackadaisical. The dining rooms, though, operate very smoothly.

Dress Code: Costa uses the term "gala" rather than formal for the dressiest night of a cruise, but does request tuxedos or dark suits for men on those evenings. Some of the slender young Italian men may wear an Armani suit with or without a tie but always manage to look dapper. Resort wear is the rule on all evenings except when gala is designated.

Tipping: Costa suggests $2.50 per person per day for the waiter/busboy team in the dining room, $1.50 per person per day for the cabin steward, and 50 cents per person per day for the maitre d'hotel/headwaiter team. Bar orders automatically have a 10 percent charge added on at the time of service.

Discount Policy: Andiamo Advance Purchase rates knock off a substantial percentage when booking and deposit are made at least 90 days ahead of sailing. On designated sailings in the Caribbean, seniors can ask for an additional $100 discount per stateroom and families of three or four occupying the same stateroom can also get a $100 per stateroom discount. Some early bookings also offer two free hotel nights after the cruise in Europe with continental breakfasts and a half-day city sightseeing tour included.

Shirley and Harry comment:

"Brace yourself for the five-language announcements. Safety drills seem longer than an hour episode of your favorite soap opera."

HIGH MARKS:

Δ Gala nights from Roman Bacchanal evenings, when toga is the requisite dress, to Venetian Masked Balls to Festa Italiana, a Carnival night with pizza dough tossing, Italian karaoke, bocce ball and tarantella dancing.

WEAKEST LINK:

• It's impossible to diet on a Costa ship. There are no waiters who'll aid and abet if you're dieting; "Mangia, mangia!" ("Eat, eat!") is a recurring refrain in the dining room.

The Fleet
COSTAALEGRA
Built 1969   Rebuilt: 1992

Category: Traditional
Overall Rating: ⚓⚓⚓   ***Rates:*** $$$
Country of Registry: Italy
Former names: *Alexandra*
Nationality of Crew: Italian officers, International service crew
Cruising Area: Mediterranean, Canary Islands Length of Voyages: 5, 7, 10 and 11 nights

Ship Specifics

Tonnage	28,500	Elevators	4
Length	616 feet	Decks	8
Beam	84 feet	Children's Facilities	yes
Stabilizers	yes	Fitness Center	yes
Passengers	820-1,070	Spa	yes
Crew	450	Verandahs	suites only
Space Ratio	37	Casino	yes
Crew/Passenger Ratio	1-2.4	Wheelchair Access	yes

Cabins: ⚓⚓⚓ ***Suites:*** ⚓⚓⚓ Cabins are very small but are in shipshape condition ranging from 146 to 156-square feet, with twin beds that can be made into a queen-sized bed, large portholes in the outside cabins, desk/dresser, combination safe, color TV with remote control, two nightstands with drawers, and a bathroom with circular round shower of clear, curved Plexiglas, a gray marble counter with basic, big mirror and good lighting. The lowest category cabins provide upper and lower berths rather than two lower beds, including six that are designated handicap accessible. Three Grand Suites measure 376-square feet each, with private verandahs, separate living room, wet bar, large portholes with forward view and mirrored walls; bedroom with wood-toned walls and queen-sized bed; separate pull-down bed for children; marble bathroom with toilet, bidet, Jacuzzi tub and separate stall shower; walk-in closet with dressing room.

Facilities for Disabled Travelers: ⚓⚓ *CostaAllegra* has eight inside cabins that are 146-square feet, not including bathrooms. Both cabin and shower doors are 31 inches with 2 inches sills. Bathrooms have roll-in showers, fold down seats and grab bars. Toilets are raised and have grab bars. There is no accessible public restroom.

Public Space: ⚓⚓⚓⚓ The stern is cropped off in a vertical wall of glass which looks strange from the outside but makes sense when you're sitting inside in the dining room or lounge looking out through all that glass. The play of light in daytime inside the public areas brings a sparkle to the whole ship. The Crystal Disco on the top deck has a painted glass floor under a clear glass dome, and the Murano Bar has its walls inset with panels of Venetian glass lit from behind. The key to the shimmering translucence is on the pool deck above, where a "canal" with a stream of water flows through. It doubles as a skylight above the bar and the light is enhanced by the sun glinting off the water.

Spa and Fitness: ⚓⚓⚓ The two-level Caracalla Spa is posh, alternating exercise machines and treatment rooms with wicker sofas and lush green plants. Facilities include a fitness area, sauna, treatment rooms and a Roman bath.

Entertainment: ⚓⚓ The sightlines in the show rooms are not very good on the *Allegra*, but the entertainment is not riveting anyhow. Shows rely more on visual than aural effects, with musical programs and concerts interspersed with variety artists like jugglers and acrobats. The Peter Grey Terhune-produced shows we've seen are pleasantly costumed and choreographed but hardly cutting edge. Still, the rows of straight, high-backed seats and the necessity of craning your neck around the many ceiling support posts in the room to see the stage will keep you awake.

Food and Dining: ⚓⚓⚓ The dining room's back wall is all glass with great views (and sometimes too much warmth and sunlight on a hot Caribbean or Mediterranean day). We like the special flourish the waiters bring to even the simplest tableside pasta or salad preparation. Food aboard is generally good, except for lackluster buffet breakfasts. We enjoyed such dishes as a respectable osso bucco with mushroom risotto, a light and delectable *manicotti alla Sorrentino* and a Boston lettuce and watercress salad with a lemon juice and olive oil dressing. But some touches are more Miami than Milano, with those cute deck gelati carts dishing out commercial American ice cream from half-gallon cartons and the pizza tastes more Pillsbury than Pisa.

Service: ⚓⚓⚓ There's a caring and attentive service staff aboard if guests will take the time to acknowledge them as individuals.

Junior Cruisers: ⚓⚓ A small children's center is located on the top deck, but organized activities generally overflow into the Crystal Club Disco where there's more space. Cruises during European school vacations, including Christmas and Easter, draw lots of families with lots and lots of bambini.

Itineraries: ⚓⚓⚓ *CostaAllegra* offers 11-night sailings to Spain/ Portugal/Morocco and to the Canary Islands; 10-night sailings in the Greek Isles; and five-night roundtrip cruises out of Genoa.

Overall: ⚓⚓⚓ Because of the ship's relatively small size, first-time cruisers can easily navigate their way around. Younger guests and young families find a good fit with the spa facilities, lively disco that goes until 4 a.m., and children's program with a dedicated playroom space. Older cruisers and more demanding travelers might wish more formality in the décor and service.

HIGH MARKS:

Δ A chapel where Catholic mass is celebrated daily.

WEAKEST LINK:

- The lack of privacy in cabin conversations. The walls are so thin, we suggest playing your radio to mask your conversation. Of course, with so many languages spoken on board, your neighbors might not understand anything you're saying anyhow.
- Smokers who ignore the "no smoking" signs.

COSTAATLANTICA
Built: 2000

Category: Resort XL
Overall Rating: ⚓⚓⚓⚓
Rates: $$ to $$$
Country of Registry: Italy
Former names: None
Nationality of Crew: Italian officers, international crew
Cruising Area: Mediterranean, Northern Europe, Canary Islands, and Caribbean
Length of Voyages: 5, 7, 11 and 16 nights

Ship Specifics

Tonnage	84,000	Elevators	12
Length	960 feet	Decks	11
Beam	106 feet	Children's Facilities	yes
Stabilizers	yes	Fitness Center	yes
Passengers	2,112-2,680	Spa	yes
Crew	900	Verandahs	yes
Space Ratio	39.7	Casino	yes
Crew/Passenger Ratio	1-2.5	Wheelchair Access	yes

Cabins: ⚓⚓⚓⚓ *Suites:* ⚓⚓⚓⚓ From a minimum measurement of 160-square feet for a handsomely decorated inside cabin with a queen-sized or two lower beds to outside verandah cabins measuring 210-square feet and 58 suites with verandahs s that are up to 360-square feet, *CostaAtlantica's* cabins are quite comfortable for two. Some 678 cabins aboard offer private balconies and another 68 have French balconies, floor-to-ceiling glass doors that open to allow looking out at the view. Bathrooms feature one-piece molded counter and lavatory with shower and tile floor; Jacuzzi bathtubs and bidets are only in suites. Chairs (in insides) or sofa (in outsides) and a coffee table furnish the sitting area in all the cabins, and storage space is generous. Grand suites provide a dining table with chairs, full sofa, marble and mosaic tile bathroom, foyer and dressing room. Those on the aft end of the vessel on decks 4, 6, 7 and 8 provide a wraparound verandah with views on two sides.

Facilities for Disabled Travelers: ⚓⚓⚓⚓ *CostaAtlantica* has eight accessible cabins. Half are outside and cabin doors measure 38 inches. Cabins alone measure between 175 and 190-square feet. Bathroom doors are 33.5 inches wide. There is a roll-in shower with hand held showerhead and seat. There is a 5 inches threshold to get into the bathroom. There are accessible public restrooms and most public rooms are accessible.

Public Space: ⚓⚓⚓⚓ This big splashy ship is so overpowering you hardly know where to look first: at the 10-deck atrium with its glass ceiling and glass elevators; at the green glass staircase created by Murano artist Luciano Vistosi that connects the two decks of Club Atlantica; at the pair of swimming pools named Fred and Ginger; or, at the replica of the 18th century Caffe Florian in Venice. We're partial to the Paparazzi and Via Veneto Lounges, where black-and-white candid photos of film stars of the 1960s by press photographer Tazio Secciarole are on display. A superlative art collection with contemporary works from Carlo Mattioli, Paul Pennisi, Gianmaria Potenza and Maurizio Russo is displayed throughout the ship. One of the more bizarre areas is Dante's Disco, its upper level behind the lobby and the lower level aft on the lowest guest deck, with red stained glass ceilings, a glass floor lit from below and red glass demons under bell jars.

Spa and Fitness: ⚓⚓⚓⚓ The two-level Olympia Gym, aerobics room, Greco-Roman Ischia Spa and Venus beauty salon provide every facility you can imagine to stay in shape, and you have the option of taking it back home with a Techno personalized fitness program ($75) with memory card you can use again on shore in any Techno facility.

Entertainment: ⚓⚓⚓ The Teatro Caruso is a three-level showroom with high-backed red plush theater seats in the balcony, black plush seats and banquettes on the main level, Murano glass chandeliers and a fairly steep rake for the rows that seat up to 1,167 patrons at one time (although it's rarely filled at showtime). Production shows are attuned more to European tastes and, although well performed, lack dramatic and musical muscle. Occasional Italian karaoke nights are scheduled for anyone so inclined.

Food and Dining: ⚓⚓⚓⚓ The two-level Tiziano Restaurant has plenty of tables for two or four, and can turn the room into a different mood with backdrops that depict Costa ships or scenery from Europe or the Caribbean. A roaming trio serenades and frescos decorate the upper level. Menus provide five main dish choices plus a pasta specialty, three always-available alternatives (steak, salmon and tagliatelle Alfredo), vegetarian menus and a spa menu that spells out calorie, fat and carbohydrate counts. The expansive Botticelli Buffet has its own pizzeria inside but the real temptation lies in the two-level Club Atlantica ($15 surcharge) with candlelight dinners from menus by renowned Italian chef Gualtiero Marchesi.

Service: ⚓⚓⚓ The crew is cheerful, efficient and friendly in general, but sometimes seem hassled on a busy afternoon at the deck bars.

Junior Cruisers: ⚓⚓⚓ The Pinocchio children's area is not easy to find. It is located on deck 5 forward, which is otherwise dedicated entirely to cabins, but facilities and staff are satisfactory. In the Caribbean, the American kids and the European kids (mostly Italian and French) are about equal in number. Ages three to 12 are invited, but children still wearing diapers must have a parent remain with them during their stay.

Itineraries: ⚓⚓⚓⚓ *CostaAtlantica* sails the Caribbean in winter and makes seven-day roundtrips from Venice in summer, with two repositioning transatlantic spring and fall crossings.

Overall: ⚓⚓⚓⚓ This ship is a knockout, with something new to marvel over on every deck. The Caffe Florian, reproduced exactly from the original in Venice, is far more elegant than some of the guests who occupy it. If you have an aversion to vivid shades of red and orange, you might prefer to book the more sedate *CostaVictoria*. The giant putty (carved cherubs) hanging onto the wooden pillars in the dining room and the Virtual World game arcade that overshadows the wedding chapel next door are sort of weird.

Shirley and Harry Comment:

"Designer Joe Farcus put the icing on the cake with the CostaAtlantica, an almost over-the-top paean to his view of Italy."

HIGH MARKS:
- Δ The only Versace boutique we've seen at sea graces the pretty row of Via della Spiga shops.
- Δ Traveling hypochondriacs will appreciate the onboard pharmacies, but you'll need to bring along your own prescriptions.

WEAKEST LINK:
- • No fresh flowers and foliage in the Winter Garden.

COSTACLASSICA
Built: 1991

COSTAROMATICA
Built 1993

Category: Resort Mid-Size
Overall Rating: ⚓⚓⚓+
Rates: $$$
Country of Registry: Italy
Former names: None
Nationality of Crew: Italian officers, international crew
Cruising Area: Caribbean in winter, Europe in summer
Length of Voyages: 5, 7 and 11 nights

Ship Specifics

Tonnage	54,000	Elevators	8
Length	723.5	Decks	8
Beam	101 feet	Children's Facilities	yes
Stabilizers	no	Fitness Center	no
Passengers	1,300-1,782	Spa	yes
Crew	650	Verandahs	suites only
Space Ratio	41.53	Casino	yes
Crew/Passenger Ratio	1-2.2	Wheelchair Access	yes

Cabins: ⚓⚓⚓ *Suites:* ⚓⚓⚓⚓ The standard insides measure 175 square feet and the outsides 200. The lowest-priced categories provide upper and lower berths instead of two lower beds but most cabins aboard have twins that convert to queen-sized. Bathrooms are marble with built-in hair dryers, showers and full-length mirrors. Hanging and storage space is less ample on the *Classica* than the *Romantica*. Oversized portholes instead of windows add a stylish look but let in less light. Burled briarwood furniture on the *Romantica* is especially decorative. The *Classica* has 10 spacious suites, each with private verandahs, separate living room, bedroom with queen-sized bed, marble bathroom with Jacuzzi tub and separate stall shower, and measure 580-square feet.

On the *Romantica*, the spa was moved so that the top deck forward area is used for mini-suites and suites, making a total of 16 suites (580-square feet) and 18 smaller but elegant mini-suites (340-square feet). Butler service, mini-bar, terrycloth robes and reclining deck chairs on the verandahs lend extra luxury. Floor-to-ceiling glass windows on the *Romantica's* deck 11 forward suites are drop-dead dramatic.

Facilities for the Disabled: ⚓⚓ *CostaRomantica* and *Classica* each have eight accessible cabins. Both ships have four outside cabins, and four inside cabins. All are 175-square feet, not including bathrooms. Cabin doors are 31 inches wide and have a 2 inch sill. Bathroom doors are 31 inches wide when open. There are roll in showers with hand held showerheads and fold down seats. The toilets are raised and have grab bars. There are no accessible public restrooms.

Public Space: ⚓⚓⚓ We can't warm up to the bare marble floors in the dining room and on the stairwells. They're so noisy that the lifeboat drill sounds like changing classes at Woodrow Wilson Junior High. The elegance that marble, tile, brass, polished wood, fountains and sculptures lend also adds a hard surface and cold ambiance. This said, we do admire the design of the public areas, the shops with their oversize porthole display windows, and stunning deck areas with cocoon chairs lined with blue and white striped cushions. The buffet restaurants on both ships resemble a basic cafeteria, however, and the show lounges with their high-backed wooden stalls rising in tiers look like a combination of a Roman amphitheater and London's Old Bailey.

Spa and Fitness: ⚓⚓⚓ Located forward on the *Classica* and amid-ships on the *Romantica*, the 6,500-foot Caracalla Spa has an exercise room, sauna, steam rooms and whirlpools, plus spa treatments such as seaweed body wraps, facials and herbal therapy massages. A walking and fitness track is located on the topmost deck.

Entertainment: ⚓⚓⚓ In Europe where five language announcements predominate, shows are less verbal and less production-oriented, with perhaps a small company of opera singers brought aboard in port or variety performers such as jugglers, magicians or acrobats. The production shows miss the cutting edge style that characterizes the entertainment aboard big American-based ships.

Food and Dining: ⚓⚓⚓ Meals are served at two sittings, with dinner at 6:15 and 8:30 in the Caribbean, 7 and 9 in Europe. Breakfasts are always open sitting, meaning you're shoe horned into the next two empty chairs at a large table, and lunch times are assigned only on days at sea as a rule. The dining rooms change magically in the evenings with the addition of painted scenic backgrounds of ancient Pompeian villas or Renaissance towns, created by a scenic designer for the La Scala Opera House in Milan. There are a lot of tables for two on these ships. The pasta is always good, and the vegetarian dishes are quite tasty. We were not thrilled by the buffet display, but the outdoor café aft on deck 10 is a charming spot to dawdle over coffee or a glass of wine.

Service: ⚓⚓⚓ While your charming waiter may have just as likely come from Riga or Rijeka as Roma, he is usually eager to please but may need some more language classes in English.

Junior Cruisers: ⚓⚓⚓ There is a designated youth center next to the suites on deck 10, but hardly adequate to contain the numbers of exuberant children aboard in summer months.

Itineraries: ⚓⚓⚓⚓ The *Classica* cruises the Greek Isles on 7- and 11-night sailings in summer, while the *Romantica* sails in Russia, the Baltics and Norway in summer, with spring and fall Atlantic repositioning between Genoa and Copenhagen and fall cruises in Spain and Portugal. In winter the *Classica* will be in South America while the *Romantica* will be in the Caribbean but will be marketed strictly for Europeans.

Overall: ⚓⚓⚓+ Improved textured ceilings have managed to lessen the sound from the marble dining room floors and the crew seems to drop fewer dishes than they did at first. These ships are still being marketed more heavily to Europeans than Americans; they're not posted to the Caribbean in winter.

HIGH MARKS:

△ An invitation to spend the day on deck, with wicker cocoon chairs, sidewalk café tables and chairs, splashing fountains and cushioned lounge chairs.

WEAKEST LINK:

- Small cabins without much closet space
- No alternative dining room

Marcia Levin Comments:

"The main restaurant is one of the noisiest at sea."

COSTAEUROPA

Built: 1986   Refurbished: 1989, 2002

Category: Traditional
Overall Rating: ⚓⚓⚓
Rates: $$$$
Country of Registry: Italy
Former names: Homeric, Westerdam
Nationality of Crew: Italian officers, international crew
Cruising Area: Northern Europe, Greek Islands, and Canary Islands
Length of Voyages: 9 to 14 nights

Tonnage	53,872	Elevators		7
Length	798	Decks		9
Beam	95 feet	Children's Facilities		yes
Stabilizers	no	Fitness Center		yes
Passengers	1,494	Spa		yes
Crew	615	Verandahs		no
Space Ratio	36	Casino		yes
Crew/Passenger Ratio	1-2.4	Wheelchair Access		yes

Ship Specifics

Cabins: ⚓⚓⚓ *Suites:* ⚓⚓⚓ The big disappointment for people accustomed to the big new ships is the lack of private verandahs, but the cabins themselves are spacious and comfortable with even minimum insides measuring almost 200-square feet. In the lowest cabin categories, which offer showers but not tubs in the bathrooms, the two lower beds cannot be put together into one queen-sized, but it can be done in some insides on deck 7 and upper category outsides. Five suites and 18 mini-suites, as well as many upper-end cabins, do provide commodious bathtubs with showers. Suites also offer a double sofa bed to sleep two additional guests, while mini-suites have a single sofa bed in the living area for an additional sleeping space.

Facilities for Disabled Travelers: ⚓⚓⚓ The *CostaEuropa* has four accessible cabins that range from 157 to 280-square feet. There are two inside cabins and two outside cabins. Cabin doors are 31.5 inches with a one inch sill at the entrance, which can be ramped if required. The bathroom doors are 34 inches wide with no sills. They have roll-in showers with fold down seats, hand held showers and grab bars. The toilets are 18 inches high with grab bars and the sinks are 31 inches high. All the public areas and decks are accessible. There are accessible public restrooms on the restaurant deck.

Public Space: ⚓⚓⚓⚓ What was so wonderful about the ship when Holland America operated it as the *Westerdam* were the two spacious Lido buffet restaurants that took full advantage of HAL's expansive buffets. On the *Europa*, the Sirens Grill and the larger Andromeda Restaurant serve buffet breakfast and lunch and dinner occasionally. The Solarium atop the ship with its charming pool and sliding glass dome roof is appealing year-round in any weather. There's a good sense of comfort throughout, making this ship ideal for longer itineraries and cooler-weather destinations.

Spa and Fitness: ⚓⚓⚓ The Nereidi spa and fitness center is functional if not glamorous, but there's plenty of massage and sauna space.

Entertainment: ⚓⚓⚓ The show lounge covers two decks, but the balcony area sightlines are not very good, meaning guests trying to see the show below will probably need to stand. Big, cushy theater-style seats on the main level provide a much better area to sit.

Food and Dining: ⚓⚓⚓⚓ The lower-deck Orion restaurant was designed and created at a time when ship dining rooms were located low on the vessel and amidships for optimum comfort in rough seas. Tables are close together and the ceiling design lends to accent the noise level. The two buffet restaurants are the Andromeda Restaurant and the smaller Sirens Grill on the upper decks. These are open sometimes for dinner but there is no designated alternative restaurant on board.

Service: ⚓⚓⚓ Expect the usual Costa service: Italian and other European and Filipino cabin and dining room stewards. Since the line has expanded so rapidly, there may be a problem with English among some of the newer recruits, many of whom come from Eastern Europe.

Junior Cruisers: ⚓⚓⚓ A small Kids Club located next to the beauty salon and across from the casino provides the line's usual child care. A Parents Night Out program allows adults to park the kids free for two nights a week; the kids get pizza or a children's buffet while the parents get a romantic dinner alone.

Itineraries: ⚓⚓⚓⚓ Costa is utilizing the *Europa* on longer-than-usual itineraries year-round, with sailings in the Baltic, Russia and Norwegian fjords in summer, including one 14-night North Cape sailing, with seasonal repositioning sailings between Genoa and Canary Islands sailings in winter.

Overall: ⚓⚓⚓ This ship fits well into the Costa fleet because the larger-than-average cabins with sofa beds and pull-down berths accommodate larger families. The drawback is the limited space provided for children, since the weather in some of the northern destinations is not always conducive to deck activity. On the other hand, the dome-covered Sirens deck and pool provides an all-weather getaway.

HIGH MARKS:

Δ The extra dining room space on the upper deck allows buffet dining on some evenings, but is not considered a designated alternative restaurant.

WEAKEST LINK:

• No private verandahs.

COSTATROPICALE
Built: 1982   Refurbished: 1998, 2001

Category: Traditional
Overall Rating ⚓⚓⚓⚓
Rates: $$$
Country of Registry: Italy
Former names: Tropicale
Nationality of Crew: Italian officers, international crew
Cruising Area: Mediterranean, Spain, South America
Length of Voyages: 5, 7, 8 and 9 nights

Ship Specifics

Tonnage	36,674	Elevators	8
Length	672	Decks	10
Beam	85 feet	Children's Facilities	yes
Stabilizers	no	Fitness Center	yes
Passengers	1,022	Spa	yes
Crew	550	Verandahs	suites only
Space Ratio	36	Casino	yes
Crew/Passenger Ratio	1-2	Wheelchair Access	yes

Cabins: ⚓⚓⚓ *Suites:* ⚓⚓⚓ Twelve suites with private verandahs, 312 outside cabins measuring around 185-square feet each and 187 slightly smaller inside cabins mean there's plenty of space inside and, in most, two lower beds convert to a queen-sized. Hair dryers and safes are provided in each. Many cabins sleep four. Bathrooms provide shower only in standard cabins, but all the bathroom furnishings appear to be brand-new. The suites have Jacuzzi tubs, shower ssitting areas and private verandahs, but in some the view is partially obstructed by hanging lifeboats.

Facilities for Disabled Travelers: Ship has 11 wheelchair accessible cabins in a few categories, including insides. Cabin doors are 31.5 inches with a one inch sill at the entrance, which can be ramped if required. The bathroom doors are 33 inches wide with no sills. Bathrooms have roll-in showers with fold down seats, hand held showers and grab bars. Most public rooms are wheelchair accessible.

Public Space: ⚓⚓⚓⚓ The tremendous improvement of the most recent remodeling has turned the formerly weary *Tropicale* from Carnival into the sophisticated, elegant *Costa Tropicale* by what can only be magic. We marveled at every public area, often not recognizing at first what this or that space used to be. The old Exta-Z disco has been converted into the Bahia Club and Restaurant, a Brazilian-accented alternative restaurant, while a pretty little library has been tucked into the lower level end of the old Islands in the Sun Lounge.

Spa and Fitness: ⚓⚓⚓⚓ A major upgrading of the gym with new equipment-plus a full roster of beauty and spa services has improved the quality without expanding the size of the fitness center.

Entertainment: ⚓⚓⚓ While the show lounge has been brightened up with new furnishings, the support posts around the room and the slight rake mean sightlines are still marginal. The Duke Piano Bar is reminiscent of Joe Farcus' piano bars that are real pianos, except in this case the keys are spread across the ceiling. A glamorous Casablanca Lounge with movie posters from the popular film replaces the old casino bar, and the original casino has been retained with new furnishings. A new production show called "Tropicalia" was created for the ship by Valerio Festi.

Food and Dining: ⚓⚓⚓⚓ The Bahia Club and Restaurant is a bright, appealing room with a dance floor in the center for dancing between courses in this alternative Brazilian restaurant with surcharge. The main dining room is handsomely decorated but retains mostly big tables for six and eight with assigned seating. In South America, the dining hours are 7:30 and 9:30 p.m. We thought the food aboard was delicious.

Service: ⚓⚓⚓⚓ We found the dining room service especially good and the staff friendly across the board. American guests may want to seek out top Italian management or the Filipino service personnel for the best English speakers; some of the new eastern European staff were polite and fluent in Italian, but unskilled in English.

Junior Cruisers: ⚓⚓⚓ A children's playroom and wading pool are located aft on deck 7; the ship employs the full Costa Kids Club program.

Itineraries: ⚓⚓⚓⚓ *Costa Tropicale* is intended primarily for European travelers in the Mediterranean, but the interesting itineraries, especially the winter Brazilian program in 2003 that visits the chic little island of Buzios should attract some Americans as well.

Overall: ⚓⚓⚓⚓ Despite this ship's vintage, the virtual makeover has turned it into an appealing, stylish vessel that suddenly seems warm and intimate compared to some of the gigantic new ships. A lot of Italian honeymooners were aboard during our visit and seemed to be having a wonderful time.

INSIDER TIP

I don't know whether you have to show proof, whatever that would be, that you are honeymooning in order to take advantage of Honeymoon Drink packages for $59.80. Package includes two tropical drinks in souvenir glasses, a bottle of sparkling wine in the cabin and up to 16 drinks from the bar list. A boys and girls card for $39.10 buys 20 nonalcoholic drinks from sodas to milk shakes and slurpees.

WEAKEST LINK:

- No windows in the dining room.

CostaVictoria

Built: 1996

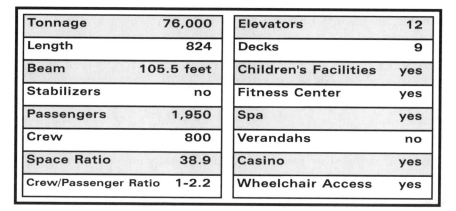

Category: Resort XL
Overall Rating: ⚓⚓⚓⚓
Rates: $$$
Country of Registry: Italy
Former names: None
Nationality of Crew: Italian officers, international crew
Cruising Area: Caribbean, Mediterranean, transatlantic
Length of Voyages: 5, 7 and 16 nights

Ship Specifics

Tonnage	76,000	Elevators	12
Length	824	Decks	9
Beam	105.5 feet	Children's Facilities	yes
Stabilizers	no	Fitness Center	yes
Passengers	1,950	Spa	yes
Crew	800	Verandahs	no
Space Ratio	38.9	Casino	yes
Crew/Passenger Ratio	1-2.2	Wheelchair Access	yes

Cabins: ⚓⚓⚓ *Suites:* ⚓⚓⚓ Standard outside cabins, depending on the deck, have either an outsized porthole or a large window, and twin beds that can be made into queen-sized beds. There is plenty of hanging and drawer space for garments, even in the smallest inside cabins, which measure 150-square feet. Outside cabins are also 150-square feet, and mini-suites measure 301-square feet. On the down side, none of the cabins or suites has a private verandah. The five suites, each 430-square feet, contain sitting and dining areas, whirlpool bath, separate shower, refrigerator, and pull-down beds for additional family members. They are located forward, just below the wheelhouse, for a captain's-eye view. Furnishings are quite attractive and the housekeeping was excellent when we were aboard.

Facilities for Disabled Travelers: ⚓⚓ The *Victoria* has six accessible cabins that measure 175-square feet. The bathroom is not included in the measurement. All are inside cabins. Doors are 31 inches wide and there is a two inch sill. Bathrooms have roll-in showers, fold down seat, and grab bars. There are no accessible public bathrooms. Most public rooms, however, are accessible.

Public Space: ⚓⚓⚓⚓ The Concorde Plaza, designed by Sweden's noted architect Robert Tilberg, is hands down the most elegant nightclub at sea. The forward, glass-walled lounge fills four aft deck areas in cool contemporary style with a generous, even prodigal, use of space. A waterfall cascades against the back wall, an all-glass elevator offers a dramatic alternative to the curving stairways that connect the upper areas, and a sleek bar is set against a glass window wall. The Capriccio Bar's terrazzo walls are covered in Chagall-like murals in celery green, sienna and gold, colors that are harmoniously repeated throughout the ship.

Spa and Fitness: ⚓⚓⚓ The Pompei Spa and Fitness Center has a handsome indoor pool surrounded by wicker chairs, sauna, Turkish bath, thalassotherapy and hydrotherapy, as well as a full selection of beauty and massage treatments.

Entertainment: ⚓⚓⚓ The Festival Show Lounge seats 621 in curved main floor and balcony rows of comfortable armchairs. Shows with a multimedia format and cheery humor mark an improvement over the feather-clad dancing girls that used to molt all over the stage during Costa musicals.

Food and Dining: ⚓⚓⚓ The food can be good to excellent when guests take the time to study the menus and confer with waiters. The best results come from ordering pastas, Italian dishes, soups, breadsticks, bruschetta and salads. Fish is expertly and delicately prepared, but pastries and desserts are sometimes heavy-handed. The Sinfonia and Fantasia restaurants are prettily decorated with wall murals and large glass windows, and the open air Terrazza Café shaded with a white sailcloth roof offers a sunny, if sometimes breezy, spot to breakfast. The top deck Ristorante Magnifico by Zeffiironi ($15 surcharge), overseen by chef Paolo Belloni, emulates Genoa's famous restaurant founded in 1939. In the daytime it doubles as the Tavernetta Lounge.

Service: ⚓⚓⚓ Graceful and friendly, the Italians and their assistants from other countries manage to display la bella figura in the age-old fashion.

Junior Cruisers: ⚓⚓⚓ The Peter Pan Children's Room on deck 6 and a teen club on deck 12 with video games, Internet connections and disco dance floor entertain both age groups while keeping them separated.

Childcare is offered during shore excursions and late at night (between 11:30 p.m. and 1:30 a.m.) by advance arrangement.

While the line attempts to control overactive children, we still noted this announcement to parents in a daily activity sheet: "Please supervise your children. Make sure they do not use the elevators alone if they are under 12 years of age, they should not play in the Casino, they should not run around in the corridors and lounges in the afternoon when other guests could be resting, children should not use the Jacuzzis or dive into the swimming pool, the Tennis Court is not to be used by children under 14 years of age, make sure that they do not run and shout on the dance floors." That, alas, says it all.

Itineraries: ⚓⚓⚓⚓ *CostaVictoria* cruises the Canary Islands and/or the Caribbean in winter, the Mediterranean in summer.

Overall: ⚓⚓⚓ This is a classic, handsome vessel with good to excellent food and service, but is much less a design tour de force than the *CostaAtlantica*. Still, in the long run, the understated elegance of the *Victoria* may outlast the bright, gee-whiz looks of the *Atlantica*. The two ships, by the way, are not sisters. The sister ship of the *CostaVictoria* would have been the *CostaOlympia*, but the unfinished hull was sold by Bremer Vulkan, the German shipyard that went into bankruptcy before the *Olympia* could be built. So the hull was purchased by Norwegian Cruise Line to become the *Norwegian Sky*; NCL added private verandahs to many of the cabins.

HIGH MARKS:

Δ "Parents Night Out" lets parents leave their children at a supervised buffet or pizza party so they can enjoy a quiet dinner alone; hours are 5 to 11 p.m., and there is no charge.

Δ An onboard pharmacy fills prescriptions and also stocks some basic over-the-counter medications.

WEAKEST LINK:

• No cabins with private verandahs.

Crystal Cruises

2049 Century Park East, Suite 1400, Los Angeles, CA 90067
(310) 785-9300 – www.crystalcruises.com

California-based Crystal Cruises was founded in 1988 for the purpose of operating luxury ships. The line is a subsidiary of the Japanese-based NYK Line (Nippon Yusen Kaisha) but operations, marketing and sales personnel are American on shore and European on board ship. Even before its inception, NYK hired experienced American shipping personnel to spearhead the company. The first ship in the fleet was the 49,000-ton *Crystal Harmony* in mid-1990, which was greeted with instant applause by sophisticated and experienced cruisers.

Its second vessel, *Crystal Symphony*, completed in 1995, is a virtual twin in some respects, but there are slight changes in configuration of cabins which makes them more comfortable and in public space which improves passenger flow. Word-of-mouth and clever advertising to luxury-minded travelers turned the company into a hot product. So hot, that Crystal walks away with all of the prestigious awards in the luxury cruise category. In 2002, the company took top awards not only for cruises, but also for on board services – the spa, entertainment, food and amenities. A leading posh magazine rated Crystal in the same category as luxury resorts.

In July 2003, the line will welcome its newest ship, the 68,000-ton, 1,080-guest *Crystal Serenity*, featuring a higher space-per-guest ratio than her sister ships. Plans include expanded areas for spa services and other athletic, cultural and intellectual pursuits. Within a range of luxury accommodations, the line will increase the number of penthouses and enlarge its deluxe staterooms with verandahs. Approximately 85 percent of all outside staterooms and suites will offer private verandahs.

Crystal's success is unusual in that some of the amenities are contrary to what luxury passengers have come to expect. Instead of the traditional single sitting on luxury ships, Crystal has two sittings in the dining room, but added two optional specialty restaurants and a self-serve restaurant to offer guests more dining options. Those optional restaurants started by Crystal have become a trend on most major cruise lines, luxury to resort, large and small.

Who Sails Crystal Cruises? Travelers accustomed to luxury or who want a taste of the good life; sophisticated urban guests who are willing to pay for the service, food, and ambiance that goes with real luxury. Most of the guests are American couples in the over 55 age range, but the vessels are attracting an increasing number of younger honeymooners and professionals who have made it – empty nesters who say, "Now, it's my turn."

Lifestyle: Contemporary luxury at its best without pomp and ceremony. Vessels are spacious and guest-friendly, but not familiar. There's no cattle call for special events. Guests are left to do their own thing at a leisurely pace without frenzy.

Dress Code: Crystal guests like to change from casual daytime wear to dressy evening attire. Per week, there are two to three formal evenings and most men are in tuxedos, ladies in very dressy long or shorts outfits. Two or three informal evenings when men wear jackets with ties and casual doesn't mean jeans and tee shirts. "Dressy casual" is more accurate. Crystal guests are heavy packers and bring their sequins and jewels on board.

Shirley and Harry Comment:
"People who don't like to dress up in the evening should choose another cruise line."

Dining: There is a single dining room and two sittings on each ship. Tables are a good distance from each other and the set up is flexible. Table size can be changed from large to small, depending on requests made prior to sailing. Food is excellent with a wide choice of menus. The likes of caviar and lobster are considered normal fare and tableside cooking, special orders and special dietary requests are handled in a routine fashion. There are two optional dining rooms on each ship. Italian on both; Chinese on *Symphony*, Japanese on *Harmony*. Fresh vegetables, fish and fruits are served throughout even lengthy voyages. This is made possible by a "Fine Tuned Cooling System' developed by NYK. It is a series of huge vaults capable of storing perishables at carefully predetermined temperatures for more than two weeks. In addition to perishable foods, the storage bins carry a supply of fresh flowers that are used generously throughout the vessels.

Service: Throughout both vessels, service in all dining rooms and in cabins is impeccable, courteous, pleasant and helpful. Also correct and proper. Special services include laundry and valet, a concierge to book or reconfirm tickets, make reservations and to be generally helpful. A recent survey which awarded "the best" to Crystal wrote, "Hand-making 100,000 chocolate truffles annually, serving 80 pounds of caviar per voyage, fluffing 3,920 feather pillows twice daily, shining 21,600 pairs of shoes a year, polishing more than 400 Riedel Bordeaux wine glasses each day and 3,600 feet of brass handrails three times every day and night are just a few of the details distinguishing the World's Best Service aboard Crystal Cruises."

Tipping Policy: Waiters and room stewards expect to receive $4 per day per person and assistant waiter, 2.50. In penthouses, $4 per day to the butler. Tip the Maitre d' at your own discretion and 15 percent is automatically added to bar and wine tabs. All gratuities may be added to your ship account and charged to a credit card.

Past Passenger Perks: Captain's Club is offered after the first Celebrity sailing. It's the only past passenger club that charges a fee ($35 per family). Benefits include promotional packages, special fares on specified sailings, cabin upgrades in some cases and in general follows the rule - the more you sail with Celebrity, the more perks. Members receive priority embarkation, pre-sailing optional restaurant reservations, and an invitation to a private party. Other perks: sail five or more cruises and you earn an upgrade; sail six or more times and you also receive priority status for on board reservations.

Discount Policy: Early booking discounts normally allow up to 25 percent off brochure rates, depending on the sailing. From time-to-time, Crystal offers other special rates. The lowest in 2002, which cannot be considered a "normal" year, was a savings of 60 percent on a 12-night Mediterranean itinerary. That put rates down below Premium and into the $$$$ and $$$ category. The discount, however, came with a caveat. It did not apply to Penthouse Deck. That's the location of all of the suites.

The Fleet

CRYSTAL HARMONY**
    Built: 1990 Refurbished: 2000, September 2002

CRYSTAL SYMPHONY
    Built: 1995 Refurbished: 2001

Category: Luxury
Rates: $$$$ to $$$$$
Overall Rating: ⚓⚓⚓⚓⚓++
Country of Registry: Bahamas
Former Names: none
Nationality of Crew: Norwegian/Japanese officers; European hotel & dining staff

Cruising Area: Worldwide

Length of Voyages: 7 to 104-night World Cruises

Ship Specifics

Tonnage*	49,400	Elevators	8
Length	791	Decks	8
Beam	99 feet	Children's Facilities	yes
Stabilizers	yes	Fitness Center	yes
Passengers	960	Spa	yes
Crew	545	Verandahs	yes
Space Ratio	52	Casino	yes
Crew/Passenger Ratio	1-1.76	Wheelchair Access	yes

__Symphony__ – Tonnage: 51,004

Cabins: ⚓⚓⚓ **Suites:** ⚓⚓⚓⚓ *Crystal Harmony* cabins were refurbished and reconfigured in late 1997 and again in 2000. Colors were lightened and brightened. Average outside staterooms are 215-square feet and have large picture windows, queen-size or twin beds, a sitting area, televisions, VCR, full tub and shower combination, refrigerator, personal safe. Minimum outsides have portholes instead of windows and are excellent buys. Three top decks have private verandahs, but some are partially obstructed on deck eight. There are a few inside cabins with similar amenities, but measure 183-square feet which is larger than some outsides on similarly priced vessels.

Crystal Symphony cabins are similar with some exceptions. Configuration is better and makes them seem much larger. Another big difference is that all cabins are outside and all have picture windows. About 57 percent have private verandahs and measure out to 246-square feet. Staterooms without balconies are about 202-square feet. Penthouse Deck is where you'll want to be if you can afford it on either ship. It pays to splurge! On each ship, six white-gloved butlers tend to guests in 64 suites which range from 367-square feet for a "normal" suite to Penthouse Suites at 491-square feet and two Crystal Penthouses with super spacious measurements of 982-square feet. Penthouse guests, in addition to normal amenities, enjoy a complimentary stocked bar, larger personal safes, specially prepared delivered daily at about 6 p.m. hors d'oeuvres and a butler to serve meals, snacks or what have you.

All cabins are equipped with TV/VCR, two hair dryers, terrycloth bathrobes, beds that can be maneuvered to fit queen or single requirements and that are outfitted with comfy duvet covers. Telephones feature private voice mail and internet access in suites. All cabins also have a personal safe and stocked mini-fridges.

Facilities for Disabled Travelers: ♫♫♫♫ Crystal ships were designed to be accessible for the physically challenged with ramp access to most decks and public areas. Elevators can accommodate standard-size wheelchairs (22.5" wide). *Crystal Harmony* and *Crystal Symphony* each have four accessible staterooms. The two smaller cabins on Seven Deck are 290-square feet and the two suites are 350-square feet. Cabin door width is 32 inches and all have roll-in showers with benches. All decks are accessible, including public restrooms, which are conveniently located. Wheelchair guests must be accompanied by an able bodied companion.

Public Space: ♫♫♫♫ The pivotal public area on both ships is the Crystal Plaza, the central, two-story atrium lobby, with a water sculpture descending from the skylight ceiling to the marble floor. Deck 6 is home to most of *Crystal Symphony's* public rooms, including the showrooms, cinema, casino, library, business center and computer lab, alternative restaurants and the Avenue Saloon. My favorite on *Harmony* is the Palm Court which has new carpeting, vintage club chairs and other details that keep the Mediterranean villa-type environment. In other areas, there are bars, lounges, observation lounge, piano bar, two showrooms, a cabaret and nightclub, and the only casinos at sea operated by Caesars Palace with Las Vegas odds at the tables. Add a library on each ship with over 2,000 books, a movie theater, photo shop, designer boutiques, gentlemen hosts, and a lot more and you have a picture of what the Crystal environment is like.

The intimate Connoisseur Club to match the one on the *Symphony* was built next to the Avenue Saloon. The Galaxy Lounge has a dramatic new look and the Palm Court

Spa: ♫♫♫♫ *Fitness:* ♫♫♫♫ Each ship hasan ocean-view Crystal Spa offering aerobic instruction, a complete line of exercise equipment and a personal fitness trainer. One large swimming pool, one indoor/outdoor pool, two Jacuzzis, full Promenade Deck for walking and jogging; paddle tennis court, table tennis and shuffleboard courts. The 2002 renovations totally reconstructed the spa and beauty salon in a style similar to what was introduced on the *Symphony* renovations. There are seven treatment rooms for services ranging from a frangipani hair and scalp treatment to an aromatherapy foot massage. The design follows Feng Shui principles, the ancient practice of balance and harmony. The new dry float bed suite contains an innovative sensory bed to create a feeling of weightlessness. This one is recommended for couples. The Fitness Center has also been enlarged to accommodate larger classes. Yoga and Pilates instruction is complimentary. New equipment also has been installed.

Entertainment: ⚓⚓⚓⚓ Like everything else on board, entertainment is first class, though classic in many respects. There's dance music before and after dinner and into the late night. First run movies are shown in the real movie house. There are production shows and professional entertainers, cabaret acts, name comics and entertainers, well-known lecturers and bridge experts. Daytime actives are toned down, but there's enough to keep you busy if that's what you want. On Crystal, it's a matter of options and choices. Crystal's enrichment program is offered on every cruise and includes a noted historian, anthropologist, politician, author, screen star, geographer or geologist who lectures on regions in which the ship is sailing or on subjects from health to economics and beyond.

Food and Dining: ⚓⚓⚓⚓ Both ships feature a variety of dining options including a main dining room with two sittings and two alternative dinner restaurants at no additional cost. The extraordinary cuisine that is a Crystal hallmark is offered in the elegant Crystal Dining Room, located in the heart of the ship just off the Crystal Plaza. The rooms are beautifully appointed with sweeping ocean views by day and a romantic ambiance at night. Menus are extensive and special orders are encouraged.

Food service is available around the clock. The casual topside Lido offers complete buffet-style breakfast and lunch. There are hamburgers, hot dogs, pizza and turkey burgers available on decks, as well as an ice cream bar, again at no additional charge. There are traditional late night buffets, tea time and the Bistro for cappuccino and pastries for late risers, and snacks throughout the day.

The Lido Cafes serve buffet breakfast and lunch in a restaurant-like setting with the self-taken out of service. Menus are extensive with omelet stations at breakfast and a carvery at lunch. Themed buffets are staged on sea days. The indoor outdoor Trident Grill serves burgers (hamburgers, steak, chicken, vegetable) and wraps and other grill fare all afternoon. Ice cream is available at the Trident Bar and the Palm Court is the daily venue for afternoon tea. Twice during the cruise, Trident Café becomes an informal restaurant. Room service is available 24-hours a day and that includes full dinners off the menu, served course-by-course.

Special Dietary Requests: Although there are no problems with vegetarian, low fat, low salt which can be accommodated on board, Crystal prefers notification of all requests prior to embarkation, particularly requests for kosher food. Kosher food is always available and is part of Crystal's inventory. Although, there is no separate kitchen, Crystal has about 25 items that can be prepared kosher-style and served on new plates with new utensils. A wide selection of desserts is also available. Food is cooked on board, except for soups. Clergymen, including a rabbi, are on board for special holidays and on longer than 12-day cruises.

Optional Restaurants: ⚓⚓⚓⚓ Both *Harmony* and *Symphony* have Italian restaurants named "Prego' and offer elegant dining and regional Italian cuisine that puts my favorite Italian eatery in Venice to shame. *Crystal Harmony's* second optional restaurant, Kyoto, features sophisticated and traditional dishes created by renowned Japanese chefs. On *Crystal Symphony*, Jade Gardens offers Asian cuisine with a contemporary flair.

There is no surcharge for these restaurants, but a gratuity of six dollar per person is recommended. Reservations are required and they fill up within two days into the cruise but patience pays off. There are always some last minute cancellations after guests read the evening's menu in the main restaurant and decide it's too good to miss.

Internet Access: ⚓⚓⚓ Several of the computers aboard *Crystal Harmony* and *Crystal Symphony* offer Internet access. Guests can send or retrieve e-mail using their own Internet e-mail system or Internet service provider, including MSN, Yahoo, Earthlink and America Online for a fee of $1.25 a minute, with a 10-minute minimum. Guests also retain the option of sending/receiving e-mail through the ships' e-mail service at a cost of three dollars each. For both services, there is a nominal one-time set-up fee of $5. Printing, workshops and group instruction are complimentary. Laptop computers are available for rent. Private instruction is also available. Internet access is available in all suites.

Junior Cruises: ⚓⚓⚓ While there aren't a lot of kids on Crystal ships, they do get families during holiday seasons. Facilities for kids are limited. There's Fantasia, a playroom with Sony play stations, and counselors who occupy children with activities ranging from art to exercise, does offer parents some respite. Kids of all ages are welcome, including infants. There's a small playroom topside and some electronic games, but no supervised program unless the number of children warrants a counselor. The ship caters to children when they are on board, but it doesn't really encourage having them sail, except on Alaska cruises when families who prefer luxury cruising bring the kids along to get them used to the good life.

Itineraries: ⚓⚓⚓⚓ From a seven-night Los Angeles round trip on the *Crystal Symphony* to 10 and 11-day Panama Canal transits to 13 to 16-day South America cruises on the *Crystal Harmony* to 19-day Orient cruises to 106-day World Cruises, Crystal ships cover the globe.

Overall: ⚓⚓⚓⚓⚓++ We don't often give five plus plus anchors, but when a ship gets top scores in every area, it deserves outstanding mention The sister ships, *Crystal Harmony* and *Crystal Symphony*, are two of the most spacious and luxurious vessels cruising the world. Their unique size allows for smooth sailing and a wide range of innovative facilities, generous amenities and elegant accommodations. The highly rated liners feature grand lounges, a lavish spa outfitted in accordance with the principles of Feng Shui, extensive exercise facilities, the only Caesars Palace at Sea afloat, and the innovative Computer University@Sea, expansive decks, two pools, award-winning cuisine and entertainment, and exquisitely-appointed staterooms, more than half of which offer private verandahs.

The Crystal product is superb and beautifully designed but not intimidating. Décor is subdued elegance with contemporary touches. Colors are soft and there's nothing in your face. A sense of pride in the product is displayed by the crew and it carries over to guests. Everything is custom designed from the fine linens, huge fluffy bath towels to the crystal and china to the elegant oriental carpets on white marble floors. Crystal provides a classy and an elegant cruise experience.

HIGH MARKS:

Δ It doesn't matter how much a person is worth, it's nice not to be charged for ice cream, a drink in the casino, caviar in the dining room or in your cabin or suite.

Δ The Palm Court on the *Harmony*. The fine rattan furniture, abundant greenery and quiet décor is an escape to a villa in the south of France and it's easy to forget that this setting is on a cruise ship.

Δ The Lucite pianos in the bar outside restaurants.

Δ The Crystal Attitude which makes everyone part of the family.

Δ The social hosts who make cruising fun for single women travelers.

WEAKEST LINKS

- The small bathrooms in staterooms. They may be "normal-size" on some ships, but on luxury vessels like *Harmony* and *Symphony*, they are tiny.
- And, the closets. Heavy packers need to have clothes pressed halfway through a voyage. Size comes with a caveat. Ten deck, which is exclusively suites, has good size marble bathrooms and walk-in type closet. We all know that there's no free lunch. You get what you pay for. The question is – would you rather sail in a smaller cabin with a tiny bathroom on Crystal, or a larger cabin and larger bathroom on a ship that offers much less in other areas? It's all a matter of choice.

(Preview)
CRYSTAL SERENITY

Inaugurates service June 2003

Registry: Bahamas
Nationality: Norwegian and Japanese Officers, International Crew

Ship Specifics:

Tonnage	68,000	Elevators	11
Length	820 feet	Decks	14
Beam	99 feet	Children's Facilities	yes
Stabilizers	yes	Fitness Center	yes
Passengers	1,080	Spa	yes
Crew	800	Verandahs	yes
Space Ratio	63	Casino	yes
Crew/Passenger Ratio	1-1.3	Wheelchair Access	yes

Itinerary: *Crystal Serenity's* inaugural season will begin in July 2003 with a series of Western Europe and Mediterranean cruises through October. She will cross the Atlantic for the first time, sail the Caribbean, transit the Panama

Canal, and conclude her first year of service with a Mexican Riviera holiday cruise roundtrip from Los Angeles.

OVERVIEW

Currently under construction at Chantiers de l'Atlantique in St. Nazaire, France, *Crystal Serenity* will boast an even greater space-per-guest space ratio than her sister ships *Crystal Harmony* and *Crystal Symphony*. Among the ship's unique features:

Eighty five percent of outside staterooms and suites will offer private verandahs and there will be 100 Penthouse accommodations which will be 37 percent larger than they are on ships in the current fleet. Five choices of dinner venues, will include a sushi bar and casual evening deck menus in the Italian and Asian specialty restaurants and in the Crystal Dining Room, Entertainment venues include the Galaxy Lounge, Stardust Club, and Caesars Palace at Sea Casino, disco for dancing, Hollywood Theatre cinema and conference center, Connoisseur Club, Avenue Saloon and more.

Crystal's full-service spa will be 40 percent larger on the new ship with more treatment rooms, an expanded gym and aerobics studio. The ship will retain its outdoor lap pool and add two outdoor whirlpools, a second indoor/outdoor pool, a second paddle court, a full promenade and a sports deck

Crystal Serenity, the line's largest ship, will feature a lot of contemporary amenities, like a boardroom with wine-cellar, and an extra paddle tennis court. There will be a second pool -- of the indoor/outdoor variety -- and additional facilities for kids, similar to the Fantasia children's playroom and Waves teen center.

Cunard Line Limited

5201 Blue Lagoon Drive, Miami, FL 33178
(305) 463-3000 – www.cunard.com

By some strange coincidence of history, Cunard, which was the first company to provide regular transatlantic steamship service, is now the last. The first Cunard vessel was the tiny 1,154-ton paddlewheel steamer *Britannia*, which made her maiden transatlantic voyage in 1840. The last is the 67,107-ton *Queen Elizabeth 2*, which for 30 weeks each year carries guests across the Atlantic between Europe and America. Between the first ship in 1840 and the *Queen Elizabeth 2* today, a vast armada of Cunard cruise vessels plied the Atlantic. Cunard Line at one time had 11 ships in the fleet during the 152 years in business and has operated more than 175 ships. Today, the company has two vessels, soon to be three when the *Queen Mary 2* joins the fleet in 2004 and takes over the transatlantic run. Cunard sold the two boutique-type ships, *Sea Goddess I* and *II*.

Samuel Cunard conceived the idea of regularly scheduled transatlantic steamship service in the late 1830s. It was his belief that ships could run on schedules like trains, without dependence on wind and sail and that steamships could offer regular, advertised service. He was convinced ships could sail on specified dates, from specified ports to specified destinations.

For its time, it was a historic and monumental concept. It proved to be an idea whose time had come. Not only did Cunard have the vision, but he also had the ability to bring it to fruition. Samuel Cunard was a Halifax merchant with American roots. As a young man he worked in shipping in Boston and supposedly sailed on Fulton's early steamboat, the *Clermont*. He prospered in various enterprises, including shipping, and was a mature man of 53, already successful and relatively wealthy, when he embarked on his new enterprise.

The basic plan, which was successful for the next 100 years, was to have steamships operating in tandem so that regularity could be assured. He began with four near-sister ships, the *Britannia*, *Arcadia*, *Caledonia*, and *Columbia*. These vessels could make the Atlantic voyage in 14 days at eight and a half knots and maintain a weekly departure schedule from Liverpool.

As the speed of ships increased, fewer vessels were required and the ultimate dual service was reached with the *Queen Mary* and *Queen Elizabeth* making transatlantic crossings in less than a week and carrying nearly 2,000 voyagers per sailing. Today, the *Queen Elizabeth 2* makes the voyage eastbound in five days and westbound in six (the time change and docking schedule accounts for the difference).

In the glory days of transatlantic voyages, Cunard ships were household words. There was the *Aquitania*, *Mauretania*, *Berengeria*, *Luisitania*, *Carmania*, *Franconia*, *Queen Mary* and *Queen Elizabeth*. The Cunard advertising slogan, "Getting there is half the fun," was known throughout the world and is still used by some companies today.

In an earlier period, Cunard switched from wooden paddlewheel ships to iron-hulled, screw-driven vessels. The first of these was the *Andes* in 1852. She was a little larger than the *Britannia* and had a "stupendous" apartment 55 feet long. In 1856, Cunard built the famous *Persia* and, because the screw propeller was not yet proven, used a paddlewheel. The *Persia* was the largest ship in the world at the time. She was 390 feet long and 3,300 gross registered tons. The *Servia* was built in 1881. She was a "massive" 7,392 tons and was the first Cunarder to be fitted with electric lights. Among the many Cunarders to come along were the 12,950-ton *Campania* in 1893, the first Cunard ship with two propellers; the *Carmania*, in 1905, which opened a new era in sea propulsion when she became the first turbine-driven ship in the fleet.

The last great transatlantic liner, the *Queen Elizabeth 2*, entered service in 1969. She was designed to be a luxury Atlantic liner for half of the year and a cruise ship the other half. She is the last bastion of a mode of travel and way of life that, for most of the world, can only be experienced vicariously. In 1987, the *Queen* had her engines changed and other up-dates were accomplished to the tune of about $165 million. Additional refurbishment was completed in 1997 and major improvements were made in 2000 and in 2001.

In the mid-1980s, Cunard, was owned by Trafalgar House, one of Britain's huge conglomerates, when it purchased the *Vistafjord* and *Sagafjord* from Norwegian American Lines and the *Sea Goddesses* from Sea Goddess Cruises. Each operated at first as separate divisions. All of that has changed. The *Sagafjord* and *Sea Goddesses* were sold and are no longer part of the Cunard fleet.

Cunard is a different company today from what it was even a few years ago. Trafalgar sold all of its interests to a Finnish conglomerate and ship building company, Kvaerner-Masa, that decided to get out of the cruise business. Because of a conflict of interest with its core industry, the company sold Cunard in its entirety to Carnival Corporation where Cunard has become an important part of the largest cruise company in the world and again operates as a separate division.

Cunard was reorganized and its growth assured with Carnival's commitment of more than $800 million to build the *Queen Mary 2*, which will enter service at the end of 2003. This signals a new era for Cunard and probably a new era in transatlantic crossings.

Until the *Queen Mary 2* joins the fleet, Cunard continues to operate the *Queen Elizabeth 2*, affectionately referred to as the *QE2*, and the *Caronia*.

Who Sails Cunard Line? Hard to tell because the ships are so different. Americans are in the majority on many sailings, but ages vary. Younger couples on the *Queen Elizabeth 2*, older on the *Caronia*. The ships attract sophisticated travelers who are not usually first-timers. They buy luxury and they pay luxury prices. Or they have budget or mid-incomes and are realizing a dream when they sail the *QE2*. Surprisingly, long voyages attract a higher percentage of singles. On my world cruise last year, Americans were in the minority. Most of the passengers were from the U.K. and Australia.

Lifestyle: Traditional shipboard leaning toward the sophisticated, but not intimidating. The fleet has two different types of ships and each has a different life style. The *Queen Elizabeth 2* is more urban with different ambiance almost determined by dining rooms to which passengers are assigned. *Caronia* is country club and you belong if you want Old World type of luxury.

Dress Code: On Cunard ships, during the day, the rule is to be as informal as you like. Dress in the dining room is casual. Shorts and swimsuits are not appropriate, but acceptable, in the self-service rooms. Evenings are casual when ships are in port and informal when ships are at sea, except for four formal evenings per two-week cruise when men are requested to wear a tuxedo or dark suite. Women usually wear long evening clothes or cocktail dresses. Most nights, informal or formal, guests dress up, depending on the dining room they are in. Men need jackets, and usually ties, every night in the Queens and Princess grills.

Queen's Grill is never really "casual." Even on nights designated "casual" or "resort casual", gentlemen wear jackets.

Dining: Both ships have primarily single sitting dining. On *QE2*, four of her five restaurants (Queen's Grill, Princess Grill, Britannia Grill and Caronia), have assigned single sittings and guests may dine between posted hours. The fifth restaurant, Mauritania, has two sittings with set hours for – you guessed it – guests who purchase the lowest price cabins.

Special Dietary Requests: Cunard ships can accommodate just about any request, but the company wants to be notified at least six weeks prior to sailing. Vegetarian, low fat, low sodium, low calorie items are on every menu, but requests for kosher food are handled differently. Many of the kosher dishes are prepared on board, but when TV-type dinners are used they are catered by Mendelson, Empire or Manischewitz for different products. The on-board menu consists of about 25 items and it's up to the guest whether meals are served on special plates with special utensils. Some of the on board preparations may not meet strictly kosher requirements, so guests should check with Cunard before they board and with the chef immediately after boarding. Priests, ministers and rabbis are on board during World Cruises and for special holiday sailings.

Service: While it differs on each ship and in each dining room on *QE2*, overall service is top-notch with attention to detail on ever level, albeit at different levels.

Tipping Policy: Gratuities to room stewards and dining room staff are included in cruise fares for full world cruise guests and those on extra long segments. Recommended tipping on other sailings is an overall $13 dollars per day, per person for Grill restaurants and $11 in other dining rooms. Caronia recommends $9 a day, per person. A 15 percent tip is automatically added to bar and wine tabs.

Discount Policy: A 20 percent early booking discount off published fares is available on *QE2* and *Caronia* for deposits made up to 90 days before sailing. There is an additional 50 percent discount off the second cruise when cruises are back-to-back. Single supplements are waived on selected voyages Business or First Class air is included on selected sailings for passengers in suites and Category 'A' accommodations. On *QE2* transatlantic crossings, special companion fares are offered. Same offers apply for *Caronia*. There also are past guest savings and other seasonal discounts.

Past Passenger Perks: Once you complete your first Cunard voyage or crossing on the flagship *QE2* or *Caronia*, you are enrolled automatically in the Cunard World Club. In addition to traditional membership benefits, including onboard parties, Cunard World Club members receive savings of 10 percent on every future cruise. These savings may be combined with other programs such as Early Booking Savings. If you have sailed any of the sister lines in the Carnival Corporation fleet - Carnival, Costa, Holland America, Seabourn Cruise Line, Windstar you are entitled to these benefits as well.

Savings may be combined with other savings programs. There are recognition gifts when guests meet 100, 300, 500, and 1,000-day milestones. Club members are invited to special events exclusively for Cunard World Club members hosted by the Captain. On board bookings of future cruises come with an additional five percent discount. Add all the discounts and it pays to be loyal to Cunard!

The Fleet

CARONIA

Built: 1973   Refurbished; 1994/2000

Category: Traditional
Rates: $$$$$
Overall Rating: ⚓⚓⚓
Country of Registry: United Kingdom
Former Name: Vistafjord
Nationality of Crew: Norwegian officers; International service staff
Cruising Area: Caribbean, Europe, Pacific, South America
Length of Voyages: 8 to 57 nights

Ship Specifics

Tonnage	24,492	Elevators	6
Length	628	Decks	7
Beam	82	Children's Facilities	no
Stabilizers	yes	Fitness Center	yes
Passengers	677	Spa	yes
Crew	379	Verandahs	yes
Space Ratio	35	Casino	yes
Crew/Passenger Ratio	1-2	Wheelchair Access	yes

Cabins: ⚓⚓⚓ *Suites:* ⚓⚓⚓⚓ All cabins and suites were beautifully refurbished during the last renovation. Brighter colors lightened the vessel without disturbing traditional features. All of the accommodations have new bathrooms and are equipped with new locks, personal safes, refrigerators, hair dryers, VCR, caller I.D. on telephones and a beeper system for calling stewards. Of the 379 staterooms, 86 percent are outside, 11 are suites, 71 are designated for single occupancy and two are double-deck Penthouse apartments. Stateroom sizes range from 68-square feet (used for single occupancy) up to 872-square feet (Penthouse apartments). All double occupancy cabins have twin beds convertible to queen and are covered with European duvets, have minibars, television with multi-language channels), terry robes, 110/220 volt outlets and marble tiled bathroom with tub and/ or shower.

The two Penthouse apartments have floor-to-ceiling windows, Bang & Olufsen entertainment centers, CDs and books, stocked bar, huge sitting areas with sofas, coffee tables and over-stuffed chairs, walk-in closets, marble bathrooms with whirlpool tubs and separate showers, private gyms, sauna and verandahs with whirlpools. Cabins have adequate storage and closet space, especially generous in the suites. Inside cabins are small, but have a cozy feeling; outside cabins are well configured, but have lost some of the British country-look.

Cabin and suite amenities include fruit baskets, soft terrycloth robes and high quality bathroom amenities.

Facilities for Disabled Travelers: ⚓⚓ Six cabins can accommodate wheelchairs. Doors are about 31 inches wide with sills. Bathrooms have 3 inches sills, but stewards will provide ramps. Only the top decks are not accessible. Other public rooms are accessible.

Dress: This ship appeals to a dressy upscale crowd. On formal nights, men wear tuxedos or a dark suit while women wear everything from formal ball gowns to sequined pantsuits. If they have it, they bring it – diamonds and all. Informal nights also require jackets and ties for men and women wear cocktail attire. Casual night means no ties or jackets required for men. Most wear slacks and a long sleeved shirt or sweater. Women wear skirts or slacks with a blouse or sweater or other suitable attire.

Public Space: ⚓⚓⚓⚓ Refits and renovations included a new shopping area, bookstore, bar and a computer center, plus new carpeting and upholstery throughout. Regency Shops recreates the look of a fashionable London boutique and features exterior walls of beautiful floor-to-ceiling cherry wood and glass display cabinets. The Book Store offers Cunard logo items and sundries and is adjacent to the clubby Library. The new White Star Bar, named for Cunard's earlier partner line, features a window wall running the entire length, but it's the nautical memorabilia collection that fascinates guests. Much of the ship' décor reflects a remarkable tribute to the old White Star Line. It is evident in photos, posters and artifacts. It enhances *Caronia's* Old World charm and hospitable British style.

A new cyber-era Computer Learning Centre has 10 computer terminals and offers classes, business and e-mail communication services. There are other lounges, bars and gathering places, but the busiest is the card room.

Spa: ⚓⚓⚓ ***Fitness:*** ⚓⚓⚓ The small fitness room houses exercise equipment consisting of treadmills, Stairmasters, a rowing machine and Lifecycles. Aerobics and aqua-aerobics classes are offered. There's a golf driving range, jogging track around promenade deck, shuffleboard and table tennis. A second pool is indoors on the lowest guest deck and is the focal point for the ship's Spa, which includes a whirlpool.

Entertainment: ♩♩♩ The ship has always had a very conservative image and she emerged from the recent reconstruction with entertainment more in line with contemporary British preferences. The former Club Viking has become the Piccadilly Club, an indoor/outdoor disco with a British personality. The impressive Ballroom that seats 700 has been given a major face-lift. The room is used for evening entertainment and dancing, as well as for British High Tea. Garden Lounge also has new carpeting and upholstery in bright floral designs and wicker-looking white furniture adds to the garden look. On some ships it would be known as the "observation room" because of its floor-to-ceiling windows curving 180 degrees around the entire forward end of the deck.

There are nightly shows that may be mini-versions of a Broadway musical or an operetta. There are individual professional performers who shuttle between Cunard vessels and activities organized by the cruise staff. There are bridge tournaments, classical concerts and hosts are on board to dance with single ladies. The afternoon highlight may be a lecture on the Impressionists in the Garden Lounge and evenings may be filled with a spectrum, from Bach to ballet to Broadway cabaret.

Casino: ♩♩ The small but clubby Casino offers quarter and dollar slot machines (each also accepts bills up to $100 in denomination), plus blackjack and roulette tables.

Food and Dining: ♩♩♩♩ The Caronia Restaurant has been renamed The Franconia in tribute to an earlier Cunard Liner. It is large enough to take care of all guests in a single sitting. There are tables for two, four, six and eight. Elegant crystal and china, starched table covers and napkins, polished silver – all enhance menus that are extensive. Special requests are filed promptly and the menu accents regional cuisine. Dining has been enhanced by the addition of outdoor seating adjacent to the Italian Tivoli Restaurant, an alternative venue for 40 guests (Tivoli's indoor tables convert to felt-covered game tables for morning bridge games). The Lido Café is near the outdoor swimming pool and this is where guests come for daily breakfast and lunch buffets. *Caronia* is one of the few ships that stills serves a grand Midnight Buffet in the dining room. Stateroom service is available on a 24-hour basis. And, it's still white-gloved service throughout the vessel.

Service: ♩♩♩♩ Personal, excellent service is provided in all areas of the ship. Special attention is paid to the cadre of loyal past guests who request specific waiters. Waiters, on the other hand, discern preferences quickly and there's no need to request a condiment more than once. It will be on your table waiting for you at every meal.

Junior Cruises: ⚓ There are no separate facilities and the ship does not lend itself to the patter of little feet. However, a counselor will be on board should the number of children warrant, which doesn't happen very often.

Itineraries: ⚓⚓⚓⚓ Current schedules call for her to sail in on varied cruise lengths in the Mediterranean from Barcelona to Venice in April and May, then move to Northern Europe for seven and 14 day cruises between Amsterdam and Copenhagen from June through August, then return to the Mediterranean itinerary until December when she will sail for one 16 day cruise to the Caribbean.

Overall: ⚓⚓⚓ Just say the word "Caronia" to a Brit and it conjures visions of posh luxury. But the name Caronia is nearly unknown in North America, so Cunard is focusing marketing and sales on the U.K. and in Europe. However, as the *Vistafjord*, the ship has a loyal American following that will fly to Europe, or wherever, no matter what the name on the hull reads. *Caronia* was reflagged to sail under the registry of Great Britain where she was built almost 30 years ago.

Now sporting the line's distinctive black hull, topped by a white superstructure and a single mid-ship Cunard-red funnel, *Caronia's* profile is a sleek reminder of the Old Days. On the inside, the nostalgia continues throughout the ship's public spaces.

Caronia was designed to sail smoothly through rough transatlantic crossings, as well as calmer Caribbean waters, with speed, style and elegance for her 665 guests. *Caronia* is for travelers who prefer graciousness and a level of unobtrusive service in the British tradition, reflecting not only the past but also the best of the present.

The *Caronia* is a classy traditional ship that was reborn after about $15 million worth of recent cosmetic improvements. Her quality standard is high and the new features have put her back into the hearts of a loyal following. Most guests are ship travel buffs who like to return to friendly faces and familiar surroundings.

HIGH MARKS:

Δ Bavarian Brunch that takes passengers to a simulated Bier Stube in Munich.

Δ Space ratio and service ratio

WEAKEST LINKS:

- To fit into this clubby ship, you have to dress to the nines. Also, not bad if you want to open the vault and take the family jewels to sea.
- Most American men balk at wearing a tie on casual nights. European men, on the other hand, find it hard to part with their ties.

QUEEN ELIZABETH 2

Built: 1969   Refurbished: 1996/ 2001

Category: Traditional/Luxury
Rates: $$ to $$$$$$
Overall Rating: ⚓⚓⚓ to ⚓⚓⚓⚓
Country of Registry: United Kingdom
Former Name: none
Nationality of Crew: British officers; International service staff
Cruising Area: Transatlantic, Europe, North America, and World Cruises
Length of Voyages: Six to 106 days

Ship Specifics:

Tonnage	70,327	Elevators	13
Length	963	Decks	13
Beam	105	Children's Facilities	yes
Stabilizers	yes	Fitness Center	yes
Passengers	1,800	Spa	yes
Crew	1,000	Verandahs	yes
Space Ratio	39	Casino	yes
Crew/Passenger Ratio	1-1.8	Wheelchair Access	yes

INSIDER TIP

The ship was built as a three-class ship and what you pay determines where you sleep as well as where you eat. Accordingly, cabins come in varying sizes and designs. Ambiance improves along with your cabin as you move up the ladder. The last two renovations have brought the ship up considerably in every area. All areas have been redecorated, plumbing has been changed and upgraded and air conditioning is fairly constant throughout the ship Accommodations vary in size, depending on the price category. Minimum priced cabins do not compare with Queen's Grill staterooms. As for the lowest grade restaurant, Mauritania, surprisingly, the menu is basically the same but service levels and special requests are more limited. On the plus side, all passengers enjoy the same entertainment, and except for the Queen's Grill Lounge, all of the same lounges. Hence, different ratings for different accommodations and restaurants.

Cabins: ⚓⚓ *Suites*: ⚓⚓⚓⚓ Cabins are priced and relate directly to the four dining room levels. Queens Grill accommodations range from penthouse-style Grand Suites to Ultra Deluxe staterooms. All are outside, have large bathrooms with tubs and showers, walk-in closets, refrigerators and sitting areas. The newer cabins have verandahs. Suites have butler service and room service by Queens Grill chefs is available to all Grill guests. Princess and Britannia Grill guests have spacious deluxe cabins with ocean views, bathrooms with tubs and showers, walk-in closets, sitting areas, televisions and other amenities. Caronia guests are in outside cabins that have tubs and/or showers, televisions and some amenities. Mauritania passengers are in either inside or outside small staterooms with small tubs or showers in bathrooms and televisions.

The smallest cabins are 100-square feet! They look more like budget-ship accommodations than what you would expect to find on the *QE2*. All cabins have either locked drawers or personal safes.

Facilities for Disabled Travelers: ⚓⚓ There are four new wheelchair accessible cabins but it is difficult to use all of the elevators. Some are old and doors are not wide enough to accommodate any size wheelchair. To reach the hospital, the only elevator is small and there is a step on some decks. There are steps connecting decks to elevators on other decks. Wheelchair passengers learn the ropes early on and don't seem to have a problem getting around.

Public Space: ⚓⚓⚓⚓ Each renovation (and there have been about 10) added or subtracted a room or two, so all elevators do not lead to the same decks. Surprisingly, however, she's an easy to know vessel. Configuration is traditional and there's lots of space. The only time there's a crowded feeling is when a "name" entertainer is on board and performs twice. The lounge is not large enough to hold half of the guests, even when there are two performances. Otherwise, there's plenty of space and usually empty places in every lounge and around every bar. Other exceptions are around black jack tables. There could be more because the manifest, particularly on transatlantic crossings, is made up of very sporty passengers. There are three swimming pool (two outdoor and one indoor), six cocktail lounges, a shopping arcade, a library filled with wonderful books in several languages, kennels which are only used on transatlantic voyages, medical and dental services, a 20-car garage, 30 public rooms in all and too many other features to list.

Spa: ⚓⚓⚓ *Fitness*: ⚓ The Fitness Center is located at the very bottom of the ship so there are no windows and air conditioning could be improved. The room is divided by the indoor swimming pool that is rarely used, so exercise classes are crowded and the area is not conducive to working out. I found it claustrophobic. The Spa and Hair salons are on an upper deck, but are also without windows. World Cruise guests accustomed to gyms offered on new ships may be disappointed.

Golf classes are also offered and there's a full promenade deck for walkers and joggers, a basketball court, golf driving range, laser skeet shooting, putting course and the usual shuffle board and table tennis.

Entertainment: ⚓⚓⚓⚓ A full range of day and evening activities and entertainment are scheduled with outstanding individual performers brought on board for just a few days at a time. In addition, the *QE2* specializes in theme cruises and lectures series on Atlantic crossings and world cruises. For example: The "Newport Jazz Festival At Sea" featuring world-renowned jazz legend Kenny Burrel; George Plimpton's International Literary Festival on Atlantic crossings; Bill Cosby and Tommy Tune are on the schedule and celebrity lecturers include Tom Keneally, author of "Schindler's List.

Food and Dining: ⚓⚓⚓ to ⚓⚓⚓⚓ Passengers purchase the restaurant as well as their cabin and are assigned accordingly to one of the five restaurants. Menus are basically the same in all dining rooms but service is more personal in the top restaurants. Off-the-menu choices may not be available in other than Grill restaurants where chefs go practically overboard to fill special requests. In all fairness, the recent renovation improved the Mauritania tremendously. It is a very pretty restaurant with good space between tables. The Queen's Grill was also updated and, while reviews are mixed, that always happens when changes are made.

There are tables from two to 10, but there are more tables for two in Grill restaurants. The Queen's Grill successfully rivals shoreside's finest restaurants. Princess and Britannia Grill guests have the same menu but in a different environment. The Lido offers informal dinner service for guests preferring a more casual atmosphere.

INSIDER TIP

If you are a Grill Room guest, expect formal wear suggestions almost nightly. Grill guests bring their finest on long cruises. I have a friend who alternates world cruise sailings annually between the *QE2* and another ship. She empties the bank vault and takes her jewels along with 45 long gowns.

Junior Cruises: ⚓⚓⚓⚓⚓ The ship has great, supervised facilities for children from infancy to teen-age levels. There are trained British nannies on board, an indoor and outdoor children's pool, computer room, video arcade and a playroom. There are very few children on long cruises, but the juvenile population increases during summer transatlantic voyages and young mothers would like to take the nannies home.

Itineraries: ⚓⚓⚓⚓⚓ World Cruise annually, transatlantic crossings and cruises as short as three-nights round trip from Southampton. Average cruises are 10 to 14-days in the Caribbean, Northern Europe and sometimes the Mediterranean. The Christmas-New Years Caribbean 14-day voyage is very popular and many families return annually.

Overall: ⚓⚓⚓⚓⚓ The *Queen Elizabeth 2* is in a category of its own and cannot be compared with other floating destinations or transportation. She is a sophisticated city afloat and until the *Queen Mary 2* is launched, remains the only supersized ship with complete hospital, medical and dental facilities, a 500-seat theater and enough space to allow most of the guests to dine at the same time. Her recent refit brought her up to and beyond many of the features and amenities available on new ships.

There is only one traditional *Queen* and sailing her is an experience not duplicated on any other ship. Sure, she shows her age in places. Don't we all? But her face lifts have removed some of the signs. Bathrooms have been completely rebuilt with new fixtures, marble in deluxe, Italian tile in others. *Queen Elizabeth 2* addicts say she's like a grand old European hotel that remains ageless.

HIGH MARKS:

△ Old World ambiance

△ New World amenities, plus plush towels and terry robes.

△ Social hosts who dance with single ladies

△ Single cabins at special rates

△ Heritage Trail with its Cunard memorabilia

△ The only real ballroom at sea

△ Stewardesses who look like French maids with white caps and aprons over short black outfits.

WEAKEST LINKS:

• The "No Smoking" signs are virtually ignored by passengers and crew. You may be seated in a "no smoking' area in the Queen's Grill for one segment of a cruise, and are surprised to find yourself in a smoking area for the following segment. Seems the segments are enlarged to meet smokers' demands. The same thing happens in lounges. Passengers move the ashtrays around to suit themselves and ignore "no smoking" signs and the staff just ignores smokers and non-smokers.

• The claustrophobic aerobics and gymnasium. The area is so far down, it's hard to find and when you get there, you can't wait to leave.

Preview
QUEEN MARY 2
Built: 2003/2004

Category: Luxury Liner

Rates: $$$$ to $$$$$$

Overall Rating: not rated

Country of Registry: U.K.

Nationality of Crew: British Officers; International service staff

Cruising Area: Transatlantic most of the year; Caribbean, South America, Mediterranean cruises.

Length of Voyages: 6 to 70 day and longer

Ship Specifics:

Tonnage	150,000	Elevators	22
Length	1,132	Decks	17
Beam	131	Children's Facilities	yes
Stabilizers	yes	Fitness Center	yes
Passengers	2,520	Spa	yes
Crew	1,253	Verandahs	yes
Space Ratio	59.5	Casino	yes
Crew/Passenger Ratio	1-2	Wheelchair Access	yes

(The following information is based on preliminary news releases and on the newly released brochure)

Overall: Reservations are being accepted and Cunard is reporting an overwhelming demand. For obvious reasons, it is too early to rate the *Queen Mary 2*.

Cunard's (and the world's) next, and possibly last, ocean liner, *Queen Mary 2*, will be the largest, longest, tallest and widest passenger ship ever constructed. Standing beside this majestic vessel at quayside, visitors will behold a structure as tall as a 21-story building. She will be over a 100 feet longer than the Eiffel Tower is tall, and more than four city blocks in length. If she were afloat in the pool at the foot of Niagara Falls, her stack would rise over 20 feet above the rim.

For more than 60 years, there has been a Cunard "Queen" sailing the oceans. *Queen Mary 2* will be the first such liner built in a generation and the worthy heir to the company's 160-year heritage. As envisioned in an artist's rendering, she will embody all the thoroughbred characteristics of her ancestors: the generous thrust of her raked prow, the stepped superstructure both fore and aft, the lean dimensions that allow for greyhound speed traversing the North Atlantic. Seen from the outside, she will look like what she is, a purpose built craft for sailing rapidly between points on the globe.

Within her hull, however, *QM2* will have a multitude of delights as spectacular and pleasurable as they are innovative and ingenious. Stepping aboard, guests will enter a realm of sweeping spaces and grand designs, the likes of which have not been seen for decades. They will enjoy a generosity of spaciousness that rivals or surpasses that of ultra-luxury small ships. They will stroll the broad, one-third mile-long teak promenade deck that encircles the entire ship. The Lobby will tower over three decks high, graced with a sweeping grand staircase and what promises to be monumental works of art.

Guests will travel in accommodations that vary from the merely commodious to the shamelessly extravagant. The standard cabins measure 194-square feet, and most will include an eight-foot balcony. In all, 75 percent of the ship's cabins have verandahs. Five duplex apartments are all the way aft, overlooking the sea from two-story glass walls. With over 1600 square feet, included in the two levels will be private gyms, verandahs and butler service.

Accommodations for disabled travelers will be offered in various category grades, including interior and sea view staterooms for a total of 30 specially equipped cabins.

As on *QE2*, accommodation selected by the guest will be matched with a dining venue. Higher categories will dine in Grill rooms and lower categories will share an opulent dining room, again towering over three decks high, with its own grand staircase and tiered seating to create both open and intimate dining spaces.

To fill days at sea, onboard activities will be staged in a number of innovative venues. Seven multi-purpose classroom facilities which can be sized to accommodate varied size classes will make up a "College At Sea," with expert instruction in a wide variety of subjects such as computer skills, languages, art and wine appreciation, cooking and more. An auditorium will feature a section that will adapt to become a full-scale planetarium where star shows, courses on celestial navigation and other visual spectacles can be presented. *QM2* will have a large library, a bookshop and a coffee shop. Like *QE2*, *QM2* will boast a true ballroom with an orchestra for dancing. A "first" at sea is the Canyon Ranch SpaClub that will occupy 20,000-square feet on two decks. The SpaClub also will offer a full menu of Canyon Ranch beauty services for both men and women. The area will include one of the ship's five swimming pools, and together with the adjacent Winter Garden, will provide a health, fitness and a relaxation area of over 25,000 square feet.

Numerous smaller lounges, alternative dining venues and specialized rooms will also welcome travelers during the crossings.

Itineraries: Inaugural season will begin in late December 2003 with a few short Caribbean sailings from Miami. *Queen Mary 2* will sail 14-day South America itineraries through mid-March, then begin her continuous series of transatlantic crossings between New York and Southampton, interspersed with 10 to 14 day Mediterranean and Northern Europe cruises.

Reservations: Cunard is accepting reservations and reporting overwhelming demand. Everyone wants to be the first to sail the newest liner afloat. Guests who sailed Cunard vessels during the 18 months prior to the opening of reservations were given priority status and that should fill the ship for the first few years.

INSIDER TIP

Cunard loyalists are disappointed that *Queen Mary 2* will not be making world cruises. She's too big to transit the Panama Canal. For the predictable future, the venerable *Queen Elizabeth 2* will continue to circumnavigate the globe while the *Queen Mary 2* does her own thing. On another point, if you are wondering what the difference is between a liner and a cruise ship, here's the best answer we can come up with, although Webster says the words are interchangeable. In the world of sea travel, a liner is generally a vessel built for speed and used primarily for transportation. Its secondary purpose may be interchangeable with cruise ships, as we know them. Cruise ships are primarily vacation-oriented and secondarily provide transportation between, not to specific destinations.

Delta Queen Steamboat Company

1380 Port of New Orleans Place,New Orleans, LA 70130

(800) 774-7550 – www.deltaqueen.com

This company has seen it all. It has survived with a determination that is historic in itself. And, each time when it looked like the last chapter, Delta Queen Steamboat Company made a come back and wrote another chapter in American river history. The latest misadventure took place shortly after 9/11. The New Orleans based Delta Queen Steamboat Co. was owned by American Classic Voyages which went into bankruptcy. The ships went on the auction block. For awhile, it looked like there were few bidders, but an angel in the form of Delaware North Companies (DNC) threw Delta Queen Steamboat a lifeline and was the successful bidder for three of the paddle wheelers- Delta *Queen, American Queen* and *Mississippi Queen*. The fourth vessel, the *Columbia Queen*, went to American West Steamboat Company.

Delaware North Companies not only saved the Mississippi steamboats, but is committed to preserving the legacy of steamboatin' for visitors from around the country and around the world. Headquarters will remain in New Orleans, along with the reservations, sales center and land based operations. Most of the former employees are back on the job and Delta Queen Steamboat Company is back in business with three vessels plying American rivers.

Our nations' heritage river boats are in good hands. Delaware North Companies with over $1.6 billion in revenue is one of the largest privately owned companies in the United States and possibly the largest hospitality and food services company in the world. DNC, as it is known, manages Visitor Services at Yosemite National Park and a long list of premier hotels, resorts, convention centers and attractions. You'll recognize most of the names which include the Boston Fleet Center. The chairman of the company owns the Boston Bruins.

The *Delta Queen* traces its roots in river history back to 1890 when the Gordon C. Greene Co. was founded to operate packet steamers on the Ohio and Mississippi rivers.

The period from 1811 to the turn of the century was the era of the paddlewheel steamboat in America, and more than 10,000 of these fascinating vessels plied the nation's rivers.

Steamboats were directly responsible for a period of unprecedented progress, accelerating the development of the American frontier. The great inland waterways became the main highways, and everything from livestock to fine furniture would be waiting on the banks for shipment. Within a few years after introduction of the steamboats, river villages grew into small towns, towns became cities, and the course of American history was changed forever.

Then, as now, the magic of Steamboatin' held a special place in the hearts of the American people. Since 1890, The Delta Queen Steamboat Company has continued the uniquely American tradition of Steamboatin' at its best, offering memorable journeys on America's historic rivers. Journeys just like they used to be, or a reasonable facsimile, draw travelers from all over the world.

Any discussion of ships must include the *Delta Queen*, and her younger sisters, *Mississippi Queen* and *American Queen*. The romance of Mississippi River cruising was kept alive a few years ago by nostalgic riverboat enthusiasts. An exceptional woman, Betty Blake, who became president of the company, spearheaded the movement. She was a personal friend who died a number of years ago, content in knowing she will always be remembered for her successful efforts to keep the tradition of river boating alive on the Mississippi for future generations. She will also be remembered for many other things, such as her warm personality and her addiction to ships. It was her petition to Congress that saved the *Delta Queen* and exempted the vessel from 20th century safety requirements.

The *Delta Queen*, a venerable 80-year-old, first operated on overnight trips between Sacramento and San Francisco. After serving as a U.S. Navy Yard ferryboat on San Francisco Bay during World War II, she was picked up at auction by Tom Greene, then president of the Greene family company. Captain Greene had her towed across 5,000 miles of open sea to New Orleans, then sailed her under her own power to Pittsburgh, where she was remodeled and outfitted for passenger service. On June 30, 1948, she made her maiden voyage on the Mississippi River with a round trip between Cincinnati and Cairo, Illinois.

When new safety-at-sea regulations were passed about 20 years ago, it took six exemptions and a special Act of Congress to save the *Delta Queen*. Those exemptions have been extended and will protect the vessel through 2008. The *Delta Queen* is considered an authentic, fully restored masterpiece and was entered in the National Register of Historic Places in June 1970.

When new safety requirements made the *Delta Queen's* future uncertain, company management decided to build a paddlewheeler which would meet new construction requirements and at the same time, would be the largest and most spectacular riverboat ever built. James Gardner (designer of the *Queen Elizabeth 2*) was commissioned to create the exterior, and internationally known Welton-Beckett designed the interiors. She was built in Jeffersonville, Indiana, where about 5,000 steamboats were constructed in the 19th century.

The *Mississippi Queen* inaugurated service on July 25, 1976, from Cincinnati. Her final cost was $27 million. She offers her guests luxury and comfort while keeping close touch with traditions created by her ancestors. Moldings, mirrors, polished steel and brass, plush carpeting throughout reflect the opulence of great steamboats of the past.

The *American Queen* was built in the same shipyard and began service in 1995 retracing the route of the 1811 journey by the *New Orleans.* Like everything else, the cost of building a paddlewheeler keeps going up. The *American Queen* cost $65 million and, like her sister, is decorated with authentic antiques and replicas.

Who Sails Delta Queen Steamboats? Vessels are geared to the over 50 year old crowd and that's what you find on board. Almost all passengers are Americans from the mid-section of the country, followed by travelers from California and Florida. For the most part, they have cruised the big ships and now come back again and again for river cruising. Non-Americans on board are especially impressed and enjoy this look at American rivers and the cities and towns that border them. Multi-generational families plan reunions on board, but there are no children's facilities and the few teenagers traveling with families seem to spend most of their time learning about the river from crew members.

Lifestyle: Riverboat cruising is an art in itself and takes some adjustment to the stillness interrupted only by the methodical plop as the paddle wheeler meets the river. Boats seemingly glide along the river past shoreside scenery that creates a gradually changing picture postcard kaleidoscope. River cruising is totally different from ocean going cruising and boats differ greatly from cruise ships anywhere in the world.

Dress Code: Passenger's should know in advance that they will spend most of their waking hours out on deck. Dress is casual with a couple of dress up nights, but leave the black ties and sequins at home.

Dining: Food is all American, Cajun flavored New Orleans cuisine. Low calorie fare has been added to regular menus and special dietary requests are possible but should be ordered in advance of sailing. There are two sittings in the dining room and riverboats are probably the only vessels on which first sitting is in greater demand than second. They are probably also the only floating resort where first sitting is at 5:30 p.m. Breakfast and lunch are buffet with table service available. Dinner is served at assigned tables. There are very few tables for two. Most seat six or eight.

Service: Young American waiters and waitresses are enthusiastic and anxious to please. They like their jobs and are friendly and proud of the vessel.

Tipping Policy: Waiters and cabin stewardesses expect $3 to $3.50 per person, per night. About $2 to assistant waiter; $5 per person for the cruise to the Head Waiter. Gratuities at bars and lounges are automatically added to your bill.

Discount Policy: Delta Queen Steamboat Co. is in an admirable position. Vessels sail at close to 90 percent occupancy year around, so discounts and special fares are not offered very often. Airfare is included on most cruises of seven nights and longer providing you book your cruise and deposit at least eight months in advance of sailing. Children cruise free in some staterooms on *Mississippi Queen* and *American Queen*, when sharing the cabin with two full-fare adults. January and February are good months to catch a bargain. In 2002, the company offered two-for-one pricing on *Mississippi Queen* and *American Queen*.

INSIDER TIP

New owners bring new pricing and as we go to press, rates are lower than I have seen them in many years. Ships resumed sailing with a very short lead time to advertise that the company was back in business. This forced rates down to as low as $125 a day, putting them in the budget class. Brochure rates are more than twice those amounts. Average six -night cruises on *Delta Queen* with river views were quoted on the Internet for $1,145 and $1,175 on *Mississippi Queen*.

Theme Cruises: Theme cruises continue to be a mainstay of paddle boat cruising. Examples are the "Music of the River" under the direction of Dr. John Edward Hasse, Curator of American Music at the Smithsonian Institution's National Museum of American History. Dixieland jazz, blues, gospel, rockabilly, country and western are just a few of the sounds that reverberate. Mark Twain Vacations celebrate Tom Sawyer Days in Mark Twain's home town of Hannibal, Missouri with tours of Twain's boyhood home and the Mark Twain Museum. In the Good Old Summertime Vacations recreate the heyday of ice cream socials, boardwalk carnivals and band concerts. Several voyages focus on Big Bands with nostalgia in the forefront, You'll foxtrot, lindy hop, boogie and jitterbug to the unique sounds of the late thirties and forties. Three great orchestras will be on board on a rotating basis to provide the big band sounds.

INSIDER TIP
What's the difference between a boat and a ship? Good question with many answers. A riverboat captain I know says, boats have flat bottoms and smaller drafts so they can sail more shallow waters. Ships have deeper drafts which force them to sail in deeper waters. They also have shaped bottoms. The explanation I like best comes from Captain Feruccio Rocconi, a former senior officer with Sitmar Cruises and now retired in California. He says a boat is what you head for when the ship is in trouble. In other words, if the vessel carries lifeboats, it's a ship. Webster, however, says ships are "large seagoing vessels." Boats are "small vessels that travel on water." There's no definition as to what constitutes a "large" or a "small" vessel. Best advice, however, is don't call one of those superliners a boat in front of her captain. It's a definition a lot of cruise directors use to get a laugh, but it was printed first in a quote by Feruccio in the 1975 edition of The Total Traveler."

HIGH MARKS:
- Δ The rivers
- Δ Old fashioned American hospitality in every port
- Δ A smooth ride without vibrations
- Δ A lesson in American history and geography
- Δ Theme cruises with emphasis on jazz, big bands, 50s and 60s music,
- Δ Cajun culinary cuisine and the good-old-summer time.
- Δ Rocking chairs and porch swings
- Δ A post office on board. All Delta Queen boats are official U.S. Post Offices. Mail cards or letters on board and they will be postmarked with the name of the vessel.

WEAKEST LINKS:
- • No doctors on board
- • No casinos

INSIDER TIP: In this era touting bigger is better, cruising on one of the Delta Queen boats is a time-stopping experience. Sailing up the lazy river is a sure way to lower blood pressure, rejuvenate the body, refresh the mind and brush up on American geography lost somewhere between high school and the rush of growing up.

Note: We have not been on board since the company resumed operations under the new ownership, so we're not rating the subjective areas (food, service, entertainment) of the ships, although the organization is known for high quality. Based on the reputation of Delaware North Companies and its commitment to continuing the heritage and standards of the company, travelers should not hesitate to sail these vessels. Having said that, the overall ratings reflect the boats and what they offer, not the food, service or entertainment.

The Fleet
AMERICAN QUEEN
Built: 1995

Category: Boutique-Adventure
Rates: $$$ - $$$$
Overall Rating: ⚓⚓⚓⚓⚓
Country of Registry: United States
Former Name: none
Nationality of Crew: United States
Cruising Area: Mississippi and Ohio Rivers
Length of Voyages: 2 to 8 nights

Ship Specifics:

Tonnage	3,707	Elevators	2
Length	418 feet	Decks	6
Beam	89.4 feet	Children's Facilities	no
Stabilizers	no	Fitness Center	limited
Passengers	436	Spa	no
Crew	222	Verandahs	yes
Space Ratio	n/a	Casino	no
Crew/Passenger Ratio	1-2	Wheelchair Access	yes

Draft: 8.6 feet

Cabins: ⚓⚓⚓⚓ **Suites:** ⚓⚓⚓⚓ Seven grades of cabins range from outside luxury outside suites to minimum priced smaller cabins. In between are deluxe cabins with small private verandahs. There are no inside cabins. All cabins and suites are furnished in the same Victorian mode with printed chintz and lots of gingerbread. Small by cruise ship standards, they are very comfortable; sort of like visiting at your grandmother's house. Texas Deck has 27 cabins that open onto the forward portion of the wrap around deck; 22 aft cabins with large windows and five with private verandahs overlooking the paddle wheel.

Facilities for Disabled Travelers: ⚓⚓⚓⚓ There are nine cabins outfitted to accommodate disabled guests. There are two elevators and almost all of the ship is disabled-friendly. Average-size wheelchairs will fit through doors. Just watch out for ramps at different stops. The crew will help with embarkation and disembarkation in ports along the rivers. There are no problems shoreside because you are in the U.S. and all facilities comply with Americans with Disabilities Act.

Public Space: ⚓⚓⚓⚓⚓ The *American Queen* looks like she's right out of a movie. The pilot house is topped by a lacy, ornate cupola and a shiny weathervane strikes a familiar chord. One almost expects a river gambler dressed in tails, cigar in hand, greeting passengers at the gangplank. Instead, they are greeted by antebellum dressed staff members offering refreshing drinks. At the bow of the boat, a sweeping exterior staircase ushers guest up to the second-level Cabin Deck. At the top of the stairs, an entrance foyer separates the Gentlemen's Card Room – a leather-type, book-lined masculine retreat – from the ladies' parlor, a demure Victorian drawing room where well coifed ladies bent over intricate needlepoint would feel right at home. Past the parlor and card room and leading to the Purser's Lobby is the antique filled Mark Twain Gallery overlooking the dining room and providing comfortable sitting for reading or relaxing. The vessel is a comfortable mix of Victorian grace and gilded gingerbread. Wallpaper is an eclectic mix of floral patterns and non-coordinating colors, the way it was in those days.

There is a self service laundry and a one-person beauty shop for shampoos, haircuts, manicures or facials. Complimentary post cards are available and mailed for you. The company pays the postage.

Spa and Fitness: ⚓⚓ There's a mini-fitness room with three machines and a small pool topside. The sunning area is quite nice, but few people use it. They much prefer the wide decks for evening relaxation and the variety of activities during the day.

Entertainment: The Grand Saloon is the venue for live entertainment in the evenings and variety of activities during the day. Conceived to look like a small opera house in a prosperous river town in the late 1800s, the Grand

Saloon features a tall proscenium stage and is flanked by private boxes on the mezzanine level.

Entertainment is all "G" rated. Daytime activities do not include bingo or horse racing. A special day could be a good old fashioned picnic out on deck complete with weight guessing, hoop throwing, archery contests, cotton candy, ice cream, straw hats and a bathing beauty contest won by a vivacious great grandmother. Classic films are shown regularly in a room which is also used to accommodate small meetings and conferences. One of the highlights is the Riverlorean who relates tales about the rivers we never heard in school.

Food and Dining: Standardized throughout the fleet, food is of high quality, well prepared and beautifully presented.

Junior Cruisers: ⚓ No facilities, but a trip on America's rivers is a good geography lesson.

Itineraries: ⚓⚓⚓⚓ *American Queen* cruises round trip from New Orleans and from New Orleans to Cincinnati and between ports like Memphis, St. Louis and Nashville.

Overall: ⚓⚓⚓⚓ Modeled after the grand steamboat palaces of the 19th century river boating era, *American Queen* is a blend of vintage appeal and modern design. The vessel is the result of three years of intensive research in order to produce an authentic replica. As the last steamboat built in the 20th century, the vessel was designed to include the best features of boats dating back to 1878, albeit with modern convenience unheard of in the old days – like running water and flushing toilets.

American Queen's 4500-ton paddlewheel is propelled by steam, although the technology when out of fashion at about the same time as high-button shoes. She should be required sailing for every visitor to the United States and for every traveler. It's an experience you are not likely to ever forget.

The *American Queen* combines nostalgia and tradition, Sitting in a rocking chair on the front porch (that's right, the rocking chairs are on the front porch), it's easy to understand Mark Twain's fascination with the river. It's very easy to settle back and commune with America's past and our own.

INSIDER TIP

I am convinced that a cruise on America's rivers should be mandatory for every school-age kid in the country. In fact, it should be included in every travelers' itinerary, including those of us who know Europe better than we know our own country. Seeing America's heartland by riverboat is a true picture of America. It's not the skyscrapers of downtown U.S.A. or the jazz and pizzazz of Las Vegas or Atlantic City or Mickey Mouse or Miami Beach. It's the soul of America and the kindness of Americans we all tend to forget.

HIGH MARKS:

Δ The largest collection of Tiffany-style stained glass lamps in the world

Δ The most wonderful front porch. Look for me in a rocking chair out on The Front Porch of the Americas.

Δ Chart Room, Captain's Bar, Engine Room Bar, Calliope Bar

Δ For reminding me that we had locks in the Ohio River before they built the Panama Canal. (And, I was born and raised in Ohio)

WEAKEST LINKS:

- No doctor (See Insider Tip)
- Menus could use a few more choices.
- Special dietary requests are hard to get

INSIDER TIP

American Queen and her older sister-river boats do not carry doctors on board. Captain Tom said that vessels cruising inland waterways do not have to worry about the same things as ocean going vessels. He explained that because of proximity to shore and ports every day, the company decided not to carry doctors or nurses. When a medical emergency occurs, the vessel radios for a medical evacuation helicopter to rendezvous and the patient is frequently in the hospital within a shorter time than it would take in some communities. It is not unusual for the river boat to "hang a tree" which means move the gangplank out and disembark passengers. That's river talk for throwing a line around a tree to tie-up along shore.

DELTA QUEEN

Built:1925-1927 Refurbished: 1994

Category: Boutique-Adventure
Rates: $$$
Overall Rating: ⚓⚓⚓⚓
Country of Registry: United States
Former Names: none
Nationality of Crew: United States
Cruising Area: Mid-American rivers
Length of Voyages: 2 to 12 nights

Ship Specifics:

Tonnage	3,360	Elevators	0
Length	285 feet	Decks	4
Beam	60 feet	Children's Facilities	no
Stabilizers	no	Fitness Center	no
Passengers	174	Spa	no
Crew	87	Verandahs	no
Space Ratio	n/a	Casino	no
Crew/Passenger Ratio	1-2	Wheelchair Access	no

Cabins: ⚓⚓⚓ *Suites:* ⚓⚓⚓⚓ All 87 cabins and suites are outside and feature views of riverbank. Many of the cabins open to the outside promenade that's been called the 'Front Porch of America." Cabins are snug, but their personalities make up for short comings-tasseled floor lamps, brass wall sconces, and wooden window shutters that lift up. Some cabins have racks, others small closets. Every cabin is different, Some have twin beds, and others queen. All are air conditioned and have private facilities which is no mean feat for a vessel this age. Some have a sink in the bedroom, not the bathroom, Upper-category cabins are furnished with authentic antiques. Bathtubs are the four-legged kind and some toilets have chain pulls.

Facilities for Disabled Travelers: ⚓ *Delta Queen* is not one of the boats recommended for disabled travelers. First off, there is no elevator and the dining room is down a flight of stairs. Then, nothing on the ship has been adapted for wheelchairs. If river cruising interests you, select one of the other vessels in the fleet.

Public Space: ⚓⚓⚓ The best space is outdoors, but there are several good roosting places inside as well. The Betty Blake Lounge is a softly lit parlor filled with armchairs and sofas, writing desks, bookcases and famed memorabilia. A portrait of Mark Twain and old prints line the walls. The Forward Cabin Lounge is where coffee and ice tea is always available and it's where passengers gather for a drink and card playing. The Grand Staircase with ornate bronze filigree railing and paneling connects the decks. The Texas lounge is a favorite hang out for spicy Cajun Bloody Marys, hot fresh popcorn and a sing-a-long which starts with one passenger and before you know it, there's a dozen or more joining the song fest.

Spa and Fitness: ⚓ There's a small area; a very small and dark area.

Entertainment: Where else can one fly a kite from the Sun Deck, tap out a tune on a vintage steam calliope, and dance the night away after meals are finished and the dining room set up for a show which is staged nightly? Theme cruises follow the same pattern as on the larger vessels, but are somewhat limited because of facilities.

Food and Dining: The Orleans Dining room on Main Deck turns into a nightclub after dinner, with a show and dancing. But during meal hours, it is a New Orleans restaurant, particularly for dinner.

Itineraries: ⚓⚓⚓⚓ Year around on two to 12-night cruises on the Mississippi, Ohio, Tennessee, Cumberland, Arkansas, Achafalaya Rivers.

Overall: ⚓⚓⚓⚓ The *Delta Queen* is not only a national Historic landmark, she's an American treasure. She is an outstanding example of the thousands of paddlewheel steamers that once thronged our great American waterways. She's the genuine article, a-one-of-a-kind star-spangled slice of Americana, filled with Tiffany-styled stained glass, brass fittings and rich polished woods. Her ambiance is warm and engulfing. The environment is a trip back in time. The vessel has developed a loyal following that was heartbroken when it looked like curtains for the *Delta Queen*. They will likely resume their annual cruise on *Delta Queen*.

HIGH MARKS:

Δ Her speed which is about six to eight miles per hour

Δ The steam calliope which bellows tunes when you least expect them

WEAKEST LINKS:

- The feeling that you have to face the real world on the last day of the cruise when you walk down the gangway with your hand luggage.

MISSISSIPPI QUEEN
Built: 1976   Refurbished: 1996

Category: Boutique-Adventure
Rates: $$$ to $$$$
Overall Rating: ⚓⚓⚓⚓⚓
Country of Registry: United States
Former Names: none
Nationality of Crew: United States
Cruising Area: Mid-American rivers
Length of Voyages: 2 to 11 nights

Ship Specifics:

Tonnage	3,364	Elevators	2
Length	382 feet	Decks	6
Beam	68 feet	Children's Facilities	no
Stabilizers	no	Fitness Center	yes
Passengers	414	Spa	no
Crew	156	Verandahs	yes
Space Ratio	n/a	Casino	no
Crew/Passenger Ratio	1-2.6	Wheelchair Access	yes

Cabins: ⚓⚓⚓⚓ *Suites:* ⚓⚓⚓⚓ All of her 207 staterooms and suites feature rich, warm, 19th century style furnishings and many cabins have coveted private verandahs from which to watch river banks go by. There are 72 inside cabins which measure a mere 123-square feet, but again, décor and ambiance make up for size. All have private bathrooms and modern amenities camouflaged with antiques and replicas. Furnishings have a 19th century country-inn look.

Facilities for Disabled Travelers: ⚓⚓ There is only one cabin outfitted to accommodate disabled guests. There are two elevators but not all of the public areas are disabled-friendly. Average-size wheelchairs will fit through doors. Just watch out for ramps at different stops. The crew will help with embarkation and disembarkation in ports along the rivers. There are no problems shoreside because you are in the U.S. and all facilities comply with the Americans With Disabilities Act.

Public Space: ⚓⚓⚓⚓ Modern conveniences have been incorporated and the vessel has a small outdoor pool and Jacuzzi and a number of cruise ship amenities, lounges and bars, and a self-service launderette. Favorite places are the two-storied Paddlewheel Lounge, with its 1890's-style saloon décor, huge picture windows overlooking the river and the blend of ragtime, Dixieland and banjo music. Furnished largely with antique furniture and vintage artwork, photographs and books, the vessel has the grace of a fine antebellum home. *Mississippi Queen* also has a small conference and meeting room, library and theater.

Spa and Fitness: ⚓⚓ The boat has a beauty salon offering hair styling and massage and daily exercise classes, plus a small area equipped with a few machines.

Entertainment: The two-story Grand Saloon showroom has private box seats on the mezzanine and reflects the opulence of an 1890s opera house. Entertainment is similar to the other boats —jazz, big band, theme cruises and the outdoors.

Food and Dining: The J.M. White Dining Room has stunning chandeliers and a magnificent view of the river through expansive windows. Following the same pattern as other vessels in the fleet, dinner is a five course affair but choices are limited.

Junior Cruisers: ⚓ No separate facilities.

Itineraries: ⚓⚓⚓⚓ 2 to 11 night cruises from New Orleans and between ports on the Mississippi, Ohio, Cumberland and Tennessee Rivers.

Overall: ⚓⚓⚓⚓ With a big red paddlewheel, tall black stacks and a golden-piped calliope, the *Mississippi Queen* is a colorful reminder of a time when America's rivers teemed with floating palaces. Outfitted in high Victorian style during a five-year, $5.5 million refurbishment, the paddlewheeler flaunts 1890s elegance as well as an array of modern amenities. She offers everything the other two boats have but has developed her own following. Lounges are larger and itineraries differ.

HIGH MARKS:

Δ The Grand Staircase topped with a trompe l'oeil ceiling of cherubs frolicking among the clouds

Δ The largest calliope on any vessel

WEAKEST LINK:

- Not enough accommodations for disabled travelers.

Peter Deilmann Cruises

1800 Diagonal Road, Suite 170, Alexandria, VA 22314

(800) 348-8287 – www.deilmann-cruises.com

Peter Deilmann Cruises operate one ocean-going cruise ship in addition to its 10 river vessels and a sailing yacht. While the main marketing target is to German-speaking tourists, some British and American travelers have discovered this upscale company with an active American sales office.

Who Sails Peter Deilmann Cruises ? German-speaking passengers, mostly upper-income couples and singles from their mid-40s to 60s, predominate, although there is always a small core of English speakers on all their vessels.

Lifestyle: Sumptuous interiors and excellent food characterize all the Deilmann vessels, with antiques and original art work from the owner's personal collection.

Dress Code: Traditional dress codes predominate. On the *Deutschland*, the line's cruise ship, men are expected to wear tuxedos, dinner jackets or dark suits on formal evenings and a jacket and tie on all other evenings aboard. Women are always in elegant or casually elegant attire. Daytime wear is casual, but definitely upscale resort-style casual, not Kmart casual.

Dining: Cuisine is continental, with local and regional specialties also offered. Smoking is not permitted in the dining rooms. When the *Deutschland* is full, there are two sittings with assigned tables, otherwise only one sitting at assigned tables. When the ship is not full, passengers are able to move around and sit with new friends. The dining room staff is happy to rearrange seating to please passengers and to encourage camaraderie. On the river vessels and yachts, single sitting meals at assigned tables are the order.

Tipping: Recommended gratuities are $13 a day per person, with $5 recommended for cabin steward and dining room waiter and $3 for the bus boy. Drink gratuities are automatically charged at time of service.

Shirley and Harry Comment

"Deilmann owns and operates all its own vessels instead of chartering them as many river vessel operators do, giving the company more control over the décor and operation".

The Fleet
DEUTSCHLAND
Built: 1998

Category: Traditional
Overall Rating: ⚓⚓⚓⚓⚓
Rates: $$$$
Country of Registry: Germany
Former names: None
Nationality of Crew: German
Cruising Area: Worldwide
Length of Voyages: 10 to 136 nights

Ship Specifics

Tonnage	22,400	Elevators	3
Length	574 feet	Decks	6
Beam	82 feet	Children's Facilities	no
Stabilizers	no	Fitness Center	no
Passengers	513	Spa	yes
Crew	260	Verandahs	yes
Space Ratio	43.66	Casino	no
Crew/Passenger Ratio	1-9.7	Wheelchair Access	yes

Cabins: ⚓⚓⚓ *Suites:* ⚓⚓⚓⚓ Most of the 288 cabins are outsides, and some offer third and fourth pull down berths. The smallest of the inside cabins is 142 square feet. Outside cabins and suites boast large picture windows, but there are no private verandahs. A large number of cabins – 46 insides and 17 outsides are designated for single occupancy. The 18 suites measure from 239 to 382-square feet, the Owner's suite is the largest, followed by the

Grand Suite (319-square feet) and the Honeymoon Suite (312- square feet). Only the Owner's and Grand Suites (8001 and 8002) offer private verandahs. All cabins include telephone, mini-bar, color TV, radio, hair dryers, and bathrobes, available on request. Only the suites offer tubs; the rest are fitted with very large tile showers decorated with tile murals. Furnishings are handsome in a classic fashion; all have sitting areas, which in the lowest price categories means that one of the two lower beds makes into a sofa for the daytime.

Facilities for Disabled Travelers: ⚓ There is only one wheelchair accessible cabin. Most of the public rooms are accessible. There is no accessible public restroom.

Public Space: ⚓⚓⚓⚓ The three-deck atrium is ornamented with a Tiffany glass dome. The Milie Marleen Salon is furnished with gold and green tub chairs and sofas in a reverse pattern of green and gold. The four tiers of passenger decks aft are covered in natural teak, with white chairs and tables trimmed with yellow cushions and cloths, topped with yellow, gray and white striped umbrellas. One of the details that is particularly impressive is the fact that the deck loungers are covered with royal blue mattresses that have the ship's name embroidered on them in gold.

Spa and Fitness: ⚓⚓⚓⚓ Two spa areas, an indoor freshwater pool and an outdoor saltwater pool take care of all-weather swimming, while a gym, sauna and around-the-ship promenade deck on deck 9 and an enclosed promenade on deck 7 for walking, offer other exercise possibilities. There's an outdoor relaxation area with traditional wood lounges adjacent to the spa

Entertainment: ⚓⚓⚓ The primary entertainment area is the Kaisersaal, the "Emperor's ballroom" or "the special room," as the staff calls it, which is all red velvet and gilt with red carpet and gold fleur-de-lye. Sightlines are marred by the support columns and the stage is nearly the same floor level as the seats. A balcony ring around the upper level is reminiscent of box seats at the opera. Zum Alten Fritz, "Old Fritz's," is a pub-bar with leather banquettes, wrought iron bar, brass urn lamps and etched corner mirrors that lend it a Viennese air. Entertainment includes operatic and classical music, show dancers, magicians and music for dancing.

INSIDER TIP

The entertainment is ⚓⚓⚓⚓⚓ if you speak German: ⚓⚓⚓ if your only language is English. That applies to comedians and lecturers. Music is international. We found individual performers to be of concert quality and outstanding talents.

Food and Dining: ⚓⚓⚓⚓ There are three restaurants aboard, with two meal sittings in operation when the ship is full. The 300-seat Berlin is the table d'hote menu restaurant, with ornate wood-backed chairs with tapestry seats, oil paintings and murals on the wall. The elegant alternative restaurant is the 100-seat Vier Jahreseiten (Four Seasons) that requires a reservation and makes no surcharge for its a la carte menu. On the top deck is an outdoor grill where chefs sizzle meat for snacks and sandwiches, and inside is a self-service buffet spread with soup, several hot main dishes, a salad bar and a dessert bar that includes ice cream made aboard the ship. Menus are international and special orders are accommodated.

INSIDER TIP

Don't let the name "*Deutschland*" put you off and don't expect Schnitzel or sauerbraten on the menu. Passengers are very sophisticated and the menus are more French, than German. We had to special order some of my favorites — red kraut, for example and Wiener Schnitzel.

Service: ⚓⚓⚓⚓ In a word, excellent. Very correct also applies. It is European style service and an efficient pursers desk makes this a comfortable ship for well-traveled passengers from anywhere in the world. Americans who prefer a more casual approach may be intimidated, but they shouldn't be, Waiters want to hone their language skills and practice their English with Brits and American passengers.

Junior Cruisers: ⚓ While there is a designated space on deck 4 that can be utilized as a children's playroom, we would not recommend this ship for kids, unless they are the rare seen-but-not-heard breed of youngsters.

Itineraries: ⚓⚓⚓⚓ ++ The *Deutschland* goes almost everywhere in the world with a mix of exotic and traditional destinations. The ship spends the January through April period on a world cruise, followed by Mediterranean and Northern Europe itineraries, and offers some exotic itineraries in late fall.

Overall: ⚓⚓⚓⚓⚓ Designed to salute the glittering 1920s and the Art Deco era, the *Deutschland* is dazzling with its rich, wood-paneled interiors and lavish attention to detail. Oil paintings from the owner's private collection, gilded classic statuary, expensive burl woods, charming murals, and sparkling crystal and glass are everywhere. About the only thing a luxury-loving passenger could carp about is the dearth of private verandahs.

INSIDER TIP

There were eight guests from English speaking countries – four Americans, two Canadians and two Brits on my cruise last year. I discovered that many of the German passengers spoke English better than I speak German, but they did not initiate a conversation. Once I spoke to them in German, they were warm and friendly. When I explained that my husband didn't speak the language, they quickly switched to English. The Captain invited the English speaking guests to a small cocktail party. One would imagine that we would form a click, but it didn't happen. We didn't team up because we were on board for the German experience. If we had wanted to sail with Americans or Brits, we would have chosen a different ship. We did meet for cocktails a few times and compared notes. At the end of the voyage, I asked whether they would sail the *Deutschland* again. Six said they would not hesitate to come back and they planned to sail the Dielmann river fleet on their next vacation. The dissenter was my husband who was uncomfortable sailing in a foreign environment. My vote? I would happily sail the *Deutschland* around the world. But, remember I speak German.

High Marks

Δ The *Deutschland* is equipped with a kidney dialysis station in the ship's hospital.

Δ The courtesy displayed by passengers and crew is a pleasant reminder of good manners. Be prepared to respond to "Guten Tag" ("Good day"), saying "Please" or "You're welcome" (Bitte) and "Thanks" ("Danke") or you'll be considered rude.

Δ The on board shop carries the best quality designer labels that I have ever seen on a ship. The prices? A lot less than I would pay at Saks Fifth Avenue.

WEAKEST LINK:

- All announcements, although there were few, are made in German, so English speaking guests are left wondering about what's going on.
- German guests, who make up about 80 percent of the manifest, have a tendency to verbally lose patience when a lecturer translates in English.

Disney Cruise Line

210 Celebration Place, Suite 400, Celebration, FL 34747
(407) 566-3500 – www.disneycruises.com

Disney Cruise Line was established in June 1994 as a division of the Walt Disney Company. It's sole purpose is operating cruise ships designed for vacations that match visits to Disney complexes. The company lined up seasoned cruise line veterans to operate the new company and commissioned two 85,000-ton vessels to be built in the Fincantieri Shipyard in Trieste, Italy. To the delight of Mickey Mouse-addicts, the ships fit the Disney profile perfectly.

From its inception, Disney Cruise Line's goal was to build vessels reminiscent of luxury liners of the 1930s and '40s, but with all of the amenities of cruise ships, particularly in entertainment, technology and materials.

The cruise division was new to the expectations of cruise passengers when *Disney Magic* was inaugurated in 1998. The company has learned a lot about cruising in the years that followed. To its credit, both ships have been fine-tuned and now offer more traditional cruise features without sacrificing any of the Disney amenities customers expect. By the time *Disney Wonder* came on line, the company had learned that a cruise is not exactly the same experience that guests expect in Disney-run hotels.

Disney ship are all about imagery. Even the ships' names-Disney Magic and *Disney Wonder* stir the imagination and create the image of what to expect on board. The design, concept and organizational team was in place for more than three years before the *Disney Magic* made her first voyage. Programs were tweaked. The cast changed on board and on shore and the company has emerged as a mainstream cruise operator with some very unique features.

INSIDER TIP
Disney ships home port in Port Canaveral, Florida, an hour's ride from Orlando. Cruisers who buy the complete package – air, cruise and Disney World hotel -receive transfers included in the package. Those opting for just the cruise, can buy transfers for $50 a piece, round trip. I'm not sure it's worth it for a family of four who can take a taxi between the airport and ship for about $55 for all of them. Those guests who opt for the hour bus ride from Orlando Airport to Port Canaveral view an introductory video that offers a tour of the ship and its facilities. If you decide to drive to the port, it is worth mentioning that parking is $21 for a three-night cruise, $28 for four-nights and $49 for seven nights, payable in advance in cash only. Credit cards are not accepted.

Who Sails Disney ships ? Anyone who enjoys a visit to one of the parks, a Disney movie and families of all ages. Disney is offering wedding and honeymoon packages and anticipates a large number of couples on first, second and/or repeat honeymoons. For the most part, there are families with kids, lots of kids.

Lifestyle: Casual and unstructured, except for assigned meal hours. It's family style throughout. The schedule is traditional cruise ship with lots of Disney whimsy added.

Dress Code: Casual wear day and evening, except for dining in the optional gourmet restaurant where jacket and ties are requested, not required.

Dining: Three dining rooms on each ship with two sittings in each, as well as an optional Italian restaurant and an informal grill serve passengers. To vary the dining experience, passengers are assigned a rotation for nightly meals between the three unique themed restaurants. Passengers are given a table number which is the same number in all three restaurants. Configuration in all three is almost mirrored for passenger convenience and familiarity. The same waiters, in different uniforms (or costumes, as the case may be) in keeping with the restaurant's theme, serve them. Guests who prefer not to rotate have the option of eating in Palo, a reservations-required, adults-only Italian restaurant, the casual Topsider Buffet or in their cabins

Special Dietary Requests: ⚓⚓⚓⚓ All requests should be made at the time cruises are booked, but there's no problem if you decide on board to go vegetarian, low salt, low calorie or low cholesterol. Kosher food is available for both lunch and dinner. Food is prepared on land through the same caterer used by the Walt Disney World Resort. Selection is wide and includes fish, chicken, meat, vegetarian and other special dishes. If you wait until you board, you may not have as many kosher items to select from. Meals are prepared and served on plastic plates, but may be converted to dining room dishes when requested.

Tipping: Recommended is $3.50 per day per person to dining room servers (known as waiters on other ships); $2.50 to his assistant; $3.50 to stateroom host/hostess (room steward/ess); and $2.50 for a three-night and $3.00 per person for a longer cruise to the Dining Room Captain. A 15 percent gratuity is automatically added to bar, beverage, wine and deck service tabs. All gratuities may be charged to your shipboard cruise card.

Discount Policy: The Disney Cruise Line vacation may be purchased as a seven-day package or as a three-or four-night cruise. The one-week holiday includes the three-or four-nights at the Walt Disney World Resort followed or preceded by the three-or four-night cruise. Package rates also include air from most cities, transfers between airport, ship and hotels, unlimited admissions to theme parks and port charges. Cruise and air packages also are available.

Passengers who make their own air arrangements and purchase only the cruise deduct $250 from brochure rates. In this competitive marketplace, Disney is offering discounts similar to other lines that appeal to families. Most of the discounts apply to cruise only rates and do not include air.

The Fleet
DISNEY MAGIC
Built: July 1998,
DISNEY WONDER
Built: Spring 1999

Category: Resort XXL
Rates: $$$
Overall Rating: ⚓⚓⚓⚓ +
Country of Registry: Bahamas
Former Names: none
Nationality of Crew: European officers, International service staff; American cruise staff and children's counselors
Cruising Area: Bahamas
Length of Voyages: 3, 4 and 7-nights

Ship Specifics:

Tonnage	85,000	Elevators	12
Length	964 feet	Decks	11
Beam	106 feet	Children's Facilities	yes
Stabilizers	yes	Fitness Center	yes
Passengers	1,800	Spa	yes
Crew	945	Verandahs	yes
Space Ratio	47	Casino	no
Crew/Passenger Ratio	1-2	Wheelchair Access	yes

Cabins: ⚓⚓⚓⚓ ***Suites:*** ⚓⚓⚓ Of the 875 staterooms, 75 percent are outside and 44 percent of those have private verandahs. Special features include family-size staterooms, some accommodating up to five persons, but for the sake of comfort, guests should come in small sizes. Average cabins range from about 170-square feet for minimum priced insides to outsides of 220-square feet. A large number of staterooms connect which increases the number of options available to families. Bathrooms are separated into two small rooms (a sink and shower and/or tub in one and a toilet and sink in the other). This feature continues to receive rave revues, particularly by families. Cabins are tastefully decorated, sofas convert to beds and a Murphy-type bed comes down from the ceiling for an additional person. All beds convert easily from almost king-size to twins.

Facilities for Disabled Travelers: ⚓⚓⚓⚓ Disney offers accessible staterooms and suites in various categories from inside minimums to deluxe suites equipped for guests with disabilities. Features include: ramped bathroom thresholds, open bed frames, added phones in the bathroom and nightstand, bathroom and shower handrails, fold-down shower seats, hand-held shower heads, lowered towel and closet bars, and Emergency Call Buttons. All staterooms are non-smoking. Listening Systems are available in the main theaters and show rooms. Closed captioning is available for stateroom televisions. American Sign Language interpretation is available for live performances on designated cruise sailings. Stateroom Communication Kits containing door knock and phone alerts, phone amplifier, bed shaker notification, a strobe light smoke detector, and a Text Typewriter (TTY) are available. Transfer tiers are provided at one of the swimming pools. Sand wheelchairs are available at Castaway Cay. Guests requiring a wheelchair for the entire cruise must either bring their own chair, or notify the cruise line as far in advance as possible.

Public Space: ⚓⚓⚓⚓ About half of the 10 decks are devoted to public space, the remainder to staterooms and suites. Both ships have three-story atrium lobbies with sweeping grand staircases, From quiet lounges and intimate bars to family type rooms centered on entertainment, ships have a lot to offer for almost every age group. The Promenade Lounge is meant to be an adults only bar and lounge with music. Sports fans hang out in the Sky Box. There are three swimming pools tailored to create separate areas for adults, children and those looking for a more active water experience.

Much of the interior décor is Art Nouveau and many of the rooms, like Parrot Cay, the children's facilities and staterooms have became instant Disney Cruise Line hallmarks.

Spa and Fitness: ⚓⚓⚓⚓ The spa is so extensive and surprisingly so popular, it's hard to get a massage appointment, particularly for massages offered in a hut on Castaway Cay, Disney's private island. Treatments in the normal spa are anything but normal. Try the Rain Forrest and you'll make a friend for life. Vista Spa & Salon covers 9,000-square feet and overlooks the ocean. While all of the usual treatments offered in the Steiner-operated spas are on the menu, there are some unusual ones like the Gentle Sauna where 140-degree dry heat is distributed from under the floor, or the Aromatic Steam Room where chamomile extracts are used to cleanse the skin and refresh the mind.

INSIDER TIP

Castaway Cay deserves special mention. Every cruise line with a private, or semi-private island claims it to be "Fantasy Island," but none comes close to what Disney has created on Castaway Cay. First off, the company spent an estimated $6 million to dredge the harbor, develop a 3,000-foot channel and build a pier so Disney ships pull alongside and passengers are free to go back and forth without tenders. Then, Disney imagineers took the natural wonders of the island and built tramways, palm-shaded walkways, hideaways and rustic shelters to look like they had been there for hundreds of years. Tropical foliage, native to the island, was maintained as was an old runway once used by drug runners and now used as a walkway and roadway for trams taking passengers between family beaches and enlarged adult-only beaches. There are special areas for kids and no shortage of lounges or umbrellas, beverage stations and picnic huts or shops. Every Disney cruise stops at Castaway Cay and even if you hate the beach, you should walk off the ship and take a look at what imagination, lots of work and tons of money can do to a neglected island paradise.

Entertainment: ⚓⚓⚓⚓ The same shows and choreography are on both ships. Shows feature magnificent sets, original music, lighting and startling illusions. The premier showplace is The Walt Disney Theatre, a 975-seat, three-deck high showplace. Three family-oriented Disney inspired musicals are offered during a three-and four-night cruise and an additional afternoon show, "Island Magic' on seven-night cruises. All are "G"-rated family-oriented, which is great for kids but leaves adults traveling without children with an after-dinner choice of a movie or the Promenade Lounge.

Catering to three distinct markets - children, families and adults, is not easy. Adults seem to get the short end as most of the ship is devoted to entertainment to please the kids (of all ages) Beat Street on *Disney Magic* and Route 66 on *Disney Wonder* are adult entertainment districts, designed with the premise that "everyone moves to a different beat." The area is restricted to over 13-year olds but it's hard to keep them out.

Shirley and Harry Comment:

"We're still waiting for Disney to come up with some new productions shows so repeat adult passengers who like this line will find something new to do after dark."

Food and Dining: ⚓⚓⚓⚓ Innovative and hard to accomplish, both ships offer a dine-around program. Designed to give guests variety in dining and venue, it works, although there were skeptics. Here's how the routine works. For example, the first night could be in Animator's Palate, a black and white room which magically, yet slowly goes through color changes. The second night might be in the casually elegant continental-style Lumier's, which is decidedly French-flavored. The third night would then be in casual-styled Parrot Cay, an island inspired restaurant with emphasis on tropical cuisine. All three restaurants cater to special dietary requests and children's menus. Still another eating option is offered in "Lido" area for buffet breakfast and lunch.

Adults have a fourth dining option and it's the best. Located topside with 270-degree ocean views, Palo is an outstanding Italian restaurant. Décor is of warm woods and Venetian glass and an open kitchen with a pizza oven is off center stage. Palo offers intimate dining at window-side tables of from two to six or eight. Menu is classic Northern Italian with the opportunity to sample a selection of appetizers and entrees served in small or entrée size portions.

Marcia Levin Comments:

"Other than Palo, food is geared to children's appetites and adults may find it mediocre."

INSIDER TIP

Dinner in Palo takes you out of Disney and into another world. Reservations are required, so run, don't walk, to the Passenger Service Desk to make reservations. If have to choose a night to forego one of the other restaurants, pass on Parrot Cay and go there for open sitting lunch instead.

Service: ⚓⚓⚓⚓⚓ It's hard to find fault with service by a multi-lingual staff who also speak excellent English. Stateroom service has improved to expected levels.

Junior Cruisers: ⚓⚓⚓⚓⚓ Disney's Oceaneer Adventure provides a shipboard program offering activities from 9 am to 1 am, supervised by some 50 counselors. Spanning nearly an entire deck, activities and facilities offer dozens of age-specific activities in an area that is nearly 10 times the size of what other cruise ships offer. Kids ages three to eight have a program designed for them at Disney's Oceaneer Club. It is a play space created for younger kids with plenty of area to run, climb and explore. Kids from nine to 12, have Disney's Oceaneer Lab, featuring high-tech fun including electronic games played on giant video walls and interactive computer activities. Teens have their own space and activities. Highlights include a two-hour teens-only disco twilight boat ride in Nassau harbor, a four hour island special triathlon that includes kayaking, snorkeling, biking, lunch and games and the midnight one hour gathering topside when teenagers have the deck practically to themselves.

Flander's Reef Nursery is designed to take care of infants and toddlers of from 12 weeks to three years. Capacity is extremely limited and babies are admitted on a first reserved basis. Baby-sitting is available until midnight and parents are charged $6 per hour for the first child in the family, $5 per hour for additional children.

INSIDER TIP
Children have 16,000 square feet devoted to their activities. More than 40 counselors are on board to supervise activities for the younger children and the teens seem to find their own friends and activities and hang out together. If you are traveling with infants under three years of age, plan to spend a lot of time with them or bring your own baby sitter. Accommodations in the nursery fill up quickly and baby sitting charges can really add up.

Itineraries: ⚓⚓⚓⚓ If you buy the Disney package, you should know that your choice of cabin category will determine hotel accommodations at the Disney Resort. Buy a suite on the ship and you'll probably stay at the posh Floridian Hotel. *Disney Wonder* sails from Port Canaveral on three and four night cruises visiting Nassau, Bahamas and Disney's private Bahamian island, Castaway Cay. *Disney Magic* sails one-week cruises with calls at Castaway Cay Key West, Grand Cayman and Cozumel.

Overall: ⚓⚓⚓⚓+ Disney ships are five anchor products, but their appeal is limited, so Total Traveler Critics rated the ship ⚓⚓⚓⚓+. The ships were designed for families, singles, seniors and honeymooners but, it hasn't exactly worked out that way. Unless you are a devoted Disney fan and wear Mickey's ears on your baseball cap, you may not find enough to do, if you are over 25 years of age. Comments are not intended to take anything away from the product that families love. The kids are busy and mom and dad get a chance to talk, or whatever.

The ships are beautiful. From the outside, it's hard to distinguish between *Disney Wonder* and her sibling, *Disney Magic*. The vehicular approach to the Disney Terminal affords passengers an awesome photo opportunity of a classic beauty in the style and with the profile of a traditional liner similar to one we could have seen some 30 years ago, The ship dominates the harbor with her black-blue hull, gold stripes, double smokestacks (one is just for show), glistening lacquered white superstructure and raked bow. Stylized characters hang off the stern. On *Disney Magic*, Donald Duck and his nephew Huey have replaced Goofy hanging over the stern and Mickey has changed his personality on the bow from Sorcerer Mickey on the *Magic* to Steamboat Mickey on the *Wonder*.

The bigger than life, Mickey greeting guests on the *Magic* has been replaced on *Wonder* with a larger than life Little Mermaid, described as "a reminder of life above and beneath the sea." But, kids of all ages need not fear that Mickey has disappeared from the vessel. He and other Disney characters are interwoven into so many details, like glass windows, and sculpted molding, it would take longer than a cruise to count the many famous ears on the ship.

While the *Magic* emulates traditional grand liners of the 20th century with grand staircases and classical oversized portholes, the *Wonder* is more opulent with a three-story atrium lobby enhanced with curly sycamore wood columns with glowing glass capitals and wave railings in polished bronze and nickel. The lighter colors and mellow artwork give the lobby a welcoming feeling.

INSIDER TIP

The Disney cruise-land package was designed with hopes that it would turn into a "hassle free vacation" with no baggage handling once passengers check-in at hometown airports." It doesn't quite work that way. Passengers who purchase a complete Disney package (air, hotel, transfers and a cruise) have a single check-in at the newly built Disney Cruise Line Terminal at Port Canaveral or at the hotel, whichever comes first. The hotel key is also the cabin key, which simplifies matters quite a bit. Here's how the package works, assuming you take the cruise first. You are met and you are escorted to the bus, while your pre-tagged baggage is taken to your cabin. You check in at the beautiful pier and board the vessel, and your pictures are taken for the ship and hotel I.D. card. At the end of the voyage, you are bussed to your hotel and your luggage catches up with you later in the day. Reverse the process if you are taking the cruise first.

HIGH MARKS
- Δ The children's program and facilities
- Δ Palo Restaurant is a trip to Italy in the midst of family tumult
- Δ A massage on the beach at Castaway Cay is heavenly

WEAKEST LINKS:
- • No casino
- • Repetitious production shows. Even my 12 year old grandson fell asleep
- • No midnight buffet or snacks, no fruit bowls in cabins, or chocolates on your pillow.

First European Cruises

95 Madison Avenue, New York, NY 10016

(888) 983-8767 – www.first-european.com

First European Cruises is the New York marketing arm of Festival Cruises (a name that was already registered but not in use in the United States when the line opened its New York office in 1997). Festival was founded in 1993. It is a Greek-based cruise line with a major European passenger following.

Like other European-based cruise lines, Festival began with renovated vintage vessels – first *Azur*, then *Bolero* (the former *Starward* from Norwegian Cruise Line, now under charter to Spanish Cruise Line, a Festival joint venture) and *Flamenco* (the former *Star/Ship Majestic* from now-defunct Premier which sailed briefly as the *Southern Cross* for Britain's CTC Cruise Lines but should not be confused with the *Southern Cross* that sailed as the *Azure Seas* for many years.). But unlike other European-based lines, Festival quickly placed newbuild orders and was the first on the block with a brand-new ship, *Mistral*, which debuted in 1999.

Since then, the company has added *European Vision* (June 2001) and *European Stars* (2002), sister newbuilds that carry 1,500 passengers each. Notably, the *European Vision* hosted VIPs from around the world at the recent G8 summit in Genoa.

The three original ships, *Azur*, *Bolero* and *Flamenco*, are traditional vessels, while the three new ships, *Mistral*, *European Vision* and *European Stars*, fall into the Resort contemporary category.

While the Mediterranean, both Eastern and Western, and the Aegean are the primary cruising areas, Festival's ships also sail in the Caribbean, Northern Europe, the Canary Islands and Morocco, as well as offering repositioning transatlantic cruises seasonally.

Who Sails First European Cruises? Although most of First European's passengers are European, some North Americans also gravitate to the ships, as many as 20 percent of the passengers on certain sailings. But CEO George Poulides says, "Overall, 98 percent of our passengers are European." The age and country of origin swing from almost entirely young European families during the summer months to older Europeans and some North Americans in the Caribbean. On the *Mistral* in the Eastern Mediterranean, we sailed with a mix of passengers from 19 different countries; the average age was 45-50. Most recently, on the *European Vision* in the Western Mediterranean, the mix was mostly Italian and French families, young to middle-aged Austrians, older French and British couples and singles, and a sprinkling of other nationalities of all ages.

Lifestyle: First European Cruises follows the traditional cruise ship lifestyle, with assigned dinner sittings (open sitting is usually in effect at breakfast and lunch), pre- and post-dinner concerts and small production shows, and activities such as crafts classes and aerobics classes scheduled throughout the day. There are shore excursions, shops, a small casino,

Dress: Two gala (read "formal") nights a week are scheduled, and passengers are requested to don dress-up clothes. "Cocktail dresses for ladies and a dark suit or blazer for gentlemen are appropriate, a tuxedo is optional," according to the English language brochure, but the Europeans apparently don't read this, and in the summer may show up in almost anything.

Dining: The food is good to excellent. On the new ships, grill restaurants on the new ships are standouts. Like on the *Queen Elizabeth 2*, passengers who buy designated upper category cabins may dine in these restaurants when space is available. It's complimentary for them, but there's a surcharge for other passengers. A buffet restaurant and separate deck grill are also aboard.

Tipping: No printed policy exists, simply the statement that tipping is an individual matter. Expect to tip $9 to $10 or so per person per day. Tips are presented in cash, usually the night before disembarkation, to restaurant and cabin stewards. Drink gratuities of 15 percent are added to the bill at time of purchase.

Discount Policy: Early booking discounts of 15 percent per person are offered for bookings made 120 days prior to departure. Off season and other special are advertised regularly and air from New York or other gateway, is frequently included in these "specials."

Shirley and Harry Comment:

"In the Mediterranean, passengers are accustomed to getting on and off in any of several ports during a weeklong cruise, whereas Americans are usually booked on a set city-to-city sailing. Be prepared for the constant embarkation and disembarkation of passengers and baggage."

The Fleet

AZUR

Built: 1971   Refurbished: 1994

Category: Traditional
Overall Rating: ⚓⚓⚓
Rates: $$
Country of Registry: Panama
Former names: Eagle, *The Azur*
Nationality of Crew: European officers, international crew
Cruising Area: Eastern Mediterranean, Aegean
Length of Voyages: 7, 10, 11 and 14 nights

Ship Specifics

Tonnage	15,000	Elevators	3
Length	466 feet	Decks	7
Beam	72 feet	Children's Facilities	yes
Stabilizers	n0	Fitness Center	no
Passengers	720	Spa	yes
Crew	330	Verandahs	no
Space Ratio	21	Casino	yes
Crew/Passenger Ratio	1-2.18	Wheelchair Access	yes

Cabins: ⚓⚓⚓ *Suites:* ⚓⚓⚓ Even the lowest-priced inside cabins are fairly spacious, with two lower beds and enough room to change your mind. There are plenty of quads with two upper berths in both insides and outsides. Furnishings include a desk/dresser with chair, perhaps two chairs in some of the upper categories. Windows are on the small side, slightly larger than a porthole and square. A dozen suites, slightly larger, provide a tub as well as shower, along with a mini-bar.

Public Space: ⚓⚓⚓⚓ Passengers, who have known this ship for years when it sailed for Paquet and later for Chandris Fantasy Cruises, are surprised and delighted at how spiffy it looks after its makeover for Festival/First European. Colors are bright and perky, especially the yellow umbrellas and striped lounge cushions on the pool deck. There's even an indoor volleyball court.

Spa and Fitness: ⚓⚓ A workout room with gym equipment, a sauna and massage room make up the spa and fitness offerings on board, along with a volleyball court. A small beauty salon takes care of hair, nails and facials.

Entertainment: ⚓⚓ The usual variety artists perform in the Azur Lounge with its karaoke facilities. A small casino and disco, plus a second lounge and a cinema fill out the entertainment venues.

Food and Dining: ⚓⚓⚓ Deck buffets are surprisingly tasty and well displayed aboard the *Azur*, and dinners are served at two sittings, 6:30 and 8:30 at assigned tables in the Riviera Restaurant.

Service: ⚓⚓⚓ The same professional European-style service is offered on the *Azur* as on First European's other vessels.

Junior Cruisers: ⚓⚓ A children's playroom on the sports deck of the Azur is adjacent to the indoor volleyball court, and a supervised activity program for kids is scheduled during summer and holiday sailings.

Itineraries: ⚓⚓⚓⚓ The *Azur* cruises the Eastern Mediterranean in winter and the Aegean in summer.

Overall: ⚓⚓⚓ While it's a fairly dense vessel, with five of the seven passenger decks housing cabins, the *Azur* has some traditional cruise ship niceties from the early 1980s such as a cinema, two swimming pools and two major lounges. For anyone who wants to cruise the Aegean at a bargain fare on a medium-sized ship with echoes of the old ocean liner days, the *Azur* will fill the bill.

HIGH MARKS

Δ The Rialto Cinema is a really proper cinema with a balcony and raked theater seats.

WEAKEST LINK:

• A shortage of deck chairs even on port days. Europeans get up early and stake out the best chairs because they've already done the Greek Isles and they are on board to soak up the sun.

EUROPEAN VISION
Built: 2001
EUROPEAN STARS
Built 2002

Category: Resort Midsize
Overall Rating ⚓⚓⚓⚓
Rates: $$$
Country of Registry: Italy
Former names: None
Nationality of Crew: European officers, international crew
Cruising Area: Aegean, Mediterranean, Caribbean, transatlantic repositioning
Length of Voyages: 7, 11 and 17 nights

Ship Specifics

Tonnage	58,600	Elevators	6
Length	823 feet	Decks	10
Beam	94 feet	Children's Facilities	yes
Stabilizers	no	Fitness Center	no
Passengers	1,500	Spa	yes
Crew	711	Verandahs	yes
Space Ratio	39	Casino	yes
Crew/Passenger Ratio	1-2.10	Wheelchair Access	yes

Cabins: ⚓⚓⚓ *Suites:* ⚓⚓⚓⚓⚓ The 132 top category mini-suites are exceptionally good. They measure 236-square feet each, with an entry foyer, sitting area with sofa, matching chair and coffee table; bedroom with queen-sized or twin beds, TV, mini-refrigerator, walk-in closet, bathroom with a deep tub and shower, and a teak-decked private verandah with chairs and table. Booking a mini-suite guarantees a table assignment in the grill restaurant rather than the larger dining room. Standard inside and outside cabins are about half that size, 140-square feet each. Each cabin on the *European Stars* has Internet connections. On both ships you'll find a mini-refrigerator, hair dryer, safe, two chairs, desk/dresser, nightstands and twin beds that can be converted to queen-sized. Bathrooms in the standard cabins have showers but no tubs. Toiletries are quite nice, superior to many American contemporary resort and even premium lines. Storage space is adequate to generous in both the bathrooms and cabins.

Public Space: ⚓⚓⚓⚓ The coffee cafes on both ships take inspiration from Italy. On the *European Vision*, the Caffe San Marco with photo murals of St. Mark's Square in Venice surrounds the atrium, while on the *European Stars*, it's a replica of Rome's Antico Caffe Greco on Via Condotti. A miniature golf course wrapped around the funnel, a rock climbing wall, and special areas such as a cigar lounge with an excellent air filtering system and a cozy pub with Stella d'Artois on draft make these ships stand out from the crowd. Deck areas are clean and trim, with light teak, striped loungers and twin swimming pools. Top decks house Virtual Reality game rooms, a golf simulator and tennis, basketball and volleyball courts.

Spa and Fitness: ⚓⚓⚓ Le Terme Healthy & Beauty Center on *European Stars* and Atlantica Spa on *European Vision* are located forward on an upper deck. A large gym houses body-building equipment and a 24-foot rock climbing wall (10 euro, about $9, for 30 minutes) is staffed by an instructor who gives lessons to beginners. A walking/jogging track with nonskid surface is located on the top deck.

Entertainment: ⚓⚓⚓ In the European fashion, the entertainers are sometimes called animators. A cast of 12 singer-dancers perform predictable shows such as a pirate production with sailors dancing hornpipes and a James Bond gangster adagio. One evening, a musical group called "artists of the *European Vision*" saluted "The Best of Abba" in a well-meaning but often off-key tribute to the Swedish pop stars from the 1970s. In the dining rooms, a strolling violinist performs kitschy melodies, to the delight of most passengers.

Food and Dining: ⚓⚓⚓ When it's good, it's very, very good. The rest of the time, it's good enough to hold its own with any of the competition. In the grill restaurant (Pergola on the *Vision*, da Giacomo on the *Stars*) you can get lunch and dinner pasta specials that are not on the menu. This is where you can have some of best pasta with pesto in Italy. The grill restaurant is open by advance reservation to passengers who are seated in the main dining rooms at a surcharge of 19 euros (around $17). Breakfast is offered at open sitting in the main dining rooms, where you're likely to hear three languages at a table for six. Lunch is available in reserved restaurants on two sittings, or you can opt for the buffet and deck grill. Besides a pasta station, you'll find a pizzeria, grilled steak or chicken, focaccia, salads and fresh fruit 24 hours a day. Dinner hours are 6:45 for the first sitting, 9:15 for the second in Europe. Limited room service menus offer hamburgers, sandwiches, soups, salads, fruit and cheese.

Service: ⚓⚓⚓ The service is much better in the grill restaurants than in the main dining room, where it sometimes tends to be perfunctory. Cabin stewards, most of them Filipino, were always helpful and courteous.

Junior Cruisers: ⚓⚓⚓ The good news is that there is an excellent children's playroom on board with a professional staff. The bad news is that not all the parents of the 250 children on our cruise took advantage of it. (We were on during the last week of the summer school holidays in Europe. The crew said the following week would be much quieter.) A teen club with video games and a jukebox is near the disco on an upper deck.

Itineraries: ⚓⚓⚓⚓ The ships offer seasonal one-week itineraries in the Aegean and Mediterranean. The rest of the year finds the *European Vision* in Caribbean in winter, while the *European Stars* sails year-round in the Mediterranean.

Overall: ⚓⚓⚓ When you're aboard for a while, you realize these are big ships masquerading as small ones, and you rarely feel overwhelmed. Public spaces such as the purser's lobby and pool deck are expansive, but outdoor areas fill up quickly on a sunny summer day. North Americans who enjoy traveling with people from other countries, especially seeing Europe with Europeans so you can practice a language other than English, will like this pair of vessels a lot.

HIGH MARKS:

Δ The line has a "no-announcement" policy, which saves a lot of confusion and noise in five languages.

Δ Smoking is not permitted in the dining rooms and show lounge.

WEAKEST LINK:

• It does get crowded, particularly at embarkation and debarkation.

• Slow moving buffet lines

FLAMENCO
Built: 1972 Refurbished: 1997

Category: Traditional Budget
Overall Rating: ⚓⚓⚓
Rates: $$
Country of Registry: Bahamas

Former names: *Southern Cross, Star/Ship Majestic, Sun Princess, Spirit of London*
Nationality of Crew: Greek officers, international crew.
Cruising Area: Baltic, Russia, Norwegian fjords; Canary Islands, Morocco.
Length of Voyages: 6, 7, 8, 10, 11 and 14 nights

Ship Specifics

Tonnage	17,270	Elevators	4
Length	536 feet	Decks	7
Beam	81.4 feet	Children's Facilities	yes
Stabilizers	no	Fitness Center	yes
Passengers	900	Spa	yes
Crew	450	Verandahs	no
Space Ratio	19.18	Casino	yes
Crew/Passenger Ratio	1-2.57	Wheelchair Access	yes

Cabins: ⚓⚓ ***Suites:*** ⚓⚓⚓⚓ Standard cabins are on the small side with thin walls and showers only. Most have two lower beds, one against each wall with a small table or nightstand between them, and a desk/dresser with chair. There are four suites aboard, all with sitting areas, tub and shower in the bathrooms and a mini-bar/refrigerator. For the price, they're not bad at all. The décor is quite attractive and the housekeeping excellent.

Public Space: ⚓⚓⚓ The thing that stands out about these vintage vessels in First European's fleet is the care and attention that has been given them in refitting and decoration. The Riviera pool and surrounding deck is appealing with well-kept teak, and the Satellite Café on the same deck provides buffet lunches and snacks. A two-level cinema in the bowels of the ship is a tip-off to the vessel's age.

Spa and Fitness: ⚓⚓ There's a small spa and fitness center next to the beauty salon, and a sports deck aft on the same deck as the dining room. Daily programs offer aerobics, pool games and other exercises.

Entertainment: ⚓⚓ The show lounge is vintage, with no rakes or other features to improve sightlines. Entertainment is less lavish than that offered on the new ships, with more variety acts that depend on sight rather than sound, - spoken or sung production shows.

Food and Dining: ⚓⚓⚓⚓ The Satellite Café on pool deck serves light meals and snacks during the daytime, while assigned sitting in the Galaxy Restaurant takes care of dinner. Tables are large and close together, but the food itself is usually well prepared and nicely served. Dinner hours are usually 6:30 and 8:30.

Service: ⚓⚓⚓⚓ Service aboard is quite good European style with international waiters and cabin stewards.

Junior Cruisers: ⚓⚓⚓ A children's Dolphin Club with supervised program is popular in summer with young cruisers. Kids four to 11 have a get-together early in the cruise, as well as daily tea time, exercise classes, arts and crafts, movies and deck games.

Itineraries: ⚓⚓⚓⚓ The *Flamenco* sails in summer from Kiel, Germany, into the Baltics, Russia and the Norwegian fjords, and in winter cruises to the Canary Islands, Spain and Morocco from Genoa.

Overall: ⚓⚓⚓ The *Flamenco* offers what the line calls "Discovery Sailings" with attention focused on a variety of destinations and cultural experiences at bargain prices. With early booking discounts, you can take a 10-night cruise for as little as $460 per person, double, in the Canaries in early January.

Shirley and Harry Comment:

"The Flamenco was the original "Love Boat"; when the ship was Princess's Sun Princess, the pilot of the long-running TV series was filmed aboard. Only after production cranked up did the Pacific Princess become the ship most identified with the series."

WEAKEST LINK
• Smoking permitted in every indoor dining area.

MISTRAL
Built: 1998/1999

Category: Resort Mid-Size
Overall Rating: ⚓⚓⚓⚓
Rates: $$$
Country of Registry: France
Former names: None

Nationality of Crew: European officers, international crew
Cruising Area: Aegean, Western Mediterranean
Length of Voyages: 7 nights

Ship Specifics

Tonnage	48,000	Elevators	4
Length	708 feet	Decks	8
Beam	95 feet	Children's Facilities	yes
Stabilizers	no	Fitness Center	yes
Passengers	1,200	Spa	yes
Crew	450	Verandahs	yes
Space Ratio	40	Casino	yes
Crew/Passenger Ratio	1-2.66	Wheelchair Access	yes

Cabins: ⚓⚓⚓ **Suites:** ⚓⚓⚓⚓ The 80 verandah suites measure 235-square feet each, with queen-sized or twin beds, sitting areas with sofa, chairs, built-in desk/dressers, televisions with VCRs, mini-refrigerators, marble baths with tub and showers, walk-in closets and private verandahs. Booking a suite guarantees a table assignment in the Rialto Grill restaurant rather than the larger L'Etoile dining room. Standard inside and outside cabins are about half that size, 140-square feet each. Each cabin has a mini-bar, hair dryer, safe, two chairs, desk/dresser, nightstands and twin beds that can be converted to queen-sized. Bathrooms in the standard cabins have showers but no tubs. Toiletries are quite nice, and storage space is generous in both bathrooms and the cabins.

Public Space: ⚓⚓⚓⚓ The eight decks are named for European cities – Paris, Rome, London, Brussels, Athens, Cannes and Madrid – and public rooms take their names from notable areas within each city, such as the Caffe Greco, Via Condotti, Il Borsalino Piano Bar and Via Venetto on Rome deck. Deck areas are clean and trim, with light teak, striped loungers and twin swimming pools.

Spa and Fitness: ⚓⚓⚓ The Sporting Club offers thalassotherapy, massage treatments and a gym with a full range of equipment. The beauty salon is in the same area. A tennis court is located on the top deck.

Entertainment: ⚓⚓⚓ While the casino is considerably smaller and the production shows not as lavish as those aboard some of the megaships, passengers who like stylish surroundings, tops-optional sunbathing and leggy dancers from French nightclubs such as Lido de Paris, will find much to enjoy. The show lounge is nonsmoking, offering a respite from the numerous European smokers.

Food and Dining: ⚓⚓⚓⚓ The Rialto Grill sometimes serves menus from Michelin-starred chefs and members of Grandes Tables de Monde. Passengers assigned to the larger dining room may request reservations in the grill when space is available but will pay a surcharge (19 euros, around $17). The main dining room serves dinner at two assigned sittings, 7 and 9:15. Breakfast (with a six-language menu) is offered at open sitting in the main dining rooms, in the cabins or at a buffet restaurant called La Croisette. Lunch is available at a reserved restaurant table on two sittings on sea days or at the buffet and deck grill. Tea is served in La Croisette, and midnight buffets and 1 a.m. sandwiches are also on the agenda.

Service: ⚓⚓⚓ The service is much better in the grill restaurants than in the main dining room, where it sometimes tends to be rushed. Cabin stewards, most of them Filipino, are always helpful and courteous.

Junior Cruisers: ⚓⚓⚓ North American passengers will find some bonuses in enrolling their children in the kids' program on board, where (during our cruise at least) they learn circus skills from professional clowns from Cirque du Soleil, then perform in a children's show on the last night of the cruise. A teen's club is next door to the children's area on the spa deck.

Itineraries: ⚓⚓⚓⚓ The *Mistral* offers set seven-night itineraries in the Aegean and Mediterranean year-round.

Overall: ⚓⚓⚓ Passengers like the idea of having two dining rooms, with a smaller, more elegant one allocated for passengers in verandah suites.

Shirley and Harry Comment:

"It's may be a bit snobby on our part, but we do feel passengers who pay more for accommodations deserve extra perks. The Mistral is our favorite of the line's vessels."

High Marks

Δ The line's "no announcement" policy, which saves a lot of confusion and noise in five languages.

Weakest Links

• You won't find smoking in the dining rooms or show lounge, but you will find it everywhere else.

Holland America Line

300 Elliot Avenue, West, Seattle, WA 98119

(206) 281-3535 – www.hollandamerica.com

Holland America Line marks its 130th year in business in 2003 and there aren't many companies in the travel industry that can say that. In 1993, the company became a wholly owned subsidiary of Carnival Corp, but it continues to operate independently and offers a totally different cruising style from its parent company.

The company's long history has influenced passenger shipping history from its very beginnings. Since 1872, when the first *SS Rotterdam* sailed on her maiden voyage from The Netherlands to New York City, at last count, there have been 140 Holland American vessels in service. The early links between Holland and America began a rich heritage and partnership.

Today, Holland America has a modern, integrated 12-ship fleet, slated for additional expansion. Officers are mostly Dutch, but some are British. The crew is from Indonesia and the Philippines.

Holland America is unique in the industry with its "no tipping required" policy. Passengers may sign for on-board purchases and even pay with a personal check in most cases. The vessels all offer informal daytime food services, and there are no-smoking areas on all Holland America dining rooms.

Holland America's fleet is not cut from a single pattern, but the ships share many of the amenities that have become the company's hallmark. Huge bouquets of fresh, fragrant flowers are everywhere. Priceless antiques and artwork line the halls. Each ship features a teak promenade that completely encircles the vessel, which means there will always be room for sunset watching at the rail.

Interesting to note that never in its long history has the company had such a diversified fleet. And, never has the Holland America fleet been so attractive. Passengers have a choice from the classic and intimate ms *Noordam, Maasdam* and her sister *ms Veendam, ms Statendam* and *ms Ryndam* to the elegant flagship *Rotterdam* and her sister *ms Amsterdam*. Then, there's *ms Volendam* and her sister *ms Zaandam*, first in a new series. She will be followed in 2003 by *ms Oosterdam*. In a class by itself is the ms *Prinsindam* (ex *Royal Viking Sun, Seabourn Sun*) the newest ship in the fleet which entered service in June 2002.

Holland America continues to adhere to company traditions even in the naming of its vessels. All of the new ships are named for past vessels with a glorious history in the HAL fleet. Some have been renamed five and six times, but all have names ending in "dam."

Talking of oldies, the first *Rotterdam* was an iron vessel carrying eight passengers in first class, 380 in steerage, plus 1500 tons of cargo. Two young Dutchmen commissioned the ship because they wanted to make sure she would remain in Rotterdam as her homeport. That maiden voyage was so successful, a new company was formed--Netherlands-American Steam Navigation Company. It became Holland America Line in 1896.

Westours is a major subsidiary of HAL's extensive involvement in tourism and it specializes in land operations in the Western U.S., Alaska, and Canada. It operates seven hotels, four-day boats, and a motor coach fleet of nearly 200 vehicles. Westours' operations in the Yukon and Alaska have set industry standards for 45 years. Deluxe escorted motor coach operations in the Canadian Rockies were expanded in 1985 to include helicopter rides from Banff, and golf at Jasper Park Lodge.

Flagship of the Holland America fleet is the new *Rotterdam VI*, which inaugurated service in November 1997. Holland America vessels sail world wide, from one-week Caribbean and Alaska cruises, to longer voyages around South America, through the Panama Canal, Hawaii and around the world on 100 day cruises.

Who Sails Holland America? Here's another surprise. HAL is not just for older passengers. In fact, new and very contemporary vessels are attracting a large number of couples under 35 years of age. Interesting to note that 80 percent of HAL passengers are divided evenly between the under 35, 35 to 55 and the over 55 segment. Families make up about 15 percent and singles under 10 percent of most voyages. The demographics change and lean toward older passengers on long and longer world cruises. Passengers are upscale, like to dress up more than once a week, and are generally sophisticated travelers who want comfortable style in their environment. First time cruisers rapidly become Holland America followers, which now has one of the largest repeat passenger numbers in the industry.

Lifestyle: More traditional than contemporary, vessels combine, for example, Old World white gloved high tea with high tech hardware. Ships are spacious and offer something for everyone in every age group. It's hard to find a passenger on board any ship who hasn't sailed a Holland America ship or whose parents didn't sail one. Vessels do not remind you of condominiums or hotels that went to sea. They are ships, albeit upscale with amenities in the same style. There's more than a touch of class in décor and art works, but there's also a friendly family feeling. Classy, but not stuffy is a simple phrase that describes Holland America's on board ambience.

Lifestyle is as easy and as stress-free as getting around the ship. On some ships, an escalator provides convenient access upward to staterooms on Lower Promenade for passengers embarking on Main Deck. And, from that point, even first time cruisers just follow the flow.

INSIDER TIP FOR DISABLED TRAVELERS:

Holland America Line has installed the industry's first system of comfortable transfer between ships and tenders; and between tenders and piers for Disabled Travelers using wheelchairs. Called the Shore Tender Accessibility Project, the system addresses a common challenge facing wheelchair guest wishing to go ashore when tenders are used. The guest's wheelchair is locked into place on a lift that runs on an inclined track from the top of the gangway to the tender. A ramp on the tender allows the chair to be wheeled directly aboard and locked into place atop a specially designed scissor-lift. The lift is then raised to provide the guest a clear view through the tender's window. Dockside, the tender has a hydraulic leveling system than can be adjusted to allow for differences in height up to 23-inches between the dock and the tender, allowing the wheelchair to be rolled directly off the tender and onto the dock. On board, guests may request TDD equipment, amplified telephones, visual alert alarms, bed vibrating alarms, closed caption decoders on televisions, and flashing light door buzzers.

Dress Code: Sophistication goes along with more traditional dress suggestions, but even on Holland America, dress codes are being relaxed. On a seven- night cruise, it is safe to pack for two formal, two informal and three casual evenings. Passengers on World Cruises can expect to dress up more often. On Caribbean cruises, plan on one less informal and one additional casual evening.

Dining: There are two sittings on every ship, plus Lido-type areas and 24-hour cabin service. The newest ships in the fleet also have optional restaurants available by reservation, but without an additional charge. Main restaurant menus are fairly standard throughout the fleet, and offer a wide variety of main courses, appetizers, desserts and of course, lavish midnight buffets.

Also available on deck and in Lido areas is a variety that reaches from hot dogs and hamburgers at the Terrace Grill to the ethnic treats of the pasta and taco bars around the swimming pools. Smoking is not permitting in any of the dining areas on the ships.

Special Dietary Requests: Vegetarian, low calorie, and sugar free items are available on menus or can be ordered on board. However, Holland America requests that all special dietary requests, Kosher in particular, be made in advance of sailing. Kosher food is available at dinner and lunch (by advance arrangement) and ships have many approved Kosher items, for example cereals, on board. Kosher lunch and dinner is catered by Weberman Caterers and there is a full menu of choices. Passengers requesting kosher meals in advance are provided with an extensive menu from which to select and Holland America will board the selections. Kosher food is served in the original container, unless the guest requests otherwise. Clergymen, including rabbis, are on board during holiday periods and on longer than 10-day cruises. Religious services are usually held in cinemas

Optional Restaurants: All of the newer vessels have Italian-themed small restaurants that require reservations. There is no surcharge and in keeping with Holland America policy, no gratuities are recommended.

Tipping Policy: "Not required' is the official recommendation which leaves most passengers in a state of confusion. Americans, in particular, seem to be infected with a tipping syndrome and we feel awkward not giving financial tokens of appreciation. If you must tip, plan on a little more than half of what you would normally tip on other ships (about $2 to waiter and room steward; half to assistant waiter per person, per day). No one will refuse the gratuity. No gratuities are added to bar and wine bills, so if you're the tipping type, you might want to take care of the server at the time service is rendered.

Past Passenger Perks: Once you sail a Holland America ship, you're a member of the Mariner Society. Perks include recognition during your cruise for days at sea, on board private cocktail parties, small gifts on every sailing, and special rates on sailing designated as "Mariner Cruises. Past passenger status on Holland America extends to frequent cruiser benefits on sister company vessels – Carnival, Costa, Cunard, Seabourn and Windstar.

Discount Policy: Listed in brochures in the column next to regular fares is one called "ES" that takes 25 to 40 percent off brochure rates for early bookings which vary by destination. These discounts are capacity controlled, which means if you book late, they may or may not be available. There are also selected sailings on which past passengers receive hefty discounts and off season sailings that are advertised as low as two-for-one.

INSIDER TIP

Traveling alone? You may want to take advantage of Holland America's program for singles. Agree to share a stateroom with another nonsmoking guest of the same sex, and you pay only the per-person, double-occupancy rate, guaranteed. If the company can't find a partner for you, you cruise solo at the agreed upon double occupancy fare. There's no promise you'll find a new and dear friend--but the company says "Single Partner Program alumni have gotten along so well that they're known to rebook for another cruise together."

The Fleet

AMSTERDAM
Built: 2000

ROTTERDAM VI
Built: 1997

Category: Traditional Premium
Rates: $$$$
Overall Rating: ⚓⚓⚓⚓⚓
Country of Registry: The Netherlands
Former names: none
Nationality of Crew: Dutch and English officers; Indonesian service staff
Cruising Area: world wide
Length of Voyages: 7 to 106 nights

Ship Specifics: Amsterdam & Rotterdam

Tonnage*	61,000	Elevators	12
Length	708 feet	Decks	10
Beam	95 feet	Children's Facilities	yes
Stabilizers	yes	Fitness Center	yes
Passengers*	1,380	Spa	yes
Crew	647	Verandahs	yes
Space Ratio	43.5	Casino	yes
Crew/Passenger Ratio	1-2.1	Wheelchair Access	yes

Rotterdam Tonnage: 62,000 – Passengers: 1316 Rotterdam

Cabins: ⚓⚓⚓⚓ ***Suites:*** ⚓⚓⚓⚓ (Both ships are nearly identical in stateroom accommodations. Description applies to both). The ships are so spacious that even inside cabins are large and comfortable at 186-square feet. Standard outsides measure only 10 feet more while the 120 deluxe cabins have private verandahs. Called mini-suites, they are 284-square feet, including comfortably sized verandahs. Two full decks are devoted to suites in three categories. Mini-suites have many of the same perks found in full suites, such as a whirlpool bathtub, mini-bar, VCR and refrigerator. Top of the line accommodations are on Concierge Deck which is totally devoted to giant suites measuring 563-square feet, including large verandahs. Two Penthouse Suites are a whopping 1,120-square feet and have party-size verandahs. All of the suites have king-size beds (which can be separated into two singles), whirlpool baths, dressing rooms, complimentary stationary, canapés nightly, complimentary dry cleaning and pressing and full meal service en suite. Occupants have other special perks. They have exclusive use of Concierge Lounge for reading, tea service, late coffee and croissants or just for an elite hang out or private party. Other perks for suite passengers include preferred seating in dining rooms and at embarkation and debarkation.

The majority of cabins are in the "standard" category. They are extremely comfortable, nicely furnished and designed to make maximum use of space. All have personal safes that operate with keys, not the combinations or credit-type used on most new ships. Most bathrooms have tubs and showers, a quality selection of amenities, and good storage space. Designed for long world cruises, standard cabins have four closets and lots of drawer space. Curtain dividers section off cabins, so there's a sitting area with a sofa and desk and another curtain divides the room from the entranceway.

Steven Faber Comments:

"Rotterdam's suites are a great choice, even for those for whom the extra expense is a budget buster. Besides the obvious benefits of extra space and amenities, the private lounge for suite passengers is a god send. The concierge is the point person for avoiding lines endemic to shipboard life."

Facilities for Disabled Travelers: ⚓⚓⚓⚓ There are 17 cabins and four suites designated as wheelchair accessible. Entrance doors are 36-inches wide with no sills. Bathroom doors are 26-inches wide, also without sills. Showers are roll-in and measure 30 by 58-inches. They have hand held shower heads as well as grab bars. The toilet is 16-inches with raiser available on request. Cabin light switches are 40-inches and the bed is 20 inches from the floor. Two mini-suites are equipped for the physically challenged.

INSIDER TIP

The *Amsterdam* has 50 suites, compared to 36 on *Rotterdam* which came on line earlier. That tells the story about Holland America alumni. Suites sell first and wait lists on many sailings are common. HAL passengers have apparently reached a stage in life where they want the best and are willing to pay for it.

Public Space: ⚓⚓⚓⚓ While the two ships share most of the same features – the overall layout, the popular Explorers Lounge, the Italian-style Odyssey optional restaurant, the Crow's Nest to name a few - the *Amsterdam* seems to push the envelope a couple of steps in décor, design and amenities. With no sacrifice of traditional amenities and ambience which sets Holland America apart from other cruise lines, *Amsterdam* is lighter, brighter and has a livelier feel. Woods are several shades lighter and colors are warmer and elements appeal to a broader demographic range. The changes are not a put down of the *Rotterdam* which has the most magnificent art collection afloat.

Most of the differences are not noticeable to the casual viewer. Only passengers who have sailed the *Rotterdam* would notice that the stern outside pool was moved a deck higher on the *Amsterdam*. Both ships have the Java Café which offer complimentary coffees and cappuccino, with cookies, of course. There's also the traditional Half Moon and Hudson Rooms for meetings and private parties as well as card playing, the Erasmus Library, a casino and the 165-seat Wajang Theater which offers freshly popped corn at the entrance and some of the newest films. The theater is also used for religious services, lectures and as additional meeting space for groups. The various public rooms provide both intimate and social atmospheres.

Spa and Fitness: ⚓⚓⚓⚓ The fitness and aerobics areas share common space but are designed not to interfere with each other. Equipment is so up to date, instructors are on hand to help use them. Fully equipped, in addition to every kind of work out and weight machine possible, there are eight treadmills which are in almost constant use on sea days. All of the equipment faces out to the ocean. The spa area on *Amsterdam* was reconfigured to expand fitness facilities, which now include rowing machine, recumbent bikes, cross trainers and additional massage rooms. The Ocean

Spa offers a full range of treatments and the beauty salon looks like it was designed for Madison Avenue. It's worth a visit to the area, if only for a look at the magnificent paintings.

Entertainment: ⚓⚓⚓ The 557-seat Queen's Lounges are the ships' two-level show rooms with comfortable seating and good sight lines from both levels. Color the rooms theater-like with bright shades of purple with red and blue accents. To enhance production shows and individual entertainers who take center stage nightly, the room has a revolving stage and a cannon system that shoots confetti for added affect. The entertainment format for evenings introduced on the *Rotterdam* continues on *Amsterdam*. Focused on Broadway, a team of 10 performers stage three full-scale production shows with lavish costuming and lively dancing. Special effects and advanced stage technology result in good entertainment that keeps the audience attention through finales. On other nights, individual performers – magicians, comedians and the like take center stage. On special voyages, there are concert pianists and other musicians. Daytime activities are the usual cruise ship events – bingo, horseracing.

Food and Dining: ⚓⚓⚓⚓ When it's time to eat and that's often on every cruise ship, *Amsterdam* and *Rotterdam* offer a number of choices, virtually around the clock. Breakfast and lunch are "open" with service hours posted daily in the main restaurant, which is a two-deck room with tables accommodating from two to 12, all spaced outside of eavesdropping range. Most tables are either round or oval-shaped, which makes for easier conversation in a low noise level. environment.

Dinner menus offer a choice of five appetizers, two hot and one cold soup, two salads, five entrees, plus a list of "always available" items like chicken, steak and salmon, one vegetarian choice and six or seven tempting desserts. I rate restaurants on how well they prepare fish, which I consider the trickiest to serve without being overcooked, or undercooked. The *Amsterdam* and *Rotterdam* galleys passed the tests with flying colors. Salmon, mahi mahi, grouper and tuna were as good as they get. My husband tests the meat quality and preparation and he also gave the galleys high marks.

For quickie lunch or brunch and late breakfasts, the self serve Lido restaurants on Holland America have always been outstanding. Open for breakfast, lunch and dinner, there's a meat carvery at lunch time, eggs to-order at breakfast, in addition to an elaborate and extensive variety of foods. Hamburgers, hot dogs and Mexican specialties are offered on deck and then there's the do-it-yourself ice cream section that finishes off lunch and teatime for most passengers.

Optional Restaurants: ⚓⚓⚓ For a change of pace and a really out-standing dining experience, passengers should sample the Odyssey Restaurant, Holland America's answer to alternative dining options. It's a trip to Italy, or if you're lucky to the best Italian restaurant in your hometown. The elegant restaurants have a contemporary pan-European flair, with warm burl wood and a red, black, gold and cream décor. On *Amsterdam*, a series of paintings showing Italian country landscapes with surrealistic overtones of gardens, terraces and the ocean; even cows under umbrellas decorates the walls. On *Rotterdam*, it's photos of the restaurant as it could have looked back 50 years or so. Fine artworks line the passageway outside the restaurants.

But it's not the décor we should talk about when we mention the Odyssey Restaurants; it's the food and service. Reservations are required in order to dine in the 88-seat rooms which serve a special menu created by Chef Reiner Greubel, Holland America's corporate executive chef. The menu stays the same throughout a voyage, but daily specials are offered. It's hard to decide between Osso Bucco and Linguine with grilled prawns and when it comes to dessert, my suggestion is to try the sampler – a little bite of everything. Optional restaurants are also open for lunch and lighter fare is offered. There's no additional charge for the Restaurant.

On *Rotterdam* the Venetian-themed Odyssey transports passengers to an exclusive eatery in Venice. Reservations are required and passengers are well advised to make them as soon as they board the ship. Odyssey was hard pressed to accommodate all of the passengers on a one week cruise.

Service: ⚓⚓⚓⚓ The ambience on these ships is warm; the service is friendly and correct. It's hard to find anything to complain about because the Indonesians and Filipinos are so anxious to please. About 70 percent of the staff has worked on other Holland America ships. Many have been with the company for more than a dozen years and I talked to several second generation employees. The Filipinos are particularly good in bars and by the second night remember your name and preferences and have your drink ready by the time you sit down.

Junior Cruisers: ⚓⚓⚓ The aft section of one deck is designed as a children's area with a playroom for younger kids. There is a teenage room that include a jukebox, dance floor, giant television screen and video games. On longer voyages when few children are on board, the room is sometimes used by early morning risers for a quick cup of coffee. There are counselors on Alaska cruises with supervised programs for all ages, including special shore excursions for kids only.

Overall: ⚓⚓⚓⚓⚓ *Amsterdam* and *Rotterdam* are not extended versions of older Holland America ships. They are a new class of ships for HAL and the overall design is substantially different from its Statendam-class predecessors. However, many of the successful elements of that four-ship series have been incorporated into the new flagship. Layout of the public rooms is similar and the *Rotterdam* and *Amsterdam* also have three deck central atriums, but there are other differences. They are larger, and have an additional staircase and elevator lobby. Counting the atrium steps, guests are never more than about 130 feet from a staircase and elevator lobby. Another improvement which may not be noticed at first glance is the increase of four inches in height in every stateroom. Holland America ships are well known as floating museums and *Amsterdam* and *Rotterdam* outdo previous collections. Impressions start with the three-deck oval-shaped atrium, appropriately named Times Square on *Rotterdam*. Focal point is the clock, not just any clock, but THE clock. Built specifically for the *Rotterdam*, it reaches through the atrium and contains an astrolabe, an Astrological clock, and 14 working clocks from around the world

Amsterdam and *Rotterdam* are at the top of the premium class of ships, although the hardware qualifies for luxury category. The ships compete very well when it comes to facilities, but the software falls a little short in a couple of areas. Forgive those minimal shortcomings, and you sail in luxury at affordable premium category rates.

Itineraries: ⚓⚓⚓⚓⚓ The *Amsterdam* replaces the *Rotterdam* on the 2003 World Cruise. During the winter season, *Rotterdam* sails on 10-day cruises between Fort Lauderdale and Costa Rica before sailing transatlantic to begin 12-day Europe cruises. In the fall, the *Amsterdam* does a series of seven and 10-day Eastern Canada-New England Cruises before returning to the Caribbean for 10-day Panama Canal voyages.

Shirley and Harry Comment:

"There's a strong sense of quality and value for money. Gezellig is the Dutch term for a warm and cozy ambience."

HIGH MARKS:

Δ The replicas of Terra-cotta warriors discovered near Xian, China, in 1974. Well modeled and proportioned, figures each have different features and facial expressions.

Δ The 17th century tapestry in the upper level of La Fontaine Dining Room, the cellos and violas hanging on the back wall in the Explorers Lounge, the bone 19th century ship model mounted in a glazed ebony wood case in the Crow's Nest, the large showcase of 17th century "Tosei-gusoko," miniature warriors in battle gear with armored sleeves and shin guards, and the 19th century stone fruit vases and of course, the series of *Rotterdam* paintings of the vessel's ancestors from the 1873 *Rotterdam I* through the present *Rotterdam VI*.

WEAKEST LINKS:

- No refrigerators in cabins below mini-suite level. Passengers in lower priced cabins can have a refrigerator put in the cabin for a $3 per day charge
- Continental breakfast only in cabins. Suite passengers may order a full breakfast.
- No robes if you're not in a suite.

Steven Faber Comments:

"Holland America's omission of a caviar bar, or at the very least, caviar service available as an extra cost item."

NOORDAM
Built: 1984

Category: Traditional
Rates: $$$
Overall Rating: ⚓⚓⚓⚓
Country of Registry: The Netherlands
Former names: none
Nationality of Crew: Dutch and English officers; Indonesian service staff
Cruising Area: Alaska, Caribbean, Panama Canal and Pacific
Length of Voyages: 7, 10, 15, 17 nights

Ship Specifics:

Tonnage*	33,930	Elevators	7
Length	704 feet	Decks	10
Beam	88 feet	Children's Facilities	yes
Stabilizers	yes	Fitness Center	yes
Passengers*	1,214	Spa	yes
Crew	566	Verandahs	no
Space Ratio	28	Casino	yes
Crew/Passenger Ratio	1-2.15	Wheelchair Access	yes

Cabins: ⚓⚓⚓⚓ *Suites:* ⚓⚓⚓⚓ Cabins are comfortably configured so passengers have a feeling of space although square footage ranges from small to good sized with minimums measuring 152-square feet and average cabins close to 180-square feet. Standard cabins all have sitting areas with sofas and all outside cabins have tubs and/or showers. Insides have showers only. There is good storage space and accommodations are nicely furnished in soft colors. Unfortunately, a number of outside cabins on Boat and Navigation decks are partially obstructed by life boats so an inside may be a better buy on those decks. Each ship features 20 mini-suites offering a sitting area, refrigerator and an additional sofa bed. Suites are handsomely decorated and spacious but are among those facilities with partially blocked views of the ocean.

Facilities for Disabled Travelers: ⚓⚓⚓ *Noordam* has four accessible outside cabins that measure 219-square feet. Cabin doors are 29-inches with no sill and bathroom doors are 34-inches wide with no sills. They have roll-in showers with fold down seats, hand held shower heads and grab bars. Sinks are 31-inches high and toilets are 18-inches high. Disabled travelers have reported problems with these cabins. They say the entrance to bathrooms has an incline.

Public Space: ⚓⚓⚓⚓ From bow to stern, the *Noordam* is full of lounges and restaurants-14 in all-some cozy, some grand, most with expansive floor-to-ceiling windows that put you at one with the sea. You'll especially like the Crow's Nest--your window to the world way up top on the Sun Deck; and the Lido Restaurant, the hallmark of every Holland America Line ship, with its adjoining outdoor terrace and swimming pool. Priceless antiques and art-work line the halls. The *Noordam's* collection is largely from the other side of the globe, with priceless vases and statues from China, Japan and Indonesia. *Noordam* has five lounges including the two-deck showroom Admiral's lounge,

Piet Hein Lounge, Explorers Lounge and the Horn Pipe Club nightclub with its Shanty Bar and the ever popular Crow's nest on Sun Deck. There's a full casino, a 230-seat theater used for lectures, meetings and religious services, card rooms, library and other rooms suitable for private parties.

Spa: and Fitness: ⚓⚓⚓ A 15-foot wide teak deck encircles Upper Promenade Deck, affording space for running or walking. The Ocean Spa fitness center is well equipped and the spa offers all of the usual massage and sauna services. Scheduled supervised aerobics classes are held regularly. Company has a Passport to Fitness program on all of its ships to encourage passengers to participate in activities. The more you attend, the more tee shirts and similar paraphernalia you are awarded at the end of the cruise.

Entertainment: ⚓⚓⚓ Entertainment seems to be geared to older passengers who tend to retire earlier. Entertainment is not one of Holland America's strong points. There are plenty of activities to keep passengers busy-bingo, lectures, movies, singers and dancers, but evening shows fall short of professionalism.

Food and Dining: ⚓⚓⚓ Menus are fairly standard on most of the Holland America ships and there is careful attention given to passenger requests. There are usually five main courses to choose from and passengers dine in two sittings at assigned tables in the main dining room for dinner. Breakfast and lunch are open sitting. The Lido restaurant features an extensive buffet for casual dining at breakfast and lunch and opens out to the outdoor Lido Terrace.

Service: ⚓⚓⚓ Attentive everywhere by an accommodating staff anxious to please. Cabins and suites have fruit bowls refilled daily and everyone gets a canvas tote bag,

Junior Cruisers: ⚓⚓ A supervised program is offered based on demand, but there is a children's activity room and baby sitting can be arranged. However, these ships are not recommended as highly for families as some of the others in the Holland America fleet.

Itineraries: ⚓⚓⚓⚓ Sailings are seasonal. During summer months, the ship is in Alaska sailing between Vancouver and Seward on one week voyages *Noordam* makes transition 15 to 17-night cruises through the Panama Canal and spends the rest of the year sailing from Fort Lauderdale to the Western Caribbean.

Overall: ⚓⚓⚓ Decor picks up on the Dutch West India company, established in Amsterdam in 1603 to forge commercial and cultural ties between Holland and the New World. Display cases throughout public rooms feature artifacts of that period-authentic navigation instruments, maps, historical notes of the period. *Noordam* is the oldest in the fleet and is holding her own against competing ships belonging to the same company. There are small sitting areas where you would least expect to find them and a comfortable ambience prevails throughout the ship.

Steven Faber Comments:

"Contrary to Holland America's reputation as being nightlife free zones, the discos on the last couple of nights of a cruise become the turf of younger middle-age divorcees and most of the off-watch senior officers. The ships are hardly dead. Around midnight, especially on embarkation day, the staff often can be found performing impromptu in lounges devoid of passengers. One might find a jazz combo forsaking light jazz standards for a cutting edge jam session, or a cocktail waitress belting out a popular song backed up by a lounge pianist."

HIGH MARKS:

Δ The extensive 18th and 19th century art collections

Δ The make-your-own ice cream sundaes

Δ Self service laundry rooms.

WEAKEST LINKS:

• Age, in ships as in everything else, does make a difference

• Outside cabins on the lowest decks, or any of the aft cabins on the bottom two decks are not the best choices. The ships has had a vibration problem which has been corrected to some extent, but is still evident in the last 10 cabins at the back of the ship on lower decks. Also, watch out for partially obstructed cabins in which life boats block either the top of the window or the bottom.

MS MAASDAM
Built: 1993
MS RYNDAM
Built: 1994
MS STATENDAM
Built: 1992

MS VEENDAM
Built: 1996
MS VOLENDAM
Built: 1999
MS ZAANDAM
Built: 2000

Category: Premium
Rates: $$$$
Overall Rating: ⚓⚓⚓⚓⚓
Country of Registry: The Netherlands, except *Veendam* which is registered in the Bahamas
Former names: none
Nationality of Crew: Dutch and English officers; Indonesian service staff
Cruising Area: Alaska, Caribbean, Canada, Mexico and Europe
Length of Voyages: 7 to 16 nights

Ship Specifics:

Tonnage*	55,000	Elevators	8
Length	720 feet	Decks	10
Beam	101 feet	Children's Facilities	yes
Stabilizers	yes	Fitness Center	yes
Passengers*	1,266	Spa	yes
Crew	602	Verandahs	no
Space Ratio	44	Casino	yes
Crew/Passenger Ratio	1-2	Wheelchair Access	yes

Cabins: ⚓⚓⚓⚓⚓ *Suites:* ⚓⚓⚓⚓⚓ Standard staterooms have two basic color schemes-peach or blue and both are "feel good" colors. Customized prints for curtains and bedspreads feature elaborate floral batik patterns reflecting the line's historic connection with Indonesia. All staterooms have sofas and 70 percent have sofa beds to accommodate a third person. Cabins and suites are among the largest at sea. Standard outside staterooms measure about 196-square feet; insides only slightly smaller at 186-square feet. Deluxe outside staterooms are a comfortable 50-square feet larger and have private verandahs large enough for a lounge chair. Sixteen of the deluxe staterooms connect allowing families to create their own suites. Less than one-third of the cabins are inside.

Suites are awesome. The "owner's suite" at 1,126-square feet would spoil most of us for life. Friends who can afford the price called it the "ultimate experience." They had all of their meals in their private dining room.

For those of us who think a 600-square foot cabin with verandah is plenty luxurious, the ships have 28 of these suites. Each suite and deluxe stateroom has a private verandah, a VCR, whirlpool bath and minibar. All staterooms are equipped with sofas, hairdryers, individually controlled air conditioning, telephones, multi-channel music system, and flexible sleeping arrangements-queen-size or twin. Fifty-two staterooms have connecting doors and six staterooms are equipped to accommodate wheelchair passengers.

Facilities for Disabled Travelers: ⚓⚓⚓⚓ *Maasdam. Ryndam,* and *Statendam* each have six accessible cabins that range in size from 188 to 219-square feet. Cabin doors are 34-inches wide with no sills. Bathroom doors are 34 inches also with no sills. They have roll-in showers with fold down toilet seat, hand held shower heads and grab bars. Toilets are 18-inches high with grab bars and sinks are 32-inches high. *Veendam* and *Zaandam* each have 22 accessible cabins in several price categories, including suites. Cabin doors are 36-inches wide, but bathroom doors are 25-inches wide. There are no sills. There are roll-in showers which are 30x58 inches, hand held shower heads and grab bars. Sinks are 36 inches high and the toilet is 16-inches with raiser available on request. All cabin switches are at a height of 40-inches and the bed is 20-inches from the floor.

Public Space: ⚓⚓⚓⚓ Passengers cruise in Old World ambience blended with contemporary design, convenience and high tech elements. Holland America comes through on promises and ambience. It all comes together with a back drop of fine polished woods, etched glass and mirrors, European marbles and tiles, and a smiling crew to emphasize that welcome. Ships combine the best of traditional ships with some pretty fancy amenities and come up with top of the line premium cruising at very good prices. Décor of public areas reflects the company's maritime involvement with different parts of the world. Each ship boasts art that should be viewed in galleries.

Spa and Fitness: ⚓⚓⚓⚓ The spas offer all of the usual treatments and the gymnasiums are equipped with excellent work out machines. Runners and joggers appreciate the wide teak deck that encircles Lower Promenade Deck. The track is wide enough to afford space for comfortable wooden deck chairs, as well as for the athletically inclined.

Located aft of the Lido Deck swimming pool are British sculpture Susanna Holt's five bronze dolphins, which have become a hallmark on this deluxe series of Holland America newbuilds. The group of bottlenose dolphins is finished in a bronze, gray and aqua patina, and stands more than 12-feet high and weighs almost two tons. A second swimming pool is located one deck below Lido on Navigation Deck.

Entertainment: ⚓⚓⚓⚓ While not up to the standards and quality of the rest of the on board amenities, there's something going on all the time – the usual bingo, horse racing, fun and games. Evenings are something else. Holland America has changed entertainment formats and is now presenting three production-type shows during a 10-night cruise; two during a one week voyage. Shows are geared to 20's, 30's and 40's enthusiasts and remain strictly "G" rated.

Food and Dining: ⚓⚓⚓⚓ Dining rooms are spectacular on all of the ships in this series of vessels. The double-deck restaurants span Promenade and Upper Promenade Decks and seat 657 on two levels connected by a pair of grand curved staircases. A music ledge on Upper Promenade overlooks the main floor and provides a venue for a string quartet to serenade during dinner hours. Windows on three sides offer views of the sea off the stern of the vessel. Adjacent to the upper dining room are two private dining areas-the King's Room and the Queen's Room, each seating 44.

With open sittings for breakfast and lunch, most passengers use the Lido for those meals, so dinner is a special nightly occasion. Menus are extensive and have been upgraded in the number of choices. Marketing to younger passengers and to children, there are special menus for youngsters, a vegetarian menu and "light" items nightly as dinner choices.

It's hard to experience hunger pangs on a Holland America ship. Food service is continuous. Cabin service is on a 24-hour basis. The Lido has extended hours. Tea is served in several places during afternoon hours and in case you can't wait for a real meal, there are food carts spread around the pool area with salad bars, tacos, hamburgers and a lot more.

Service: ⚓⚓⚓⚓⚓ Holland America's not-so-secret weapon is the crew. Attentive, polite, anxious to please and always smiling, the Indonesians and Filipinos add to the ambience and enjoyment.

Junior Cruisers: ⚓⚓⚓⚓⚓ All six vessels cater to families and have devoted considerable space for children's activities. Supervised programs are in place for three age groups and daily activities include golf putting, dance lessons and theme parties. Teens have a separate disco and staff members hold dance lessons. There is a video arcade and activities for junior cruisers include pizza parties and other events.

Itineraries: ⚓⚓⚓⚓ *Maasdam* sails from Fort Lauderdale on 10 to 14- night cruises in the Caribbean and through the Panama Canal during winter, spring and fall when she moves to the Mediterranean and Northern European cruises. *Ryndam* goes on 7 to 11-night sailings in Alaska during summer months then moves to 10-night cruises round trips from Fort Lauderdale to the Southern Caribbean. *Statendam* alternates Eastern, Western and Southern Caribbean on 10-night round trips from Fort Lauderdale during winter months, then moves to one-week Alaska cruises from May through September.

Veendam sails round trip from Ft. Lauderdale on 7 to 13-night cruises in the Eastern Caribbean, then moves to Vancouver for May through September sailings. Volendam and Zaandam follow similar schedules.

Overall: ⚓⚓⚓⚓ Holland America is an old hand at producing "Dutch Masterpieces" in ships which somehow seem to get better and better. Although sextuplets in basic design and configuration, each vessel seems to establish her own identity and personality on her maiden voyage. Ships incorporate popular features and designs found on slightly older sisters of the sea, but each introduces new elements and features that create a unique style. Subtle differences in color, artwork, upholstery and decor individualize the vessels.

Holland America believes in tradition and carries the family name of vessels that sailed before the new generations of ships. The *Ryndam* is the third ship to bear the name. The *Statendam* is the fifth. *Maasdam, Volendam* and *Veendam* are the third ships with the same name.

HIGH MARKS:

Δ The warm and friendly atmosphere.

Δ The Flemish chest on the *Ryndam* and the 18th century Italian screen.

Δ Also on the *Ryndam*, the Alaska theme in the Crows Nest.

Δ The Jacob's ladder sculpture in the atrium of the *Veendam*. A monumental piece of sculptured glass created by Luciano Vistosi of Murano, Italy.

Δ The 26-foot Italianate fountain on the *Statendam* and the *Maasdam's* centerpiece-a green glass sculpture by the same artist from Murano.

Δ The thousands of frosted Venetian glass morning glories that fill the ceilings in dining rooms called Rotterdam on all the ships.

△ The escalators for easy access to upper levels.

△ The fresh popcorn available to movie goers at the entrance to the theater.

WEAKEST LINK

• Production shows have improved, but are still slow moving. So slow, that half the audience has either left or is sleeping when the final curtain falls.

• No refrigerators in lower priced cabins. Rent them, if you like, for $3 a day!

Peter Knego Comments on Zaandam:

"Often bland food and uninterested waiters in the Lido."

MS PRINSENDAM
Built: 1988   Refurbished: 2002

Category: Luxury
Rates: $$$$
Overall Rating: ⚓⚓⚓⚓
Country of Registry: The Netherlands
Former Names: Royal Viking Sun; Seabourn Sun
Nationality of Crew: Norwegian officers; Indonesian staff
Cruising Area: Pacific Rim
Length of Voyages: 14- 40 days

Ships Specifics:

Tonnage*	38,000	Elevators	4
Length	674 feet	Decks	8
Beam	95 feet	Children's Facilities	yes
Stabilizers	yes	Fitness Center	yes
Passengers*	794	Spa	yes
Crew	443	Verandahs	yes
Space Ratio	47.8	Casino	yes
Crew/Passenger Ratio	1-1.8	Wheelchair Access	yes

INSIDER TIP

When ships change names, ownership or management, there's always an element of doubt that surfaces in the minds of consumers. In this case, put those nagging doubts to rest! Our favorite *Royal Viking Sun* was transformed into the *Seabourn Sun* and now has a third life as the ms *Prinsendam*. She has emerged better than ever. She is now part of the Holland America family that has embraced her image and added amenities designed to enhance her elegant personality. When she was built as the *Royal Viking Sun*, she set the stage for a new era of ultra-luxury cruising with features and amenities unique in the emerging and rapidly changing marketplace of 1988. When she became the *Seabourn Sun*, she had a $15 million renovation, the spa was expanded, new facilities added and she carried on the traditions set when she sailed as *Royal Viking Sun*. Under the Holland America banner, she is again fresh out of a multi-million dollar refit and she looks as good as new. In fact, *Prinsendam* is a good example that even excellent products can be improved, freshened up and come to market as an even more excellent product.

Cabins: ⚓⚓⚓⚓⚓ *Suites:* ⚓⚓⚓⚓⚓ This ship was built for 100-day cruises and everything is spacious. Staterooms are exceptionally large and beautifully appointed, average cabins measure about 270-square feet, smallest suites are nearly twice that size and deluxe suites are two-room apartment-sized. Each has a walk-in closet, remote control television, VCR, safe and a refrigerator. There's a choice of tub/shower, or shower in comfortable marble bathrooms. Almost all single beds convert to queen-size. More than 60 percent of the cabins feature floor-to-ceiling windows and 38 percent have private verandahs. All but 19 are outside cabins.

Butlers serve the elegant penthouse suites and there is an owner's suite the likes of which I would like to cruise some day. It's in the category of "if you have to ask how much, you can't afford it."

The *Prinsendam* features a new type of accommodation with addition of 14 staterooms, 10 of which are "lanai" cabins. These staterooms, constructed in space formerly used as a lounge on Promenade Deck aft, have private lanais and share a private, covered deck and a hot tub. Lanai guests have privileges at the Neptune Lounge, the concierge lounge open to occupants of suites on Sports and Lido decks as well. The additional staterooms upped passenger capacity in twin bedded cabins by 28.

Public Space: ⚓⚓⚓⚓ During the transformation, the ship was Holland Americanized with changed names and redesign of public areas. Among major changes are conversion of the former Compass Rose Room to an Explorer's Lounge and a specially commissioned sculpture for the central atrium. More than $350,000 worth of modern art and antiques were installed to supplement existing artworks. The *Prinsendam* has a new Ocean Bar, an Art Gallery, a new Internet Center, a revamped show lounge and a reconfigured dining room to accommodate two dinner sittings. All of the public rooms are spacious. There are five lounges, a card room, smoking room, library, and all of the Holland America hallmarks – a Java Bar Cage, Crow's Nest high atop the ship, and major changes in the Queen's Lounge show room to permit expanded entertainment. There's the Wajang Theater with the popcorn machine at the entrance which has been moved to a more convenient location. The theater is used for lectures, meetings and religious services, as well as showing of current films. There's a casino and an 11-computer station Internet café. Internet access also is available in cabins and suites.

Spa: ⚓⚓⚓⚓ ***Fitness:*** ⚓⚓⚓⚓ This area was completely reconfigured and updated into a spacious and very "new' spa and gymnasium before she began sailing as *Seabourn Sun*, so it didn't need improvements. The extended deck provided the space for a Spa du Soleil in this aft section. It is a complete facility rivaling elite health clubs. The Spa is enhanced by Mediterranean sculptures and soft colors. There are private spa rooms ranging from the massage rooms to my favorite Rasul Chamber, which is a series of treatment rooms for couples that provides a memorable experience. The Fitness Center has also been expanded with new toning and cardio-vascular equipment.

Entertainment: ⚓⚓⚓ With a larger stage and new lighting, entertainment on *Prinsendam* is not restricted by size and offers scaled down Las Vegas and Broadway-style production shows and other variety entertainment. Daytime activities are enhanced with lecturers, bridge tournaments, and most of the favorite day time activities expected on Holland America ships. The Explorers Lounge has astring ensemble and there's music at afternoon tea time in several venues.

Food and Dining: ⚓⚓⚓⚓ *Prinsindam* features a new alternative restaurant, a new Lido Restaurant and a reconfigured dining room which has been resized. La Fontaine Dining Room retains its large windows and spaciousness, but has switched to traditional Holland America-type two sittings. Menus are in the Holland America tradition but based on a recent cruise, have been tweaked quite a bit. There were choices in five different courses as well as careful attention to special requests. The Lido Restaurant has also turned HAL-style with two serving lines and full buffets in a casual environment for breakfast, lunch and dinner. The Terraces serves hamburgers and other casual fare.

Optional Restaurant: ⚓⚓⚓⚓ The new Odyssey Restaurant, featuring international cuisine and Mediterranean décor is in an area formerly occupied by the forward portion of the dining room, Reservations are suggested but there is no charge for this a la carte restaurant. Opposite the Odyssey, guests are offered complimentary hot hors d'oeuvres before dinner in the traditional Ocean Bar, a HAL trademark, featuring a bandstand and dance floor.

Junior Cruisers: ⚓ There's not much space for kids and it is not a ship I would recommend for small children. The itinerary doesn't lend itself to bringing the kids, but there will be supervisors during school periods or when the number of children booked warrants a counselor and a program.

Itineraries: ⚓⚓⚓⚓ *Prinsendam* explores exotic Asia and the South Pacific on voyages of 18-days and longer which can be combined into more than 60-days without repeating ports. During summer months, *Prinsendam* will sail in the Mediterranean and in Northern Europe.

Overall: ⚓⚓⚓⚓ Holland America is calling the *Prinsendam*, the "Elegant Explorer" and the name fits the vessel. *Royal Viking Sun* and *Seabourn Sun* followers will find everything we loved about the ship and a lot more. The *Prinsendam* is an exceptional example of improving something most of us thought didn't need improving. She is really beautiful and just as spacious as ever. The new staterooms are an elegant touch and the old staterooms are being refurbished as the ship sails.

INSIDER TIP

Prinsendam doesn't really fit into any Holland America category. She belongs in a separate category for the line, one that probably will not be followed by other vessels in the growing fleet. There's little chance another Elegant Explorer like *Prinsendam* will be built. by any cruise line. She's one of kind. In her previous lives, the ship developed an exceptionally large and very loyal following of passengers who sailed her no matter where she went. As the *Prinsendam*, those followers filled her during the 2002 inaugural European sailings. No cruise-a-holic ever gives up on favorites. My best advice; if you want a luxury experience at premium prices and exotic itineraries, consider the *Prinsindam*. You won't be disappointed.

INSIDER FYI

What's in a name? *Prinsendam* follows a tradition of ship names dating back to Holland America's founding in the 19th century. The name *Prinsendam* has been around for a while. The first ship with that name sailed in 1973 on Far East and Alaska itineraries through 1980. The name translates to "princes" ship, with "dam" being the familiar HAL passenger name suffix that has been used since the late 1800s."

HIGH MARKS:

Δ For keeping the elegance of *Royal Viking Sun*

Δ The complimentary cappuccino and cookies in the Java Café

Δ The wide teak deck that encircles Lower Promenade Deck

Δ Cleopatra Slipper Bath which massages the body with forceful jets from neck to toe in the Spa du Soleil.

MS ZUIDERDAM
Built: December 2002
MS OOSTERDAM
Built: June 2003

Category: Premium
Rates: $$$$
Overall Rating: Not Rated
Country of Registry: The Netherlands
Former Names: none
Nationality of Crew: Norwegian officers; Indonesian staff
Cruising Area: Alaska, Caribbean, Europe
Length of Voyages: 7,10, 12 days

Ships Specifics:

Tonnage*	85,000	Elevators		14
Length	951 feet	Decks		11
Beam	105.8 feet	Children's Facilities		yes
Stabilizers	yes	Fitness Center		yes
Passengers*	1,848	Spa		yes
Crew	800	Verandahs		yes
Space Ratio	46	Casino		yes
Crew/Passenger Ratio	1-2.3	Wheelchair Access		yes

INSIDER TIP

Holland America's *ms Zuiderdam* began her inaugural season in the December of 2002, and she is an attention getter, The first of a new class of cruise ships aptly called the Vista Series, the ship is forward-looking in both design and spirit. *Zuiderdam* entered service after we went to press, so no ratings are available. The descriptions are based on advance information furnished by Holland America.

Here's a preview:

More outside staterooms with ocean views and private verandas. More amenities, including Internet/e-mail data ports in every stateroom. Of the 924 staterooms, only 136 will be insides. Others will be 165 standard outsides, 461 deluxe outsides 100 superior suites, 60 deluxe suites and two Penthouse suites, all with private verandahs. Expanded spa facilities, three sparkling pools, and 7-day cruises through the Eastern Caribbean.

SOME OF THE NEW FEATURES INCLUDE:

Δ Exterior elevators vertically transversing 10 decks and providing panoramic views from either side of the ship.

Δ A new "cabaret-style" show lounge, complementing a three-level main show lounge.

Δ Expanded spa facilities; Internet café and coffee corner; Internet/e-mail data ports in all stateroom

Δ Club HAL children's facility, with indoor and outdoor areas;

Δ Concierge lounge for the exclusive use of suite guests;

Δ Dining options, including a two-level main dining room, a casual "round-the-clock" cafe, and an alternative restaurant

Δ Two interior promenade decks

Δ A covered exterior promenade deck encircling the ship

Δ Large Lido swimming pool beneath a retractable magradome

Δ A dedicated disco and the signature "Crow's Nest" observation lounge/nightclub

Δ Extensive multi-million-dollar art collection

Δ Expanded facilities for the physically challenged (A total of 28 wheel chair-accessible staterooms in various categories; Dedicated elevator for wheelchair users to assist with tender embarkation; two tenders equipped with wheelchair-accessible platforms; Accessible areas at the bar counter and other public desks, wherever possible -All public rooms will be accessible.

MSC Italian Cruises

420 Fifth Avenue, New York, NY 10018

(800) 666-9333 – www.msccruisesusa.com

MSC Italian Cruises is the new name for Mediterranean Shipping Cruises, founded in 1992, based in Naples and part of a 30-year-old privately-held shipping company with headquarters in Switzerland. Now with four ships, MSC itself has been around a long time under various names, including Lauro in the 1980s when it was the operator of the ill-fated *Achille Lauro* and then Star Lauro prior to becoming MSC.

The *Melody* is the former *Rhapsody Atlantic* from now-defunct Premier Cruises, the *Rhapsody* is the former *Cunard Princess* and the *Monterey* is an American-built ship that formerly sailed for now-defunct Aloha Pacific Cruises in the late 1980s. A fourth vessel, *Symphony*, the former *Enrico Costa* of Costa Cruises, is posted year-round in South Africa for cruises to East Africa and the Indian Ocean.

A 60,000-ton newbuild is currently under construction at France's Chantiers d'Atlantique and expected to enter service in the spring of 2003. The company also has an option on a second ship for 2004.

MSC Italian Cruises is the largest privately-owned Italian cruise line and the only cruise line capitalized in Italy.

Who Sails MSC? Guests are European, primarily Italians, along with South Africans (on the *Symphony*) and a growing number of North and South Americans, particularly in the Caribbean, where English speakers may make up to half the guest manifest. They are mostly couples, ranging in age from mid-40s to 70s, with some honeymooners and families with children to bring down the average age demographics. The line is proud of the fact that they have made cruising more affordable and appealing to middle class Europeans when it used to be the holiday for only the upper classes.

Lifestyle: MSC Italian Cruises sails with Italian officers, Italian waiters and Italian chefs, although cabin stewards and cleaning staff may be international, so you can expect plenty of pasta, cajoling and charm. Shipboard life follows the traditional cruise pattern.

Dress Code: While the classic, vintage ships of MSC are less formal than some, men are asked to wear jacket and tie on formal nights. "Neat, casual wear" is called for every evening after 6 p.m.

Dining: Expect Italian cuisine with pasta featured at both lunch and dinner. Dinner is served at two assigned sittings, 7 p.m. and 8:45 p.m. Room service and buffet breakfasts are offered; lunch is available both at a buffet and in the restaurant with open seating. Smoking is not permitted in the dining rooms.

Special Dietary Requests: Most ships can accommodate salt-free, low-carbohydrate, kosher, or other diet preferences. However, this request must be made in advance, so be sure to advise your travel agent. All special dietary requests must be made at least 45 days prior to departure date.

Tipping: Suggested tips are $7 a day per person, with $3.50 for the waiter and bus boy, $3 for the cabin steward and 50 cents for the maitre d'hotel. 15% service charge is added to bar tabs at the time of service.

Discount Policy: Both Caribbean itineraries aboard the *Melody* can be combined at a discount for a 22-day cruise of the Caribbean, Panama Canal and West Indies. Florida passengers can get a $49 motor coach service to and from the ship from more than 20 cities in the state.

Shirley and Harry comment:

"Security aboard today's MSC ships is extremely stringent. It's one of the most security-conscious cruise lines in the business, as we can personally vouch from attempting to board as visitors in port when we were carrying all the proper credentials and permission from the home office."

The Fleet
MELODY
Built: 1982   Refurbished: 1996

Category: Budget-Traditional
Overall Rating: ⚓⚓⚓
Rates: $$
Country of Registry: Panama
Former names: Star/Ship, Atlantic, Atlantic
Nationality of Crew: Italian and international
Cruising Area: Mediterranean, Canary Islands, Morocco and Caribbean
Length of Voyages: 7, 11, 17 and 22 days

Ship Specifics

Tonnage	36,500	Elevators	4
Length	671 feet	Decks	8
Beam	89 feet	Children's Facilities	yes
Stabilizers	no	Fitness Center	no
Passengers	1,064-1,350	Spa	yes
Crew	535	Verandahs	no
Space Ratio	n/a	Casino	yes
Crew/Passenger Ratio	1-1.98	Wheelchair Access	yes

Cabins: ⚓⚓⚓ *Suites:* ⚓⚓⚓⚓ Cabins average around 185-square feet so even the insides seem fairly spacious. A number provide additional upper berths for families, a density first created for Premier Cruises, so two adults and as many as three children can share one modestly-priced accommodation. The six suites offer large sitting areas with sofa and chairs, queen-sized bed, mini-refrigerator, TV and bathroom with tub and shower. The décor is handsome and the ships are spotlessly clean.

Facilities for Disabled Travelers: ⚓⚓ Five cabins are designated wheelchair-accessible, but in a ship this age, don't expect wheelchair turnaround space in cabins and bathrooms. Not all of the public rooms are wheelchair accessible.

Public Space: ⚓⚓⚓⚓ Ship buffs will adore the Blue Riband Pub, named for the award given the ship crossing the Atlantic in the shortest time. You can browse through framed photos of the vessels holding the record. The Riviera Terrace makes a nice place to have tea or breakfast with its sliding transparent dome roof and tables set with white linen cloths, flowers and wicker chairs. The Junkanoo Club has as undulating bar with 17 rose ultrasuede barstools, a dance floor, raised side levels and a thrust bandstand.

Spa and Fitness: ⚓⚓ A top deck jogging track and a small fitness area and beauty salon with beauty salon and massage room are located on the next deck down amidships.

Entertainment: ⚓⚓⚓ Two different musical groups entertain on board, presenting deck music from 5 to 6, and the Junkanoo Club has live music in the evenings. The casino is unusually large for a European ship, reflecting its days with Premier Cruises. Cabaret acts including a magician perform in the Club Universe show lounge.

Food and Dining: ⚓⚓⚓⚓ A typical dinner menu offers a choice of three appetizers and two soups, pasta and risotto, along with fish, veal, turkey breast, steak, vegetables, salads and desserts. Dinner is served at assigned tables in the Galaxy Restaurant at two seating times, 6:30 and 8:45 in the Caribbean, 7 and 9 in the Mediterranean. The restaurant is located on a lower deck with portholes instead of windows; the ship was originally built as a trans-Atlantic and cruise vessel for now-defunct Home Line that went out of business when the ship was new. The Satellite Café serves buffet meals with additional seating in the Sunrise Terrace and on the deck. A rolling gelato (ice cream) cart usually turns up at teatime on the pool deck; mid-morning croissants are served between 10 and 11 for late sleepers.

Service: ⚓⚓⚓⚓ The Italian waiters and bus boys make mealtimes a celebration; Indonesian and Filipino cabin stewards are fast and friendly when cleaning your stateroom.

Junior Cruisers: ⚓⚓⚓ As you would expect from a ship that operated for Premier Cruises, the children's area is expansive. A large children's recreation room is located on Premier deck with a wading pool adjacent. While the ship offers a children's program in summer in the Med, none is provided during the winter in the Caribbean.

Itineraries: ⚓⚓⚓⚓ The *Melody* sails into the Panama Canal on its winter cruises from Ft. Lauderdale, going into Gatun Lake and through the Gatun Locks, then comes back out on the Atlantic side rather than making a transit. These cruises alternate with itineraries into the West Indies and Bahamas, so a guest can book two 11-night sailings back-to-back at a discount and have a lovely 22-day winter vacation for as little as $2,590. In summer, the ship cruises the Mediterranean.

Overall: ⚓⚓⚓ While not new, the ship is sparkling clean and nicely decorated. The ship can be booked at a real bargain price. The line compares its 11-night Caribbean prices with other cruise lines' seven-night fares. Wines by the bottle are also reasonably priced.

HIGH MARKS:

Δ Pricing that goes easy on the budget

Δ Great itineraries

WEAKEST LINK:
- The ship library has a limited number of books in several languages
- along with a plaintive sign, "Please return books when finished." There
- should be a companion sign, reminding guests to buy books in port, if
- they didn't bring them along for the ride.

MONTEREY

Built: 1952   Refurbished: 1988, 1996, 1997

Category: Traditional
Overall Rating: ⚓⚓⚓   *Rates:* $$$
Country of Registry: Panama
Former names: Free State Mariner
Nationality of Crew: Italian officers, international crew
Cruising Area: Mediterranean, South Africa
Length of Voyages: 10, 11, 14 and 22 nights

Ship Specifics

Tonnage	20,046	Elevators	2
Length	563 feet	Decks	8
Beam	80 feet	Children's Facilities	yes
Stabilizers	no	Fitness Center	no
Passengers	576	Spa	yes
Crew	200	Verandahs	no
Space Ratio	35.8	Casino	yes
Crew/Passenger Ratio	1-2.88	Wheelchair Access	yes

Cabins: ⚓⚓⚓ *Suites:* ⚓⚓⚓ The extensive remodeling that turned the *Monterey* from a U.S.-flag vessel sailing for Aloha Pacific into a Panamanian-flag vessel sailing for MSC also made public areas throughout and cabins, in particular, much softer and more luxurious than under the sometimes hard-edged requirements for the American flag. Some standard inside and outside cabins have the peculiar folding bed/sofa combination that, while well upholstered and perfectly comfortable, still manages to look like bunks. Bottom-category cabins have upper and lower berths instead of two lower beds. All beds are twins unless a double or queen-sized is specifically requested. Four lavish suites are located forward on promenade deck with separate sitting area, bedroom and bathroom with tub and shower.

Public Space: ⚓⚓⚓ The most recent renovations and remodeling gave a shiny new look to the public areas but many of the most popular features – spa, casino, disco and cinema – are located deep in the bowels of the ship. The superstructure itself is dated but very solid; it was built at Sparrows Point Shipyard in 1952 as the *Free State Mariner* cargo vessel. It then turned into the *Monterey* in 1956 for cruise-type service between San Francisco, Honolulu, Auckland and Sydney. It was laid up in 1978 and came out of mothballs in 1988 to be refitted for now-defunct Aloha Pacific Cruises. MSC bought it at auction in Honolulu after Aloha Pacific went into bankruptcy.

Spa and Fitness: ⚓ A small fitness center down on deck A has a few exercise machines, but on Boat deck a full walking and jogging track circles the ship. A tennis and volleyball court is also on the top deck; a sauna, beauty salon and massage services are available.

Entertainment: ⚓⚓⚓ Films in several languages, including English, are scheduled daily in the cinema. Production shows are much simpler on these multi-language mid-sized ships, with showrooms on the same level as the audience seating, so with the chorus girls, you see the "t" but not the "a."

Food and Dining: ⚓⚓⚓ Dining rooms are nonsmoking. Breakfast is served in the dining room at open seating and at the buffet. Dinner is served at two sittings at assigned tables. The food is classic cruise cuisine with an Italian accent.

Service: ⚓⚓⚓⚓ Italian waiters make the dining room service special, although they sometimes seem to be in a hurry at lunchtime. A crew of only 200 serves the 576 guests aboard.

Junior Cruisers: ⚓ A very limited children's program is offered on board when the number of youngsters warrants it; there is no dedicated space for kids.

Itineraries: ⚓⚓⚓⚓ Winter cruises in South Africa include 22-day repositioning voyages between Genoa and Durban offer fascinating ports of call. In summer, the ship cruises the Eastern and Western Mediterranean and Canary Islands.

Overall: ⚓⚓⚓ While the ship has admirable features - size and stable ride - it has shortcomings for families. It is perhaps best for older folks looking for affordable new destinations on longer sailings.

HIGH MARKS:

Δ Croissant service on checkout morning.

Δ The mid-afternoon gelato cart.

WEAKEST LINK:

• Age does matter. It's hard to erase the telltale signs on a 50-year-old ship.

RHAPSODY

Built: 1977   Refurbished: 1991, 1995

Category: Traditional
Overall Rating: ⚓⚓⚓
Rates: $$
Country of Registry: Panama
Former names: *Cunard Princess*
Nationality of Crew: Italian officers and international crew
Cruising Area: South America in winter, Mediterranean in summer
Length of Voyages: 5, 7, 11 and 18 nights

Ship Specifics

Tonnage	16,852	Elevators	2
Length	541 feet	Decks	9
Beam	76 feet	Children's Facilities	yes
Stabilizers	n/a	Fitness Center	yes
Passengers	576	Spa	yes
Crew	200	Verandahs	no
Space Ratio	231.98	Casino	yes
Crew/Passenger Ratio 1-3		Wheelchair Access	no

Cabins: ⚓⚓⚓ *Suites:* ⚓⚓⚓ Cabins are smallish with thin walls but all have two lower beds. Bathrooms are also rather small with showers but no tubs until you get to the mini-suites. We'd prefer to call the 20 mini-suites on board deluxe cabins but they do provide a sitting area. Two suites are relatively spacious with queen-sized beds, long desk/dresser/counter and sitting areas. The bathrooms have tubs. Only the suites are furnished with TV sets.

Public Space: ⚓⚓⚓ We never cared for the ship when she was the *Cunard Princess* but after all of the renovations, we like the *Rhapsody* better. MSC designers have turned the relatively stodgy public rooms into more glamorous bars and lounges. The 8 Bells indoor/outdoor nightclub works well in warm climates since there is an adjacent aft deck that can handle overflow. A cinema seating 135 is located on Deck Five aft taking up what could be appealing space.

Spa and Fitness: ⚓⚓ A sauna, gym, massage room, and beauty salon are supplemented by deck paddle tennis, golf driving and scheduled exercise classes. A dedicated workout fiend might feel short-changed.

Entertainment ⚓⚓ The casino is quite small with a row of what the British call "fruit machines" and a few gaming tables. The largest dance floor is in the Showboat Lounge where the stage for shows is also located. A piano bar dominates the Top Sail Lounge on the top deck.

Food and Dining: ⚓⚓⚓⚓ The classic continental menus always offer pasta and usually risotto, but you'll find old standbys such as lobster Thermidor, beef Wellington and roast duckling, along with Caesar salad and Vesuviana ice cream cake, better-known in American waters as Baked Alaska.

Service: ⚓⚓⚓⚓ The Italian dining room staff and international cabin stewards do a nice job with service, correct without being cloying.

Junior Cruisers: ⚓ A children's program is promised and a kiddie pool is located next to a pair of Jacuzzis but there is no designated playroom area for kids.

Itineraries: ⚓⚓⚓⚓⚓: The *Rhapsody* cruises in South America in winter and the Mediterranean in summer.

Overall: ⚓⚓⚓ Almost everything about this ship is routine except for the itineraries. Prices are very low and quite fair for the quality of food and service aboard, and the ship is always clean and fresh-smelling.

HIGH MARKS:

Δ It's an easy ship to get around for a first-time-cruiser

Δ Passengerswill find the *Rhapsody* to be a friendly vessel.

Δ Menu offerings make up for some of the ship's weakest links.

WEAKEST LINK:

• Not enough room in the swimming pool for doing laps.

• Cabin service menus are limited

Norwegian Cruise Line

7665 Corporate Center Drive, Miami, FL 33126
(305) 426-4000 – www.ncl.com

Norwegian Cruise Line is in the forefront of the new cruise revolution, introducing the much-ballyhooed Freestyle Cruising in the summer of 2000 aboard the *Norwegian Sky* and quickly putting it in place throughout the fleet (except for the *Norway*). The timing was right. Freestyle Cruising is aimed at younger cruisers who dislike old cruise habits: assigned mealtimes and tables, dress codes and regimented disembarkation by deck or color code.

"No good resort tells you when to eat, where to sit and what to wear," NCL president Colin Veitch said when announcing the new system. "None of them send you over to dine at a large table full of strangers." So NCL decreed that there would be no assigned meal sittings, only a shadow of a dress code (resort casual), pooled tipping at a fixed daily rate ($10) automatically added to the bill unless the guest arranges otherwise, and disembarkation at the guest's convenience.

Back in 1966, Caribbean cruising virtually began with the company, then called Norwegian Caribbean Lines and founded by Knut Kloster and Ted Arison. Their effort was geared to creating a cruise product that was casual, one-class cruising in the Caribbean in contrast to the more formal, class-oriented tradition of world cruises and trans-Atlantic crossings. The partnership broke up in 1972. Kloster retained the company and begin a rapid expansion of the line, while Arison went off to found a rival brand, Carnival Cruise Lines.

In the 1980s, NCL bought and later absorbed two San Francisco-based cruise lines, Royal Viking Line and Royal Cruise Line. In 1998, NCL bought Orient Lines and in February 2000, both NCL and Orient were acquired by Asian cruise giant Star Cruises plc of Malaysia.

Today NCL offers a greater variety in ship size and design than rivals Carnival, Royal Caribbean and Princess Cruises. Its fleet was assembled in bits and pieces over the years rather than being ordered in a series of identical hulls like those that are sailing the other lines. The *Norway*, the senior vessel in the fleet, was acquired in1979. Built in 1962 as the *France*, she was the last of the great French Line vessels and was laid up for five years after the decline of trans-Atlantic service. Two massive renovations have not completely obscured the graceful lines and charming onboard ambiance of the ship.

The *Norwegian Sea*, built as the *Seaward* in 1988 as the last vessel to come out of Finland's Wartsila shipyard before it was turned into Kvaerner Masa-Yards, still carries relics of the typical Norwegian cruise ship of the period: small cabins with twin beds (once fixed, now able to be moved together into a queen-sized bed) and level show lounges with lots of posts obscuring the sightlines.

Norwegian Dream and *Norwegian Wind* were built as the *Dreamward* and *Windward* in 1992-93 and "stretched" in 1998 to increase capacity. The *Norwegian Majesty* was built in 1992 as the *Royal Majesty* for new-defunct Majesty Cruise Line and was also "stretched" in 1999. The *Norwegian Sky* was built in 1999 on the hull of what was to have been the *CostaOlympia*.

The *Norwegian Sun* was built as sister ship to the *Sky* but with numerous improvements in cabin size and with more private verandahs. The *Norwegian Star* was originally designed for parent company Star Cruises, but was switched to NCL for year-round service in Hawaii when new legislation outlawed gambling equipment aboard any ship based in the islands. There was still time for the uncompleted ship to be altered. Instead, the designated gaming area was turned into a seagoing department store.

Who Sails Norwegian Cruise Line? For years, NCL promoted its connections to professional sports teams, theme cruises like the Norway jazz festival, and its scaled-down versions of Broadway shows, so it's hardly surprising to note sports and music fans, lots of young couples from the heartland, yuppies and Baby Boomers on board these ships. In the interim, theme cruises have been discontinued and professional sports stars downplayed. Freestyle Cruising has added still more first-time cruisers and couples who might otherwise book a Caribbean resort. Families with children are attracted to the children's programs aboard, while weddings aboard continue to gain in popularity.

Lifestyle: Freestyle Cruising dominates the lifestyle aboard all the ships except the *Norway*, which promotes a "return to the genteel days of traditional cruising with impeccable service, elegant appointments and formal dining." How's that for having your cake and eating it too? Aboard the rest of the fleet, dining venues are open from 5:30 p.m. to midnight and guests may arrive whenever they wish. However, since most arrive between 7 and 8:30, when lines sometimes form, it might be a good idea to reserve in advance, especially if you want a table for two.

Dress Code: While you're not required to dress up on certain evenings as you once were, there is still one evening designated "optional formal," meaning formal wear is required in one main restaurant while the others stick to casual resort wear. What this means (according to the brochures) is something akin to a pair of khakis and a polo shirt (presumably worn by either sex) and skirt and blouse or sundress (presumably limited to female passengers). Jeans, T-shirts, shorts, cut-offs, tank tops and bare feet are not allowed in any of the restaurants at dinnertime. No shirt, no shoes, no seven-course meal.

Dining: With the introduction of Freestyle Cruising, NCL also added more eating venues on board all the ships, but don't be startled to see surcharges in effect in some of the restaurants. Generally speaking, the food aboard is quite good and often fresh and inventive. We also notice menus are morphing into fusion foods. On the *Norwegian Sky,* for instance, one Thursday lunch (which went on into the late afternoon hours) was a mix of Southwestern and Cajun cuisine, with offerings such as Cajun potato salad with andouille sausage, pasta with black beans and cilantro, Southwestern succotash, baby shrimp salad, and Mexican coleslaw. A classic NCL tradition is the Chocoholic Buffet at midnight one night during each cruise.

Special Dietary Requests: Vegetarian, low salt, sugar free and light cuisine are no problem because they are part of the regular menus. When it comes to kosher foods, the company wants to be notified preferably at the time final payment is made or at least 30 days before sailing. Kosher food is available at all meals. Food is catered by Mada'n Kosher Foods in Dania, Florida. There are multiple selections offered at each meal. Food is on dishes or plastic, depending on the guest's choice. The policy is standard throughout the fleet.

Tipping: Gratuities in the amount of $10 per person per day are automatically added to cabin charges, plus the usual 15 per cent added at time of service on bar beverage bills. If you want to add more or pay less, you must go to the purser's desk and have them make the appropriate correction. The staff will also take cash.

Past Passenger Perks: Membership in Latitudes is automatic once you have sailed NCL. Perks include a quarterly publication, onboard amenities, including delivery of the New York Times fax (which other guests have to pick up at the Purser's Desk), cocktail reception, and special Latitude sailings where members receive a $200 shipboard credit and upgrades based on the level of membership. If you cruise often with NCL, you may work your way up to free hotel stays and shore excursions. You are also the first to know about "special deals." Latitude members also receive bridge and galley tours, special check-in counters, early boarding and up to 30 minutes free time at the ship's Internet Café.

Discount Policy: Early Bird Fares are early booking savings applied to cruise-only bookings; the line does not specify how many days in advance constitute early booking. NCL does a lot of regional advertising and rates are down into the budget category.

Shirley and Harry Comment:

"If you prefer traditional cruising with assigned seating times and table, and waiters who get to know your serving preferences during the cruise, all you have to do is ask. You can request an assigned table for two or for several like-minded fellow guests to join you in a traditional dining room seating arrangement."

The Fleet
NORWAY

Built: 1962   Refurbished: 1980, 1990, 1993, 1999

Category: Traditional
Overall Rating: ⚓⚓⚓⚓
Rates: $$$
Country of Registry: Bahamas
Former names: *France*
Nationality of Crew: Norwegian officers, international service staff
Cruising Area: Caribbean
Length of Voyages: 7 days

Ship Specifics

Tonnage	76,049	Elevators	11
Length	1,035 feet	Decks	12
Beam	110 feet	Children's Facilities	yes
Stabilizers	yes	Fitness Center	yes
Passengers	2,032	Spa	yes
Crew	1,000	Verandahs	yes
Space Ratio	37.42	Casino	yes
Crew/Passenger Ratio	1-2.03	Wheelchair Access	yes

Cabins: ⚓⚓ *Suites:* ⚓⚓⚓⚓ Numerous renovations over the years and the addition of two upper decks several years ago added a lot of suites and private balconies to the *Norway* but thickened her sleek profile. Since she was built in the days before modular cabin construction became the rule, the idiosyncratic cabins are a hotel manager's nightmare. One travel agent told us of booking two cabins in the same price category for two clients who were friends; the cabins turned out to be totally different sizes with different furnishings. Some of the lowest-price cabins on board offer upper and lower berths, not desirable for fussy or elderly folks or romantic-minded couples. The lowest category we'd recommend for budget travelers is a deluxe inside with two lower beds, category I and II in the current brochures. Some outside cabins have portholes and others windows, some have two lower beds that don't connect and some have double or queen-sized beds. All outside cabins except the standards provide mini-refrigerators. Suites and penthouses get concierge service.

The top-of-the-line Sun Deck forward owner's suites 001 and 002 have wrap-around balconies with tables and chairs large enough to lunch or entertain outside, along with separate living room and bedroom, bath with Roman tub and hot tub, separate shower, double vanity and guest bathroom.

Facilities for Disabled Travelers: ⚓⚓⚓ Guests confined to a wheelchair must bring their own collapsible wheelchair. Doors on the 11 staterooms designated as accessible range from 35 inches to 39 inches wide. None of the staterooms have pre-installed equipment, but the Courtesy Department can supply hearing-impaired equipment. Eleven cabins are wheelchair accessible

Public Space: ⚓⚓⚓⚓ We have certain favorite spots aboard the *Norway* that, fortunately, never seem to change. One is the Club

Internationale, which looks like the kind of sophisticated New York nightclub that existed only in movies like "The Thin Man," where Nick and Nora Charles wore formal attire and sipped martinis or champagne. Elegant green and gold silk tapestry covers the chairs and banquettes, and original light fixtures from the 1960s still adorn the walls and ceilings. Another favorite area is the pair of enclosed promenade decks, one called Fifth Avenue and the other the Champs Elysees. Lined with shops, lounges, an Internet Café and library, it seems chic night and day, even without the charming little ice cream table and chairs that used to line the deck.

Spa and Fitness: ⚓⚓⚓ The Roman Spa offers sybaritic beauty days in 6,000 square feet of indulgence from steam rooms and saunas to hydrotherapy baths and massage. The Olympic Deck Fitness Center is open 24 hours a day for restless sleepers who need a workout; the basketball court is just outside on the aft deck.

Entertainment: ⚓⚓⚓⚓ The Saga Theater is a real theater with rows of seats, good sightlines to the stage and no drink service, more like a small Broadway house than a cruise stage. The quality of the production shows is consistently good. NCL pioneered the concept of staged mini-versions of Broadway musicals instead of revue-type shows or variety acts. Also fun to watch are the Sea Legs Revue shows with lots of jokes, songs and dances and high-kicking chorus girls. Checkers Sports Bar with big-screen TV is a throwback to the old days of sports-themed sailings.

Food and Dining: ⚓⚓⚓ While the traditional cruise pattern of assigned tables and dining times is followed aboard the *Norway*, the cutting edge cuisine typical of the line has also found a place. A recent lunch, for instance, began with meat-filled potstickers, a choice of hot red bean soup or cold mangospacho (a version of gazpacho made with mangoes), fresh grilled perch, basil-flavored polenta over spinach and a to-die-for Cajun carrot cake with caramel sauce and a side of butter pecan ice cream perched atop a crisp wafer cookie.

Service: ⚓⚓⚓ The old-timers aboard the ship are still proud of its history and style, but some of the new waiters, especially in the buffet service areas, could use a little more training.

Junior Cruisers: ⚓⚓⚓ Troll Land is the name still painted on the door of the children's playroom, which opens off the enclosed promenade on starboard side, conveniently close to the ice cream parlor. Inside walls are covered with bright, fanciful murals. Another larger designated play area is located higher up on Fjord Deck.

Itineraries: ⚓⚓⚓⚓ The *Norway* continues to cruise year-round in the Eastern Caribbean, sailing every Sunday afternoon from Miami and calling in St. Maarten, St. John, St. Thomas and at NCL's private island, Grand Stirrup Key.

Overall: ⚓⚓⚓⚓ The *Norway* is akin to the singer in the Broadway show "Follies" who belts out the tune, "I'm Still Here." We were told several years ago that the ship would leave the NCL fleet (to be re-assigned to parent company Star Cruises) in late 2001, but she's still here. Particularly popular with honeymooners, the ship offers a number of attractive upscale cabins and suites with bright, airy glass walls and private balconies; don't make the mistake of booking a dark, tiny, low-priced cabin just to save a few dollars.

INSIDER TIPS

You can poke around the *Norway* and discover vestiges of the old France in spite of all the changes made over the years. Look for original round or oval mirrors and built-in dressers in the staterooms, and decorative murals etched on aluminum in an era when it was thought ships would get rid of all the wood on board. The Windward dining room is the former first-class Chambord restaurant. The former library with its graceful ceiling details has been turned into a perfume shop. If you can sneak backstage at the theater, you'll see that the former chapel, complete with different doors from first and second-class areas of the ship, has been turned into a wardrobe room for costumes.

HIGH MARKS:

Δ The elegant new suites with two bathrooms.

WEAKEST LINK:

- The outdoor Lido area. It's either too hot to eat outdoors or it's raining and uncomfortable. If it's a sunny day, the lines tend to be long.
- Charges for ice cream on the deck. Sure, it's a designer brand, but who cares?
- The shabby carpeting in some of the public rooms.

Shirley and Harry Comment:

"The charming Café de Paris, the sidewalk café that used to be located on the enclosed promenade decks called Fifth Avenue and Champs Elysees, has disappeared. Staffers say the U.S. Coast Guard decided the pretty wrought iron chairs and tables obstructed the deck in case of an emergency. Now you can stroll along the avenues but can't sit down for a drink or a coffee."

NORWEGIAN DREAM
Built: 1992   Refurbished and stretched: 1998
NORWEGIAN WIND
Built: 1993   Refurbished and stretched: 1998

Category: Resort XL
Overall Rating: ⚓⚓⚓⚓
Rates: $$$
Country of Registry: Bahamas
Former names: *Dreamward* and *Windward*
Nationality of Crew: Norwegian officers, international service staff
Cruising Area: Alaska, Canada/New England, Caribbean, Europe, Hawaii, South America, South Pacific
Length of Voyages: 7 to 16 days

Ship Specifics

Tonnage	50,746	Elevators	7
Length	754 feet	Decks	10
Beam	94 feet	Children's Facilities	yes
Stabilizers	no	Fitness Center	yes
Passengers	1,748	Spa	yes
Crew	700	Verandahs	yes
Space Ratio	n/a	Casino	yes
Crew/Passenger Ratio	1-2.49	Wheelchair Access	yes

Cabins: ⚓⚓⚓⚓ *Suites:* ⚓⚓⚓⚓ A dozen new owner's suites were added on the Sun Deck of both ships during the stretch, each with its own verandah shielded on one side by the suite wall, lending more privacy than the normal private verandah offers. With a separate bedroom and a living room with double sofa bed, four adults can sleep in comfort, with a fifth Pullman bed also available for the occupant who draws the short straw. Families should consider these suites instead of booking two adjoining outside cabins since they get the added bonus of a private verandah, concierge service, refrigerator, stereo with CD player and both tub and shower.

A half-dozen 175-square-foot penthouses are located forward on decks 8, 9 and 10 with floor-to-ceiling windows, queen-sized beds, sitting area and refrigerator, plus that lovely concierge service. All the cabins aboard are fairly spacious, with the smallest insides measuring around 150-square feet, and have duvet covers, TV sets and bathrooms with shower and hair dryer.

Facilities for Disabled Travelers: ⚓⚓⚓⚓ Each ship has 13 staterooms designated as accessible. They are insides and outsides. Both cabin and bathroom doors are 33 inches wide and range in size from 193 to 220-square feet. Both doors have 1 inch sills. Some of the cabins have tub/shower combinations and roll-in may be difficult. There are fold down seats in showers, grab bars and toilets are 15 inches high. Elevator doors are 34 inches and 36 inches wide. Most of the public rooms are accessible.

Public Space: ⚓⚓⚓⚓ Except for the terraced indoor and outdoor areas such as the sunbathing rows on deck and the stepped-down glass-windowed dining rooms on the aft end of the ships, the décor aboard *Norwegian Dream* and *Norwegian Wind* is predictable, with lounges filled with endless rows of upholstered or leather-like tub chairs in color combinations only a Norwegian could love. Singles of all ages will like the long row of wooden stools at the Topside Bar on the Sun deck by the pool, a perfect pick-up spot. Couples can cool off in the Wet Bar with its underwater stools, and those guests wanting a game of Scrabble can always slip away to the coffee bar and game room on the International Deck. The *Norwegian Wind* casino is handsomely decorated with whimsical life-sized portraits of flappers on the wall.

Spa and Fitness: ⚓⚓⚓⚓⚓ A large upper deck gym and fitness center includes beauty salon, massage and treatment rooms, gym and saunas, and just overhead is the basketball/volleyball court and exercise course.

Entertainment: ⚓⚓⚓⚓ The always-professional entertainment produced for NCL by producer Jean Ann Ryan and others includes production shows, variety shows, cabaret acts and lounge performers with music for listening or dancing. Lucky's Piano Bar has been known to harbor a sing along or two now and then.

Food and Dining: ⚓⚓⚓ The terraced dining rooms – Sun Terrace and the larger Terrace – make dining a pleasure with their theater loge tiers only one table wide. The alternative restaurant called Le Bistro takes advantage of a formerly routine small dining room, turning it into an elegant sidewalk café framed with draperies against a brass railing that separates it from the flow of traffic between dining rooms. The food continues the pattern of NCL's fusion-accented cruise cuisine except in Le Bistro, which serves French-style "gourmet" food. The Lido buffet in the Sports Bar and Grill can get crowded at popular hours or port day breakfast time.

Service: ⚓⚓⚓⚓ The crew to guest ratio is less favorable on these stretched ships than on the Norway or the big new ships.

Junior Cruisers: ⚓⚓⚓ Teens will be happy to know their area includes a video arcade and is on a separate deck well apart from the children's area. Activity groups are divided by ages two-to-five, six to 12 and 13-17. Group babysitting is available for kids from two-to-12 in the Kid's Crew area. Children under two may not participate in the Kid's Crew program.

Itineraries: ⚓⚓⚓ The *Norwegian Dream* cruises South America in winter, Europe in summer, repositioning to Canada/New England in autumn and south to the Caribbean in November and back to South America again in December. The Norwegian Wind spends summer in Alaska and winter in Hawaii, making 10- and 11-day cruises from Honolulu that also call at Fanning Island in the Republic of Kirabati (pronounced keer-ah-bahs).

Overall: ⚓⚓⚓ When this pair of 1,748-guest ships debuted in the early 1990s, they carried only 1,246 guests and seemed to us a nice size for a cruise ship, big enough to offer a lot of options without overwhelming people who don't want to travel with crowds of other people. While the stretching has not destroyed the stylish terraces all over the ship, the extra 500 guests do seem to add to the clutter at the breakfast and lunch buffets in the Sports Bar and Grill. But the renovation enhanced the very attractive glass-windowed amidships dining room called Four Seasons, enlarged both the spa and casino, and added a new Dazzles nightclub/disco near the casino.

Steven Faber Comments:

"Stretching Norwegian Wind and Dream was one of NCL's more ill-conceived decisions. Two intimate, nicely sized, personal vessels were turned into overcrowded flow nightmares in the name of economy."

HIGH MARKS:

Δ The delightful dining rooms aboard really spotlight Freestyle
   Dining options.

Δ Breakfast in the Sun Terrace or The Terrace.

WEAKEST LINK:

The increased density of the ship that the stretching procedure added has lessened the space ratio from 32.9 to 29, and at the same time decreased the service ratio from one crew member for each 1.75 guests to one crew member for each 2.49.

NORWEGIAN MAJESTY

Built: 1992   Refurbished and stretched 1999

Category: Resort Mid-Size
Overall Rating: ⚓⚓⚓
Rates: $$
Country of Registry: Bahamas
Former names: *Royal Majesty*
Nationality of Crew: Norwegian officers, international service staff
Cruising Area: Canada/New England, Caribbean, Europe, South America
Length of Voyages: 9 to 16 days

Ship Specifics

Tonnage	40,876	Elevators	4
Length	680 feet	Decks	9
Beam	91 feet	Children's Facilities	yes
Stabilizers	yes	Fitness Center	yes
Passengers	2,032	Spa	yes
Crew	1,000	Verandahs	no
Space Ratio	27.95	Casino	yes
Crew/Passenger Ratio	1-2.35	Wheelchair Access	yes

Cabins: ⚓⚓⚓ *Suites:* ⚓⚓⚓⚓ Most of the accommodations on board offer two lower beds and, except where designated on the deck plan, they can be pushed together to form one queen-sized bed. Certain designated cabins, however, provide a double bed or queen-sized bed. On the inside double cabins, a handsome mirror fills the spot where a window would be, successfully presenting the illusion of space and light, brightening the room inside. This is a plus since most of the inside and outside standard cabins are on the small side. All cabins provide duvet bedcovers, TV sets, safes and bathroom with shower and hair dryer. If you want a bathtub, you'll have to book a suite.

Owner's suites are comfortably spacious with separate sleeping and sitting areas and floor-to-ceiling bay windows, full bath with tub and shower, and concierge service.

Facilities for Disabled Travelers: ⚓⚓ The ship has four accessible outside cabins. Cabin and bathroom doors are 33 inches wide with no sills. Bathrooms have roll-in showers, hand held showerheads, fold down seats and grab bars. All decks are accessible and there are accessible public restrooms.

Public Space: ⚓⚓⚓⚓ There's a relaxed, casual atmosphere on board that appeals to many younger guests. At 38,000 tons, the ship is small enough to easily find your way around, even on a three-day cruise. All the public rooms you would expect are there. Some can be opened and combined, making it flexible for meetings and convention charters.

Spa and Fitness: ⚓⚓⚓ The Body Waves Spa fills a large section of Promenade Deck with saunas and massage rooms, aerobics, gym and beauty salon. In addition, guests can jog or walk completely around the ship on Promenade Deck, an increasingly rare privilege with today's ship designs. It's easier to count laps when you don't have to turn around; five laps equals one mile.

Entertainment: ⚓⚓⚓ The Palace Theatre programs some sophisticated evening entertainment, including production shows, and in the daytime there's live music for dancing on deck.

Food and Dining: ⚓⚓⚓ When she was the *Royal Majesty*, this ship was one of the first to offer a smoke-free dining room at sea back in 1992. Today it continues to provide an appealing ambiance, along with the varied new NCL cuisine and the freewheeling dining hours and options. Indoor and outdoor tables await the self-service buffet guests at breakfast and lunch, while evening options range from the romantic Le Bistro (reservations required and surcharge applied) to the Seven Seas and the Four Seasons dining rooms. Ice cream and pizza are offered outdoors on the Piazza San Marco aft on deck 10.

Service: ⚓⚓⚓ On the crew/guest ratio, there's an extra one-third guest added to the two guests each crew member should be serving, so don't be surprised if a room service request is a little slow arriving.

Junior Cruisers: ⚓⚓⚓ The Kids Korner playroom has an adjacent splash pool and sundeck outside that lets children enjoy their own version of a Caribbean cruise with squealing and splashing with newfound friends under the supervision of professional youth counselors. Teens are left to enjoy a big video arcade opposite the Internet Café.

Itineraries: ⚓⚓⚓ Predictable three-, four- and seven-day sailings appealing to first-time cruisers and honeymooners include Bermuda in summer on a seven-day roundtrip cruise out of Boston and two cruises a week from Miami into the Bahamas and Mexican Caribbean in winter.

Overall: ⚓⚓⚓ As with the *Norwegian Dream* and *Norwegian Wind*, the *Norwegian Majesty* added capacity for 500 additional guests when it was stretched in 1999 with the addition of a 112-foot section added to its middle. Built for warm weather cruising, the ship offers a fair amount of sunbathing space on deck, along with two pools (one of them smallish) and two hot tubs. In a break from tradition, the show lounge is located aft rather than forward, and the spa is relatively large for a ship this size. The *Norwegian Majesty* is especially good for young cruisers, first-time cruisers and honeymooners. With seven restaurants and 11 bars and lounges, there's always somewhere to go.

HIGH MARKS:

△ A larger-than-average number of lounges and restaurants with regal
△ Names left over from the days with now-defunct Majesty Cruise Line:
△ Royal Observatory, Royal Fireworks and Café Royale.

WEAKEST LINK:

• No private verandahs aboard the *Royal Majesty*, although 20 suites offer bay windows with views fore and aft.

NORWEGIAN SEA
Built: 1988

Category: Resort Mid-Size
Overall Rating: ⚓⚓⚓
Rates: $$
Country of Registry: Bahamas
Former names: *Seaward*
Nationality of Crew: Norwegian officers, international service staff
Cruising Area: Bahamas, Canada/New England, Caribbean
Length of Voyages: 3 to 14 days

Ship Specifics

Tonnage	42,000	Elevators	6
Length	710 feet	Decks	9
Beam	93 feet	Children's Facilities	yes
Stabilizers	yes	Fitness Center	no
Passengers	1,518	Spa	yes
Crew	1,000	Verandahs	no
Space Ratio	27.95	Casino	yes
Crew/Passenger Ratio	1-2.4	Wheelchair Access	yes

Cabins: ⚓⚓ *Suites:* ⚓⚓⚓ The bottom-of-the-line cabins aboard are quite small although they have two lower beds, some of which can be pushed together to make a queen-sized bed. Pay close attention to the deck plan details where sleeping facilities are which are spelled out. All cabins provide duvet bedcovers, TV sets, safes and bathrooms with shower. Some accommodations, mostly suites, offer tubs. The four owner's suites face forward with a captain's eye view of the sea and 280 to 360-square feet of space. The deluxe suites on Norway Deck offer sleeping and seating areas for three, as well as a mini-refrigerator, tub and shower. All the suites provide concierge service.

Facilities for Disabled Travelers: ⚓⚓ Four inside cabins have been designated as wheelchair accessible. Cabin and bathrooms doors are 33.5 inches wide and do not have sills. Bathrooms have roll-in showers, hand held showerheads, fold down seats and grab bars. Toilets are 16 inches high and have grab bars. All decks are accessible and there are accessible public restrooms.

Public Space: ⚓⚓ The two-deck Crystal Court lobby provides a dramatic entrance for boarding, as well as offering a cool dark refuge when coming in from the dazzling tropical sunlight. Oscar's Piano Bar is a lively getaway; both Stardust Lounge and Cabaret Lounge boast big dance floors and live music. Boomer's Disco fills an appropriately large space aft on deck 8. Gatsby's Wine Bar is a chic room that is often booked for weddings in port and sometimes set up charmingly for a wedding lunch. Seeing it arranged this way, we've never understood why it wasn't turned into a second alternative restaurant, perhaps Italian or a steakhouse, since there is a galley nearby. The adjacent Le Bistro is an alternative restaurant serving familiar celebration-night-out French/American cuisine.

Spa and Fitness: ⚓⚓⚓ A top-deck fitness center (open 24 hours) and net-enclosed driving range, plus an all-around-the-ship jogging track on the promenade deck and an aft sports deck with basketball/volleyball court, access generous exercise options. Two swimming pools and two hot tubs are on the pool deck and a beauty salon and barbershop on Main Deck

Entertainment: ⚓⚓⚓⚓ Production shows, variety shows and cabaret acts are regularly scheduled, along with live music for dancing in the lounges nightly.

Food and Dining: ⚓⚓⚓⚓ This ship was built in 1988 when nobody could imagine guests wanted to eat in a lot of different venues during a cruise; there are two dining rooms, plus an alternative surcharge restaurant (Le Bistro) and a self-service buffet, the Big Apple Café, on Lido deck with indoor and outdoor seating. The menus reflect the same expansion of recipes typical of the line since it introduced Freestyle Cruising.

Service: ⚓⚓⚓ Again, a low service ratio means two and a half guests instead of only two share a single crewmember.

Junior Cruisers: ⚓⚓ The Porthole Children's Center is actually an inside room about the size of three inside cabins on a lower deck   Teens will find a video arcade aboard.

Itineraries: ⚓⚓⚓⚓ The *Norwegian Sea* sails to The Bahamas from New York in summer, with four days at sea and two ports of call; to Canada/New England in the fall with a Colonial America repositioning cruise between Montreal and Miami; then spends its winters in the Caribbean and spring in Bermuda.

Overall: ⚓⚓⚓ The biggest fault we find with the *Norwegian Sea* is its general lack of teak deck areas. Instead, in many areas, guests are walking around on indoor/outdoor carpet or painted metal deck surfaces. Also, years of doing three-and four-day cruises have left some wear and tear; while the ship is clean and well cared-for, the outer decks have a used look in some areas. The guest space ratio – the amount of public space figured mathematically on a numerical basis – is also the lowest in the NCL fleet. First-time cruisers, however, will find a lot to like from the Freestyle Cruising dining options to the casual garb.

HIGH MARKS

Δ   Everything Under the Sun department store and drugstore on the *Norwegian Sea* is handy to pick up anything you forgot to pack; if you're short on cash, hit the ATM machine in the lobby.

WEAKEST LINK
- No private verandahs
- Too few staff to serve so many

NORWEGIAN SKY
Built: 1999
NORWEGIAN SUN
Built: 2001

Category: Resort XL
Overall Rating: ⚓⚓⚓⚓
Rates: $$$
Country of Registry: Bahamas
Former names: none
Nationality of Crew: Norwegian officers, international service staff
Cruising Area: Alaska, Caribbean, Panama Canal
Length of Voyages: 7 to 16 days

Ship Specifics

Tonnage	77,104	Elevators	12
Length	853 feet	Decks	12
Beam	108 feet	Children's Facilities	yes
Stabilizers	yes	Fitness Center	yes
Passengers	2,002	Spa	yes
Crew	1,000	Verandahs	yes
Space Ratio	38.5	Casino	yes
Crew/Passenger Ratio	1-2	Wheelchair Access	yes

Cabins: ⚓⚓ *Suites:* ⚓⚓⚓⚓ Standard cabins are around 150-square feet on the *Norwegian Sky*, small but adequate. Each contains twin beds that can be pushed together to make a queen-sized bed with duvet, love seat, small coffee table, chair and desk/dresser with mini-refrigerator. Bathrooms are compact with showers only. There is a dearth of drawer storage space and the hangers are the I-don't-trust-you types that clip into a metal ring. Our cabin aboard our first cruise on the *Norwegian Sky* was the smallest "superior deluxe double stateroom" we've ever occupied on a ship, prettily decorated but so tiny you had to go out in the hallway to change your mind.

The *Norwegian Sun* carries 100 more outside cabins than the *Sky*, and basic insides measure 176-square feet. The wardrobe hanging and drawer space has also been expanded somewhat on the *Sun*. Owner's suites boast private verandahs with hot tub, a living room with queen-sized sofa bed and pull-down single berth in addition to the queen-sized bed in the separate bedroom. Butler and concierge service is included.

Slightly less expensive are the penthouse suites with private verandahs that are located forward or aft on the ship; on the *Sky* the aft ones are larger than the forward ones if you don't mind staring at where you've been instead of where you're going. In these suites, there is a whirlpool tub in the bathroom, and a sitting area instead of a separate living room. You still get butler service, however. On the *Sun* there are also a pair of suites forward on Viking Deck with wraparound verandahs, as well as mini-suites, a notch down in price from the penthouse suites.

Facilities for Disabled Travelers: ⚓⚓⚓ The *Sky* has six inside accessible cabins while the *Sun* has 20, four of which have private verandahs. Cabin and bathroom doors are 35 inches wide without sills. On *Sky*, cabins are a mere 147-square feet, which hardly affords turn around space. Both ships have roll-in showers, hand held showerheads, fold down seats and grab bars. There is knee clearance under the sink.

Public Space: ⚓⚓⚓⚓ Ships have three-deck atriums with glass elevators and two-deck theaters. The undulating Topsiders Bar on the pool deck has to be the biggest Happy Hour at sea with 48 barstools. Both ships offer a cigar room and a Martini menu that lists 30 concoctions they call Martinis, not one in the classic gin or vodka version. The closest a fussy drinker could come to a real Martini would be to order the Cajun Martini and tell them to hold the jalapeno.

Spa and Fitness: ⚓⚓⚓⚓ Body Waves Spas on both ships offer a 24-hour Fitness Center, massage and treatment rooms, saunas, a big aerobics room, steam room and a range of beauty services. In addition, there is full promenade jogging track, along with golf driving range and basketball and volleyball court.

Entertainment: ⚓⚓⚓⚓ It was aboard the *Sky* that we saw the Jean Ann Ryan production saluting Sir Cameron Mackintosh called, "Hey, Mr. Producer," one of the best shows we've ever seen at sea. A version of it called

"Encore Mr. Producer" plays aboard the *Sun*. Energetic dance shows called "Sea Legs Revue," a music show with a Latin accent and an evening of jazz and pop favorites are also sometimes on the agenda. Dazzles night club/disco features the longest bar at sea and is busy until 5 a.m. Windjammer piano bar and lounge has sing-alongs, while the Sports Bar offers big-screen live and videotaped broadcasts of sports events.

Food and Dining: ⚓⚓⚓⚓ The *Sun* offers nine restaurants; the *Sky* (which was built before Freestyle Cruising was created) has six. The *Sky* offers Asian and Italian dishes in the Ciao-Chow Restaurant, plus signature pizzas at lunchtime, and Le Bistro serves Mediterranean food. A Cajun/Southwestern buffet is a typical lunchtime offering in the Garden Café, which also features a kid's buffet daily from 5:30 to 6:30 p.m. tucked into one corner with small-sized tables and chairs and a lower-than-average buffet counter. Horizons of Italy ($10 per person cover charge) serves cooked-to-order

Italian specialties in one of the most elegant dining rooms at sea, a long narrow room reminiscent of the Orient Express train, with tables for two by the window and a row of raised banquettes for four against the wall. The *Sun* has two main restaurants, one of which observes a dress code on formal nights and can be reserved for traditional seating with assigned time, table and wait staff for guests who prefer this. Also on board are Le Bistro for French food, Il Adagio for Italian, Ginza for sushi and teppanyaki, East Meets West California/Hawaii/Asian fusion food, Pacific Heights light cuisine on pool deck, the 24-hour Garden Café, and Las Ramblas Tapas Bar and Restaurant. Some of these require a reservation and carry a surcharge. The real dish-dropper, however, is a live lobster tank aboard the *Sun*, a reference back to parent company Star Cruises, whose Aquarius introduced the very first live fish and lobster tank at sea.

Service: ⚓⚓⚓⚓ NCL has introduced motivational training for staff members. One hotel director from the line told us, "The time is over when you can get hotel-trained people (for cruise ships); you train them on board now."

Junior Cruisers: ⚓⚓⚓⚓ Kids will find an outdoor deck area and children's pool on the top deck, as well as an indoor playroom forward on deck 7. Teens have their own Teen Club by day that turns into a disco for teens only every night. The Video Zone provides interactive video games and simulators.

Itineraries: ⚓⚓⚓⚓ The *Norwegian Sky* spends the summer in Alaska and the winter in the Caribbean, with Panama Canal transits offered on the repositioning sailings. The *Norwegian Sun* stays year-round in the Caribbean, with seven-day roundtrips out of Miami on exotic Western Caribbean itinerary that adds Belize and Roatan in Honduras's Bay of Islands to the classic route.

Overall: ⚓⚓⚓⚓ This pair of almost-sister ships began with the *Norwegian Sky*, whose maiden voyage in August 1999 which also included an eclipse of the sun off the English coast. The *Sky* was built on an existing hull that had been created for the *Costa Olympia*, sister ship to the *Costa Victoria* but cancelled by Costa after the German shipyard that built it declared bankruptcy. The *Norwegian Sun*, which debuted in September 2001, carries the same number of guests in a slightly larger gross registered tonnage; the cabins are bigger and there are more penthouses and private balconies aboard, as well as more Internet Café terminals. You don't need a tuxedo – or even a tie – on these ships, but if you want to dress up for the captain's welcome-aboard night, you can party with other dressed-up folk in a designated dining room.

Peter Knego Comments:

"Norwegian Sun seems to be a ship with an identity crisis. Is she Asian or Western? Initially conceived for Star Cruises as an expanded version of their SuperStar Leo, she was completed for NCL's Hawaiian service. Color schemes and colors seem to work against each other in many of the public rooms."

HIGH MARKS

Δ Freestyle Disembarkation usually clears the ship by 10:15 a.m.; room service breakfast is offered up to 9 a.m. By 11:30 a.m., new guests usually begin embarking, although their cabins may not be ready for occupancy. They are free to relax in the public rooms, have a drink in the bar or a snack at the buffet, a huge improvement over sitting in a folding chair in the terminal, waiting until 2 p.m. to get on board.

WEAKEST LINK:

• The paucity of storage space in the cabins on the *Norwegian Sky* (later remedied on sister ship *Norwegian Sun*) shows up more strongly in Alaska where you need extra space for sweaters and warm clothing.

NORWEGIAN STAR
Built: 2001
NORWEGIAN DAWN
Built: 2002

Category: Resort XX
Overall Rating: ⚓⚓⚓⚓⚓
Rates: $$$
Country of Registry: Bahamas
Former names: none
Nationality of Crew: Norwegian officers, international service staff
Cruising Area: Hawaii, Fanning Island in the Republic of Kirabati, Caribbean
Length of Voyages: 7 days

Ship Specifics

Tonnage	91,000	Elevators	12
Length	965 feet	Decks	15
Beam	105 feet	Children's Facilities	yes
Stabilizers	yes	Fitness Center	yes
Passengers	2,240	Spa	yes
Crew	1,100	Verandahs	yes
Space Ratio	40.6	Casino	yes
Crew/Passenger Ratio	1-2.03	Wheelchair Access	yes

Cabins: ⚓⚓⚓ *Suites:* ⚓⚓⚓⚓⚓ The less expensive accommodations measure around 150 to 170-square feet, adequate but not spacious. All include two lower beds that can be pushed together to make one queen-sized bed, a divided bath with large shower, color TV with remote control, mini-refrigerator, safe, hair dryer and coffee and tea maker. All suites and mini-suites plus 372-standard staterooms offer private balconies. The suites and mini-suites range from 229-square feet to 5,802-square feet. The biggest are a pair of jaw-dropping garden villas, each with its own living room, dining room, and three separate bedrooms, each of which has a luxury bathroom with glass walls facing the ocean, a private rooftop terrace and garden with gazebo, outdoor dining table, whirlpool spa and sunbathing area. This could be the ultimate luxury getaway for a small family group or friends.

Facilities for Disabled Travelers: ⚓⚓⚓⚓ There are 20 cabins and suites designated for wheelchair guests. Four have private verandahs; four are outsides and the rest inside cabins. Cabin and bathroom doors are 35" wide. There are roll-in showers with grab bars.

Public Space: ⚓⚓⚓⚓ There's something for almost everyone on the *Norwegian Star*, everything from the Havana Club with its hand-rolled premium cigars and cognac to the Java Café with espresso, cappuccino, frozen coffees and pastries. An eight-deck-high atrium with glass elevators and a three-deck theater with the ambiance of a European opera house add a sort of grandeur. The Galleria is a great department store covering 8,417 square feet and selling everything from logo T-shirts and tiny souvenirs to brand-name watches and jewelry. E-mail users can keep in touch 24 hours a day at one of 17 computer terminals in the Internet Café. Swimming pools are more purpose-built than aboard most ships, with the Barong Spa lap pool for exercisers, the Oasis Pool for lounging under sun umbrellas with drinks in hand, and the Splash Down Kids Pool just for children.

Spa and Fitness: ⚓⚓⚓⚓ The Barong Spa Center, operated by Hawaii-based Mandara Spa, provides both eastern-style and western-style beauty and health treatments, in-spa treatments and simultaneous in-suite massages for couples. They also claim to have the largest indoor lap pool at sea, 27 feet long and 13 feet wide, as well as Japanese pools, saunas, steam rooms, Hydro bath, Jacuzzi and juice bar. Exercisers will find a 24-hour fitness center with treadmills and other machines. On the Sports Deck are two driving ranges, volleyball and basketball court, and soccer area. A "boxercise" area boasts a bouncy "sprung" wooden floor to aid the action.

Entertainment: ⚓⚓⚓⚓ Three lavishly staged production shows are featured on each cruise, including "Asia Cirque" with a company of Chinese acrobats and "Music of the Night," a salute to Andrew Lloyd Weber. Karaoke rooms, an English pub with sports bar big screen TV, a German beer garden and a nightclub and disco open until 5 a.m. also provide diversions.

Food and Dining: ⚓⚓⚓⚓ The 10 restaurants on board include two large dining rooms, the opulent Versailles and the cool and elegant Aqua, each with its own unique menu; the Market Café buffet and the Blue Lagoon Food Court, each open 24 hours a day; La Trattoria, a casual red-checkered tablecloth Italian evening eatery tucked into a corner of the Market Café; and Las Ramblas Tapas Bar & Restaurant, serving Spanish-style snacks and dishes.

These restaurants are free to guests and only La Trattoria requires an advance reservation.

Three eateries serve dinner with surcharges that start at $10 per person: Endless Summer, a big airy restaurant serving Hawaiian food; Ginza, a Japanese/Chinese/Thai restaurant with sushi bar and teppanyaki room; and Le Bistro, with traditional French dishes and tableside service. Lastly, there is the SoHo Room, offering high-end contemporary cuisine on an a la carte basis or a fixed meal for $14 without wine, $25 with a glass of wine served with each of three courses. Live lobster from the tank is $25 and caviar $22 per portion. For anyone who's still hungry, there are ice cream bars, hamburger grills, a German Biergarten with beer, cocktails and Bavarian food such as weiss wurst and pretzels, indoor and outdoor bars and lounges of all descriptions from an English pub with a giant sports TV screen to a karaoke circus flanked by a pair of smaller private karaoke rooms that seat 10. Use of the private rooms requires the purchase of a drinks package.

Service: ⚓⚓⚓⚓⚓ The *Norwegian Star*, purpose-built for Freestyle Cruising, finally shows how well the new pattern can work – but it puts a lot of pressure on staff when everyone wants to dine in the same venue at the same time. Fortunately, the extensive on-board training while the ship was en route from its European shipyard to its Honolulu base has helped make the staff aboard the Norwegian Star probably the most polished team in the fleet.

Junior Cruisers: ⚓⚓⚓⚓⚓ Families will like the enormous children's center, an indoor play area with separate "Snooze" and "Flicks" rooms, and a sheltered outdoor deck with several waterslide kiddie pools and pint-sized spa pools. In the buffet restaurant, there is a special children's dining area with a low-level serving counter and kid-sized tables and chairs.

Itineraries: ⚓⚓⚓⚓⚓ *Norwegian Star* cruises year-round in Hawaii, with a foray down to Fanning Island in the Republic of Kirabati (pronounced keer-ah-bahs) once every cruise. This 600-mile trip provides a full day at sea en route to Fanning and another full day at sea on the way back. Because of U.S. cabotage legislation, the *Norwegian Star*, a foreign-flag ship, is not permitted to sail between U.S. ports unless there is also a call at a foreign port. Fanning Island fills the bill, and makes an interesting visit to an unspoiled, real-life tropical island as opposed to the lush and luxurious fantasy islands of Hawaii. The other ports visited during the cruise are Kona on the Big Island and Nawiliwili, Kauai; guests may board either Sunday in Honolulu or Friday in Kahalui, Maui, and disembark a week later in the same port. Sometimes the port of Fanning Island has to be cancelled when bad seas do not permit guests to go ashore.

The *Norwegian Dawn*, due in December 2002, is scheduled to make seven-day Caribbean cruises alternating Eastern and Western Caribbean itineraries.

Overall: ⚓⚓⚓⚓ The *Norwegian Star* is a truly impressive cruise ship, comparable to even the most mind-boggling new vessels. With the luxury of a different restaurant to dine in every evening (and three still left over for lunchtime), nobody should worry getting bored or feeling trapped. The showy vessel is so wide at 105 feet that it can just barely slip through the Panama Canal, and, in the casual spirit of the islands, a guest never has to don a tie, let alone a tuxedo.

HIGH MARKS
Δ A small wedding chapel aboard may be booked for marriage ceremonies when the ship is in port.

WEAKEST LINK:
• No casino. Ships based in Hawaii year-round are not permitted to have gaming machines aboard, even if they are covered up and never used. However the Norwegian Dawn will carry a casino.

Orient Lines
7665 Corporate Center Drive, Miami, FL 33126
(800) 333-7300 – www.orientline.com

Founded in 1992 and owned by Gerry Herrod, former chairman of Ocean Cruise Lines and Pearl Cruises (both now out of business), the company was purchased by Norwegian Cruise Lines about three years ago. Although part of a large conglomerate (Star Cruises owns NCL and Orient was in the purchase package), it remains destination oriented. Where the ship goes is primary for its guests. As the name of the company and name of its first ship, *Marco Polo*, implies, the Pacific was its original venue, but it has expanded to the Mediterranean during summer months, the Antarctic during late December through early February, and back in familiar waters the rest of the year.

The company packages cruises with pre-and post-hotel stays, which most guests purchase. Orient Lines is now a two-ship fleet and has developed a loyal following of guests who want the small ship experience.

Who Sails Orient Lines? Depends on the itinerary, but not too many first time cruisers. Most guests read the itinerary first and then look at shipboard amenities. Most are North Americans. In the Mediterranean, it's a general mix of age groups leaning toward the over 55 segment. In Antarctica, it's more adventurous travelers and in the Orient, the ship again appeals to experienced travelers in the older segment.

Lifestyle: Easy going, with a touch of sophistication. Guests are friendly and it's not unusual to strike up an interesting discussion with a fellow voyager, then discover he was the former ambassador to one of the countries you will visit or a movie actress who looks and acts like a real person in real life. Everyone on board has a common interest - the itinerary - so it's easy to get to know a good number of guests within a couple of days.

Dress Code: Plan on two dress-up, three informal (jacket and tie) and the remainder resort-casual evenings. Very few men bring tuxedos along on adventure style cruises. Dark suits, ties and jackets are appropriate. Daytime wear is casual jeans-style, suitable to the ports of call.

Tipping Policy: The line recommends $10 per day per person divided between waiters, room stewards and bus boys Tips to the head waiter and others are optional, although 15percent is recommended for bar and wine tabs.

Past Passengers Perks: The company has a multi-tiered Polo Club. Incentives make it worthwhile to fill out the forms when you sail Orient for the first time and become a member. Among perks are two-for-ones not advertised to the public. On board credits, based on the length of the cruise, complimentary shore excursions, a free hotel night, payment of on board gratuities and an invitation to a "members only" party on future cruise.

Discount Policy: Orient Line package rates include economy air, transfers, pre and post hotel stays and some sightseeing. You can purchase the cruise without any of the trimmings, but it's hard to beat the company's all-inclusive rates. Early booking discounts range from five percent on Antarctica cruises to 25 percent on Passage to India voyages. Group rates mean further reductions.

INSIDER TIP:

Orient Lines offers some of the lowest single occupancy rates in the industry. The company charges a 25 percent surcharge over the per person, double rates so expect to see a higher than average percentage of single travelers in their own cabins. The line has social hosts on board to dance with women traveling alone.

The Fleet
MARCO POLO

   Built: 1965   Refurbished: 1993

Category: Traditional
Rates: $$$
Overall Rating: ⚓⚓⚓⚓
Country of Registry: Bahamas
Former Names: Alexandr Pushkin
Nationality of Crew: Scandinavian officers; Filipino service staff
Cruising Area: World wide
Length of Voyages: 7 to 32 nights

Tonnage	22,080	Elevators	4
Length	678 feet	Decks	8
Beam	77 feet	Children's Facilities	no
Stabilizers	yes	Fitness Center	yes
Passengers	800	Spa	yes
Crew	350	Verandahs	no
Space Ratio	27	Casino	yes
Crew/Passenger Ratio	1-2.2	Wheelchair Access	yes

   Ship Specifics:

   Cabins: ⚓⚓ *Suites:* ⚓⚓⚓⚓ Cabins are decorated with warm, light woods and furniture, tasteful fabrics and pastel wall-to-wall carpeting. Compact, but comfortable, a "D" category (outside superior) for example measures about 10 by 15 feet with twin beds, two chests of drawers, large windows, five-foot closets, telephones, TV and music, bathrooms with showers, built-in hair dryers and well stocked amenity kits.

An average outside cabin measures 140-square feet and insides are about 10-square feet smaller. Mini-suites are larger but have awkward shapes. The two Owner's Suites will spoil you for life. They have a huge living room with wrap around windows, queen-size bed and more storage and closet space than two people can fill on a three-week voyage, not counting purchases along the way. Category 'A" deluxe outsides are a better buy than mini-suites, but watch out for partial obstruction. Some of the lower-priced cabins have portholes and twin beds that cannot be reconfigured into queen-size sleeping arrangements.

Facilities for Disabled Travelers: ⚓⚓ There are two cabins with wheelchair accessible bathrooms and but it may be difficult for physically challenged guests to get around in ports and on the ship.

Public Space: ⚓⚓⚓ She's a quiet ship with colors schemed to relaxation. Almost all public rooms are on Belvedere Deck amidships and afford views of the sea. Lounge space is more than ample for even a full complement of passengers and there are quiet and secluded corners in the least expected places. The Polo Lounge is a popular day and night gathering spot where a pianist is in residence. The Ambassador Lounge forward is a conventional showroom but is not sloped, so seats in the back take some neck stretching. There's also the Palm Court, a favorite for reading and English tea, a well-stocked library, limited shopping arcade and a casino. Above Raffles is the Charleston Club, one of the most attractive rooms on the ship. It has a polished metal ceiling and panoramic views of the sea.

Spa and Fitness: ⚓⚓⚓ The Health and Beauty Center is high up and is larger and with better facilities than on some up-market vessels. Operated by the Steiner group, it has sophisticated workout equipment, a sizable aerobics area, sauna and a triple Jacuzzi. In all, there's a pool and three Jacuzzis.

Entertainment: ⚓⚓⚓ There is no lack of entertainment or shipboard activities. There are interesting and informative lecturers who discuss the geography and politics of the cruising area. Ethnic performers are brought on board in just about every port. On selected sailings, there are informal special-interest seminars on a variety of topics. In Antarctica, a top team of naturalists, biologists and geologists join a noted expedition leader.

Food and Dining: ⚓⚓⚓ The Seen Seas Restaurant is a sophisticated dining room that seats guests in two sittings at tables from two to eight. The food is surprisingly good with menus that emphasize fresh ingredients and light fare. Presentation is picture-pretty and food ranges from good to excellent. Five course dinners nightly offer varied choices but there is usually a specialty of the region on the menu. Raffles is the Lido-type self serve restaurant that is also the venue for special optional Oriental Dinner nights. There is no additional charge, but reservations are required and a $5 per person gratuity is added to your ship account.

Special Dietary Requests: Vegetarian and low-calorie option are always on the menu and special requests are honored. Company must be notified of the request, especially for kosher cuisine 60 days before sailing. Kosher foods are selected from a long menu in advance of sailing. Meals are catered on shore.

Service: ⚓⚓⚓⚓⚓ The ship is staffed by Filipinos who love their jobs and show it in the way they address every guest; in the way they pay attention and remember food and beverage preferences; in their mannerisms - friendly, but not too friendly; in the way they smile and in the pride they take in their ship and in their jobs.

Junior Cruisersv ⚓ This is not a ship with itineraries I would recommend for young children. I would however, recommend it for over 12 years old who would appreciate the various cultures and experiences offered by itineraries.

Itineraries: ⚓⚓⚓⚓ From February through April Australia and New Zealand; May through October Mediterranean; November to mid-December Africa; remainder of the year in Antarctica. Cruise lengths run from one week to 36 days and voyages can be combined.

Overall: ⚓⚓⚓ The *Marco Polo* is the right size for destination-based ships. She's no mega-liner with 2,000 guests, but neither is she a boutique vessel that is slow to reach destinations. She has speed that allows more time in port. The vessel is a happy blend of graceful design with an Italian-style and Oriental touches. Her hull can withstand heavy weather conditions and the superstructure has decidedly German influences. She's well suited for unusual itineraries and offers a combination of some of the best aspects of cruising combined with exciting itineraries and value-packed pricing.

HIGH MARKS

△ The low cost of shore excursions. A full day excursion in Bangkok sells for $51, including lunch.

△ Multi-lingual hostesses to translate for non-English speaking passengers.

△ The family atmosphere that carries over between crew and guests.

△ A collection box. The *Marco Polo* crew sponsors a home for abused and abandoned children in Manila.

△ Zodiac landing craft for use in remote destination, such as Antarctica, and two-high speed tenders for other ports.

△ A helicopter landing-pad on the top deck.

WEAKEST LINK

• Showroom is showing her age and is on the shabby side.

• She's getting older, but aren't we all?

INSIDER TIP

Originally built in an East German shipyard for the Soviets in 1965, she was built to serve as an icebreaker and carry troops. Herrod paid about $25 million for her and spent another $75 million transforming her into a modern liner. It took almost three years and the ship was renamed the Marco Polo after the famed Venetian merchant-adventurer who sailed many of the same waters now being explored by Marco Polo passengers.

CROWN ODYSSEY
Built: 1988

Category: Traditional
Rates: $$$
Overall Rating: ⚓⚓⚓⚓
Country of Registry: Bahamas
Former Names: Crown Odyssey, Norwegian Crown
Nationality of Crew: Norwegian officers; international service staff
Cruising Area: Caribbean, and South America
Length of Voyages: 7 to 14 nights

Ship Specifics

Tonnage	34,250	Elevators	4
Length	614 feet	Decks	10
Beam	92.5 feet	Children's Facilities	no
Stabilizers	yes	Fitness Center	yes
Passengers	1,050	Spa	yes
Crew	470	Verandahs	yes
Space Ratio	27	Casino	yes
Crew/Passenger Ratio	1-2.2	Wheelchair Access	yes

Cabins: ⚓⚓⚓⚓ ***Suites:*** ⚓⚓⚓⚓ *Crown Odyssey* has some of the best staterooms and suites at sea. Almost 80 percent are outside cabins. Minimum inside cabins measure 154-square feet, while the luxurious Penthouse Deck apartments are a whopping 650-square feet and come complete with private verandahs and amenities. Storage space is plentiful with 12 to 17 drawers and two closets even in minimum-priced cabins. There are 65 suites in varying sizes on two decks. They come in four categories with small variations in rates. Some have bay windows opening to three-sided views of the sea with sofa and chairs in the bay area. Standard cabins are close to 200- square feet, and four cabins were specifically designed to accommodate wheelchairs.

King-size beds and oversize verandas are on Penthouse Deck, a semiprivate deck with 10 apartments. Bathrooms throughout are oversized by premium-ship standards, and amenities are plentiful. All cabins and suites offer robes and slippers. A large percentage have tubs as well as showers.

Public Space: ⚓⚓⚓ The double-deck atrium is the ship center, where guests have a tendency to congregate. Focal point is a marvelous brass sculpture representative of the world, with some of its complicated insides cleverly revealed. There are bars, lounges, shops, piano bar, sunning areas, rooms to dance in, card room, and lots of elbowroom. Public space, like the rest of the ship, makes extensive use of glass, brass, copper, and pale rosy shades accented with deeper taupe and mauves, plus velvets, and textured fabrics. Extensive use of mirrors and wide stairwells adds to the feeling of spaciousness.

Spa and Fitness: ⚓⚓⚓ The ship is a fitness buff's delight. There are wide teak decks for walking without sidestepping obstacles, two whirlpools, and a shallow pool, not to mention the main pool. There's even an indoor swimming pool, a rarity on ships built after the 1960s. Down on the lowest deck is the Greek-Roman-style spa and fitness center, which has two good-size Jacuzzis flanking the indoor pool. There's a well-equipped gymnasium, sauna and massage rooms.

Entertainment: ⚓⚓⚓ Entertainment is NCL-style, which means three production or Broadway-type shows and individual acts on other nights. Lecturers are a major part of the entertainment because it's interest in itineraries that brings guests on board.

Food and Dining: ⚓⚓⚓ The Seven Seas dining room has two sittings and provides what might be compared with a three-star restaurant experience with varied menu choices and excellent service. New menus offer a wide range of choices with five main courses, plus other options. There's a complete calorie-counted menu at lunch and dinner, and special dietary requests are accommodated with little notice. There's also a children's menu.

Happily, the company still uses the beautiful china and crystal from the ship's previous life and has retained the configuration of the dining room with its tables of from two to eight, spaced at a distance outside of eavesdropping range.

Service: ⚓⚓⚓ The staff and crew are among the friendliest and most accommodating. They seem to take special pride in the product and go that extra step to please guests. The crew is attentive but not overly friendly, concerned but not solicitous.

Junior Cruisers: ⚓⚓ Depending on demand, counselors are boarded and a program is developed, but the ship is not set up for great numbers of children and is not recommended for under-15-year-olds.

Itineraries: ⚓⚓⚓ *Crown Odyssey* sails a long Mediterranean spring/summer season, then comes trans-Atlantic to Fort Lauderdale and begins South America cruises. The vessel does a series of Antarctica cruises, visits Buenos Aires, Rio de Janeiro, Chile and the Amazon. In March, she heads back to Europe sailing the northern countries before moving back to the Mediterranean.

Overall: ⚓⚓⚓ When she was built as the *Crown Odyssey*, the vessel was ahead of her time. She incorporated many of the features on ships built a decade after her completion. As the *Norwegian Crown*, she was an excellent alternative to megaship cruises. Designed to carry upscale guests, she was outfitted to provide high levels of comfort and plush surroundings. The ship was designed by the well-known team of Agni and Michalis Katzourakis, who are widely acclaimed for fairly conservative colors and styles. After 15 years in service, the vessel remains fresh and attractive. Like the decor, onboard art is exceptional and timeless. Traces of former Greek ownership are still in evidence. The vessel homogenizes these classical themes with modern styling and near-authentic Art Deco touches.

INSIDER TIP

The *Crown Odyssey* is an excellent value. Savings of about 40 percent are available for early bookings, and every year when the ship repositions, there are some very low rates offered. Look for even more spectacular offerings in 2003 and beyond. If sailing the Amazon or Antarctica is in your dreams, opt for one the bay window staterooms. But, book early. Antarctica voyages sell out quickly. You won't regret it!

HIGH MARKS:

Δ Itineraries that offer Antarctica in comfort.

Δ Beds that feel more like hotel accommodations than berths

Δ Top of the Crown, with its 360-degree panoramic view of the sea and ports of call

WEAKEST LINK:

• The sound proofing in the main restaurant leaves much to be desired.

P&O Cruises

Richmond House
Terminus Terrace
Southampton, SO14 3PN, UK
44-1224-572615 – www.pocruises.com

Peninsular and Oriental Navigation Company (P&O) is the oldest and largest of the British shipping companies. Founded in 1837, three years before Samuel Cunard founded his company, India-bound travelers in the 1840s traveled overland across the Suez before the Suez Canal was built. During the 19th century, sea voyages were considered therapeutic, and by 1898, a P&O poster was advertising a 60-day pleasure cruise to the West Indies.

The word "posh," according to legend, was derived from the cabin reservation stamped P.O.S.H., meaning "Port Out, Starboard Home" for those traveling between England and India who demanded the coolest staterooms in the days before air conditioning.

The company pioneered service in many areas of the world and added a tone of luxury and "snob appeal" to sea travel. During the past century, the company offered service on ships such as the *Viceroy of India* in 1929. All first-class cabins were singles that connected with each other, but private baths were not available in most. The company was also involved in budget-minded immigrant trade to North America and Australia. Interesting to note that PandO claims to have been the first to offer leisure cruising back in 1844, but other continue to dispute the claim.

In 1974, P&O acquired Princess Cruises, bigger and better known in the U.S. than its parent; the two companies "demerged" in 2000. P&O Cruises, now a division of P&O Princess Cruises plc, is marketed primarily in the United Kingdom with a pair of sister ships, *Aurora* and *Oriana*, as well as the *Arcadia*, which leaves the fleet in the spring of 2003 to become the *Ocean Village*, and the *Oceana*, (the former *Ocean Princess*), transferred into the *P&O* fleet in late 2002. Joining in the spring of 2003 will be the *Adonia*, formerly the *Sea Princess*, built in 1998.

In addition, P&O Princess Cruises plc has five other subsidiaries – Swan Hellenic, operating the 360-passenger *Minerva* for English-language expedition cruises; *Ocean Village*, scheduled to operate the former *Arcadia* for casual, contemporary cruises aimed at the British market; the *Australia*, along with the *Pacific Sky* (the former *Sky Princess*) for the Australian market; *AIDA*, with two ships in operation and a third due in 2003, all targeting the German youth market; *A'ROSA*, with the *A'ROSA BLU*, a conversion of the *Crown Princess*, and a second ship, a conversion of the *Regal Princess*, due in 2004. *AIDA* and *A'ROSA* do business in Germany under the name Seetours International.

Who Sails P&O? Primarily the British, who have been sailing with P&O since the 1840s, but also a sprinkling of other English-speakers, including Americans, Canadians, Australians, New Zealanders and South Africans.

Lifestyle: Classic traditional cruising as perfected by the company that virtually invented it.

Dress Code: Traditional, and stubbornly upheld by the British, who may run around all day in cotton frocks or undersized bathing suits and even terrycloth robes, but who are sticklers for correctness when black tie is required in the evening.

Dining: Unlike Cunard ships, which have adjusted to American-style cuisine and meal patterns with only a faint whiff of the original, P&O still serves kippers, kidneys and finnan haddie for breakfast and kedgeree and curries along with a roast, called a joint, for lunch. Afternoon tea is the fourth major meal of the day, even when casually served in the cafeteria, and high tea (using the term correctly) is a light supper, most often served to the children on board at 5:30 p.m. The British like to see the full array of silverware to be used for the meal spread out in front of them at the beginning, unlike the continental Europeans, who deliver the utensils separately before each course. The "sweet" or "pudding" always comes before the savory (cheese, marrow, smoked oysters on toast or chicken livers grilled with bacon) that finishes the meal.

Tipping: Gratuities are spelled out in a leaflet found in the cabin; the suggested total amount averages around $9 a day per person. Optional tips for the buffet restaurant staff are pooled and divided among them by the manager.

Discount Policy: On some cruises, early booking discounts are offered, but there are seasonal special offerings. The world cruise this year was offered at about a 50 percent discount.

INSIDER TIP:

This is cruising as it used to be, with fancy dress parades and guest talent shows, quoits competitions on the aft deck and a quiet, European-style gaming room with the noisy slots allocated to a soundproofed room next to the pub.

HIGH MARKS:

Δ Families find P&O marvelous for the British nannies and the evening childcare.

WEAKEST LINK

• For the American palate, the lunch buffets on P&O ships are often soggy rather than crisp and fresh

The Fleet

AURORA

Built: 2000

ORIANA

Built: 1995

Category: Premium
Overall Rating: ⚓⚓⚓⚓+
Rates: $$$
Country of Registry: United Kingdom
Former names: None
Nationality of Crew: British officers, international crew
Cruising Area: The world
Length of Voyages: 3 to 90 days

Ship Specifics

Tonnage	76,000	Elevators	10
Length	845 feet	Decks	10
Beam	76 feet	Children's Facilities	yes
Stabilizers	yes	Fitness Center	yes
Passengers	1,870	Spa	yes
Crew	850	Verandahs	yes
Space Ratio	32.34	Casino	yes
Crew/Passenger Ratio	1-2.2	Wheelchair Access	yes

Cabins: ⚓⚓⚓ *Suites:* ⚓⚓⚓ The *Oriana* has only one deck of cabins with private verandahs, while the *Aurora* has three decks of them. The standard inside and outside doubles are 150-square feet with two lower beds, love seat or sofa, desk/dresser, TV, safe, mini-refrigerator, tea- and coffee-making facilities and hair dryers. On the *Aurora* only, the standard double with verandah measures 175-square feet. Mini-suites of 325-square feet offer two lower beds that convert to queen-sized, separate sitting areas with sofas and two chairs, dining table with chairs, private verandah with loungers, chair and tables, bathroom with whirlpool tub and shower, and trouser press and ironing board. Suites vary from 400 to 445-square feet, with all the furnishings of the mini-suite plus a larger verandah and special butler services. Storage space is generous as befits ships utilized for around-the-world cruises.

Facilities for Disabled Travelers: ⚓⚓⚓ Eight designated wheelchair-accessible cabins on each ship measure 257-square feet. Doors are wide enough to accommodate an average size wheelchair. Bathrooms meet requirements and all of the public rooms are accessible.

Public Space: ⚓⚓⚓⚓ Guests feel like they have just walked into a British country house hotel when they stroll into the public lounges on these ships. Coffee is served quietly and politely to people sitting reading or quietly chatting. Deck space is expansive, with plenty of amidships lounging space, a five-deck aft area with plenty of quiet nooks for chatting, dozing or reading, and top deck lounging and sunning spots. The pub-like tavern on the *Oriana* and the French-style 24-hour bistro on the *Aurora* are popular gathering spots, and a lot of area is devoted to dancing, reading and writing.

Spa and Fitness: ⚓⚓⚓⚓ A complex of art nouveau-accented Oasis spa facilities is located on Lido deck, amidships on the *Aurora* and slightly forward on the *Oriana*, with a full range of beauty and spa services. The *Aurora* also provides a large gym and aerobics center on Deck A, one deck below Lido, with an indoor pool and whirlpool with retractable sky dome.

Entertainment: ⚓⚓⚓ The magnificent Theatre Royal on the *Oriana* looks like a London West End theater, with an orchestra pit under the stage and rows of red velvet theater seats. Here and in the Curzon on the *Aurora* is where production or variety shows are staged; smoking or drinks are not permitted. Dancing is one of the most popular evening entertainments aboard, with dedicated dance floors in several lounges; you'll see couples elegantly dancing the fox trot, waltz, quick step and Latin rhythms early to mid-evening, then switching over to disco at midnight.

Food and Dining: ⚓⚓⚓ If you are an anglophile, you'll love the indulgent, million-calorie British buffet breakfasts with English-style bacon, eggs, baked beans, grilled tomatoes and mushrooms, kippers, black pudding and fried toast. A big handsome cafeteria area called the Conservatory on the *Oriana*, the Orangery on the *Aurora*, offers a casual tea as well as buffet breakfasts and lunches, while the classic dining rooms serve two breakfast, lunch and dinner sittings at assigned tables. In the evenings, first seating is at 6:30, second seating at 8:30. A children's tea (supper) is served at 5:15 nightly in the buffet restaurant. Occasional theme buffets are also held in the cafeterias in the evenings when it used as an alternative to the dining rooms. Expect classic dishes from roast beef with Yorkshire pudding to jam roly-poly and bread-and-butter pudding and even haggis for Robert Burns' birthday on one winter sailing.

Service: ⚓⚓⚓ Service aboard is good to excellent, quiet and unobtrusive but correct.

Junior Cruisers: ⚓⚓⚓ These ships offer what many consider to be the best care and programs for children at sea. The space devoted is generous. Besides the kiddie pool next to the enclosed indoor play area, there is a full-sized shallow aft pool devoted to kids 12 and under only, and an enclosed outdoor play area. A large indoor playroom for children nine and under has a TV room, computer center with video games and all sorts of crafts activities. Children under two may use the room only with one parent present, and the counselors do not change diapers. Children can have a supervised early supper in one of the dining rooms at 5:15, after which they can be dressed for bed and cared for in the night nursery at no extra charge until midnight, so parents can enjoy a quiet dinner and evening entertainment options. A teens' lounge/disco and an adjacent video game room is reserved for those 10 and older. The playroom is open from 9 a.m. until 10 p.m. and the night nursery from 6 p.m. until 2 a.m. The teen club operates until around midnight normally.

Itineraries: ⚓⚓⚓⚓ Both ships usually offer a world cruise between January and late March or early April, followed by Mediterranean and Northern Europe sailings. Ports of call combine the familiar and the exotic in an appealing blend.

Overall: ⚓⚓⚓+ We can imagine veteran American cruisers – particularly those who still mourn the loss of Royal Viking Line and Royal Cruise Line – would find these dignified vessels very much to their liking. The line's strict adherence to dress codes and decorum and the absence of frequent public announcements and frenetic promotions for bingo games and art auctions are quite soothing. Best of all, they look like ships instead of floating hotels, resorts or shopping malls.

HIGH MARKS

Δ Quoits and shuffleboard tournaments, games of whist in the large card rooms

Δ A cinema, a resident theatre company, concerts and afternoon cricket competitions – it's cruising British style.

WEAKEST LINK:

- It takes Americans a few days to understand the language spoken by the staff and crew. It also takes that long for the crew to understand us. I think they speak English, but the dialects are confusing, particularly when they speak quickly.
- It's not much fun to be the only ones in the lounge not laughing at the comedian.

INSIDER TIP

Read the ratings on these ships differently than you would on other vessels. To appreciate the vessel, think British and expect to vacation in tune with their lifestyle. Americans have difficulty understanding the fast patter of the comedian, and even some of the waiters. The ships are ⚓⚓⚓⚓⚓ but for Americans, they rate ⚓⚓⚓⚓

Princess Cruises

24305 Town Center Drive, Santa Clarita, CA 91335-4999

(310) 553-1770 – www.princesscruises.com

Like Alexander the Great, Princess Cruises needs new worlds to conquer. In mid-2002 it was operating a fleet of 11 ships with four more due by the end of 2004. Since the vessels already operate throughout (and around) the world, including newly introduced Antarctic sailings due to begin in 2003, the line has taken another tack. It is initiating several alternative cruise companies with niche target markets and repositioning some of the present tonnage into other areas.

Princess Cruises began as a quirky little California-based upstart in the winter of 1965-66, when entrepreneur Stan McDonald chartered the 6,000-ton *Princess Patricia* from Canadian Railways and offered cruises along the Mexican Riviera from Los Angeles to Acapulco. In the early days, according to one travel writer review, "the standard dessert was canned peaches" and the décor "on a par with a good, clean $7-a-night room in a venerable but respected Toronto hotel."

But the line grew rapidly, soon chartering three additional vessels: two from Costa and a third, renamed *Island Princess*, from Norway's Fearnley and Eger. Princess soon caught the attention of London-based Peninsular and Orient Steam Navigation Company, better known as P&O. The giant cruise line brought its new *Spirit of London* to the west coast in the winter of 1972-73, but failed to make a dent in Princess's popularity. So in 1974, P&O acquired Princess and set about upgrading the fleet hardware.

Under the new owners, the *Island Princess* was purchased outright from Fearnley and Eger, along with its sister ship *Sea Venture*, which was renamed *Pacific Princess*. The *Spirit of London* was transferred to Princess and renamed *Sun Princess*.

In 1975, TV producer Doug Cramer came up with a TV series idea called "The Love Boat" that he wanted to film aboard a cruise ship. While he used the *Sun Princess* for the pilot, the *Pacific Princess* became the ship most closely associated with the series. The glitz and glamour from the series rubbed off on the line (and vice versa) and life began imitating art when actor Gavin MacLeod, who played Captain Stubing on the series, continued as spokesman for Princess for a number of years.

Continuing its "if you can't beat 'em, buy 'em" theory, Princess/P&O acquired rival Sitmar Cruises in 1988, adding three existing vessels and one almost-completed new ship to the fleet, bringing the total up to nine.

Pending transfers at this writing: *Crown Princess* has been transferred to *A'ROSA* Cruises and is sailing as *A'ROSA BLU*, targeting the German-speaking traditional cruise market. Sister ship *Regal Princess* is tentatively scheduled to be transferred to the same company in 2004. With the departure of the *Pacific Princess*, scheduled to leave the fleet in November 2002, and the transfer of the *Ocean Princess* and *Sea Princess* to parent company P&O as the *Oceana* and the *Adonia*, Princess should again have a scaled-down fleet of 10 vessels in 2004.

Princess and P&O officially "demerged" in 2000. For more information about the new parent company P&O Princess Cruises plc, see P&O (see the company profile).

The most distinctive contribution Princess has made to big-ship cruising came with the debut of its 1,950-guest *Sun Princess* in 1995 and the even-bigger *Grand Princess* in 1998. The line accomplished the near-impossible – making big ships feel like smaller ships for the guests aboard.

Princess fans have two new types of vessels to anticipate in the near future. The 88,000-ton Coral class vessels include the *Coral Princess*, due in late 2002, the Island Princess, due in mid-2003, and the Diamond class ships, the 113,000-ton *Diamond Princess*, due in mid-2003, and the *Sapphire Princess* due in mid-2004.

Who Sails Princess Cruises? Everyone who loved "The Love Boat" on TV; longtime brand-loyal cruisers over 45, both couples and singles; families with children or three-generation family-reunion cruisers; young couples drawn to the eat-at-any-hour food plan and the full gamut of entertainment and activities; brides and grooms who want a romantic wedding ceremony in the shipboard chapel, followed by a honeymoon aboard.

Lifestyle: With a new slogan, "Princess, where I belong," the line promises to be almost everything to every cruiser, and comes surprisingly close for everyone except travelers that don't like big ships with lots of companions. The big new ships in the Grand Princess and Sun Princess-classes will suit anyone looking for a resort vacation with scuba lessons, midnight snacks and dancing on the deck, as well as pleasing those who crave the classic cruise experience. Personal Choice Dining, for instance, allows a choice of dining where, when and with whom you please, as opposed to arriving at a set time at a reserved table where the waiters and the other passengers are familiar friends. Princess guests run the age gamut – families with infants and toddlers who will find babysitting and organized play; teens who have a full range of activities designed just for them; first-time cruisers who'll enjoy the ease with which they can mix and mingle with fellow guests; young couples and singles who want a less-structured cruise environment but still like to dress up occasionally; vacationers who want a respite from stressful jobs and want to spend hours relaxing in the spa; single women who want to meet handsome Italian officers in dress uniform; older women who still want remnants of the classic cruise experiences they remember from the 1970s; and older couples taking a graceful turn on the dance floor.

INSIDER TIP

Princess has a special wheelchair transportation gangway mechanism called the Caterpillar Step that simplifies embarkation and debarkation in ports worldwide. Accessibility in Alaskan ports use buses that have lift-equipment for sightseeing.

Dress Code: There are usually two formal nights a week, and Princess guests do bring their most glittery outfits to show off. You'll see many more tuxedos or white dinner jackets than conservative dark suits, and women are usually bejeweled and sequined. If a gentleman forgets his tuxedo, he can rent one on board most Princess ships. Daytime clothing on board can be quite casual, and a bathing suit is fine on deck so long as you remember a shirt or cover up to throw on when you're walking through the rest of the ship.

Dining: Personal Choice Dining allows guests to specify ahead of time which style of cruise dining they prefer, an open choice of times and venues or the traditional assigned table and time. Usually one dining room on each ship is designated to the traditional assigned seating, the other or others to Personal Choice dining. If a guest changes his mind during the sailing, he can easily switch from one to the other. The Horizon Court offers food 24 hours a day in two separate buffet areas where breakfast gradually turns into lunch, lunch into teatime and snack time, then dinner going on to a full waiter-served meal for prowling night owls at 2 a.m., which blends into continental breakfast around 6 a.m. Children's menus are always available, as are low-fat, low-calorie menus, vegetarian menus and simple steak or seafood dishes grilled to order. In the dining rooms, you can always find a freshly made pasta dish as well as traditional and trendy main dishes and tableside preparations. Alternative restaurants (with a surcharge) include Southwestern and Italian cuisine on the Grand Princess-class vessels and charming pizzerias (no surcharge) on the Sun Princess-class ships. Don't miss the once-a-cruise Pub Night if you enjoy fish 'n chips and beer around midnight.

Peter Knego Comments:

"For the price, it's hard to find fault with Princess. Cuisine is uneven, but some of the pastas are among the best at sea. Food ranged from excellent to so-so."

Special Dietary Requests: Low fat, low calorie, vegetarian and simple steak or seafood dishes are always available in dining rooms. Requests for kosher meals must be made in advance of sailing. Food is prepared on shore and is catered b Schreiber. Choices of main courses, desserts, appetizers and soups are extensive. Meals are served on plastic plates. A limited supply of kosher meals is always in stock. Religious services are held with clergymen on board for all holiday sailings.

Tipping: With the advent of Personal Choice dining, Princess ships reverted to a policy of automatically charging tips of $10 a day per person for food and cabin service to your on-board account. Beverage service carries a 15 percent gratuity levied at time of service. Any adjustments you wish to make in the amount should be done at the purser's desk onboard.

Past Passenger Perks: You're member of the Captain's Club after your first cruise. In addition to lapel pins marking milestones (5th to 100th voyage), past guests are eligible for upgrades on selected voyages and members-only deals.

Discount Policy: Early booking discounts and Love Boat Savers fares are available on all sailings in designated cabin categories and/or for cruises booked before a specified date. Acknowledging that 2002 was not a "normal" year, we anticipate that "normal" may not return for a few years.

INSIDER TIP

In late 2002, Princess advertised cruises at 1975 rates. A Venice to New York 12-day crossing was advertised for $999! True, it was a repositioning cruise, but there are other "deals" in the Caribbean and even Alaska advertised for a little more than $100 a day. Those prices are for minimum accommodations, but if price is your determining factor, check around. If your travel plans are flexible, you could luck into a phenomenal deal

WEAKEST LINK:

When you start unpacking in your cabin, you may notice that some of the usual Princess amenities such as bathrobes, a shower cap and a bowl of fruit are missing. To save money and avoid wasting fruit or having to launder unused robes, the line has changed its policy: you still get them, but you need to request them from the housekeeping staff so they know you really want them.

Shirley and Harry Comment:

"The main problem aboard Princess ships these days is the absence of largesse. The bean counters are beginning to influence the cruise experience even when the intentions are good. Asking for a fruit bowl from housekeeping is a deterrent "

The Fleet

GRAND PRINCESS
Built: 1998

GOLDEN PRINCESS
Built: 2001

STAR PRINCESS
Built: 2002

Category: Resort XXL

Overall Rating: ⚓⚓⚓⚓⚓

Rates: $ $ $

Country of Registry: Bermuda

Former names: none

Nationality of Crew: British/Italian officers, international service staff

Cruising Area: Alaska, Canada/New England, Caribbean, Europe, Mexican Riviera

Length of Voyages: 7 to 15 days

Ship Specifics

Tonnage	109,000	Elevators	14
Length	951 feet	Decks	16
Beam	104.6 feet	Children's Facilities	yes
Stabilizers	yes	Fitness Center	yes
Passengers	2,600	Spa	yes
Crew	1,100	Verandahs	yes
Space Ratio	41.92	Casino	yes
Crew/Passenger Ratio	1-2.4	Wheelchair Access	yes

Cabins: ⚓⚓⚓⚓ *Suites:* ⚓⚓⚓⚓ Standard cabins are fairly spacious with the smallest insides measuring 160 square feet, standard outsides up to 210-feet, and verandah cabins from 215 to 255 square feet. Each contains two lower beds that convert to one queen-sized bed, mini-refrigerator, generous closet space, personal safe, TV, and bath with shower. Mini-suites with private verandahs are 325 square feet, with lots of built-ins with desk/dresser space and compartmentalized storage.

Suites measure 515 to 800 square feet and include all the furniture in cabins plus seating areas, granite-topped consoles with two TV sets, walk-in closets and bathrooms with whirlpool tubs. The most posh accommodations are the grand suites (one on each ship) with separate sitting room, wet bar and bathroom with whirlpool tub. Two family suites on each ship can sleep up to 10 family members if four are children or eight people if all are adults. These have two bathrooms and two self-contained staterooms that connect through a living room.

Facilities for Disabled Travelers: ⚓⚓⚓⚓ *Star* and *Golden* each have 27 and *Grand* has 25 accessible cabins in categories ranging from minimums to two mini-suites. Entrance and bathroom doors measure 35 inches with no sills. Bathrooms have roil-in showers with grab bars, hand held showerheads and fold down seats. All public facilities are accessible including the swimming pool.

Public Space: ⚓⚓⚓⚓ The top five decks house the entertainment and public areas - the nightclub/disco and its glass-enclosed moving sidewalk 150 feet above the sea, the open decks and swimming pools, the children's and teen areas, gym, spa, sports areas and 24-hour Horizon Court food service. You'll also find a swim-against the tide lap pool, a nine-hole putting green and a pair of golf simulators that allow you to "play" one of the world's top courses for a fee of $20 per half hour. The major indoor public areas are on decks 5, 6 and 7, and include the Princess Theater, an enormous show lounge that fills two decks forward, the Vista Lounge with cabaret shows and variety acts, and the Explorers Lounge, a large multi-level bar with an imaginative African-themed décor that is spoiled by the constant display of Art Auction paintings propped all over the furniture and leaning against the walls.

Spa and Fitness: ⚓⚓⚓⚓ The spas, operated by Steiner of London, are large on all three ships, but the Lotus Spa on the *Star Princess* adds additional space by moving the teen area to the aft end of the same deck near the kids' spaces. Asian-inspired treatments such as the popular Chakra Stone Therapy, a massage with oils and heated stones ($158 for 90 minutes) have been added to the usual beauty, sauna and massage services, thermal suite, aerobics room and exercise gym. In the gym, 11 treadmills have sign-up sheets for reservations. The best time to use the equipment without waiting is very early in the morning, in the evenings, or when the ship is in port.

Entertainment: ⚓⚓⚓⚓ Dynamic new production shows with a cast of 19 and a seven-piece orchestra continue to support the line's reputation for excellent entertainment; "Da Beat" and "Dance!" are the titles aboard the newest ship, *Star Princess*. With state-of-the-art technical facilities, the Grand Princess-class ships can recreate almost any special effect you'll see on Broadway or in Las Vegas. Big stages are fitted with multi-deck flies for raising and lowering scenery, and casts include Chinese acrobats and adagio dancers from Russian ballet, with each production show presented on two different evenings. The total number of entertainers aboard these ships is 22, plus 30 musicians playing in the different lounges. You'll find music for fast or slow dancing, piano bar sing-a-longs, karaoke, game shows, classical music concerts, lecturers, lifestyle enhancement programs and current and classic feature films screened frequently both in the theater and on the cabin TV sets.

Food and Dining: ⚓⚓⚓ The favorite Italian dishes aboard Princess ships – lunch and dinner pasta specialties, risotto, minestrone – remain on the dining room menus, along with classic shipboard presentations. Corporate executive chef Alfredo Marzi continues to introduce new California-inspired dishes and cutting-edge cuisine for the new, younger Princess guests. You could actually sail aboard one of these megaships and never go near the dining rooms for a week, because the 24-hour Horizon Court dishes up breakfast and lunch buffets and casual sit-down dinners until 2 a.m., and the deck food stations include hamburgers and hot dogs, pizza and Haagen-Daz ice cream (you have to pay for the ice cream because it's from a shipboard concession).

Alternative Restaurants: ⚓⚓⚓⚓ A bonus with the Grand Princess–class ships are the two alternative restaurants, a Southwestern café with a mélange of Mexico, New Mexico, Texas, Arizona and California flavors (a surcharge of $8 includes a free giant Margarita) and Sabatini's Trattoria, with all-you-can-eat Italian food served in a dizzying progression of courses until you want to shout, "Basta!" ("Enough!") At Sabatini's, the surcharge is $15 for the dinner or for a caviar-and-seafood brunch on days at sea. Reservations are required for both alternative restaurants. Since space is at a premium, it's a good idea to make them on the day you board to be sure you get the evenings you want.

Marcia Levin Comments:
"The Italian specialty restaurants are superb. Well worth the $15 per person surcharge."

Service: ⚓⚓⚓ The explosion of new ships at Princess has meant rapid hiring and intensive training for a number of new hotel personnel, many of them from Eastern Europe. Under the pressure of simultaneously acquiring cruise service skills and articulate English, some of the newer waiters seem overly serious and nervous, but they soon relax into the camaraderie. Upper level jobs such as maitre d'hotel and dining room captain are still held primarily by Italians, some of whom are Sitmar veterans. and some from Home Line and even the Italian Line. They are professionals who offer excellent service along with a generous dollop of flirtation with the ladies. The Filipino cabin stewards are efficient and friendly as always.

Junior Cruisers: ⚓⚓⚓⚓ Princess has made tremendous strides in the area of family cruising in the last five years. The area turned over to junior cruisers, both kids and teens, is huge, especially on the third ship in this series, *Star Princess*. On a mid-March sailing, there were 200 kids aboard, with some 500 expected for the upcoming Easter and Passover holidays. They are divided by age groups into three -to-five year-olds, six and seven year-olds, eight-to-12 year-olds and, in the Off Limits Teen Center, 13-to-17 year-olds. Each age group has its own activity and social area; small children also have a kiddy swimming pool and enclosed outdoor play area. Minimum age is three for participation in supervised activities.

Itineraries: ⚓⚓⚓⚓ The size of this trio of ships means none of them can pass through the Panama Canal, so they are divided between oceans for their itineraries. The *Grand Princess* stays year-round in the Caribbean, the *Golden Princess* cruises in Europe and the Caribbean and the *Star Princess* is in the Pacific Ocean, dividing her time between winter sailings from Los Angeles along the Mexican Riviera and summers in Alaska.

Overall: ⚓⚓⚓⚓ For one golden moment of glory between the *Carnival Destiny* and Royal Caribbean's *Voyager of the Seas*, the *Grand Princess* was the world's largest cruise ship. But for many fastidious travelers, this is a dubious distinction. Biggest is not always best, so we'll cheer Princess for showing us how to plan a big ship that feels like a smaller vessel. Designer Giacomo Mortola and interior designer Teresa Anderson endeavored to break large areas into smaller, more intimate spaces. A more subdued three-deck atrium lends to the illusion. Embarkation, baggage handling and disembarkation work smoothly because of two embarkation stations, one forward for guests with forward cabins, and one aft serving the other half. Three exits facilitate orderly disembarkations for shore excursions. While we like some details more from other Princess ships – the larger cabins on the *Regal Princess*, the elegant styling aboard the *Royal Princess*, the elegant winter garden pizzeria on the Sun Princess-class ships – the Grand Princess-class has a lot to offer the average cruiser.

INSIDER NOTE

We took a taxi from our hotel to board the *Grand Princess* in Istanbul. As we approached, the taxi driver said, "You have arrived at the largest hotel in Turkey." He should have added, "One of the best."
:

HIGH MARKS:

△ You can get married at sea in the romantic chapel on board with the captain himself officiating. The ships are registered in Bermuda, so the vows are legal under Bermuda Maritime Law but the ship must be 12 or more miles from shore when the ceremony is held.

△ If you worry about the ship's size and keeping track of your spouse or kids on board, you can rent walkie-talkies for the week.

△ You can buy fresh flowers by the stem or in an arrangement for your cabin or as a gift from a flower kiosk in the foyer near the deck 6 purser's desk.

△ You can book your shore excursions online at www.princesscruises.com, before you leave home to be sure you get one of the sought-after helicopter tours in Alaska or all-day excursions in Europe. The tours are not paid for in advance and may be cancelled after you board the ship with no cancellation fee. Booking via the Internet, shore excursion staffers tell us, allows guests to get immediate confirmation for space on tours.

△ Long queues waiting to get into the captain's welcome-aboard cocktail party are no longer the case on these ships. Instead, Princess hosts a real cocktail party that spills out over four decks and can be entered and exited from anywhere. The captain introduces his officers from a balcony overlooking the main lobby and atrium.

WEAKEST LINK:

• We really miss the delightful inside pizzerias that are so pleasant for lunch aboard the Sun Princess-class ships. Instead, on the Grand Princess-class ships, we get only a pool deck pizzeria that has tepid slices of previously baked pizza under a warming lamp. Somehow even two alternative restaurants with surcharges can't make up for it.

REGAL PRINCESS
Built: 1991 Refurbished: 1995, 2000

Category: Resort XL
Overall Rating: ⚓⚓⚓⚓
Rates: $ $ $ $
Country of Registry: United Kingdom
Former names: none
Nationality of Crew: British/Italian officers; International Service Staff
Cruising Area: Australia, New Zealand, Hawaii, Alaska, Orient/Asia (China, Japan, Thailand, Vietnam, India, Indonesia), Canada/ New England
Length of Voyages: 9 to 30 days

Ship Specifics

Tonnage	70,000	Elevators	9
Length	811 feet	Decks	12
Beam	105 feet	Children's Facilities	yes
Stabilizers	yes	Fitness Center	yes
Passengers	2,600	Spa	yes
Crew	630	Verandahs	yes
Space Ratio	44.02	Casino	yes
Crew/Passenger Ratio	1-2.5	Wheelchair Access	yes

Cabins: ⚓⚓⚓⚓⚓ *Suites:* ⚓⚓⚓⚓⚓ Cabin size is outstanding on the *Regal Princess*.. Even a standard inside double, smallest and cheapest lodging on the ship, is a generous 190 square feet. Each cabin contains amenities that used to be found only in suites – mini-refrigerators, remote-control color TV sets, guest safes and walk-in closets. A total of 184 cabins open onto private verandahs. Most spacious are the 14 top-of-the-line suites, each as big as an apartment, with a large verandah, dressing room and walk-in closet, bedroom with queen-sized bed, sitting room with stocked mini-bar and refrigerator, and large marble bathroom with tub and shower, plus an adjoining second half-bath also accessed from the foyer.

Facilities for Disabled Travelers: ⚓⚓⚓⚓ *Regal Princess* has 10 accessible cabins, six inside and four outside. Size ranges from 228 to 289-square feet. Cabin doors are 33 inches wide and bathroom doors are 31 inches. There is a ramped sill in the bathroom, roll-in shower with a seat, hand held showerhead and grab bars. The ship is equipped with a pool lift for those with mobility impairments. All decks are accessible and there are conveniently located accessible restrooms.

Public Space: ⚓⚓⚓⚓ When the *Regal Princess's* profile and upper deck public areas were designed more than a decade ago by Italian superstar architect Renzo Piano, the intention was to create a "dolphin-browed" cruise ship with a distinctive profile plowing through the water. A beautiful open space in the interior of the domed dolphin brow was framed into what Piano called "the inside of a whale" with polished, rounded, bone-colored ribs arching from ceiling to floor, framing wide curved glass windows. The silky eggshell finish of the glossy plaster ribs dominated the room that would be called The Dome. This was before the vessel was finished, furnished and filled with potted palms, clanging slot machines, leather chairs and cocktail tables. In an effort to make the space serve as three different areas – casino, observation lounge and evening cocktail bar with dancing – it ended up short-changing all three functions. Far more appealing are the sophisticated lounges on the promenade deck: the Adagio with its murals recalling the 1920s and 30s; the next-door Bengal Bar with wicker chairs, lazy ceiling fans and echoes of the British Empire; the Bacchus wine-and-caviar bar; and, the Stage Door, the scene for white-glove afternoon teas and high-decibel late hour disco.

Spa and Fitness: ⚓⚓⚓ Although all the basics are here – beauty shop, sauna, steam and massage rooms, treatment rooms, a spacious aerobics room and fully equipped gym – most of them are relegated to a windowless lower deck the way spas used to be before they became major revenue-producing elements on board ships. These days, when exercising with a sea view through big windows on an upper deck has become the norm, the *Regal Princess's* little spa seems claustrophobic. Maybe they could move it up to The Dome and put those noisy slot machines and potted palms down below.

Entertainment: ⚓⚓⚓⚓ The International Show Lounge covers two decks and offers curved balcony theater-style seating as well as cocktail tables and chairs down front on the lower level. Production shows are staged here, along with the rollicking "Pub Night" once a cruise and variety "Showtime" productions with singers, jugglers and comedians. The huge stage doubles as a dance floor between shows. Three production shows incorporating live video projection play on board, "Shake, Rattle & Roll," "Give My Regards" and "Country Roads."

Food and Dining ⚓⚓⚓⚓ Because the charming Palm Court dining room with its pastoral murals is the only large sit-down restaurant on the ship, Personal Choice dining is not an option aboard the *Regal Princess*. Here, as on the *Royal Princess*, traditional shipboard patterns hold sway. There is, however, an alternative bistro-style restaurant added to the Lido buffet area with a more casual evening menu. The Bravo Pizzeria is also located on an upper deck, beside the colorful Characters Bar with its zany drink concoctions.

Service: ⚓⚓⚓⚓ The dining room staff is primarily European, the hotel cabin staff Filipino, and service is generally very good except for newcomers who are still learning English and how to find their way around the ship. The bar staff can be breezy or brusque, depending on the individual's mood.

Junior Cruisers: ⚓⚓⚓⚓ The Youth Center has allotted a lot of space at one end of the top deck, with more new facilities added for both kids and teens. Babysitting is available in the evenings from 10 p.m. to 1 a.m. as well.

Itineraries: ⚓⚓⚓⚓⚓ The *Regal Princess* spends summers in Alaska and winters in Asia and Australia/New Zealand. In the fall it visits Canada/New England, and during the Christmas holidays cruises Hawaii.

Overall: ⚓⚓⚓⚓ The *Regal Princess* just happened to fall into that transition zone in cruise ship design that still relegated the spa to the nether regions below deck, expects guests to be very happy night after night at the same table in the same restaurant, and fails to realize that putting in lots of private verandahs at the beginning costs very little compared to the revenue they return.

HIGH MARKS:

- Δ This ship is for people who enjoy art-filled surroundings. They will revel in the murals that fill the vessel.
- Δ Cabins size erases any claustrophobic hesitations passengers may have about cruise ships.

WEAKEST LINK:

- • The dreary exercise facility. You won't find a sea view from the spa.

ROYAL PRINCESS
Built: 1984   Refurbished: 1995

Category: Traditional
Overall Rating: ⚓⚓⚓⚓
Rates: $$$
Country of Registry: United Kingdom
Former names: none
Nationality of Crew: British officers; international service staff
Cruising Area: Antarctic, South Africa, West Africa, South America, Panama Canal, Europe
Length of Voyages: 9 to 21 days

Ship Specifics

Tonnage	45,000	Elevators	6
Length	757 feet	Decks	12
Beam	106 feet	Children's Facilities	yes
Stabilizers	yes	Fitness Center	yes
Passengers	1,200	Spa	yes
Crew	520	Verandahs	yes
Space Ratio	37.5	Casino	yes
Crew/Passenger Ratio	1-2.4	Wheelchair Access	yes

Cabins: ⚓⚓⚓⚓ *Suites:* ⚓⚓⚓⚓ All cabins are outsides on this classic vessel which introduced the revolutionary design in 1984. Mechanical equipment and crew service areas are relegated to the inside of the cabin decks and cabins are all lined up with windows facing the sea. Of the 600 cabins, 150 have private verandahs. All boast tubs, showers and refrigerators, as well as twin beds that are easily converted to a single queen-sized bed. Be aware that some of the lowest priced doubles may have the view partially obstructed by hanging lifeboats. You'll usually get enough daylight to tell day from night and enough sky to gauge the weather outside before leaving your cabin. These cabins, on Baja and Caribe decks, are designated specifically on the deck plan, so you won't arrive at the ship only to find you have very little view.

The most romantic cabins aboard are the two penthouse suites with whirlpool tubs for two in a tile-and-marble bathroom, a dining room where your butler will serve your dinner any night you want to eat in, and a living room big enough to entertain half a dozen friends.

Facilities for Disabled Travelers: ⚓⚓ There are four accessible outside cabins. Cabin and bathroom doors are 33.5 inches wide with ramped bathroom thresholds. Bathrooms have roll-in showers with seats, hand held showerheads and grab bars. All decks are accessible and accessible restrooms are conveniently located. Elevators have Braille numbers and audio floor indicators.

Public Space: ⚓⚓⚓⚓ The curved staircase allows a grand entrance into the foyer, but even more impressive (and an ideal photo spot) are the five aft decks, terraced and covered in natural teak, which once served as the location for a wedding scene between Lana Turner and Stewart Granger on "The Love Boat." In the daytime, a favorite is the Horizon Lounge, designed as a sort of aft observation lounge with disco in the evenings, but in the late morning it's usually a quiet and welcoming spot to curl up with a good book without missing any of the scenery. Guests meet and congregate in the upper-level Princess Court and lower-level Plaza in the atrium. A spacious card room serves the numerous bridge players that seem to gravitate to the *Royal Princess*, and a well-stocked library across the way supplies reading material if you didn't bring along any of your own. The Crown Casino is smaller and less gaudy and less noisy than most shipboard casinos these days. The *Royal Princess*, in fact, seems quieter and more elegant than her younger sisters.

Spa and Fitness: ⚓⚓⚓ This was one of the first spas to be located high atop a ship with wraparound glass windows and a nearby lap pool for exercising. A full promenade around the ship (rare these days) gives you the opportunity for a brisk stroll to stay trim and healthy. Two whirlpool spas on deck adjacent to one of the swimming pools allow a leisurely soak.

Entertainment: ⚓⚓⚓ Besides production shows in the six-level International Lounge with raised, thrust stage, *Royal Princess* offers variety and magic shows, headlined singers and plenty of space for dancing: in the Horizon Lounge, on deck, in the large Riviera Club and in the International Lounge. Some passengers find the self-service laundry room on board an entertainment venue. Many acquaintances have been struck up in here that blossomed throughout the cruise and sometimes even later.

Food and Dining: ⚓⚓⚓ The two-level Continental Dining Room is reached by silvery elevators or handsome stairs leading down from the Riviera Deck. Traditional cruise meal patterns are followed, with two assigned sittings each night for dinner, instead of the Personal Choice Dining options on the larger Princess ships. The Lido self-service restaurant, however, has been converted into a 24-hour dining venue with bistro service by reservation in the evenings.

Service: ⚓⚓⚓⚓ It may be the ship's size or its generally graceful ambiance, or even the guests it attracts, but service always seems better here than on any of the other Princess vessels.

Junior Cruisers: ⚓⚓⚓ Kids and teens definitely take a back seat to their elders on the *Royal Princess*. Because the emphasis from the beginning was on seasoned cruisers, mostly older couples and singles, facilities for junior cruisers are less than ample. Child counselors are assigned to the vessel whenever the number of children booked warrants it, but we'd recommend potential guests look for a ship with around-the-clock childcare, or book one of the Grand Princess-class ships instead.

Itineraries: ⚓⚓⚓⚓+ With retirement of the *Pacific Princess*, the *Royal Princess* became the smallest ship in the fleet and suddenly ended up with the longest and most exotic itineraries, including a first-ever Antarctic sailing for the line. The ship sails between Cape Town and Buenos Aires in January, calling at Tristan da Cunha and selected spots on the Antarctic Peninsula, as well as Cape Horn, Tierra del Fuego, Port Stanley in the Falkland Islands and Montevideo, Uruguay. Prior to that itinerary is a scheduled cruise along the coast of rarely visited West Africa. The ship also visits other South American ports, transits the Panama Canal, and in summer visits the British Isles, Scandinavia and Western Europe.

Overall: ⚓⚓⚓ This ship is still the favorite in the Princess fleet for those who like smaller vessels and traditional cruise patterns. The natural teak decks provide generous strolling, lounging and games space, and the top deck Horizon Lounge opens up splendid views in three directions (four if you count a good look at the amidships deck sunbathing areas). Christened by the late Princess Diana when the bloom was still on the royal family and termed at the time "the most advanced cruise ship ever built," the *Royal Princess* continues to present a seamless blend of classic liner and contemporary cruiser with the best features of each. Her sense of grace and dignity, her accessible size, and her comfortable cabins, all boasting bathrooms with tub and shower, mean this vessel should continue to be a favorite for years to come.

HIGH MARKS

Δ The beautiful portrait and photos of the ship's godmother.
Royal Princess is the only cruise ship to be christened by
Princess Diana.

Δ An elegant and intimate cinema that makes an ideal getaway for a
matinee or evening screening of a new film.

WEAKEST LINK:

• You won't find Personal Choice dining offered, because the ship
has only one major dining room

SUN PRINCESS
Built: 1995
DAWN PRINCESS
Built 1997
SEA PRINCESS
Built 1998

Category: Resort XL
Overall Rating: ⚓⚓⚓⚓
Rates: $ $ $
Country of Registry: United Kingdom
Former names: none
Nationality of Crew: British/Italian officers, international serving staff
Cruising Area: Alaska, Caribbean, Mexican Riviera, Panama Canal,
Tahiti, Hawaii
Length of Voyages: 7 to 22 days

Ship Specifics

Tonnage	77,000	Elevators	11
Length	856 feet	Decks	14
Beam	106 feet	Children's Facilities	yes
Stabilizers	yes	Fitness Center	yes
Passengers	1,950	Spa	yes
Crew	900	Verandahs	yes
Space Ratio	39.48	Casino	yes
Crew/Passenger Ratio	1-2.1	Wheelchair Access	yes

Cabins: ⚓⚓⚓⚓ *Suites:* ⚓⚓⚓⚓ While the cabins aboard are perfectly lovely, they just aren't as large as comparable categories on the *Regal Princess*. Nearly 70 percent of the cabins, 410 to be precise, have private verandahs. The bottom-priced inside and outside cabins start at 135-square feet with twin beds that can convert to queen-sized, mini-refrigerator, TV set, in-room safe, hair dryer, terrycloth robes (by request) to use during the cruise and tile bathrooms with shower. Guests who want a bathtub (or two TV sets instead of one) should book a mini-suite or suite; these range from 374 to 754-square feet. Both mini-suites and suites offer separate bedrooms and sitting rooms, two TV sets, refrigerators, spacious closets, and bathrooms with tubs and separate stall showers, but the suites also offer a dining area with a table and four chairs, as well as a much larger balcony than mini-suites. Families will find 300 additional upper berths for children or adult friends or family members.

Facilities for Disabled Passengers: ⚓⚓⚓⚓ Each of the ships has 19 accessible cabins (seven outsides and 12 insides) measuring from 213 to 305-square feet with 33-inch wide entrance and bathroom doors, no-sill bathrooms and plenty of roll-around and chair-turning space inside. All decks are accessible and so are public restrooms that are conveniently located.

Public Space: ⚓⚓⚓⚓ We fell in love with the *Sun Princess* at first sight—when she was still under construction at the Italian shipyard Fincantieri. The magnificent marble lobby with its patisserie tucked into one corner and its grand staircases sweeping up toward the shopping galleria on a second level and an airy open lounge with piano on the third level is breathtaking. The spacious library offers cushy leather "listening chairs" to hear a favorite CD or a bestseller on tape. The clubby Wheelhouse Bar is a favorite evening getaway for a drink and dancing before and after dinner, and the casino is situated in such a way that guests can easily avoid passing through it and thereby escape the noisy slots and cigarette smoke.

Spa and Fitness: ⚓⚓⚓⚓ The spa, aft on an upper deck, is set up for pampering with high-tech gym, aerobics area, saunas, indoor/outdoor pool and spas and 11 treatment rooms offering everything from massages to aromatherapy. On the pool deck a large lap pool is flanked by whirlpool spas and a second rectangular pool is set up for water volleyball.

Entertainment: ⚓⚓⚓⚓ Special production shows have been designed for each of these ships to take advantage of the state-of-the-art theater stage. At the same time on the same evening. there is a variety or cabaret show in the fan-shaped Vista Lounge. Both programs run for two nights so passengers get a chance to see them.

Food and Dining : ⚓⚓⚓⚓ Personal Choice Dining is alive and well on these ships, with two elegant dining rooms decorated with murals appropriate to the theme. The *Dawn Princess*, for instance, has canal murals in the Venetian dining room and the countryside around Florence in the Florentine dining room. Each ship also has a charming pizzeria that resembles a winter garden with verdigris green garden chairs, tile-topped wrought iron tables and a glass-fronted kitchen where you can watch your pizza cooked to order. The 24-hour food service in Horizon Court serves early-to-late buffet breakfasts, lunches, teatime snacks and bistro dinners with table service.

Optional Restaurants: ⚓⚓⚓⚓ On Sun-class ships will you find the Sterling Steakhouse (we suspect an insider pun since the chairman of the board for Princess when these ships were built was Lord Sterling and the steaks are served from special cuts of Angus beef from the famous "Sterling Silver" brand). In the Caribbean and on the Mexican Riviera, the 70-seat steakhouse serves dinner under the stars, while in Alaska it is usually set up inside a special area of the Horizon Court. A tray of raw steaks is presented, and passengers choose from rib eye, New York strip, porterhouse and filet mignon. Barbecued chicken is also offered. There is an $8 per person surcharge.

Marcia Levin Comments:

"Making daily dinner reservations under Freestyle Dining Plan can be a hassle. You are better off taking assigned seating, then eat in the other restaurants by reservation."

Service: ⚓⚓⚓ Service varies from ship to ship and cruise to cruise, but the main difference that separates the new Princess ships from the old ones is that they need more experienced cruise personnel than are available in the current market; the training has to be accelerated to phase in new staff members.

Junior Cruisers: ⚓⚓⚓⚓ Kids have their own lollipop-bright Fun Zone on an upper deck with outdoor play space and splash pool securely fenced off from the rest of the deck, along with indoor playrooms and supervised babysitting available in the evenings. The separate teen areas are called, depending on the ship, Cyberspace, The Fast Line or Wired, with video games and a giant TV screen.

Itineraries: ⚓⚓⚓⚓ All three ships cruise Alaska in summer. *Dawn* and *Sea Princess* sail the Caribbean in winter, with Panama Canal and Hawaii on repositioning cruises. The *Sun Princess* sails from Los Angeles to the Mexican Riviera in winter.

Overall: ⚓⚓⚓⚓ The best thing about this handsome trio of sisters is that Princess makes big seem smaller once you get on board, with spaces divided into intimate areas rather than massive football fields. So far the large size of the vessels hasn't been responsible for sending agoraphobic guests screaming into the night. Instead, the ships are planned to capitalize on getting away from regimentation, but at the same time having a full complement of things to do at almost any hour of the day or night. For anyone who worries about getting bored or feeling enclosed on a cruise, these are the ships for you. Outstanding art collections ($2 to $3 million a ship) and plants and landscaping ($1 million a ship) enrich and enhance the surroundings, but, unfortunately, the Art Auction for-sale pictures are spread all around the vessel as if the line needs to recoup their art expenditure as soon as possible.

HIGH MARKS:

- Δ The dive program that promises to turn a landlubber into a certified diver in one week. The $299 course includes instruction and videos, four pool dives, four open-water dives and an SSI Scuba certification kit.
- Δ Internet Cafes and business centers with rental laptops let guests keep up with e-mail at 75 cents per minute.

WEAKEST LINK:

- Nowhere to be found are the expected Princess amenities such as bathrobe or shower cap laid out in the cabin bathroom or a bowl of fresh fruit on the coffee table when you check in. The good news is that you can still have them for free; you just have to call housekeeping and request them.

LATE NEWS

Princess Cruises purchased two former Renaissance ships, the R3 and R4, renamed them and inaugurated their sailings in December 2002. The 688-passenger R3 premiered as the "new" *Pacific Princess* – not to be confused with the original love boat, which left the Princess fleet this October, The R4 became the *Tahitian Princess*. According to Princess, both vessels, which originally entered service in 1999, are "well suited to offer many of the Princess' Personal Choice Cruising options including a wide variety of dining choices such as a 24-hour Lido and Italian and American steakhouse specialty restaurants" The ships have a total of 344 staterooms – 317 of which are outside and 232 with private balconies, as well as 10 suites, 52 mini-suites and three cabins that are wheelchair accessible. Other features include eight bars, a library, card room, casino, and spa and fitness facilities.

Tahitian Princess sails year-round Tahiti and South Pacific cruises. The ship operates three itineraries, with a total of 50 departures roundtrip from Papeete, with calls at Bora Bora, Moorea and Raiatea. Other itineraries include French Polynesia/Cook Islands sailings that explore ports of Huahine and Raratonga and feature overnight stays in both Papeete and Bora Bora; French Polynesia/Samoa cruises to Pago Pago and Apia; and French Polynesia/Marquesas voyages to Nuku Hiva and Hiva Oa. A full range of pre and post Tahiti packages are available.

The *Pacific Princess* operates on a split deployment, sailing half the year throughout French Polynesia and the wider Pacific region for Princess Cruises, and the other half for P&O Cruises' Australia brand. Specific itineraries for the Pacific Princess were not available when we went to press.

Special introductory prices for 10-day *Tahitian Princess* sailings begin at $799 per person, double occupancy. Year-round competition for these newcomers includes Radisson Seven Seas Cruises' *Paul Guaguin*, Windstar Cruises' *Wind Song* and Bora Bora Cruises' *Moana Bora*, *Haumana*, *Tia* and *Tu Moana*

Radisson Seven Seas Cruises

600 Corporate Drive, Suite 410, Fort Lauderdale, FL 33334
800-477-7500 – www.rssc.com

Founded as Radisson Diamond Cruises in 1989 by a group of multinational investors, the company's first vessel was the *Radisson Diamond*. Seven Seas was founded in 1989 and owned by K Line (Kawasaki Kisen Kaisha, Ltd.), a major shipping force in Japan. Together with the highly respected Norwegian shipping company I.M. Skaugen of Oslo, K Line formed Seven Seas Cruise Line as a management company based in Singapore. In 1990, the company acquired the former *Starship Explorer*, and after refurbishment, renamed her *Song of Flower*. *SSC Radisson Diamond* was the first passenger-ship to utilize the twin-hull principle.

Radisson Seven Seas Cruises is a wholly owned cruise division of Radisson Diamond Cruises and Seven Seas Cruise Line. The January 1995, the merger of Radisson Diamond Cruises and Seven Seas Cruise Line formed Radisson Hospitality Worldwide, a division of the Carlson Hospitality Group, Inc., which operates, manages, and franchises a number of international chains, including T.G.I. Friday's restaurants. Carlson belongs to Minneapolis-based Carlson Companies, Inc., one of America's largest privately held corporations and a major force in the travel industry. Carlson was founded by Curtis L. Carlson, who continues to serve in an active role as chairman.

Radisson Seven Seas Cruises grew to a fleet-wide capacity of 2,224 luxury berths with the debut in March 2001 of the 700-guest *ms Seven Seas Mariner*, the world's first all-suite, all-balcony suite cruise ship. The line operates and markets the highly rated 350-guest *ssc Radisson Diamond*, and the five star180-guest *ms Song of Flower*. The 320-guest, 19,200-ton *ms Paul Gauguin* entered service in Tahiti and French Polynesia in 1998, and is the most deluxe cruise ship ever to be based there year-round. The line also markets select voyages of the deluxe, 184-guest *ms Hanseatic*, a luxury adventure cruise ship.. The 700-guest, *ms Seven Seas Voyager*, currently under construction, is scheduled for delivery in 2003. Like the *Seven Seas Mariner*, she will be an all-suite, all-private verandah vessel.

Radisson is the fourth largest luxury line, operating and marketing ships that have been consistently rated as "the best" in national surveys.

Who Sails Radisson Seven Seas Cruises? Travelers are generally in the 45 and up age bracket, well educated and well traveled, with household incomes in the $150,000 and up range. They are not usually first time cruisers, although there are always a few who start at the top when they try a cruise vacation. Radisson cruises are not for travelers who prefer Las Vegas as a vacation destination. It is for travelers who want the best in every element that makes a luxury cruise – itinerary, food, service and fellow travelers of like interest and means.

Radisson's passengers are extremely well-traveled and well-heeled. They want to cruise to off-the-beaten-path destinations in an exclusive and attentive environment. On European itineraries, there's almost a split down the middle between Americans and Europeans. Radisson passengers are likely to be more interested in enrichment programs than production shows, more anxious to explore new areas than inventory the shops on St. Thomas.

The *Paul Gauguin, Hanseatic* and *Song of Flower* are filling about 60 percent of their manifests with couples between the ages of 35 and 55. Passengers are older on the *Radisson Diamond, Mariner* and *Navigator*.

Lifestyle: Sophisticated country club, rather than cruise ship-style. Classy, but Each ship has a limited number of passengers, so mixing and mingling opportunities abound. Everyone looks familiar after a day or two, and conversations start easily at bars and lounges.. Passengers are mixing with fellow travelers of like mind and purpose, and there's that luxury feeling of belonging to the same "club."

Dress Code: Elegant casual is recommended for most evenings, with a couple of formal nights on every sailing. Daytime is resort casual, but don't expect to see cut-off jeans and sleeveless Tee shirts.

Food and Dining: All the vessels, except for the *Paul Gauguin*, offer single dining rooms with open seating. *Paul Gauguin* has two dining rooms. Dining hours are extended and usually range from 7 to 10 p.m. for dinner; tables from two to eight or more are available. Passengers show up for meals at a time that suits their preference within scheduled hours, and the headwaiter shows them to the size table requested, but not necessarily the same table at every meal.

Special Dietary Requests: Vegetarian, low salt, sugar free and low calorie items are on all of the menus, but requests for kosher meals must be made in advance. Prior to sailing, passengers are furnished with a five page list of foods, from appetizers to calorie-laden desserts. On board, they are given a special menu listing their choices. They select their courses and choices on board from a menu made up of the list they submitted to Radisson. Proper plates and utensils are served in the same manner as guests who are dining off the regular menu.

Junior Cruisers: Radisson vessels are not designed to handle children and there are very few on board, except for families during school holidays. These are the ships you sail when you don't want to be surrounded by children. These are the ships you sail when you become an empty nester or grandma offers to keep the kids.

Tipping Policy: A no-tipping policy is in place on every vessel and service personnel do not expect a gratuity. A 15 percent tip is added to your ship account for bar, spa and other personal expenses.

Past Passenger Perks: Seven Seas Society is multi-tiered. When you sail the second time, and thereafter, you're invited to special "Society" events, and recieve gifts such as logo wear and Faux Faberge eggs. Radisson's most cruised Society members were invited to sail without any charge on *Seven Seas Mariner's* shakedown cruise where they were given hard hats and invited to assess the ship. The cruise line is planning to make a similar offer to its top customers when the *Seven Sea Voyager* enters service this year.

Discount Policy: Early-booking discounts of about 25 percent and special seasonal offerings of as much as 50 percent are available. Substantial savings of more than 50 percent are available when two sailings are combined. Even luxury lines like Radisson run sales and when they do, they offer exceptional value. Last year (2002) saw discounts that included upgrades to Business Class air for a minimal amount, two-for-ones and other prices that shouted bargain, "we've got to go". With the stock market doing a yo-yo dance, there's a good chance rates in 2003 will imitate 2002.

HIGH MARKS:

Δ There's no call to bingo. In fact, there are no calls for anything.

Shirley and Harry Comment:

"We particularly enjoyed the peace and silence inside the ships where there is a delightful absence of the ubiquitous elevator music that fills most ships."

The Fleet
HANSEATIC
Built: 1993 Refurbished: 1995

Category: Boutique-Adventure
Rates: $$$$$
Overall Rating: ⚓⚓⚓⚓
Country of Registry: Bahamas

Former Names: none
Nationality of Crew: German officers; international service staff
Cruising Area: Alaska, Antarctica, South America, and the Orient
Length of Voyage: 7 to 25 nights

Ship Specifics

Tonnage	9,000	Elevators	0
Length	402 feet	Decks	4
Beam	59 feet	Children's Facilities	no
Stabilizers	yes	Fitness Center	yes
Passengers	184	Spa	yes
Crew	125	Verandahs	no
Space Ratio	56	Casino	no
Crew/Passenger Ratio	1-1.3	Wheelchair Access	yes

Cabins: ⚓⚓⚓⚓ **Suites:** ⚓⚓⚓⚓ The *Hanseatic* is the most luxurious of the new breed of exploration vessels. There are 90 spacious staterooms, each one measuring 236-square feet. All offer ocean views and most have huge picture windows. Each stateroom has a separate sitting area, marble appointed bath with full size tub and shower, hair dryer, spacious closets, individual temperature controls, color television with VCR, radio, and refrigerator stocked with non-alcoholic beverages upon embarkation. Four deluxe suites measure 475-square feet and include a walk-in closet as well as a larger entertainment area and separate sleeping area.

Luxury-size cabins, which would be called suites on other ships, offer high-quality cruise ship amenities. The four suites are twice the size, and butler service is offered in suites as well as in deluxe cabins. Most staterooms have single beds, which cannot be made into queen-size.

Facilities for Disabled Travelers: ⚓ Two cabins are listed as handicapped accessible, but without an elevator and accessibility to all public rooms and explorations of ports of call, travelers with disabilities would do better on a different ship.

Public SpaceOverall: ⚓⚓⚓⚓ There's a main lounge with a dance floor and bar, an observation lounge topside, a card room, boutiques, and a theater that also serves as a lecture hall.

Entertainment: ⚓⚓⚓⚓ There's a team of lecturers on every voyage, and they serve as the main source of entertainment-called enrichment on exploration voyages. Talks by naturalists, biologists, zoologists, and other scientists are scheduled daily and sometimes several times a day when the ship is at sea. For evening diversion, there's a piano bar with a vocalist, and films are shown in the theater and on closed-circuit television. For most passengers, the exotic, unusual ports of call are enough entertainment.

Dress: Passengers have been-there, done-that and are a sophisticated group who dress up for dinner more often than on other adventure-type vessels. "Elegant casual" is the way the brochure puts it for evening

Spa and Fitness: ⚓⚓⚓ More than adequate for the small number of passengers. There is a top-deck facility with exercise equipment and a spa, plus a good selection of body and hair treatments. There's also a glass-enclosed whirlpool and a swimming pool.

Food and Dining: ⚓⚓⚓⚓ The Marco Polo restaurant serves three meals a day at a single sitting. Configuration of the room allows just about everyone to have a view of the ocean from a window table. Menus are extensive, and there's a self-serve salad bar for lunch and dinner. An informal café serves light breakfast and lunch, including salads and hamburgers. Room service offers en suite dining,

Service: ⚓⚓⚓⚓ A multilingual young European crew is exceptionally friendly and service-oriented.

Junior Cruisers: ⚓ There are no specific facilities for children, and very few children under 16 sail the Hanseatic.

Itineraries: ⚓⚓⚓⚓+ Exceptional. Two-week Alaska sailings from Nome include calls at a port in Siberia, cruise of the Bering Strait, and visits to St. Matthew Island, Dutch Harbor, and Kenai Fjords National Park in Alaska before arriving in Seward. A 17-night cruise from Valparaiso, Chile, calls at Isla Mocha, Puerto Montt, Casto, Laguna San Rafael, Ana Maria Glacier; cruises the Magellan Strait; then calls again in Chile at Punta Arenas; transits Drake Passage; visits Paulet Island, the Antarctic Sound and Antarctic Peninsula, Deception Island, South Shetland Islands, and cruises around Cape Horn before arriving in Ushuaia, Argentina. Itineraries change annually, and voyages in the Orient and around Japan are just as enticing.

The ultimate adventure is to go beyond the point where one cannot go."
Bruce Chatwin

Overall: ⚓⚓⚓⚓ That was the opinion of the late explorer who penned that thought while exploring Patagonia. Perhaps that's what motivates us to travel in regions of the earth visited infrequently by mankind. The eagerness to know the unknown, to satisfy one's curiosity and to explore both vast spaces and minute worlds differentiates us from other species.

The 9,000-ton *ms Hanseatic* boasts the highest possible ice-class rating for a passenger vessel and the most luxurious amenities of any adventure ship. Onboard, guests enjoy all the amenities of the finest luxury vessel, an extensive lecture program and access to the world's most remote destinations. She all but circumnavigates the globe with exploration cruises in the Arctic and Antarctic and seasonal operations in lesser-visited regions such as the Spitsbergen Archipelago, Iceland and Greenland.

INSIDER TIP
Travelers yearning for exotic ports of call without sacrificing luxury will love the *Hanseatic*. Many landings are by zodiac and include first-time visits by travelers who come by ship. The vessel has luxury amenities and is priced to include air, sightseeing, and gratuities. Her shallow draft allows for cruising in rivers never before navigated by passenger craft. The Hanseatic is also pricey and attracts mostly Germans; the rest of the manifest is made up of other Europeans and North Americans.

HIGH MARKS:
   Δ The luxurious lifestyle unusual on an adventure-type ship
   Δ The fabulous itineraries that will move even land lovers to non-touristy places.

WEAKEST LINK:
   • No doctor or nurse on board

MS PAUL GAUGUIN
   Built: 1997

Category: Boutique-Luxury
Rates: $$$$

Overall Rating: ⚓⚓⚓⚓
Country of Registry: Wallis & Futuna Islands
Former Names: none
Nationality of Crew: French officers; international service staff
Cruising Area: French Polynesia
Length of Voyage: 7 nights

Ship Specifics

Tonnage	18,800	Elevators	4
Length	513 feet	Decks	7
Beam	71 feet	Children's Facilities	no
Stabilizers	yes	Fitness Center	yes
Passengers	320	Spa	yes
Crew	206	Verandahs	yes
Space Ratio	59	Casino	yes
Crew/Passenger Ratio	1-1.1	Wheelchair Access	yes

Cabins: ⚓⚓⚓⚓ *Suites:* ⚓⚓⚓⚓ Except for 14 porthole cabins on the lowest deck, all accommodations have large picture windows or private verandahs offering ocean views. Each measures between 200 and 249-square feet and has queen or twin beds, marble-appointed bathrooms with tubs and showers, terry robes, hair dryers, televisions, refrigerators stocked with soft drinks, and personal safe. Suites range from 300-square feet to over 500-square feet with the same features as staterooms, plus additional services.

Public Space: ⚓⚓⚓⚓ Extensive for a ship this size. In the stern, there's a retractable marina, from which passengers can step off to go water skiing, surf-boarding, snorkeling, scuba diving, or kayaking. In addition to the main lounge, there's also the Connoisseur Club, with comfortable leather chairs, that serves as a retreat for after-dinner cognacs, liqueurs, and cigars. Both present music and entertainment nightly. A special feature is the Fare (pronounced foray) Tahiti Gallery, stocked with books, videos, and other informative materials on the art, history, and culture of the islands and on the life and work of Gauguin. The piano lounge, La Palette, is bound to be a favorite gathering area.

Entertainment: ⚓⚓⚓ The itinerary is enough to satisfy most entertainment needs. Besides the vessel is in port many evenings and during the day, so passengers prefer to disembark and explore the local hang outs. However, for those who stay on board, there is dance music, a piano bar, small casino, and lecturers to help them understand the history and culture of the region.

Spa and Fitness: ⚓⚓⚓⚓ A full-service spa is operated by world-famous Carita of Paris and includes complete beauty service. The well-equipped fitness center has all types of weights and machines.

Food and Dining: ⚓⚓⚓⚓ Single open-sittings in two restaurants features Continental and French cuisine. Jean-Pierre Viago, a two-star Michelin chef, inspired menu selections. In addition, there's an outdoor Bistro grill and 24-hour room service. Salad bars are superb and make use of local fresh vegetables, fruit and freshly caught fish. Your dinner may have been swimming in the clear waters a few hours before you dine.

Service: ⚓⚓⚓⚓ Close and very personal. It's the type of ship where everyone knows your name on the first morning aboard. There's a level of sophistication in keeping with the Polynesian atmosphere.

Junior Cruisers: ⚓⚓ Forget about them. Leave the kids at home. There are no facilities or programs for little ones.

Itineraries: ⚓⚓⚓⚓ Seven-night round-trips from Tahiti to Bora Bora, Raiatea, and Mooreain the Society Islands, and overnight visits to Rangiroa and the remote Tuamotu Archipelago.

Toby Salzman Comments:
"Absolutely, the best ship for a sybaritic one-week escape."

Overall: ⚓⚓⚓⚓ Everything seems to be geared to the serenity associated with the places that inspired Gauguin's art and persuaded author James Michener to call these "the most beautiful islands on earth." The vessel offers a luxurious Polynesian experience, with added touches, like complimentary wine at dinner. Three original Gauguin sketches are under glass in the Fare Tahiti room, and decor emphasizes regional cultures.

INSIDER TIP

The *Paul Gauguin* is the overwhelming The Total Traveler Critics Choice for the Best Ship for Romance These mavens recommend *Paul Gauguin* for couples – married, or otherwise, lovers, significant others. Even if you weren't in a romantic mood when you embarked, you will disembark holding hands. I can personally vouch for the affect *Paul Gauguin* has on romance. I have a grandson whose parents sailed *Paul Gauguin* on their honeymoon. His middle name is "Paul."

SSC RADISSON DIAMOND
Built: 1992

Category: Boutique-Luxury
Rates: $$$$
Overall Rating: ⚓⚓⚓⚓⚓
Country of Registry: Bahamas
Former Names: none
Nationality of crew: International officers and staff
Cruising Area: Europe, Caribbean, and South America
Length of Voyages: 3 to 19 nights

Ship Specifics

Tonnage	20,295	Elevators	4
Length	415 feet	Decks	12
Beam	105 feet	Children's Facilities	no
Stabilizers	yes	Fitness Center	yes
Passengers	350	Spa	yes
Crew	192	Verandahs	yes
Space Ratio	58	Casino	yes
Crew/Passenger Ratio	1-1.8	Wheelchair Access	yes

Cabins: ⚓⚓⚓⚓ *Suites:* ⚓⚓⚓⚓ There are no inside cabins. Every passenger has an ocean view. Standard cabins measure 243-square, feet including balconies, which is on the small side for what the brochure calls mini-suites, but large if you think of them as staterooms. Accommodations without balconies have the same measurements and provide that much more living space. Instead of sliding-glass doors, they have bay windows. All staterooms have large windows or sliding-glass doors, single beds that can convert to queen-size beds, sofas, dressing tables, good-size closets, refrigerators, and personal safes. Bathrooms have tubs and showers and come equipped with robes, plush towels, and high-quality amenity kits. Suites are 522-square feet and have very comfortable sitting areas and king-size beds. Bathrooms have all the amenities offered in standard staterooms, plus Jacuzzi tubs. All staterooms and suites have a stocked mini-bar. with the initial stock offered on a complimentary basis and refills at shipboard prices.

Facilities for Disabled Travelers: ⚓⚓ Two cabins are designated as wheelchair accessible. Cabin doors are 34.5 inches wide and the bathroom door is much wider (38.25 inches). Bathrooms have roll-in showers with grab bars and sinks are 33 inches from the floor. Cabins are 244 square feet. All of the public rooms and elevators are accessible.

Public Space: ⚓⚓⚓ Because this ship was originally designed to accommodate conventions and meetings rather than individual travelers, an unusually large portion of the public space is devoted to servicing large groups. There is, however, sufficient lounge and deck space to afford one of the highest space ratios in the industry. There are two main lounges: Windows, a multilevel lounge used for multiple purposes, and the Club, which is a combination supersize piano bar and lounge. The Conference Center doubles as a center for art auctions, lectures, and movies. There's also a library, a business center, a pool, and good sunning areas.

Spa and Fitness: ⚓⚓⚓ Facilities are scaled down to suit the small number of passengers, but there is an aerobics studio, a well-equipped fitness center, and a hair salon. Spa treatments are available. There's a swimming pool and a retractable marina aft, which is opened for swimming and water sports when ports and weather permits.

Entertainment: ⚓⚓⚓ This is not the type of ship for production shows and lavish entertainment. There is an excellent band in Windows with a good singer or other cabaret-style performer. Dancing is the evening entertainment. Choices are limited, but there's always camaraderie around the piano bar or the casino. Windows becomes a disco for late-nighters. Afternoons are not regimented, but there are lecturers and special guests who conduct seminars.

Food and Dining: ⚓⚓⚓⚓ The restaurant is one of the most beautiful at sea, and the dining experience is a highlight. Dining is at tables from two to ten or more. Wine is complimentary at dinner. Menus for every meal are extensive featuring regional specialties and international delicacies. Special orders and requests are graciously accommodated.

The alternative restaurant is topside and corresponds to what would be a Lido area on other ships, but it is like no other Lido. There are separate stations for different types of foods - salad, pasta, meat, vegetables, and grills. Called "The Grill," in the evening, the room becomes a gourmet Italian family-type restaurant with a set eight-course menu. It's managed by an Italian couple, and eating there is like eating in a small, elegant restaurant in Milan under the stars listening to the strains of violins. Reservations are required.

Service: ⚓⚓⚓⚓ Excellent and correct. Although you don't have the same waiter or waitress for each meal, they are professional and treat passengers as special guests. Room stewardesses are of the same caliber, and stateroom service is swift and tables are beautifully set for room service. Passengers are addressed by name. Service is personal, but without being overly friendly.

Junior Cruisers: ⚓ If you're bringing small children, find a different ship. There are no separate facilities, but surprisingly, families of all age ranges are on board during summer months.

Itineraries: ⚓⚓⚓⚓ During winter months, the *Radisson Diamond* sails in the Caribbean, usually from San Juan, on three, four, seven, and 10-day cruises. Some voyages include the Panama Canal, which she just barely squeezes through because of her width. The rest of the year is spent in Northern Europe, the Mediterranean, and North Africa, cruising out of various ports on 4-to-15-day itineraries. Transatlantic sailings take about 19 days.

Overall: ⚓⚓⚓⚓ Interior design conveys an immediate sense of indulgence and comfort with its subtle blending of contemporary and Art Deco styles. Silks from Thailand enhance traditional brass and woods, leathers from Italy, and plush upholstery. *Radisson Diamond* is the world's first and only major cruise ship to utilize the submerged twin-hull principle. By placing the propulsion machinery in the hulls beneath the water line, not only does the 26-foot draft add to the ship's stability, but engine and propeller noise and vibration are greatly minimized. A *Radisson Diamond* cruise is for passengers who don't want to stand in line, who want to eat when they're ready, and who enjoy exotic ports of call at leisure.

INSIDER TIP

In case, you're wondering, SSC stands for semi-submersible craft. The main structure is above water level and rides on top of two hulls. These hulls, which are submerged, contain the machinery, thus largely removing noise and vibration from public rooms and staterooms. The design, known as SWATH (Small Waterplane Area Twin Hull), has been around for some time, but Radisson claims a refined design. A SWATH ship offers a relatively small water-plane area compared with a monohull vessel.

HIGH MARKS

Δ The photo opportunity—a ship with a hole in the middle

Δ A very smooth ride

Δ The welcoming bottle of champagne in every cabin

Δ The well-stocked, complimentary mini-bar

Δ No bingo

WEAKEST LINKS:

- No midnight buffet, but who needs it? You dine when you have dinner and we rarely got out of the restaurant until after 10 p.m.
- No self-service laundry, but the laundry service offered on board was excellent – fast and not overpriced.

MS SEVEN SEAS MARINER
Built: 2001
MS SEVEN SEAS VOYAGER
Built: 2003

Category: Luxury
Rates: $$$$$
Overall Rating: ⚓⚓⚓⚓⚓++
Country of Registry: France
Former Name: none
Length of voyages: Six to 108 days
Cruising Area: The World, South America, transpanama, summer in Alaska.

Ship Specifics

Tonnage	50,000	Elevators	5
Length	709 feet	Decks	8
Beam	90 feet	Children's Facilities	yes
Stabilizers	yes	Fitness Center	yes
Passengers	700	Spa	yes
Crew	445	Verandahs	yes
Space Ratio	71	Casino	yes
Crew/Passenger Ratio	1-1.3	Wheelchair Access	yes

Suites: ⚓⚓⚓⚓⚓ There are no inferior accommodations on *Seven Seas Mariner*. They are all outside suites and every one has a verandah. But, they differ in size and range from very comfortable to big, bigger and biggest. Suites measure from about 301-square feet to 1,580-square feet. Measurements include balconies and regardless of size, all have European king-size beds which can be configured into twins, walk-in closets, marble appointed bathrooms with tubs and showers, plush terry robes, hair dryers, TVs and videos, refrigerators stocked with soft drinks replenished daily, complimentary in suite bar set-up of choice alcoholic beverages which can be exchanged for your favorites, combination safes, Judith Jackson amenities replaced daily and attentive butler service in top category suites.

Designed by renowned marine architect Peter Yran & Bjorn Storbraten of Oslo, Norway who also designed suites on Seabourn and Silversea, so there is a similarity in configuration. A sitting area with sofa, chairs and a desk fronts on the balcony, divided from the bedroom area by drapery. Stateroom decor combines smooth, light-toned woods with rich fabrics in pale green, burnt orange and gold tones. Decorative art hangs on the walls above each bed.

The Master Suite has two bedrooms, two balconies and two and a-half baths. In between those giant suites there are Penthouse Suites at 449-square feet; Horizon suites at 522-square feet, Seven Seas suites with 602-square feet; Seven Seas aft suites with a total of 697-square feet with one of the largest verandahs taking up 135 of those square feet. All of the suites are outstanding, but the top three categories will be hard for other lines to duplicate. In addition to oversized bathrooms with separate glass enclosed showers; they have an additional bathroom with everything duplicated from the larger facility, except for the tub and shower. They also have the luxury of butler service, nightly surprise trays of canapés, and other amenities. The Grand and Mariner suites range in the 700-square foot area, while the two Master Suites double everything. All of the suites are matched in size and beauty by the attentive service by stewardesses and stewards.

Facilities for Disabled Travelers: ⚓⚓⚓⚓⚓ There are six accessible suites. Cabin and bathroom doors are 46 inches wide. Bathrooms have roll-in showers with grab bars. Balconies have a one and a half inch threshold for which stewards will provide ramps.

Public Space: ⚓⚓⚓⚓⚓ Public rooms are large, decorated in soft blues, tangy oranges and beige tones and somehow manage to blend from room-to-room. Among unique features are the way major rooms, like the Horizon Lounge, which is the second show lounge and is used for a number of activities, leads to a covered deck terrace. Or, the way the outside covered terraces in the Veranda lead into the air-conditioned interior space. Or, my favorite Garden Café outside the library. Wicker tables and chairs in small groupings are separated by hanging Japanese bonsai trees bringing a casual outdoor atmosphere indoors for relaxed reading, conversational groups, or just ocean watching.

Most of the pubic rooms are on decks five, six and seven, with one of the most attractive and probably romantic rooms on deck 12, the Observation Lounge. Huge window walls afford a 180-degree view of the ocean from the ship's bow. Comfortable seating and quiet music encourage evening dancing and listening as well as daytime ocean watching. Deck 5 is anchored forward by the lower level of the Constellation Theatre and aft by the main restaurant, Connecting the decks is a bank of three glass elevators that go up to the top deck and overlook the open atrium area. A second set of elevators is forward and the angled steel and wood staircase offers another connection between decks.

Decks 6 and 7 are entertainment and dining venues. An open library is available around the clock amidships and operates on an honor system with a good selection of current and classic books and videos. Computer center has 14 multi-media stations. Staffed during specified hours, computer classes and assistance are offered. Charge is a nominal 75 cents per minute.

Spa and Fitness: ♨♨♨♨ Sports Deck features more on-board facilities for active vacationers than any other ship in the Radisson fleet. Facilities include a paddle tennis court, golf driving range (with protective netting), shuffleboard courts and a jogging track that circles above the pool deck below. Three whirlpools at one end of the Olympic size pool front the top of the atrium.

I would be remiss not to specifically mention the Judith Jack Spa as one of the best at sea.. Trained and skilled therapists staff the noteworthy operation. They "promise" to relieve stress and a few wrinkles in a variety of treatments, including a massage by two masseuses. The usual menu of thalassotherapy, aromatherapy, massage, steam room and sauna facilities as well as a full range of beauty and grooming services are just a few of the treatments offered amid the most soothing surroundings imaginable. Interesting to note that in keeping with Radisson's no-gratuity policy, there's no line for gratuities on the bill guests are asked to sign for services.

The adjoining Fitness Center features all the latest gym equipment with treadmills, rowers, cycles, free weights and weight machines. There's also a separate aerobics room, and the spectacular views through the floor-to-ceiling windows are as invigorating as any workout.

Entertainment: ⚓⚓⚓⚓ There's large casino, a disco which went until 2 a.m. on my cruise, conference rooms, Star Night Club for pre-and post-dinner dancing, and hosts for dancing with single female passengers. Then, there's the Connoisseur Club, reminiscent of a venerable London Club with expansive leather armchairs that invite you to relax, savor a martini or brandy or just the enjoyment conversation brings. Cigar aficionados can check the climate-controlled humidors to purchase their special smoke.

When the sun sets, entertainment moves to the two-tiered Constellation Theater, home to full-scale productions.. There are so many lounges and venues that there's never a crowd. Multiple lounges feature live music and dancing. The *Mariner* offers every daytime activity listed on megaship daily programs, but with a difference. Instead of 200 or 300 passengers in attendance, each attracts from 20 to 50 fellow passengers. A typical sea day lists a morning stretch class, bridge lecture, an enrichment lecture, bingo, wine tasting an introduction to digital photography. And, those were pre-lunch choices. Afternoons listed an art auction, shuffleboard, golf contest, documentary movie, computer class, blackjack tournament and team trivia, accompanied by one of the best high teas as sea.

Toby Salzman Comments:

"If you think you may hate cruising, book the Seven Seas Mariner. Great for upscale travelers, yet not extravagantly priced. The Mariner is intimate enough so that you never feel crowded."

Food and Dining ⚓⚓⚓⚓ Notably unique on the *Mariner* is the fact that it is the largest ship afloat to offer single open-seating dining in every one of her four restaurants. This makes the choice of each night's dining destination a most pleasant quandary. Which means guests sit with whomever they please. They dine whenever and wherever they wish, even in their suites, where selections from the ship's main restaurant can be ordered during dining hours in addition to 24-hour room service menu, which incidentally is served quickly on tables set by the server.

The Compass Rose is the *Mariner's* largest and most elegant restaurant. At tables gleaming with polished silver and fine china, guests dine on an ever-changing potpourri of selections ranging from the latest fusion creations and exotic taste combinations to traditional favorites such as prime rib or lobster. Selections for the health conscious are more simply prepared fare for times when overworked taste buds need a respite. At Latitudes, the smallest restaurant, chefs have creative latitude and menus could be an eclectic ethnic mix from the four corners of the world served in a single night's menu, depending on the chef's mood. The reservations-only hideaway features special cosmopolitan cuisine in an intimate setting

La Veranda's wonderfully evocative Mediterranean fare reminds one of a tempting little bistro in Provence or an inviting family-run trattoria in Parma. Think of aioli, fresh garlic dancing in sizzling olive oil and seafood so fresh you'd think they'd just hauled the catch over the stern. The atmosphere is casually elegant, and the cuisine is obviously prepared with loving care. During the day, La Veranda also provides self-service buffet breakfasts and luncheon at multiple stations, which are behind closed doors when the sun sets.

Signatures is the only restaurant at sea to be created and operated by chefs wearing the white toque and blue riband of the Cordon Bleu of Paris, the most prestigious culinary authority in the world. The ambience is classically and elegantly French, of course.

Service: ⚓⚓⚓⚓ Service is as good as it gets. Even though you may dine in a different restaurant nightly, waiters somehow know your name and your favorite drinks and have them ready when you arrive. This is particularly impressive in the restaurants that require reservations. Room service is quick and correct and service in every restaurant is impeccable.

Junior Cruisers: ⚓ Although families sail during school holidays, there's no facility dedicated to kids and I doubt many under 16-year olds would find enough to interest them on board.

Itineraries: ⚓⚓⚓⚓ *Mariner* took over the 2003 World Cruise from *Seven Seas Navigator* for January to mid-May. She'll then transit the Panama Canal and sail on Alaska cruises before returning to Fort Lauderdale for a series of round trip Caribbean cruises.

Overall: ⚓⚓⚓⚓++ The *Seven Seas Mariner* boasts the 100-seat "Signatures," Le Cordon Bleu's first and only permanent restaurant-at-sea; exclusive Le Cordon Bleu Classe Culinaire des Croisières workshops offered to guests on select cruises; four dining venues with the main dining room offering single, open seating; an exclusive Judith Jackson Sea Spa featuring specially trained therapists skilled in Jackson's celebrated aromatherapy; "Club.com," an 18-computer Internet café and classroom; and pod propulsion systems for virtually vibration-free cruising.

In spite of her size and spacious interiors, there's a warm and welcoming feeling throughout the vessel. Soft and rounded edges, woods in various shades lending depth to fabrics in soft pale blues, turquoise and brushed gold and burnt orange contribute to the ambiance. Large and small lounges blend and flow into other areas enhanced with marble, fine art, etched glass and textured fabrics. The result is a ship designed to fit luxury guests' lifestyle. Even at first glance, passengers know *Mariner* is special and they know that they are embarking on a luxury adventure. They enter into a graceful atrium that soars eight decks, are greeted by a friendly staff and promptly escorted to the ship's suites in glass-enclosed elevators. It's the first major clue that this ship is a combination of style and impeccable service.

When Radisson introduced *Seven Seas Navigator*, the company established a new standard for luxury cruise ships. *Mariner* fit right into the Radisson Seven Seas profile that signaled the lines' success at the top of the market for the past decade. The all-balcony, all-suite vessel is winning high marks and building a loyal following. The company is doing it right.

From embarkation to disembarkation, passengers experience the ultimate in seagoing luxury. Passengers arriving before the announced embarkation hour embark and are shown into the showroom for snacks and drinks while suites are readied for occupancy. On disembarkation, passengers with later flights are not rushed off the vessel..

INSIDER TIP

When it comes to price, after viewing typical suites in every category, best buy on the ship is probably one of the Penthouse Suites. The eight suites in this category are priced at a per diem of about $40 to $50 per person more per day and offer 50 percent more space than standard suites. Double prices for top suite categories, but one occupant on my cruise thought the "price was right" and rebooked the same suite for a back-to-back 30-day South America cruise in late January.

We particularly like the perks offered to full world cruise passengers - overnights in five star port hotels in Bangkok and in Cambodia for a visit to Angor Wat, dinners at four-star restaurants in Hong Kong and a list of other goodies.

Seven Seas Voyager: Here's an advance look at the 490-guest *Seven Seas Voyager* that joins the RSSC fleet in May 2003. *Voyager* is offering inaugural cruises in Western Europe and the Baltic. The *Voyager*, the world's second all balcony-suite vessel, will be a sister ship to, but not an identical twin of, the *Seven Seas Navigator*. The vessel at 49,000 tons is close to the *Mariner* size, but she will only carry 490 passengers, which is closer to the *Navigator* capacity. Voyager incorporates the best features of both.

The new vessel will have a space ratio of 70, which makes her one of the most spacious vessels ever built. Minimum suites are sized at 356 square feet and that does not include the verandah. Four main dining venues will be featured, including the 110-seat Le Cordon Bleu. The ship will also feature some of the more popular elements of the *Seven Seas Navigator* and take them further up the luxury scale. *Navigator* boasts ultra-spacious marble bathrooms with separate showers and full bathtubs.

The 2003 inaugural season will be spent in Northern Europe and the Mediterranean. In November 2003, *Voyager* will sail across the Atlantic for a couple of Caribbean round trips from Fort Lauderdale, before heading through the canal for West Coast sailings and Alaska cruises in 2004.

SEVEN SEAS NAVIGATOR
Built:1999

Category: Luxury
Overall Rating: ⚓⚓⚓⚓⚓
Rates: $$$$$
Country of Registry: Bahamas
Former Names: none
Nationality of Crew: European
Cruising Area: South America, Caribbean, Alaska
Length of Voyages: 7 to 50 days

Ship Specifics:

Tonnage	33,000	Elevators	5
Length	560 feet	Decks	8
Beam	81 feet	Children's Facilities	no
Stabilizers	yes	Fitness Center	yes
Passengers	490	Spa	yes
Crew	324	Verandahs	yes
Space Ratio	67.3	Casino	yes
Crew/Passenger Ratio	1-1.5	Wheelchair Access	yes

Suites: ⚓⚓⚓⚓ There are no cabins, or if like to call them state-rooms, there aren't any of those either. This is all-suite vessel which should not be confused with Seven Seas Mariner, which is an all-suite, all-verandah vessel.. The Navigator has 245 suites. The smallest is 301 square feet. The largest is 1,174-square feet, including the verandah. Rich damasks and sumptuous silks in the shades of sand, terra-cotta and taupe surround you with eye-pleasing color and body-easing comfort. The soft fabrics are set off by furnishings in warmly finished woods and floors of intricately veined marbles.

Each suite has a European king-size bed or twin beds, separate living room area, mini-bar stocked with select beverages, walk-in closet, TV/VCR, and bathroom with full tub and separate shower. All suites have sweeping ocean views and nearly 90 percent have private balconies. Ten suites are also interconnecting, which, when two are combined, offer a maximum of 1,529 square feet of living space. The large bathrooms have glass-enclosed showers and full-size tubs. A six-foot-wide mirror extends over the sink, which has plenty of space for toiletries. Amenities are high quality and replenished as quickly as they are used.

Facilities for Disabled Travelers: ⚓⚓ There are four accessible suites in convenient locations. Cabin door is 34.25 inches wide. The bathroom door is 38.25 inches wide with a sill can be ramped by the room steward, there are roll-in shower with a bench, hand held shower head and grab bars. The vessel does not accommodate electric wheelchairs or scooters. Access to some outside decks may be difficult because of high doorway sills.

Public Space: ⚓⚓⚓⚓+ Glass-walled elevators rise through three decks of airy lounges, shops, clubrooms and restaurants. Streamline style of the 1930s is very much in evidence, with furnishings that fit the mood. Every room is designed so the guest travels in ease. Artwork varies, but the sensuous curves of an Erte drawing sets the mood. No space is dedicated to a specific period or style. *Seven Seas Navigator* is decidedly modern. The two tiered Seven Seas Show Lounge is the main venue for entertainment and special events. The lounge has stadium-style seating. Galileo's Lounge is topside and offers spectacular views. Other public rooms include a library with a good selection of books and videos, a computer room with Internet and mail capabilities. The ship is so spacious, most public rooms can accommodate the entire passenger complement without a rush for seats.

Entertainment: ⚓⚓⚓⚓ For a ship this size, entertainment is outstanding. Similar to the programs offered *Seven Seas Mariner*. Lecturers, dance classes, bridge games, There's a good size casino, a disco, small conference rooms, a night club for pre and post-dinner dancing, and hosts to socialize with single female passengers. When the sun sets, entertainment moves to the two-tiered Seven Seas Show Lounge, home to scaled down production shows and featured entertainers. With so much space and so few passengers, there's never a crowd. Lounges feature live music and dancing. The *Navigator* offers every daytime activity listed on megaship daily programs, but with a difference. Instead of 2000 or 3000 passengers, there are only 490 attending functions, when the ship is completely full.

Food and Dining: ↧↧↧↧↧ Like other vessels in the fleet, *Navigator* features a single open sitting, so passengers are free to dine when and with whom they want to break bread. Complimentary wines are served with dinners and there's no charge for soft drinks. The Compass Rose dining room offers an extensive selection of appetizers, soups, salads, pasta and desserts. There's a separate dessert menu with calorie-laden temptations. Breakfast is served in the Compass Rose as well as in the Portofino Grill which has a picture perfect buffet featuring multiple options, including an egg station. Lunch is just as impressive in the Grill or the restaurant. In addition, the Pool Grill offers hamburgers, hot dogs, veggie burgers, fries. Suite service is around the clock and the menu doesn't leave anything out, including full course dinners. The Grill becomes an optional Italian restaurant on several evenings, depending on the length of the cruise.

Spa and Fitness: ↧↧↧↧↧ The spa is not super sized, but it has the latest workout equipment an there's no need to sign up to use the treadmills. The spa is operated by Judith Jackson, a name well known to shoreside spa enthusiasts and it is different from Steiner-operations on other ships. Attendants don't seem to be in a hurry, nor do they try to sell products. Treatments run the gamut from a normal Swedish massage to exotic aromatherapy treatments. The fitness center faces the ocean and has a separate aerobics room for classes or individual exercise. There are two levels of very comfortable lounge chairs for sun worshippers, Two whirlpools and two showers are around the saltwater pool.

Junior Cruisers: ↧ There are no dedicated facilities for children and few couples bring the kids. Frankly, Radisson would not be my first pick for under 16 year olds.

Itineraries: ↧↧↧↧↧ The *Mariner* has taken over the *Navigator's* world cruise, so *Mariner* will do a 50-day cruise around South America, Holiday cruises from Fort Lauderdale, transit the Panama Canal and then sail to Alaska

Overall: ⚓⚓⚓⚓⚓+ *Navigator* is devoid of endless corridors of cabin doors, noisy, crowded reception areas and bothersome announcements. Atmosphere is calm and quiet, with excellent food and service and itineraries that feature exotic ports of call and experiences. The overall ambience is country club-style. Radisson has managed to produce the ambience luxury guests look for in a cruise vacation. When you sail *Navigator*, like the rest of the fleet, everyone knows your name. The ambience is befitting the style of a small prestigious hotel serving guests who are more like old friends than simply names and numbers. After the first day, no one asks for your cruise card to charge your bar bill.

Even luxury travelers appreciate what may seem like small perks – complimentary wines with dinner in all restaurants, no charge for soft drinks anywhere, guest's choice of two bottles of alcoholic beverages for cabin use and the low Internet (75 cents per minute) charges. Shore excursions are competitively priced. All is calm and all is quiet, befitting the style of a small prestigious hotel serving guests who are more like old friends than simply names with numbers.

HIGH MARKS

Δ Cabin and closet space as well as amenities make she ship perfect for longer cruises.

SONG OF FLOWER
Built: 1986   Refurbished: 1989/2001

Category: Boutique-Luxury
Rates: $ $ $ $ $
Overall Rating: ⚓⚓⚓⚓⚓
Country of Registry: Norway
Former Name: *Explorer StarShip*
Nationality of Crew: European
Cruising Area: Asia and Europe
Length of Voyage: 6 to 14 nights

Ship Specifics

Tonnage	8,282	Elevators	2
Length	410 feet	Decks	6
Beam	53 feet	Children's Facilities	no
Stabilizers	yes	Fitness Center	yes
Passengers	172	Spa	yes
Crew	144	Verandahs	no
Space Ratio	48	Casino	yes
Crew/Passenger Ratio	1-1.2	Wheelchair Access	yes

Cabins: ⚓⚓⚓⚓⚓ ***Suites:*** ⚓⚓⚓⚓⚓ All accommodations have ocean views and, except for minimum cabins with portholes, they have large windows. Cabin size ranges from 172 to 330-square feet. Decor is in soft peach and blues, and amenities are extensive. Every stateroom is equipped with two lounge chairs, video player, generous storage and closet space, locking drawers for valuables, well-stocked and constantly replenished refrigerator. Guests are welcomed in staterooms with hats for men, caps for women, plush robes, high-quality amenities in bathrooms, and huge umbrellas for that unexpected downpour. Suites, converted from two cabins in *Explorer* days, have two full bathrooms (one with mini-size tub, the other with shower only), and separate living rooms and bedrooms. Suites are roomy at over 400-square feet. Beds are either twin or queen-size in nearly all cabins.

The category that sells out first is "B" on Observation Deck. These are newer 321-square-foot cabins with larger bathrooms (full-size tubs) and private verandahs

Facilities for Disabled Travelers: ⚓ There are no cabins or suites designated as wheelchair accessible. .

Public Space: ⚓⚓⚓⚓ Three good-size traditionally furnished public rooms include the topside Observation Lounge, with its busy bar and comfortable chairs for ocean watching, afternoon tea and socializing; the active main lounge, which is tiered with a marble dance floor and stage; and the nightclub, which doubles as a disco and a venue for high tea. There's also a small casino, very well-stocked library, golf driving cage, and swimming pool.

Entertainment: ⚓⚓⚓ Daytime hours are not heavily scheduled with activities. Most passengers prefer it that way, but there are lectures for those seeking information about world events and/or regional history and culture.

There's dance music in the evenings, a vocalist, a piano bar, and the evening highlight is the elegant dinner. There's also a resident group of four talented singers and dancers.

Spa and Fitness: ⚓⚓⚓ A small gymnasium has a few machines, Jacuzzi, sauna, and spa offering beauty and hair treatments.

Food and Dining: ⚓⚓⚓⚓⚓ Dining is a highlight, second only to itineraries. Food is excellent in quality, taste, and presentation. The 172-seat Galaxy dining room takes care of all passengers in an open-sitting arrangement, with two-hour periods set aside for each of the three meals. Table size ranges from two to 10.. Breakfast and lunch are buffet-style in the dining room, with the option of menu selections and table service. Dinners are special—impeccable, attentive white-glove service, fresh flowers, and starched linen. Weather permitting, the outdoor Café and Grill on Sun Deck serves short-order and buffet breakfasts, grilled sandwiches, and buffet lunches. Cabin service is on a 24-hour basis.

Service: ⚓⚓⚓⚓ Passengers are addressed by name from embarkation to debarkation. Service is friendly and quick. Special requests are handled immediately.

Junior Cruisers: ⚓ There are no special facilities or programs, and few children sail the *Song of Flower*, although cabins and suites can easily accommodate a third and even fourth passenger.

Itineraries: ⚓⚓⚓⚓ Six-to-14-day cruises seasonally in India, the Red Sea, Arabia and the Far East including China, Burma, Vietnam and Indonesia, with summers spent exploring classic Mediterranean, Scandinavian, Baltic Republics and Northern European destinations.

Overall: ⚓⚓⚓⚓ The *Song of Flower* competes head-on against *Seabourn* and *Silversea*, but she's more like a larger *Sea Goddess* incorporating some features deliberately ignored by the competition. She's Old World luxury with New World amenities offered in a subdued, understated environment. Welcoming and classy rather than stuffy. She's a vessel that says "old money" based on atmosphere, ambience, and passenger manifest, but no one talks about money.

The yacht-like *Song of Flower* is on the plain-side and does not come up to the aesthetic qualities of her competitors, yet she is extremely popular and fills on most voyages. When compared to other ships her size, she comes up short on décor and facilities, but her loyalists wouldn't sail another ship no matter what the inducement may be. *Song of Flower* has a certain something that appeals to that "old money" crowd mentioned earlier. Scandinavian refinement and destination-intensive, passengers were irate when she was taken out of service for six months after 9/11 because her itinerary put her in areas where safety was questionable. Radisson received more complaint letters from passengers who feared her future was doomed. She's back in service and the faithful are filling her beds.

INSIDER TIP

On our first evening on board, we shared our dinner table with a delightful couple from London, who we later learned carried an impressive title in front of their name. Self-introductions were first name, a trend that carried throughout the vessel. Within a couple of days, the ambience had homogenized into a club-like environment. If you are adventurous and well-heeled and won't hesitate to brave the seas in any weather, you will board the tender (*Little Flower*) for 25 minutes to see the castle at Isle of Skye; or similar hard to reach places. Passengers have a tendency to drop ship names instead of celebrity names. *Song of Flower* is for the traveler who can afford the best, but is too polite to return a dish that isn't quite to his or her taste; the kind of guest who dresses for dinner, but not in beads and spangles; a CEO who refuses to wear a tie in your country club and still looks like he emerged from the pages of GQ with a wife from off the pages of Town and Country. If you fit that profile, the *Song of Flower* is the ship for you.

HIGH MARKS:
- Δ Exotic itineraries
- Δ Laid back atmosphere
- Δ Suites with two bathrooms

WEAKEST LINK
- There's only so much we can do and how many face lifts it will take to look the way we want to look. *Song of Flower* is starting to show her age.
- She's plain vanilla flavor and travelers who like some color will not enjoy the ship

Regal Cruises

300 Regal Cruises Way, Palmetto, FL 34220
(941) 723-7300 – www.regalcruises.com

Regal Cruises was founded by the owners of the New York-based mass-market national discount travel company, Liberty Travel, in 1993. Its single cruise ship is the old *Caribe I*, which it acquired from Commodore Cruise Line and promptly renamed *Regal Empress*. The company calls itself "the world's smallest cruise line" and is currently headquartered in St. Petersburg, Florida.

Who Sails Regal Cruises? Ship buffs who like old ships, young couples and singles who want to party, couples over 50 who want to gamble, retirees on a tight budget and anyone who cares less about ship amenities than they do about the ocean. Who shouldn't go would probably give a better picture. This ship is not for travelers who expect a classy state-of-the-art cruise ship and first-time cruisers who want to test the waters. The *Regal Princess* could turn them off cruising.

Lifestyle: Casual, casual, casual. Expect crowds in most areas and lots of lines for everything.

Dress Code: Except for restrictions on tank tops and shorts in the dining room, just about anything goes, although Regal suggests jackets and formal nights.

Dining: There's plenty of food and it's almost impossible to go hungry, but don't expect lobster or caviar. The day starts with early-bird coffee, continues with three meals at two sittings in the dining room, teatime, and Pietro's Pizza Palace, which also serves hot dogs and Cuban sandwiches.

Tipping Policy: Waiters and room stewards expect $3.50 per person per night; busboys, $2. Other gratuities suggested for services as rendered.

Discount Policy: Early-booking savings, but rates are so low it is not necessary to look for a discount, although they are offered on some itineraries and soft sailings. Advertised specials are as low as $80 per day, per person.

INSIDERS TIP

Seasoned travelers do not sail this ship, but you find retirees who like to cruise on a very low budget.

The Fleet

REGAL EMPRESS

Built: 1952   Refurbished: 1995

Category: Budget
Rates: $ $
Overall Rating: ⚓⚓
Country of Registry: Bahamas
Former Names: Caribe I, Olympia
Nationality of Crew: International
Cruising Area: Mexico and Northeastern United States/Canada
Length of Voyages: 2 to 10 nights

Ship Specifics

Tonnage	22,979	Elevators	3
Length	611 feet	Decks	8
Beam	79 feet	Children's Facilities	no
Stabilizers	yes	Fitness Center	yes
Passengers	1,160	Spa	yes
Crew	396	Verandahs	no
Space Ratio	23	Casino	no
Crew/Passenger Ratio	1-3	Wheelchair Access	yes

Cabins: ⚓⚓ *Suites:* ⚓⚓ Minimum cabins are closet-size at 105 square feet, but they do have two lower beds and budget travelers on a two-night cruise may find them adequate. Up a step are cabins with small portholes that can accommodate a third person, but again, with lots of togetherness. "Mini-suites" are about 180 square feet and have double beds and two windows and are really a good buy for this type of ship. They sell for about $110 per night in the Caribbean, a little higher on Canada/New England cruises. Suites are not plush, but they are almost twice the size of cabins, and it is not unusual to find them occupied by four singles. They have mini-refrigerators and sofas that convert, but there are only two of them and they sell quickly.

Public Space: ⚓⚓ Very little has been done to the ship since it changed ownership, so there are some nice features that go back about 40 years. Open deck space, although very crowded when the ship is full, brass on staircases, paneled library, very large and noisy casino, lounges and bars, and a theater. There's also a piano bar.

Spa and Fitness: ⚓⚓ There's an equipped gymnasium, a spa offering the usual services, exercise classes, two whirlpools, shuffleboard, skeet shooting, and swimming pool.

Entertainment: ⚓⚓⚓ There's plenty to do. Commodore Club; a piano bar; the Mermaid Lounge, with its etched glass and music; Grand Lounge, where evening mini-production shows and individual entertainers perform; and the usual daytime activities of bingo, horse racing, and participation games. The busiest room on the ship is the casino which draws from a large number of Floridians who want to gamble.

Food and Dining: ⚓⚓ Dining room is old-style and has some original oil paintings and murals depicting New York and Rio. Most tables are for six or more. Portions are generous, but food is not up to what should be served on a cruise ship.

Service ⚓⚓ Less than what it could be, but better than expected on this type of budget ship.

Junior Cruisers: ⚓ Limited facilities and programs for the large number of children on weekend cruises or during school holidays.

Itineraries: ⚓⚓⚓ From November to May, *Regal Empress* sails from Port Manatee, Florida, on two-and five-night cruises to Cozumel, Mexico, and the Caribbean, with longer cruises scheduled during holiday periods. During other months, she cruises on one-week voyages from New York to Bermuda and on 12-night Canada-New England cruises, also from New York.

Overall: ⚓⚓ She's a tired old ship, but her prices are about the cheapest at sea. It is possible to sail her for as little as $60 a day on some cruises and that's cheap! The ship has an interesting history and cruise-a-holics who like old ships find her interesting. Some of the woods, the Art Deco touches, and etched glass are reminiscent of the ship's grander past. Originally built in 1953 as the *Olympia* for long two-class cruises, she was reconstructed and refurbished in 1983 for short Caribbean cruises and sailed as "the happy ship" for Commodore. Each refurbishment changed the vessel, and she is now an eclectic mix of Art Deco, brass, plastic, and modern pieces of furniture. She is also a high-density ship, with a lot of passengers crowded into rooms with limited space.

HIGH MARKS

Δ The very low prices make it cheaper to cruise than to stay home.

WEAKEST LINKS

- No cabins for disabled travelers
- Crowded casino. Get there early to find a seat at a blackjack table.

Shirley and Harry Comment:

"Vessel is chopped with 'you can't get there from here' layouts that make getting around difficult. Passengers flock to the ship because the price is right and they do have a lot of fun"

Renaissance Cruises
(Out of business since October 2001)

Royal Caribbean International

1050 Caribbean Way, Miami, FL 33132
(305) 536-6573 – www.royalcaribbean.com

In 1969, three Norwegian shipping companies, I.M. Skaugen, Gotaas Larsen and Anders Wilhelmsen, founded Royal Caribbean Cruise Line for the purpose of offering year-round seven and 14-day cruises out of Miami. Today, Royal Caribbean is a publicly traded company on the New York Stock Exchange and one of the major players in the cruise ship industry, with a total of 16 ships scheduled to be in service by mid-2003.

In 1997, the company acquired Celebrity Cruises, which has retained its separate brand name even in the midst of being folded into the greater corporate entity.

The constant parade of dazzling new ships from Royal Caribbean always reminds us of one of the most fascinating phenomena of late 20th -century life, the mall. That vast enclosed emporium of shops, bars, theaters and restaurant has become a meeting place for teenagers and a weekend and evening destination for the young and upwardly mobile. In a sheltering, climate-controlled environment, surrounded by glittering options for spending money, people get dreamy-eyed and slow-moving – especially when they happen to get in a buffet line in front of you.

Royal Caribbean ships always seem to make two different statements, offering two contrasting lifestyles on one ship – the dazzling, come-hither bright lights and sense of action to attract young and first-time cruisers, coupled with cool, sophisticated public rooms and lavish suites to please upscale repeat passengers.

Who Sails Royal Caribbean? Middle America (and that includes middle Canada as well) is the backbone of the RCI passenger roster, and the standard issue embarkation costume for both male and female passengers heading out on a Caribbean cruise is chinos or khaki Bermuda shorts with a neat logo polo shirt (from J. Crew or Land's End). Families with new clothes, new cameras and fairly well-behaved children mingle with young couples, middle-aged couples, slow-moving seniors traveling with friends and relatives, and animated Latin Americans chattering in three languages and ignoring No Smoking signs. RCI passengers are younger than many other lines can claim, especially on the gigantic Voyager class, where the average passenger age appears to be 35 to 40.

Passenger loyalty is a big factor with RCI passengers, many of whom see no reason to switch brands so long as their favorite keeps building new ships and offering good deals. More Europeans are aboard as well, particularly the British, who have sampled the new Vision-class ships in Europe and like the bigger, glitzier vessels. Gal pals who leave their husbands at home, gay couples who don't flaunt it and sedentary seniors with wheelchairs or canes will also find themselves comfortable and cared for on RCI ships. First-time cruisers fare very well on board with a staff that politely explains everything from the way the cabin toilets flush to which server in the dining room is responsible for pouring water and coffee.

Facilities for Disabled Travelers: Royal Caribbean provides special services for passengers with special needs. The newer ships are more accessible with wider corridors that will accommodate wheelchairs. In addition, through Special Needs Desk, mobility impaired passengers receive early embarkation. On all ships, one swimming pool and Jacuzzi have been equipped with a hydraulic lift. An accessible tender system will be completed on all ships in mid-2003. there are accessible blackjack tables, and accessible cabins and suites on all ships.

Lifestyle: In a word, "active." While there are sedentary couples on board, the high profile passengers are energetically walking or jogging around the sports deck, working out in the gym, sunbathing by the pool, dancing in the disco late at night and joining in the ship tours, exercise classes, scaling the rock-climbing walls on Voyager-class vessels, ice skating, in-line skating, playing miniature golf on simulated courses and shopping like there's no tomorrow. These young and young-at-heart passengers like to access the Internet and pick up or send out e-mail with RCI's 24-hour Internet centers.

Dress Code: While the dress code has eased up a little, RCI still ostensibly follows the traditional cruise ship pattern, with assigned tables at two sittings, two formal nights a week where "tuxedos or jacket and tie" are requested for men, and where "casual" does not mean one can wear shorts and Tee-shirts into the dining room in the evening. Other than the two formal nights a week, there are two other dress codes, "casual" – dresses or slacks and blouses for women, sports shirts and trousers for men (jeans are not encouraged) – and "smart casual" – dresses or pantsuits for women, jacket added to trousers and open-necked shirts for men. You can rent a tuxedo from the cruise line if you wish; ask your travel agent when booking.

Dining: Non-threatening, special occasion food is produced on a rotating set menu that is similar if not identical on the different ships. There is a wide variety and good range of choices, and the preparation is capable if not inspired. A typical dinner begins with three appetizers, three soups, one pasta, four entrées including one red meat, one white meat, one seafood and one vegetarian, a low fat, low calorie ShipShape menu and a clutch of desserts including cakes, pies, ice cream, sorbets and frozen yogurt.

The relationship between RCI passengers and their food is a close one, and most of them are never far away from the buffet. After a day of water sports and a beach barbecue at Coco Cay or Labadee (the line's private island beaches), they hit the teatime snacks with a vengeance. There are alternative restaurants on the newer ships and an all-day buffet service on all the vessels. Room service from an in-cabin menu is offered 24 hours a day. Johnny Rockets, a California-based retro-style hamburger-and-shake shop is found on the Voyager-class ships.

Special Dietary Requests: Vegetarian and low calorie dishes are on every menu, but salt free, sugar free and kosher must be requested in advance of sailing. Kosher meals are catered by Weberman Kosher Caterers. The food is prepared and packaged on plastic plates, then re-heated on the same packaging and brought to the passenger completely sealed. Meals are then served on regular china with a doily separating the package from the plate.

INSIDER TIP

Most travel agents don't remember to tell you that even if you book a minimum priced cabin, you can have some of the perks offered to suite passengers for a relatively small amount of money and a lot of fun. I discovered it when we were booked in a less than great cabin and I read the material sent with the tickets. Called "Crowning Touches", you have a bottle of Dom Perignon champagne and canapés waiting in the cabin when you arrive, terry bathrobes for two (which are yours to take home), a massage or facial, Moet and Chandon along with breakfast for two delivered to the cabin when ordered, nightly pre-dinner canapes, and a nightly tray of sweets. Also included in the package are a formal 8x10 portrait in an engraved silver-plated frame, an invitation to visit the bridge and limousine transfers between airports and the ship, which sure beats taking the bus. Break the price down and the champagne and robes cover the price of $399 for the two of you. For the budget-minded, there's a slimmed down package for $170 that doesn't include the robes.

Tipping: Passengers tip their stewards in the traditional fashion, by putting cash in an envelope and giving it to the server on the last night aboard ship. Figure $3.50 a day per person for the cabin steward, $3.50 for the dining room water and $2 for the assistant waiter. Headwaiters expect $2.50 per person for a three-, four- or five-day cruise, more for a seven-day cruise. A 15 per cent tip is added to each bar beverage check at the time of purchase.

Past Passenger Perks:: To become a member, you need to be at least 18 years old and have cruised at least once with Royal Caribbean International. You are then eligible to enroll in the Crown & Anchor Club. Membership is tiered. The more you cruise with Royal Caribbean, the greater the perks. In addition to an invitation to a private onboard event, you get a robe to use during your cruise. Cruise 10 times and you may get to keep the robe. You also get priority check-in, special price offers, special rates on suites and verandah cabins and a special place on the priority list when a sailing is sold out.

Discount Policy: Early booking discounts are available and advertised special in low season, in particular move rates down a couple of notches.

INSIDER TIPS

Thee long-running (and highly popular) ShipShape program awards cruise dollars for every exercise class or sports activity on board that a passenger participates in, even line-dancing class, and cruise dollars may be redeemed for cruise line logo items at the end of the cruise. The more dollars you collect, the nicer the bonus gift.

WEAKEST LINK:

- *Shirley and Harry Comment: "RCI could use some upgrading of Lido buffets. Less could be more. Less choice, more quality."*

The Fleet
NORDIC EMPRESS
Built: 1990

Category: Resort mid-size
Overall Rating: ⚓⚓⚓⚓
Rates: $$$
Country of Registry: Liberia
Former names: none
Nationality of Crew: International
Cruising Area: Bermuda, Caribbean
Length of Voyages: 4 to 7 days

Ship Specifics

Tonnage	48,563	Elevators	7
Length	692 feet	Decks	12
Beam	100 feet	Children's Facilities	yes
Stabilizers	yes	Fitness Center	yes
Passengers	1,600	Spa	yes
Crew	671	Verandahs	yes
Space Ratio	30.35	Casino	yes
Crew/Passenger Ratio 1-2.38		Wheelchair Access	yes

Cabins: ⚓⚓⚓⚓ ***Suites:*** ⚓⚓⚓⚓ For an RCI ship of this vintage, the cabins are comfortable and well-designed, but not spacious. Even the lowest-priced standard inside doubles offer compact, livable space with two lower beds that can be put together into one queen-sized bed, a desk/dresser with stool or chair, hair dryer, closet-circuit TV, phone, tile bath with shower and generous shelf space. Insides are imaginatively decorated with pictures and vertical fabric-and-Plexiglas strips framing wall sconces instead of the usual blank wall covered by curtains. The 56 ocean view staterooms with private balconies and small sitting areas are the best accommodations aboard, except for a few suites. Honeymooners should try to book the Royal Suite for optimum luxury and privacy.

Facilities for Disabled Travelers: ⚓⚓ Four cabins are designated accessible for wheelchairs, two inside and two outside. Cabins with 117-square feet for the inside and 139-square feet for the outside are tight fit for wheelchair turn arounds. The square footage includes the bathrooms which have roll-in showers with fold down seat, hand held shower heads and grab bars. Cabin and bathroom doors are 32 inches wide. Toilets are 17.5 inches high with grab bars and the sinks are accessible. There are no sills and most public rooms are accessible.

Public Space: ⚓⚓⚓⚓ Passengers are impressed with the dramatic nine-deck atrium on the *Nordic Empress* with its Centrum staircase and cascading waterfall, a perfect place for a photo op. The cozy Carousel Pub is a nice place for a pre-dinner cocktail, and the two-deck Carmen dining room is placed aft with a big window wall facing the sea. Royal Caribbean's signature Viking Crown Lounge is perched 11 decks above the ocean for a dazzling vista by day and a turn on the dance floor by evening. You'll find plenty of shops aboard, plus a gigantic casino, two-deck show lounge and cabaret-style shows in the High Society Lounge aft. There's also a computer work station with 14 terminals in the purser's square.

Spa and Fitness: ⚓⚓⚓ The ShipShape Center features a spa and gym, as well as treatment and massage rooms, and there is a beauty salon adjacent to the shopping areas. Be sure to participate in the ShipShape onboard activities to win enough cruise ship dollars to get a logo Tee-shirt or visor. Designated ShipShape low-calorie and/or low-fat dishes are on every menu for fitness-minded passengers.

Entertainment: ⚓⚓⚓⚓ The Strike Up the Band Showroom is filled with comfortable, overstuffed chairs and banquettes which, in the balcony, become a problem. There are so many exuberantly undulating brass railings among the scalloped curves and levels in the balcony that aisles are narrow and access difficult. We've seen some late-arriving passengers vaulting over the back of an empty sofa to get into a seat. Production shows are high quality, well costumed and choreographed, and other lounges around the ship provide live music for dancing or singing along in the evenings.

Food and Dining: ⚓⚓⚓ The menus are virtually the same throughout the fleet in the main dining rooms, with dinners offering three starters, three soups, one salad, one pasta and six main dishes, ShipShape and vegetarian plates, plus daily standards such as broiled salmon, grilled chicken and Caesar salad. The usual buffet breakfasts and lunches, as well as a casual dinner from 6:30 to 9:30 p.m. that combines buffet and table service is offered every evening, no reservations necessary, in the Windjammer Buffet.

Service: ⚓⚓⚓ The passenger service ratio is one crew member for every two and one-third passengers, not quite up to the ideal one for two.

Junior Cruisers: ⚓⚓⚓ Adventure Ocean is designed for toilet-trained toddlers from the age of three. No diapers are permitted, even the pull-up types. Age groups are divided into three to five, six to eight, nine to 11, 12-to14 and 15-to-17. In the playroom, a slide dumps giggly kids into a sea of brightly colored plastic balls. In a cave-like television room padded with carpeting, videos are screened, and after-hours group babysitting (for toilet-trained children over three) or in-cabin babysitting (for children from six months up) can be arranged. Cost is $6 to $8 per hour. A children's menu is offered, and on designated evenings, children and young people participating in the Adventure Ocean program may join their friends and the youth counselors for a kids' dinner.

Itineraries: ⚓⚓⚓ The *Nordic Empress* sails the Western Caribbean from Tampa on seven-night itineraries visiting Grand Cayman, Belize and Cozumel

Overall: ⚓⚓⚓ We've always felt this ship from its debut was ideal for honeymooning couples. Royal Caribbean does a good job of tactfully informing first-time cruisers about protocol so that everybody looks as if they know their way around. The welcome-aboard program is well-orchestrated as the cruise staff introduces who does what around the ship, the services and prices of the shipboard concessions such as spa and beauty services, photographer and casino, and youth counselors to explain activities and sign-in rules. The pool deck was designed for use at night as well as in the daytime, with dramatic evening lighting and covered gazebos that can be used as bandstands or dance floors. Umbrellas and sailcloth-covered pavilions provide shade during warm days when the ship is in port. This is a quieter, gentler version of a party cruise.

HIGH MARKS

Δ A special Mardi Gras itinerary is offered in the Western Caribbean in March that visits New Orleans and Yucatan's Progreso.

WEAKEST LINK:

• Sightlines for the shows are not good in parts of the Strike Up the Band balcony Try to arrive early to get a good seat.

SOVEREIGN OF THE SEAS
Built: 1988

MONARCH OF THE SEAS
Built: 1991

MAJESTY OF THE SEAS
Built 1992

Category: Resort XL
Overall Rating: ⚓⚓⚓⚓
Rates $$$
Country of Registry: Norway
Former names: none
Nationality of Crew: International
Cruising Area: Bahamas, Caribbean
Length of Voyages: 3 to 7 days

Ship Specifics - Sovereign

Tonnage	73,192	Elevators	13
Length	880 feet	Decks	14
Beam	106 feet	Children's Facilities	yes
Stabilizers	yes	Fitness Center	yes
Passengers	2,250	Spa	yes
Crew	840	Verandahs	no
Space Ratio	32.5	Casino	yes
Crew/Passenger Ratio	1-2.67	Wheelchair Access	yes

Ship Specifics - Monarch & Majesty

Tonnage	73,941	Elevators	11
Length	880 feet	Decks	14
Beam	106 feet	Children's Facilities	yes
Stabilizers	yes	Fitness Center	yes
Passengers	2,350	Spa	yes
Crew	822	Verandahs	yes
Space Ratio	31.46	Casino	yes
Crew/Passenger Ratio	1-2.85	Wheelchair Access	yes

Cabins: ⚓⚓ *Suites:* ⚓⚓⚓⚓ After they created these cabins, they should have broken the mold. While Royal Caribbean's traditional standards always dictated cabins somewhere between small and compact, these tiny accommodations measure a tight 127-square feet in the lower cabin categories. Inside are twin beds in an L-shaped configuration, one chair, a small TV set, a tripod glass-topped table with a brass wastebasket set under it like a base (we once tried to chill champagne in it but were sternly upbraided by a Bahamian cabin stewardess), a built-in cabinet with four drawers, a closet with one full-length and one half-length hanging area plus drawers and a safe, and a small tidy tile bathroom with shower. The company's official doctrine at the time was that passengers spend as little time as possible in their cabins and would prefer lavish space in the public rooms and deck areas. The Royal Family Suites (#1549 on the *Monarch* and *Majesty*) sleep five (if they're relatives or really, really close friends) with a private verandah, sitting area, master bedroom and bath and second bedroom with two lower beds, a pull down berth and small bath with shower only.

Facilities for Disabled Travelers: ⚓⚓ *Monarch* and *Majesty* each have two inside and two outside accessible cabins. The insides are 119-square feet which is not enough space for wheelchair turnarounds. Outsides are 157-square feet. Cabin and bathroom doors are 30 inches wide. They have roll-in showers with fold down seats, hand held shower heads and grab bars. *Sovereign of the Seas* has six accessible cabins designed for wheelchair maneuverability. Cabin dimensions are the same. Most areas of the ship are accessible except for the swimming pool, upper level of the Windjammer café and the Champagne bar. There is one accessible public restroom near the Purser's office.

Public Space: ⚓⚓⚓ When *Sovereign of the Seas* debuted in 1988, we were awestruck. We wrote, "In the five-story open lobby, brass-trimmed glass elevators glide up and down, their gleaming reflections glancing off marble walls. People walking past pause to lean against a brass railing to look far below at a white baby grand piano where a man in a red jacket is playing light classics beside three fountain pools. Almost every major city in America has one of these grand hotels with majestic staircases and soaring, ethereal space. The only difference is, this one is scheduled to sail off into the sunset at 5:30."

To help passengers navigate their way around the ship, cabins were all positioned forward and the public rooms aft so that passengers could make their way vertically from, say, the cocktail bars to the dining room to the show lounge to the casino, and horizontally from their cabins to the public areas.

Spa and Fitness: ⚓⚓⚓ We figured once on the *Sovereign of the Seas* that if you walked from a cabin on B deck forward to the sports deck for a morning exercise class, you would travel the full 880-foot length of the ship and then up 11 decks. (With a stroll like that, who needs exercise?) Nevertheless, if you need more, there's a ShipShape Center, saunas, massage and treatment rooms, beauty salon and gymnasium, plus a two level sports deck high atop the ship. Around the full promenade deck on *Sovereign of the Seas*, three-and-half laps is one mile, seven laps is two. It's the same on all of the ships in this class.

Entertainment: ⚓⚓⚓ Happily only a short stroll separates the chorus girls from the cheesecake, and you can hoof it easily from the pair of amidships dining room to the show lounge one or two decks above (depending on your dining rooms assignment). As befitting a line that names its public rooms after musical shows, the entertainment itself is usually quite good, from the bands that play in the dance lounges to the big production and variety shows on the main stage.

Food and Dining: ⚓⚓⚓ Each of the three ships has two dining rooms, a two-level Windjammer Café which provides breakfast and lunch buffets and an alternative restaurant in the evenings that combines buffet and table service for passengers who want to dine in casual dress on a dress-up night. The Touch of Class Champagne Bar on promenade deck is tucked away between the library and the card room on all three ships. Room service that includes hot foods, is provided on a 24-hour basis; cabin breakfast includes the possibility of hot egg dishes.

Service: ⚓⚓⚓ While the service staff aboard is friendly and efficient, the ratio of one crew member to almost three passengers is not ideal.

Junior Cruisers: ⚓⚓⚓ Kids are divided into age groups —three to five, six to eight, eight to 12 and 13-to-17. Teens have their own soft drink bar, video games center and disco with light show. Little kids must be three or over and toilet-trained to take advantage of the Adventure Ocean program of supervised activities and to be enrolled in evening babysitting. In-cabin babysitting for infants can also be arranged but must be reserved at least 24 hours in advance ($ 6 per hour)

Itineraries: ⚓⚓⚓⚓ *Sovereign of the Seas* and *Majesty of the Seas* offer three- and four-day itineraries departing Port Canaveral on Thursdays and Sundays (*Sovereign*) or Fridays and Mondays (*Majesty*) into the Bahamas, visiting Nassau and the private island beach at Coco Cay. On the four-day itinerary, *Majesty* also visits Key West. *Monarch of the Seas* makes four- and five-night cruises into the Western Caribbean from Ft. Lauderdale, with calls in Key West and Cozumel on the four-day itinerary, adding Costa Maya, near Cancun, on the five-night program.

Overall: ⚓⚓⚓⚓ While these ships are not identical, they are close enough to be sisters and were built in a four-year period by the French shipyard Chantiers d'Atlantique. At their debuts they were the largest cruise ships in the world, carrying more than 2,000 passengers each, an astonishing number at the time. Now, in comparison to the glittering, gigantic newer megaships in the line, they seem a bit stodgy and dowdy. At one time, *Sovereign* and her twin sisters *Majesty* and *Monarch* might have been dubbed Marriott of the Seas, because from the moment the youngish, often first-timer passengers boarded, they had the sense of arriving at a major resort for a Caribbean vacation that just happened to be aboard a cruise ship. That sense of hotel and vacation rather than ship and cruise has continued to be stressed in RCI advertising and continues to attract the multitudes.

HIGH MARKS

Δ As the first 2,000-plus passenger megaships, these ships still deserve special attention. They introduced heavier soundproofing materials between cabins, three-dimensional Plexiglas ship directories to help passengers find their way around, and a soaring sense of space that took ships into a new dimension.

WEAKEST LINK:

• Walking a long corridor seems unavoidable in the deck plans that put cabins forward and public rooms aft. It's also a long way to an elevator when your cabin is all the way forward, no matter which deck you occupy.

LEGEND OF THE SEAS
Built: 1995

SPLENDOUR OF THE SEAS
Built: 1996

GRANDEUR OF THE SEAS
Built: 1996

RHAPSODY OF THE SEAS
Built 1997

ENCHANTMENT OF THE SEAS
Built 1997

VISION OF THE SEAS
Built: 1998

Category: Resort XL
Overall Rating: ⚓⚓⚓⚓⚓
Rates: $ $ $
Country of Registry: Norway and Liberia
Former names: none
Nationality of Crew: International
Cruising Area: Alaska, Canada/New England, Caribbean, Hawaii, Panama Canal, Australia, New Zealand, Tahiti, Europe, Mexican Riviera, South America.
Length of Voyages: 3 to 15 days

Ship Specifics

Tonnage	78,490	Elevators	11
Length	916 feet	Decks	11
Beam	105 feet	Children's Facilities	yes
Stabilizers	yes	Fitness Center	yes
Passengers	1,800-2,000	Spa	yes
Crew	660-760	Verandahs	yes
Space Ratio	38.4	Casino	yes
Crew/Passenger Ratio	1-2.5	Wheelchair Access	yes

Tonnage -	Enchantment & Grandeur	74,140
	Legend & Splendour	69,130
	Rhapsody & Vision	78,491
Length -	Enchantment & Grandeur	916 ft
	Legend & Splendour	867 ft
	Rhapsody & Vision	915 ft

Cabins: ⚓⚓⚓ ***Suites:*** ⚓⚓⚓⚓ With these ships, the 127-square-foot Royal Caribbean standard cabins on the *Sovereign, Majesty* and *Monarch* expanded to a still-compact 138-square feet, but added many more private verandahs, which expands the space somewhat. On the first of the series to appear, *Legend of the Seas*, we occupied a cabin described as "Larger Outside", which begged the question, Larger than what? Basic inside and outside cabins on these ships have two beds that convert to queen-sized, a sofa/loveseat sitting area, color TV and tile baths with shower. Families should consider booking one of the four royal family suites with two bedrooms, two bathrooms, private verandah and walk-in closet and a living room, sleeping four in luxury or eight in relative comfort by using pull-down berths and a sofa bed. Top digs on the Vision-class vessels is the royal suite, one on each ship, with a huge living room with baby grand piano, refrigerator and wet bar, sitting area and separate dining area, marble bathroom with whirlpool tub, entertainment center, vanity area, walk-in closet and dressing room, and big private balcony.

Facilities for Disabled Travelers: ⚓⚓⚓ Each ship has 14 accessible cabins. Entrance and bathroom doors measure 32 inches with minimized raised sills. Accommodations are inside and outside and are located close to elevators. Cabins have roll-in showers, detachable shower heads, benches, lowered sinks and vanity and no sills at the bathroom entrance. Almost all of the public rooms are accessible and door leading out to decks work automatically.

Public Space: ⚓⚓⚓⚓ The six ships in RCI's Vision class vie with the eight vessels in Carnival's Fantasy class for crowd-pleasing variety and personality in each of the otherwise identical designs. Artwork throughout the RCI fleet is admirable, and the references to pop culture multiple. In the Schooner Bars, for example, identical on all the ships with their ship models, wood floors and rope ladders, the James Bond 007 Martini is listed on the menu as, "shaken, not stirred, Martinis are forever." While the Schooner Bar is the same on all the vessels, each Casino Royale carries a different décor. On *Enchantment of the Seas*, huge carved pirate heads stare down, and the entrance is over a glass floor with golden fish, pirate booty, baubles, bangles and beads underneath. As with the Carnival ships, a sense of fun relaxes the awesome lobbies and atriums.

Spa and Fitness: ⚓⚓⚓⚓ The spas aboard the Vision ships are as handsome as any in the cruise industry. Adults should count on spending a lot of time in the Solarium (children are not permitted, but Royal Caribbean has no plan to keep them out), inviting spa areas with pools covered by a retractable dome, mosaic tile floors, benches and statuary resembling a Roman bath. Inside are all sorts of treatment rooms and beauty services, and anyone who took Latin in high school can have fun figuring out the phrases that adorn the marble walls. A large glass-walled gym has treadmills, free weights and stationary bikes with race course software.

Entertainment: ⚓⚓⚓ Besides production shows, the entertainment includes music for listening or dancing in several venues at the same time – a piano bar in the Schooner Bar, a trio in the Champagne Terrace playing jazz and standards, ballroom dance music from an orchestra in the big aft lounge, and a loud, flashing disco dance floor in the Viking Crown Lounge (aboard *Splendour of the Seas*, it's set in a stylized Viking ship; on *Enchantment of the Seas,* it's in natural woods with sharp lime-green and royal blue decor.)

Food and Dining: ⚓⚓⚓ Two-level dining rooms serve mainstream special occasion food, plus spa options, vegetarian menus, a choice of six main dishes and a collection of rich desserts.

Service: ⚓⚓⚓ Dining room service, particularly from European waiters, both male and female, is generally quite good, although some of the more serious-minded recent arrivals from Eastern Europe are still working on their English and smiling skills. The usual full ranging RCI menus are in effect, but the theme dinners – Italian night, French night, Caribbean night – have gotten more sophisticated.

Junior Cruisers: ⚓⚓⚓⚓ Adventure Ocean welcomes kids three to 17, with a staff of experienced youth counselors and supervised activities divided into four different age groups. In an enchanting setting, three-to-five year olds may do face painting or ring toss, castle building or bean bag games. Six-to-eight year olds follow scavenger hunts and craft balloon animals. Voyagers nine to 12 get movie nights, karaoke and other cool things, while Navigators 13 to 17 have dance parties, talent shows, midnight basketball and adventure science. A video arcade and disco are dedicated just to teens.

Itineraries: ⚓⚓⚓⚓ The *Legend of the Seas* cruises the Pacific, sailing in Alaska, the Mexican Riviera, Hawaii, Australia and New Zealand. *Enchantment of the Seas* alternates seven-day Eastern and Western Caribbean cruises from Ft. Lauderdale year-round. *Grandeur of the Seas* makes Western Caribbean seven-day cruises out of New Orleans year-round, calling in George Town, Grand Cayman and Cozumel and Progreso, Mexico. *Rhapsody of the Seas* sails the Western Caribbean from Galveston, visiting Key West, Belize City and Cozumel in winter, then cruises Canada/NewEngland in summer and fall. *Splendour of the Seas* sails seven-day European itineraries in the Mediterranean from a Barcelona base in summer and repositions to South America in winter. *Vision of the Seas* cruises Alaska and Canada in summer, with seasonal Hawaii and Panama Canal repositioning sailings in the spring and fall, and spends the winter sailing to Baja and the Mexican Riviera.

Overall: ⚓⚓⚓⚓ The six Vision-class ships were built in two shipyards, Finland's Kvaerner Masa-Yards and France's Chantiers d'Atlantique, and all debuted within a time span of only three years. The aim was to create nimble ships slightly smaller than the previous trio of megaliners but with a faster cruising speed. This would allow passengers a longer time in port or shorter transits between ports, making these vessels marketable in port-intensive areas with a special appeal to first-time or destination-oriented cruisers. While all are sisters in the general sense, they are actually three sets of identical twins in the light of specific measurements. Some of the most interesting differences between the vessels can be found in the stairwells, where carefully chosen collections of art provide a mini-museum show every time you walk up or down the stairs instead of taking the elevators.

These ships were called "the ships of light" from their conception, with some two acres of glass on every ship. The two-deck dining rooms have all-glass walls, the Viking Crown Lounge wrapped around the funnel is almost all glass, and a glass-walled café that doubles as observation area is high atop the ship and forward. People who cruise on glass ships should always take along their sunglasses.

HIGH MARKS

Δ *Legend of the Seas* and *Splendour of the Seas* carry 18-hole miniature golf courses that measure 6,000 square feet aft on the top deck. They are serious and dignified, not silly and cartoonish. Instead of the usual windmills and castles, you'll find artificial heather, miniature trees, sand traps and small bronze sculptures of Scottish golfers. Glass baffles shelter the course from winds and halogen lights permit night games.

Richard Faber Comments:

"I find the ambience on Vision class ships far more inviting and stimulating than the stark, institutional décor of some higher priced ships. However, these ships need better cuisine, better alternative dining venues, more personalized service and better shore excursions."

WEAKEST LINK:

- The intention to keep solariums as "adults only" areas is excellent, but it doesn't work out that way. While most of the lounge chairs are occupied by adults, there's no one in charge of the space who has the guts to remind parents that kids have their own space and are not permitted in solariums. As a result, on every Royal Caribbean sailing I have been on, the "adults only" area has always had kids, albeit not in large numbers, but enough to eliminate the "quiet" from the area.

VOYAGER OF THE SEAS
Built 1999
EXPLORER OF THE SEAS
Built: 2000
ADVENTURE OF THE SEAS
Built: 2001
NAVIGATOR OF THE SEAS
Built: 2002

Category: Resort XXL
Overall Rating: ⚓⚓⚓⚓⚓
Rates: $ $ $
Country of Registry: Liberia
Former names: none
Nationality of Crew: International
Cruising Area: Caribbean
Length of Voyages: 7 days

Ship Specifics

Tonnage	142,000	Elevators	14
Length	1,020 feet	Decks	15
Beam	157.5 feet	Children's Facilities	yes
Stabilizers	yes	Fitness Center	yes
Passengers	3,114	Spa	yes
Crew	1,185	Verandahs	yes
Space Ratio	45.6	Casino	yes
Crew/Passenger Ratio	1-2.6	Wheelchair Access	yes

Cabins: ⚓⚓⚓⚓ *Suites:* ⚓⚓⚓⚓⚓ These ships are so revolutionary there's even a new kind of cabin unfamiliar to cruisers (except those who have sailed P & O ships or Scandinavian ferries). They would normally be termed insides because they don't overlook the sea; instead, they provide bay windows with window seats overlooking the Royal Promenade. They're called atrium staterooms, and have two lower beds that convert to queen-sized, bath with shower, mini-bar, hair dryer, vanity area, color TV, radio and phone. Some 765 cabins offer private verandahs. Four royal family suites that sleep up to eight with two bedrooms, two baths, private balcony and living room are available, as well as the lavish royal suite with baby grand piano, wet bar, dining room, living room, marble bath and private verandah

Marcia Levin Comments:

"Promenade view rooms offer little privacy if drapes are open. They are really inside cabins with a fancy name."

Facilities for Disabled Travelers: ⚓⚓⚓⚓ There are 26 wheelchair accessible staterooms, except on the *Voyager*, which has 18. Cabins are almost divided equally between insides and outsides. Entrance and bathroom doors are 32 inches wide with no sills. They have roll-in bathrooms with hand held shower heads. Cabins are nicely laid-out which enables good maneuverability. Alert kits for hearing impaired are available. Public rooms are accessible and most doors leading out to decks are automatic.

Public Space: ⚓⚓⚓⚓ The heart of these ships is the Royal Promenade on decks 5, 6 and 7, a magnificent enclosed promenade similar to London's Burlington Arcade, three decks high, wide enough for three lanes of automobile traffic and longer than two football fields. Packed with people at all hours, the controlled-climate promenade offers sidewalk cafes, an English or Irish pub, a sports bar, an Art Deco deli, boutiques, a general store, an elegant champagne bar, a cigar club and impromptu parades by costumed clowns and stilt-walkers. The discos on these ships are also worth writing home about. Called variously The Vault, The Chamber, The Dungeon and Jester's, each is located in a vast but claustrophobic two-deck space with heavy overtones of gothic. The Chamber on *Explorer*, for instance, is a castle with gargoyles, stained glassed windows with vaguely sadomasochistic themes, medieval bar chairs, bats hanging from the ceiling and spooky lights reminiscent of the haunted house in Disneyland. (The stained glass windows caused a couple of passengers on our sailing to mistake it for the chapel.)

Spa and Fitness: ⚓⚓⚓⚓ A 25,000-square-foot two-deck spa, gym and solarium with swimming pool, massage and treatment rooms, aerobics center and spa pools promises to keep you shipshape. If you don't like gyms and machines, you can get a full workout having fun on the basketball/volleyball court, rock-climbing wall, in-line skating track, miniature golf course and ice skating rink.

Entertainment: ⚓⚓⚓⚓ Entertainment aboard is varied and very professionally produced. The real headliner is the ice show (free, but tickets are required to allow everyone a chance to get a seat), although headliner guest stars (Norm Crosby was aboard our cruise) are also promoted. Fourteen singers and dancers take part in a splashy production show, two variety shows are also scheduled, and any night you can hear live bands around the ship offering a smorgasbord of sounds from Latin and calypso to piano bar, dance music by the show band, strings, country western, karaoke and disco. There's a hugely popular pub on the Royal Promenade as well. Finally, on these ships we find an inspired change in the top deck Viking Crown Lounge that has characterized all the RCI ships since the long-gone *Song of Norway* in 1970 and is too often a yawn-producing, under-utilized space until disco time. The revised design turns the space into separate lounges including a jazz club, a sports bar and a forward observation area.

Food and Dining: ⚓⚓⚓ Foodies may quibble with some of the preparation of shipboard meals – galleys serving more than 10,000 meals a day cannot be expected to turn out gourmet cuisine – but no one can complain about the variety of menu and venues, including an intimate Euro-Italian restaurant, a self-service ice cream bar, a casual dinner grill, a sidewalk café with all-day pizza, a 24-hour diner (Johnny Rockets) with great hamburgers, a casual dinner grill, 24-hour room service and an all-day buffet.

Optional Restaurant: ⚓⚓⚓⚓ A quiet, candlelight dinner for two is possible in the romantic Portofino Restaurant by making advance reservations and paying a $20 per person surcharge. Children under 13 are not permitted, and the restaurant suggests allowing two hours for the multi-course dinner. Reserve as soon as possible after boarding for the best choice of times; we found the best night to go is the first night out since most passengers haven't gotten around to reading their programs yet. If you want to lunch at the wildly popular Johnny Rockets without standing in line, go right at noon on the first port day of the cruise when everyone else is ashore. You'll still have time to go ashore on your own in the morning or later in the afternoon.

Service: ⚓⚓⚓⚓ While the well-trained longtime crew members aboard maintain RCI's often-praised service, veterans of many cruises will notice the sometimes frantic efforts of newer staffers to keep up.

Junior Cruisers: ⚓⚓⚓⚓ Just for kids, Adventure Ocean has indoor and outdoor attractions from computers to splash pools and beach toys, plus wild and wacky science laboratories. Teens have their own Optix nightclub, handily adjacent to Johnny Rockets with its indoor and outdoor booths. All ages have supervised activities throughout the day and evening. We have only one quibble – the Adventure Beach kids pool and playground is designed to be open so parents can watch the kids play, but it's also not separated enough from the rest of the deck traffic, so a bunch of adults may end up in there as well.

Itineraries: ⚓⚓⚓⚓ If the itineraries for these gigantic ships seem monotonous, it's because they're bigger than some of the islands in the Caribbean and can only dock in certain ports. The *Voyager of the Seas* sails every Sunday year-round from Miami into the Western Caribbean, calling at Labadee, RCI's private beach in Haiti; Ocho Rios, Jamaica; George Town, Grand Cayman; and Cozumel, Mexico. *Explorer of the Seas* alternates Eastern and Western Caribbean itineraries from Miami, sailing every Saturday and visiting San Juan, St. Maarten, St. Thomas and Nassau on the Eastern schedule, and Labadee, Ocho Rios, George Town and Cozumel on the Western. *Adventure of the Seas* sails designated Sundays from San Juan to Aruba, Curacao, St. Maarten and St. Thomas, and on other Sundays to St. Thomas, Antigua, St. Lucia and Barbados. *Navigator of the Seas,* which enters service at the beginning of 2003, is scheduled to alternate Eastern and Western Caribbean cruises sailing every Saturday from Miami and visiting Nassau, St. Thomas, San Juan and Labadee on Eastern itineraries, Labadee, Ocho Rios, George Town and Cozumel on Western itineraries.

Overall: ⚓⚓⚓⚓⚓ These are the world's largest cruise ships – at least until the new *Queen Mary 2* arrives for Cunard Line. Carrying more than 3,000 passengers, they offer all sorts of eye-catching novelty features from ice skating rinks to rock climbing walls. But to dismiss them as overgrown gimmicks would be a disservice to what is a dramatic break-through in cruise ship design. Here at last is a vessel that should lure the last of the reluctant young non-cruisers because it has, from a seagoing point of view, nearly everything anyone could want. There's no sense in being trapped with nothing to do. On a seven-day cruise, even the most active passengers would barely tap the options. Too big to transit the Panama Canal, the ships are anchored with a three-deck dining room aft and a three-deck theater forward. Decks 11 through 15 carry open decks with swimming and spa pools, sports and sunbathing areas, decks 5, 6 and 7 house the Royal Promenade, and decks 2, 3, 4 and 5 are where you'll find the three-deck dining room, the show lounge, casino, shops, business and conference center, ice rink and various bars and lounges. Rarely have we seen a more alluring ship to separate passengers from their expendable budgets.

HIGH MARKS ON EACH SHIP:

△ Wedding chapel
△ An ice-skating rink
△ A rock-climbing wall
△ A weird and spooky disco,
△ A crew musical parades in outlandish costumes.

WEAKEST LINKS:

• Unfortunately, you have to share all the wonders of these ships with the other 3,113 passengers and popular events can get crowded.
• You'll also have difficulty finding your cabin at first. Because of the width, there are as many as five cabins across in some passenger areas, so you must study the deck diagrams by each elevator to be sure you head in the right direction.

RADIANCE OF THE SEAS
Built: 2001
BRILLIANCE OF THE SEAS
Built: 2002

Category: Resort XXL
Overall Rating: ⚓⚓⚓⚓⚓
Rates: $ $ $
Country of Registry: Liberia
Former names: none
Nationality of Crew: International
Cruising Area: Alaska, Canada/New England, Caribbean, Europe, Hawaii, Panama Canal
Length of Voyages: 7 to 12 days

Ship Specifics

Tonnage	90,090	Elevators	9
Length	962 feet	Decks	12
Beam	106 feet	Children's Facilities	yes
Stabilizers	yes	Fitness Center	yes
Passengers	2,100	Spa	yes
Crew	859	Verandahs	yes
Space Ratio	42.9	Casino	yes
Crew/Passenger Ratio 1-2.44		Wheelchair Access	yes

Cabins: ⚓⚓⚓⚓⚓ *Suites:* ⚓⚓⚓⚓⚓ More than half the cabins on board have private verandahs that add additional space and breathing room. A definite step up in size are the cabins. Even the most basic insides, at 166- square feet, are a far cry from the early days of Royal Caribbean, when a couple in a standard cabin sitting opposite each other on twin beds had to interlock knees. Six are family staterooms that sleep up to six in 319-square feet with lots of togetherness. A notch up in class are the three royal family suites that sleep up to eight in 584-square feet that includes two bedrooms, two bathrooms, a sitting room with sofa-beds and a private verandah. A royal suite fills 1,001-square feet, big as a small apartment, with huge private balcony, separate bedroom with king-sized bed, living room with baby grand self-playing piano, entertainment center, dressing room and walk-in closet with vanity, bathroom, mini-bar, wet bar, hair dryer and closed circuit TV. Just down in size and style are four other suite categories from 362 to 512-square feet.

All cabins are furnished with interactive TV set, telephone, computer jack, vanity tables with space for laptop computers, mini-bar/refrigerator, hair dryer, convertible double/single hanging closet and bedside reading lights. Passengers who book the upscale cabins on deck 10 also have concierge service and access to a concierge club similar to a concierge floor in a land hotel.

Facilities for Disabled Travelers: ⚓⚓⚓⚓ There are 26 accessible cabins in a variety of categories. Entrance and bathroom doors are 32-inches wide. There are no sills.. Bathrooms have roll-in showers with detachable shower heads, grab bars and fold down seats. Public rooms are accessible, and accessible restrooms are conveniently located.

Public Space: ⚓⚓⚓⚓ A nine-deck atrium draws a gee-whiz reaction from boarding passengers, but during the cruise, the average cruise passenger may come to appreciate the appealing, comfortable and clubby public areas. Books, Books & Coffee serves espresso and lattes with cookies and pastries, sells best-selling and classic books, and even offers a couple of computer stations with which to browse your e-mail. (A dozen other terminals are located in Royal Caribbean On-Line on deck 5). A 24-hour library with a good selection of books provides easy chairs and an honor check-out system if you want to take a book back to your cabin. Even non-spa fans are knocked out by the striking solarium on *Radiance of the Seas* with its "waterhole" pool covered by a retractable glass canopy and guarded by a trio of 16-foot elephants flanked by waterfalls and luxuriant tropical foliage. (The African elephants are replaced by Indian elephants and a "days of the raj" theme on *Brilliance of the Seas*.) And the Colony Club is a handsome collection of public rooms decorated with hardwood floors and club-style furniture, including the Bombay Club with its self-leveling pool tables and the glass-walled Singapore Sling's bar with a full aft view to the sea.

Spa and Fitness: ⚓⚓⚓⚓ Besides the glamorous solarium pool and loungers, you'll find massage and treatment rooms, gym, aerobics area, thermal suite, beauty salon, men's and women's locker rooms and full fitness center. Note that some of the exercise classes may carry an additional surcharge and that passengers under 16 are not permitted in the spa and gym. Out on deck is a nine-hole miniature golf course, golf simulator, sports court, jogging track and rock-climbing wall. Best time to get a turn on the rock-climbing wall is first thing in the morning, as soon as it opens.

Entertainment: ⚓⚓⚓⚓ The production show "Welcome to Our World" was created especially for the *Radiance of the Seas*. It features a cast of 12 singers and dancers, beautifully costumed and choreographed with a bit more verve and bare flesh than previous RCI production shows. Comment from the audience was mixed, so by the time you see it, it may be toned down. Current films are shown in the theater as well.

Food and Dining: ⚓⚓⚓⚓ In lieu of the Johnny Rockets diner on the Voyager class ships, you'll find the raffish little Seaview Café on a top deck near the teen area with late-morning to late-night snacks, including nachos, jalapeno poppers, burgers, onion rings, pizza and fish 'n chips. Expect the usual vast Windjammer Café for breakfast, lunch and casual dinners and the glittering dining room with a two-level grand entrance stairway. If you want to spend a quiet evening in, order from the 24-hour room service menu and dine in your cabin or on your verandah.

Optional Restaurants: ⚓⚓⚓⚓⚓ We especially like the alternative restaurants on board. Chops Grille is a glamorous steakhouse with tables for two by the window and a menu of steaks, chops, chicken and fish, shrimp cocktail, Caesar salad, crab cakes, onion soup, clam chowder, creamed spinach, home fried potatoes, fried onion rings and strawberry cheesecake. There's even a bottle of specialty steak sauce on every table created by RCI executive chef Rudy Sodamin, (and conveniently for sale in the shop on board), Portofino is an Italian restaurant with pretty pink tablecloths, a mural of Siena's Palio medieval horse race on one wall, and a full roster of favorites from antipasto to tiramisu. Both restaurants require advance reservations and carry a $20-per-person cover charge.

Service: ⚓⚓⚓ Service is cheerful but can be a little muddled. One morning at breakfast we ordered eggs over easy with sausage, then casually added, " – oh, and some potatoes." The diligent waiter, who had painstakingly written all of it down, returned with a plate of eggs and sausage with hash browns -- and two boiled potatoes on the side.

Junior Cruisers: ⚓⚓⚓⚓ These are very good ships for families with children. Like most, the children's program, Adventure Ocean, is divided into different age groups, but unlike most, each age group has its own separate venue with appropriately-sized furniture, toys, computers and games. Group babysitting for any child registered in the Adventure Ocean program, toilet-trained and three or over, is offered nightly for a fee. The Optix Lounge for teens has its own disco dance floor, soda bar and computer stations. Vividly-painted cut out fish ornament a children's pool and an adjacent pool area designated for teens.

Itineraries: ⚓⚓⚓⚓ Since these ships have more flexibility and are faster and somewhat smaller than the Voyager class, expect to see them in more cruising areas. The *Radiance of the Seas* sails in Alaska and the Pacific Northwest in summer and the Caribbean in winter. *Brilliance of the Seas* sails 10- and 11-day itineraries from Miami into the Caribbean in winter, and cruises Northern Europe and Canada/New England in summer.

Overall: ⚓⚓⚓⚓ *Radiance of the Seas* and sister ship *Brilliance of the Seas* are the classiest, and most elegant vessels Royal Caribbean has ever built. While the Vision-class vessels used a lot of glass, the Radiance-class ships seem to be made entirely of glass. From the outside glass elevators that look out to the sea to a green glass staircase leading down into the atrium lobby, you look up and see nine decks looking down at you. Unlike the behemoths in the Voyager-class, these ships can pass through the Panama Canal, meaning more destinations and itineraries can be offered.

HIGH MARKS

Δ The Bombay Billiard Club has a trio of self-leveling pool tables outfitted with a gyro to compensate for ship motion. Even if the ship should list to one side in a storm or heavy seas, the table gyroscopically adjusts and the balls remain where they were instead of rolling.

WEAKEST LINK:

• We're still grappling with the new "men in black" concept RCI introduced on Radiance of the Seas, wherein the hotel director becomes a "general manager" assisted by a "vacation services director" and "human resources manager," and members of what used to be called the cruise staff are "recreation specialists." What ever happened to the purser with the gold stripes on his sleeves? We miss him.

Royal Olympic Cruises

805 Third Avenue, New York, NY 10022
(800) 872-6400 – www.royalolympiccruises.com

Royal Olympic Cruises was founded in 1995 with a merger of two historic family-owned Greek lines, Epirotiki Cruises and Sun Line. Epirotiki had started in shipping some 150 years ago while Sun Line was founded in 1957. The Keusseoglou family of Sun Line sold their company stock in late 1999 to another historic shipping company, Cyprus-based Louis Cruise Lines Ltd., which is today the majority owner of Royal Olympic Cruises. The line operates seven or eight cruise ships during the Eastern Mediterranean season. The *Stella Oceanis* usually sails under charter and is not included in the brochure. The two newest vessels, *Olympia Voyager* and *Olympia Explorer*, also cruise in the Caribbean and South America in winter.

Prior to the merger, Epirotiki was the largest cruise line in Greece and has been prominent in shipping since the end of the last centry. Since the company introduced Greek island cruises, Epirotiki has carried over 4.5 million passengers to the Greek islands and the Black Sea and well over a million on oceans of the world.

Sun Line Cruises prior to the merger focused primarily on exotic destinations in the Mediterranean and South America, and the line offered an intimate atmosphere, enrichment lectures and classic ships. First vessel in the fleet was the *Stella Maris I*, used exclusively for Aegean cruises from Piraeus.

With changes in passenger preferences and in the industry at large, the merger made a lot of sense to both companies. The new company, Royal Olympic, carried 73,000 passengers on its six ship during the first year of consolidated operations. The company then launched an aggressive building campaign to strengthen its position in the market with new purpose built ships. Some of the older vessels were sold and new ships. *Olympia Explorer* in 2002 and *Olympia Voyager* in 2000.

Who Sails Royal Olympic Cruises? In winter, guests are well-traveled, well-educated cruise veterans, most but not all middle-aged, more than half from North America, the rest Europeans and South Americans. There are more than a few single older women who like the attention they get from the Greek waiters and the dance hosts. There are also culture groupies of both sexes and all ages who follow popular lecturers notable from the pages of National Geographic. In summer, the average age drops and the countries of origin increase as a mix of vacationers utilize Greek Island cruises as a part of a summer tour package.

Lifestyle: Traditional cruise patterns dominate with assigned dining at two sittings and after-dinner entertainment that is understandable in five languages. In winter, a sedate, lecture-oriented crowd explores the Caribbean and South America; in summer, a younger, livelier crowd tours ruins all day and discos half the night.

Dress Code: Traditional codes prevail, with two formal nights a cruise in winter, sometimes only one in summer, when dress aboard is more casual. On longer cruises, several nights a week may be designated informal (meaning jacket and tie are requested for men). The rest are casual, which means long pants, not shorts, and shirts with a collar. One night a cruise is Greek night, when casual attire in shades of blue and white, the colors of the Greek flag, are expected.

Dining: Greek dishes are always delicious. Lunch buffets usually include a good mix of salads and cooked vegetables served at room temperature. Dining room breakfasts and lunches are served at open sittings (meaning you're whisked into the next two empty chairs at a large table), while dinners are served at assigned tables with two sittings, 6:30 and 8:30.

Tipping: Recommended tips total around $9 a day per person, divided into $3 for the cabin steward or stewardess, with the remaining $6 going into a pool divided among the remainder of the ship's personnel according to Greek Seamen's Association rules. Bar tabs automatically have a 10 percent gratuity added on at time of purchase.

Discount Policy: Early Booking Savings up to 45 percent are offered on a capacity controlled and varying deadline basis. Brochures list early-booking discounts of 30 percent for 14-day cruises, up to 50 percent on 28-day voyages, and up to 15 percent for short cruises. Discounts vary, depending on the ship. Royal Olympic offers excellent fly-land and cruise packages. For example, a 12-night Athena Tour package, including round-trip air from New York, three nights with breakfast in a first-class Athens hotel, full-day tour to Delphi with lunch, sightseeing tour of Athens, transfers and baggage handling, plus a seven-night cruise of the Greek islands and Turkey, was advertised for a minimum rate of $2,130. Rates increase slightly during high season in May, September, and the first half of October.

HIGH MARKS

Δ Low prices on well-organized shore excursions

INSIDER TIP
While a Greek Islands cruise sounds romantic, savvy travel agents rarely book one for honeymooners since the hot summer tours, sometimes two in one day, are so exhausting.

The Fleet
OLYMPIA EXPLORER
Built: 2002
OLYMPIA VOYAGER
Built: 2000

Category: Resort Mid-size
Rates: $$ to $$$
Overall Rating: ⚓⚓⚓
Country of Registry: Greece
Former names: None
Nationality of Crew: Greek officers, international crew
Cruising Area: Aegean, Caribbean, Central and South America
Length of Voyages: 3 to 58 days

Ship Specifics

Tonnage	25,000	Elevators	4
Length	590 feet	Decks	6
Beam	84 feet	Children's Facilities	no
Stabilizers	no	Fitness Center	yes
Passengers	836	Spa	yes
Crew	360	Verandahs	yes, suites only
Space Ratio	29.9	Casino	yes
Crew/Passenger Ratio	1–2.32	Wheelchair Access	yes

Cabins: ⚓⚓⚓ *Suites:* ⚓⚓⚓ Most guests occupy a small cabin around 140-square feet. They are outsides with windows or portholes, twin beds that can be converted into queen-sized, plus a chair and corner desk/dresser, a second chair and a small round table, hair dryer, safe and mini-refrigerator, plus adequate hanging and drawer storage for a fairly long cruise.

On the *Voyager*, only the top 12 sky suites (375-square feet) offer private verandahs. An additional 16 suites (215-square feet) provide a bay window instead. Bathtubs and sitting areas are also restricted to the suites. Sky suites also offer butler service. On the *Explorer*, the same 12 sky suites provide private verandahs, but an additional 12 deluxe suites (265-square feet) also have small verandahs. Furnishings are attractive

Facilities for Disabled Travelers: ⚓⚓ Each ship has four accessible cabins. Entry and bathroom doors are wide enough to accommodate a small wheelchair. Bathrooms have roll-in shower with hand held shower heads, grab bars and other required amenities. Most public rooms are accessible.

Public Space: ⚓⚓⚓ Designer Michael Katzourakis created most of the public rooms with clean, classic lines and an absence of fuss and furbelow. The handsome lobby is a circle of white marble with a second deck atrium above, flanked by a small casino and cigar room. The Ulysses Walk meanders through the heart of the ship from the casino past the shops, library and card room into the main bar, where a singer-pianist is on duty much of the day and evening, alternating with trivia quizzes, small meetings and Greek language classes. A museum wall along one side of the walk frames classic Greek artifacts or copies in Plexiglas cases. The sleek disco forward atop the ships and the pool deck aft with pizzeria and pool bar keeps daytime traffic moving outdoors as the Ulysses Walk does inside.

Spa and Fitness: ⚓⚓⚓ The Jade Spa, operated by a Greek company, offers a variety of treatment packages priced from $90 for an aromatherapy facial, half-hour massage and Vichy body shower to a serenity package for $218 that includes a 45-minute aromatherapy massage, thalassotherapy spa bath, cleansing facial, French spa pedicure and foot massage. Located amidships on the top deck, the spa also sells Ahava beauty products from the Dead Sea.

Entertainment: ⚓⚓⚓ The main lounge is the venue for daytime concerts and lectures and small, tasteful evening production shows with six cast members modestly, but prettily costumed. Cabin TV sets play feature films and documentaries throughout the day and evening on two channels.

Food and Dining: ⚓⚓⚓ Traditional two-sitting meals are served in the dining room with at least one Greek specialty featured at every dinner. Afternoon pizza snacks are served on deck, and tea and finger sandwiches, cookies and pastries are presented in the main lounge. Breakfast and lunch is available at both a buffet with indoor and outdoor seating and in the dining room at open seating. Since shore excursions are important to most passengers, you should plan to arrive early for the buffet on tour days. A special Mediterranean vegetarian menu is also available.

Service: ⚓⚓⚓ When a Greek waiter is in a good mood, nobody can be more charming, but there are occasions, particularly at open seating breakfasts and lunches in the dining room, when a "head 'em up, move 'em out" attitude prevails and they seem very bossy.

Junior Cruisers: ⚓ There are no dedicated children's areas on board, although cabins that sleep four are available.

Itineraries: ⚓⚓⚓⚓ The ships cruise the Eastern Mediterranean and Aegean in summer, the Caribbean, Central and South America in winter.

Overall: ⚓⚓⚓ The concept of the fastest ships in the world is impressive, allowing a seven-night itinerary in the Eastern Mediterranean that can hit two continents, four countries and eight ports of call, but the reality is that in rough seas (at least during our Central and South American sailing) the ship's motion under full speed is so extreme that open decks are off limits and the elevators may be shut down for several hours at a time.

HIGH MARKS

Δ The hospital on board is quite impressive for a ship of this size, with examining room, operating room, patient ward, x-ray room and pharmacy.

Δ The low prices in the spa.

WEAKEST LINK

• The motion of the ocean takes over in rough seas when the ship is going at full cruising speed.

ODYSSEUS
Built: 1962   Refurbished: 1988, 1995

Category: Traditional
Overall Rating: ⚓⚓
Rates: $$
Country of Registry: Greece
Former names: *Aquamarine, Marco Polo, Princessa Isabel*
Nationality of Crew: Greek officers and dining room, international hotel crew
Cruising Area: Aegean, Eastern Mediterranean
Length of Voyages: 3, 4, 6 and 7 nights

Ship Specifics

Tonnage	12,000	Elevators	1
Length	483 feet	Decks	7
Beam	61 feet	Children's Facilities	no
Stabilizers	no	Fitness Center	yes
Passengers	448	Spa	yes
Crew	200	Verandas	no
Space Ratio	26.78	Casino	yes
Crew/Passenger Ratio	1–2.24	Wheelchair Access	no

Cabins: ⚓⚓ *Suites:* ⚓⚓ While the lowest category cabins provide upper and lower berths rather than two lower beds, all are fairly spacious as vintage Greek ships go, most around 140-square feet. The so-called suites (you get two chairs or a sofa along with two lower beds in around 200-square feet) provide tubs as well as showers in the bathrooms. On the lowest guest deck, there are a fair number of cabins both fore and aft without connecting corridors or elevator service. We're unable to describe the bedspreads, since we never saw ours; the beds were usually covered with what looked like beige army blankets, and there were no extra bed pillows. Bathrooms are on the rudimentary side.

Public Space: ⚓⚓⚓ The primary public room deck is Jupiter, with a main lounge forward, a cocktail lounge, casino, library, card room and nightclub amidships and a pool and deck area aft. The Solarium is a sheltered sun tarp on Kronos deck aft for serious baskers.

Spa and Fitness: ⚓⚓ The fitness center on the top deck has a sauna, massage room, gym, fitness club and beauty salon.

Entertainment: ⚓⚓ Local folkloric groups or singers sometimes come aboard in port. There's usually a musical duo or trio for dancing and some variety artists.

Food and Dining: ⚓⚓⚓ The lunchtime Greek deck buffets are usually delicious and you can always get a Greek salad whether it's on the menu or not. The dining room is adjacent to the buffet restaurant so you can check out the lunch menu and the buffet alternatives at the same time.

Service: ⚓⚓⚓ The crew is very friendly, and service is good, except for brusque manners sometimes in the dining room on open seating.

Junior Cruisers: ⚓ There's no dedicated children's area on board, but if children are sailing, some attempt at a program or activities is made.

Itineraries: ⚓⚓⚓⚓⚓ There are always interesting itineraries, even on the three and four day sailings roundtrip out of Piraeus. Longer sailings visit Istanbul and the Bosphorus.

Overall: ⚓⚓ We wish we could be more enthusiastic about this ship, but last time we were aboard was with a large European medical group on convention. They smoked and chatted on their cell phones incessantly, but away from the ship everything was fine because the shore excursions weren't crowded.

HIGH MARKS

Δ The *Odysseus* has plenty of open deck space.

Δ Itineraries make up for short falls in other areas

WEAKEST LINK

• No private verandahs anywhere on board

• Be prepared for small cabins

OLYMPIA COUNTESS
Built: 1976   Refurbished: 1986, 1988, 1997

Category: Traditional
Overall Rating: ⚓⚓
Rates: $ $ $
Country of Registry: Greece
Former names: Cunard Countess
Nationality of Crew: Greek officers and dining room, international cabin staff
Cruising Area: Greek Islands, Turkey
Length of Voyages: 3 and 4 days

Ship Specifics

Tonnage	18,000	Elevators	2
Length	537 feet	Decks	7
Beam	75 feet	Children's Facilities	no
Stabilizers	no	Fitness Center	yes
Passengers	814	Spa	yes
Crew	350	Verandahs	no
Space Ratio	22.11	Casino	slots
Crew/Passenger Ratio	1–2.32	Wheelchair Access	no

Cabins: ⚓⚓ *Suites:* ⚓⚓ Cabins are small-really small–with some as little as 125 square feet, but even the insides, except for two tiny ones on Venus Deck, offer two lower beds. Outside cabins on the lower decks have portholes instead of windows. Suites are around 215-square feet with two lower or one queen-sized bed, a small sitting area and bathroom with tub and shower. Outside cabins on the lower decks have portholes instead of windows.

Public Space: ⚓⚓⚓ A cinema, show lounge, secondary lounge with dance floor, a small casino with slots only and an inviting pool bar are pretty much the story here but there is an indoor coffee verandah and a large out-door buffet area on deck.

Spa and Fitness: ⚓⚓ A fitness area with sauna, gym and paddle tennis court are supplemented by a small beauty salon and spa on a lower deck.

Entertainment: ⚓⚓ The usual summer entertainment in the Eastern Mediterranean, with some dance music in the evenings, a handful of slot machines, and an indoor/outdoor nightclub and entertainment.

Food and Dining: ⚓⚓⚓ The dining room is noisy with large tables and a low ceiling. Tables are assigned at two fixed sittings. Buffet service is also available on deck for breakfast and lunch. The Greek dishes are the best, both on buffets and on the menu.

Service: ⚓⚓⚓ Friendly waiters and nice cabin stewards can do a lot to make your cruise special if they don't get overworked and short-tempered.

Junior Cruisers ⚓⚓ A small children's playroom is set aside next to the library, but shore excursions fill the days on these short cruises, so you really don't need activities for the kids.

Itineraries: ⚓⚓⚓ The ports of call are tried and true with great shopping, historic ruins and the customary leadership from what we call the Athens School of Incomprehensible Guides. The ship makes roundtrip three-and four-day sailings from Piraeus, but ports can be crowded at the peak of the season.

Overall: ⚓⚓ It's a good choice for a budget-minded family with older children in tow (small ones couldn't handle the pace and shore excursions). The prices are so moderate for the cruises, particularly the fares for a third and fourth guest in a cabin, that a family of four could book two adjacent inside cabins for little more than crowding all four in the same cabin with two pull down upper berths.

HIGH MARKS

Δ The ship is so small, it's easy to find your way around, a boon for guests on these short cruises.

WEAKEST LINK

• This is one of those ships that never built a loyalist following even when she was new. Nothing has changed. Nothing is outstanding. Only the itinerary is memorable. If you can't afford anything better, cruise for the itinerary and don't expect the romance of the to take over.

STELLA SOLARIS
Built: 1953   Refurbished: 1971, 1994

Category: Traditional
Overall Rating: ⚓⚓⚓
Rates: $ $
Country of Registry: Greece
Former names: Stella V, Cambodge
Nationality of Crew: Greek officers and dining room, international hotel crew
Cruising Area: Aegean
Length of Voyages: 3, 6 and 7 days

Ship Specifics

Tonnage	18,000	Elevators	3
Length	544 feet	Decks	8
Beam	72 feet	Children's Facilities	no
Stabilizers	no	Fitness Center	no
Passengers	628	Spa	yes
Crew	320	Verandahs	no
Space Ratio	28.66	Casino	yes
Crew/Passenger Ratio	1–1.96	Wheelchair Access	no

Cabins: ⚓⚓⚓ ***Suites:*** ⚓⚓⚓ The four bottom-price cabins have upper and lower berths and an inconvenient location that requires taking a flight of stairs up one deck to get to an elevator. But most of the accommodations on board are fairly spacious, and all the others are elevator accessible. All (except the four above) are furnished with two lower beds, built-in desk and dresser, stool, bathroom with tub and shower, and, in some, the possibility of booking adjoining cabins. The 34 top suites are quite spacious, with sitting area, sofa and chairs, coffee table, built-in wood cabinetry, and the option of a queen-sized bed or twins, huge walk-in closet and bathroom with tub and shower.

Public Space: ⚓⚓⚓ Almost all the public areas are located on one deck – a piano bar aft with wide window wall behind it, then the main lounge, with raised seating on the sides. Amidships is a reception lobby and small shop, then a very handsome New York-style bar with leather sofas and banquettes, and forward is the dining room. For many years, the décor never changed, although the fabrics were refreshed periodically. The wife of the former owner of the ship did the decoration and never found the need to change anything over the years. A tiny card room is one deck up, and on the top deck is the Lido bar and buffet restaurant, along with the pool deck with its two overlapping pools surrounded by a seating height rim.

Spa and Fitness: ⚓⚓⚓ The 2,600-foot Daphne Spa was added a few years ago to supplement the beauty salon. It puts more emphasis on massage and beauty treatments than on gym machines.

Entertainment: ⚓⚓ These days the entertainment aboard is tamer than it used to be. We remember a week in the Aegean when we watched everything from a Spanish flamenco troupe to a belly dancer and a comic violinist. When the ship sailed in the winter in the Caribbean, Central and South America, there were scholarly lectures and classical concerts, but those are down-pedaled now that the vessel only does short summer sailings out of Piraeus.

Food and Dining: ⚓⚓⚓ We used to love the homemade Greek yogurt and Mt. Hymettus honey in the dining room at breakfast time and gained weight every time we went aboard from eating too many of the crisp, hot, freshly made potato chips. Now the cooking is more in line with other Royal Olympic vessels with Greek dishes featured on buffet and at lunch and dinner in the dining room. The buffet restaurant on Lido deck serves a modest but tasty array of dishes at lunchtime.

Service: ⚓⚓⚓ Many of the guests on the longer winter cruises used to come back year after year because they adored a particular Greek waiter or steward or the Captain. Many of those charmers have, unfortunately, retired by now, and those that are still working are sometimes brusque to the short-cruise guests.

Junior Cruisers: ⚓ There's no dedicated area for children on board.

Itineraries: ⚓⚓⚓⚓ The three-day roundtrip cruise from Piraeus visits five different ports in the Greek Islands and Turkey. Six-and seven-day itineraries call in Istanbul, Kusadasi, Patmos, Mykonos, Rhodes, Heraklion and Santorini. The ship no longer cruises in the winter months.

Overall: ⚓⚓⚓ This was such a wonderful ship in its day, with its 28-foot draft and steam turbine engines, its long, leisurely sailings in winter with Latin dance bands and notable enrichment lecturers. It's still a comfortable vessel to take for a budget Greek Islands cruise.

HIGH MARKS

Δ For Greek island hopping, the ship beats flying from island to island. The ship goes to four or five islands, sometimes two in one day. It's impossible to cover that much territory in that short a time by air. A few hours is all you need to explore the smaller islands and do a little handicraft shopping.

WEAKEST LINKS

- Nothing to rave about although she was a great ship in her day.
- She is on the shabby side.

Shirley and Harry Comment:

"We miss those freshly made potato chips in the Grill Room that went the way of other amenities that are no longer offered" Ethel Comments: "I miss the fun we had in the Greek Taverna."

TRITON

Built: 1971   Refurbished: 1993

Category: Traditional
Overall Rating: ⚓⚓
Rates: $$
Country of Registry: Greece
Former names: *Sunward II, Cunard Adventurer*
Nationality of Crew: Greek officers and dining room, international hotel crew
Cruising Area: Aegean
Length of Voyages: 3, 4 and 7 nights

Ship Specifics

Tonnage	14,000	Elevators	2
Length	486 feet	Decks	7
Beam	71 feet	Children's Facilities	no
Stabilizers	no	Fitness Center	no
Passengers	676	Spa	yes
Crew	300	Verandahs	no
Space Ratio	20.7	Casino	yes
Crew/Passenger Ratio	1–2.25	Wheelchair Access	no

Cabins: ⚓ ***Suites:*** ⚓⚓ The standard cabins on board measure from 95-square feet up to 133, while the suites are 219-square feet. All cabins except a couple of very tiny "loss leaders" with upper and lower berths (included to indicate a low bottom price) have two lower beds that can be put together into a queen-sized bed. They're fairly narrow, with the beds and nightstand filling the width of the room. Bathrooms have showers only, except in those designated as suites, which also have tubs. The latter measure around 13x17 feet and include a small sitting area.

Public Space: ⚓⚓⚓ The public areas are clean and attractive. The top deck observation lounge called " 9 Muses Nightclub" is over the bridge with a captain's eye view through extensive glass windows. A covered deck bar amidships does double duty as a midday respite from too much sun and a deck party place with disco stage at night.

Spa and Fitness: ⚓⚓ There's a jogging track on Ouranos deck that goes around the ship. Fitness buffs will have to do with a small fitness center, massage and sauna aft on Apollo deck and the Adonis Beauty Salon on *Venus* deck. Hmm, if Adonis comes from *Venus*, where does Mars fit in?

Entertainment: ⚓⚓ There's a big casino, left over from this ship's days in the Caribbean for Norwegian Cruise Line, plus a cinema, a covered outdoor nightclub area and a small main lounge with tables crowded together. The usual entertainment, which is to say, not much.

Food and Dining: ⚓⚓⚓ The Horizon Dining Room, light and bright with windows all around, serves dinner at assigned tables at two sittings, 6:30 and 8:30. There's also a buffet restaurant called Café Brazil that serves breakfast and lunch. Stick to the Greek specialties, and plan to have an early dinner ashore in Mykonos, since the ship stays there until 10 p.m

Service: ⚓⚓⚓ The staff is usually friendly and efficient.

Junior Cruisers: ⚓ There are no designated facilities for children on board.

Itineraries: ⚓⚓⚓⚓⚓ The usual what's-not-to-like Greek Islands cruises of three-and four-nights, plus some seven-night forays into the Western Mediterranean that can be boarded in Piraeus or in Rome's port of Civitavecchia.

Overall: ⚓⚓ The *Triton* is a surprisingly sleek-looking ship with some interesting budget-priced itineraries for first-time visitors to the Aegean. The pool and deck areas are inviting and the casino is big enough to please Americans, something most Greek ships don't offer.

HIGH MARKS

Δ Thanks to its former service with NCL, the *Triton* offers cabins where the beds can be instantly converted from twins into one queen-sized unit.

WEAKEST LINK

- This ship was never considered "great" and it hasn't changed over the years even with changes in ownership.
- The *Triton* is over 30 years old; that's old for a ship that hasn't been brought up to the 21st or even 20th century standards we expect in cruise ships.
- No playroom for kids, no library for adults and no self-service laundry, but there isn't time to use them anyhow in these port intensive intineraries

WORLD RENAISSANCE
Built: 1966   Refurbished: 1978, 1987, 1991

Category: Traditional
Overall Rating: ⚓⚓
Rates: $$
Country of Registry: Greece
Former names: Renaissance, Homeric Renaissance
Nationality of Crew: Greek
Cruising Area: Aegean
Length of Voyages: 3, 4, 6 and 7 nights

Ship Specifics

Tonnage	12,000	Elevators	1
Length	492 feet	Decks	7
Beam	69 feet	Children's Facilities	no
Stabilizers	no	Fitness Center	no
Passengers	474	Spa	yes
Crew	230	Verandahs	no
Space Ratio	25.31	Casino	yes
Crew/Passenger Ratio	1–2.06	Wheelchair Access	no

Cabins: ⚓⚓⚓ *Suites:* ⚓⚓⚓ Except for some small cabins with upper and lower berths at the bottom rungs of the price categories, accommodations aboard this ship provide two lower beds and bathrooms with showers. Mid- to upper-level outsides are 165-square feet, while suites measure an average of 275-square feet. Only suites have bathtubs and separate sitting areas.

Public Space: ⚓⚓⚓ Public areas are spread out throughout this ship, unlike most of the vintage vessels in the Royal Olympic fleet. The dining room and purser lobby are on Dionysius deck, the disco and one swimming pool aft on *Venus* deck, the main lounge and shop on Apollo deck, a second pool and sunbathing deck aft on Hera deck and a gymnasium on Jupiter deck high atop the ship.

Spa and Fitness: ⚓⚓ A beauty parlor does double duty as a spa (meaning facials and other spa beauty treatments) while the aforementioned gym on the topmost deck is for workout time.

Food and Dining: ⚓⚓⚓ The dining room serves dinner at assigned tables at two sittings and has windows for a brighter atmosphere. Greek specialties are highlighted at lunch and dinner. The main lounge serves as the Lido buffet restaurant with additional seating out on the deck.

Service: ⚓⚓⚓ As we've said elsewhere, when it's good, it's very very good, but when it's brusque, it's bad.

Junior Cruisers: ⚓ There is no designated childcare facility on board.

Itineraries: ⚓⚓⚓⚓⚓ The same Aegean port-intensive itineraries are offered as on the line's other vintage ships. If it's Tuesday, it must be Patmos.

Overall: ⚓⚓ The line operated the *World Renaissance* for years, then sold it to Indonesia's Awani and bought it back several years ago to replace the larger *Olympic*, which carries twice as many guests. The *World Renaissance* fits more comfortably into Royal *Olympic*'s vintage fleet. The intimate size, large deck area and subdued emphasis on bars and casinos are more appealing to European travelers, whereas Americans would probably prefer the *Triton* or the *Stella Solaris*, which offer similar itineraries.

WEAKEST LINK

- The ship itself. There are better choices for Americans even in the Royal *Olympic* fleet

Seabourn Cruise Line

6100 Blue Lagoon Dr. Ste 400, Miami, FL 33126
(305) 464-3000 – www.seabourn.com

Seabourn Cruise Line was founded in 1987 by Norwegian industrialist, Atle Brynestad. It was designed with the sole purpose of developing a cruise product with specific appeal to a clientele of discriminating leisure travelers. Joining Brynestad in those early days was Warren S. Titus, a well-known cruise ship executive and one of the founding fathers of Royal Viking Line. Their plan was to provide experienced travelers with nothing less than the best cruise experience in the world. In 1992, Carnival Cruise Lines purchased an interest in the company and then acquired the rest of the company in 1999.

The founding team came up with the concept of cruise ships no larger than 10,000 tons and carrying no more than 212 guests, thereby providing one of the highest space ratios in the cruise industry at that time. The

Seabourn Pride went into service in 1988 and was followed by the *Seabourn Spirit* about a year later. In 1996, Seabourn acquired the *Seabourn Legend* (ex-*Queen Odyssey* and ex-*Royal Viking Queen*), a vessel built from the same mold and nearly identical to the other two ships.

Who Sails Seabourn Cruise Line? The successful doctor, lawyer and merchant chief. Not to mention the CEO who want to cruise without crowds, without lines and without hassle. On board, there's a large cadre of Royal Viking followers and travelers who do not concern themselves with price and always book first-class air. Guests come from all over the world. They are most likely to be couples ranging in age upward of 35 on short cruises; upward of 55 on voyages of 14 days and longer.

Lifestyle: Plush and laid-back. No regimentation, not even at embarkation or debarkation. It's whatever the guest wants to make it. Cruising Seabourn-style more closely resembles vacationing in an elegant villa in the south of France than cruising as we have come to know it today. Special treatment begins at embarkation with white-gloved stewards escorting guests to suites from dockside. While at first blush the lifestyle seems stuffy and guests do not go out of their way to mix and mingle, there's a warm, fuzzy feeling that comes with being in the same boat with those in the same economic and usually social status, if you will forgive words that sound snobbish.

Dress Code: Becoming more relaxed and casual, but not in the sense of most other ships. People who pay these prices like to dress and there are more formal nights suggested when almost every man is tuxedo-clad and most women are in long dresses enhanced by fabulous jewelry. Suggested dress codes depend on length of voyages and itineraries. On an African safari cruise, dress will be more casual. On a long Pacific or European cruise, it will be dressier. Clothing suggestions are included in ticket packets, which incidentally are real leather and come in magnificent boxes. Daytime wear is resort-type casual. Casual on Seabourn means everything up to sequins and feathers.

Dining: Like the rest of the decor, elegant. This is restaurant dining at its best. A single, beautifully furnished restaurant on each ship is large enough to accommodate all guests in a single restaurant-style sitting. Guests show up at the restaurant at times that suit them with extended meal hours and are seated at a table size of their choice by the headwaiter. Menus on all the ships are similar and extensive. Off-the-menu requests are encouraged, and tableside preparations are the norm. Caviar for all three meals, if that's what makes your cruise.

Tipping Policy: No tipping is permitted or accepted anywhere on the ships, not even in the beauty shop or spa. I tried and the tip was politely turned down

Past Passenger Perks: You can take advantage of the lower fares offered repeaters through Seabourn Club even if you are booking your first Seabourn cruise. The only caveat is that you sailed one of the Carnival Corp family of companies – Carnival Cruise Lines, Holland America, Windstar, Cunard or Costa. As a Seabourn Club member, you are invited to a private party hosted on board by the captain and are recognized with jeweled pin on milestone cruises (100 to 2000 days) The big incentive to belong to the Club is that free up-to-two-week cruise after sailing Seabourn ships for 140 days. Signature Value Sailings program gives members a 50 percent reduction in rates. On my Northern Europe sailing last year, there were five couples sailing "free"!

Discount Policy: Seabourn doesn't like the word "discount." Doesn't seem to fit the image, but there are special offerings that take the edge off some of the pricing. Advance purchase can save about 10 percent. Bring another couple along and save another 10 percent. Combine cruises and save about 25 percent or more. There also are savings for repeat guests and seasonal offerings that allow substantial price reductions. Rates are high, but if you are luxury-minded and are looking for value, remember that the price includes all gratuities, drinks (alcoholic and nonalcoholic), economy air, some shore excursions, and the pampered experience of a lifetime.

HIGH MARKS
  Δ No tips means no tips. Gratuities are not accepted even in the hair dressing salon and the spa.
  Δ No bingo and no photographers in your face.
  Δ No loudspeaker announcements
  Δ An extensive selection of books and videos

WEAKEST LINKS
  • If there's an affinity group, no matter how small, they tend to take up a lot of the limited space.
  • Unless you are outgoing and are not timid about starting a conversation with strangers, you may disembark not having met anyone other than the person you boarded with. Guests who want to meet people should hang out at the bar, which is two deep from about 7:30 to 9 p.m.

The Fleet

SEABOURN LEGEND
SEABOURN PRIDE
SEABOURN SPIRIT

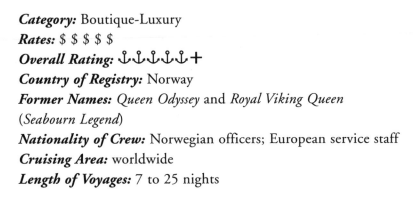

Built: 1998, 1989, 1988   Refurbished: 1999/2000

Category: Boutique-Luxury
Rates: $ $ $ $ $
Overall Rating: ⚓⚓⚓⚓⚓+
Country of Registry: Norway
Former Names: Queen Odyssey and *Royal Viking Queen*
(*Seabourn Legend*)
Nationality of Crew: Norwegian officers; European service staff
Cruising Area: worldwide
Length of Voyages: 7 to 25 nights

Ship Specifics

Tonnage	10,000	Elevators	4
Length	439 feet	Decks	6
Beam	63 feet	Children's Facilities	no
Stabilizers	yes	Fitness Center	yes
Passengers	204	Spa	yes
Crew	100	Verandahs	owners' suite
Space Ratio	49	Casino	yes
Crew/Passenger Ratio	1–2	Wheelchair Access	yes

Suites: ⚓⚓⚓⚓ There are no cabins. Everyone sails in a suite. All accommodations are from standard to super deluxe Regal Suites, but there's nothing standard about any of the suites. Standards measure 277-square feet; super suites are 575-square feet. Beautifully furnished, each suite has a king-size bed that can convert to twins, a large sitting room with television and VCR, and a stocked bar with each guest's favorite alcoholic and nonalcoholic beverages restocked as needed. And there's more: a sofa, comfortable chairs, a writing desk with personalized stationary, and a coffee table with adjustable height for en-suite dining. There is a walk-in closet and private safe, as well as hand-cut crystal and a five-foot picture window. In some suites, the picture window has been converted to French balconies, which are rails where the glass door used to be. They are not verandahs, because there is no place to stand or sit. Guests who don't like air conditioning can now open the doors and let the sea air into the suite.

Furnishings are soft and silky. The large marble bathrooms have tubs, showers, and double sinks on the *Pride* and the *Spirit*. Only Owner's Suites have real private verandahs.

Facilities for Disabled Travelers: ⚓⚓⚓ Each ships has four suites designated for disabled. They are about 277-square feet with entrance doors 33 inches wide with no lip. Bathroom doors are 28.5 inches wide with a four inch lip. Room stewards can provide ramps. There's a roll-in shower and grab bars. Seabourn joins other small ships in rules that do not allow seeing-eye dogs and guests must furnish a doctor's letter before suites are reserved for disabled.

Public Space: ⚓⚓⚓⚓⚓ The three-deck atriums set the tone for the vessels. A double circular stairway with etched-glass balustrades and brass railings connects the decks. There's a lot of subdued glamour and very little glitz. On each ship, there are observation lounges topside offering 180-degree ocean views, two main lounges, a library equipped with best-sellers and videos, a small swimming pool, good sunning areas, an outdoor bar, and three Jacuzzis.

Spa and Fitness: ⚓⚓⚓⚓ Completely equipped fitness center, scheduled classes, and individual training, plus a full spa offering a wide variety of treatments.

Entertainment: ⚓⚓⚓⚓ The entertainment has been expanded but remains geared to the sophisticated traveler who avoids the neon atmosphere of the smoke-filled nightclub. A talented pianist-vocalist entertains during pre-dinner cocktails and a cast of four headlines after-dinner cabaret-style shows. There's a small band that plays for dancing in the observation lounges and showrooms. Daytime entertainment is as you like it; there's no typical cruise ship schedule. Lecturers are world-renowned and most guests attend these sessions.

Food and Dining: ⚓⚓⚓⚓ Seabourn prides itself on food and service and the many awards earned by the company pay tribute to its achievements. Open seating for three meals with menus so extensive it's difficult to find something else to request. It's hard to find anything missing from menus, which are on a three-week rotation, so it's unlikely to find menus repeated.

However, if the guest has a favorite item, the chef will be happy to prepare it. There is also a theme dinner on each cruise and the Veranda Cafés for casual breakfasts, lunches Bistro-style dinners. These cafés are not to be confused with Lido areas on other ships. You select your own food or have a waiter bring it to you and you are seated at tables set with fine linen and silver. You never ever have to carry your own tray. There's a dinner dance in the dining room on every cruise, which is a highlight. Suite service is near perfect and is not limited to a set menu. I know guests who craved caviar at 2 a.m., and that's what they got within 15 minutes of placing the order.

Service: ⚓⚓⚓⚓++ Impeccable and correct. Main courses arrive simultaneously for everyone at the table; silver covers are removed ceremoniously so everyone eats at the same time. Restaurants are handsome rooms on the lowest levels of the ships. Stewardesses will pack and unpack for guests and assist in anyway possible. I traveled alone and my stewardess showed up every evening to zip up that troublesome zipper at the back of the dress. What's more, she was there waiting for me when I returned to the cabin at midnight, ready to help pull that zipper down. That's service way beyond anything expected.

Junior Cruisers: There are no special facilities. In the course of several cruises, I saw only one infant and two children under 12 on board. The parents of that infant had won one of those mega lotteries and were taking two years off to see the world and brought the nine-month-old toddler along. They said they had more baby-sitting volunteers than they could use in 14 nights.

Itineraries: ⚓⚓⚓⚓ Worldwide. Exotic and short Caribbean sampler cruises. *Seabourn Legend*: January through March, 14-night cruises to Australia and French Polynesia. In the Mediterranean on 7-, 10- and 14-night cruises through October, when she sails from Fort Lauderdale on three-night samplers and 10-, 14- and 16-night Caribbean cruises through December. *Seabourn Pride*: After an 18-night January sailing from Fort Lauderdale to Valparaiso, Chile, she begins a series of 13-night Chilean Fjords cruises, then moves across the Atlantic for 13- and 14-night Northern Europe itineraries before returning to New York in September for 12- and 14-night sailings to New England and Canada. In November and December, she sails 10-night round-trip Caribbean cruises. *Seabourn Spirit*: In the Far East on 14-night sailings from January through April, when she moves to the Mediterranean on 7-, 10- and 14-night sailings before returning to the Orient in November.

Overall: ⚓⚓⚓⚓++ Rating Seabourn ships is very difficult because its competitors - Radisson Seven Seas Cruises and Silversea Cruises - also offer outstanding products in the same category. Loyalists find differences and there are some features that can be compared and should help travelers make the decision. Unless you are in one of the top suites, Seabourn does not have verandahs and the second factor is onboard atmosphere, which is somewhat more formal on Seabourn ships than on the competition. Once you have sailed one of these small vessels, it's going to be difficult to accept any other form of cruising, providing you can afford the tab. Seabourn delivers a superb product with excellent itineraries and newly added perks.

HIGH MARKS
- Δ The reduced single supplements on selected sailings
- Δ Concorde flights at much reduced rates
- Δ Shore excursions included on most exotic itineraries
- Δ Complimentary beverages throughout the ship – alcoholic and non-alcoholic

WEAKEST LINK
- • The product is so good, there's nothing to complain about.

SeaDream Yacht Club

2601 S. Bayshore Drive, Coconut Grove, Florida 33133
(305) 856 5622 – www.seadreamyachtclub.com

SEADREAM I
Built: 1984   Refurbished: 1997/Refit 2000
SEADREAM II
Built: 1985   Refurbished: 1997/2002

Category: Boutique Luxury
Rates: $ $ $ $ - $ $ $ $ $
Overall Rating: Not Rated
Country of Registry: Bahamas
Former Names: SeaGoddess I, SeaGoddess II
Nationality of Crew: European
Cruising Area: Caribbean & Mediterranean
Length of Voyages: 3 to 14-days

Ship Specifics:

Tonnage	4,260	Elevators	1
Length	344 feet	Decks	4
Beam	47 feet	Children's Facilities	no
Stabilizers	yes	Fitness Center	yes
Passengers	110	Spa	yes
Crew	89	Verandahs	no
Space Ratio	37	Casino	yes
Crew/Passenger Ratio	1–1.3	Wheelchair Access	no

SeaDream Yacht Club is a new venture by Norwegian Arle Brynestad, founder of Seabourn Cruise Line and Larry Pimentel, former president of Cunard-Seabourn. Both were involved with the initial introduction of the Sea Goddesses. The concept is yachting in an "open and unstructured ambience" where there are no clocks, no crowds, no lines and no stress. Yachting features an open and unstructured ambience allowing guests to sail in a free-form holiday. Brynestad and Pimentel say SeaDream is "a yacht company, not a cruise line."

So why include them in a cruise book? Because the vessels have been synonymous with boutique luxury cruises. Call it what you will, they are mini-size cruise ships and renovations and concept doesn't change them. Another reason to include them is the large following the vessels developed over the years.

INSIDER TIP

We are not rating the experience, food or ambience since the project is new to the market and we have not had enough feed back to make accurate comments.

Who Sails SeaDream? High-income travelers who want the comforts of a private yacht and are willing to pay the price. The ships are chartered frequently by small groups and families for special occasions – birthdays, anniversaries, etc.

Cabins and Suites: ⚓⚓⚓⚓ They may be described as "suites" but they warrant a more accurate description of "deluxe outside cabins." At 195-square feet including bathrooms, they are comfortable in spite of size. Sixteen of the staterooms are called Commodore Club and are twice the size at 390-square feet. Appointments were refurbished in light shades. They have televisionsVCRs, refrigerators stocked with liquor and soft drinks, personal safes, hair dryers and mini-bars. Each has a small full bathroom with tub and shower but the amenities almost make up for size. They are stocked with very high-grade toiletries, lots of very thick towels and soft terrycloth robes. There is enough closet space for clothes, but not enough if you bring scuba and diving gear, which are popular activities since the vessels cruise warm weather ports. A few cabins have a removable wall and can be combined for more space. Add about 50 percent to the fare for that comfort. A limited number of staterooms have been designated for single occupancy.

Public Space: ⚓⚓⚓ There are private alcoves for sunning, a large screen golf simulator, a Marina at the stern where guests can launch kayaking, water skiing, tubing, snorkeling and sunfish sailing. The Main Salon near the lobby is where all indoor scheduled activities take place. That could include an aerobics class, a lecturer or a cooking demonstration. It's also the place for pre and post-dinner dancing and where guests get to know each other. The Club Salon, one deck up, is the only other public lounge. There are ample deck space and lounge chairs to catch the sun. Other indoor amenities include a piano bar and all accommodations are Internet-ready.

Spa: ⚓⚓⚓ *Fitness:* ⚓⚓⚓ There's a mini-spa and new equipment for workouts. Sports activities are high on guest activity lists. Vessels have platforms in the stern that can be lowered to the sea for snorkeling, swimming and other water sports. Ships carry speedboats, rubber rafts and windsurfing boards.

Entertainment: There really is no organized entertainment as we know it based on life aboard a cruise ship. There's a trio for dancing, sometimes a singer. But that's it. The entertainment is in dining and in the ports the ship visits. There's a complimentary open bar policy. Shore excursions are included in cruise fares. Vessels are so small that can enter just about any harbor and they visit exotic ports where other ships cannot go. There are beach parties, barbecues, scuba expeditions, snorkeling off remote islands, and wonderful secluded beaches.

Dress: There is no formal dress code. It's no tux "for guys, no gala gowns for gals."

INSIDER TIP

Everything on the vessel is mini-sized to accommodate less about 100 guests. This is cruising in a yacht without the worries of ownership. In spite of its size and because of the small number of guests, there is never a crowd anywhere, never a line; there's always a feeling of privacy and spaciousness.

Service: With a ratio of almost one crew member for every guest, service should be outstanding

Food and Dining: There's a single dining room with open seating, so guests can dine alone or with others and table sizes are flexible. Preliminary reports indicate that food is incredibly good and is comparable to a fine restaurant in France. Beverages are included and there seems to be an unending supply of Mumm's champagne served in tall fluted crystal glasses. Menus are extensive and regional specialties are offered. The staff makes special requests seem ordinary and fills them without a fuss.

Junior Cruises: Don't bring them along. This is a cruise for adults who want to get away from the kids. That is unless you charter the whole vessel which some families do.

Itineraries: *SeaDream I* and *SeaDream II* sail to small Caribbean islands where cruise ships cannot enter during winter months. Spring, summer and early fall are spent in the Mediterranean. Itineraries are flexible. Vessels overnight in some ports.

Overall: The SeaDream vessels look and exude the feeling one might have in a small, chic European hotel. Oriental carpets cover terrazzo floors in her small atrium lobby. Décor features rich Scandinavian woods, natural fabrics and original art. They are not for everyone. It takes a certain kind of traveler to appreciate the unstructured atmosphere the vessel maintains in really close quarters.

Silversea Cruises

110 East Broward Boulevard, Fort Lauderdale, FL 33301
(954) 522-4477 – www.silverseacruises.com

Founded in 1992 by the former owners of Sitmar Cruises, Silversea Cruises has climbed to the top of the "best of the best" Condé Nast Traveler's list. Silversea vessels were conceived and designed for luxury cruising in a style reminiscent of cruising of old, as described by writers and poets. The company realizes that the fantasy of our imaginations includes cocoon-like atmosphere where service is anticipated and rarely has to be requested; where our every wish is interpreted as a command, where dining rooms present fine linen and china and superb food. And, of course, the ships sail to exotic, interesting destinations. All this and more in an unhurried, slow-paced environment with some entertainment as diversions to enrich the mind and spirit.

Silversea Cruises must have read my ideal ship list because their products come close in every respect and even exceeds them in some. A unique feature is that more than half of the suites on the all-suite vessels offer private verandahs. There are other special features. The company offers complete packages with air, pre-hotel nights, some shore excursions, transfers, port charges, and special shore events included in a single price. There's no charge for drinks, alcoholic or soft. Rates are not cheap; when you put all the components together, you'll find the cost of sailing a Silversea ship is high, but not excessive considering the quality and extras.

Who Sails Silversea Cruises? Anyone who can afford the price tag. Although most of the guests are Americans, the rest come from every corner of the world. The guest list can range from the CEO of a watch company in Switzerland to British royalty to a U.S. technology genius to my family doctor who was so impressed with the product, he and his wife booked a cruise to China for 2003.

One thing is certain: People in a certain income tax bracket like to sail with people in the same bracket. You'll find them on Silversea ships. There are some singles on every sailing, but most of the manifest comprises couples from 40 years of age on up. Most people under 40 can't afford to go and, if they can, you can bet it's old money or they were smart and sold their Internet company in 2000.

Lifestyle: The impressive oversize silver-toned brochure is a good indication of what to expect on board. When a company spends that much money on printing, you know it will not be watching the pennies on board. Posh, but not pushy. Relaxed, but not lazy. Active, but only as active as you like. Friendly, but not familiar. Hospitable, but not presumptuous. From receipt of the elegant brochure to debarkation, each person is treated like a special guest.

Onboard ambience is whatever guests want, and that's what they get. If it's conversation or interaction with fellow guests, that's easy in the intimate lounges. True, some guests come aboard to get away from conversation, but try not talking at a wine tasting, or a cooking demonstration or a discussion of one of the stimulating lectures. There's a certain something that comes with being in the same boat with your peers, be it in social or economic status.

Dress Code: Daytime finds guests in casual resort wear, the type one might wear on a casual night on lower priced vessels. Attire for evenings is dressy for the most part. Tuxedos, long dresses and expensive jewelry are common sights. Itineraries play a major role in determining suggested dress. If you have spent the day climbing the Great Wall in China, recommended dress is usually jackets but no ties required. A complete list of suggested clothing is included in documentation, which arrives in a timely fashion.

Dining: Silversea's emphasis on fine food and wine is evident from the first moment guests step aboard. After being greeted by white-gloved attendants with flutes of chilled champagne, they are escorted to their suites, where a bottle of champagne is waiting. Single restaurants serve guests in extended hours on an open-sitting basis. See "Food and Dining" below for details.

Special Dietary Requests: Silversea should be notified when you make your booking, but the creative culinary staff has no problem coming up with vegetarian, low fat, sugar free, low calorie. Requests for kosher cuisine can be handled on board, but you'll have more choices for five course meals if you or your travel agent contacts the line and puts your request in writing.

Tipping: Silversea has a no-tipping policy; no gratuities are accepted anywhere on the vessel, including the spa.

Past Passenger Perks: It pays to sign up for membership in the Venetian Society. Perks are worthwhile. Membership comes with an automatic 5 percent discount, which goes to 10 percent when you have sailed 100 days or more. You also receive milestone pins and after 500 days on Silversea, you're entitled to a free 14-day cruise, then another free one week cruise for each additional 150 days on board. You are also the first to know about special rates on cruises designated as "Venetian Society." There are shipboard credits, complimentary onboard laundry service and other goodies.

Discount Policy: Even super-luxury ships run specials and offer savings, but they are never called discounts. Silversea offers exclusive perks and savings to repeaters. There are early-booking savings of 15 percent depending on how early you book and savings of up to $5,000 per couple when cruises are combined. Pre- and post-cruise packages are also available at substantial savings. On certain sailings, air upgrades to Business Class range from free to $1,995 per person.

Silversea's all-inclusive fares are probably the most comprehensive in the industry. Even on some selected sailings, they include round-trip air, pre-cruise deluxe hotel stay, all transfers and porterage, all beverages including superior wines and spirits, all gratuities, all port charges, and "The Silversea Experience," a special shoreside excursion offered on selected sailings.

INSIDER TIP

Silversea has introduced "Personalized Voyages," a revolutionary new way to cruise. It allows guests to custom design their own cruise vacation. Set to debut on *Silver Cloud* in 2003, guests will be able to determine the length of their voyage based on their own travel wishes – embarking and disembarking by choice from a selection of over 200 ports. Similar to a luxury resort stay, guests sailing *Silver Cloud* decide when they want to check in and check out. Guests may cruise as long as they want to with a minium of five nights. Here's how it works: You study the *Silver Cloud* 2003 brochure, pick the segment of any cruise that interests you, book it and take care of your own air. The traditional option is also in place. Rates will be quoted on a per diem basis. Insiders are skeptical that the system will work because it has never been tried before on a cruise ship. On a liner like the *Queen Elizabeth 2*, passengers embark and disembark in almost every port and the industry is watching to see if it can work on a cruise ship.

HIGH MARKS

Δ No packed buses on shore excursions (guests are limited to 35 on 55-seat buses)

The Fleet

SILVER CLOUD
  Built:
SILVER WIND
  Built: 1995/1996

Category: Boutique-Luxury
Rates: $$$$$
Overall Rating: ⚓⚓⚓⚓⚓+
Country of Registry: Bahamas (*Silver Cloud*); Italy (*Silver Wind*)
Nationality of Crew: Italian officers; European service staff
Cruising Area: Worldwide
Length of Voyages: 7, 12, 14, and 16 nights

Ship Specifics

Tonnage	16,800	Elevators	4
Length	524 feet	Decks	6
Beam	70 feet	Children's Facilities	no
Stabilizers	yes	Fitness Center	yes
Passengers	296	Spa	yes
Crew	196	Verandahs	yes
Space Ratio	57	Casino	yes
Crew/Passenger Ratio	1-1.5	Wheelchair Access	yes

Suites: ⚓⚓⚓⚓ Accommodations are all suites, but they come in several sizes on both ships. The smallest, at 240-square feet, are the Vista suites. Veranda Suites measure 295-square feet including the balcony. The largest, the Grand Suite, measures 1,314-square feet. In between the smallest and largest are the Silver Suites and a one-bedroom Royal Suite, both of which sell out faster than the lowest priced Vista Suites. All accommodations are decorated in shades of turquoise, peach, and blue and accented with lots of grained wood. Suites without verandahs are on the lowest deck and have five-foot panoramic windows, but 75 percent of the 148 suites have private verandahs. Each suite features a marble bath with a full-size tub, a walk-in closet, a cocktail cabinet that is continuously stocked with passenger preferences, personalized stationary, and high-quality bathroom amenities restocked twice a day. There's a special tranquility in all the suites and super luxury in the 541-square-foot Silver and 827-square-foot Owner's suites.

Public Space: ⚓⚓⚓⚓ More than guests expect on this size ship. Each ship has a tiered Venetian Show Lounge, which sets the vessels apart from other all-suite ships; a spacious main bar that spans the full width of the ships; a small casino; card and conference rooms; a well-stocked library that is always open for borrowing books and videos; an outdoor pool and bar; two whirlpools; a wrap-around track for joggers and walkers; and an Observation Lounge and bar with window walls that afford 180-degree ocean views. It's the place for quiet reading, afternoon tea and snacks, pre-dinner cocktails, or viewing when ships leave or arrive in ports. The Bar is the most popular room on board; it's where guests meet, talk and get acquainted.

Spa and Fitness: ⚓⚓⚓⚓ There's a scheduled program of aerobics and other exercise classes in an area separated from the well-equipped, but sometimes crowded fitness area. The full service spa offers hair and beauty treatments.

Entertainment: ⚓⚓⚓⚓ Here again, Silversea offers much more than guests expect. There's the live music of a small orchestra, a trio, or pianist in all the lounges during pre-and post-dinner hours and entertainment nightly in the Venetian Show Lounge. A resident cast of four or six talented performers stage cabaret-style shows and there are individual acts on other nights. There's something going on every night. Daytime schedules vary and could include backgammon, wine tastings, and culinary demonstrations. Some cruises are themed. Good examples are culinary extravaganzas and the National Geographic Traveler Series, which features unusual shore excursions and on board lecturers who are world-famous experts in history, culture, photography, and adventure travel.

Food and Dining: ⚓⚓⚓⚓ On each ship, the main dining venue, is simply named "The Restaurant." The open-sitting policy allows passengers to dine with companions of their choice or at a table for two if they prefer. Tables are set with crisp Frette linens; service is on fine Limoges china and crystal-with Christofle silverware. International and eclectic menus are complemented by a selection of fine wines. Master chefs from Le Cordon Bleu Academy have joined Silversea's chefs and sommeliers to create what experts have rated as the best cuisine at sea. In fact, it's hard to find a shoreside restaurant that equals the quality, presentation, and taste, including the wines, for less than $125 per person for a typical dinner. Caviar, lobster, delicate French dishes, tasty and unusual vegetarian dishes: all are available and served readily. Also available are specialty items like Roast Quail with Truffle Sauce.

Tableside preparations are the norm and special requests are honored routinely. Food is served around the clock. En suite service is available for every meal and happily there's a fresh pasta dish prepared in front of you in Terrace Café during lunch hours. Choices are great and assistance is available at every turn. There are dessert stations, pasta stations, egg stations in the morning and service for those who don't want to stand and select their food. They are really alternative restaurants that are open on some evenings for special theme-night dinners.

Service: ⚓⚓⚓⚓ Stewardesses go more than that extra mile. They'll sew on a button, press out the wrinkles, unpack and pack for you, and change the linen and robes daily. The café staff at the Italian restaurant is mostly Italian; the traditional warmth and caring attitude reminds us of the Sitmar days.

Junior Cruisers: ⚓ There are no separate facilities for children and very few small kids are on board. During holiday periods, it's not unusual to find a few preppy teenagers traveling with their parents.

Itineraries: ⚓⚓⚓⚓ *Silver Cloud* sails 8-to-16-day voyages in South America from January through March. She then moves to Africa and Mediterranean for 10- and 16-day sailings until June, when she begins 11- and 12-night Northern Europe cruises before returning to Montreal in September for a series of New England and Canada 10-day cruises. In October, the *Silver Cloud* sails on an 8-day Caribbean and Panama Canal cruise before making a 16-day Hawaii voyage and a return to French Polynesia and Far East cruises.

The *Silver Wind* was taken out of service shortly after 9/11, She is scheduled to resume sailing in mid-2003. She normally spends November through March in Africa and the Pacific Rim, then moves to 8-, 11-, and 14-night cruises in the Mediterranean before returning to the Pacific.

Overall: ⚓⚓⚓⚓+ Everyone has a dream boat, and in my 30-some years of cruising, I have found just a few that come close to filling my wish list, which includes a spacious suite, sophisticated dining without regimentation, exotic and not over-visited ports; a staff offering excellent personal service that's friendly but not familiar; a relaxed yet refined atmosphere; a choice of entertainment and fellow guests who don't necessarily show up in black tie every night but who are dressed appropriately for the evening, Silversea vessels come really close to that ideal. Of course, price is a factor. You get what you pay for and Silversea does not short-change value.

SILVER WHISPER
Built: 2001
SILVER SHADOW
Built: 2000

Category: Luxury
Rates: $$$$$
Overall Rating: ⚓⚓⚓⚓+
Country of Registry: Bahamas
Nationality of Crew: Italian deck/ International staff
Cruising Area: Europe, South America, Caribbean, Asia
Length of Voyages: 10 to 100 days

Ship Specifics:

Tonnage	28,258	Elevators	5
Length	610 feet	Decks	10
Beam	81.6 feet	Children's Facilities	no
Stabilizers	yes	Fitness Center	yes
Passengers	388	Spa	yes
Crew	295	Verandahs	yes
Space Ratio	74	Casino	yes
Crew/Passenger Ratio	1-1.3	Wheelchair Access	yes

Suites: ⚓⚓⚓⚓ Design and configuration of the vessels puts suite accommodations forward and public rooms aft on five decks. It makes getting around easy and familiar after the first hour on board. Guests have a choice of with or without verandahs. Big, bigger or biggest. On *Silver Shadow* and *Whisper*, choices are greater then on the smaller ships. About 82 percent of the suites have private verandahs and each of those 134 suites measures a healthy 345-square feet. Vibrant fabrics blend with honey-colored cabinetry and all have comfortable seating areas separated from sleeping areas by a curtain. Marble bathrooms with two sinks, full size bathtubs, separate showers and walk-in closets with personal safes are some of the features.

Vista Suites offer the same amenities but without the 68-square foot verandah. Instead, a five-foot window frames the sea and cabins are actually larger at 287-square feet. Also, lower priced and a good buy for travelers who say they don't use a verandah.

Going up a notch are two Medallion Suits at 621-square feet and 13 Silver Suites at 701-square feet. Going up a few more pegs are the two Owners Suites at 1,208-square feet, two Royal Suites at 1,312-square feet, four Grand Suites at 1,409-square feet. As expected, these are spacious, elegant accommodations that open out towards the sea with verandahs sized for parties. They are beautifully furnished and can be combined to sleep six.

All suites enjoy some of the same amenities – the Italian Frette linen, soft down pillows, marble bathrooms with telephones, Bulgari toiletries personalized stationary, refrigerator and stocked bar, videocassette player and plush robes and towels.

Public Space: ⚓⚓⚓⚓ Increased space allowed the company to add several public areas not featured on the other ships. With a space ratio of 74, currently the highest at sea, there is plenty of elbow room. On the other hand, there are lounges, bars and card rooms for those times when camaraderie is welcome. Take The Bar, for example. A favorite on the *Cloud* and *Wind*, it has been enlarged and seats 109 guests. It becomes an immediate gathering spot for pre-dinner and late evenings. The Athenian Show Lounge has seating for 356, so there's no reason to rush through dinner to find a seat for the one-show scheduled every evening. It's a multi-tiered music hall cleverly designed to give every guest the best seat in the house. Seats are theater-style chairs and each row is dotted with small tables to hold complimentary cocktails, soft drinks or coffee during shows.

Other rooms worthy of mention include the 55-seat Observation Lounge, which was one of my favorite venues. Located forward of The Spa, the lounge spans the bow of the ship. Designed for socializing with friends, broad easy chairs face out to the sea, a table with current books and magazines provide diversions while a sparkling wall of glass follows the curve of the ship's bow and affords views without boundaries. During afternoons, tea is served and there's water and juice bar. When the sun sets, the Lounge becomes a full service bar with soft music for easy listening.

There's a swimming pool and dance floor outdoors. Two whirlpools are at the rear of the pool, each elevated and topped by a canvas structure. Teak tables and chairs with canvas umbrellas surround the pool's port and starboard sides, A jogging track runs the entire outside edge of the deck above, which also has the traditional shuffleboard area.

The Computer Center shares space with the Library. Four computer stations provide Internet access on a 24-hour basis. The library is stocked with hundreds of volumes and a good selection of videos for in-cabin use. The Conference and Card Rooms can accommodate 58 guests and occupy a quiet niche forward of The Humidor on Deck 7. The casino was inspired by the grand casino of Monte Carlo, albeit in miniature. A contemporary chandelier and gaming tables dominate the center of the room with slot machines tucked into alcoves. The winsome atmosphere carries over into the adjoining Casino Bar.

Spa and Fitness: ⚓⚓⚓⚓ The spa takes up almost all of the 10th deck and is operated by Mandara Spas. As the name implies, décor, ambience and treatments have Oriental influences that stress relaxation of the mind and body. Cool colors blend with the sky and sea and a Pacific Island mood permeates the environment. The overall effect comes close to what one would expect in a plush seaside resort in Bali. Undersized gymnasiums on *Cloud* and *Wind* have been more than tripled in size and there was no sign up necessary for equipment use. The fitness center is separated from the aerobics area and includes treadmills, step machines, cross trainers, weights and separate changing rooms for men and women.

Entertainment: ♆♆♆♆♆ With a larger ship, the show room was expanded to include a larger stage to enable the company to increase entertainment. There is some form of entertainment in the show room every evening. A resident team of dancers and singers present mini-production shows. Daytime activities are highlighted by lecturers, cooking demonstrations and wine tasting seminars. Major "names" booked for future sailings include Michael Crawford, which is really impressive.

INSIDER TIP

There's a tendency to associate luxury cruising with dressing to the nines. That's not the case on Silversea. During a 10-night voyage, evenings on port days were "resort casual" or "informal" and only two nights were "formal." A nice touch was that guests adhered to suggested dress codes throughout evenings and "formal" did not mean bangles and beads. Most women wore dinner suits and dresses, long and short. Smart dress was the way I would describe the dress code.

Food and Dining: ♆♆♆♆♆ One of the highlights on a Silversea cruise is the open seating policy that allows guests a choice of dining venues and dining companions. The Restaurant is the main dining venue. It has a seating capacity of 424, which exceeds the total guest capacity and allows for tables of from two to 10. Guests enter through a formal hall leading into The Restaurant is crowned with three grand chandeliers, making it the most formal and most elegant room on the ship. Candle lit and fresh flower centerpieces adorn each table.

The Terrace Café is an indoor-outdoor casual restaurant with multiple self-serve stations with waiters standing by as guests make selections. It is rare to see a guest carrying a tray, A nice feature is that waiters take guests to tables, then unload the trays and set the table a though it was a full service restaurant. Location of the Terrace Café allows for 180-degree views and a wall of floor to ceiling windows that bring the outdoors inside. Tables seat from two to six. The far, port side corner features buffet stations serving hot and cold breakfast and lunch favorites. By day, hearty buffets with grills and pasta stations high-light the fare. The room becomes an informal bistro featuring Italian, French and Asian specialties served tableside in the evening. Menus are prefixed by region and reservations are suggested.

Silversea has more than doubled its complimentary wine selection and fea-tures 25 new white wines and the same number of new red wines from around the world. Impressive vintages include bottles from France, Italy, Germany, New Zealand, Australia, Chile, Argentina and the U.S. I suppose a wine con-noisseur could have come up with a special vintage reques,t but most guests were quite happy with the selections offered.

Junior Cruisers: ⚓ There is no space dedicated for children.

Itineraries: ⚓⚓⚓⚓ Mediterranean and Northern Europe during sum-mer months; long Pacific and South America voyages during the rest of the year

Overall: ⚓⚓⚓⚓+ Although almost twice the size of the first two ships in the fleet, the feeling of intimacy is not lost on *Silver Shadow* or *Silver Whisper*. She delivers the same aura of "exclusivity" as the smaller vessels plus amenities only possible on larger ships. Like their sister-ships, *Silver Cloud* and *Silver Wind*, granite, marble, rich woods and brass are used to their best advan-tage by Italian craftsmen, although she was designed by Peter Yran and Bjorn Storbraaten, Oslo-based architects whose credits include designs of competing vessels. The beauty of the ship is in the understated design elements and the simplicity of open spaces. Contrary to current ship design trends, large walls are not covered with paintings, so art pieces used to enhance a room, blend into the area rather than dominate the scene.

Silver Shadow and *Silver Whisper* are two of those ships on which guests plan their return voyage before they pack their luggage to disembark. They elegant, yet casual in an up-scale resort sort of way; spacious without loss of the intimacy offered on the two smaller ships in the fleet. A crew of 295 serves 388 very fortunate guests, so service is hard to duplicate on any vessel.

HIGH MARKS

Δ Debarkation is a breeze. Guests with late flights or who just don't want to be rushed are invited to stay on board for lunch and/or until 4 p.m. to enjoy the vessel. We had a flight at 3 p.m. and when we debarked at 1 p.m., there was a car waiting to take us to the airport and a driver who assisted with check-in at the airport.

WEAKEST LINKS

- Corridors are on the narrow side and there were always service carts and maids cleaning rooms no matter the time of day. I don't know whether that was due to the lack of regimentation on board so guests just opted to sleep later on sea days or to some being served in cabins, but it was a distraction.

- And, I did miss the Silversea Experience, which is now offered only on special sailings. It is a surprise shore event hosted by Silverseas. During previous cruises it has been a private ballet performance in St. Petersburg, a wedding in Turkey, reenactment of a Civil War battle in Savannah at a fort outside the city, private wine tasting events in the Bordeaux region of France and special caviar and vodka black tie event in the Hermitage in St. Petersburg (Russia).

INSIDER TIP

Mandara is an example of alliances made between Silversea and high-end international companies specializing in specific areas. The company collaborated with Moet & Chandon to create one of the signature rooms, Le Champagne, adjacent to the bistro-style Terrace Café. The room accommodates up to 24 guests and is primarily an intimate venue for wine tastings but it can be used for private cocktail and dinner parties. Another alliance was made between Silversea and Davidoff, purveyor of fine cigars and luxury goods. A highlight of the partnership includes Davidoff's participation in the design of the cigar clubs and humidifying rooms aboard *Silver Shadow* and *Silver Whisper*. The Humidor by Davidoff", as the clubs are named, are in the style of traditional English smoking clubs with seating for 25.

The World of ResidenSea Ltd

Regent Center West, Building No. 3, Suite D
P.O. Box F-40967 Freeport, The Bahamas
U.S.(305) 264-5090 – www.residensea.com

The World of ResidenSea is a new concept in the ever evolving cruise industry. The company calls it "the world's first resort community at sea continuously circumnavigating the globe." The concept was conceived and developed by Norwegian Knut U. Kloster, Jr., former chairman of Royal Viking Line and Norwegian Cruise Lines, and a member of a well known shipping family. Other maritime veterans and industry executives lent their expertise and knowledge to the project which after several years of planning and re-planning has launched its first ship, *The World of ResidenSea*.

The plan is to sell 110 spacious, fully furnished and equipped apartments which owners can call "home", or place into a rental pool with the other 88 guest suites available for reservations in the high end cruise and vacation market.

Original plans were downsized, but the project is alive and apparently doing well. Sales and reservations offices have been opened in the U.S. and in several foreign countries. The company has big plans and is considering construction of a twin vessel which would double the size of the one ship fleet.

The best way to describe the concept is to detail on the company's first ship.

THE WORLD OF RESIDENSEA
Built: 2002   Registry: The Bahamas

Category: Luxury
Rates: $$$$$$
Maximum speed: 18.5 knots.
Length of cruises: 5 to 365 days
Itineraries: The world

Tonnage	43,000	Elevators	8
Length	644 feet	Decks	12
Beam	97.8 feet	Children's Facilities	no
Stabilizers	n/a	Fitness Center	yes
Passengers d/a	396	Spa	yes
Crew international	320	Verandahs	yes
Space Ratio	over 100	Casino	yes
Crew/Passenger Ratio	1–1	Wheelchair Access	yes

Who Sails/Buys ResidenSea? The company says that 40 percent of the apartment owners and guests come from the United States, 60 percent from Europe and the rest from all over the world. *ResidenSea* apartment owners have one thing in common. They are rich, really rich, have multiple homes, maybe New York, Palm Beach, or the French Riviera. It is doubtful that many of the purchasers will sail continuously, but there are people on every major cruise ship who have given up land-based homes and spend the entire year on board ship cruising wherever. When we say rich, we mean spending $2 million for the smallest apartment on *The World* and more than $6 million for one of the larger units. Those prices do not include annual maintenance which starts at about $60,000 or food, gratuities, sightseeing, etc.

The people who buy apartments are those who can afford to stop the world and live in a fantasy environment not available on land. The renters (a.k.a. cruise passengers) are and will continue to be luxury cruisers who have tried every luxury brand and want to rub elbows with the rich and "famous."

Lifestyle: I must admit, it is unique. With one staff member for every passengers, service must be as perfect as it gets. Spaciousness is overwhelming and cannot realistically be compared to any other ship. Based on early reports, *The World* is more like a global village at sea. Owners and guests are sophistacted travelers who have been everywhere and seen everything. The *World's* community enjoys the privacy and camaraderie of the most discriminating private club.

INSIDER COMMENT

When I try to visualize the space ratio, I can only compare it with living on an island with 400 other people and 400 service staff waiting to jump at a single request. Some of the glitzy magazines have highlighted Fisher Island which is reached only by boat and only by residents and invited guests. Look for Fisher Island on the starboard (right) side as your ship sails out of the Port of Miami. The middle of the island is park land and two golf courses. Residents live along the outer beach and ocean perimeter. Sailing *The World* would be something like living on Fisher Island. Most of the homes are shuttered during nine months of hot weather and I can only guess that the same will happen on *The World*.

Suites: Cruise passengers choose from 88 luxuriously appointed guest suites, ranging in size from 259 to 648-square feet with 84 percent featuring a private verandah. Whether you choose a Libretto, Adagio, Concerto or Sonata Suite, all have the following amenities in common: two single beds or a queen-size bed, sitting area, entertainment center, refrigerator and cocktail cabinet, writing desk, dressing table and marble bathroom with separate tub and shower. Fine Frette bed linens and down pillows, luxurious bath amenities, complimentary in-suite beverages — nothing has been overlooked in making your stay aboard *The World* a world-class experience. Your suite on *The World* is your base for world exploration. It's designed to be a special place to retreat to after a busy day on board or ashore.

Apartments: Called "The Ultimate Indulgence", range from 1,106 to 3,242-square feet and sell for prices that reach well over $6 million. Each apartmentwas created by one of four internationally prominent designers. Owners have a choice that reflects personal design sensibilities. Rhapsody suites are effortlessly elegant yet warm and inviting. Dignified stripes pair with cheerful florals and patterned carpets. Rich woods, classic paneling and deeply comfortable furniture contribute to an interior that has timeless elegance. Continental apartments combine antiques with sumptuous fabrics to create a suite that could be in any international city from Rome or Hong Kong to Monte Carlo. The design includes stone floors and upholstered walls, Baltic, Russian and French-style furniture, mixed with Chinese lacquer. Contemporary apartments have a sense of space in furniture, fabrics, lighting and colors selected for their innate capacity to blend into a contemporary atmosphere. Maritime residences have the aura of a private sailboat, enhancing an intimacy with the sea not available on land. "They combine the nautical with the contemporary," explains architect/designer Peter Yran. When owners are not in residence, most are available for rental by cruise passengers. Expect to pay about $1,000 per day, per person, but that includes meals and the works.

Facilities: Two swimming pools, a jet pool, jogging track, paddle tennis court and a full-size tennis court. Unique onboard golf faciltes include two full shot driving ranges, golf simulators, a real grass putting green and four full-time pros on staff. *The World's* 6,545 square-foot spa, health and fitness center and beauty salon are operated by renowned Swiss spcialist, Clinique La Prairie. Offering aerobics and workout areas, private training, exercise machines, saunas and treatment rooms.

Food: Interesting to note that apartment owners pay for their meals or cook-in, or have room service. There's Freddy's Deli where they find everything from baked beans to Beluga caviar. Residents have to provide for themselves, down to the toilet paper, but they do get daily maid service, if they pay for it and each apartment is equipped with a microwave oven. There are four restaurants serving everything from Thai to Mediterranean cuisine or, if you don't feel like "going out", there's in-suite dining. A la carte dinners run around $75 per person for a three course Asian fusion meal with wine in the top restaurant. Guests who reserve in the same manner as they would any cruise ship have the advantage of an all-inclusive rate.

Entertainment: This should be in the "facilities" section because what is offered is almost overwhelming: Learning Center at Sea, continuous series of seminars and presentations on history, geography, the arts. There is a theater that offers concerts, dramatic presentations and films. The ship spends more time in port, so resident golf instructors accompany guests to top courses everywhere. *The World* guests have interchangeable privileges at major private country clubs in every sector of the universe.

Rates: It's almost in the "if-you-have-to-ask, you-can't- afford-it -category." *The World* offers all-inclusive "value." Rates for apartments begin at around $1,000 per person, per day. Suites run around $750 per person, per day. When you book a pre-planned voyage, virtually everything will be taken care of for you - suite accommodations on board, roundtrip economy air transportation from select U.S. and Canadian gateway cities, transfers, gratuities and port charges. Even beverages, including an extensive selection of fine wines and spirits are complimentary throughout the ship. All-inclusive value means you can relax and focus on the rewards of your in-depth travel experience.

INSIDER TIP

If you must try *The World*, take heart. Introductory offers ran about $500 a day per person and I wouldn't be surprised to see similar offers in 2003. You should know that all-inclusive doesn't include for example, a half hour of golf on the simulator which runs about $50, a half hour massage is $60; and shore excursions run higher than on other luxury ships.

Itineraries: *The World* will be home to the owners of 110 luxurious private residences who are free to "come home" at any scheduled port and be aboard for any period of time. The same flexibility is available to guests of *The World's* 88 guest suites when they participate in an innovative program called Tailored Time Fares. With this unique pre-purchase program, you may purchase 30, 60, 100, 200 or 300 days on board *The World* in Adagio, Libretto, Concerto or Sonata Suites. Over 24 months, you may use your days at sea in any combination you choose for custom vacations of your pre-purchased design. Itineraries follow world events – Carnivale in Rio, World Cup Races in Auckland, etc. and the ship spends more time in exotic ports of call.

On *The World*, you don't have to choose between a vacation on land and a vacation at sea. You can have them both. Almost any vacation activity you can think of can be combined with your days on *The World*. Plan an extended golf vacation in Spain and Portugal, then join the ship at a later-scheduled European port. Take a hiking holiday in Chile, then join *The World* as it sails north along the west coast of South America. Disembark for the land portion of your vacation at any scheduled port, then rejoin the ship at a later-scheduled port. And of course, only the days you are on the ship are debited from your pre-purchased days.

INSIDER TIP

The World and its concept is too new to rate. We have not had enough feedback to rate the ship or the concept. This is one of those ships we classify as "limited appeal," but in this case at the very high end of the spectrum. It should be in a special category –"Dreams."

Windstar Sail Cruises
300 Elliot Avenue West, Seattle, WA 98119
(888) 796-3679 – www.windstarcruises.com

Windstar Sail Cruises was the first company to feature sail-powered cruise ships. Karl Andren, owner of Circle and Day Line Cruises in New York City, and his London partner, Jacob Nielsen, founded the company in 1984. The idea was to provide an alternative to traditional cruising for younger passengers. Holland America acquired a 50 percent interest in Windstar in 1987 and purchased the remainder in 1988. Subsequently, Carnival Corporation purchased Holland America Line/Westours and its Windstar division.

Windstar operates four 440-foot, 150-guest, four-masted computerized sailing vessels, the *Wind Star*, *Wind Song*, and *Wind Spirit*, and the former *Club Med I*, now named *Wind Surf*. Itineraries are as spirited as the concept. Vessels sail Caribbean and Mediterranean waters and *Wind Spirit* will return to Tahiti in 2003.

Who Sails Windstar Cruises? The young at heart who love the sea and to whom dressing up is putting on a silk shirt and slacks for the captain's party and those who want the quiet of a sailing night, the relaxed atmosphere without engine noises or vibrations. Many have given up their private craft in favor of leaving the driving to the professional crew. Surprisingly, there are very few singles on board Windstar. Couples between the ages of 35 and 55 and over 55 make up most of the guest list. About 80 percent are Americans, even on European voyages. Guests are well traveled and have sailed most of the big ships, but they return again and again to Windstar.

Lifestyle: Very laid-back and resort casual. In a fast-paced world, a Windstar voyage seems to stop the clock. This is unregimented leisure in surroundings that offer yacht-like comfort and luxury. Windstar guests share common preferences: the serendipitous over the routine, the freedom of exploration over regimented schedules, the exotic, less-frequented areas of the world rather than the usual well-traveled routes. Guests are best described as adventuresome, experienced, upscale, sophisticated, and discerning.

Dress Code: Jackets and ties are never required, but no shorts, jeans, sneakers, or Tee-shirts at dinner meals, please. Elegant casual is subject to individual interpretation, but no one shows up in cruise-style evening wear at dinner.

Dining: Open-sitting dining with extensive menus in both the restaurant and indoor-outdoor cafés.

Tipping Policy: As is the policy on other Holland America-owned vessels, no gratuities are required. But on a recent Caribbean voyage, the cruise director offered the information that gratuities given to the waiter would be divided among the rest of the staff, which left most of us in a quandary since we had a different waiter almost every night. We didn't know whom to tip, so we left about $5 a day per person with the headwaiter and asked him to take care of tipping for us.

Past Passenger Perks: Incentive to belong to the Foremast Club is a newsletter and an automatic discount off of early booking fares.

Discount Policy: There are early-booking discounts that could add up to about 35 percent off fares. Special sailings, particularly in the Caribbean, for as low as two-for-ones, and offers in the Mediterranean that also reduced rates by about 50 percent.

HIGH MARKS
Δ The feeling that comes with slow motion
Δ The sails flapping in the wind
Δ Silence out on deck

WEAKEST LINK
• No elevators on the three smaller vessels

The Fleet

WIND STAR
Built: 1986 Refurbished: 1996

WIND SONG
Built: 1987 Refurbished: 1997

WIND SPIRIT
Built: 1988 Refurbished: 1998

Category: Boutique-Adventure
Rates: $ $ $ $
Overall Rating: ⚓⚓⚓⚓
Country of Registry: Bahamas
Former Names: none
Nationality of Crew: British and Norwegian officers; Indonesian and Filipino service staff
Cruising Area: Caribbean, Mediterranean, French Polynesia
Length of Voyages: 7 nights

Ship Specifics

Tonnage	5,250	Elevators	no
Length	440 feet	Decks	4
Beam	64 feet	Children's Facilities	no
Stabilizers	no	Fitness Center	yes
Passengers	148	Spa	yes
Crew international	88	Verandahs	no
Space Ratio	36	Casino	yes
Crew/Passenger Ratio	1–1.6	Wheelchair Access	no

INSIDER TIP

These vessels are sail-cruisers with five masts, seven triangular, self-furling, computer operated sails. Booms are motor-controlled with high-tech sensor input to trim the angle of the sail. Angle of heel is kept at a maximum of six degrees by a computer-controlled hydraulic stabilizing system in the engine room.

Cabins: ⚓⚓⚓⚓ *Suites:* ⚓⚓⚓ There's only one Owner's Suite; it's just a little larger than the cabins. But it is sold at about 35 percent more than average cabins so it's not worth talking about. Cabins, however, seem small at first blush, but configuration is so good it makes them feel larger than 180-square feet. There's an extraordinary amount of storage space for sports equipment that guests bring on board. All the cabins are alike and make maximum use of space. Twin beds convert to doubles and have twin portholes, television, VCR, and mini-bar stocked with beverages which when consumed are charged to your ship account. Bathrooms are some of the best at sea for a ship this size. The teak and mirrored rooms are compact, but showers are twin-sized. They were built so water doesn't slosh over to the bathroom floor. Supersized towels are plush and matching robes are the only ones I have ever purchased for use at home. High-quality amenities are replaced daily.

Public Space: ⚓⚓⚓⚓ Interiors are in keeping with sleek exteriors. Leathers, soft colors, nautical artifacts, artworks and paintings, large windows, and natural fabrics create an upbeat yachty atmosphere. Guests joke about the small swimming pool, but swimming off the aft platform in clear waters makes up for it. There's a Jacuzzi, a very popular outdoor bar, comfortable sunning chairs, a lounge with a dance floor, a small casino, a boutique, well-stocked libraries, and quiet space indoors and outdoors.

Spa and Fitness: ⚓⚓ A minimally equipped gymnasium and a full-service spa, albeit both sized to match the number of guests who will use the facilities.

Entertainment: ⚓⚓⚓ Dance music in the main lounges, sometimes piano music on deck, and water-sports activities, which is what most guests want. Windstar vessels are warm-weather cruisers, so a typical day may start with a dawn diving excursion to feed the sharks, a snorkeling exploration off an uninhabited island, and a quick tour of the local sights. The afternoon could be filled with water skiing, banana boating, and fishing off the stern. By the time dinner is finished, most guests prefer a moonlight stroll on deck and are too tired from the day's activities to do much more than retire to their cabins.

Food and Dining: ⚓⚓⚓⚓ Main dining rooms accommodate all guests at one sitting, which contributes to the intimate ambience. Menus change daily for lunch and dinner, and there's usually an outdoor barbecue one night with items like grilled tuna, steak and chicken. Light menus are offered and special requests are honored. But the chefs take advantage of local fresh fish and vegetables-these are the specialties. Dining rooms are open only for dinner. Breakfast and lunch are served or self-served in the cafés topside at indoor or outdoor tables. There's always a great salad bar, fresh fruits, and made-to-order specialties. Award-winning chefs supervise cuisine in the open-sitting dining room and many dishes are unique to the West Coast. Cabin service is also available.

Service: ⚓⚓⚓⚓ Warm, friendly, and very personal. Staff gets to know guests very quickly and everyone is addressed by name.

Junior Cruisers: ⚓ No special facilities or programs.

Itineraries: ⚓⚓⚓⚓ The *Wind Star* sails seven-night cruises from Barbados to Caribbean islands from January through March, then she leaves for the Mediterranean for one-week cruises from Nice to the Italian Riviera. She returns to Barbados in early November. *Wind Spirit* sails on one-week cruises from St. Thomas from January to April, then leaves for a summer sailing between Rome and Istanbul before returning to the Caribbean in early November. *Wind Song* spends winters sailing one-week cruises from Puerto Caldera, Costa Rica, to nearby islands, then returns to seven-night cruises from Rome to the Riviera.

Overall: ⚓⚓⚓⚓ These are motorized luxury sailing vessels with shallow drafts that allow them to visit small and very interesting places. They were built specifically for the upscale, active traveler who is not content with sedentary life aboard a traditional cruise ship. They are similar to the Sea Goddess concept of luxury-yacht-like experiences, but with a difference. They provide an alternative for the active water-sports lover. Each vessel carries its own Zodiac, an inflatable launch for water skiing and beach landings; water skis; windsurfing boards; small sailboats; parasailing and scuba gear; and snorkeling and deep-sea fishing equipment. These are ships in motion. Guests are always doing something, and itineraries are designed so vessels visit ports during the day and sail at night.

HIGH MARKS.

- Δ Being greeted by the captain at the bottom of the gangway. He personally welcomes every guest.
- Δ The crisp uniforms worn by the service staff.
- Δ The unusual shore excursions.

WEAKEST LINK

- No elevators

WIND SURF
Built: 1990   Refurbished: 1998/2001

Category: Boutique-Adventure
Rates: $$$
Overall Rating: ⚓⚓⚓⚓⚓
Country of Registry: Bahamas
Former Name: Club Med I
Nationality of Crew: British and Norwegian officers; Indonesian and Filipino service staff
Cruising Area: Caribbean and Mediterranean
Length of Voyages: 7 nights

Ship Specifics

Tonnage	14,745	Elevators		2
Length	617 feet	Decks		7
Beam	66 feet	Children's Facilities		yes
Stabilizers	yes	Fitness Center		yes
Passengers d/a	312	Spa		yes
Crew	163	Verandahs		yes
Space Ratio	47	Casino		yes
Crew/Passenger Ratio	1–2	Wheelchair Access		yes

Cabins: ⚓⚓⚓⚓⚓ *Suites:* ⚓⚓⚓⚓⚓ The 125 cabins are nearly identical to those on other Windstar ships, but it's the 31 suites that measure 376-square feet that are attracting a lot of attention. They were created by removing a wall between standard cabins and making one suite out of two cabins. One cabin became a bedroom and the second one became a full size sitting room. The suites have two full baths and that's a big advantage. Color scheme for the carpets, duvet and pillow covers, drapery and chair coverings is in geometric patterns ranging from deep reds to light beige, accented by teak wood, fine linen wall coverings and original art.

However, the best suite on board is not shown on deck plans. It's a two room Owner's Suite on Bridge Deck left over from *Wind Surf's* previous life. Decorated in Art Deco fashion, it is plush with a king-size bed, real living room, but only one bathroom. It's away from the rest of the cabins and suites and is really special. It's available for purchase but the rate is not in brochure.

Cabins throughout are identical, each with two portholes. At 188-square feet, they are very comfortable. Queen-size beds convert to twins and storage space is more than enough to stow gear for the most avid sportspersons. There's a small sitting area with a dresser that doubles as a desk, lots of drawers, closets and cubby holes that I didn't find until checking for leftovers on debarkation day. Bathrooms are a joy. Teak floors, dual head showers in semi-circular enclosures that don't allow for wet floor, vanities, hair-dryers, terry robes, plus plush and plentiful towels and lots of storage space for toiletries.

Every cabin has an unobstructed view of the ocean, TV/VCRs, mini-bar/refrigerator, telephone and private safe. Lively colors of the sea brighten the rooms. Although cabin food service is available, it is rather difficult since there is only one chair in each cabin. On the smaller sail-ships, there are two chairs and a pull out shelf which doubles as a table. High quality amenities are packaged in rope bags for cabins and in baskets, which include a few additional goodies for suite guests.

Facilities for Disabled Travelers: ⚓ High ledges and elevators and doorways are not wide enough to accommodate physically challenged travelers in wheelchairs. There are no cabins or suites outfitted to accommodate the disabled, although there were a couple of passengers in wheelchairs on my last cruise. They said that the crew was extremely helpful, but they skipped the ports of call. They came on board for the sailing experience.

Public Space: ⚓⚓⚓⚓ Public rooms were reconfigured and redesigned to keep the *Wind Surf* in line with facilities on the rest of the fleet. The Restaurant takes up the forward section and leads into the Wind Surf Lounge with the Casino tucked into a separated corner. Center of the deck is dominated by the Library and is lined by promenades on both sides with large glass walls. Library is well stocked with videos, but under stocked with reading material. The Signature Shop, pool, sunning area and the Pool Bar are located forward.

Wind Surf Lounge is large enough to accommodate all of the guests in a single Captain's party. Raised on both sides, color tones are taupe and blue, but the room is dominated by a square atrium with a skylight surrounded by artwork wisely retained from the ships previous life. While the size of the lounge is impressive, sail-cruise type guests usually head up to the Compass Rose Room to cluster for drinks and camaraderie.

Toby Salzman Comments:

"With full ship charters representing 20 percent of the company's business and incentive groups accounting for about six percent, the 2,095-square foot Conference Center is an important facility. Located down on Deck 0, it is a full service facility with bar and food service as well as electronic meeting services."

Spa and Fitness: ⚓⚓⚓⚓ The WindSpa is the largest on any boutique size ship and takes up 10,000-square feet of precious space. The spa is as complete as a spa can be at sea and since each of the massage rooms was a cabin in the ship's previous life, each has a shower and bathroom for privacy. Health, exercise, pampering and purification treatments, aerobics, a series of daily yoga classes, aqua-aerobics, and stretch classes are offered from 7 am to 10 pm to make allowances for guests returning late from shore.

Steiner Transocean Limited operates the spa with a staff of 20. Packages may be pre-purchased and range in price from $259 to $699 per person. Pre-booked packages receive priority in appointments and that's important on a ship this size where everyone has a single purpose – to pamper him or herself. The new glass-enclosed fitness center has $80,000 worth of state-of-the-art workout equipment. The WaterSports Platform is five times larger than anything like it at sea. Weather permitting, there's wind surfing, water-skiing, scuba diving, kayaking, and very popular Zodiacs and launches that take guests to nearby reefs and island beaches in the Mediterranean and Caribbean. A very helpful staff of four experienced divers supervises the water sports program.

Entertainment: ⚓⚓⚓ Guests who sail *Wind Surf* are a mixed group. They may be first time or repeat honeymooners, lawyers, doctors, television and screen personalities, CEO's and retirees who have traveled the world and are not looking for a Las Vegas experience or a heavy entertainment schedule. So, *Wind Surf* doesn't give them glitz. Emphasis is on sports, beaches and the outdoors. But, there is a casino, a band in the Wind Surf Lounge and a trio in the Compass Rose Room. Guest lecturers cover regional topics. The nightly routine calls for the host or hostess to talk about the following day's port of call. Other than optional shore excursions in every port, guests are on their own.

Food and Dining : ⚓⚓⚓⚓ This is one of *Wind Surf's* special pleasures. Size also allowed for three dining venues: the Restaurant, an alternative Continental-French-style Bistro and a traditional self-service Lido-like eatery named The Verandah for indoor and outdoor dining.

I would be remiss if I didn't comment on what is the best deck "barbecue" at sea I have ever seen in all my years spent on ships. Held at least once each cruise, the deck area becomes a backyard barbecue with multiple grills offering lobster, crabs, clams, oysters, chicken, steak and I could go on and on. It rivaled my previous favorite "barbecue" staged on a private beach on a Sea Goddess cruises.

The 272-seat main Restaurant is sculpted around the windows with the galley taking up the center. A highlight for me in all three dining venues was the emphasis on fresh foods-vegetables, fruits and fish-prepared with a light hand in imaginative recipes. Of course, there are the usual beef dishes, duck, pork, lamb and poultry. Desserts were outrageous and specialty drinks like cappuccino were available at every meal without additional charges.

Dining is similar to other Wind Star ships where The Restaurant is only open for dinner. The Verandah serves breakfast and lunch. Menus in the Restaurant usually offer a choice of three or four appetizers, two soups, two salads and four or five entrees and at least a half dozen desserts. There's a "light" calorie menu and vegetarian choices at every meal. The wine list offers California and European vintages in varying price categories and there's a $12 per person "Chef's Suggestion" of three different wines in three ounce glasses to accompany dinners

Junior Cruisers: ⚓ You also won't find more than a few children, if any. There are no dedicated children's facilities.

Overall: ⚓⚓⚓⚓ Larger by far than her older siblings, *Wind Surf* has all of the special amenities offered by the other Windstar ships, but brings new features and dimensions to the sail-cruise experiences. First off, she's spacious and that's something few sailors expect on this type of vessel. With a whopping space ratio of 47, she's right up there with top luxury ships. Increased size also allowed for increased spaciousness representing a whopping increase of 30 percent over her siblings. *Wind Surf* carries 312 guests as compared to 148 on her smaller sister vessels.

Itineraries: ⚓⚓⚓⚓ Summer in the Mediterranean, winters on one-week cruises between Miami and Costa Rica.

INSIDER TIP

Much as I enjoyed *Wind Surf* and the other sailing vessels in the fleet, in all honesty, *Wind Surf* is not for everyone. Like her siblings, *Wind Surf* would not be the vessel of choice for single travelers. While there were a few single guests on board, I would not recommend it for singles unless they are outgoing and do not rely on shipboard entertainment for the pleasures of cruising. There is very little group activity, other than water sports events

HIGH MARKS

- Δ Some of the best food and service at sea
- Δ The suites with two bathrooms
- Δ The feeling that comes with cruising with all of the sails blowing in the wind

WEAKEST LINK

- • Not much to do on board after dinner. It's either a movie in your cabin, a chance to beat the odds in the casino or quiet conversation with your significant other and new friends.

Major companies and their vessels, which focus marketing on North American passengers, are profiled in depth in "The Shipping Companies and Their Ships" Chapter, but there are hundreds of other vessels sailing in waters around the world. They provide entirely different experiences in different lifestyles. They visit different ports and more exotic places. They come in all shapes and forms, and they sail on all bodies of water deep enough to accommodate them. They appeal to many of the same passengers who sail the big ships, but they have greater appeal to passengers who choose not to cruise the Caribbean, for example. But all of these vessels—freighters, cargo liners, riverboats, flat-bottom boats, and sailing ships—have one thing in common with mega liners and classic liners: They all float, albeit at a different pace.

Lesser known, regionally popular vessels and their itineraries are highlighted in this chapter. These vessels are no less attractive, nor do they offer less to passengers. They are "different" from what we have come to expect from Caribbean cruise ships, and they are developing loyal followings. For example, cruising the Nile is a memorable experience and quite easily arranged. Sailing on a barge through Europe's canals is impossible on a large ship, but delightful on a vessel carrying four passengers. What follows is a sampling of vessels the adventurous traveler will enjoy.

While the cruise industry in North America has been growing steadily during the past 30 years, ship travel lagged behind in Europe and Asia. That is until a few savvy travel companies decided to play catch-up and entered the cruise business. Now the expansion rate in both Europe and Asia is proceeding at a faster pace than it did in the United States during the 1970 heydays.

The Greek islands and Mediterranean ports have been favorite cruising grounds for many years, and Greek shipping companies are coming to the front of the line with ships of varying sizes. Also growing are fleets of smaller vessels in North America. Boats have shallow drafts to allow for exploration of North and South America's beautiful waterways never included on cruise ship itineraries. With increases in visitors to China, for example, the Yangtze River has more passenger vessels visiting historic sites than ever before in shipping history.

Most of these companies offer early booking discounts of five to 25 percent. Not all companies are represented in North America, but information should be available through travel agencies. Addresses are listed when available. Also, don't be surprised by small charges for room service and afternoon tea or coffee or by gratuities being automatically added to your ship account.

European ships, river boats and barges are reviewed by Shirley Slater and Harry Basch. Ships that compete seasonally in the Caribbean or are marketed in North America are profiled in "Cruise Companies and Their Ships" Chapter and are rated against other ships in the same price and size category. In all fairness, ships marketed primarily in Europe or the Pacific are not rated because amenities, lifestyle and services are geared to those specific markets.

Major European Cruise Companies

And Their Ships

By Shirley Slater and Harry Basch

CLASSICAL CRUISES
132 East 70th Street
New York, NY 10021
(212) 794-3200
www.classicalcruises.com

Classical Cruises offers Mediterranean, Aegean and Northern European cruises with an emphasis on history and culture that are marketed to the general public as well as college alumni and affinity groups who may charter the entire vessel. They have a fleet of small, yacht like ships – *Callisto*, *Pegasus*, *Sun Bay I* and *Sun Bay II* – that carry from 34 to 92 passengers.

Onboard lectures prepare passengers for forays into the historic ports of call with those same lecturers, with free time allowed to pursue individual interests. Often, the ships stay in port into the evening, allowing time for dinner ashore if a traveler wishes, although the food aboard the vessels is usually quite good. Complimentary wine and beer are often included with meals and a hotel overnight before the cruise as well as tours and shore excursions are also included in the base fare, which begins at around $500 a day per person, double occupancy. Airfare is not usually included.

Cabins are all outsides with windows or portholes, and prettily furnished. On the brand-new *Sun Bay II*, suites with private verandas are available. Most sailings are 10 to 14 days.

FRED. OLSEN CRUISE LINES

PO Box 342

New York, NY 10014

(800) 688-3876 (EuroCruises)

www.fredolsencruises.co.uk

This family-owned cruise line was founded in Norway in 1848 when the three Olsen brothers started an international shipping company. Today the cruise line division is based in Ipswich, Suffolk, UK, while the remainder of the company's wide range of businesses is still headquartered in Oslo.

The cruise company operates three ships, the 442-passenger *Black Prince*, built for Olsen in 1966; the 761-passenger *Black Watch*, formerly *Royal Viking Star*; and the 729-passenger *Braemer*, the former *Cunard Dynasty/Crown Dynasty*.

Fred. Olsen ships have a large following in the UK, with many repeat passengers, primarily couples and singles in the upper middle ages, and are picking up more North American passengers who prefer a classic cruise experience on mid-sized ships. The vessels cruise year-round in the Mediterranean, Northern Europe, Canary Islands, Caribbean, Norwegian Fjords and Arctic Circle, the Baltic, Africa and India, and offer a circumnavigation of South America.

Lifestyle on board is more like an English country house hotel than a floating resort/shopping mall. Entertainment is cabaret-style and includes musical revues, British comedians, live music for dancing and educational and enrichment lectures. Gentleman hosts travel on every Fred. Olsen cruise to dance with single ladies. Singles are also in demand for bridge competitions, which can get fierce.

Designated single cabins without enormous surcharges are available, as well as inside and outside double cabins. Suites with private verandas are offered aboard *Black Watch* and *Braemer*, and a limited number of wheelchair-accessible cabins are available on all three.

The *Black Prince* was the first ship equipped with a Marina Center that could be floated on the ocean surface as a base for water sports. The *Black Watch* offers golf packages with onboard tutorials and four rounds at famous courses in Europe and the Caribbean, depending on the ship itinerary. All three ships have fitness centers and beauty salons with full spa services. A children's program is also available during summer and holiday cruises, with a designated playroom on the *Black Watch*.

HAPAG-LLOYD

399 Hoes Lane
Piscataway, NJ 08854
(800) 334-2724
www.hapag-lloyd.com

Hapag-Lloyd represents a merger between two legendary German ship-ping and cruise lines, Hamburg-Amerika or HAPAG (an acronym for Hamburg-Amerikanische Packetfahrt Actien-Gesellschaft), founded in 1856, and North German Lloyd, which began service between Germany and America in 1958. The two companies merged in 1931 and today concentrate on both cargo-shipping and cruises that are designed primarily for the German-speaking market.

The line operates four ships, the 408-passenger *Europa*, built in 1999; the 420-passenger *Columbus*, built in 1997; and the expedition vessels *Hanseatic*, built in 1993 and carrying 184 passengers, and the *Bremen*, built in 1990 and carrying 164 passengers. All have German as the official language on board and the euro as official currency, although whenever English-speaking passen-gers are booked, English is added to the announcements and a daily program is printed in English.

The *Europa* is a highly-rated luxury ship that attracts upscale German-speaking couples of all ages and sails all over the world, with an official around-the-world cruise offered every January. Minimum size for accommo-dations is 290 square feet and goes up to 645 square feet. All accommodations are suites, most with private verandas and a private e-mail connection. Already having undergone one major refit, the ship now provides a conference room where the casino used to be and a larger spa facility.

The *Columbus* aims at a more mainstream market, again primarily German-speaking except in summer when it cruises the Great Lakes under the aegis of Great Lakes Cruise Company in Ann Arbor, Michigan.

The *Bremen* and *Hanseatic* are familiar vessels to American expedition travelers, because one or both have been chartered out for English-speaking Antarctic cruises marketed by Radisson Seven Seas Cruises.

Average per passenger per day rates are $450 for the Europa, $375 for the *Hanseatic*, $300 for the *Bremen* and $180 for the *Columbus*.

HEBRIDIAN ISLAND CRUISES LTD.

Griffin House, Broughton Hall
Skipton, North Yorkshire BD23 3AN, Britain
(800) 659-2648
www.hibridean.co.uk

This pair of charming Scottish ships really looks as if they should be members of Relais & Chateaux or the seagoing version of the Royal Scotsman luxury train. The 49-passenger *Hebridian Princess* has been cruising for the company for more than a decade; the 80-passenger *Hebridian Spirit* joined in 2001.

Cabins are individually decorated in Scottish style with plenty of plaids and floral chintzes, with extra cushions, cushy chairs and reading lamps and the food aboard is prepared in such small portions that it tastes more like one would find in an elegant country house hotel than a cruise ship. Single cabins are available on both vessels. A "no tipping" policy is in effect, and shore excursions, use of bicycles, fishing tackle and gym equipment on board, and all soft drinks and bottled water are included. An all-British crew in a high ratio of crew to passenger is aboard, making service superlative. The *Hebridian Princess* does not sail at night but rather ties up at a berth on shore.

Areas cruised include the Mediterranean, Aegean, Adriatic, Scandinavia, the Baltic and the North Atlantic.

KRISTINA CRUISES

The Cruise Broker
PO Box 342
New York, NY 10014
(800) 688-3876
www.kristinacruises.com

This two-ship Finnish family-owned line cruises to St. Petersburg and other ports in the Baltic, the coast of Western Europe, the Norwegian fjords and the Mediterranean with the 200-passenger *Kristina Regina* and the smaller *Kristina Brahe*. The lifestyle aboard is a mix of cruise ship and Scandinavian ferry, particularly notable in the narrow cabins (doubles begin as small as 72 square feet and singles at 43 square feet). Duty-free shops almost overwhelm public areas for cruise passengers, but meals are served at a single seating, shore excursions are sometimes included in the basic fare, and the ship usually docks close to the center of the city.

The *Kristina Regina* combines the atmosphere of intellectual adventure with relaxed and informal cruise style with music in the evenings, movies and dining that is a mixture of Finnish and American (think reindeer and turkey). An English-speaking Finnish crew provides friendly service in the two single-seating dining rooms.

There is no swimming pool aboard, but the ship has a small sauna. No Finnish vessel could sail without a sauna.

Peter Knego comments:

"One of the few twin-funneled ships in service (although the forward unit is a dummy). *Kristina Regina* was built in 1960 for Stockholm ferry service. She was converted into a cruise ship in 1981 and refurbished in 1997."

MY TRAVEL GROUP PLC (FORMERLY AIRTOURS)

1011 East Colonial Drive
Orlando, FL 32803
www.mytravelco.com

This travel company, also known as Sun Cruises with headquarters in Manchester, England, was affiliated with Carnival Corporation when it was Airtours. It markets primarily in the United Kingdom, and presently counts four ships in its fleet, the 791 passenger *Seawing*, the former *Starward* from Norwegian Cruise Line; the 1,062-passenger *Carousel*, the former *Nordic Prince* from Royal Caribbean; the 1,100-passenger *Sundream*, the former *Song of Norway* from Royal Caribbean; and the 1,400-passenger *Sunbird*, the former *Song of America* from Royal Caribbean. The ships cruise primarily in the Mediterranean and Northern Europe, with some Caribbean sailings in winter.

Packages are the thing with this company, which also markets most of the familiar cruise lines in North America. On board style is British, meaning dress follows the requested dress code, cuisine offers big British breakfasts, elevenses or mid-morning snacks, luncheon, afternoon tea, dinner and midnight buffet. More passenger participation – karaoke, costume parades, passenger talent shows – and fewer production shows make up the entertainment calendar.

Passengers are mostly British or come from Northern European countries. Americans looking for inexpensive vacations in Europe and the Mediterranean will be comfortable on any of these ships. The company prides itself on offering the lowest available advertised rate and guarantees it within 29 days of booking.

Dress code is European casual which is dressier than American's version of casual. No tuxedos are required, but most men show up at dinner in jackets and ties. Recommended gratuities are slightly lower than on U.S. based ships.

NORWEGIAN COASTAL VOYAGE

405 Park Avenue, Suite 904
New York, NY 10022
(800) 3223-7436
www.coastalvoyage.com

Formerly known as the Bergen Line, this division of the company markets year-round voyages along the west coast of Norway between Bergen in the south and Kirkenes in the north aboard 11 coastal steamers. It's the so-called Hurtigrutun or Quick Route. While Norwegians use it as ferry service from point A to point B, tourists from countries as diverse as Japan, Mexico, Canada, the United States and many parts of Europe take the full 1,250 nautical miles for the spectacular scenery and the chance to get acquainted with Norwegians following their line of work. Schoolchildren, midwives, mail, cargo and commuters sail between ports and islands along the route.

The number of ships is always 14; when a new one comes on line, an old one is retired. The present fleet is headed up by the newest pair, the "millennium ships" introduced in 2000, the *Finnmarken* and the *Trollfjord*. They are modern ships with suites, some boasting balconies and Jacuzzis, inside, outside and wheelchair accessible cabins, fitness center with sauna and squash court, and numerous bars, cafes and restaurants. Categorized as "new ships" are the *Nordnorge, Polarlys, Nordkapp, Nordlys, Richard With* and *Kong Harald*, with suites, junior suites, inside, outside and handicap-designated cabins, along with plenty of lounges, bars and restaurants, fitness centers and conference rooms.

The *Vesteralen, Narvik* and *Midnatsol* are "mid-generation ships," less lavish in design and with simpler accommodations than the previous vessels, while the *Nordstjernen* and *Lofoten* are "traditional ships" with the atmosphere of the historic coastal ships. Finally, there is the *Brand Polaris*, an Arctic ship with the highest ice class rating, and the *Polar Star*, an ice-breaker converted to expedition ship, which can go into the Arctic ice. Both *Brand Polaris* and *Polar Star* cruise to Greenland and Spitsbergen.

The Nordnorge also offers cruises to Antarctica and the Chilean Fjords between November and February. Daily departures on the Norwegian coastal voyages are offered each way, and every one-way seven-night voyage calls at 34 different ports. Escorted land packages are also available. There is no tipping aboard the vessels.

Discounts for seniors are in effect on most sailings, and no single supplements are required in shoulder season and off-season. Repeat passengers who previously cruised in summer can also get a 20 per cent reduction in shoulder or off season.

All but the *Bran Polaris* and *Polar Star* have car-carrying capacity and take from 184 to 1,286 passengers. Rates vary with season and also depend on the age of the vessel. Newer ships command higher rates. About half of the passengers are Norwegian. Vessels are very popular with retirees, but remember retirement in most European countries begins at age 50 in many cases.

INSIDER TIP

Cabins are closet sized on the older ships sailing as ferries. Don't expect a cruise ship. These coastal vessels are transportation for locals and overnight experiences for tourists. Food is not up to minimal cruise ship standards. My week on the *King Harald* was a first in many respects. I bought food at the kiosk. However, if seeing dozens of fjords, sometime two, three or four in one day interests you and you need coastal transportation, it won't cost you an arm and a leg. There are train-style reclining lounge chairs for ferry passengers who use the vessel for transportation.

E.B.

SAGA INERNATIONAL HOLIDAYS

222 Berkeley Street
Boston, MA 02116
(800) 952-9590
www.sagaholidays.com

The comfortable and much-loved *Sagafjord*, which sailed for Cunard for many years, has been turned into the *Saga Rose*, dedicated to mostly-British passengers over 50 and sold directly to the public rather than through travel agents. The ship cruises in Northern Europe, the Mediterranean and around the world.

This classy, vintage ship has a high passenger space ratio and some very attractive suites with private verandas. Singles will find a number of dedicated cabins for one without the horrendous surcharge some ships make. With 54 singles, 25 inside doubles, 221 outside doubles, 12 wheelchair-accessible cabins and 17 suites, there's something for everyone.

Most of the public rooms are on one deck, so it's easy to navigate around the vessel except for one nightclub area tucked away on an upper deck with its own back elevator. Average per day rates are around $400, but you can save about half if you buy the complete air-sea-hotel package from SAGA.

INSIDER TIP

Don't expect to board the plush *Sagafjord* of old. Most passengers have no idea they are sailing on a vessel with a glorious history. One may stumble on traces of yesteryear, but on a recent inspection I found little to remind me of the ship I once knew. Passengers should buy this ship for the almost all-inclusive bargain price. They'll get a comfortable ride and visit interesting ports of call. With 90 percent of the passengers over 65; some going up into the 80's and 90's, shore excursions are planned at a slow, very slow pace.

E.B.

SOCIETY EXPEDITIONS

2001 Western Avenue, Suite 300
Seattle, WA 98121
206-728-9400
www.societyexpeditions.com

Similar in style to Lindblad Cruises, Society Expeditions' main thrust was to organize archaeological tours for special interest groups. The company has expanded beyond that purpose but still keeps all itineraries as adventures. Vessels are small enough to maneuver in shallow waters so passengers can explore remote areas of the world. The 96-passenger *Society Explorer* holds many firsts in the world of exploration cruising. She is the ship that has sailed the farthest south and north of any vessel other than icebreakers. The 139-passenger *World Discoverer* made the first successful west-to-east transit of the Northwest Passage.

Society Expeditions Cruises, Inc. is owned by Heiko Klein, a German tour and travel operator, and Abercrombie & Kent, a tour company specializing in luxury expedition travel. Jointly, they operate the two expedition vessels that cruise the Antarctic between November and February, then sail to remote destinations for adventure cruises.

SWAN HELLENIC

631 Commack Road, Suite 1A
Commack, NY 11725
(877) 219-4239
www.swanhellenic.com

This company, a division of P&O, has been providing educational European tours to the British public since the 1920s, and began Greek ship-based tours in 1952 when the war-torn country of Greece had little tourism infrastructure. Everyone from the Archbishop of Canterbury to the Deputy Keeper of the British Museum has taken a turn talking about mythology, history, archeology, geology, astronomy, military history, marine biology, art, drama and music.

The elegant 400-passenger *Minerva*, introduced in 1996, brought a fresh, younger attitude aboard as well as a few more North American passengers. The *Minerva II* replaces the original in 2003.

Meal sittings are open, with passengers free to arrive within a time frame and sit where and with whomever they please. There is a no-tipping policy as well. Dress aboard is casual during the daytime but a bit dressier for the evenings, with two formal evenings each cruise where dinner jackets are requested for gentlemen. (Suits or jacket and tie will pass muster, however.)

Smoking is not permitted in cabins or dining rooms, or during lectures. When cruising in Muslim countries, no alcohol is served on the ship in deference to local custom. Although some wheelchair access is available, the number of wheelchairs is limited for each sailing. Passengers are expected to be "fit and healthy," says the brochure. Shore excursions are included in the fare.

THOMSON CRUISES

Greater London House
Hampstead Rd.
London NW1 7SD, England
44-20-7387-9321
www.thomson-holiday.com

This British tour company operates two ships, the 1,198-passenger *Emerald* and the 1,050-passengers *Topaz*, with open sittings at mealtime and all-inclusive bar packages. The *Topaz* has some single cabins along with standard and deluxe insides and outsides. The ship has two restaurants, four bars, two lounges, a disco, whirlpool, swimming pool, beauty salon and massage treatments, shops, children's playroom, teen club and gym.

The *Emerald* also provides two restaurants, five bars, two lounges, a disco, casino, two whirlpools, a swimming pool, beauty salon, shops, children's playroom, fitness center, sauna and massage rooms and library. Cabins on the *Emerald* include standard insides, standard outsides with portholes, superior cabins with two lower beds or a double bed, many with pull down third berth and sofa bed. Premier cabins offer double beds, mini-refrigerator, and sitting area.

Cruising areas include the Mediterranean, Aegean and Canary Islands. Shipboard lifestyle follows the traditional pattern with two formal nights that request dinner jackets or jacket with tie for men. Entertainment includes production shows, cabaret and variety performers and live music for dancing.

Peter Knego Comments:

"The *Emerald* is one of those ships with interesting previous lives. She was originally built as the *Santa Rosa* and sails today in a vastly rebuilt state as Louis Cruise Line's *Emerald*, under charter to Thomson Cruises. Her sister vessel, *Santa Paula*, was bombed out in Kuwait in 1990 where she was used as the Ramada Al Salaam Hotel. At 24,851 tons, the *Emerald* carries 1,162 passengers. Her capacity and configuration date from her conversion to Regency Cruises' *Regent Rainbow* in 1992."

(The following two companies market exclusively to German-speaking passengers.)

AIDA CRUISES

Frankfurter Strasse 233
Neu Isenburg 63263 Germany
49-6102-811000
www.poprincesscruises.com

Affiliates of P & O Princess Cruises plc and marketing under the Seetours International label in Germany, AIDA Cruises currently operates two ships, *AIDAcara*, launched in 1996 as the *AIDA Clubship*, and the new *AIDAvita*, delivered in 2002, targeting the German youth market.

A third ship, the newbuild *AIDAaura*, will be added in 2003. The *AIDAcara* carries 1,190 passengers while the *AIDAvita*, like the upcoming *AIDAaura*, carries 1,270. AIDA passengers with an average age of 43 are active and sports-minded. The lifestyle on board is patterned after upmarket clubs and resorts.

The new *A'ROSA* label utilizes the former *Crown Princess*, transferred in 2002 to become the 1,590-passenger *A'ROSA BLU*, and her sister vessel *Regal Princess*, and is scheduled to join in 2004. These ships will cater to the German premium market but with a more traditional style cruise pattern.

P & O Princess Cruises plc estimates an increase of 43 per cent in German passenger cruise days by 2005.

DELPHIN CRUISES (SEEREISEN)

Postfach 100407
Offenbach am Main, 63004 Germany
(800) 688-3876
www.delphin-kreuzfahrt.de/magazin.htm

Delphin Cruises (Delphin Seereisen in Germany) operates the 466-passenger *Delphin*, a handsomely furnished cruise ship that sails in summer in Northern Europe and the Mediterranean and in winter all around the world. The ship is the former *Kazakhstan II* from Black Sea Shipping that was renovated in 1994. Standard cabins are fairly spacious as are the Junior Suites and the top suites feature a separate living room and dressing room with bedroom and bath. Older passengers will need to use the elevators since stairs throughout the ship are very steep

Sailing Vessels

North America, Europe, Pacific

Not all vessels with sails are alike. Some only accommodate a dozen people, others several hundred. Some have a captain and one or two crew while others are full-scale cruise ships with a large crew and a full range of amenities.

Many small sailing vessels are old historic ships, virtual floating museums. Their accommodations are simple. Service is simple. What you do on board is up to you. Vessels usually sail during the day, making several stops at towns or beaches, then anchor at night. There may be sunfish, windsurfers, dinghies or kayaks on board, or you can swim or snorkel. You can take a turn hauling lines if you wish, and get sailing tips at the helm. Cooking is often done on a wood-burning stove, and dinner served buffet-style on deck. Usually there is one lobster bake with a driftwood fire on shore. Smoking is never permitted below. Young children usually are not permitted, except for special family voyages.

Large sailing ships have the excitement of sailing plus the amenities and entertainment of a cruise ship. There is a full service dining room with waiters, tenders for shore excursions, and often sunfish, kayaks and other water sports. Some of the large sailing ships are casual, others are more formal. None have wheelchair access, and most have no elevators.

Cabins are all outsides with windows or portholes, and furnished like your friend's yacht. On the brand-new *Sun Bay II*, suites with private verandas are available. Most sailings are seven, 10, or 14 days.

CLUB MED CRUISES

75 Valencia Avenue, 9th Floor
Coral Gables, FL 33134
(305) 443-0659
www.clubmed.com

This one-ship cruise line is an offshoot of the well-known Club Med Vacation Villages. The 376-passenger *Club Med 2*, built in 1992, cruises the Mediterranean in summer and the Caribbean in winter. (The *Club Med 1* was sold to Windstar Cruises back in 1998 to become the *Wind Surf*.)

A 617-foot sail-cruiser, the ship is a five-masted vessel with seven computer-controlled sails that are used sporadically during the cruise, sometimes in tandem with the motors.

The social staff aboard consists of 64 to 77 GO's ("gentils organisateurs"), a sort of free-wheeling social staff that usually seem to get first dibs on the best seats at the bar and all the most popular sporting gear that is carried in and launched from an aft marina deck when the ship is at anchor.

Passengers are the same people who frequent the adult Club Meds, young to middle-aged singles and couples, families with children over 10 (under 10 is a no-no), honeymooners, water sports fans and destination-oriented young vacationers from Europe and America.

Meals are casually served at open sittings in the food venues aboard, which include a sit-down dining room, a buffet dining room and a deck grill that is also sometimes hauled ashore for beach picnics. Wine (vin very ordinaire) is usually complimentary by carafe, with additional premium wines available for purchase. Dress is very casual and entertainment by the GO's is akin to shows put on in grandpa's barn by Mickey Rooney and Judy Garland in the old MGM movies.

SEA CLOUD CRUISES

32-40 North Dean Street
Englewood, NJ 07631
(888) 732-2568

One of the most magnificent sailing vessels in the world is the classic *Sea Cloud,* built in 1931 as a private yacht for financier E. F. Hutton and his wife Marjorie Merriweather Post, the cereal heiress. The popularity of the cruises that sell out year after year encouraged the building of the *Sea Cloud II,* a modernized, slightly larger replica that was launched in 2001.

The ships sail in the Caribbean, Mediterranean, British Isles and Baltic, some of the time under charter by such prestigious organizations as New York's Metropolitan Museum of Art. The owners and operators are German with an American marketing office in New Jersey. Both vessels are registered in Malta. The owners' suites on the 69-passenger *Sea Cloud* still contain the gold faucets, marble fireplaces (nonworking) and French canopy bed, while the comparable suites on the 96-passenger *Sea Cloud II* have many of the same features. All the cabins are outside on both vessels. On the original, some of the less expensive cabins are small, but shipshape, containing only two built-in beds with storage drawers underneath and a dresser with four drawers. On Sea Cloud II, even the less expensive cabins are somewhat larger with a sitting area.

On the original, the main deck is natural teak with brass trim, glossy wood-paneled walls and polished benches, above which you can watch young sailors, male and female, climb the rigging to set the 30 sails of the four-masted bark in the time-honored fashion. On the replica, you have virtually the same experience.

STAR CLIPPERS

4101 Salzedo St.
Coral Gables, FL 33146
(305) 442-0550
www.starclippers.com

(Star Clippers' ship profiles are included in the "Cruise Companies and Their Ships" Chapter)

WINDJAMMER BAREFOOT CRUISES

P.O. Box 12
Miami, FL 33119
(800) 327-2601
www.windjammer.com

Captain Mike Burke organized the company in 1947, and he says they keep alive the tradition of great sailing ships. Cruises are called "barefoot adventures." Shipmates need not lend a hand, but most end up assisting with handling the masts. Burke buys his sailing ships from the estates of the likes of Onassis, Vanderbilt, Guinness and the Duke of Westminster. He says he buys them when they are in disrepair, and then fixes them up.

Windjammer cruises are not for everyone. They appeal to youngish (under 25 year old and few adventurous older) travelers looking for "barefoot" informality, a spirit of adventure, and a cruise with absolutely no regimentation and as little clothing as is absolutely necessary.

The Windjammer fleet consists of six sailing vessels that, according to Burke, make up the largest fleet of tall ships in the world. The supply ship, *Amazing Grace* has accommodations for 94 passengers. The flagship, the four-masted schooner, *Fantome*, is a 282-foot barkentine originally built for the Duke of Westminster as a private floating palace. Purchased by Onassis as a wedding gift for Prince Rainer and Princess Grace, it was somehow never delivered. The 676-ton vessel accommodates 128 in cabins with private baths. Homeport is Nassau, and she sails the second and fourth Tuesdays every month.

Others in the fleet are the *Flying Cloud* (400 tons) positioned in the British Virgin Islands; *Polynesia* (430 tons) positioned in St. Maarten. The *Mandalay* and the *Yankee Clipper* (327-tons) are positioned in the West Indies. Incidentally, the *Yankee Clipper* was acquired from the Vanderbilt estate and had been used extensively on scientific explorations and long voyages. Originally built by the German industrialist Alfred Krupp as his personal yacht, she was confiscated by the United States as a war prize

WINDSTAR CRUISES

300 Elliott Ave. W.
Seattle, WA 98119
(800) 258-3229
www.windstarcruises.com

(Windstar Cruises' ships are profiled in "Cruise Companies and Their Ships" Chapter)

River Cruises in Europe

By Shirley Slater and Harry Basch

The rivers of Europe invite travelers to sail along historic and storied routes of the Rhine, the Danube, the Volga, the Elbe, the Thames, the Po, even Shakespeare's beloved Avon, stopping along the way for wine tastings in the Moselle, shopping in Austria, folk dancing in Hungary, to see the circus in Moscow, the opera in Verona's open-air Roman arena or the pottery makers of Delft.

Unlike group land tours, which tend to be made up primarily of Americans, the river boats attract a number of Europeans, who may often outnumber North Americans. You're socializing with a more cosmopolitan crowd, and may even have an opportunity to practice saying hello, goodbye, please and thank you in another language.

While some of the river boats we've sailed aboard are more lavish than others, all have offered a unique close-up look at a lovely part of Europe, delicious meals, friendly service, regional wines and a silk-smooth ride.

Americans accustomed to the paddlewheel steamboats of Delta Queen and American West may be taken aback at the lack of furbelows on the European river boats. They often look squat and undistinguished without the rakish red paddlewheel and tall black funnels we're accustomed to. Americans familiar with the American passenger river boat *RiverBarge Explorer* will find the European vessels more familiar.

They offer a smooth ride and shallow draft, sociable open decks where passengers spend much of the day watching the scenery along the riverbanks, and the same care and attention to meals and service as any cruise ship. Menus may not be as expansive – you may have only two choices per course instead of three or four – but all meals are usually included on river boats, unlike many of the European ferries. Most often, a single fixed menu is offered with a choice of two main dishes.

While some shore side entertainment will be brought aboard in port, don't expect much beyond shore excursion lectures, port videos and teatime and after-dinner music. Sometimes an optional evening excursion to the circus, opera, theater or ballet may be offered.

Cabins are generally on the small side, with two lower beds or a double or queen-sized bed (ordered at the time of booking since most do not switch back and forth). Sometimes one of the two beds is made up as a sofa during the day. Bathrooms are compact, usually with shower but no tub. There are very few private verandas on river vessels, but some have French doors backed up by a wrought iron rail that open to let in fresh air and let passengers look out to see the scenery. A lounge, dining room and deck lounging area and bar are always aboard, sometimes with a small swimming pool, sauna, fitness center, boutique and/or beauty salon.

Few, if any young children are aboard most of Europe's river vessels, with the exception of KD River Cruises, which offers discounts and even free passage on designated sailings for children four to 14.

We sailed KD's Rhine River itinerary recently aboard the *Deutschland*, a 182-passenger vessel that is part of the line's new Exclusive (sic) Package Program, started when that venerable company merged with rapidly growing Viking Line in 2000. Exclusive means that the fare includes all shore excursions plus beer, house wine and soft drinks, and German sparkling wine at breakfast. Passengers on Viking and KD vessels are mostly German and British, with a sprinkling (on our cruise) of Americans, Austrians, Swiss, French, Italians, Russians, Romanians, South Africans, Mauritians, Portuguese and Spanish. Menus and announcements come in three languages, as do guided bus tours in the cities along the Rhine.

The lifestyle aboard KD River Cruises is casual, with meals at assigned tables at a single seating. Self-service buffet continental breakfasts can be expanded with hot dishes available on order. Lunch offers a copious salad bar, soup, a choice of two main dishes and dessert, while dinner is a course-by-course affair of appetizer, soup, salad, a choice of three main dishes, dessert, and fruit and cheese.

We sailed the Po River in Northern Italy aboard the new Peter Deilmann river vessel Casanova with more upscale, dressed-up passengers, most of them German-speaking. Deilmann's are the most luxurious of the river cruises in our opinion, along with the classic *River Cloud I* and *II* from Sea Cloud Cruises. Deilmann river boats are graciously furnished in classic antique-style furniture with original oil paintings from the owner's own collection. Eleven different boats almost equally elegant, including the brand-new *Frederic Chopin*, sail on the Rhine, Rhone, Danube, Po, Elbe, Saone, Oder, Main and Moselle, along with the Main-Danube Canal.

Other major river boat companies include Abercrombie & Kent, catering primarily to a North American market with upscale luxury river boats and canal barges.

Intrav, a division of the same Swiss company that owns and operates Clipper Cruises; and Elegant Tours and Cruises, which markets the lavish new *River Cloud* that cruises the Seine and the waterways of Holland and Belgium, and *River Cloud II* that sails the Po River.

Uniworld, a California-based company offering European river cruises designed exclusively for American travelers, and Grand Circle Travel, with a fleet of its own river boats designed to the match of tastes of American passengers, also promises you'll travel exclusively with other Americans if you're reluctant to see Europe with the Europeans.

Postcards from the River

The Rhine . . . is a tantalizing mix of Wagner's Ring Cycle and "The Sound of Music" as the boat floats past fairytale castles, haunting ruins, villages of half-timbered houses and rows of vineyards marching over steep hillsides. The best part of each day is when we sit on deck in a comfortable lounge chair by the rail with a picture map of the river so we can identify each one of the three dozen historic castles and castle ruins on the banks of the Rhine. No other river in Europe has such dramatic scenery surrounding its castles, churches and medieval town gates.

The Elbe . . . is so quiet as we move along the river; we can hear the birds singing in the nearby trees when our windows are open. From our mooring in the Czech Republic village of Decin, we can see a fairytale castle on the hill. A brass oompah band in bright costume greeted us on our return from a day in Prague with some loud and lively tunes, and sometimes a barmaid with a tray of beer steins and an accordionist kick off an impromptu party on deck. Along the river we have seen ducks, swans, geese, a few storks, even a blue heron, and once we glimpsed deer standing stock-still in a misty green meadow.

The Danube . . . the "beautiful blue Danube" ranges from steel blue to dark gray to, on occasion, muddy brown – "It's always blue when you're in love," a Viennese lady on board tells us – It waltzes past lush green hillsides and castle ruins that date from the Crusades, through the vineyards of Austria with their crisp young white wines, along the borders of the Czech Republic, Slovakia and Hungary to Budapest with lots of music and wine, romantic ruined castles and majestic abbeys.

The Po . . . inspires us to warble the song from "Kiss Me Kate" that begins, "We open in Venice, we then play Verona, then on to Cremona . . ." and so on, through Mantua, Padua and Parma. Not in the song but very much a part of the cruise is glorious Bologna, our favorite city of Venice and a new discovery from this cruise, the colorful-canal-lined town of Chioggia, a sort of poor man's Venice on the Adriatic, where we docked in the heart of town on a bustling market day to spend the entire afternoon and evening.

The Seine . . . the picturesque charm that attracted artists and tourists more than a century ago remains in the coastal village of Honfleur with its colorful fishing boats casting reflections in the harbor, narrow old buildings clinging to the hillsides and fishwives selling seafood fresh from the boats. When you travel along the Seine from the sea to Paris, you follow the river's broad, lazy loops and scribbles through the rich green countryside, watching the soft colors and shapes give way to the stark angularity of the 12th century stone at the ruins of Richard the Lionhearted Gaillard fortress, and pausing in the village of Giverny to visit Monet's home and gardens where you can stand on a wisteria-covered Japanese bridge and watch the changing light and color around the water lilies in the slow-moving waters below.

The Volga . . . during the summer's "white nights", the sun is still shining when you come out of the theatre in St. Petersburg at midnight and you can haggle with street vendors selling nesting dolls and embroidered blouses from the Tsarist era. The "Golden Ring" itinerary goes from Moscow north to the Volga-Baltic Canal, then along Lake Ladoga, the Svir River and Lake Onega into St. Petersburg, home of the Hermitage museum, the Catherine Palace and St. Isaac's Cathedral, with side visits to Petrodvorets and its lavish summer palaces.

The following are some of the companies offering river cruises in Europe:

ABERCROMBIE & KENT

1520 Kensington Road,
Oak Brook, IL 60521
(800) 323-7308
www.abercrombiekent.com.

Four river boats, 22-passenger *Princesse Royale* in Belgium and Holland, 50-passenger *Chardonnay* cruising between Dijon and Lyon in France, the new 50-passenger *Provence* between Lyon and Arles, and the 50-passenger *Anacoluthe* cruising from Paris to Joigny.

ELEGANT CRUISES

24 Vanderventer Ave.
Port Washington, NY 11050,
(800) 683-6767
www.elegantcruises.com.

The *River Cloud* offers elegant river boat cruises in Holland, Belgium, Hungry and Austria, while the *River Cloud II* concentrates on the Po River in Italy.

GRAND CIRCLE TRAVEL

347 Congress Street
Boston, MA 02210

A fleet of 10 river boats carrying between 120 and 164 passengers cruise the rivers of Holland, Germany, France, Austria and Hungary.

INTRAV

7711 Bonhomme Ave.
St. Louis, MO 63105
www.intrav.com.

The company operates a wide range of river boats carrying from 32 to 240 passengers cruise on the Danube, Elbe, Ilssel, Maas, Main, Morsel, Neckar, Neva, Rhine, Rhone, Saone, Seine, Svir, Vltava and Volga rivers.

KD RIVER CRUISES OF EUROPE

2500 Westchester Ave., Ste.113,
Purchase, NY 10577
(800) 346-6525
www.rivercruises.com.

This division of Viking Cruises has seven river boats cruising the Rhine, Moselle, Main, Elbe, Danube, Rhone, Saone, Seine, Volga, Svir and Neva. Special longer cruises go from Amsterdam to Budapest or Vienna.

PETER DEILMANN CRUISES

1800 Diagonal Road, Suite 170
Alexandria, VA 22314
(800) 348-8287
www.deilmann-cruises.com.

Deilmann's ten elegant river barges offer seven and 14-night cruises in Germany, Austria, Hungary, Serbia, Romania, France, Poland, Czech Republic, Italy and Holland.

UNIWORLD

Uniworld Plaza
17323 Ventura Blvd.
Los Angeles, CA 91316
(800) 733-7820
www.uniworld.com.

A fleet of 11 river boats carrying 80 to 240 passengers cruise the rivers of Germany, Holland, Belgian, France, Portugal, Spain, Italy, Austria, Czech Republic, Hungary, Serbia and Bulgaria.

VIKING RIVER CRUISES

21820 Burbank Boulevard
Los Angeles, CA 91367
(800) 323-7308
www.vikingrivercruises.com.

Viking has ten 150-passenger river boats and offers 9- to 16-day land/river packages in Holland, Belgium, Germany, France, Italy or Russia.

European Canal Cruises

By Shirley Slater and Harry Basch

The captain of the *QE2* is not likely to offer you a turn at the wheel, and you won't hop off Celebrity's *Summit* in the Panama Canal for a hike or a bike ride along the towpath. Big cruise ships are like seagoing deluxe hotels, lavishly appointed, self-contained cities.

But just as travelers seek out little country inns and bed-and-breakfast establishments in off-the-beaten-track locations, cruise passengers seek alternative cruises that provide a comfortable and relaxed journey while retaining all the luxury food and service to which they are accustomed.

A perfect antidote to the if-it's-Tuesday itinerary is a leisurely, luxurious cruise aboard a hotel barge in Europe. While the historic Burgundy Canal is the most popular for both hotel and self-drive barges, the Nivernais Canal, the Rhone Canal, the Canal du Midi in Provence, the Champagne and the Alsace-Lorraine area are also popular barge destinations.

Instead of eight countries in seven days, you'll get a close-up relationship with a few towns, a couple of vineyards where you'll taste wines with the winemaker himself, a minor chateau or two, perhaps a dinner in a Michelin-starred local restaurant and breakfast every morning on still-fresh-from-the-oven croissants and brioche, fetched by a staff member who bicycles from the barge mooring up to the nearest local bakery.

Lolling lazily on the deck sipping a glass of champagne, you see the countryside at eye level, waving at farmers in dazzling canary-yellow fields of rapeseed and fishermen in blue work smocks dozing along the canal side as you glide past, almost close enough to touch the scarlet poppies and wild iris, lavender lupine and feathery white Queen Anne's lace that bloom there. Life

587

on a hotel barge is as lighthearted as a floating house party with a dozen congenial friends. There are usually bicycles aboard, one for each guest, so when you feel curious or energetic, you can disembark at one of the locks and ride along the towpath or explore nearby villages and countryside

On our most recent sailing aboard French Country Waterways' Liberte, we shared the barge with three other American couples about our age, plus a remarkable crew of four, two British and two French, who did everything without ever looking frazzled. Mark was the captain who steered the barge, did most of the bartending, introduced the dinner wines to us each evening and took care of the bright blooms that decorated the barge deck.

Natalie picked us up and delivered us back to the Hotel Meurice in Paris, took us on drives and excursions and worked as matelote (sailor) in between, hopping on and off the barge to tie us up at every lock. We wondered why so many dogs gathered every time we approached a locktender's cottage until we saw Natalie feeding tidbits of leftover ham to them, as well as tossing bread to the swans on the canal. Severine picked out our local wines and cheeses, (at least three of each cheese at lunch and dinner and two wines at each meal. We had the equivalent of a graduate course by the end of the cruise. Jane was our chef, preparing exquisite meals from local seasonal products – lunches of vegetable salads and fresh fruit served under umbrellas on the sunny deck and course-by-course dinners in the wood-paneled dining room that began with fresh grilled foe gras or cold tomato soup, grilled duck breast or salmon with fresh ginger, a warm tart with homemade apple sorbet or a chocolate mousse with banana pecan ice cream.

Days are easy and effortless, with time to read, work crossword puzzles, chat or doze, perfect for people who want to let city-jangled nerves slow down to a gentle, contented purr. Our cabins were shipshape but comfortable, with built-in beds and cabinetry, plenty of storage, an air conditioner, windows that open and close, and a tiny bath with shower and toilet. There was the option of taking a hot-air balloon over the vineyards, setting down in a field in the last rays of the setting sun to find a crowd of friendly French has gathered to greet you. By the time the champagne was uncorked, everyone was chattering in a mix of fractured French and English. Moments like these last forever in our travel memories.

There are a few things you should know about barges and barging through these exotic rivers. Some barges have 15 as a minimum age for children, except on charter sailings. Barges are really not for babies or toddlers. There are no play areas or places they can get away from the other passengers, and barge galley crews are usually too busy to prepare separate, less sophisticated meals for kids.

We cruised once with two well-behaved young teen-aged boys from Australia who never created problems for the other passengers. If you have small children and you want to cruise the canals, consider renting and handling your own boat (see below) or booking a small charter barge with two or three other families with children and take turns looking after the kids.

Barges are small, but not claustrophobic. Passengers spend a lot of time on deck or in the main lounge rather than the cabins (perhaps because they are usually small), and every barge we know carries bicycles along for side jaunts. You can disembark at any of the many locks and get back on later down the line if you want to go jogging or walking, as well as bicycling.

The prices may seem fairly high compared to some Mediterranean cruise ships but consider the extras that are not included on a regular cruise. The average price per day for barge cruises runs from around $250 to $450 per person while a Mediterranean cruise on a contemporary vessel or new mega ship costs around $300 a day. On a barge, almost everything is included - cocktails and wines, all shore excursions except hot-air ballooning, transfers to and from the barge from Paris in most cases, and bicycles for use anytime. Some barge cruises also include a gourmet dinner at a top-rated restaurant on shore. A few barges may charge for cocktails, but wine with meals is always included.

As for languages, there's no need to speak French unless you want to ask directions or have conversations in the villages or with the lock tenders along the route. Your barge captain and crew are fluent in English, and in some cases are British.

Life aboard a barge is casual. Daytime clothing can be jogging suits, jeans or shorts, whatever is comfortable and appropriate to the weather. In the evenings, you may want to change into something dressier but still casual. A necessity is good walking shoes for the towpath and bike rides. If you plan to go ballooning, layer your clothing for early morning flights, since the weather warms up when the sun gets higher in the sky. If your itinerary includes a meal at a gourmet restaurant, take along a dress-up outfit.

Pack lightly, even if you plan to tour Europe extensively and spend only a small part of you vacation time on the barge. If you have more than two suitcases, you may want to consider storing some of your luggage on shore, perhaps at one of the hotels you'll be using. If you stay at any hotel, in Paris and are booked to come back there the barge cruise, the concierge will store baggage and have it waiting for you on your return. Amenities will not be the same as in a deluxe hotel or on a large cruise ship. Generally you'll find electrical connections but they'll usually be 220 volt with 110 connections limited to electric razors. Some companies provide hair dryers in the cabins. Barge operators may request conservation of fresh water, which means shorter showers.

Not all barges are alike. In the beginning, the novelty of the experience managed to supercede the sometimes basic accommodations – upper and lower bunks and bathroom down the hall – but now you'll find all-suite barges in some cases, and all the hotel barges we've seen have en suite private bathrooms with toilet and shower. It's a favorable sign when the barge brochure shows photographs of the cabins. They're usually located on a lower deck near the waterline so your window will give you close-up views of canal banks and the insides of locks when you negotiating them.

Barge passengers usually linger over drinks and dinner, with after dinner drinks in the dining room or on deck. But, since barges tie up at night in a village or town, you may want to walk in to a nearby café or disco. Conversation is the major pastime aboard most barges. People who enjoy this sort of vacation find they're in the company of like-minded people who have a lot in common with them.

The following are some of the companies that book barge cruises for European canals and rivers. If there seem to be an inordinate number of them, be aware that many of the barge owners may use several marketing companies to sell their sailings.

ABERCROMBIE & KENT

    1520 Kensington Road

    Oak Brook, IL 60523,

    (800) 323-7208

    www.abercrombiekent.com.

Twenty-three barges on canals in France, Holland, Belgium, England and Ireland, featuring wine-tasting, golfing programs in Scotland and England, antique and opera charters.

CONTINENTAL WATERWAYS

    1 Promenade du Rhin

    BP 41748, 21017

    Dijon Cedex, France

    (800) 323-7308

    www.continentalwaterways.com.

Sixteen barges on canals in France, Holland and Belgium featuring wine tastings, family cruises, golfing in France and balloon options. Book through

Abercrombie & Kent (800) 323-7308, Ewaterways (800) 546-4777, or The Barge Broker (800) 275-9794.

ELEGANT CRUISES

24 Vanderventer Ave.
Port Washington, NY 11050
(800) 683-6767
www.elegantcruises.com.

Three barges in Burgundy, Provence and the south of France, plus Scotland which offers golfing packages.

EUROPEAN WATERWAYS

35 Wharf Road
Wraysbury, Staines
Middlesex TW19 5JQ, England
(800) 394-8630 in US
www.gobarging.com.

Six barges with itineraries in France, England, Ireland and Scotland

FRENCH COUNTRY WATERWAYS

PO Box 2195
Duxbury, MA 02331
(800) 323-7308
www.fcwl.com.

Five barges ply the canals of Burgundy, Nivernais, Loire, Lateral a l'Aisne in the Champagne region, and the Marne au Rhin in Alsace-Loraine. The barges are marketed exclusively by the owner company and feature wine tastings and special dinners at Michelin-starred restaurants.

Self-drive Barges

A rapidly-growing segment of canal traffic is aboard self-drive barges. If you're resourceful enough to make your own minor repairs, want to plan your own itineraries and prepare your own meals, by all means consider the less expensive option of renting a barge.

No experience is necessary, say the rental agencies, and you don't even need a license. Instead, you get a guide and a manual, and are checked out on the boat with a demonstration before you take over.

Crown Blue Line, for instance, rents canal boats and barges in France, Holland, Germany, Ireland, Scotland and Italy with dozens of different models that sleep from two to 12. All are fully equipped with bedclothes and towels, cooking utensils, cutlery and glassware. You'll find a refrigerator, sink, cooker with oven grill, bathroom with shower and toilet, hot and cold running water and heating system. Figure on about $725 a week for a basic model sleeping two during the shoulder seasons of early spring and late fall to some $5,000 for a deluxe model that sleeps 10. You can even arrange for your boat to be stocked with a starter kit of groceries. Call them toll-free at (888) 355-9491 for a free color brochure or log onto the website, www.crown-holidays.co.uk.

EXPEDITION VESSELS

Society Expeditions
1520 Kensington Road
Oak Brook, IL 60521
(800) 548-8669
www.societyexpeditions.com

Similar in style to Lindblad Cruises, Society Expeditions' main thrust was to organize archaeological tours for special interest groups. The company has expanded beyond that purpose but still keeps all itineraries as adventures. Vessels are small enough to maneuver in shallow waters so passengers can explore remote areas of the world. The 96-passenger *Society Explorer* holds many firsts in the world of exploration cruising. She is the ship that has sailed the farthest south and north of any vessel other than icebreakers. The 139-passenger *World Discoverer* made the first successful west-to-east transit of the Northwest Passage.

Society Expeditions Cruises, Inc. is owned by Heiko Klein, a German tour and travel operator, and Abercrombie & Kent, a tour company specializing in luxury expedition travel. Jointly, they operate the two expedition vessels that cruise the Antarctic between November and February, then sail to remote destinations for adventure cruises.

WORLD EXPLORER CRUISES

555 Montgomery Street
San Francisco, CA 94111
(800) 854-3835
www.wecruise.com

C.Y. TUNG and the Seaways Foundation own World Explorer Cruises. It has one ship in the fleet, and it promotes voyages as learning experiences. World Explorer purchased the *Enchanted Seas* from Commodore Cruise Line and is operating it as the *Universe Explorer* in the tradition of the line, which is as a floating classroom. The 23,500-ton vessel has had many lives. Built in 1958 as the *Brasil*, she has sailed as the *Volendam, Monarch Sun, Island Sun, Liberte, Canada Star* and *Enchanted Seas* as well as the *Queen of Bermuda*. The 739-passenger *Universe Explorer* has been reconfigured somewhat and has an improved fitness center and an expanded library.

Lectures are the daytime entertainment. She sails on two week Alaska cruises during summer months and to South America in December and January. During the rest of the year, she is a floating university for students attending the Semester at Sea program operated under the auspices of the University of Pittsburgh and the Institute for Shipboard Education. Students are joined by a minority of adult passengers who want continuing education as they circle the world. Priced moderately for non-students, tuition is on the high side. Passengers are more interested in experiencing foreign cultures than in Broadway shows.]

Peter Knego Comments:

"The vessel is beautifully maintained and her spartan decor combines remnants of her American origins, new soft fittings, and some items from the *Universe* (ex *Badger Mariner, Atlantic,* and *Universe Campus*) which was scrapped in early 1996). She has had more careers and name changes than just about any other passenger ship afloat. She has a remarkable assortment of cabins in varying configurations and sports a 15,000 volume library, the largest afloat. Half of the year, *Universe Explorer* circumnavigates the globe as a floating university for the Seawise Foundation's Semester at Sea program, but sails for World Explorer Cruises in Vancouver-based Alaska service during the summer and makes an occasional winter Caribbean cruise. Even with the new mega ships cutting fares, they are still twice the amount World Explorer charges. The *Universe Explorer* sails at capacity. Her unique enrichment lectures programs help keep this ship popular."

PACIFIC RIM CRUISES

Kumgang Cruise
www.kumgang.ke

The company is owned by Hyundai Motors and operates three ships between North and South Korea, which is counter to what with have been reading in the press about relations between the two Koreas. Basically voyages are between ports in the two countries. Passengers are almost all Korean, with a small percentage of Japanese and others from Pacific countries. Ships are all former cruise ships and very little has been done to change configurations. Big change is in cruise style which is Korean-style.

Hyundai Kumgang is the former *SuperStar Capricorn, Golden Princess, Birka Queen, Sunward* and *Royal Viking Sky*. The *Hyundai Pongnae* is the former *SuperStar Sagittarius* and *Sun Viking*. The *Hyundai Pungak* is the former *Island Princess* and *Island Venture*.

North Americans will not be comfortable in this all-Korean environment unless they speak Korean.

INSIDER TIP

It is difficult to get information in English about Kumgang Cruises. I recommend www.cruise.com. It specializes in cruises (and information on unique cruises in non-touristy areas of the world. The site has links to small boat operators whose vessels cruise unique and adventurous rivers and ports. Examples are: African Safari Cruise Club, Blue Lagoon Cruises in Fiji, Bora Bora Pearl Cruises in Tahiti, Captain Cook Cruises which cruise the Great Barrier Reef and Fiji, Kangaroo Explorer Cruises in Queensland, Siamcruise Company in the Andaman Sea and Vietnam, Songline Cruises of Indonesia, Spice Island Cruises in Bali and other small companies with vessels that accommodate on average about 25 passengers.

STAR CRUISES

391B Orchard Road #13-01
Ngee Ann City, Tower B
Singapore 0923
65-226-1168
www.starcruises.com

Star Cruises is to the Pacific Rim what Carnival Cruise Line is to the Caribbean. An upstart company that started in 1993 with a single ship, it is now the fourth largest cruise line in the world. It purchased Norwegian Cruise Line and Orient Lines a couple of years ago and is in newbuild mode for all of its divisions. The company is effectively putting the Pacific region on the map as a key international cruise destination. It was the first in the region to initiate regular cruises from Singapore for a growing number of locals as well as for Japanese, Chinese and Thai travelers. Star Cruises is setting its sites on the Australian and North American markets.

Star Cruises was founded by hotel and casino executive Eddy Lee. Their first two ships were converted Swedish passenger ferries, *Star Aquarius* (former *Athena*) and *Star Pisces* (former *Kalypso*). Demand for Pacific "fun" cruising was so great, they bought the Cunard *Crown Jewel* and both the *Aurora I* and *Aurora II*, small luxury vessels leased by Classical Cruises from a German Bank. The company also purchased the *Sun Viking* from Royal Caribbean International. The vessel was renamed *SuperStar Sagittarius*.

Star Cruises presently operates eight cruise vessels in the Pacific Rim. They are *Star Pisces*; *SuperStar Aries, SuperStar Gemini, SuperStar Leo* and *SuperStar Virgo*; and the *MegaStar Aries, MegaStar Taurus* and *SuperStar Capricorn*. The second Libra-class new building - *Norwegian Dawn* (formerly *SuperStar Scorpio*), is 91,000-tons and is sailing in the Norwegian Cruise Line fleet.

The Cruise Ferries brand which was launched in 2001 currently operates the *m.v. Wasa Queen* offering cruise-ferry services between Hong Kong and Xiamen (China).

Crews are Scandinavian on the decks and Asian in service staffs. Star Cruises introduced all-inclusive pricing to Pacific area home ported vessels. Rates differ between the three types of vessels, but to most passengers from the Pacific region, they consider them lower than flying to a land-based resort. However, seasonal reductions are inevitable. Average Daily Rates run around $200 to $360 a day, per person. There have been advertised specials that cut those rates in almost half.

Itineraries are of great interest to North Americans and European travelers. Depending on season and the ship, there are three and four night Gulf of Thailand Cruises that sail round trip from Laem Chabang (Bangkok) to Ko-Kong (Cambodia).

Also, round trip from Singapore to Bangkok with stops in China on three to seven-night cruises and three night Singapore to Phuket voyages.

Star Cruises' marketing emphasis has been on the Asian market, but with the planned opening of offices in the United States and London, there will be aggressive marketing. Rates are attractive and itineraries are interesting, but the few Americans who have sailed report a totally different cruise experience with a lot of entertainment focus on gambling.

On board lifestyle is very busy with planned activities and a lot to do. With most of the passengers from Asian countries, it is safe to assume that passengers will vacation on board Asian-style, which means many families – young and old. Gambling casinos are large and very crowded.

Asian travelers consider casual attire suitable for most occasions. "Smart casual" attire is required in the specialty restaurants. For shore visits, it's casual wear. (Note: Skimpy beachwear is inappropriate in Muslim countries) Comfortable walking shoes or sandals are a must (but remember to remove them at the door if you are visiting temples). Of course, a swimsuit, sunglasses, sunscreen lotion, and a beach towel are staple items. Bring sportswear or gym gear if you are planning to play golf, tennis, or workout. And, needless to say, bring a camera and lots of film.

INSIDER TIP
Most Asian passengers dress up for dinner, but not in tuxedos and long gowns. It's more likely that the women will wear colorful local finery which could include kimonos or those magnificent long dresses.

Most foreign currencies are accepted on board at prevailing exchange rates. The onboard currency will be that of the country where the ship is based. Singapore dollars for cruises out of Singapore, US dollars for cruises out of Bangkok. Most major c credit cards (Amex, Visa, Diners, Masters, and JCB) are accepted, along with traveler's checks, but not personal checks.

The multi-lingual staff hails from 26 nations and they all speak English. There's a "no tipping policy" but it is loosely enforced. Not included features are shore excursions, optional dining in some restaurants, items of personal nature such as beverages, phone calls, shop purchases, laundry, beauty treatments, hairdressing, massage services, medical services, port charges, government taxes and fees.

Star Cruises started the freestyle dining trend. Eat when you want, almost where you want and with whomever you want. All meals are included during the cruise at the main dining restaurants. Or, opt for the alternative restaurants at charges of from $10 to $20. Reservations are required.

INSIDER TIP

Star Cruises has almost a class system for passengers. The cabin or suite that you book determines your status. Balcony Class passengers with a Red Access Card (stateroom key) may dine at selected restaurants and may also enjoy set meals as well as a la carte menus that are available at a moderate charge except during the Gala Dinner. Admiral Class passengers enjoy all of the Balcony Class privileges. World Class have all of the above, plus priority in reservations for meals and private invitations to the Captain's table.

Reports indicate that the food is good, in fact very good. Menus which were expanded to keep pace with the increased number of International passengers from other than the Pacific and Orient regions now feature international-type cuisine with greater choices. Regardless of price paid for a vacation, Asians expect very good food and service which they say Star Cruises delivers.

OCEANIC CRUISE LTD.
5757 West Century Boulevard, Suite 390
Los Angeles, CA 90045
www.oceaniccruises.com

Owned by the Japanese SMI Group (Shoa), Oceanic Cruise was formed in 1989 to operate and market the 120-passenger *Oceanic Grace*. Definitely a high-end luxury product and priced to reflect the ambience, the vessel offers a gentle mix of Oriental and Occidental flavors. The 5,050-ton boutique-quality ship was built in 1989 and is in the Seabourn-Silversea class. The staff is bilingual, and both Japanese and American specialties are offered in the dining rooms. Itineraries make a one-week around-Japan circle and offer the unique opportunity to visit some of Japan's remote villages. Almost all the passengers are high-income Japanese couples ranging in age upward from 40.

China

Yangtze River cruising is about as exotic as it gets. In Chinese, it is called Chagjiang, meaning "Long River." It has been a 4,000-mile lifeline of China as it rises from the Tibetan plateau and plunges through mountain passes to form a border between Hubei and Hunan before reaching the plains of Jiangsu and Shanghai. The scenic river is the cradle of Chinese civilization.

It is the great commercial highway of China, and passenger ferries, commercial barges, and now cruise boats provide a busy traffic pattern. Passenger ships began sailing the Yangtze in the early 1980s with vessels equipped for American passengers. Favorite itineraries include The Three Gorges (Qutang, Wu, and Xiling). Shore excursions offer trips to the many tributaries, local villages, and historic towns.

More than 25 ships offer cruises through the Gorges. Most are owned by government authorities and a few by local companies. Most are marketed through the China Changjiang Cruise Company, a joint venture between Chinese and Hong Kong companies. Ships operate on regular itineraries during the season, which runs from March through November. They offer three-, four, and five-night cruises either upstream or downstream from Wuhan.

HOLIDAY INN/ASIA PACIFIC
33 Canton Road, Tower 3, 20/F
Kowloon, Hong Kong

The company operates two vessels managed on a Crown Plaza level by Holiday Inns. Boats are fast and accommodate 156 passengers in near-cruise-ship style with all the trimmings. Well, almost all.

ORIENT EXPRESS CRUISES
1155 Avenue of the Americas
New York, NY 10011
(800) 524-2420
www.orientexpres.com

The name of the ship is enough to describe the experience. How does *Road to Mandaly* sound? The vessel has 70 cabins and is being offered as a counterpart to the famous Orient Express. It runs between Mandalay and Pagain and is generally sold as part of a China package. The ship was redone in 1996 and now serves all passengers in a single seating.

REGAL CHINA CRUISES

57 West 38th Street
New York, NY 10018
(800) 270-7245
www.regalcruises.com

The company operates three 289-passenger vessels designed and built specifically for Yangtze River cruising. *The Princess Sheena, Princess Jeannie,* and *Princess Elaine* are the longest on the river and are headquartered in Nanjing. Five decks high, they have most of the amenities of a mini-cruise ship, but there is a great deal of onboard emphasis on Chinese culture. Regal China Cruises is a joint Sino-American venture.

SMARTOURS

501 Fifth Avenue, Suite 812
New York, NY 10017
(800) 337-7773
www.smartours.com

This is a fairly new company specializing in China and Yangtze River cruises. It offers an 18-night Yangtze River cruise aboard the *Yangtze President,* round-trip air from Los Angeles, intra-China flights, ground transportation and transfers, deluxe and superior first-class hotels, all outside cabins, all shore excursions, local guides, and most meals on selected departure dates for as low as $2,299 per person. The *Yangtze President* is one of the newest and nicest of the ships sailing the river. Launched in 1995, it is fully air-conditioned and has all outside cabins facing the river, lower beds, and private baths. There are two restaurants, a bar, lounge, sauna, small fitness center, and limited entertainment, which no one minds. It's the Yangtze River that provides the entertainment.

INSIDER TIP

It's hard to beat the price and the all-inclusive features of the China packages offered by this company.

VICTORIA CRUISES

5708 39th Avenue
Woodside, NY 11377
(800) 3348-8084
www.victoriacruises.com

Victoria Cruises operates four vessels, *Victoria I, II, III* and *IV*, which look more like Mississippi riverboats than Chinese anything. Each accommodates 154 passengers. A new series of vessels, Victoria 21st Century, Victoria Three Kingdoms, and Victoria Dragon, began operating on three- and six-day cruises on the Yangtze. They are geared to North American travelers and are as luxurious as they get in this region. They entered service in 1996.

COASTAL AND RIVER CRUISE LINES
(Wherever there's a river, there are boats in operation. Here is a sampling of what's available)

ADVENTURE ASSOCIATES

913150 Colt Road, Suite 110
Dallas, TX 75240
(972) 907-0414
www.metropolitantouring.com

The company represents Galápagos Cruises and its vessels, the *Isabel II* and the *Santa Cruz*. Both offer one-week or shorter cruises to the Galápagos Islands.

ALASKA MARINE HIGHWAY

Box 25535
Juneau, AK 99802
(800) 642-0066
www.dot.state.ak.us

The company operates ferries along the coast and takes on passengers and RVs for overnights or for point-to-point travel.

AMAZON TOURS AND CRUISES

Requena 336
Iquitos, Peru
(800) 423-2791
www.amazontours.net

The company is one of the largest operators of cruises to the Galápagos Islands. Seven vessels rotate on three-to-seven-night cruises. Accommodations are tight, but cruises are very popular with ecology-minded travelers.

ST. LAWRENCE CRUISE LINES

253 Ontario Street
Kingston, Ontario, Canada K7L 2Z4

The company operates one-way voyages on the 64-passenger *Canadian Empress*. This is scenic cruising through the international seaway, the Thousand Islands, and the Ottawa River. Cabins are small, but they are all outside and the views are spectacular.

Nile Cruising

Travelers bent on exploring Egypt with a view from the Nile have a choice of navigable craft ranging from a felucca to a 185-passenger vessel. Cruises range from three to six days with an occasional 10 days between Cairo and Luxor. I do not recommend the longer cruise unless you are an Egyptologist.

Standards for luxury are different from what we North Americans have come to expect. Vessels have improved in recent years, however, and there is more competition for passengers these days. It's hard to recommend a single company, but there is a choice.

I visited a number of crafts and sailed two in recent years. With an increase in the number of Nile riverboats, sanitary conditions and accommodations have improved.

There are startling similarities between all Nile riverboats. Because of highs and lows on the river, boats are styled like barges, with flat bottoms for maneuverability. Shore excursions are included in the total price. Cabins are usually very small, except on some of the newer boats operated by hotel companies. These offer sumptuous suites.. The best time to cruise is when the weather cools off (late October through March, maybe early

April). Food is from fair to mediocre, at best. Ships are not always spotless, but are okay for up to five days on board. When I was in Luxor last year, many of the Nile boats were laid up because of a shortage of tourists. It is impossible to know which boats will be sailing in 2003. Travel agencies should have the information.

INSIDER TIP

If you decide to cruise the Nile, there are a few things you should know. It is not uncommon for travelers on the Nile to suffer stomach upsets, so several notes of caution should be sounded. Come prepared with anti-diarrhea medication. The boat's nurse is quick with injections (for a charge), which works for most passengers. Do not drink the water offered on board ship. That includes water in the dining room and in the cabins. The ship lounge is happy to sell large, sealed bottles of mineral water for three dollars each. We discovered the same size bottles and brands sold at stands at all stops along the Nile for 50 cents. Consumption of fluids is a must in this hot, dry climate, and our 10 glasses of water a day added up quickly. In lounges, drink local beer. It is good, thirst-quenching, and a lot cheaper than other alcoholic beverages.

If you are a fussy eater, food could be a problem. The morning eggs were of the powdered variety, the no-choice noon meal was usually lamb, and dinner was always the same—a buffet with rice, a noodle dish, and lamb; occasionally a second meat dish was served. Desserts were pretty good. In all fairness, we were not on one of the newer "deluxe" boats.

Again in fairness, the antiquities of Luxor, Abu Simbel, and Aswan made up for the inconveniences on the boat. My favorite in every port, after the monuments and tombs, was a leisurely horse-and-carriage ride through local markets.

ABERCROMBIE & KENT INTERNATIONAL

1520 Kensington Rd, Suite 212
Oak Brook, IL 60523
(800) 323-7308
www.abercrombiekent.com

Company operates two vessels, *Sun Boat III* and *Sun Boat IV*. Each has 42 cabins and sails on five to eight night cruises between Luxor and Aswan seasonally.

MENA HOUSE OBEROI HOTEL

Pyramid Road Giza
Cairo, Egypt
(800) 223-4978 (Misr Travel handles bookings in U.S.)
www.oberoirhotels.com

Boats are operated by the Oberoi Hotels. *Sheherayar, Shehrizah, Oberoi Philae* and *Nephitis* are considered deluxe. The *Oberoi Philae* looks like a paddlewheeler. There are private balconies for Nile viewing, and large windows in cabins and suites. It's probably the dressiest product on the Nile. Men are required to wear jacket and ties in the restaurant for dinner. Ships sail between Luxor and Aswan on three to six-night cruises

NABILA NILE CRUISES

605 Market St., Suite 507
San Francisco, CA 94105
(415) 979-0160
www.nabilatours.com

Company operates one of the largest fleets with six vessel that offer three, four and seven-night cruises between Luxor and Aswan.

SONESTA INTERNATIONAL HOTELS

200 Clarendon St
Boston, MA 02116
(617) 421-5400
www.sonesta.com

Company has three ship operates on four to six night Nile cruises between Luxor and Aswan. The most deluxe are the *Sun Goddess* which has four suites and the *Egyptian Moon Goddess* which has 54 junior suites and two presidential suites.

Adventurous travelers, curious about the sea, ships and out-of-the-way places, dream of freighter and cargo voyages. Show me a dreamer and I'll show you someone planning (and hoping) for a slow boat to China—a leisurely sailing to a distant island with a strange-sounding name. Talk with half the cruise ship passengers sailing the seas in a reasonable facsimile of luxury and I'll bet they'll say, "Some day, I'm going to take a freighter cruise around the world." They should know that what they have on board that cruise ship is not what they are going to get on board a freighter, providing they are among the fortunate few who succeed in getting space on a cargo liner, which is often confused with freighters.

Freighter travel is not for everyone. It's for people who want to stop the world and get off for a spell. Freighters are for dreamers who visualize slow boats to no place in particular, around the world in general. Freighters are for loners who yearn for the peace that comes with solitude and lazy days at sea. Freighters are not for travelers who lean heavily on cruise directors and planned activities. Freighters will be daily and nightly disappointments for passengers who look forward to lavish buffets, service and companionship.

To dyed-in-the-wool freighter fans, amenities of old liners are nothing compared to the aura of romance and adventure found on working cargo ships. Although today's freighters, like their sister ships designated "cruise," may be a far cry from the tramp steamers of yesteryear that picked up and discharged their cargo at random, they still have the timeless appeal of a Hemingway novel. To those of us who sail vicariously on the rusted buckets that carried Somerset Maugham across the South Seas, the lure of freighter travel is still a powerful draw.

INSIDER TIP

I use the words "freighter," "cargo liner" and "tramp steamer" almost interchangeably. This is a good point at which to clarify differences in what we commonly call "freighters."

Containerships are the most common on the seas today. Larger containerships serve intercontinental trades. Smaller ones, usually referred to as feeders, feed the larger ships with containers. General Cargo and Refrigerated Cargo (Banana) Ships carry goods like large machinery, steel plates, lumber, etc. and are built in various shapes and forms to accommodate a variety of goods. These ships often spend more time in ports unloading which is an advantage for passengers who find themselves with plenty of time to explore.

Mail and Supply Ships connect local communities, such as the Marquesas Islands in French Polynesia or along the coasts of Norway and Labrador, bringing mail and supplies. Typically the voyages take two to four weeks with short and frequent port calls, from one hour to one day, and most of the passengers on board are local commuters. The British Royal Mail Ship, *St. Helena*, makes longer trips from the U.K. to South Africa as well as to the Ascension, Canary and St. Helena Islands. And, while the Windjammer's fleet of tall ships sails around the Caribbean Islands, the *Amazing Grace* shuttles between the islands carrying passengers as well as supplies.

Trampers have unreliable itineraries. They are mainly bulk-carriers, carrying general cargo, loose grain, coal and other ores in holds below deck. They often have only one or two passenger cabins.

Cargo vessels are the most common of freight carrying vessels. Although seagoing lifestyles have changed dramatically, there are still fleets of passenger-carrying cargo vessels. They offer a special shipboard experience appreciated by a dedicated following convinced that passage by freighter is the ultimate trip. If you want this kind of experience, you had better hurry. Cargo passenger ships may well be the real travel bargains of today, but the choice is narrow and opportunities are limited.

The days of $50 per diems on freighters are gone. Freighters are no longer cheap, but they are relatively inexpensive compared to what cruise ships, even budget priced, charge for similar itineraries. A freighter, for example, will not be cheaper than a plane to the same destination, but it will be a lot more fun and take a lot more time to get there. Add the plane fare with the cost of hotels and food and the total will turn out to be that freighter bargain you were looking for.

The long, leisurely days in port offered by boom-loading freighters have been replaced by the short unloading time it takes to move containerized freight from ship to shore or the reverse. True, the traveler can still almost completely stop time on board a freighter, but a quick look at the way ships of the future are heading will probably make this type of clock-stopping another chapter in books filled with tales of the good old days of sailing.

By name alone, freighter-passenger and cargo-passenger vessels separate themselves from cruise ships. By profile, they also differ drastically. Unfortunately for freighter lovers, during the past three decades the number of dual-purpose ships has declined dramatically and there's a distinct possibility this type of vessel will soon become totally obsolete. There is some good news. More cargo vessels seem to be taking on from two to four passengers.

So what's the difference between freighters and cargo liners? Freighters are usually smaller versions of cruise ships when it comes to tonnage. Accommodation of cargo-handling gear changes the silhouette and the super-structure is smaller. Oceangoing dry-cargo liners usually have gross tonnage between 5,000 and 12,000 and have been specifically designed for cargo. The term "liner" is applied to a ship that operates on regular service between ports. If you're wondering how a tramp steamer got its name, wonder no more. "Tramp" was applied to a ship employed on charter to take cargo from port to port, at any time, anywhere in the world. The cargo liner, referred to as a freighter in some countries, generally has four or five holds and is designed for easy discharge of cargo. The way the ship rides is dependent upon the weight distribution of cargo, so ships are designed to carry the heaviest loads amidships.

According to the International Conventions and Conferences on Marine Safety, a passenger-carrying freighter or cargo liner is a vessel principally engaged in transporting goods but licensed to carry passengers as well. The most common definition of a passenger freighter is a vessel that carries cargo and takes from two to 12 passengers along for the ride. Cargoliners generally carry goods and from 20 to 100 passengers. Freighters and cargo liners have other features in common. Cargo is most important on these ships. Cargo governs the ports visited and the length of time in port. Cargo pays the tab and builds company profits. Passengers ride along at the convenience of the company and, some say, to keep sea traditions alive. More and more shipping companies are opting to convert valuable space occupied by passengers into non-eating, non-service-demanding cargo.

Although your dreams of freighter travel may resemble heaven, there are disadvantages you should know about before you opt for this means of sailing the seas.

Know Before You Book Passage

Freighters do not usually operate on definite time schedules. Some never call at the ports listed in brochures. Ports of call depend on the call of the cargo. Changes are often made mid-sea and it is difficult for passengers to pre-arrange a visit with friends in any port. Ports of call are added and subtracted according to loading and off-loading requirements.

There are and age restrictions on freighters. With 12 or less passengers, freighters do not carry doctors, and each company sets its own requirements and age limitations. Everyone over 65 is usually required to have a medical health certificate testifying to good physical and mental health. Most companies spell out specifics clearly in their brochures. They will accept "no one with a history of heart disease or other serious organic problems; no one who may require continuous medical or personal attention; nor handicapped persons dependent on canes, crutches or wheelchairs." Some companies have an age limit of 76, others of 79. Very few have no age limitations. Check restrictions before booking.

Freighter travel is not for children. Most companies discourage or refuse to accept them as passengers. This is an easy-to-understand rule. Imagine 11 senior-aged passengers climbing the rails after 45 days at sea with a hyper under-10-year-old.

On the plus side, freighters generally take rough seas very well. Cargo-carrying vessels are broad-beamed with low superstructures. This, combined with heavy cargo below the water level, acts as a stabilizing influence. Even in rough seas, with decks awash, cargo keeps the vessel down and reduces the motion of the ocean.

Every passenger goes first class on a freighter because cargo pays the ship's operation expenses, making freighter travel one of the best bargains in the marketplace. Rates are on a per day, per person basis, but most companies have found there's little profit in carrying passengers.

Because freighters operate on indefinite schedules, if a voyage is sold as a 60-day cruise and it takes 70 days before the ship delivers you back to a home-port, there's no extra charge for the additional days. On the other hand, if you paid for 60 days and you're back at home port in less time, companies refund a per diem amount based on the number of days you missed on board ship. Cargo-carrying vessels heading for a scheduled port may be rerouted mid-ocean because a lucrative freight-hauling contract has been negotiated and is waiting to be picked up halfway around the world.

Since freighter travel requires a lot of time and less money, average age of passengers is in the high 60s to mid-70s. Don't expect 12 swingers cruising around the world. Freighter passengers are more apt to get high on a round of bridge than a clandestine meeting with a ship's officer. During summer months, average age is lower because many teachers plan ahead for this less expensive route to the world.

INSIDER TIP

A single woman will not be accepted by most freighter companies for a voyage on which she is the only female booked. Call it what you like but I call it unfair.

Which Freighter Cruise?

Where do you want to go? In addition to the leisurely pace of getting there, a freighter cruise is taking you to a faraway area of the world. Your choice of destinations will determine the length of the voyage and sometimes the flag and registry of the vessel. You won't be hungry on the ship. The flag flying from the mast usually indicates the ethnic background of the crew; chances are good that if the flag is Greek, the moussaka will be excellent.

Naturally, the longer the cruise, the more ports on the itinerary. But remember, containerized cargo liners do not—repeat, do not—spend much time in port. Huge loading cranes lift the containers from trucks to ship or vice versa, and longshoremen work around the clock. Time is money and that's what freighter and cargo hauling is all about.

A freighter cruise doesn't come with a guaranteed itinerary, but you will know which area of the world you will be sailing. Select the ship going to the Orient, if that's where you want to go, or to the Mediterranean, if those calm, blue waters intrigue you. You may not visit all the Greek islands, but the ship will pull in at a couple of the larger islands.

Along with the area of the world, consider the time you want to spend. Then combine both time and area with ethnic preferences and you'll come up with one or two ships worthy of further investigation.

INSIDER TIP

If you are looking for more time in port, select bulk-loading ships. It takes longer to move the cargo. Containerized vessels have speeded required loading and unloading time, so time in ports is shorter. Semi-containerized ships are a compromise.

Booking Passage

Not all travel agents are informed about freighters and few want to spend the time it takes to complete a confirmed booking on a freighter. Professional agents will tell you they cannot spare the time needed to keep abreast of ever-changing freighter schedules and availability. Thus, most of the advance planning and research is up to the traveler. Since time for freighter travelers should be discretionary or at least not listed as a priority, you should be willing to spend some of it checking availability, itineraries and ships.

Freighters do not advertise voyages to the public and schedules are not published frequently. Select when you want to travel but be flexible. The itinerary of your choice may force you to change your plans to meet the ship's schedule.

Most of the more popular freighter voyages are booked at least a year in advance. The traveler willing to sail on short notice has an excellent chance of being on board when the ship leaves port. That's why I say freighter travel is for the traveler whose lifestyle is flexible. Cancellations come up all the time and, prior to sailing, freighter companies do call travel agents who register their clients on waiting lists.

If you decide to do your homework and write directly to the freighter company, request brochures with layouts of the ship, up-to-date fares and cabin availability. They will reply with first-available sailing dates and you'll understand the importance of far-in-advance planning. If there is no space on the sailing of your choice, ask to be wait-listed, even if you are forced to cancel your plans later on. You are not required to pay a deposit until space is confirmed on a specific voyage. As with every rule, this one also has exceptions. A few companies do require substantial deposits when space is requested. When that happens, be sure to purchase cancellation and trip-interruption insurance so if you must cancel the trip or return in mid-voyage because of health reasons you will not lose all your money.

If you decide to be wait-listed, be prepared with passport, required documentation and inoculations. You may receive a telephone call a few days before sailing saying space is available. You should also request space from more than one company. Second and third choices avoid disappointment.

Ports of Embarkation

Certain freighters, like cruise ships, have homeports and other ports where they embark cargo and passengers. Frequently, even though your space on the voyage has been confirmed, the ship will not confirm your port of embarkation. You will be notified a few weeks before sailing of the port and embarkation times. If you arrive in the port city before embarkation day, be sure to contact the ship's port agent and advise him of where you can be reached in case of a last-minute change.

Passenger-carrying freighters sail from Albany, Baltimore, Charleston, Los Angeles, Miami, Milwaukee, New Orleans, New York, Norfolk, Philadelphia, Portland, San Francisco, Seattle, Tacoma, Vancouver and Wilmington. You can and should get the port agent's name, address and telephone number from the freighter company when you receive your passage tickets and instructions.

INSIDER TIP

Do not buy non-refundable airline tickets. I suggest one-way airline tickets, then an e-mail from the ship for your return flight. Your port of embarkation is not necessarily your port of debarkation. In most instances, freighter companies reserve the right to return you to your country of origin but not necessarily to the same city. Check the conditions of your passage.

Life Aboard a Freighter

Travel by freighter doesn't mean you'll be roughing it in any sense of the word. There's nothing "tramp" about this type of travel. True, it is less structured and less formal than cruise ship travel, but amenities in many forms compensate. Freighters carrying 12 or fewer passengers cruise at speeds comparable to other ocean going vessels and many have attractively decorated passenger areas. The decor is not as plush as on some cruise ships, yet not as drab as on others. A specific area is set aside for passenger use and there is always a small lounge for recreational activities. This room sometimes doubles as the dining room. Passengers are free to roam the decks except for restricted areas and are free to mix with officers.

Cabins: All cargoliners have outside cabins with facilities. Cabins are generally sold on a per person, double occupancy basis. Cabins are equipped with twin beds (not bunks), table or writing desk, sometimes a small sofa, a chair, and two closets. Newer ships have tubs as well as showers. There is no room service but cabins are cleaned daily and organized by a steward. Freighter cabins are generally larger than on newer cruise ships, perhaps not as lavish, but just as comfortable.

Facilities: There is always a lounge and/or bar and a small library. Deck chairs and steamer rugs are provided without charge. There is plenty of deck space even on container ships for lounging, walking and exercise. Some freighters even have swimming pools. Valet/laundry service is not provided but most ships have a washer and dryer for passenger use. Ships are heated and air-conditioned. There is no beauty shop, no barbershop and no ship store. Passengers are usually permitted to purchase essentials at the crew shop.

Eating on Board: You'll notice I didn't call this "dining." Passengers eat with the officers and the quality of the food varies from ship to ship. Generally, it is not gourmet dining but it is first-class and service is good. Food-service hours are much earlier than on cruise ships. There is no cabin service but an open pantry is available at most hours and is stocked with do-it-yourself sandwich makings, fruits and beverages. Because passengers eat what the officers eat, food depends on the tastes of the captain. Passengers have reported sailing with captains who have French-trained chefs cooking up gourmet delights. Normal meal hours on a freighter are: breakfast from 7:30 a.m. to 8:30 a.m.; mid-morning tea or coffee; lunch from 11:30 a.m. to 12:30 p.m.; tea at 3 p.m.; happy hour at 5 p.m. for cocktails and conversation; and dinner around 6 p.m. Special diets cannot be accommodated. There is usually a choice of main courses (perhaps three or four) but don't expect caviar and lobster. All passengers eat at one seating.

Drinking on Board: Freighters have well-stocked bars or cocktail lounges and drinks are priced lower than on cruise ships. Wine is reasonably priced and sometimes served with meals at no cost. There's no rule against a bottle in the cabin if you are so inclined.

INSIDER TIP

Containerized vessels mean decks covered with containers and, unless you select your cabin carefully, you could spend the voyage with a view of a container instead of the sea. Study deck plans and make sure your cabin doesn't face fore (the bow of the ship). That's one area always filled with containers.

Ship Safety and Sanitation: All ships boarding passengers in U.S. ports must comply with U.S. Coast Guard and Safety of Life at Sea regulations. U.S.

Coast Guard officers inspect vessels and the same stringent rules applied to cruise ships apply to freighters. This is also true of U.S. Public Health inspections. You'll find galley ratings for cleanliness in the same listings that include cruise ships. Very few freighters or cargo liners pass U.S. Public Health inspections with flying colors. The galleys are clean but they are not set up in the style outlined in these inspections. For instance, galleys on board freighters are too small to have the required footage between edible and nonedible supplies. I wouldn't worry about sanitation on board freighters. Passengers are in very close contact with the captain and if conditions are good enough for him and his highly paid officers of the sea, they are good enough for me.

Entertainment: You're on your own, so you and the other passengers better like each other. Bring plenty of reading material and brush up on your bridge and backgammon. There is no entertainment planned except for movies two or three times a week. The crew sometimes puts on a farewell show and the passengers sometimes entertain the crew. But there's work to do on board a freighter and officers and crew retire early. So do passengers.

Tipping: The only two crewmembers that passengers are obliged to tip are the waiter and the room steward. Some lines recommend a gratuity as low as $1 a day for each; others recommend you split about one percent of your total fare between the two.

What to Wear: Casual is the key word. Dress for the weather and comfort. Men should wear jackets and ties when officers dress but, on most freighters, this happens only once during the voyage. Leave the tuxedo and gowns at home. Women can get away with almost anything but favorites include jeans, skirts, dresses and jackets. Jewelry, furs and long dresses are out of place on board freighters. Bring wash-and-wearables and leave the short shorts at home.

Cruise Lengths: Some freighters carry passengers only on a round-trip basis; others traveling the Atlantic, for instance, carry passengers for 10 days into one or two ports in either direction or round-trip; still others permit passengers to break long voyages and fly back from certain ports. There also are freighter voyages that practically circumnavigate the globe. It's the ultimate bargain in an around-the-world cruise that could last five or six months.

Itineraries and schedules: vary greatly, so it is impossible to print a complete guide. It would be outdated before the book could gather a speck of dust on the shelf. At the end of this chapter is a list of typical voyages with names and addresses of freighter lines and freighter/cargo liners sailing from U.S. ports on a fairly regular basis. Some freighter voyages have been known to last 120 days; others terminate after a week.

Rates: Although not as inexpensive as in the old tramp-steamer days, freighter travel averages out at between $85 and $150 a day, depending on the ship, facilities offered and accommodations. Cost can go as low as $50 a day and as high as $250.

What to Bring on Board: Bring items such as cosmetics, shampoo, hair dryer, transformer, adapters, film, scotch tape, paper clips, rubber bands, string, pens, playing cards, an alarm clock, a room freshener (if odors bother you), a sewing kit, scissors, cleaning fluid, laundry soap and a washcloth. And, lots of books! Ships have what they call a "slop chest"—a small store that carries basics such as toothpaste and shampoo. Freighters are not equipped to supply passengers with some of the "necessities" of life available on cruise ships.

INSIDER TIP

Bring a few extra passport photos along. They'll come in handy if the ship puts in at an unannounced port and visas are required. The port agent will come aboard and take care of those arrangements if it becomes necessary. Also, carry on your favorite brand of aspirin, writing paper, and lots of reading material. Don't forget a supply of traveler's checks and you'll find a stack of single dollar bills handy on board ship and in ports. You can bank them with the purser while at sea. Of course, bring all your prescription medicines and written prescriptions, sunglasses and your usual travel gear. You might want to bring a pocket-size dictionary if the ship's crew speaks a language you don't.

In Port: Unlike cruise ships, there is no social director to brief you on what to do and see once the ship ties up in a strange port. So good guidebooks are a must. Buy one covering the general area of your voyage and then map your sightseeing plans for the day ashore. Some of your fellow passengers might like to join you and sometimes the ship's officers plan a sightseeing tour and invite passengers to participate. The ship's port agent is generally on hand to greet you on arrival and will assist with sightseeing plans; but remember, freighters do not dock at passenger terminals. The assigned dock for your freighter could be a couple of miles from where passenger ships land. Tourist-information agencies are usually located at the passenger dock or pier, so scrounging for information may become a problem.

To be prepared, write to the tourist offices of the ports listed in the original scheduled itinerary. Request maps, tours, taxi and bus routes, and prices. Most will be happy to load you down with information. Another approach is to talk with the crew on board the freighter. They probably call at the same ports regularly and will be delighted to share little-known, offbeat restaurants and retreats with you. I'm told that crew tours are great. They are inexpensive because the total cost of the bus and guide is divided among participants. It is not a money making proposition for the ship but more a matter of morale boosting.

Ports visited by freighters are sometimes smaller, little known and usually still unspoiled by cruise ship passengers who visit by the hundreds and thousands. "Unspoiled" also means less expensive for shopping and sightseeing. If shopping interests you, check with crew members. They know the best stores and best values. Before arrival, the captain announces time in port. He will post the hour by which all passengers must be back on board. This does not mean the ship will sail at the exact time. She may sail six hours later if more cargo arrives so you should keep checking back with the port agent. All ships will furnish local-contact telephone numbers and addresses prior to allowing passengers to leave.

INSIDER TIP

Don't waste time in port; it's probably your most precious commodity. If you decide on public transportation, be sure you know where the bus or streetcar is going and when it is returning. The worst thing you can do is to get lost in a country where there are few English-speaking visitors. And, as with cruise ships, if you miss the boat, you're on your own! Best advice is to subscribe to TravelTips, a magazine devoted to travel by freighter and cargo liner, P. O. Box 580218, Flushing, NY 11358 (www.traveltips.com) and to contact Freighter Travel News, P. O. Box 12693, Salem, OR 97309 (www.freighterworld.com). Both companies specialize in freighter travel and have availability information readily available. You will notice that many of the freighters use those companies to handle bookings and information.

Ships of the Freighter World

A Sampling

All rates quoted are per person, double occupancy, and based on round-trip unless otherwise specified. Daily rates quoted are approximate and subject to change.

BANK LINE

Freighter World Cruises
180 South Lake Avenue, Suite 335
Pasadena, CA 91101
(800) 531-7774
www.aws.co.uk

Registry: Isle of Man. Age limit: 82. Officers are British and Polish. Crew is from Poland and Bangladesh.

Facilities on board are first-class. Passenger areas are spacious. Most popular voyages for Americans are on the *Arunbank, Foulebank, Speybank* and *Teignbank.* Ships are cargo vessels that carry bulk and containers, as well as 12 passengers on each. There are monthly departures from Dunkirk, France, for around the world cruises that last about 120 days. Vessels sometimes leave from a southeastern U.S. port and sail to South Africa, then Brazil, before returning to Savannah. The round-the-world itinerary is booked long in advance because it is sensational.

Ships were built in the 1983 and in 1986 refurbished to carry 12 passengers each. Segments of 26-to-64-days are sometimes available on world voyages. Rates run about $112 per day.

BLUE STAR LINE

TravelTips
16307 Depot Road
Flushing, NY 11358
(800) 531-7774
www.traveltips.com

Registry: Bahamas. Age limit: 79 (65 and older must have medical certificate).

Based in the United Kingdom, the company is one of the oldest that carries passengers on its freighters and cargo liners. Three of its vessels, *America Star, Queensland Star* and *Sydney Star,* offer passenger service to Australia and New Zealand from the U.S. east coast. Each has four double and two single cabins equipped with private baths. Public areas are air-conditioned. There is a lounge, bar, laundry room and outdoor saltwater swimming pool on every ship. Rates are from $97 to $117 per day.

The *Argentina Star* and *Columbia Star* are cargo ships that travel from the west coast of the US and New Zealand and the six cabins have the same amenities as the rest of the passenger-carrying fleet. The *Melbourne Star* carries 10 passengers and offers 45-day round trips from the U.S. west coast on a similar run to Australia and New Zealand. Although final destinations on all of these vessels are the same, interim ports vary according to cargo requirements.

COLUMBUS LINE

Ost-West Str 59-61
Hamburg, 20457 Germany
www.columbusline.com
Freighter World Cruises
(800) 531-7774
www.freighterworld.com

Registry: Germany, Age Limit: 79, Ships have German crews. Company operates the *Columbus Canterbury* that accommodates two passengers. It is a modern containership that houses passengers in a large air-conditioned owner's suite.

There's an elevator, swimming pool. Vessel sails from Savannah, Georgia, and usually returns to Philadelphia. Destinations are in Australia and New Zealand. Per person, double occupancy runs about $7,000 for the voyage which is an average per diem of a little over $100.

EGAN OLENDORFF LINE

P.O. Box 2135
Luebeck, D-23509 Germany
(800) 531-7774
www.oldendorff.com

Registry: Liberia. Age Limit: 79, Each ship has space for eight passengers. There are no elevators. The *Tasman Challenger* and *Tasman Crusader* are sister vessels built in 1982. Cabins have shower or bath and mini-refrigerators. There's a bar and lounge. Ships sail 61-day round trips around Asia and the Pacific, departing from Auckland, New Zealand. Rates vary slightly, but average per diem runs about $82.

The *Tasman Explorer* and *Tasman Voyager* were built in 1987 and also carry eight passengers. They are semi-containerized and call on ports similar to the other vessels in Asia. Five cabins have closets, refrigerators, showers or tubs. Three have double beds. There's a lounge for passengers and officers, outdoor swimming pool, gym and a laundry. Per diems for the 46-day voyage average $80.

MARITIME REEDERI

180 S. Lake Ave, Ste 335
Pasadena, CA 91101
(800) 531-7774
www.freighterworld.com

Registry: Germany. Age limit: 79. Newest in the fleet is *Columbus Coromandel* built in 2000. There are two single cabins, and a large Owner's Suite, with twin beds, a living room, good storage space, as well as a refrigerator, a dining room and lounge, outdoor pool and covered deck space. Average per diem for 47-day voyages is $107.

The *Columbus Florida* also has space for four passengers and sails from the U.S. West Coast to Australia and New Zealand, but itineraries may vary from ship-to-ship. This cargo vessel can accommodate three passengers in two comfortable cabins and one in a single cabin. There is no elevator, but there is a lounge and covered deck space.

Other vessels in this company's fleet that accommodate passengers include the *Columbus Pacific* built in 1996. It travels to rainforests and banana plantations near the Equator and the beach areas around Valparaiso from the U.S. West Coast. The *Columbus Texas*, built around the same time, offers three passengers transport from the U.S. East Coast to the East Coast of South America. Voyages last about 43-days. The *Nautica 1*, built in 1983, carries nine passengers between Hamburg, Germany, and the Mediterranean. Two double cabins have upper and lower berths. The 28-day voyages run just under $70 per day, per person.

MEDITERRANEAN SHIPPING COMPANY

Sea the Difference
420 Fifth Avenue
New York, NY 10018
(800) 666-9333
www.mediterraneanshipping.com

Registry: Cypress or Panama. Age limit: 75 (physician's letter required with pre-existing conditions).

All routings may be booked one-way or round-trip. Most ships accommodate eight to 12 passengers and have indoor or outdoor swimming pools, lounges, VCR, library and games. Popular sailings from U.S. ports include 8-to-23-day round-trips from New York to South America and 18-to-23-day round-trips from Charleston to Cape Town. Company has numerous shorter and longer voyages from European ports. Rates run from $85 to $125 per day.

NAURU PACIFIC LINE

North American Maritime Agencies
100 California Street
San Francisco, CA 94111
(718) 939-2400
www.traveltips.com

Registry: Korean. No age limit. Ships carry 90 to 100 passengers and sail on approximately 40-day voyages every six weeks. Rates are in the $100 per day category depending on choice of cabin. Usual ports include Honolulu, Majuro, Ponape, Truk and Saipan; also voyages from San Francisco to the Micronesian islands.

INSIDER TIP

One of the vessels is a former Holland America Line ship and has retained much of the cruise ship atmosphere. The entire Promenade Deck is glass-enclosed public space. She has a swimming pool, library and gift and sundry shop. Air-sea arrangements are possible. Nauro Pacific Line also operates a 12-passenger ship from Nauru to Australia. Port-to-port rates are available: for example, San Francisco to Truk, from $1,645 to $2,225. Ship is the *Enna G*, designed for passenger-cruise-cargo service so she has amenities associated with passenger ships. All cabins are outside and air-conditioned and have private facilities. Nice dining room; good food and service.

P&O CONTAINERS

Strand Cruise and Travel
Charing Cross Shopping Concourse
London WC2N 4HZ U.K.
(800) 568-3262

Registry: British Age limit: 80, A division of P&O (Princess Cruises), the company operates two very well run and comfortable container vessels that sail from Tilbury, England, to South Africa and Australia on 44-to-80-day voyages. The *City of Durban* accommodates six passengers while the *Palsier Bay* holds eight passengers. Vessels were built in the late 1970s and have double cabins, lounges, TV and swimming pools. Rates run about $50 to $75 per day.

INSIDER TIP

P&O Cruise Lines operates the cruise ship *Canberra* on world cruises for about $130 a day, which is almost the same as a freighter or cargoliner, but the amenities and service are cruise ship quality. The *Canberra* is a fine older vessel with some cabins sharing bathroom facilities, but it's still a great buy for budget-minded world cruise passengers. With an average of $130 a day, some berths go for as little as $80 or even less!

Here are two good leads. These travel companies specialize in freighter travel and represent some of the freighter lines. They have last minute availability and itinerary information.

TravelTips Cruise Freighter Travel Association, 163-07 Depot Road, , Post Box 580218, Flushing, NY 11358; (718) 939-2400; www.traveltips.com

Freighter World Cruises, 180 South Lake Avenue, Suite 3335, Pasadena, CA 91101, (800) 531-7774; www.freighterworldcruises.com

Rating the Best: Ships were rated on a scale of one to 10 in all phases of the cruise product. Ships or companies with the highest ratings were selected as "The Best" for specific interests. In some instances, three ships or companies make the top list; in others it is one or two ships or companies. In all instances, ships were rated against other ships in the same price and size category. For specific details, see the ship profiles in "The Cruise Companies and Their Ships" Chapter. Where a series of ships within a company has virtually the same features and amenities, the series and company are named. (Ships are listed in alphabetical order as "The Best" which does not indicate numerical order. Categories are noted with each choice.)

The Total Traveler (TT:) Cruise Critics choices for
"The Best of The Best Ships"

Critics Choice for The Best Vacation Value
(Quotes are composites from the Cruise Critics Panel)

Carnival Cruise Lines
$$$ RESORT

"The company delivers a lot more than the brochure or the price indicates."

Holland America Line
$$$$ PREMIUM

"The company includes many features in the cruise price that others charge for on board - cappuccino, coffee, popcorn and ice cream are examples."

Princess Cruises
$$$ RESORT

"Ships offer variety in every aspect of the cruise experience; variety you could not get on shore for anywhere near the prices charged."

Royal Caribbean International
$$$ RESORT

"Voyager-class with rock climbing and ice skating rinks have put cruising into mainstream vacation options for a larger segment of the traveling public."

Silversea Cruises
$$$$$

"The company offers as all-inclusive a product as you can possibly assemble, but they do it without sacrificing choices."

Critics Choice: The Best World Cruises:

Amsterdam (Holland America)
$$$$ PREMIUM

"Veteran world cruise passengers sail the company's annual voyage. It's an extremely comfortable itinerary on a ship that offers luxury at premium rates. Itinerary goes around South America. Round trip from Fort Lauderdale."

Aurora (P&OCruises)
$$ BUDGET

"Low-priced, it is an excellent value for a circumnavigation round trip from Southampton."

Crystal Symphony (Crystal Cruises)
$$$$$ LUXURY

"An excellent ship which offers a very popular cruise itinerary that includes South America's east and west coast ports, as well as Easter Island."

Seven Seas Mariner (Radisson Seven Seas Cruises)
$$$$$ LUXURY

"The mid-size all-suite, all-verandah new ship offers multiple amenities and dining choices. Three month itinerary begins in Los Angles and terminates in Fort Lauderdale."

Queen Elizabeth 2 (Cunard Line)
$$ - $$$$$ TRADITIONAL

"The last liner of a bygone era is alive and well and very popular with repeat passengers. Some take the three month voyage annually. Rates run from budget to luxury and itineraries call for complete circumnavigations."

Critics Choice: The Most Romantic Ships at Sea:

Boutique Categories

Paul Gauguin (Radisson Seven Seas Cruises)
$$$$ LUXURY

"The Tahiti itinerary adds to the romance of the intimate and plush vessel. Quiet corners on board, and romantic settings on shore."

Silver Wind/Cloud (Silversea Cruises)
$$$$$ BOUTIQUE LUXURY

"Intimate vessels with superb suites and lots of table for two in the dining room."

Wind Spirit/Song/Star/Surf (Windstar Cruises)
$$$$ BOUTIQUE ADVENTURE

"Nothing beats the romance of evenings on deck with the huge sails flapping in the breeze. These ships are perfect for honeymoons."

Critics Choice: The Most Romantic Ships at Sea:

Larger Vessels

Carnival Spirit/Pride/Legend (Carnival Cruise Lines)
$$$ **XXL**   RESORT

"Mix, if you like, or settle into a quiet spot. Dine in the supper club, dance until the sun rises."

Dawn/Sea/Sun/Ocean Princesses (Princess Cruises)
$$$ **XL**   RESORT

"Sophisticated vessels with lots of cozy corners."

Millenium, Summit, Infinity (Celebrity Cruises)
$$$$ PREMIUM

"Private small rooms, chatty Martini Bars, tables for two."

TT: Critics Choice: The Best Ships for Seniors

Rotterdam/Prinsendam (Holland America Line)
$$$$ PREMIUM

"Seniors love Holland America and its special attention to older passengers."

Carnival Paradise (Carnival Cruise Line)
$$$ XXL   RESORT

*"This is the only large ship that prohibits smoking by passengers and crew.
The pristine air and the lively atmosphere are very popular with senior travelers."*

Caronia (Cunard Line)
$$$$ TRADITIONAL

*"Ship offers a traditional cruise experience, the way cruising used to be. Very few
steps and excellent cuisine)."*

Crystal Harmony/Symphony (Crystal Cruises)
$$$$$ LUXURY

*"The majority of guests are over 50. Ships offer high end cruise experiences in
mid-size ships. Easy to get around, savvy seniors opt for the luxury of butler
service on 10 deck."*

Seabourn Pride/Spirit/Legend (Seabourn Cruise Lines)
$$$$$ BOUTIQUE

*"Top of the line, small vessels. Dining rooms pay careful attention to special
dietary requests."*

World Explorer
$$ BUDGET

*"Inexpensive way to see the world on a budget without obsessing in airports.
Ships are senior-friendly."*

Critics Choice: The Best Ships for Disabled Travelers

Rotterdam (Holland America Line)
$$$$ PREMIUM

"This ship has 23 wheelchair accessible cabins. Holland America on all of its ships has reengineered embarkation and debarkation to make it easier and disabled guests."

Carnival Spirit, Pride, Legend
$$$ XXL   RESORT

"Accessible cabins have wide doors and elevators with tactile controls and accessible gym equipment. And, a very disabled passenger-friendly crew."

Grand-Princess, Ocean Princess
$$$ XXL   RESORT

"Ships in these series offer large cabins for disabled travelers and easy access to swimming pools, embarkation and debarkation."

Royal Caribbean Voyager-class vessels
$$$ XXL   RESORT

"Company has installed pool lifts at swimming pools."

Critics Choice: Best Companies for Kosher Food:
(See company profiles for details)

$$$	**Holland America**
$$$$$	**Radisson Seven Seas Cruises**
$$$$$	**Crystal Cruises**
$$ to $$$$$	**Cunard Line**

Critics Choice: The Best Optional Restaurants at Sea:

Carnival Spirit/Pride/Legend
$$$ XXL   RESORT

"Topside and built into the funnel, these restaurants are posh supper clubs with music and dancing high in the sky. Menu is geared to steaks and chops, but the specialty is Joe's Stone Crabs."

Millenium/Summit/Infinity (Celebrity Cruises)
$$$$ PREMIUM

"Premium Restaurants are products of renowned check Michel Roux. Food is superb and the intimate atmosphere is very much like it used to be on famous old liners."

Disney Wonder/Magic
$$$ XL   RESORT

"Unlike the rest of the ship, no one under 18 is admitted to the intimate restaurants serving excellent Italian-themed food in a romantic setting."

Critics Choice: The Best Ships for Singles
(Single rates, activities, and overall ambience determined the choices)

Carnival Cruise Lines
$$$ RESORT

"Company probably carries more singles than other line. Every ship in the fleet was nominated as "the best for singles," so take your pick. They are the "Fun Ships" and the line offers "guaranteed" single rates. It's easy to meet other singles. Ships host singles parties and events."

Crystal Cruises
$$$$$ LUXURY

"Single rates are as low as 20 percent over per person, double rates and there are gentlemen hosts on board to make sure there are no wallflowers left waiting for a dance."

Silversea Cruises
$$$$$ LUXURY

"Single supplements on selected sailings are as low as 10 percent over the per person, double rate. These ships and the supplement attract older women who want to dance with the gentlemen hosts.."

Critics Choice: Cruise Lines with The Best Entertainment at Sea:

Carnival Cruise Lines
$$$ <u>RESORT</u>

"The company continues to walk off with all of the top awards for entertainment, particularly for the spectacular production shows on every vessel. Shows are professionally produced, fast paces with dazzling costume changes and original music and choreography."

Princess Cruises
$$$ <u>RESORT</u>

"On the larger and new ships, there are two major shows almost nightly. Grand Class ships have two show lounges and timing is set so guests can take in two shows almost every night."

Norwegian Cruise Line
$$$ <u>RESORT</u>

"Newest ships in the fleet (Star and Sun) take "Freestyle Cruising" another step up with rotating shows scheduled so passengers can see them at various times. Shows offer variety and a lot of spice."

Critics Choice: The Best Spas and Gyms at Sea:

Carnival Triumph/Carnival Spirit class ships.
$$$ XXL   <u>RESORT</u>

"NauticaSpas are multi-level and are among largest afloat. Ten treatment rooms. Fresh fruit juice bar, Nautica fare is on evening dinner menus."

Norwegian Sky
$$$ XL   <u>RESORT</u>

"The Body Waves Spa is an Asian-inspired featuring ancient Japanese hands-on healing. Guests in suites may request in-cabin massages."

Royal Caribbean's Voyager class ships
$$$ XXL   <u>RESORT</u>

"Each ship has 14 treatments rooms and a solarium with a retractable roof for relaxation before or after treatments."

Prinsendam (Holland America Line)
$$$$ <u>LUXURY</u>

"Sol du Soleil spa is one of the most beautiful, low key spas at sea. The spa menu of treatments is extensive. Rasul room is where couples may privately apply detoxifying mud mixture."

Seven Seas Mariner (Radisson Seven Seas Cruises)
$$$$$ <u>LUXURY</u>

"The ship has the first Judith Jackson Spa at sea which is a lot different from other floating spas. Treatments are from the best International spas. Private areas and quiet relaxation area for use before or after treatments."

Critics Choice: The Best Cruise Lines for Families
(Based on facilities, supervision, programming for multi-generational families)

Carnival Cruise Lines
$$$ <u>RESORT</u>

"Programs and facilities for kids from ages two to teens. Group baby sitting evenings so parents, grandparents and adults can enjoy multiple entertainment venues."

Disney Cruise Line
$$$ <u>RESORT</u>

"Ships were built for kids and facilities take up most of the public space, but kids must be at least three and potty trained."

Princess Cruises
$$$ <u>RESORT</u>

"Excellent programs and facilities, but no kids under three. Baby sitting evenings and at other times so parents and grandparents can participate in activities."

Adventure/Explorer/Voyager of the Seas
$$$

"Excellent program for kids and there's plenty to do for adults ."

Holland America Line
$$$$ <u>PREMIUM</u>

"Ships with good facilities and programs include Amsterdam, Rotterdam, and Maasdam and have supervised programs for ages five and up. Just for kids shore excursions in Alaska and Caribbean."

Critics Choice: The Best Ships for Conventions and Meetings:

Seven Seas Mariner (Radisson Seven Seas Cruises)
$$$$$ <u>LUXURY</u>

"Dedicated convention and meeting space. Technical facilities for staging in the tiered theatre are state of the art."

Crystal Symphony
$$$$$ <u>LUXURY</u>

"Ship is small enough that it can be chartered. Staging is excellent."

Silver Whisper/Silver Shadow (Silversea Cruises)
$$$$$ <u>LUXURY</u>

"There's a small dining/board room, good for private meetings on corporate retreats. The conference center connects to the card room and dining/board room so there can be breakout space following conferences."

Radisson Diamond (Radisson Seven Seas Cruises)
$$$$ <u>BOUTIQUE</u>

"Good for small ship charters when corporations can only spend 5 days in the Caribbean -Ship can be "branded" with corporate logo, flag, etc."

Seabourn Pride, Spirit. Legend (Seabourn Cruise Lines)
$$$$$ <u>LUXURY</u>

"Ships are small enough for elite corporate charters and can be branded with company logo, etc.. Also, they will customize ports and itineraries for charters."

Adventure of the Seas (Royal Caribbean International)
$$$ XXL   <u>RESORT</u>

"Ships in this class have facilities on the Studio B stage for events, awards ceremonies, product launches; the latest in lighting and audio-visual techniques. Excellent meeting facilities with breakout space. Good for large corporate event charters."

Critics Choice: The Best Ships for Conventions and Meetings (continued):

Celebrity Millenium/Summit (Celebrity Cruises)
    $$$$ PREMIUM

"Ships have facilities for events, awards ceremonies, product launches requiring the latest in lighting and audio-visual techniques. Also excellent meeting facilities with technical and audio-visual facilities. Good for large corporate event charters."

Maasdam (Holland America Line)
    $$$$ PREMIUM

"Ships in this series are suited for charters; not too big, not too small. They can be branded with corporate logo, etc. Staging is good and there's plenty of meeting and conference space dedicated for that purpose."

The world's best islands are the ones
that float and move.
They're called cruise ships. "

Cruise Diva

Pick a patch of ocean or a navigable waterway in any part of the world, and there's a good chance you'll find cruise ships plying the waters. Passenger-carrying vessels sail within sight of each other in the Caribbean. They cruise the islands of the South Pacific, sail up and down North America's inland waterways, visit the exotic Mediterranean, dodge icebergs in the land of the midnight sun and Antarctica, and call at enchanting Pacific and Far Eastern ports. Almost every country in the world is in the passenger ship business.

All cruise ships offer shore excursions, inclusive sightseeing packages put together by operators on shore. Buses, vans, or taxis pick up passengers dockside, a guide explains the sights, some shopping time is allowed, and passengers are returned to their ship or dropped off in town to explore further on their own.

While a small number of cruise travelers prefer to stay on board when the ship visits a port, most passengers go ashore for the sightseeing, shopping, beaches, and a taste of local cuisine and nightlife. Ship activities are restricted during time in port, so passengers who do not disembark opt for a quiet day with meals served on a limited schedule.

There's no question that it is advantageous to make the most of hours on shore, be it a day, an evening, or a few hours. Trial-and-error sightseeing on your own may be preferable if you have several days or a week on an island, but it is an extravagant waste of time when your visit is by cruise ship and your time ashore is measured in hours. The decision facing passengers is—should you take the ship's prearranged shore excursion or sightsee on your own?

In the Caribbean, shore excursions arranged by cruise ships cost from about $25 to $50 for four hours of sightseeing. Excursions in the Mediterranean or Asian ports can run as high as $200 for a full day and under $10 for a hair-raising climb by donkey in Santorini. Excursions in Baltic countries average about $45 for half-day tours. Longer trips in which air travel is involved can run into hundreds of dollars and sometimes include hotels and meals when the ship overnights in a port. The usual shore excursion, however, is a half-day, a full-day, or an evening outing. Nightclub tours cost about $45 in San Juan and about $30 in Mexico.

The advantages of purchasing the ship's shore excursions are obvious. The tour is fully escorted (usually a cruise-staff member accompanies the tour); the guide speaks English; and there is some degree of responsibility and supervision exercised by the ship. In almost all cases, the ship acts as an agent for a land-based tour operator, adding several dollars to the price at which the tour is sold to passengers. The ship makes it very clear that it assumes no legal liability for shore excursions, but cruise lines know a bad shore excursion can spoil an entire cruise experience. Everything possible is done to make sure passengers are satisfied.

Touring the port on your own is possible almost everywhere. If there are four of you, a day's outing will probably cost less than the total of four individually purchased shore excursions. In non-English-speaking countries or islands, or where a visa is required, there's no assurance your guide will speak English or show you the most interesting places. His "yes" to your "Do you speak English?" question may be the only English he knows, and the possibility of disputes arising at the end of the tour as to price and original agreement are quite real.

Passengers' group visas (in countries where they are required—Russia, for example) enable travelers to take part in ship-sponsored shore excursions. For women traveling alone, ship-sponsored day and nightclub tours provide a sense of security and eliminate dealing with taxi fares, checks, and gratuities.

It is not a good idea to depend entirely on taxi drivers and local tour operators. In some ports, a mob of cab drivers waits eagerly for ships to dock. Many of the drivers are competent, but some lack proper training as guides, while others succumb to the temptation to overcharge or their "sightseeing" tours include visiting shops where they receive a commission for bringing passengers. Rental cars are available in most ports if you prefer seeing a place on your own, and limousines with drivers as well as rental motor scooters take up the slack for preferences at opposite ends of the spectrum.

There is no set formula for how to divide your time on an island or in a city. No rule fits every port. Some ports are scenic and tempt exploration, while others have idyllic beaches that are hard to resist. Snorkeling, sailing, fishing, cultural monuments, and museums—every port has a little of one attraction, more of another. A good tour combines the best of everything—including shopping opportunities.

Information about ship-sponsored shore excursions is usually available several months before departure for cruises lasting more than 10 days. Shorter cruises provide this information once passengers have boarded, or it is included in the ticket package about a month or so before sailing day. The information is usually detailed and includes the possible extent of physical activity involved in each tour. Some may require a lot of climbing, others walking on flat surfaces. The best way to choose is to read the brochure carefully and know your own limitations.

This chapter was not written as a guide for travelers spending days or weeks in the port city or ports of call. Travelers vacationing in hotels at these ports have more time to explore and should have more details at hand for complete enjoyment. Information on sightseeing noted in this chapter is for the cruise passenger spending about six hours in the port. Every effort has been made to inform readers of the most interesting and historic sights. For Mediterranean and North Sea ports, the average time spent in port by cruise ships was used as a basis for recommended sightseeing.

It is impossible to list every port in the Bahamas, Caribbean, West Indies, Mexico, Alaska, Canada, Greece, Israel, Turkey, North Africa, Italy, England, Holland, Denmark, Sweden, Norway, Russia, and about 50 others including newer ports in Malaysia and Vietnam; so only those most frequently visited by major cruise lines have been included. Average shore excursion prices (per person) are listed for every port, based on personal experience and on information from ships visiting these ports and from shore tour operators. Prices quoted are subject to change with very little or no notice, but should not vary more than 10 to 20 percent in an upward direction. Shore excursion prices never seem to go down, but some top-of-the-line cruise lines are including a few shore excursions in cruise packages. When that happens, the information is available prior to booking.

Exchange rates of foreign currency versus the U.S. dollar are not listed because they are volatile. What is accurate at press time could be higher or lower by the time this book reaches bookstore shelves. We have not listed names of currencies and existing money-exchange restrictions, but we do offer tips on how to get the most for your money in each country. Daily currency exchange rates are available from the purser's office on board ship. The information is usually updated at regularly scheduled port talks a day or two before reaching each port. Don't worry about converting your money for short stays on shore. Shopkeepers are happy to accept U.S. dollars, traveler's checks, and major credit cards. Never change money on the street. Use a hotel desk or currency exchange.

As a general rule, restaurant recommendations for ports are not included in *The Total Traveler Guide to Worldwide Cruising*. With only a short time in port, most passengers find the fastest and best port meal is on board ship. But in some ports, notably the Caribbean island of St. Martin, where literally dozens of fine French restaurants are available, dining on shore is one of the highlights of the visit, so restaurants may be recommended. When an eatery is considered part of the port experience, mention is made.

INSIDER TIP

Shore excursions are becoming more adventurous, and ships are offering more than the usual sightseeing and shopping opportunity in every port. Appealing to the daredevil in each of us, there are tours that offer horseback riding on the beach, drive-yourself jeep explorations, mountain climbing, rafting, helicopter sightseeing, and a myriad of other activities travelers read about and maybe dream about doing some day. When available to passengers on board ship, they are supervised and considered safe. The shore excursion manager will usually tell passengers how much physical exertion will be required, but the tours are well worth the memories they will provide.

Alaska

For more than 25,000 years, the First Peoples—the Aleuts, Tlingit, Haida, and Tsimshian—hunted, fished, and roamed throughout the vast expanses of a region they called Aleyeska, which means "the great land." In the mid-1800s, Russian and European explorers searching for the fabled Northwest Passage sighted the Alaskan coastline. Soon afterward, they established a handful of small communities along the coast so they could trade the overabundant fur pelts and lay claim to this land for the imperial czar of Russia or the kings and queens of England and Europe.

When the Klondike gold rush opened up Alaska to the rest of the world in 1889, thousands of fortune seekers literally stampeded in droves over steep, snow-covered mountain passes, across Arctic tundra, and up untamed waterways in the crazed pursuit of gold. Ten cities, including Nome and Skagway, sprang up overnight.

Alaska was a great land then and still is today, even though it is far different from the fabled land of the last major gold rush. This past century has brought most of the trappings of modern civilization. But Alaska still embodies the vitality, ambition, potential, and beauty associated with youth. Its young population is building modern cities in remote wilderness areas. Bush pilots wing over expansive reaches of land while shadowing the Aleuts still hunting in their kayaks. In this Last Frontier, Alaskans have delicately combined the contrasts and benefits of wilderness and civilization.

With 590,000 square miles, Alaska's rugged country is greater in area than one-fifth of the combined landmass of the lower 48 states. At 33,000 miles, Alaska's coastline is longer than the entire continental U.S. coastline. The state also embraces five mountain ranges that contain 19 peaks extending over 14,000 feet high. In Denali National Park, Mount McKinley rises more than 20,230 feet, making it the tallest mountain in North America. There are more than 3,000 rivers and 3 million lakes in Alaska.

The casual-country lifestyle of Alaskans is reflected in their clothing. Let the weather be your guide. Comfortable layering—Tee shirt, shirt, and cotton sweater—is acceptable. Lightweight woolens, slacks, sweaters, and water-repellent coats are suggested. Comfortable, low-heeled shoes for walking are a must. Shipboard clothing ranges from swimsuits for sunny days on deck to parkas for chilly evenings.

INSIDER SHOPPING TIPS

Shopping opportunities are similar in all ports. Fur parkas may be priced higher than in your hometown, but Alaskan Indian carvings and native artifacts are excellent souvenirs. Alaskan jade (not as valuable as Oriental) varies in form and quality from trinkets priced at a few dollars to carvings priced at several hundred dollars. Everything purchased in Alaska is duty-free for returning U.S. residents and need not be included in your customs declaration.

Party animals may find life in these small communities dull and boring, but this state is made up of rural towns that adjust to accommodate tourists during summer months. Nothing in these communities (except for a couple of dance recitals) is a put-on for visitors. You will see life as it is. Prices for food and housing are high, fishing is excellent, and the family boat is more important than the family car. The same school buses that transport kids during winter months are used for shore excursions in some places. Guides are local residents who are proud of their communities and happy to talk about life in Alaska.

INSIDER TIP

Don't expect to find sophisticated entertainment, trendy boutiques, Eskimo camps, gold mines, or the Alaska pipeline. That comes with flying around the state and spending more time than is allowed on cruise ship visits. Shore excursions vary from hour-long city tours on motor coaches to sightseeing—boat rides and daylong flying expeditions.

Shore Excursions: Ships offer full and half day escorted sightseeing in every port. Prices depend on what you select as the offerings run the gamut from river rafting to bus tours, from helicopter rides that land on a glacier, from salmon fishing to salmon "barbecues", from walks through towns and village to walks on a glacier. Cost ranges from $45 for a half day to over $200 for flights and adventurous activities.

On Your Own: Most of the piers in Alaska are walking distance from the center of town, some are city center, but you'll need to hire a car to get to the glaciers and to see some of the interior. With the multitude of escorted excursions offered by ship, unless you have a specific place you have marked as a must-see and it is not included or does not allow enough time, I recommend one of the excursions that includes most of what you want to see or do.

More Information: Alaska Division of Tourism, Box 110801, Juneau, AK 99811-0801, or www.alaska.com

Glacier Bay, just west of Skagway, is not a port of call. It is a highlight of all Canada-Alaska cruise experiences, a day spent with nature. Cruise ships slip through the Icy Strait into the awesome 50-mile-long Glacier Bay, rimmed with a score of active glaciers. Hunks of ice frequently tumble off 250-foot heights in an exciting process called calving. A ranger from the National Park Service boards every ship and explains the sights over the ship's public-address system. Glacier Bay's advancing and retreating glaciers record a history of rhythmic changes in the climate of the planet. Centuries of mild climate in the far north have alternated with long, cold periods of successive ice ages. The glaciers seen today are remnants of a general ice advance that began some 4,000 years ago. This period is sometimes called the Little Ice Age. Few of the many glaciers that once supplied the huge ice sheet still extend to the sea, but there are 11,400 square miles in Glacier Bay National Monument enclosing 16 active tidewater glaciers. Icebergs, which have cracked off from near-vertical ice cliffs, dot the waters of the bay.

No matter which glacier your ship cruises, you'll want to spend the day on deck with camera clicking. During the summer months, daylight extends to past midnight; on the longest day of the year, there are merely two hours of near darkness.

INSIDER TIP

In response to a campaign by ecologists, the number of ships cruising Glacier Bay is limited. If Glacier Bay is important to you, check brochures and sailing dates carefully. Not all ships listing Glacier Bay actually cruise Glacier Bay on every sailing. Many ships alternate cruising of Glacier Bay with Alert Bay, also quite beautiful.

Alert Bay

When English Captain James Cook first visited Cormorant Island, off the coast of Vancouver Island, he found a native population with a lot of leisure time. Timber, fish, and game were plentiful. In Alert Bay today, vestiges of the Indian culture are still seen in wood carving and weaving. The area is so small shore excursions are not offered, but the scenery is magnificent.

Anchorage

Anchorage is sometimes called "Chicago of the North." The city got its start during the Alaska Railroad construction period in 1917 and remains young at heart. Its average citizen is 28 years old, and sled-dog races are still among the most popular events in town. Anchorage retains a frontier spirit, with moose occasionally roaming city streets despite a certain hustle in the air.

Most cruise ships listing Anchorage as a port of call dock at Seward or Whittier because of the required draft. Passengers take an hour-long train or bus ride to visit Anchorage. On one-week Alaska cruises, when Anchorage is listed, ships sail between Seward (Anchorage) and Vancouver, alternating voyages in reverse. A round-trip from Anchorage to Glacier Bay would require a minimum of 10 to 14 days.

The city is easily explored by foot. Among interesting sights are the Old City Hall; the Alaska Railroad depot, with its totem poles; and a 1907 locomotive. The Oscar Anderson house, next to a coastal walking trail, was Anchorage's first permanent frame house, built by a tent-city butcher in 1915. Major civic buildings are: The Alaska Center for the Performing Arts, at the corner of 5th Avenue and F Street; the George M. Sullivan Sports Arena; and the William A. Egan Civic and Convention Center. The Anchorage Museum of History and Art presents a microcosm of the region's culture and history.

For lunch in town, try Club Paris. Decades old, it's the place where locals continue to meet. Definitely not for vegetarians; beef and freshly caught seafood are house specialties. Reservations are suggested. Several microbreweries offering a broad variety of beer and bistro menus have opened recently.

Haines

The community of Haines lies in a spectacular setting on the Chilkat Peninsula near the northern end of Lynn Canal between Rainbow Glacier and the snow-capped Coastal Range. It is not surprising that the Chilkat Tlingit first settled this beautiful location centuries ago. They called the place Dtehshuh, which meant "the end of the trail."

In 1879, the shores of Portage Cove were selected for a mission site. Two years later, the mission of Haines was established. When fur-trading days were over, Haines developed into a gold-mining supply center, and a few fishing canneries were established. Gold was discovered about 35 miles upriver from Haines, and until the mid-1920s, gold seekers sifted thousands of dollars worth of placer gold from the Porcupine River and its tributaries.

In 1903, the U.S. Army constructed Fort William H. Seward in nearby Port Chilkot. It was decommissioned in 1944 and is now the home of Alaska Indian Arts, with its striking totems, and the Raven Tribal House.

The largest concentration of bald eagles anywhere in the world can be viewed within the 4,800-acre Alaska Chilkat Bald Eagle Preserve. The eagles are drawn here each year by the late run of chum salmon, and as many as 3,500 eagles gather during the peak period.

Juneau

Along the shores of the Gastineau Channel, nestled on the skirts of Mount Juneau and Mount Roberts, is the capital of Alaska—Juneau. A modern cosmopolitan city, Juneau has risen on top of tailings from an old gold mine. Narrow, winding streets, some of which are only steep, wooden stairways, lead to homes perched precariously on the hillsides. The business of the state government is the pulse of this city, but the gold-rush days of the past are still very much a part of Juneau's spirit.

Alaska's capital contains many buildings of interest. Among them are the Alaska State Museum, Juneau-Douglas City Museum, and Governor's Mansion. There is a 13-mile bus trip on Glacier Highway to Mendenhall Glacier, a huge receding river of ice. Driving through the Mendenhall Valley, one goes through the Tongass National Forest, the largest national forest in the United States. Another interesting site is the Chapel by the Lake, from which a splendid view of the Mendenhall Glacier is reflected on Auke Lake.

Ketchikan

Ketchikan owes its beginnings to the gold rush of the 1890s, when it became the chief center of Alaska's fishing industry. But it's not fishing that brings cruise ships into the harbor. Ketchikan, just 230 miles southeast of Juneau is the largest southern town on the Inside Passage. With a population of 14,000, it is Alaska's fourth-largest city. Ketchikan is wedged between mountains and waterfront in Alaska's Panhandle and is best known for its totem poles, used by Indians to record business transactions, show social standing, and illustrate stories.

The Indian totems at Saxman Park, two miles from town, are a camera buff's delight. There are more totems in Totem Bight, about 11 miles from the city. Ketchikan considers itself the salmon capital of the world, and great schools of migrating salmon pass through the narrow straits. The waterfront is always a busy place, and a walking tour affords an interesting contrast of old and new: saloons with sawdust-covered floors side by side with modern department stores.

Ketchikan is a vibrant community with the dubious reputation as the Rain Capital of Alaska. The average rainfall is 162 inches with measurable precipitation 240 days of the year. Ketchikanners don't seem to mind the rain, but visitors are well advised to bring rain gear.

Seward

Named for U.S. Secretary of State William H. Seward, who helped in purchasing Alaska from Russia, and set at the foot of Resurrection Bay on the east coast of the Kenai Peninsula, Seward is known as the gateway to the Kenai Fjords National Park. Buildings in the downtown area are of turn-of-the-century vintage and reflect the town's origins as a supply center for seamen.

Sitka

The former capital of Russian America, Sitka is nestled at the foot of Harbor Mountain, on Baranof Island. The island is named for Alexander Baranof of the Russian-American Company, who built a trading port north of Sitka in 1799. It is situated in one of the state's most spectacular natural settings. Dominating Sitka's skyline is the snow-capped 3,200-foot cone of an extinct volcano, Mount Edgecumbe. An archipelago of small, lushly forested islands in Sitka Sound protects this small community of 8,000 from the fury of the North Pacific. Many of the residents are descendents of the Tlingit Indians. For more than 126 years, Alaska was explored and ruled by Russia. Although the United States took over in 1867, the charm of the old city is still alive in Sitka.

First called Novo Arkhangelsk ("New Archangel"), Sitka got its new name when it became headquarters of all Russian activities in Alaska. By the mid-1850s, imperial Russia's interest in her remote, vulnerable colony declined as profits from the fur trade decreased dramatically. After the Russian occupation ended, the Russian Double Eagle flag was lowered, and Alaska was turned over to the United States.

Remnants of the old days live on. The widely acclaimed, colorfully costumed New Archangel Dancers perform authentic Russian folk dances for visitors. And Sitka's friendly, red-coated tour guides proudly show you their community. Most tours include a visit to the national monument where the great battle of Alaska was fought in 1804. Other highlights include visits to the Alaska Museum and St. Michael's Cathedral, with its strong Russian motif, rich oil paintings, and large icon collection. The cathedral has been restored, and all the treasures are on display.

Sightseeing: Unforgettable is a scenic seaside drive in Sitka. Passengers on a helicopter tour experience the best view. Highlights include views of Sitka Sound, filled with evergreen-covered islands, some of which still boast abandoned World War II fortifications. Another view is of St. Lazari Island National Bird Reserve, home of the eagles. The helicopter tour lands in such inaccessible areas as the crater of Mount Edgecumbe and deserted beaches. Don't book the helicopter tour until the very last minute; sights and landings depend on weather. Should you decide to see Sitka on your own, "musts" include the cathedral and the large collection of restored totems, including the Sitka National Monument.

Skagway

The only apparent reason for Skagway's founding was that it was a convenient place from which crazed fortune seekers could get to the Klondike gold fields. Located at the northernmost reaches of the Inside Passage is the gold-rush town of Skagway, nestled in a long, narrow valley and surrounded by snow-capped mountains rising thousands of feet. Over the past decade, the town's boardwalks and original false-fronted buildings have been restored.

Once a honky-tonk boomtown, Skagway retains the flavor of its historic past as the gateway to the Klondike. Gold-rush memories linger on in the town's wooden sidewalks, unpaved streets, and turn-of-the-century frame buildings. Guides tell colorful tales of Skagway's history. Skagway's legacy began in 1887, when Captain William Moore staked his claim at the mouth of the Skagway River and built a wharf in anticipation of the stampede to the Klondike. Within days, tens of thousands of gold-hungry prospectors headed north aboard crowded steamers to stake their claims. They quickly overran Moore's homestead and laid out a new town renamed Skagway.

Sightseeing: There's a lot to see in and around Skagway. Visit beautiful Reid Falls; the famed White Pass and Yukon's narrow-gauge railroad headquarters; the Trail of '98 Museum, with its many authentic artifacts of the gold-rush era; and Gold Rush Cemetery, where villains and good guys alike are buried.

Wrangell

Wrangell is the third-oldest settlement in Southeast Alaska, and the only one with the distinction of having had flags of three different nations flying over it—Russian, British, and American—although no war was every fought over the area. It was purchased or traded from one country to another. Located at the northern tip of Wrangell Island, on Zimovia Straight, it is the well-known gateway to the Stikine River.

The area was once the territory of the Stikine Tlingit, who settled here and used the nearby river as a trade route to the interior. Three gold rushes surged through the region, and the spunky community took it all in stride. It survived two devastating fires, in 1906 and 1952, and remains a solid frontier town, with false-fronted buildings, a sheltered fishing harbor, and plenty of room to grow. Lumber is the major industry. Fishing and fish processing tie for second place.

Sightseeing: While there is not much to see, a walk to the Wrangell Museum, housed in the city's first schoolhouse, is worth the visit. One of the most important attractions is Shakes Island and Tribal House, with interior house posts more than 200 years old. Highlights of the visit to Wrangell are the hidden treasures. At Petroglyph Beach, you can hunt for over 40 prehistoric petroglyphs scattered among the rocks on the beach. It is presumed that ancient inhabitants carved these mysterious stone images as markers or messages.

Africa, Indian Ocean & South Atlantic

Cruising this area of the world is increasing in popularity. Travelers can safari in Africa, visit Gold Mines in South Africa, scuba and explore World War II shipwrecks from less visited and inhabited islands and experience diverse cultures unique to these areas of the world. No one ship sails on a regular year around schedule to specific parts in this part of the world. Cruises are seasonal and are usually part of longer voyages on which passengers may purchase the segment visiting countries in which they have specific interests. Here's a run down of the most popular ports of call.

Mumbei (Bombay), India

India is a fascinating and exotic destination. Admittedly, there is poverty, a lot of poverty, and that is unfortunate. There are homeless people and there are beggars, but there are also sights and sounds and smells that a traveler will experience no where else on earth. Mumbei is the port used most frequently by cruise ships. African and Asian traders found a port that became, and remains, the economic center of India. While African and Asian touches continue to this day, British influences are very evident.

Sightseeing: From Mumbai, ships offer overnight tours to Agra for the Taj Mahal and to Delhi. A must for first time visitors is the Taj Mahal and if the tour allows for an overnight, so much the better. Ships also offer half and full day tours around Mumbai and include the Elephant Village.

On Your Own: Taxis are relatively inexpensive, but convert dollars into local currency so there is no confusion. It will be cheaper if you negotiate for a specific time - a few hours or for the full day. Taxi drivers speak English and they know their city. They will take you to the market, the "red light" district, the high end and the low life that makes Mumbei. Be sure to include a visit to ancient Bombay - the Indo-Gothic Victoria Station and the frenetic Crawford Market. Traveling beyond that point takes you through a dilapidated, decaying area where Jews lived a couple of hundred years ago. There are several synagogues in the area, a few are still functioning. It's hard to recognize a synagogue because it could be decorated with Christmas lights. Be sure to take a guide on this kind of a tour.

More information: Government of India Tourist Office, 30 Rockefeller Plaza, North Mezzanine, New York, N.Y. 10112. www.tourindia.com

INSIDER TIP
Don't try to do Mumbei, the Taj Mahal and Delhi on your own when you arrive for a short visit. Trains and planes are always full and unless you have made pre-arrangements for a private guide and transportation, you will not have enough time. Take the ship's shore excursion even though it is pricey.

South Africa – Cape Town

Cape Town has an excellent port and its geographic location encourages ships to call here. It's a surprising city - urban, developed and sophisticated. Awaken early to take advantage of the beautiful harbor with Table Mountain as a backdrop. Cape Town dates back to 1652 and of great interest are its beaches, high mountains, fishing villages and vineyards. The Castle dates back to 1666 and is the oldest building in South Africa.

Ships offer full and half day excursions for about $45 and $60, respectively. Although everyone speaks English, escorted tours are recommended. Half-day tours take in the wineries. It takes a full day for the drive to Cape of Good Hope, but it's worth it if you go in November and early December when the protea are in bloom.

On Your Own: If four of you get together, a car for the day should cost about $25 each. Plan your own itinerary in Cape Town. You can get a good overview in a full day. Since most ships overnight in port, spend the second day browsing on your own.

Durban

Durban on the East Coast is a popular port of call. Its history has left deep scars and the area has had more than its share of conflicts. The Boers and the local Zulus, not to mention the British, were at each other in the 19th century. The 20th century witnessed other problems which led to positive changes in South Africa.

Sightseeing: Ships offer half-day tours for about $40 along the Victoria Embankment and a look at present day Durban. Most offer a full day safari to a private reserve for about $65 including lunch. We took the one-day safari last year and saw more wildlife than fellow passengers did on the three day safari. Other full day tours cost about $75 and stop at Zulu Village.

Mombassa (Kenya)

This is the most popular port for a one to three or four day safari. Take the latter and you rejoin the ship at the next port. Most ships remain in port for two days which is enough time to overnight in a game park. Cost runs about $350 per person. Ships that use Mombassa as an embarkation and debarkation point offer pre-cruise five- and seven-night safaris.

INSIDER SHOPPING TIP

Mombassa is a good shopping port for native woodcarvings, chess sets, fabrics and baskets. English is the official language, so you will not have problems bargaining with the street merchants.

More information: South African Tourist Corporation, 610 Fifth Avenue, New York 10020. Or E-mail: satourny@aol.com

Madagascar - Nosy Be

The port city is Nosy Be, which means Big Island. Confusing to passengers once they alight the tender that takes them ashore and they find a less than friendly welcome to a dusty and very humid island and a poor community waiting for them. The island's musical language remains a mix of African, Arabic and Indonesian languages. Few people speak English.

The only local product that interests tourists is a very fragrant perfume, Ylang-ylang, made from the yellow flowering trees.

Sightseeing: Not much to see. Shore excursions cost about $45 for a half day that takes passengers around the area and to Lemur Park of Nosy Komba to see some rare animals.

More information: Embassy of Madagascar, 2374 Massachusetts Ave., NW, Washington, D.C. 20008; or 1-619-481-7474

Seychelles

The Seychelles, an island nation in the Indian Ocean off the East Coast of Africa, is made up of just under 100 islands. Mahe, with about 50,000 residents, is the main island. The two other populated islands are Praslin and La Digue. The total population of the Seychelles is approximately 70,000. The people of the Seychelles, called Seychellois, are of mixed African, Indian, Chinese and European ancestry. English and French are official languages and Creole is spoken throughout the islands. Currency is the Seychelles Rupee.

More information: Seychelles Tourist Bureau, 235 E. 40th St., Room 24A, New York, N.Y. 10016.

Australia

Given the size and scope of Australia, there is no possible way to see, much less know the country during a cruise ship visit. Australia is recommended for pre-and/or post-cruise extensions. Australia is part of the British Commonwealth, and England's influence is evident in many aspects of Australian lifestyle. The real beginnings of nationhood came with the discovery of gold in 1841. A tide of immigration began and it continues to this day.

"Down under" means seasons are reversed, and the best time to cruise the waters around Australia and New Zealand is during their spring and summer periods; our fall and winter months. Prices are comparable to big city prices in the United States, and shore excursions could average about $75 for half-day and more than $150 for full day tours.

INSIDER SHOPPING TIP

If you have longed to own a fine opal, Australia is the place to buy it. Just remember, as with any semi-precious or precious stone, quality is more important than size if you are buying an investment. Otherwise, if the price is right and you like it, view your opal as a souvenir. Also, remember you pay for quality which is based on color, size and other variables.

More information: For all of the cities and attractions Australian Tourist Commission, 2049 Century Park East, Suite 1920, Los Angeles, CA 90067. Or www.australia-information.net

Adelaide

Capital of South Australia, Adelaide sits on a narrow plain between the Mt. Lofty Ranges and the Gulf St. Vincent's clear waters. The planned city features beautiful parks, play grounds and gardens, balanced with wide-open spaces. Adelaide is dubbed "City of Churches."

"Must-sees" include Cleland Wildlife Park and cuddly koalas, wombats, emus and dingoes.

Cairns

Most ships call in Cairns because of the Great Barrier Reef, one of the great wonders of the world. But there is more to this coastal city in the heart of Queensland in the north of Australia. The area enjoys tropical climate for most of the year and is a winter resort for European and Australians.

Shore excursions: The most popular is the day cruise to the Great Barrier Reef. It includes lunch, a guide, and an opportunity to snorkel with the tropical fish. There's also a glass bottom submarine ride included for passengers who like to keep their feet wet. If you only have one day, the tour is a must. Cost about $100. With an additional day, choices include a full day visit to an Aboriginal Village and a narrow gauge train ride through a neighboring forest. Cost about $85, including lunch.

INSIDER SHOPPING TIP:

A very large shopping mall is part of the main cruise ship terminal. It's an everything-made-in-Australia mall and prices are very reasonable. Best buys are trendy resort wear.

Melbourne

Built along the banks of the Yarra River, Melbourne is a city of wide, tree-lined boulevards, riverside lawns and gardens, and a compact downtown where Victorian-era buildings stand next to modern steel and glass structures. The city's mobile landmark, the Melbourne tram rumbles past the old downtown buildings just as it did during the late 19th century.

While Sydney's Opera House is best known for its exterior, VAC is renowned for its interior. It has five underground stories and innovative architectural and acoustic designs. The riverside center includes nearly one thousand acres of surrounding gardens and houses designed by famous European and aboriginal artists.

INSIDER SHOPPING TIP

Visit Queen Victoria market, which sells everything from clothes to vegetables at very competitive prices, not unlike London's Portobello Road and Covent Garden.

Sydney

Sydney is cosmopolitan, lively, and contemporary in its nightlife, theater, music, industry, and lifestyles. A modern subway line connects all the main shopping areas and main line train services. Buses are plentiful and inexpensive. Ferries or water taxis are the preferred, as well as most delightful, way to see the great harbor or relax from the hustle of the city. They leave at about 15 minute intervals from Circular Quay, which is almost alongside the new piers. Ferries also make daily harbor cruises. I always suggest a day cruise for familiarization for a close-up look at Sydney's superb waterfront area.

INSIDER TIP

While the Sydney Opera House is a "must" on every visitor's list (and it does not disappoint), the structure was built without elevators or handicapped facilities. There are steep stairways. Buses stop far from the entrance and, unless you use the stage door entrance, there's a long walk inside the building. If you happen to have balcony seats, bring binoculars. Wear comfortable shoes.

On Your Own: For an inkling of its history, walk around the Old Rocks area near the bridge to see Cadman's Cottage, the Customs House, and the two Georgian buildings. The Sydney Opera House is one of the world's architectural wonders. It has four halls where top quality drama, ballet, opera, and concerts are performed. While the Sydney Opera House looks exactly like its much-publicized image, the inside is somewhat disappointing and stark in its minimalism.

For the best view of the city, climb to a vantage point like the Harbor Bridge, or the 48th floor skywalk observation deck of Australia Square. If you associate koalas with Australia, a good place to see the furry animals is at Koala Park, fifteen miles northwest of Sydney.

INSIDER SHOPPING TIP

I'll bet few of you are aware that South Sea Pearls are mined off the coast of Australia and they are available at many jewelers in varied colors and sizes. If you're interested, remember this is a big ticket item, but costs about 35 percent of what similar quality sells for on Fifth Avenue. Most travelers think "Japan" or "Hong Kong" for pearls, but I found them less expensive in Sydney. Look for a jeweler who boasts about his years in business and shop at what looks like the most reputable. I found a jeweler In the ML Center (walking distance from the pier) whose family had been in business for 80 years in Sydney. When I had the pearls strung at home, the appraisal was so high, I purchased a black strand from the same jeweler on my next visit.

Tasmania – Hobart

Tasmania is situated off Australia's southeast coast, across the Bass Strait from Melbourne. The island is about the size of Ireland, with a population of less than half a million. Tasmanians look upon themselves as different from mainlanders. Tasmania is wetter, giving it a greener, lusher look than the rest of Australia. It is more mountainous, with alpine lakes and a rugged interior that has barely been explored in parts. The island's past also sets it apart from the mainland. It was among the first areas of Australia to be settled by Europeans, beginning in 1803 as a penal colony. Tasmania became a dumping ground for convicts who were too incorrigible for the New South Wales penal colony. Today, about a sixth of Tasmania's population can trace its ancestry directly to those convicts.

Convicts built many of the sturdy Georgian and Victorian era buildings that still stand. Thousands of British prisoners were banished to the island from 1803 to 1850. The island's fierce aboriginal resisted European settlement to the end and eventually became extinct in one of the most tragic chapters in Australia's history.

New Zealand

New Zealand is made up of two islands with some of the most magnificent and dramatic natural features in the world: the Alpine peaks of Mt. Cook and its neighbors (each over ten thousand feet), and the towering walls of majestic fjords on the South Island. Weather is similar to Australia with cruise ships calling during the summer months of October through mid-April. New Zealanders are beer drinkers, and the local beer is very good and quite inexpensive. Wines are produced locally.

INSIDER SHOPPING TIP
Good buys are limited to wood carvings and ornaments made out of greenstone, which looks a lot like jade. Sheepskin rugs and hand made wool items, such as sweaters and blankets.

More information: New Zealand Tourism Board, 501 Santa Monica Blvd., Suite 300, Santa Monica, CA 90401, or www.discovernz.co.nz

Auckland

Auckland is placed astride two seas - Waitemata Harbor and Manukay Harbor, which provide contrasting views. The town is built on sloping hills, surrounded by forests. A scenic drive above the city is recommended, while a waterfront drive displays the seaside location. Mt. Eden, behind the town, was once a Maori fort and offers a great view of the city. The War Memorial Museum is two hundred acres of gardens housing one of the best Maori collections in the world. If you're lucky and ship arrives during the World Cup Races, you'll be able to see the boats from your ship and experience the excitement that runs through the city,

Dunedin

Dunedin might well be referred to as "Edinburgh down under." Instructed to reproduce features of the Scottish capital, Dunedin's city surveyor measured and laid out the city before the colonists arrived. Thus, it is no coincidence that many of the city's streets bear the names of its counterpart, or that architecture is similar in both cities. Like its Scottish sister-city, Dunedin also is the seat of one of the country's most respected universities and bastion of a quietly sophisticated culture.

On Your Own: A walk through Dunedin should start at the heart of the city center, the Octagon, a spacious municipal garden sporting a statue of Scottish poet Robert Burns. On the Octagon, you'll find the Victorian-style Municipal Chamber built in 1878 and the Gothic revival style First Presbyterian Church built in 1873. The nearby law courts (built in 1899) and Flemish Renaissance style Railway Station (built in 1904) offer more innovative examples of various architectural eras.

Milford Sound

Milford Sound is New Zealand's most famous fjord. "Sound" is actually a misnomer, since Milford is closed at one end. The view from the head of the fjord is especially breathtaking with high granite peaks framing a glacier-covered inlet. The peaks are reflected onto the deep, dark waters of the fjord below. The area receives about three hundred inches of rainfall a year, allowing a lush carpet of ferns and small trees to prosper on the steep cliffs rising from the water.

Wellington

Since 1865, Wellington has served as the capital of New Zealand. Apart from its beauty and importance as the seat of the national government, the city also is the commercial center of a growing industrial area, a busy export port, and the North Island's communication and transport link with the South Island.

Places to visit in Wellington include the Parliament, Kelburn Park high above the city and reached via cable car, the Botanical Gardens covering sixty-three acres, and the National Art Gallery.

Bahamas, Bermuda, Caribbean, West Indies And The Panama Canal

The Caribbean islands enjoy a sunny year-round climate with temperatures ranging from an average 75 degrees in January to 85 or 90 in August. Rainy months are May through September. Recommended clothing ashore is casual, comfortable, and very lightweight. Beachwear is only acceptable on beaches. Shoes should be comfortable. A few hotel restaurants and casinos require jackets and ties in the evening.

Most islands have their own currency, but dollars are accepted everywhere as are travelers checks and major credit cards. Tipping follows U.S. custom of about 15 percent, but on some islands a service charge is added in restaurants and hotels.

The Caribbean is the most popular cruise area of the world. Itineraries change frequently and cruise lines tend to reposition ships. Almost every cruise line sailing from Florida calls at Caribbean ports. The ships are too numerous to mention, but all ships sailing from Cape Canaveral, Miami, Fort Lauderdale, San Juan and Tampa visit Caribbean islands. If the island has a deep harbor, more than one ship probably makes seasonal visits.

Cruise itineraries generally are broken down into Southern, Eastern, Western Caribbean and Panama Canal sailings Although Bermuda and the Bahamas are technically in the Atlantic Ocean and not in the Caribbean, they are included in this section because cruise lines often stop at both Caribbean and Bahamian ports and sometimes include Bermuda.

Southern Caribbean ports include: Bridgetown, Barbados; La Guaira/Caracas, Venezuela; Roseau, Dominica; St. George's Grenada; St. John/St. Thomas, U.S.V.I., Casa de Campo, Dominican Republic, San Juan, Puerto Rico. and Willemstad, Curacao. Eastern Caribbean ports include: Nassau, Phillipsburg, St. Martin; St. John/St. Thomas; Basseterre, St. Kitts, and San Juan. Western Caribbean ports include: Cozumel, Mexico (see section on Mexican ports); Ocho Rios, Jamaica; and Grand Cayman.

Sightseeing: Ships offer a wide variety of tours in every port. Many are sports oriented, others are sightseeing and shopping. Expect to pay abut $40 for a half day, about $75 for a full day with lunch.

On Your Own: Most islands are small; none offer antiquities or major attractions. They are sun and beach ports with shopping as an added attraction. They are a haven for water sports - divers go underwater, snorkelers are welcome at all the beaches, boat rentals are available. Most public beaches are a taxi ride from piers and some hotels will allow you to use the facilities for a small fee. Ask the shore excursion department on the ship about hotel beaches and what arrangements are required. Shoppers can usually walk or take a short taxi ride to the market and/or area with the most shops.

More Information: For detailed information on all ports contact Caribbean Tourism Organization, 80 Broad Street, 32nd Floor, New York, NY 10004; (212)635-9534 or www.info@caribtourism.com

Antigua

Antigua covers only 108 square miles and has a population of 70,000 residents. It is a mere 16 miles across at almost any point. Christopher Columbus discovered Antigua (the largest of the Leeward Islands) and its dependent islands of Barbuda and Redonda in 1493 during his second voyage to the New World. During the 18th and 19th centuries, Antigua served as a British naval base and was Lord Nelson's station from 1786 to 1788. The base has been restored and is a major tourist attraction. An independent state in the British Commonwealth, Antigua retains much of the charm and culture of its first mother country. St. John's is the capital city.

The island's beaches are famous--365 to be exact, offering one for every day of the year--and wonderful trade winds make Antigua a favorite with those who have sand in their shoes. Tours include visits to English Harbor, the site of Admiral Nelson's historical dockyard with its restored buildings, restaurants and small hotels. Also worth visiting are Clarence House, the governor's country house, built in 1787; Fig Tree Drive in the mountainous tropical sector of the island; the hundreds of beautiful beaches and coves protected by off-shore reefs; the Anglican Cathedral and Court House in St. John's; a sugar factory; and several old forts.

INSIDER SHOPPING TIPS

Some shops close on Thursday afternoons. Antiguan rum sells for about $10 a bottle, and locally made hand-screened print fabrics are also good value. Other good buys are English imports, local handicraft, garments made in Hong Kong, Swiss watches, pottery, and Cuban cigars (which may not be imported into the United States). Local handicrafts are also of interest to tourists and include tortoise items, ceramics, and the Mary Hat of Madras-lined linen that folds flat for packing.

Aruba

Aruba is one of those naturally air-conditioned islands blessed by year-round temperatures averaging 82 degrees. Umbrellas are unnecessary since the island has less than 20 inches of rain annually. The multi-cultural environment has encouraged several languages. Papiamento (a patois that is both spoken and written), Dutch, Spanish, and English seem interchangeable.

A small island, 15 miles off the coast of Venezuela, Aruba is a bit of Holland transplanted into the West Indies. Although the Spanish discovered the island in 1500, it is the Dutch whose influence dates from Peter Stuyvesant's arrival in 1624. Since those days, and the days of the Arawak Indians, people from more than 40 nations have settled on this coral-rock island. The architecture is a blend of Holland and the West Indies, and homes are painted vivid colors of the rainbow.

Sightseeing: Take the ship tour or do it on your own, but first time visitors should see the natural bridge on the north coast, carved from solid coral rock by the sea; William III Tower, which dates back to 1867, once served as a prison and is now a colorful "timepiece"; Mount Hooiberg for an interesting view; and Ranchostraat's Lime Kiln, a gigantic oven used in the early 1900s to make lime.

INSIDER SHOPPING TIPS
Caya G.F. Betico Croes is the main shopping street, renamed for a hero of the island's Independence movement. It was formerly called Nassaustraat (Nassau Street). Today equally good shopping is found in a couple of malls located a short walk from the port: Sonesta's Seaport Village Mall and Seaport Marketplace, which bustles with activity day and night. Good buys are Swiss watches, perfume, cameras, cashmere goods, and china. Some stores are closed from noon to 2:00 P.M. All stores are closed Sundays.

The Bahamas

More than 700 limestone islands and 2,400 cays make up the Bahamas group, which forms a 760-mile arc in the Atlantic, about 50 miles from Florida's coast. The climate is similar to that of South Florida with temperatures ranging from 60 to 85 degrees all year. The Bahamas Dollar is on par with the U.S. dollar and is used almost interchangeably.

Christopher Columbus arrived in the Bahamas on October 12, 1492, and called the original inhabitants "Indians," thinking he had arrived in India. Arawak or Lucayan Indians, in fact, populated the island. Today's population consists of descendants of English settlers, American Loyalists, and Confederates (who came here in the late 17th and 18th centuries), and slaves from Africa, (whose descendants now account for about 80 percent of the population). The residents like to call Columbus their first tourist.

More Information: Bahamas Ministry of Tourism, 150 E. 52nd St. 28th Floor, North, New York, NY 10022, or www.bahamas.com. The Ministry will furnish information on all of the islands.

The Bahamas

Freeport

This coral rock island is a result of an American financier's imagination. Unlike other islands of the Bahamas, Freeport stresses the new as opposed to the quaint and traditional, all with a Bahamian touch.

Sightseeing: Interesting day excursions should include a visit to a nearby fishing village for a look at the way the island was before 1955; the International Bazaar; Port Lucaya, with its international shops, set across from the hotel and casino bearing the Lucaya name; downtown Freeport; various golf courses; El Casino, and Garden of the Groves, a beautiful botanical garden.

INSIDER SHOPPING TIP

Prices are the same as in Nassau, but the atmosphere is international in the bazaar, which changes sidewalks and street lights in each country's area. Of interest to tourists are English imports, straw and other native work, baskets, jewelry, and some art.

Nassau

Nassau has native charm. A busy, bustling, capital city in the sunshine, Nassau is also a laid-back resort center on New Providence Island where everything in the Bahamas happens. Beaches are outstanding, particularly on Paradise Island and at Cable Beach. Climate is ideal year-round. Take either the ship excursion or hire a cab at the dock. Price is negotiable. The one-hour horse-and-buggy tour (about $15 for two) covers the Bay Street area and drivers are old-timers who take you over back roads and come up with the best stories about the good-old-days. Harbor ferryboat transportation between the dock and Paradise Island runs regularly ($3 to $4 per person). Taxis cost about $5 per person to Paradise Island. Harbor cruises to nowhere are also available for a seaside look at Paradise Island and Nassau.

INSIDER TIP
Take a ferry, a bus or taxi to Paradise Island for a birds' eye view of Atlantis, one of the most incredible resort complexes in the world. There are regularly scheduled guided tours through tunnels and waterfalls. Kids of all ages will love it and chances are good you will think about coming back for an extended land vacation.

Sightseeing: Tours sold on board ships take you to Fort Charlotte; historic old churches; Blackbeard's Tower; the Queen's Staircase; Ardastra Gardens; Paradise Island; and the multi-colored, multi-faceted Cable Beach complex.

INSIDER SHOPPING TIP
Nassau rivals St. Thomas with the number of jewelry shops, but bargains are few and far between. Perfume, liquor and cosmetics are about 15 percent less than back home, but selection is limited. A number of trendy international-type stores have opened. These include "names" such as Gucci, but prices are not an incentive to carry the stuff home unless your town doesn't have a branch of that particular store. It is possible to catch a good buy in English imports, crystal, china, woolens, and jewelry

Bahamas Private Islands

Almost every cruise line boasts a private island where passengers enjoy barbecues and beach games, water sports and a "Fantasy Island" ambience, or a reasonable facsimile, as part of the total cruise experience. A thousand or so "Out" islands in the Bahamas are called "Neighbor Islands. They have been "rediscovered" by cruise lines looking for "new" destinations and they have become "ports of call."

Called "beach parties" on uninhabited, or sparsely inhabited Bahamian Islands, passengers rate the "Robinson Crusoe" experience very high. Ships stop from four to eight hours. No shore excursions are sold, and passengers disembark by tender, except for Disney Cruise Line ships. Restroom facilities are available on all of the islands but there are few changing facilities, so wear your bathing suit, sandals and a cover-up. A buffet picnic-type lunch is served on the island by the cruise line.

Some ships recommend that you bring the ship's towels ashore, then return them to your cabin steward; others furnish towels on the island. All of the ships offer extensive water sport activities. Beaches have chairs and umbrellas for passengers intent on avoiding the sun, but there are never enough umbrellas to go around. Bring head covers.

It's an enjoyable day on islands that are unspoiled in the way the Bahamas were not too many years ago.

In the Southern Bahamas, Holland America Line has acquired Little San Salvador Island, just off the northern coast of Cat Island, where it has developed a private port of call dubbed "Half Moon Cay." In the Northern Bahamas, Norwegian Cruise Line calls on Stirrup Cay in the Berry Islands, and Princess ships do their thing at the southern tip of Eleuthera. Royal Caribbean offers its version of a beach party at Coco Cay in the Bahamas on some itineraries and at Labadee, Haiti on others.

Disney Cruises takes passengers to Castaway Cay. Formerly known as Gorda Cay, a 1,000-acre island in the Abacos, Disney has created a unique island paradise for their passengers. Unlike other islands, Disney ships pull right alongside and no tendering is required.

Costa Cruises' uses Serena Cay in the Dominican Republic for their day at the beach, and an extra dollop of fun, in the form of Dominican folk music and dancers, makes for an enjoyable day away from the ship.

All of the activities on the "private" islands are water related and all offer fun and games in the sand, and a beach barbecue supplied by the ship. Passengers who hail from mid-western cities, and to whom a day at the beach is a very special treat rate these island days as highlights of the cruise experience. All lines have supervised special events going on for children – treasure hunts, sailing, snorkeling, and even sand castle building.

Barbados

The most easterly of the Caribbean islands, compact Barbados is 21 miles long and 14 miles wide and has a population of 254,000. Feisty Atlantic surf batters its east coast, while the tranquil Caribbean bathes the white beaches of its west coast, home to most water sports on the island. Bridgetown is the island's capital, port, and commercial center, and its bustling harbor is the focus of all sights and sounds of a West Indian seaport. Harbor police wear uniforms similar to those worn in Admiral Nelson's navy. His statue decorates Trafalgar Square and St. Michael's Cathedral, where George Washington supposedly worshiped.

The Barbadians are chiefly of British (five percent) and African (95 percent) descent and speak with a soft, 18th-century inflection. Donkey carts, bicycles, and pushcarts share the roads with buses and motorcars while Barbadians sip afternoon tea on the veranda and share tidbits with the native sugar-birds.

Sightseeing: Places to see in Bridgetown include: Magazine Lane, where the Montefiore Fountain was presented to the island's people by a prominent Jewish family; the 18th century Town Hall, the former meeting place of the House of Assembly; Trafalgar Square with Lord Nelson's statue; the Barbados Museum with relics of the island's history; and St. Michael's Cathedral, rebuilt on coral rock in 1780. Don't miss the stature of Lord Nelson, in place three decades before the famed London version was created. If time permits, take the spectacular drive across the island from Bridgetown to Bathsheba on the Atlantic coast.

INSIDER SHOPPING TIPS
The best shopping buy in Barbados is local rum which still sells for under $10 a bottle at port shops. Other good buys include china, crystal, cameras, watches, cashmere, and linens, as well as native handicrafts of straw, mahogany, shell, and coral. Stores are open 8:00 A.M. to 4:00 P.M. Monday through Friday and closed Saturday afternoons and Sundays.

Bermuda

A tiny speck in the Atlantic, Bermuda is about 1,000 miles north of the Caribbean and 800 miles southeast of New York. The 150 islands of Bermuda cover 21 square miles. It's a two-season island with summer temperatures (May to mid-November) from 75 to 85 degrees; winter temperatures (mid-December to March) from 60 to 70 degrees. Covered-up casual lightweight clothing and dressier casual are recommended for evenings. Bathing suits, bikinis, and bare feet are not acceptable for street wear. Ties and jackets are required for dinner and evening activities in hotels. Bermuda is very British. Although traffic is heavier than it was a few years ago, it is still common to see a dignified gentleman in a jacket, shirt, and tie with an umbrella tucked under his arm as he rides his moped into town.

If you believe the advertising, Bermuda is for lovers. Also for golfers, tennis enthusiasts, beach goers, and island aficionados. For years, Bermuda was the private playground of Englishmen and Northeasterners who treated the island as a personal paradise, and Bermuda's government officials still act as official watchmen so too many tourists do not pollute the island.

Ships tie up at one of the three harbors - Hamilton, St. George's, or West End. The traditional port is Hamilton, the capital and the most commercial area on the island. Hamilton is also the most convenient pier. Passengers whose ship ties up at St. George's walk off the vessel into Bermuda's equivalent of Colonial Williamsburg. Located at the East End of the island, St. George's is a charming town with 17th century buildings, narrow lanes, and small boutiques. West End is the farthest cruise port from Bermuda's main attractions, but a new tourist complex is under construction in the area.

INSIDER TIP

Bermuda is far from inexpensive. A cup of coffee costs between one and three dollars, depending on where you sip. A bottle of beer runs as much as five dollars and a pack of Kodak 110 film with 12 exposures is priced around five dollars. A quick lunch in a coffee shop can top the $10 per person figure. Don't put cameras and/or other valuables (purses) in the basket attached to motorbikes (mopeds). Snatchings by fast-riding motorcycle thieves have been reported by ship passengers. The crime rate, otherwise, is very low.

On Your Own: I use the ferries that leave from Hamilton (at the end of the piers) and then take the bus back. Cost is about five dollars and it is the best sightseeing on the Island. Express bus service leaves Hamilton every 15 minutes for dockyard, a trip that takes about half an hour, or half the time of regular bus service. Visitors to Bermuda are not permitted to rent cars, but that doesn't restrict mobility. The bus system is efficient, and schedules are readily available. Ferries are more fun. They provide a mini-cruise across Hamilton harbor to Paget for one dollar each way, or from Hamilton all the way to the Dockyard for two dollars. Taxis are easy to find but expensive. But, for the price of a ride, visitors are likely to receive a sightseeing tour. Every driver I've ever encountered acted like a tour guide, or better still as someone showing off his home. Motorbikes, scooters, and mopeds are the most popular way to get around and probably the most dangerous.

INSIDER SHOPPING TIP
Best buys are for anything made in England which is imported without duty, making it "duty free" and at about 20 percent below U.S. prices. Visitors usually stock up on cashmere products, woolens from Scotland, and china from Belfast

More Information: Bermuda Department of Tourism, 310 Madison Avenue, Suite 210, New York, NY 10017. Or www.bermudatourism.com

British Virgin Islands

Scientists believe the British Virgin Islands were originally one large piece of land formed by volcanic activity. Now there are some 50-plus islands in a less-than-60-mile area containing some of the clearest water and prettiest scenery in the region.

Tortola

Tortola is known as the yachting capital of the world. The lovely trade winds and sheltered coves make it a favorite with those who travel on charter boats. But cruise ship passengers can enjoy these islands just as well. Part of the British Commonwealth today, the original settlers were Amerindian tribes: primarily the Arawak and Carib nations. Spain, Holland and France all attempted to colonize the islands but the British took over and annexed Tortola in the late 17th century.

Be sure to cover your swimsuit in town. These islands are fairly conservative. They are not known for great shopping values but for laid-back water sports, fishing and great beaches.

Sightseeing: On Virgin Gorda, ("fat virgin," in Spanish), the Baths are a sight to see and resemble nothing as much as toy blocks for a giant who disappeared without cleaning up his playthings. Marvelous clumps of granite thrown here and there--some of the boulders are taller than many houses--and when the sun shines through the rocks it's almost mystically beautiful. Road Town, on Tortola, is the capital of the B.V.I. and where most cruise ships call. See the J.R. O'Neal Botanic Garden; visit Mount Sage National Park, the island's tallest peak, or just head for a beach and enjoy the scenery.

More information: British Virgin Islands Tourist Board, 370 Lexington Ave., Room 1605, New York, N.Y. 10017, or www.bvivacations.com

Cayman Islands

Three islands make up the British Crown Colony of the Cayman Islands, known as one of the world's great diving destinations. While dress for the most part is casual, businessmen (bankers for the most part,) wear jackets and ties.

The Caymans were not as popular 100 years ago as they are today. Because of the treacherous coral reefs that surround them, more than 300 ships met their doom here, and now provide a fascinating attraction for underwater divers. Tales of buried treasure and buccaneers add romantic flavor to the history of the Cayman Islands. It's only in the last 30 or 40 years that tourists discovered these islands for their diving opportunities and off-shore banking.

Sightseeing: The greatest attractions in the Caymans are underwater. The most spectacular beach is the Seven-Mile Beach. Water attractions include Pedro's Castle, Henry Morgan headquarters in pirate days; Turtle Crawls in North Sound; wild orchids and wild parrots on Rum Point; "Hell," a weird coral formation on the north end of the island; and Georgetown, formerly a quiet capital city, now with international banks offering "numbered" and "secret" banking facilities. The most popular excursion invites you to "swim with stingrays." It's a memorable experience, especially for kids over eight.

INSIDER SHOPPING TIP

I have never found an outstanding bargain in Grand Cayman, but there are dozens of jewelry shops and some trendy boutiques have opened. Unless you are desperate to buy something, I would wait for another port to do my major shopping. British imports - china, crystal and woolens, are "duty free" but selection is limited.

More Information: Cayman Islands Department of Tourism, 420 Lexington Avenue, New York, NY 10017 or www.cayman.com

Curacao

Curacao lies just 35 miles north of Venezuela in the southern Caribbean. Trade winds are constant, and evenings are cooler. There is some rain in November and December. A Spanish navigator, Alonso de Ojeda, serving under Christopher Columbus, discovered Curacao in 1499. The Spaniards settled on the island in the early 1500s, and in 1634 the Dutch captured the island and founded a settlement. Peter Stuyvesant became governor in 1643.

On Your Own: Willemstad, the capital city, is best seen by walking across the Queen Emma Bridge (the largest pontoon bridge in the Western Hemisphere) and through its bustling streets. A canal-like inlet bisects the sparkling-clean city into what are called Punda and Otrabanda. Gabled houses in early Dutch-Colonial style are painted pastel colors, and the bay front area is characteristic of that style.

Willemstad is really a Dutch masterpiece with its waterfront-lined 17th and 18th century buildings painted in shades of yellow, lime, and blue. Architecture is strictly Dutch influenced. The city is picture-postcard pretty and is probably the most photographed in the Caribbean.

The entrance to the harbor has been renovated and is near the Governor's Palace, Dutch Reform Church (1769), and the Mikve Israel-Emanuel Synagogue, built around the same time.

Sightseeing: Among interesting places to visit are the oldest Protestant church (1759), on the square behind Governor House; the 1732 synagogue; the view from the top of Ararat Hill; the Jewish cemetery which is the oldest Caucasian cemetery in the hemisphere; the coral caverns, and the lighthouse.

INSIDER SHOPPING TIP

This is one of the better shopping ports. Curacao of Curacao, of course, is sold at five dollars a fifth. Like Aruba, Curacao is a duty-free haven, and everything from all over the world is available at fair prices - china, crystal, jewelry, watches, clothing, and perfume. Selection is greater in Aruba, but Curacao is making a giant effort to catch up. Shops in the downtown district of Willemstad are open Monday through Saturday from 8 A.M. to noon and again from 2 to 6 P.M. A few of the larger stores stay open throughout the day.

More Information: Curacao Tourist Board, 475 Park Avenue South, Suite 2000, New York, NY 10016, or Email: etdbny@dtdb.com

INSIDER TIPS

Do take the square nickels should a shopkeeper offer them in change. They are very scarce and make great souvenirs. They are still available from banks. Curacao is one of my favorite islands. If unusual beaches turn you on, don't miss the beach at the Sonesta Beach Hotel or the Holiday Inn. You can make arrangements to use the changing facilities and locker rooms for a nominal charge (sometimes, no charge depending on how busy the hotel happens to be). Be sure to bring a headscarf if you are concerned with the way your hair looks. Those tropical trade winds work on a 24 hour basis and can ruin the most lacquered look within seconds. But it's worth it! The island has 38 great beaches!

Dominica

Dominica is one of the largest of the Windward Islands, yet, apart from its capital, it is one of the least developed. It sits in the Lesser Antilles between Guadeloupe and Martinique. Extremely casual clothing is recommended for this island blessed with trade winds that keep average high temperature in the 80s and lows in the high 60s. The island is mountainous and rugged, with a tropical jungle, whose rich soil yields bumper crops of bananas, vanilla, and citrus. According to popular legend, it has as many rivers as days of the year.

Known as "Nature Island," it has 290-square miles of lush terrain and is home to numerous exotic species of rainbow-colored birds, butterflies, and flowers. It is also one of the few places that remain home to the Carib Indians, the early inhabitants for whom the Caribbean was named. About 3,000 Carib Indians live on 3,700 acres in the northeastern part of the island.

INSIDER SHOPPING TIP

Except for native handicraft, hold off for serious shopping in some of the more populated islands geared to mass tourist infiltration.

Dominican Republic

The Dominican Republic covers two-thirds of the island known as Hispaniola and shares with its western neighbor, Haiti. Cruise ships call at two ports in the Dominican Republic: Santo Domingo, the capital city, which has developed a new harbor facility and terminal with duty-free shops; and Puerta Plata on the north shore of the country. There is a city atmosphere in Santo

Domingo; and more rural around Puerto Plata.

The Dominican Republic's first tourist was Christopher Columbus in 1492. In 1496, Columbus's brother Bartholomew founded Santo Domingo de Guzman, capital of the Republic, making it the oldest European settlement in the New World. Visitors are surprised to find the Western Hemisphere's first hospital, first university, oldest street, and the oldest Cathedral. The Dominican Republic also claims a "last." Dominicans say the remains of that great explorer, Columbus, are entombed in the first Cathedral, although this claim is disputed by cities in Spain and Cuba. Restoration of historic sites is also a "first" for Caribbean islands. The historic zone has been restored to almost the way it was back in those colonial days.

Sightseeing: Among places to visit in Santo Domingo are the Basilica Santa Maria in Menor with its carvings, treasure rooms, and Columbus's tomb; the restored Alcazar de Colon built by Don Diego, Columbus's son; the Viceregal Museum with its Spanish antiquities; the Tower of Homage, the oldest stone fortress in the Americas, now a prison; Santo Domingo University; the national capital; the famous Boca Chica beach; and the fabulous new hotel-resort complexes complete with Las Vegas-style casinos.

In Puerto Plata, on the north coast, there are long stretches of beaches, an unspoiled community, the new Jack Tarr Village, a marvelous golf course, water sports, and a magnificent coastline. It is basically an agricultural countryside. For the best views and an exciting experience, try the cable car ride up the mountains behind Puerto Plata.

INSIDER SHOPPING TIP

Shopping is surprisingly good in Santo Domingo. Amber is reasonably priced. Another local stone is larimar, which is blue in color. Other good buys are mahogany carvings, pottery, ceramics, straw articles, embroidery, and paintings. Stores are open from 8:30 to noon and from 2:30 to 6:00 P.M., Monday through Saturday.

More Information: Dominican Republic Tourist Information Center, 1501 Broadway, Suite 410, New York, NY 10036 or www.dominicanrepublic.com

Grenada

Southernmost of the Windward Islands, Grenada lies 90 miles north of Trinidad. The population numbers 96,000 on an island that is only 21 miles long and 12 miles wide. Dry season is January through May, with rainy weather from June to December, but rain seldom lasts more than an hour.

Discovered by Columbus in 1498, Grenada is the largest of the three islands that comprise the Independent State of Grenada. This is where you find the famous black-and-white beaches. Only 50 yards separate the jet-black sand of the Atlantic from the pure white sand of the Caribbean. St. George's is the capital city.

Grenada is a mountainous island, laden with exotic plants and trees (cinnamon, cloves, cocoa, vanilla, ginger, nutmeg, avocado, papaya, mango, banana, and breadfruit). No one goes hungry in Grenada. Grenada's heritage is as rich as the foliage. A visit to Carib's Leap at the north end of the island is a look at one chapter in the island's history. There, Indians chose suicide over slavery and leaped to their death after a battle-stand against the French. If your ship is in port on a Saturday, visit the local market for a kaleidoscopic view of everything grown on the island. Locals come into town for chatter and communication with other locals. Bring your camera.

Sightseeing: Among interesting places to visit are the massive battlements of Fort George and Fort Frederick; Great Etang, a volcanic crater lake; the beaches at Point Saline; Annandale Falls on the Beausejour River; nutmeg processing stations; and Carriacou, a tiny island accessible by ferry. This island is famous for the abundance of spices it produces, and it is known as the Spice Island because it grows one-third of the world's supply of nutmeg. Its flag even shows nutmeg.

INSIDER SHOPPING TIP

The best shopping is in spices of all kinds, particularly those that are hard to get in other parts of the world. Spices are packaged so there is no problem bringing them into the U.S. Saffron is the best buy. It sells for a fraction of the cost in U.S. specialty food stores. Some jewelry and art objects and native handicrafts from Trinidad are also well priced. The best place to shop for spices is in local supermarkets right off the shelf for 30 to 50 cents per container. Some examples of unusual condiments are: Trinidad mustard, tonic wine, Tulong, English bitter chocolate and of course, saffron.

Guadeloupe

The island of Guadeloupe has a population of 330,000 and covers 687 square miles. The currency is the French Franc, and languages spoken are French and Creole with very limited English spoken except in tourist shops and restaurants.

Guadeloupe is shaped like a giant butterfly with the wings made by the two islands, Grand Terre on the east and Basse Terre on the west, forming the mountainous area crowned by La Soufrier at 4,813 feet. Scenery is a mix of mountains, volcanic peaks, green forests, lakes, waterfalls, and tropical flora. Pointe a Petre is the commercial port city. There are good beaches only a 15-minute ride from the pier and excellent hotels have been built. Basse Terre is the capital.

Sightseeing: The Creole architecture that reminds one of New Orleans is hard to miss. There are three very interesting museums, an 18th century fort, the sugar town of Sainte Anne and its beaches, Guadeloupe National Park with its tropical forest, Basse Terre, and if time permits, some of the neighboring small islands accessible by ferry.

INSIDER SHOPPING TIP
Shops are open the same hours as Martinique and offer the same 20 percent tax refund when payment is made in traveler's checks or by credit card. (See "Martinique" INSIDER SHOPPING TIPS.) Anything French is cheaper than back in the U.S., but selection seems better in Martinique.

More information: French West Indies Tourist Board, 444 Madison Ave., New York, NY 10017 or www.fwindies,.com

Jamaica

One of the most beautiful and diverse Caribbean islands, Jamaica attracts visitors with a variety of hotels, resort cities, scenic landscapes, and culture. Situated in the middle of the Caribbean, Jamaica is nearly 150 miles long and 50 miles wide with mountains, beaches, rivers, waterfalls, and plantations. Its population is over two million, language is English, and currency is Jamaican Dollars. U.S dollars cannot be accepted legally, but they will accept credit cards. It can be as much as 15 degrees cooler in mountain areas.

Columbus discovered Jamaica on his second voyage in 1494. Impressed by what he saw, the discoverer called his landing place "Santa Gloria," but Spaniards who came after him learned that the gentle Arawak Indians who lived on the island called it "Xamaca," which meant "islands of springs." Jamaica retains British traditions leftover from the days when it belonged to Great Britain

The native Jamaican is a mixture of millions of African slaves, European traders, and Asians who arrived here in the late 1800s. What has emerged is a people with unique accomplishments in music, culture, art, and handicraft. It is an island of contrasts with mountains and beaches, rural and urban communities, large resorts and small guesthouses. A winding coastline surrounds the island, and cruise ships, which sought other ports during Jamaica's troubled period, are again including Ocho Rios and Montego Bay ports in itineraries.

INSIDER SHOPPING TIP

Merchandise enters the country "duty free" to be sold to tourists. Duty free purchases must be sent to your ship (or to the airport). Free port items include perfume, cashmere goods, silks, Swiss watches, cameras, crystal, china, and photography equipment. Jamaican-made items are batik, carvings, ceramics, rum, and straw work. Every port city has a native market, and shops have branches with similar merchandise in all port cities.

More Information: Jamaica Tourist Board, 801 Second Ave., 20th Floor, New York, NY 10017 or www.jamaica.com

Montego Bay

Montego Bay has stood the test of time. Long before Columbus and the Spaniards arrived, Arawak Indian tribes worked and played at this spot, which is situated captivatingly on the water's edge at the foot of a range of green hills. Many Spanish colonists of the early 16th century were quick to recognize the advantages of settling there, and the English, who took over in 1655, were just as enthusiastic. Present-day visitors are no less so. Montego Bay (the Spaniards called it "Manteca Bahia", meaning "Lard Bay") is second only to Kingston in area and population. Built around a charming old town square, it has a number of churches (one dating from 1775), a town hall (1808), banks, many shops, movie houses, nightclubs, an art gallery or two, and the usual civic amenities.

Sightseeing: Interesting places to visit include Rose Hall Plantation with its time-honored legend of the "white witch", Good Hope Plantation, Montego

Bay Straw Market, Doctor's Cave (for swimming), and banana, sugar cane, and coconut plantations. Time permitting, take a leisurely ride on the Governor's Diesel Coach, which takes visitors into the heart of Jamaica with stops at interesting points along the way. And from either Ocho Rios or Montego Bay, visit Dunn's River Falls, a 600-foot waterfall shaped like a giant staircase.

Ocho Rios

Along a stretch of coral on the north-central Jamaican coast is the popular resort city of Ocho Rios, 67 miles east of Montego Bay and 58 miles northwest of Kingston. Sightseeing is the same as for Montego because they are so close. This area embraces a spectacular 42-mile expanse from Discovery Bay in the west to Port Maria in the east, with lovely holiday spots like Runaway Bay, Mammee Bay, Ocho Rios, and Oracabessa, in between.

Sightseeing: Attracted by a giant development plan which included a deep-water cruise ship harbor, the number of vessels calling at Ocho Rios has increased markedly during the past few years. The pier is within walking distance of convention hotels and resort facilities. Foremost among the area's attractions are Dunn's River Falls, which cascade down from the nearby hills, splashing into the blue Caribbean. To climb from sea level though the cascading torrents is a thrilling and memorable experience.

INSIDER TIPS

Jamaica is strict about enforcing currency exchange laws, and it is illegal to bring Jamaican dollars into or out of the country. Money must be exchanged at official exchange points (banks, hotels, and authorized exchange facilities at sea and airports of entry). Resist money exchange offers on the street. Imprisonment, fines, and a lot of embarrassment could interrupt your vacation. Also don't even think about, or pause to talk with, street vendors offering to sell you narcotics. Jamaican authorities are cracking down on these sales, and you are looking for trouble if you get involved. Vendors have been known to tip off police, and tourists find the police waiting for them at the gangplank. Be prepared for beggars using the ploy of a "sick child." They'll ask for a "dollar, please" and you'll soon discover there's a raging epidemic on the island. Some salespeople on the street and in markets can be quite aggressive. A firm "no, thank you" is usually enough to hold them at bay. Finally, Jamaica has had some problems with crime and it is best to stay with a group and off darkened side streets. A positive attitude and stride are important. Don't look like a victim!

Martinique

Martinique is the most exotic of the Caribbean's French islands. Its population of 350,000 is as French as that of the mother country. The island is 50 miles long, 22 miles wide, and covers an area of 425 square miles. There are three distinct seasons, with an average temperature of around 79 degrees: very fresh from November to April; dry and warm from April to July; and rainy from September to November. Currency is the French Franc and not everyone accepts U.S. dollars. Language is French and Creole. Martinique, like other islands, has become more casual, and it is not necessary to wear a jacket and tie at night except for very special occasions.

A French possession since the middle of the 17th century, Martinique became an Overseas Department of France in 1946 and a Region of France in 1974. After the abolition of slavery in 1848, the island was opened to immigration, and there was an influx of Hindus, Chinese, and Annamites from French Indochina.

Martinique's famous Mount Pelee erupted in 1902, in three minutes wiping out the entire population of the former capital city of St. Pierre, whose ruins are called the "Pompeii of the New World." Martinique is also renowned as the birthplace of Napoleon's Empress Josephine, and for *HMS Diamond Rock*, a ship commissioned by the British Navy in the 18th century, held out for eighteen months against the French. This is also the location of one of the island's best beaches. Fort-de-France is the capital city.

Sightseeing: A day in Martinique should include a ride through the lush rain forests, up Mount Pelee and past Martinique's brightly-colored fishing boats and villages. The Volcanology Museum of St. Pierre is devoted to the eruption of Mount Pelee, which is now considered inactive. Also worth seeing are La Pagerie, the birthplace of Empress Josephine, the countryside and downtown Fort-de-France.

INSIDER SHOPPING TIPS

Since the island is French, anything made in France is a good buy. Rue Victor Hugo is the main shopping street. Perfumes, crystal, china, Lalique, and rum are excellent values. Shops are normally closed between 12:30 and 2:30 P.M. and Saturday afternoons, except when a large cruise ship is in port. Some shops also stay open beyond the normal 6:00 P.M. closing and on Sunday morning when cruise ships are in port. There are a number of good shops in Martinique, but I have dealt with Roger Albert (the name of the shop and the name of the founder) for the last 25 five years and do not hesitate to recommend it. Roger Albert has the largest selection of French and other imported merchandise of interest to travelers. The store is reliable and prices are highly competitive. You can take advantage of a 20 percent immediate tax credit if you pay for your purchases by traveler's checks or major credit cards. Clerks are courteous. The senior Roger Albert has retired and his son has taken over operation of the huge store. He is just as enthusiastic and has a big welcome mat out for Americans. This tax refund amounts to a 20 percent reduction in prices on top of the already lower prices on items from France and makes Martinique the cheapest place to purchase your French fragrances and cosmetics. If your ship is heading for Martinique and your shopping list includes French items, save some of your purchases for this island.

More Information: French West Indies Tourist Board, 444 Madison Ave., New York, NY 10017 or www.martinique.com

Canada

Cruise season for both east- and west-coast Canadian ports runs from May through late October. July and August are considered high season in British Columbia. High season on the eastern seaboard extends through October's Indian summer. Temperature ranges from the low 50s in May to a high of up to 80°F on sunny September days. July and August temperatures generally average in the mid-60s to low 70s. The Canadian dollar fluctuates and is running about 25 percent below par with U.S. currency. English and French are the official languages in the Montreal area.

Tipping customs closely follow those in the United States, but taxi drivers seem to expect a little more than the usual 15 percent. If you check your coat, expect to tip about a dollar. It's easy to get around in every Canadian city. Public transportation is very good, and taxis are readily available.

INSIDER SHOPPING TIPS
With a weak Canadian dollar, there are very good shopping values in Canadian and British-made goods such as woolens and china. Alaskan Eskimo artifacts and artworks are popular purchases. Canadian-produced textiles also are excellent buys. Large cities with malls are the best place to shop for clothing. Locally made items are available in every port, but selection is best in larger cities, except for handicraft items. Trendy raincoats are good buys.

Depending on the port, suggested dress is comfortable, city-type clothing. Jackets are required for dinner in more expensive hotel dining rooms and restaurants. A sweater or lightweight jacket is recommended, as temperatures tend to change quickly. Comfortable walking shoes are a must.

More Information: Canadian Government Office of Tourism, 1251 Avenue of the Americas, New York, NY 10020, or www.canada.com for information on every port of call on both Canadian coasts.

INSIDER TIP

It doesn't happen very often, but often enough to put American travelers on the alert: Some merchants quote prices in Canadian dollars and take payment in U.S. dollars, figuring on a dollar-to-dollar basis. Always ask whether the price quoted is in Canadian currency. The Canadian dollar is worth less (running about 70 percent of the U.S. dollar at press time), and payment in U.S. currency should be based on the current exchange rate.

British Columbia

British Columbia is an immense, varied, and indescribably beautiful land nearly four times the size of Great Britain, over twice the size of Japan, and larger than the American states of Washington, Oregon, and California combined. It is bordered on the south by Washington, Idaho, and Montana; on the east by the Canadian province of Alberta; on the north by the Yukon and the Northwest Territories; and on the west by the Pacific Ocean and the Alaskan Panhandle.

In all British Columbia's 370,000 square miles, there are only 3.2 million people. More than half the population is concentrated in the southwest corner, living an urban life in and around the balmy lowlands of the Strait of Georgia. During Captain James Cook's last voyage in 1778, he explored the west coast of present-day British Columbia and claimed this vast area for Great Britain. Rival British and Spanish claims were finally resolved in 1790, and the British sent Captain George Vancouver to explore, map, and take possession of the land. British and American claims were settled in 1846, and the boundary was set along the 49th parallel.

Vancouver

Home to approximately 1.5 million people, Greater Vancouver is Canada's third-largest city. Equidistant from the Far East, Europe, and South America, the port of Vancouver is the busiest port on the Pacific Coast. Most of British Columbia's fishing fleet is based here. Vancouver reminds some people of San Francisco, others of Los Angeles or Toronto. For the most part, it is a city full of surprises. Americans on a first visit expect Vancouver to be colder, smaller, duller, and not quite as over powering scenically. In reality, it is a city that is sometimes damp, never dull, and always hospitable.

Vancouver has an impressive skyline. Viewed from the city marina, from Stanley Park, or from Grouse Mountain, the city at night looks like a multi-masted schooner steaming out to sea. Glitter has been added on Robson Street (also called Robsonstrasse), a three-block-long collection of Middle European shops, cafés, and restaurants. There are cafés specializing in strudel, Sacher tortes, and butter horns, the Pacific Northwest's equivalent of a sweet roll, mit kaffee. Gastown, formerly a no-man's-land of warehouses and railroad yards, has been restored in turn-of-the-century style, with cobblestone streets, squares, and alleys, in a corner of the city. Gastown was named for Gassy Jack Deighton, who built a saloon and hotel in 1867. The origin of his nickname is lost in time.

The Capilano Suspension Bridge, with its collection of totem poles, is an unusual sight, and the Grouse Mountain Sky ride transports you via aerial tramway to the highest point in the area. If you're lunching in town, sample any of the dozens of authentic Chinese restaurants in Chinatown. Even prior to Hong Kong's return to China, many Chinese began migrating to Vancouver, and the city's oriental population is supposed to be the largest of any city in the Western Hemisphere. Visit the Dr. Sun Yat Sen Garden, the only authentic classical Chinese garden outside China.

INSIDER SHOPPING TIP
Vancouver is a great city for shopping. There are several department stores, specialty shops, trendy boutiques and English imports that stock English woolens. Prices are less than in the United States on locally produced wares, comparable on designer or name-brand articles. An outstanding shopping center is the Royal Centre Mall adjacent to the Hyatt Hotel, with 70 stores under one roof.

Shore Excursions: City tour (three hours), $55; stroll through Stanley Park (leisurely paced, about three hours), $40. Metered taxis, city buses, and rental cars are available. Free round-trip transportation from the pier to Royal Centre Mall.

On Your Own: It's easy to map your own sightseeing plans. Buses run frequently and taxis are not expensive. Best way to see downtown Vancouver is by foot. It is hilly, but there are lots of coffee shops for rest stops. Rental cars are available.

Victoria

First-time visitors often find there's something special about Victoria, named for the queen who ruled the British Empire for more than 64 years. It is a historic and gracious city. In its narrow streets, 19th-century buildings line the sidewalks, and window boxes overflow with flowers. Everywhere are grand stone and brick buildings, in all manner of shapes and forms. Many are ivy-covered and turret-trimmed, with handsome columns. The capital of the province of British Columbia, Victoria is usually the first or last stop on Alaska-Canada cruises.

With the discovery of gold on the Fraser River in 1858, Victoria became the outfitting center for adventurers and miners. In 1859, it became a free port, and when British Columbia joined the Dominion of Canada in 1871, Victoria became the capital of the westernmost province.

Sightseeing: There is much to see in Victoria - Bastion Square, with its fine old buildings; the Empress Hotel, with its gleaming crystal and castle-like architecture; Beacon Hill Park; and Craigdarroch Castle, named for Annie Laurie's home in Scotland. Built in 1888, Craigdarroch was eventually raffled off for $1 per ticket. The winner could not afford the heating bills, and the castle was turned over to the city. Other points of interest are the Maritime Museum, devoted to artifacts connected with maritime history; Anne Hathaway's Cottage, a life-size replica of the thatched cottage in which William Shakespeare's wife was born; and Buchart Gardens, acres and acres of manicured gardens famous throughout the world for their incredible beauty.

Shore Excursions: City and Buchart Gardens (three hours), $50; Buchart Gardens at night (four hours), $55; grand city sights including high tea (under four hours), $60. Metered taxis and city buses are available dockside for transportation and sightseeing.

On Your Own: Take the tour if Buchart Gardens interests you. It's a long taxi ride, or rent a car at half or full-day rates. You can walk to most of the downtown attractions and don't miss High Tea at the Empress Hotel.

INSIDER SHOPPING TIP

Victoria is a nice, civilized place to shop. The people are very friendly and polite. You'll find Eskimo-carved soapstone, Alaskan and Canadian jade, Indian artifacts, and antique shops specializing in English china and jewelry. I visit gardens all over the world and have yet to find one that surpasses the beauty of Buchart Gardens. Don't miss it!

Northeast Passage – Canada's East Coast

Summer/fall cruises between New York and Montreal are increasing in popularity as more vessels schedule August through October sailings. On these Northeast Passage Voyages, ports of call usually include Boston and Bar Harbor. It's easy to get around those cities; shore excursions are not really necessary.

Halifax, Nova Scotia

The largest city in the Canadian Maritime Provinces, Halifax is Nova Scotia's capital. The city's 18th- and 19th-century buildings are part of a large redevelopment plan to preserve its heritage. Halifax has a cool maritime climate with changeable weather. Daytime high temperatures are typically in the 70s, falling to the mid-50s at night.

Sightseeing: With just a day to spend in Halifax, optional sightseeing should include a harbor cruise; an excellent way to see the city. Other places of interest include: Peggy's Cove, an artist community, in one of the many fishing villages strung out along Nova Scotia's rugged south coast about 30 miles southwest of Halifax. The Halifax Citadel National Historic Park takes up much of Citadel Hill. Founded in 1749 by Lord Cornwallis, the Citadel was built to protect the city and offers an outstanding view of the city. Dating from 1828, this large star-shaped masonry fort is one of the best surviving examples of 19th-century fortification in North America. There's also the Nova Scotia Museum, Public Gardens, Maritime Museum of the Atlantic, and the Province House, with its excellent marine-history collection that includes the historic hydrographic vessel CSS Acadia, docked at the museum's wharf.

Shore Excursions: City and museums (four hours), about $50; Peggy's Cove, including lobster lunch (six hours), $70.

Montreal

Montreal is Canada's richest cultural center and the second-largest French-speaking city in the world. When the French arrived in 1535, they found a community of 3,500 Indians, who were soon displaced and scattered. The city was called Ville Marie when it was founded in 1642, and a strong French influence is still obvious in today's Montreal.

The city has two centers: Centre Town, with its business district, restaurants, theaters, fine hotels, and shops; and Underground Montreal, a city in itself. Entered through the Queen Elizabeth Hotel, it is a network of subterranean commercial and residential complexes, known as "places" linked to the Metro system. Tours include both cities and a visit to the former Olympic village as well as a look at the St. Lambert Lock of the St. Lawrence Seaway, a 9,500-mile network of navigable waters.

Sightseeing: Other interesting sights include the Notre Dame Basilica, noted for its large altar, organ, wood carvings, and paintings; Place Jacques Cartier, with restored 19th - century houses, restaurants, flower markets, and outdoor cafés; Vieux Port, a waterfront entertainment complex; Biodome and Botanical Gardens, with over 25,000 species of flora and Dream Lake Friendship Garden, a Chinese garden in the Ming Dynasty style; Mount Royal Park, which was planned by New York's Central Park architect and offers a wonderful panorama of the city.

Shore Excursions: Full-day tour (seven hours), $50 to $85; half-day tour (three hours), $35 to $45; Biodome and Botanical Gardens (four hours), $50.

Quebec City

The city is located along an eight - mile plateau atop solid rock. The Citadel is its highest point, 360 feet above the St. Lawrence River. Quebec is the only walled city in North America and has a carefully preserved French flavor and character. Most of the beautiful 18th- and 19th -century buildings have been faithfully restored.

In truth, modern Quebec is divided. Dufferin Terrace is part of the upper town and the historic center, while the old town along the waterfront is crowded with more historic buildings, museums, restaurants, and shops.

Sightseeing: Quebec City is best explored by colorful horse - drawn carriage or by foot. Important sights include: Place Royale, a small cobblestone square at the center of Lower Town, which marks the beginning of French colonization of North America; Notre Dames des Victoires, which dates from the late 17th century and is known for its fine interior woodwork and commemorative paintings; La Promenade des Gouverneurs in Upper Town, a walkway that extends half a mile and affords a magnificent view of the St. Lawrence River; and Battlefield Park, site of the battle between General Wolfe and Field marshal Montcalm in 1759.

Special excursions outside Quebec City also are worthwhile: Ile d'Orleans is a historic island just downstream from Quebec City, and its showcase of ancestral homes is well worth the trip. Parc de la Chute-Montmorency offers a waterfall one and a half times higher than Niagara Falls.

Shore Excursions: Full-day tour (seven hours), $60; half-day tour (three to four hours), $35 to $40.

Prince Edward Island

Canada's smallest province is unique in many ways. The soil is naturally red, and sandy beaches are gloriously tinted varying hues of both red and pink. PEI (Prince Edward Island) National Park offers tempting beaches and nature trails. Lucy Maud Montgomery wrote Anne of Green Gables near Cavendish, and British influence is everywhere. Prince Edward Island's Acadian culture thrives in brightly painted homes flying tricolor flags.

Charlottetown, the capital, features restored buildings from the harbor to Euston Street. Victorian touches are everywhere, and at Province House National Historic Site, a working museum, visitors can see where founding fathers met in 1864 to discuss the federal union.

Shore Excursions: History and culture tour (under three hours), $35.

Saint John

New Brunswick is one of Canada's oldest provinces. On St. John the Baptist Day in the early 1600s, Samuel de Champlain landed at the seaside point he dubbed Saint John. Three thousand Loyalists, escaping the Revolutionary War, incorporated the city in May 1785.

Sightseeing: Be sure to see the lovely old Victorian houses on Germain and Prince William streets; visit Moosehead Brewery and the Old City Market, built by local shipbuilders with a roof resembling the hull of a ship. The Carleton Martello Tower is a stone fortification, one of 16 towers built in North America by the British as a defense against the Americans during the War of 1812. The tower was used as a fire command post for harbor defenses during World War II. Reversing Falls at the St. John River's mouth is a natural wonder. The river's tides turn back twice daily with a force claimed to equal that of all the rivers in the world. St. John is the longest river in Atlantic Canada.

Shore Excursions: Scenes of Saint John (approximately two hours), $35; highlights of Saint John (less than three hours), $40.

Panama and the Panama Canal

Panama is more than a canal, although few cruise ship visitors have the opportunity to disembark in Christobal on the East Coast or Panama City on the West Coast. Climate in the region is hot and very humid. The best months to cruise the Canal are November to April. Currency is interchangeable with the U.S. dollar, and the Balboa is of equal value. All of the 250,000 people who call Panama "home" speak Spanish, the official language, but English is spoken almost everywhere.

INSIDER SHOPPING TIP

Panama is a free zone, and if you can get off the ship, best buys are in prescription drugs which do not require a prescription. In some cases, the price difference is more than 50 percent. Take your prescription bottle with you. Sometimes the same drug is sold under a different name, but the local pharmacist will look it up and show you the different names. English bone china, Irish crystal, perfume, Oriental jade, and precious stones. Molas (colorful pieces of cloth, sewn layer by layer into a fabric used by the Cuna Indians as blouses and by Norte Americanos as wall hangings) are available for framing or for blouses and dresses.

Sightseeing: When ships do allow a day on shore in Panama, shore excursions vary with length of time in port. Cruise ships listing San Blas as a port of call do not charge for the shore excursion, which is made by ship tender. Some ships offer a train trip across the Panama Peninsula. Take it! You'll still see the Canal in operation, but you'll have a chance to see some of what Panama's interior looks like. Each area of Panama is different. The Canal and its locks top every visitor's list, but if time permits, fly over and visit the San Blas Islands for a look at an unfamiliar culture. Panama City has old buildings and museums, but the Canal Zone has developed into a bit of transplanted United States.

INSIDER TIP

When I have a choice, I prefer the westbound Panama Canal itinerary. The most interesting locks are closer to the east, and the ship passes through them during morning hours. Also, Panama City is closer to the West Side and if the ship is going to dock, I would rather spend the evening in that city than in Christobal. There is much more going on.

Panama Canal

One of the most incredible journeys possible today is one our ancestors couldn't sail because the body of water just wasn't there: the Panama Canal. For hundreds of years great explorers, from Christopher Columbus to Lewis and Clark, searched for an east-west passageway, a path of water through the American landmass. The dream was so great that what couldn't be found had to be engineered and created.

The Panama Canal today is a tranquil, eight-hour daylight journey between the Atlantic and the Pacific. The engineering marvel is a shining example of American initiative, ingenuity, and know-how. The "Big Ditch" has been around for more than six decades and is a popular route for cruise ships. Some use the Canal transit for the passage itself and do not dock on either side of the Republic of Panama. But most vessels combine the Trans-Panama experience with stops in the Caribbean and Mexico and within the country of Panama itself.

Some ships take advantage of the fact that Panama is a destination in itself. A popular diversion is a visit to the San Blas Islands. Ships anchor about a mile or so from one of the more inhabited San Blas, and passengers are taken ashore by ship tender for a tour of an Indian civilization that has changed very little during the past five or six decades. This is home of the mola. Prices are rising, but a fairly nice San Blas mola is still available for about $25.

INSIDER SHOPPING TIP

On San Blas, the rings in the nose, hoops through the ears, and colorful garb are not tourist put-ons, although they do put on a good show when cruise passengers arrive. The Indians dress that way even without visitors. True, some of the savvier are "adjusting" to large numbers of tourists, and "authentic old Molas" are being manufactured as quickly as they sell. The Cuna Indians also charge for having their picture taken. Current prices are about a $1 apiece.

More Information: Panama Government Tourist Office, 1212 Avenue of the Americas, 10th Floor, New York, N.Y. 10036, or www.panama.com

Puerto Rico – San Juan

Approximately 110 miles long and 35 miles wide, Puerto Rico lies near the middle of the curve of islands that begins with the Bahamas and ends at Trinidad, a position that has helped make San Juan, its capital, a major hub for Caribbean travel. Populated by 3.3 million, the island enjoys average summer temperatures of 86 degrees, which drop only a few degrees during winter months. Because it is part of the United States, the dollar is the official currency, but the official languages are Spanish and English. Everyone speaks Spanish, but outside of San Juan, not everyone speaks English. You'll be comfortable on shore in lightweight casual clothing with a sweater or wrap for evening. It is not necessary to dress up for nightclubs and casinos. Tie and jacket are sometimes required in hotels after 7:00 P.M, but no longer required in casinos.

San Juan, with more than 500,000 residents, is one of the oldest cities in the Western Hemisphere. Columbus discovered Puerto Rico in 1493 and named it San Juan Bautista in honor of St. John the Baptist. During the Spanish American War in 1898, American troops landed on the south coast, and Puerto Ricans refused to come to the aid of the Spanish. The Commonwealth of Puerto Rico was formed in 1952, and the U.S. flag flies alongside the Puerto Rican flag.

The Old City has been carefully and beautifully restored. The streets remain paved with the original blue-glazed blocks brought over as ballast in Old Spanish sailing ships. Seventeenth-century Spanish homes are pastel colored, and iron grillwork is everywhere. In spite of its aggressive North American business atmosphere, San Juan is very Spanish in customs and flavor. The newer sections are residential, hotel, and shopping areas.

Sightseeing: Most ships dock within walking distance of the Old City, and the best way to see this area is on foot. Vehicular traffic is bumper-to-bumper, and it is faster and less frustrating to walk. An easy tour by foot takes you to the most important historic sites. On the "must see" list are Old San Juan, the Condado section; El Morro, the 16th century fortress; San Geronimo; La Fortaleza, built in 1533, the official residence of the Governor (said to be the oldest executive mansion in continuous use in the Western Hemisphere); the Cathedral of San Juan Bautista, built in 1527; Casa Blanca, built as the home of Ponce de Leon and now a museum; burial spot of Ponce de Leon; San Jose

Church, the second-oldest Roman Catholic church in the New World; the Rain Forest (El Yunque); and the hotels, nightclubs, and casinos. Casinos in hotels are supervised by the government and operate in all of the large hotels. Minimums are still $2 at the blackjack tables. Casinos open at 8:00 P.M. Jackets (no ties) required for men at most casinos.

INSIDER SHOPPING TIP

Everything you can buy in the United States or Canada is available in Puerto Rico at slightly higher prices. Although merchants claim prices to be lower than in St. Thomas on imported items, I have not found this to be the case. They say jewelry, gold, perfumes, and liquor are priced competitively with the Virgin Islands, but I found liquor and perfume to be 10 to 30 percent higher than in St. Thomas or St. Croix. I do not consider San Juan one of the better shopping ports in the Caribbean, although some trendy jewelry and accessory boutiques have opened and are inviting cruise passengers to view their wares. Everything purchased in Puerto Rico enters the United States duty free. There are some interesting shops featuring funky jewelry (made in Puerto Rico) in the Old City.

More Information: Commonwealth of Puerto Rico, Tourism Commission, 575 Fifth Ave., 23rd Floor, New York, NY 10017, or www.puertorico.com

St. Barthelemy (St. Barts)

This lovely little island is only eight square miles and is frequented by the international jet set crowd. St. Barts is a bit of the French Riviera in the Caribbean. When you spot a rock star or television personality walking down the street, it's your first clue that this is a pricey destination. It's also quite beautiful.

Christopher Columbus hit this island (along with all the others) in 1493 and named it for his brother Barolomeo. Now, at the end of the 20th century, St. Bart's is one of the hottest and trendiest island destinations. The harbor is the proverbial picture postcard and filled with only the best and the biggest yachts.

This is the only island in the region with a Swedish accent. The capital is St. Gustavia, named for King Gustav III and, street names appear in French and Swedish. Traded by France to Sweden, in the late 19th century, but French remains the official language and the French Franc is the official currency.

The island doesn't offer a lot of sightseeing opportunities, but the Musee Municipal de St. Barthelemy is worth a visit. Take plenty of pictures because no one will believe the beauty of the island.

More information: French West Indies Tourist Board, 444 Madison Ave., New York, NY 10017.

St. Lucia

St. Lucia, the second largest of the Windward Island chain, is French in heritage, and British in character. It is a popular port of call for cruise ships, and the number arriving increases annually. It is an island free of noise and pollution, and reputable girl-watchers claim it has the most beautiful women in the Antilles. Sugar Loaf's peaks dot the island up to 3,000 feet high, and the southern approach through Soufriere lies in the shadow of two peaks, Gros Piton and Petit Piton.

There is some mystery as to St. Lucia's discovery, but there is nothing mysterious about its democracy. The Castries City Council is the oldest elected ruling authority in the English West Indies. The island is fertile all year, and rivers run down from its mountainous backbone. The capital city is Castries, which is also the commercial heart of the island.

St. Lucia's 238 miles are crisscrossed with valleys of orchids, hibiscus, roses, bougainvillea, and tropical fruit. Visit Castries Harbor, Gros Island, Sulphur Springs, and the residential Cap; see Soufriere, with the world's only drive-in volcano.

INSIDER SHOPPING TIP

There are good buys in silk-screened fabrics and native handicraft, but St. Lucia is more of an island that offers tranquility and some unusual sights than for shopping. The "downtown" shopping district is walking distance from the tender quay and there are some interesting French boutiques. I found unusual designs in sports wear and accessories, and bought them for the style, not the price.

St. Maarten/St. Martin

This small two-in-one island has enjoyed several cultures. Originally Italian, named San Martino, the island's most distant points are only 8.5 miles apart. Temperatures average close to 90 degrees year around with September the hottest, and January and February the coolest. Currency is the Netherlands Antilles Florin and, the French Franc, depending on which side you're on, but currency is interchangeable and everyone accepts U.S. dollars. Language is Dutch on one side, French on the other, and almost everyone speaks English on both sides. Casual is the word on clothing and even casinos do not require jackets or ties at night.

Spell it St. Maarten or St. Martin and you're right on both counts. What's more, the island enjoys a split personality, two languages, and two flags. Situated about 150 miles east of Puerto Rico, between the islands of Anguilla and St. Bartholomew in the Lesser Antilles, it is both a convenient and extremely popular port of call for cruise ships sailing from San Juan and the Florida East Coast.

On Columbus's second voyage of discovery in 1493, he sighted a lovely group of small islands on St. Martin's Day and promptly named the one ringed by sparkling white beaches "St. Martin." The cannibalistic Carib Indians were replaced and subdued in subsequent years for brief periods by French freebooters, Portuguese, English, Dutch, and Spaniards.

But no country claimed the island and it gained fame as a pirate hideout. Sunken wrecks of galleons bear witness to this swashbuckling past. When the Spanish finally withdrew, so the story goes, they left behind nine foreigners from their crews-four Frenchmen and five Dutchmen. Legend has it that a Frenchman and a Dutchman stood back-to-back and from a certain point on the coast started to walk around the island. They agreed to divide the land between them by a boundary drawn from the point where they had started to that at which they met. The Frenchman was a faster walker than the Dutchman who supposedly tarried too often for a sip of Old Dutch Gin. But he apparently knew what he was after. He started toward the more valuable end of the island in which the Salt Ponds are located and which has a natural deep harbor. Who got the better of the deal is still being debated. While France ended up with the larger portion in the north with its undulating terrain, Holland secured the relatively flat, richer south.

The peaceful coexistence enjoyed by these two nations for over 300 years is being enjoyed daily by visitors who come for lengthy vacations and cruise ship passengers who usually spend about eight hours in port.

The Dutch side has been Americanized to some extent and is very touristy, but the French remain committed to their heritage. While no physical border divides the island and there are no customs or immigration checkpoints, there are road signs noting the division. Today, there are two different ways to spell the name, two different currencies, two distinctive styles of architecture, and two ways of life. Probably more importantly, from the visitor's point of view, is that there are two distinct styles of cooking and the existing possibility to enjoy the best of both worlds.

Cruise ships dock at the new port which is a taxi ride from town, or they anchor offshore and tender passengers into mid-Philipsburg, the capital city of Dutch St. Maarten. There are advantages to both. Tender arrivals eliminate the need of a taxi for shopping and docking eliminates the tender schedules.

Smaller vessels, such as those in the Seabourn and Silversea fleets use Marigot, capital of French St. Martin.

INSIDER TIP

As a frequent visitor to St. Maarten, I like to leave the hustle and frenzy of the Dutch pier area and head for the tranquility of the French side. Unless pre-reserved, rental cars are hard to come by on the spur of the moment and I join ships in recommending against moped rentals. Taxis are plentiful and run continuously between Philipsburg and Marigot for about $10 per person.

Sightseeing: Among the sites are the ruins of Fort Amsterdam; Simpson Bay; Mount William Hill, for a beautiful view; the Great Salt Pond; the border crossing; Marigot; and the picturesque plantations, beautiful resort complexes with golf courses, and casinos.

INSIDER SHOPPING TIPS

Shoppers can spend the day in Philipsburg, or head to the French side. The main street in Philipsburg is crowded and the tumult reminds one of Hong Kong. There are shops that sell everything and anything the tourist is likely to buy. Jewelry store after jewelry store have a tendency to confuse all but the committed shopper. Prices are comparable to St. Thomas, but are more "negotiable" than in other Caribbean ports. This is a free-port shopping center with good buys in European imports - perfume, liquor, fabrics, crystal, china, watches, especially Delft and other Dutch or French items. Shops close between noon and 2:00 P.M, except when a cruise ship is in port.

Due east of Puerto Rico in the Atlantic and the eastern Caribbean are the three principal islands of the U.S. Virgin Islands - St. Croix, St. Thomas, and

St. John. There are also 50 smaller islands. The islands are an unincorporated U.S. Territory, and everyone born here is a U.S. citizen. Currency is the U.S. Dollar and language is English, but a lot of Spanish is spoken.

Christopher Columbus, the first tourist of record from the Old World, was greeted with a hail of arrows when he landed on the north shore of the Virgins more than 500 years ago. Today's visitor to St. Croix is more likely to be hailed by taxi drivers and shopkeepers in St. Thomas, golf carts in St. Croix, and bikini-clad scuba divers in St. John. The three American Virgins are the best known of the nearly 100 in the Caribbean, but they differ greatly in personality and terrain.

St. John, the smallest, is only 20-square miles and has been declared a national park. The park, on land donated by Laurance Rockefeller, is famous for its unspoiled tropical beauty, and cruise ships offer snorkeling excursions that take about four hours and allow time for exploring underwater coral trails. Some ships even provide box lunches for this $35 expedition.

St. Croix, the largest of the U.S. Virgins, is 84-square miles and is attracting an increasing number of cruise ship calls. Many St. Thomas shops have branch stores in St. Croix. The island is best known for its Old World atmosphere, manicured golf courses, and fine resort complexes.

St. Thomas, with only 32-square miles, manages to combine qualities of the other two islands with a 21st century calypso lilt that classifies the Virgins as "foreign." The discovery process initiated by Columbus is being repeated constantly by visitors from all over the world. Almost every cruise ship sailing the Eastern Caribbean stops there.

No one paid much attention to the lonely Virgin Islands for many years until pirates discovered the protected channels, bays, and coves and moved into them as sanctuaries for their ships. St. Thomas became a pirate base of some fame when buccaneers made their headquarters in Charlotte Amalie. The Dutch tried to take possession and finally sold out to the Danes, who took over in 1672 and operated the Virgins under the authority of the Danish West Indies Company. Denmark offered to sell the Virgins to the United States in 1869, but negotiations were not completed until 1917. The strategic position of the Virgin Islands as an outpost for the protection of the Panama Canal persuaded the United States to pay $25 million to Denmark.

Three factors contribute to the popularity of the Virgins. The climate is almost perfect, with few days below 70 or above 85 degrees. Accessibility is also an important reason. They lie in the sea-lanes and are reached quickly by plane or ship. Lastly, and probably most importantly, is the free-port status of the islands and the high customs exceptions allowed by the United States for returning residents.

Contrary to the saying, the best things in life are not free. But they are reasonable in the Virgins, the only place in the Caribbean where visiting Americans can buy $1,200 worth of merchandise and bring it home without paying duty. It has been estimated that more liquor is sold in St. Thomas on any day to cruise ship passengers than in the average city of 100,000 in a month. Uncle Sam is responsible for this phenomenon by allowing five fifths of alcoholic beverages to be included in the $1,200 allowance.

But St. Thomas is more than shops, although no visitor has ever left the island without meeting temptation on Main Street in Charlotte Amalie. More than a hundred shops are housed in 19th century restored warehouses, and their shelves are stocked with merchandise from every corner of the world.

St. Thomas sits pertly on the edge of a landlocked harbor. Homes sprawl up the hillsides that rise sharply to a height of 1,500 feet. These hillsides are actually three volcanic spurs named Frenchman's Hill, Denmark Hill, and Government Hill, but they are better known as Foretop, Maintop, and Mizzentop. A good road leads around the island and to its main settlements and points of interest but traffic patterns are a holdover from Danish times, and you're right if you drive on the left in the Virgins. Charlotte Amalie is the only city most visitors see, but its population is less than half the total of that of the island group. The Danish influence is evident in street names, and the architecture reflects influences of various occupants. There are Dutch doors, French grillwork, Spanish patios, Danish rooflines, and modern, Miami-type hotel structures.

One of the first settlers in St. Thomas was a group of Jewish refugees in 1665, the year the island was first settled by pioneers. Gabriel Milan, a Jew, was the first governor of the islands, commissioned in 1684 by King Christian V. For three centuries, the St. Thomas synagogue has been a symbol of peace, blessing, and refuge to Jewish families. Danish archives for the 1697 to 1698 period list Jacob and Diana Elias and their two children as taxpayers. A contemporary account of Jewish historical development in the Virgin Islands claims the growing community followed a wide variety of occupations, including some who participated in negotiating the transfer of St. Croix from French to Danish sovereignty. The artist Camille Pissarro and Judah P. Benjamin, who was attorney general and secretary of war and state under Confederate President Jefferson Davis, are some of the Jewish residents of St. Thomas who left their mark. In addition to the first governor, two others were Jewish. Morris Fidanque de Castro was appointed governor by President Dwight D. Eisenhower in 1950, and Ralph M. Paiewonsky was appointed governor by President John F. Kennedy in 1961 and reappointed by President Lyndon

Johnson. The Paiewonsky family continues to reside in St. Thomas and are active business, community, and religious leaders.

The synagogue has been restored over the past hundred years but maintains Sephardic architecture and customs, which call for the Ark to be placed on the east wall. Sand-covered floors are in the same tradition, which, according to Isadore Paiewonsky, "remind Jews of the exodus from Spain, like the historic Exodus over the desert to the Promised Land."

Sightseeing: Time spent in St. Thomas will be the most hectic of your entire cruise. You only have a day and there are so many tempting things to do, see, and buy, you'll be hard pressed to fit it all in. Shopping opportunities are so overwhelming that there is a lingering, nagging temptation to spend the whole day in port going shop-to-shop. But if you give in to temptation you will have missed really seeing the island.

A variety of shore excursions is sold on board ships. If you are pressed for time and have a long shopping list, consider taking one of the excursions. That will still leave ample time for shopping. The city tour, for example, takes about two hours and includes a ride through the busy city of Charlotte Amalie, a stop at Bluebeard's Castle for a drink, general orientation, and a look at some of the island's better-known beaches (about $35). For visitors who know St. Thomas, there's a tour to St. John ($80). It begins with a safari car ride to a ferry that takes you on a 20-minute ride to the neighboring island. After landing, another safari-type four wheeler takes you through the lush National Park, the famed Rockefeller resort, Caneel Bay, and for one of the most perfect snorkeling or swimming experiences anywhere in the world. This is for snorkelers and swimmers considered less than expert. The guide supplies equipment and instruction, and the adventure is enjoyed by first-time underwater explorers from eight to eighty. For more expert scuba addicts, most ships offer special scuba tours into deeper waters (about five hours, $80), but proof of certification is required. The city tour takes in all of the historic sites and, on request, will leave passengers in town at the end of the route so they can shop before returning to the ship on their own.

Megan's Beach is traditionally rated one of the 10 best beaches in the world. The island's beaches and turquoise waters are tempting even to the most devote landlubber. There are several good restaurants in town, but they are very crowded when ships are in port, so I usually hold out until I get back on board, or I settle for a fast-food place along Main Street.

INSIDER SHOPPING TIP

The nitty-gritty of a cruise visit to the Virgin Islands is shopping. St. Thomas is probably the world's largest luxury-type shopping center with so little space to display merchandise from the four corners. Some being offered at less than 50 percent of what it would cost in the country of origin. Unfortunately, a number of "shlack" stores have opened and visitors should discriminate between one-price stores and those in which bargaining can reduce prices. Number one on most Americans' shopping lists is liquor. While it is cheaper than in most places in the U.S., prices are not the bargains they were just a few years ago. I priced a designer brand of vodka and found it was not worth carrying home for a two dollar difference in price. There are specials and you will succumb, but be sure to have the store send the liquor back to the ship for you. There's no point in lugging the boxes around when liquor delivery is guaranteed to arrive on board without leakage or breakage. In the rare instance when a problem does arise (breakage or delivery is not complete), contact the purser's office immediately. Some stores have special arrangements that allow the ship's purser to replace damaged or missing liquor. Should a problem be discovered after you get home, the best approach is to contact the merchant by mail with complete information. If you have been dealing with a reputable shop, there will be a refund but no liquor. It's not allowed through the mail.

LATE NEWS

Delivery to cruise ships may now be subject to new security rules, which does not allow delivery to ships.

INSIDER SHOPPING TIP: #2:

Choices are unlimited and go from Gucci to a mom-and-pop operation. Prices on almost everything are lower than back home. Count crystal, china, camera, and perfume among the best values with prices running from 20 to 50 percent below stateside. But like everything else, perfume prices are not as low as they were a few years ago. Considering state sales taxes, perfume and cosmetics should run about 20 percent less than in the States. You'll pass shops showing a king's ransom in jewelry and watches, crystal, china, fine leather goods, cosmetics, and fragrances; not to mention fashions for men and women. You'll find names such as Omega, Concord, Corum, Bulova, Gucci, Cartier, Citizen, Seiko, Lamy Pens, Staffordshire, Orlane, and Lancome inside every door. While I do not recommend specific shops, I am reporting on personal inspections and experiences in several reputable stores. Shoppers who do not want to waste time should head directly for A.H. Riise or Little Switzerland. They have the most complete selections on the island and have several locations with headquarters stores on Main Street. You'll find the largest selections of merchandise at competitive duty free prices. You'll find contemporary jewelry as well as a collection of antique and estate pieces from around the world. They carry fine china, crystal, the newest designer fragrances and cosmetics, housewares featuring Wusthof Trident knives and Italian acrylic ware, lambs wool and cashmere sweaters, plus a liquor department at Riise for one-stop shopping,

INSIDER SHOPPING TIP: #3:

Don't end your Main Street walk until you get to the end of the street. You'll pass dozens of other shops. There's the Leather Shop for Bottega bags; Tropicana Perfume Shop with its extensive fragrance collection; Jolly Roger with a collection of pipes priced from $1.50 to $1, 500; the Scandinavian Center with its George Jensen and David Anderson collection; Blue Carib Gems selling Caribbean amber, black coral, and agates; H. Stern with a fabulous collection of jewels, the Cloth Horse with its Finnish Marimekko fabrics by the yard; and just about every European designer shop you'll find in Paris or Rome.

A new and very convenient shopping area has been built at Havensight Mall at the West Indian Company Dock, which is where most cruise ships dock if they don't tender passengers to shore. It's a restored series of warehouses and if you opted for scuba diving or snorkeling at St. John, you'll still have time to shop at the same prices and in many of the same shops that line Main Street.

More Information: United States Virgin Islands Government
Tourist Office 1270 Avenue of the Americas, New York, NY 10020,
www.usvirginislands.com

Mexico

No other country enjoys so many popular cruise ports. Mexico has two long coastlines with deep blue harbors and beautiful small cities whose residents have learned to accommodate visitors. Twice in 400 years the country was destroyed, and a new culture imposed on its people. Each upheaval left contrasts. Great pyramids sit in the middle of jungles, and Christian fiestas take over the cities during holidays. Mexico City used to float on a lake, and now has a subway system famous for its speed, efficiency, and modern art. Mexico offers long beaches, air-conditioned hotels, a beautiful countryside, and warm, friendly people.

The most popular cruise months are October through May, but ships call at Mexican ports all year. Temperature is fairly constant. During February, temperatures reach a high of 85 to 90 degrees in Acapulco, the southernmost port of call. Reported average temperatures in central and western ports are closer to the high 70s and into the 80s.

Spanish is the official language, but English is spoken in all tourist centers. Shopping is fun. For less than $25 you can buy good quality machine-made shirts, hand-made dolls, and sometimes full-sized guitars. There are also basket works, pottery and tiles, carved onyx, tin and copper works, silver jewelry, hand-blown glass, leather goods and other handicrafts in local markets and stores. Check the beautiful hand-finished and embroidered patio dresses, selling for about $65, and stateside boutiques have them priced at more than $200. Less expensive models sell for under $20, and are worth at least three times the price. They are available throughout Mexico, but I found prices and selection best in Mazatlan.

Acapulco is trendier and also more expensive. Men's hand-embroidered shirts are excellent buys, selling for about $18.

Don't hesitate to bargain everywhere, except in department stores. Mexicans are not easily offended, particularly when it comes to bargaining. If the price is set, they will say so. If not, you will both enjoy the bargaining. The only problem is in knowing, "How low is the lowest?" You'll never know until you compare purchases and prices with shipmates after you leave port.

Tipping Ashore: Taxi drivers do not expect a tip, but sightseeing guides expect about fifty pesos per person; museum guides, five pesos; and waiters are usually tipped fifteen to twenty percent of the bill, depending on the type of restaurant and service rendered.

Transportation: (See "Shore Excursions" for each port.) Taxis, tour buses, and railroad, as well as rental cars, mopeds, and cycles in most ports.

What to Wear Ashore: Comfortable, resort-type clothing. Sandals, jeans, and shorts are acceptable. As with all sightseeing, comfortable shoes are very important. All Mexican ports of call are resort areas, and informality in dress is one of the Mexican Riviera's choice attractions. Bring swimwear for beaches. Jackets are required only in very exclusive clubs and restaurants.

INSIDER TIP

Prescription drugs are sold over the counter in Farmacias. Prices are incredibly low. Pharmacists stock generic equivalents of U.S. name drugs at about 40 to 50 percent of U.S. prices. It is advisable to bring a copy of your prescription.

Mexico remains a very worthwhile travel buy. Although the peso fluctuates in value, our dollar still goes a long way. It's one country where the American gets his money's worth and then some. Cruise passengers take advantage of shopping opportunities. The exchange rate at press time was just under eight pesos to one U.S. dollar. Mexican-made products are still a bargain.

INSIDER TIP

The water in Mexico is fine for Mexicans, but visitors frequently can't tolerate it. Drink bottled drinks without ice (which is made from tap water) or buy bottled water. Tequila and Margaritas are popular and inexpensive. Bars are generally "for men only" in Mexico. Imported whiskey is very expensive, and a Scotch and soda costs more than $5 at an ordinary bar. Mexican beer is surprisingly good and inexpensive and if you must drink whiskey, ask for local brands. Price will be a fraction of imported brands.

More Information: Mexican Government Tourist Office, 405 Park Avenue, Suite 1401, New York, NY 10022. www.mexicoonline.com will furnish information on all ports of call within the country.

Popular Ports of Call

Acapulco

This is one city where visitors never have to dress. Swimsuits and shorts are the accepted uniforms of the day. No one watches a clock. Breakfast is any time after waking up, lunch is from 1:00 to 4:00 P.M., and cocktails follow a siesta. Dinner is served after 9:00 P.M. There are miles of public and hotel beaches offering every type of water sport facility. Don't miss Puerto Marques Beach during the day, Pie de la Cuesta at sunset, and a glass-bottomed boat ride around the bay. Watch high divers and parachute skiers, or rent a boat and fish for the big ones. Shops are filled with handicrafts and chic clothes. The city has many elegant restaurants and a busy nightlife and, thanks to a citywide renaissance, is getting ready for the year 2000.

An unusual way of sight seeing along the Costera, (main boulevard), is in a brightly decorated horse drawn carriage, known as a calandria, for $15 per half-hour.

Shore Excursions: City tour and cliff divers (four hours), $35. All-day tour, $65.

INSIDER SHOPPING TIP
If you like flea markets, you'll love the one in Acapulco. The area is not dangerous, but--as anywhere--visitors should be alert for pickpockets and thieves.

Cabo San Lucas

Cabo San Lucas, known as "the capes," in Baja California, Mexico, is an 800-mile sliver of Mexican territory extending south of the California border between the Pacific and the Gulf of California. Cabo San Lucas is the tip of the peninsula where the Pacific and the Gulf meet. The waters are cool, the sand and air warm, and the area has somehow managed to remain unspoiled by masses of tourists. The ground is sandy and has been called "Mexico's desert." Fishing is the main sport as well as the most important industry. It is picturesque, quiet, and relaxing. Cruise stops depend on tide and weather conditions.

New hotels have been built, and visitors bent on finding a new destination are making footsteps in the sand. Most impressive sight is the Cabo San Lucas Arch, a huge, natural stone formation made by the waters of the Pacific and the Sea of Cortes. Best seen on short boat trips.

Shore Excursions: sail and snorkel (under three hours), $34; coastal highlights of Baja California (three hours) $32, and boat tour and visit to a beach resort (under five hours), $28.

Ensenada

Humorists have a good time with Ensenada, but there is really nothing to laugh about. It's a sleepy but picturesque port located on the north end of Todos Santos Bay, less than 100 miles south of the California-Baja border. Since cruise traffic has been increasing, towns people are trying to improve facilities and new outlet stores, stores, cafes and mini-malls have opened.

The best part of Ensenada is the waterfront where you can watch fishermen haul in their catch or mend their nets. A stroll around town provides opportunities to see or buy Mexican arts and crafts at duty free prices. New perfume shops are competitively priced with Caribbean islands. Better still, since your ship will be visiting larger Mexican cities stop at a native cantina and sip a cool Margarita.

Shore Excursions: City and countryside tour (four hours), $22; tour of Domecq Winery of Calafia Valley (less than four hours), $30; Baja Bandidos horseback trail ride (three hours), $42.

Manzanillo

This quiet, remote Mexican port really puts out a warm welcome mat when cruise ships arrive. They even ring the giant church bells. Manzanillo has a series of bays and coves, narrow streets, so-so shops, coconut and banana plantations, and Mexico's plushest, lushest resort--Las Hadas.

Shore Excursions: (three hours) run around $25 and include a visit and drink at Las Hadas, where daily rates run more than $500 per person. Its guest list includes the famous and infamous, and the traveler who likes to rub elbows with celebrities, but you'll have a hard time recognizing movie stars in their natural form without make up and wearing bikinis.

Mazatlan

Mazatlan, 20 miles below the Tropic of Cancer, sits on a peninsula surrounded by seemingly endless miles of beaches and rocky cliffs. It is typical of Mexico's best - known cities in the sun. Its modern port facilities are among Mexico's busiest, and both sport and commercial fishing contribute heavily to the local economy. Long, dazzling beaches attract visitors to luxury hotels.

The colonial area in the heart of downtown is 18th and 19th century, obviously untouched by the present except for power lines and neon signs. Outdoor activities range from exploring coral pools to bird watching on small islands to shrimp feasting from vendors' carts to rides in two - wheeled carriages called "spiders."

Mazatlan is affectionately called "the fish trap," and they say marlin run up to 750 pounds. To prove the fish tales, scores of billfish are strung across arches on the dock. Most cruise ships arrange fishing parties on local yachts for passengers who just can't resist the temptation of marlin, dolphin, and shark at the end of their lines.

Pacifico is the local beer recommended as a thirst-quencher, and El Shrimp Bucket is a good place for lunch or a snack. Mariachi bands and high-spirited diners and drinkers are part of Mazatlan. It is Mexico at its leisurely best. For shopping, passengers have a choice of street vendors who set up stalls along the pier, trendy shops, or city markets.

Merchandise runs the gamut from an assortment of rebozos and rugs to fine jewelry and excellent shoes. The main Town Square is where everyone in Mazatlan meets everyone else in Mazatlan. It's a labyrinth of narrow streets and small souvenir shops. The Golden Zone is the main tourist development area with hotels, restaurants, and shops.

Shore Excursions: City tour (three hours), $35. All day tour, city and surrounding countryside, includes lunch (seven hours), $40; Fiesta evening party, $35. Deep-sea fishing, private yacht with ship group, including lunch (seven to eight hours), $100. City center is a twenty-minute walk from the pier; a $4 taxi ride.

Puerto Vallarta

The classic vision of Old Mexico, of red-tiled roofs and cobblestone streets, is a reality in Puerto Vallarta. Success hasn't spoiled this city perched on horseshoe-shaped Banderas Bay, and census takers can't keep up with growing numbers of residents and visitors.

A few donkey carts rattle over cobblestones, but a highway bypass has been completed. Lovers Lane is the malecon (sea wall), and the Guadalupe Church with its lighted, crown-shaped tower adds a fairyland atmosphere on moonlit nights.

Puerto Vallarta is a mix of cultures. There's the Cualo River where native women wash their clothes by pounding them on rocks while the other side has wide stretches of uncrowded, uncluttered beaches, luxury hotels, and American homes. Richard Burton and Liz Taylor helped put Puerto Vallarta on the map when they filmed the Night of the Iguana here.

INSIDER SHOPPING TIP

Nearby is the picturesque village of Yelapa, preserving its vanishing Indian culture. It's a good place to practice that time-honored art of bargaining for hand-crafted articles and embroidered goods. Sharpen your bargaining skills when you deal with street vendors. Shopping is convenient, and if your ship docks at the old pier, the center of town is within walking distance. From the new pier it's a ten-minute, $4 taxi ride. Siesta is between 2:00 and 4:00 P.M., and shops remain open until 9:00 in the evening.

Shore Excursions: City tour and shopping (three hours), $20. Town and country drive (four hours), $36; sightseeing and private villa lunch (six hours), $90.

Zihuatanejo

An idyllic village with a hard to pronounce name Zihuatanejo (see-wah-tan-NEH-hoh), slumbers like a South Sea paradise waiting to be discovered. North of Acapulco, it offers a Polynesian-type vacationland, complete with coral reefs, coconut plantations, and a glistening beach where outrigger canoes are drawn right up on the sand. This rustic village is so remote that the last 30 miles of road from Acapulco were paved just a few years ago, but cruise ships have provided easy access for about 15 years. The village has become a popular one-day stop for passengers on longer cruises to the more cosmopolitan ports of Mazatlan, Puerto Vallarta, and Acapulco.

Water-related activities and superb beaches head the visitor's list of things to do and see. To see, there's central market square, the Potosi lighthouse at the southern tip, Las Gatas lined with thatched shelters, and miles of colorful tropical foliage and exotic birds. Pigs, dogs, and stately Brahma cattle wander the streets between the buildings.

Shore Excursions: City and surrounding area (three hours), $35.

The Yucatan Peninsula

As cruise passenger demographics change, so do preferred itineraries. Not too long ago when passengers were mostly in the 60-plus age range, if a ship didn't call at St. Thomas, the itinerary was hard to sell. Today the hottest Caribbean itinerary includes a stop in Mexico's Yucatan Peninsula with its new and growing resort areas with infrastructures in place to welcome growing numbers of cruise ship passengers.

Cancun

Just a few years ago Cancun was an isolated and almost desolate tropical island, largely untouched since the decline of the mighty Maya Empire around the 13th century. Today it is a tropical paradise hosting thousands of visitors who come to enjoy its unspoiled beaches, crystal clear waters, and remnants of an Indian heritage.

Cancun is situated off the northeast tip of the Yucatan Peninsula, 30 miles north of Cozumel, and 200 miles east of Merida. Technically, the hotel zone of Cancun is an island. But, it is separated from the downtown mainland at each end by channels less than 100 yards across, connecting the 18-square mile Niochtupte Lagoon with the Caribbean, each crossed by a low-level bridge.

Cancun has an average of more than 200 sun-filled days a year and has less annual rainfall than the Virgin Islands or the Bahamas. It is not directly in the Caribbean's hurricane belt, although there's an old Mexican saying that hurricanes have no helm. Hurricane Gilbert made a direct hit on Cancun in 1990.

In addition to first-class and deluxe hotels, Cancun has a beautiful convention center, shopping and restaurant complexes, a small archaeological zone, and a magnificent 18-hole Robert Trent Jones golf course. The rest of the island has been designated by the government as a bird and wildlife sanctuary.

Activities are beach and water oriented. There are golf and tennis facilities and weekly (Wednesday) bullfights.

Sightseeing: A visit should include the nearby archaeological zones. The most interesting is to Tulum, about 80 miles south of Cancun, a magnificent, small, walled Mayan city on a cliff overlooking the ocean. Only two hours away, toward Merida, is one of the most impressive of all Mayan ruins, Chichen Itza. The buildings date to the Classic period, around AD 600 to

900. The site covers about six square miles. One section has the great pyramids and temples of the Maya; another was built by the Toltec, their successors who invaded the Yucatan in the 20th century.

Shore Excursions: Cruise ships offer a variety of shore excursions. Diving and snorkeling are favorites, but with only one day to spend in port, cruise ship passengers must decide between antiquities and ruins and underwater sports. But, somehow they always find time for shopping. Shore excursions to Tulum cost about $75 and a 45-minute flight to Chichen Itza--considered one of the most important archeological sites on the American continent--about $175-$200. The latter tour takes about six hours. Both are well worth the prices. Folkloric show and visit to San Gervasio ruins (under four hours) $50; while a night out on the town from Cancun is about $40; the Mayan ruins of Tulum and Xel-Ha (approximately seven hours), $80.

INSIDER TIP

Most cruise brochures lump Playa del Carmen and Cozumel together. Passengers, as well as travel agents, assume they are one and the same. They are not. In almost all cases, the ship anchors only in Cozumel, but makes arrangements for passengers to disembark in Playa del Carmen for excursions. After a bus ride, guests rejoin the ship in the late afternoon. If the ship docks in Cancun, shore excursions to Chichen Itza sites are easier to reach. Playa del Carmen is actually a tiny town 40 miles south of Cancun. It is 10 miles west of Cozumel and close enough to Tulum and Chichen Itza for a one-day excursion to one or the other, or both. Playa del Carmen has a great beach.

INSIDER TIP #2

A not to be missed attraction about 20 minutes from Cancun is in Calica. It's an archeological park built on the ruins of a Mayan village. It has an excellent reproduction of a Mayan village and offers some understanding of a culture that has disappeared. Take the river trip, which goes under excavations and ruins if you are there during daylight hours. In the evening, Calico presents the best Mexican folkloric performance showing the various cultures alive and thriving in the country. Some ships offer excursions. Calica has built a small port and some ships have scheduled stops.

Cozumel

About 15miles south of Cancun is Cozumel, pronounced "coo-zoo-MEHL," frequently called Mexico's original Caribbean playground probably because it is the country's largest island. In spite of its international fame, it is still under populated. The remains of Mayan temples and ceremonial centers still dot the island.

Cozumel was the first place in Mexico to be visited by Europeans, and at one location along the beach a plaque marks the spot where Catholic Mass was first celebrated in the country. There is only one village on Cozumel, San Miguel, with only about 2,000 hotel rooms, miles of unspoiled beaches, and some of the largest tropical fish populations anywhere in the world. With near-ly perfect weather, proximity to historic ruins, and excellent shopping opportunities, it is little wonder that Cozumel is Mexico's most popular port of call.

The island is 30 miles long and about 12 miles wide. This sun-drenched, easternmost tip of Mexico has become an "in" destination. Many inland Mayan attractions make popularity of the peninsula inevitable. With beautiful waters washing over one of the world's largest barrier reefs, the island is a special favorite with scuba divers. Although it was the first landfall in Mexico for Spanish conquistadors, it was the diving community of the world that truly discovered Cozumel.

Diving and marine life are only part of what Cozumel offers the visitor. For many cruise passengers, shopping will be the top attraction; for others it will be the artifacts and ruins of the Mayan society.

INSIDER SHOPPING TIPS

Best buys are in silver jewelry, papier-mâché decorations, dolls, Christmas decorations, men's shirts, and local handicrafts. Jewelry, perfume, tee shirt and sportswear shops line the streets. All brands manufactured in Mexico are sold in "outlet" stores and are priced well below U.S. tickets, but perfumes and cosmetics are a little more than in Eastern Caribbean ports, and a little less than in the U.S. Jewelry stores seem to follow the sea lanes and branches of almost every St. Thomas store has opened in Cozumel. I didn't find the prices or selection exciting, but apparently cruise passengers contribute heavily to the local economy.

Shore Excursions: Tour (three hours) or beach party, $35 or sail and snorkel (three hours) $40.

The Mediterranean and Black Sea

There's a special fascination associated with the timeless beauty of the Mare Nostrum and the wine-dark sea of Homer. The age-old charm of Mediterranean countries and the mystery of their ancient civilizations intrigue modern-day travelers. No cruise itinerary covers all of the ports, but many ships offer an interesting combination of cultures in these sun-drenched islands. For those who know the Mediterranean, cruising in the area is a return to familiar scenes that change so subtly it's hard to define progress. For new travelers to the area, it is a fascinating journey of discovery--minarets and winding alleyways in Cairo; the unspoiled gems of the Cyclades Islands - Delos and Mykonos; the Bay of Naples, the mysterious Black Sea and much more.

Again, the following information is geared to a short visit, during which the traveler wants to see the highlights, get a feel of the atmosphere, shop and decide whether a return visit should be planned. Shore excursion prices quoted are based on current average charges by cruise lines and are subject to change. Rates vary as much as 25 percent, depending on the ship and the quality of the tour. Don't expect air-conditioned comfort on buses or in taxis on some of the Greek islands. But, you can generally count on a warm welcome throughout the region.

Passports are usually required but inoculations are no longer necessary in most countries. (Visas are required for some countries) Shore excursion prices vary from ship to ship, but average out at about $50 for a half-day tour without lunch. Full-day tours with overnight hotel stays can run close to $250 or more.

Cruise season begins in early spring and lasts through mid-October. High season is from mid-June through September. World cruises call during winter months. The climate is mild, but evenings can cool off to the low 60s even in summer months. Highs can reach into the 90s. Shopping opportunities differ from country-to-country, but almost all stores and restaurants accept credit cards. Some do not accept U.S. dollars, so it is advisable to convert a small amount of money into local currency. Eastern Standard Time is six or seven hours behind local times depending on the season. Service charges of about 15 percent are usually added to restaurant and hotel bills.

Egypt

The Arab Republic of Egypt, lying at the crossroads of Europe, Asia, and Africa, has two faces--the Egypt with 5,000 years of history and the new Egypt with modern hotels and recreational facilities. There are two distinct seasons, with a short spring and fall. Hot weather begins in May and reaches about 97 degrees in summer, with a sharp drop in temperature after sundown. Currency is the Egyptian Pound. Language is Arabic, but English is spoken in large cities and in hotels catering to Western visitors.

Taxis are metered and inexpensive. Rental cars are available, but traffic is fierce and competitive, especially in Cairo. They are not recommended for cruise passengers with limited time. Short-term visitors do better using cabs. Outside of Cairo, horse-and-carriage transportation is available in most cities for five to $10 per hour, depending on size of the city, demand of the moment, and your bargaining ability.

INSIDER SHOPPING TIPS

Shopping is fun if you are not in a hurry. Bazaars are a delight, but sharpen your best bargaining skills. Everything is negotiable. You can find good buys in gold cartouches (pendants worn on neck chains) made to order with your name in hieroglyphics, available in 10 to 24 -carat gold and priced accordingly. Other good buys are handicrafts, cotton, carpets, and jewelry.

Dress ashore is casual, lightweight cottons and drip-dry clothing. Summer months are very, very hot, so bring a hat. (See additional tips under "Cruising the Nile.") Women who wear shorts will attract attention. Comfortable shoes are necessary.

More information: Egyptian Tourist Office, 630 Fifth Avenue, Suite 1706, New York, NY 10020, or www. idsc.gov.eg which will furnish information on all ports and cities.

Popular Ports of Call

Alexandria

Most ships that call at Alexandria allow one or two days in port. This is a seaside resort with modern facilities and ancient sites. Shore excursion options include sightseeing in and around Alexandria as well as one-day and overnight tours to Cairo, depending on how long the vessel remains in port. In Alexandria, you'll see the Graeco-Roman Museum with a collection of items dating back to the third century BC; the Serapium Temple with Pompey's Pillar; the Catacombs of Kom El Shugaffa; the residence of the former royal family; and the Amphitheater with its famed marble terraces.

Cairo

A one-day visit to Cairo allows for a small sampler of what this city and its surroundings have to offer. If this is your first visit, the three great Pyramids of Giza and the Sphinx should head your "must list." You'll probably opt for the camel ride around the Pyramids, Time permitting, see the Step Pyramid, which is about an hour's drive to Sakkara.

INSIDER TIP

If this will be your only opportunity to see the pyramids, take the tour offered by the ship which is probably docked at some port in the Suez Canal. If you have been to Cairo before, before buying the ship tour, remember that it is a long drive and a tiring day that requires a lot of walking.

The highlight of a visit to Cairo is a few hours at the Egyptian Museum with its treasures dating back five thousand years. There's the Citadel of Cairo built in 1183, the Al Azhar Mosque, the cities of the dead, the old synagogue, the Coptic Church, and a lot more. Evening entertainment ranges from a romantic felucca (native boat) ride on the Nile to Las Vegas-type revues with belly dancers and casinos in Western-style hotels.

Shore Excursions: Cairo Overnight, by air-conditioned motor coach, includes meals and visits to three Pyramids; $220; City tour, (three hours), $40.

INSIDER SHOPPING TIP

For guidance on bargaining techniques in Egypt, I pass along a personal experience. An Egyptian merchant showed me a galabea (a long, native-type dress) with the asking price of $85. I hesitated to respond and before I could counter-offer, the price dropped to $60. While I was considering how much the dress was worth, the price dropped to $50. As a starting point of the negotiations, I offered $20. When the vendor countered with $50, I stuck to my $20, rapidly developing more interest in the game of haggling than I had in the dress. Within a few minutes the galabea was mine for $20. I can't promise the same kind of success in all Egyptian markets or stores, but it is worth the effort if you don't want to overpay and want the fun of trying for the lowest price. Bargaining is expected in all stores and markets, other than five-star hotels, but it's worth a try even there. I've heard of good "discounts" in even the most exclusive places.

Malta

Malta is more than a prop in a Humphrey Bogart film. It Is a Mediterranean republic; an archipelago of six islands with a long-standing history. Malta is the largest of the islands and from the times of the Normans to Napoleon has changed hands many times. The oldest free-standing structures in the known world are megalithic temples on Malta and Gozo, dating from 3250 BC

The Knights of the Order of St. John ruled for nearly 300 years. In Valletta, the capital of Malta, it is said that 4,000 laborers and masons worked on the fortifications of the town, dividing the land into 1,125 private plots before 1571 when the Grand Master moved the Order to their new home. The town of Valletta was planned as a fortification to defend itself against the Turks.

Malta is the last bit of land belonging to the European continent that one sees before reaching the coast of Africa. English is the official language and residents are prepared for tourists, most of whom are from England and come via a seemingly steady stream of chartered aircraft.

INSIDER SHOPPING TIP

Shops are loaded with locally manufactured goods, which are produced for European designers. Hence, good buys are available in retail outlet stores, especially in men's shirts.

Shore Excursions: Valletta and Medina (Malta's main city before the creation of Valletta,) including shopping (four hours), $35; Tarxien Ruins, Ghar Dalam Caves, and Marsaxlokk Village, remains of prehistoric site older than the Pyramids or Stonehenge, (under four hours) $35.

On Your Own: It's easy to see Malta on your own. The center of town is walking distance from the pier and taxis are available in town for further exploration.

More Information: Malta National Tourist Organization in Valetta. The office is right at the end of the pier or contact www.malta.co.uk

Morocco – Casablanca

Although Hollywood's version of Casablanca has been deeply etched into the consciousness of several generations as a city of sinister intrigue and romance, the largest city in Morocco is in fact a world famous trade center. Casablanca, home to four million people, is North Africa's busiest port. Occupied by the Portuguese in 1575--who changed the original Phoenician name of Anafa to Casa Blanca or "white house,"--modern Casablanca played a key role in World War II and was one of three primary landing sites in the Allied invasion of North Africa.

Casablanca offers bazaars, crowded souks, and wonderful sun-drenched beach resorts. Language is Arabic with some English available in shopping areas. Credit cards are accepted. Currency is the Dirham.

Shore Excursions: includes City tour, Hassan II Mosque, Central Market, Habous Quarter and a photo op at Mohammed V. Square with its gardens and central fountains. Shopping time is included in shore excursions offered on board. Half day tours sell for about $35. Longer tours (about six hours) include a visit to Rabat, Morocco's capital, and the youngest of Morocco's four "imperial cities, as well as the Mausoleum of King Mohammed V, the Kasbah of the Oudaias, Medina Hassan Tower, and Mechouar of the Royal Palace. For about $50.

More Information: Moroccan National Tourist Office, 20 E. 46th St., New York, N.Y. 10017, or www.tourism-in-morrocco.com

Corsica

Corsica, "the scented isle," was discovered by the Genoese in 1492. Napoleon Bonaparte was born in Ajaccio in 1769 and was responsible for the fame of this fourth largest island in the Mediterranean Sea. Ajaccio, Corsica's major town, sits wedged between gigantic red granite mountains and the sea. It was known for its riches in the 18th century and today is popular with tourists who enjoy the Napoleonic ambiance.

There's not much to see in Corsica after seeing Napoleon's statue at the Place Austerlitz (an exact replica of the one at Les Invalides in Paris), and another of him with his four brothers at the Place De Gaulle. The beaches are Ajaccio's main attraction and they attract sun seekers from northern Europe. Beaches stretch from a narrow crescent to broad expanses.

Shore Excursions: Half day tours include a ride through the Corsican countryside, the mountain village of Cauro, and back down to the narrow country lanes as well as a brief tour of the city. Takes about four hours and costs about $40. Full day tours include Golfe de Porte, lunch in Porto and time for an independent stroll, (eight hours) $70.

More Information: French Government Tourist Office, 444 Madison Ave., New York, NY 10017or www.franceguide.com

France

Almost everything is special about France. It is the home of haute couture and haute cuisine, great writers, artists, and philosophers. The beautiful city of Paris is not all of France anymore than New York City is all of the United States. France is a country where a one- or two-day visit may not leave the visitor with the best impressions. More than one visit is required to appreciate the country.

Summer temperatures in northern France average 76 degrees. The Riviera is sunnier and warmer, with an average January temperature of 48 degrees. Currency is the French Franc and language is, of course, French. English is spoken in restaurants, shops and hotels in major tourist cities. A few shops still close between noon and 2:00 P.M. Ready-to-wear clothing, perfumes, gloves, and crystal are favorites with visitors. Department stores are good places to shop. Many stores close on Sunday and Monday. Local buses, metered taxis, and rental cars are available.

If your port of call is a city, wear city-type clothing. On the Riviera, dressy casual resort-wear is appropriate. Jackets and ties are required for dinner in nicer restaurants and hotels.

More Information: French Government Tourist Office, 444 Madison Ave., New York, NY 10017, or www.franceguide.com

Bordeaux

It's worth an early wakeup call to sail past the vineyards as the ship eases into the port of Bordeaux. Its recent surge of popularity as a port of call is due to its proximity to the Mediterranean and its 18th century elegance and atmosphere. Shore excursions usually head out to wineries and tastings, but it's the city itself that intrigues visitors. Wander on your own and sample the great fish restaurants near the wharf and be sure to see Parliament Square and the historic district, Pay particular notice to the individually carved faces around the Bourse, but you'll have to look up to see them. They are on doorways and walls and they are all different.

The French Riviera

Cannes

The city may owe its name to the abundance of reeds (cannes) in marshes long drained, but Cannes owes its rise to fame to an important English lord who sojourned in Cannes. He returned to London with nothing but praise. From then on, progress advanced rapidly and included casinos, the film festival, and resort-hotel complexes. The seaside setting, sandy beaches, and ritzy tone helped boost real estate values. If time allows, be sure to wander outside Cannes to visit the French cities of Provence, Grasse, Vence, St. Paul de Vence, or to the fairytale country of nearby Monaco.

INSIDER SHOPPING TIP

Cannes is hardly the place to do your bargain shopping. World-famous jewelers and dress designers usually offer the same merchandise everywhere else at lower prices except during a strong U.S. dollar period. High-fashion clothes carrying big-ticket numbers are good buys if you wear the labels. If you happen to be in this area in late August or September, look for sales in summer merchandise. Reductions are substantial and make shopping worthwhile.

Shore Excursions: To Nice (four hours), $80. To Cap d'Antibes (nine hours), $150, including lunch; to Monaco, (nine hours) $135 including lunch.

On Your Own: It's easy to get around. Mini-buses make a circle route of the Riviera and it is easy to get on and off if a particular town looks interesting. It's also easy to walk around Cannes on your own.

INSIDER TIP

It is unfortunate, but a warning is in order. Tourist season signals a mass migration of pickpockets along the coastal French Riviera. Thieves are professionals who work in teams using crowds and children as bait. Best advice is to leave all valuables on board ship and take only a credit card and a small amount of money in a pants pocket or concealed money belt. I have been there and am now a local crime statistic. My wallet was taken so smoothly, I didn't realize it was gone until I started to pay for lunch. The French police were great and luckily, all I lost was a few dollars and my credit cards. They caught the thief about a month later after he had run up hundreds of dollars on my AMEX card, but the aggravation of reporting lost cards was distressing. The policeman who assisted me said this was a common occurrence during summer months. He had been a victim of a band of vagrant children the day before.

Nice (Villefranche)

Smaller ships dock at the port of Nice, but larger vessels either anchor outside the harbor, or use Villefranche as the port of call. In either event, both areas are worthy of a visit. Villefranche is a charming resort village with delightful cafes and a beautiful walkway along the beach. It is a convenient access point to Monte Carlo, Nice and Cannes which are accessible by ship shore excursions or by local bus service, which is not recommended on board ships but is in reality a tour of the Riviera no matter which destination you select.

Buses stop right outside the Villefranche port terminal and an information office in the terminal will head you in the right direction. Nice is about an hour's bus ride away and takes you through some interesting small cities. The Nice bus terminal is a short walk from the Promenade des Anglais that fronts the Mediterranean and is lined with hotels and a giant casino. An early start will allow for lunch in the famous Excelsior Hotel or one of the nearby restaurants, a visit to the Chagall Museum, the flower market, and the old town. Buses run on a regular schedule, which is printed and posted at the bus stops. Price for the one-way ride to Nice from Villefranche was three dollars.

Rouen

The most popular shore excursion is the one offering a full day trip to Paris, which is understandable, if you have never been to Paris. But, Rouen is an ancient city that has more than enough to fill a day in port. It is a beautiful walled city that can be seen on foot or on a half-day tour, which will include a visit to Monet's home and gardens at Giverny. On your own, you should walk the cobblestone streets and visit the famous cathedral with its façade covered with Monet's paintings, the medieval clock and the church dedicated to Joan of Arc. It's well worth lining your ships' deck to watch the spectacular arrival and departure along a curving river lined by medieval castle ruins.

Shore Excursions: Full day with lunch and sightseeing in Paris about $150; round trip transportation to Paris (no tours) $90; Rouen sightseeing tour, $45.

Gibraltar

A self-governing British colony since 1704, Gibraltar is strategically placed opposite Ceuta. Together, they form the legendary Pillars of Hercules. Within this tiny British enclave is a wealth of scenery, history, and wildlife. Gibraltar is 1400 feet above the sea, and although geographically, it is part of the Iberian Peninsula, its geology is African. The town is noisy and very busy.

The Barbary apes are delightful and a bus ride up to see them is a diversion from the countless jewelry and souvenir shops dotting the main street. Imported toiletries and pharmaceuticals are relatively inexpensive.

Shore Excursions: Scenic tour (four hours), $50; highlights and cable car, (under three hours), $40. Fixed-rate taxis for point-to-point or by the hour (about $15 for the first hour) are available. Car ferry and passenger boats to

Tangiers take almost three hours for day excursions and cost about $55.

More Information: Gibraltar Tourist Office, Arundel Great Court, 179 The Strand, London, England WC2R 1EH, or www.gibraltar.gov.gi.

Greece

Greece combines past greatness and present vitality with a wonderful climate. It is a microcosm of the history and culture of ancient civilizations combined with the comforts of the twentieth century. Greece has one of the longest coastlines in Europe, beautiful and varied scenery from the mountains of the north, the plains of Thessaly, the rich valleys of the Peloponnese, and the golden beaches of Attica and enchanting islands. June, July, and August are considered high season.

Temperatures in Athens range from a low of 52 in April to a summer high of 90 degrees. Islands to the south of Athens average 10 to 15 degrees warmer. The currency used is the Drachma and the language is Greek, but English and French are spoken widely.

INSIDER SHOPPING TIPS

Greece is a good place to shop. Original designs in 18-carat gold jewelry are beautiful, but prices are not cheap. Look for leather goods, shoes in particular, locally woven fabrics, handmade silver jewelry, icons, and ornaments. Shops are usually closed Monday, Wednesday, and Saturday afternoons and all day Sunday. Wonderful street markets feature locally made items.

On Your Own: Buses and taxis run between Athens and the Port of Piraeus. Shore excursions are offered in Piraeus and on the islands by taxi, bus, on foot, or by donkey. Depending on the ship's time in port, a variety of tours are offered: Athens and the Acropolis (three hours), $50. Evening ashore (includes show and dinner at deluxe hotel), $80. All-day tours to surrounding areas and cities, $65 (including lunch). Public transport is good and reasonable. A taxi from port to Athens runs about $35.

City clothing is suggested for Athens; comfortable shoes for the Acropolis and other sightseeing walks. Comfortable, resort-type clothing is proper for island ports of call.

More Information: Greek National Tourist Office, 645 Fifth Avenue, New York, NY 10022, or www. eot.gr/

Athens and Piraeus

Nothing rivals the ancient classical perfection of the Acropolis in Athens. The Parthenon, the Temple of the Wingless Victory, the Erechtheum with the Caryatids supporting the porch and the Acropolis Museum are ageless in their beauty. Spreading out below these memorials to the past is an animated modern European capital--a city of striking contrasts. Other famous scenes of classic fame lie nearby: Corinth, the Temple of Poseidon at Sounion, Delphi, and Mycenae.

All ships bound for Athens arrive in its port, Piraeus, about 14 miles away. Whether you opt for the ship tour, the local bus or trolley car, or a taxi, the ride from the port takes you through smaller fishing villages and ports. You'll travel to Syntagma Square, the Tomb of the Unknown Soldier, and the Old Palace. Try to see the soldiers (Evzoni) change guard. On the way to the Acropolis (a must for both first-timers and repeat visitors), pass the Temple of Zeus, Hadrian's Arch, and the National Library, and mix with the natives at sidewalk cafes, shops, and on the streets. The "Sound and Light" at the Acropolis is excellent.

On Your Own: Athens is a wonderful city to tour on foot but wear your most comfortable shoes. Few visitors leave without climbing the Acropolis for a view of modern Athens and a feel for ancient Athens. From ancient relics to encounters with Lady Luck in 20th century casinos, Greece accommodates the visitor. There are casinos as active as any in Europe, situated atop Mt. Parnes (about an hour's drive from Athens) and on Rhodes and Corfu.

INSIDER TIP

Greek people are warm and friendly. When the lens fell out of our camera on the steps at Syntagma Square, we panicked. About to sail through those photogenic Greek Islands and no camera? How awful! The owner of a photography shop on the corner opposite the Palace not only quickly repaired our camera but also delivered it to the hotel in plenty of time for us to board ship in Piraeus.

The Greek Islands

Don't expect great sights on the Greek islands. What you'll find are peaceful retreats, left over relics rich of history. Some offer more tourist pleasures and others merely afford a chance to visit a small-unspoiled village. Most are too small for group excursions, and you can walk the island in an hour or so. When excursions are offered, they cost between $30 and $75 for three or four hours.

Corfu

This Ionian Island is not much more than great scenery and sandy beaches, with a resort center and the sixteenth-century Church of St. Spyridon, patron saint of the island. Explore Old Town, a delightful maze of tiny streets and lengthy history, and don't miss the cricket field still used one hundred years after British rule.

Crete

Heraklion is the main city of Crete, the largest of the Greek islands. It was founded by the Saracens about 1,000 BC They were followed by the Venetians, then the Turks, who held on for a couple of centuries. In 1913, Crete became part of Greece. Since most cruise ships stop here, the natives are ready for the tourists, and street shops beckon with homemade goods. Tours and sightseeing take the visitor to see the El Greco icons at the church of St. Menas, Palace of Minos at Knosses, and the Heraklion Archaeological Museum.

Delos and the Cyclades

Delos, birthplace of Apollo and Artemis, is the smallest of the Cyclades Islands and became the religious center of the Ionians. Excavations have revealed remains of temples, commercial houses, theaters, sanctuaries, and quantities of fine mosaics from those long-ago times.

Center of the Cyclades, a now deserted three-mile square rocky island, was once the wealthiest island of the Aegean with a population of over 20,000. Officially an archaeological site, Delos served as the center of the civilized world in its days of glory. Most interesting is the Alley of the Lions. Tours are offered by ships calling at Delos and at Mykonos or book a ferry on your own.

Mykonos

Mountainous and rocky Mykonos rises up from the dark Aegean Sea to a height of almost 1200 feet. A beautiful island, famous for its gleaming white windmills and neat, cube-like houses, Mykonos is considered the gem of the Cyclades.

Lifestyle for visitors and residents is tranquil and unhurried, which probably accounts for the influx of artists and jetsetters from Europe and the Americas during summer months. A "swinging island," it has a number of bars, clubs, and discos (as well as an inordinate number of beautiful people). Mykonos also is noted for its nude beaches and boutiques lining narrow and quaint cobblestone alleyways. A favorite snack is octopus with ouzo and fresh lobster meat.

Shore Excursions: Mykonos by night, party with the beautiful people, (three hours) $75.

Rhodes and the Dodecanese

The 600-square-mile island has over 26,000 hotel beds, but can hardly be called "over developed." The concentration of accommodations is in the "new" city of Rhodes and stretches along the two coasts out of the city of Rhodes for about 20 miles.

Situated on the pointed northern tip of the island, the town of Rhodes with its full-time population of 35,000 is divided into two sections: one is the colorful and interesting Old Town or medieval city "protected" by 30-foot-high, five-mile-long sandstone walls and the other is the "new city." One can walk the cobblestone streets and alleyways much as the knights of St. John of Jerusalem did centuries earlier or visit an old synagogue that withstood time and Nazi occupation during World War II.

INSIDER SHOPPING TIPS

Among the souvenirs that attract visitors are antiques, copper, modern jewelry fashioned in a workshop adjoining the store, ceramics, donkey saddles, freshly-ground coffee, fine worsted and other cloth, shoes, sandals, handbags, old goldsmiths' balances, pistols, swords, daggers, muskets, blunderbusses, hand-cranked coffee mills, brass candlesticks, replicas of icons, scarves, tee shirts, carpets, flokati rugs, marble tables, chess sets made of onyx and metal, mink coats, fur jackets, hand-made candles, birthday cakes, seafood meals, Greco-Turkish sweets, and 72-hour made-to-measure suits, among other items.

The "new" town includes the octagonal marketplace and the bustling yacht harbor of Mandraki. The latter is "guarded" by two friendly deer, the symbol of the island.

Santorini

Known as Kalliste (most beautiful) and Strongyli (round) in ancient times, Santorini is rich in history. It was thought by many scientists to have been the lost continent of Atlantis. Donkeys carry tourists up a zigzag steep trail to the village of Thera on top the precipice and a one-way ride is a tourist "must." Here you can sip local wine and stare at the cone of Greece's last active volcano.

At the village of Akrotiri a museum was built on the site where the sensational discoveries of a buried city were unearthed in 1967.

INSIDER TIP
A paved road built a few years ago leads up the mountain to Thera. Tours by taxi are available, but the donkey ride is more fun. Bargain for either a one-way or round-trip ride. And don't pay until you are safely down the mountain. If you are an animal lover and will be offended because the donkey master hits the animal to get him moving, take the taxi ride or cable car up. I didn't mind and neither did the donkey-although my animal wheezed and snorted all the way up.

Israel

One of the youngest nations of the modern world, Israel is also one of the world's oldest with a history dating back almost 6,000 years. First called the "Holy Land" in the Bible, the area is still popularly known by that name with Muslims, Jews, and Christians claiming sites that authenticate the history of their religions. Much of the former desert land, once owned by absentee landlords has been made to bloom again. The intensive irrigation projects developed by the Israelis to transform the Negev have produced technology that is now being made available to other desert areas of the world.

In normal times, cruise ships visit from May through mid-November, but some cruise ships originating in Greece and world cruises call year-around at either Haifa or Ashdod. The climate is mild in port areas, with an average low of 45 in March, and a high of 90 degrees in August in Haifa and Tel Aviv, while cooler in mountain areas. The currency used is the Israeli Shekel, but U.S. dollars are accepted almost everywhere. The language is Hebrew, but signs are also in English, which is widely spoken. Yiddish, German, Arabic, and French are also spoken.

All major stores are closed from sundown on Friday to Sunday morning. Good buys are in locally made jewelry, beachwear, copper, knitwear, religious ornaments, and diamonds of less than one carat (but shop carefully). Local and inner-city buses, metered taxis, Sheruts (shared taxis with fixed rates), and rental cars are available. Dress is casual but take a raincoat and light woolens during late fall and winter months for touring. Sturdy shoes are a necessity for exploring both in major cities and the countryside. Arms (and sometimes heads) should be covered when visiting religious sites.

More Information: Israel Government Tourist Office, 800 second Ave., New York, NY 10117. www.goisrael.com.

Haifa

Unfortunately, most cruise ships only spend two days in Israel, a country where one can spend a lifetime and still not see or understand it all. So what can you do with one or two days in Israel? With 24 hours in the Holy Land, you can see the port city of Haifa, travel by motor coach to Nazareth to see the Church of St. Joseph, Mary's Well, and other historical sites before continuing past the village of Cana to Tiberias on the shore of the Sea of Galilee. From there head to Capernaum to visit the ruins of the ancient synagogue and to the Mount of Beatitudes (the scene of the Sermon on the Mount). Return to Haifa along the shores of the Galilee to visit a kibbutz and take in a final panoramic view from Mount Carmel. With an extra day in port, Jerusalem, Bethlehem, and Tel Aviv can be added to your bird's-eye view of Israel.

Shore Excursions: Full days (without lunch), $95. Half-day city tours, $55.

Car rentals and limousines with guides are available. Inter-city bus service is excellent. Some ships offer overnight tours to Jerusalem that cost about $250 per person, double occupancy.

INSIDER TIP

If this is your first visit to Israel, don't try to see it all in 24 hours. Choose the highlights and plan to return. If Israel is a highlight of your cruise, select a ship that spends more time in port. Occasionally, ships have special itineraries. I found one a couple of years ago that spent eight days of a 14-day cruise in Israel. The ship was my hotel, and Haifa was a short walk away. In fact, the whole country was a short ride from the pier.

Jerusalem

Jerusalem has an Old City and a New City, and both are worthwhile. The Old City, with its eight-gated walls, allows for a fabulous view of the rooftops, archways, and alleys of former days. See the Western Wall, the last vestige of Solomon's Temple that is the most sacred spot on the earth to Jews. Follow the Via Dolorosa with the 14 stations of the Cross and share the reverence of Christians at the Church of the Holy Sepulchre. The Dome of the Rock is the place, tradition says, where Abraham prepared to sacrifice Isaac, and from where, Muslims believe, Muhammad ascended to heaven. The city is a city of museums, but don't miss the Israel Museum housing the Dead Sea Scrolls.

Explore the Mea Shearim quarters of the ultra-orthodox Jews, and go to the Knesset to see the floors and tapestries by Chagall.

Tel Aviv

The bustling, young city is bright and modern. The bustling scene in Dizengoff Square with its shops and nightclubs is the key to the city. Places to visit include the magnificent beach, the Tel Aviv Municipal Museum, the Haganah Museum, and the Diaspora Museum, which traces the varied histories of the Jewish people following their forced dispersion from their homeland. Then refresh yourself with a drink at one of the numerous cafes in the Dizengoff area.

Alongside Tel Aviv is Jaffa, a four thousand-year-old community. Visit the Artists' Quarter overlooking the old harbor. It has been restored to a picturesque area. Look for bargains in the flea market near the clock tower

Italy

Italy offers infinite variety in its geography, climate and people. In the north there are snow-capped mountain peaks, and in the south the palms and orange groves of Sicily. In the summer the beaches of the Adriatic and Italian Riviera are among the most popular in Europe and in the winter the Alps and Dolomites are a snow-covered playground. Then there are the great cities of Rome, Florence, Venice, and Milan, rich in historic and artistic treasures.

Cruise ships visit southern ports from March through November. Temperatures range from an average low of 46 in April to a high in the 90s in August, but it is generally mild in port areas throughout the year. Currency is the Lire, and language is Italian.

INSIDER SHOPPING TIPS

Shopping in Italy still comes with promises of good buys in shoes, handbags, all leather goods, jewelry, gloves, and glassware, but the best values are in designer clothing. The more expensive the item, the larger the differential between what the item sells for in Fifth Avenue shops. Stores in major cities remain open during lunch hours. Best buys are if your ship brings you to Italy when the seasons are changing. Discounts are huge and when I am there in late August or early September, I bring an extra suitcase.

There are good local bus systems, a subway in Rome, plenty of metered taxis, and rental cars (but watch out for wild and reckless drivers, who treat highways like the Grand Prix). Italy also has frequent strikes, so it is probably a good idea to buy the tour offered on board ship.

Depending on the area, "comfort" and "casual" are key words. Heads, shoulders, and arms should be covered on visits to churches.

More Information: Italian State Tourist Department, 630 Fifth Avenue, Room 1565, New York, NY 10020, or www.italiantourism.com

Civitavecchia (The Port For Rome)

The port for Rome is Civitavecchia, gateway to the ancient capital of the western world and center of Christianity for 2,000 years. The ride from the port city passes the Appenine Mountains to the east and the Tyrrhenian Sea to the west but it is over a four lane highway which shortens the ride to less than one hour from Civitavecchia to the Excelsior Hotel on the Via Venetto.

Rome blends old and new, ancient and modern, religious and secular in a magnificent metropolis built on seven hills and founded, according to legend, by twin brothers Romolus and Remus in 753 BC.

Vatican City is the spiritual city for close to 600 million Roman Catholics and is a miniscule sovereign state, home to the Pope, the world's largest church and impressive St. Peter's Square. The Vatican mints its own coins, prints its own stamps, and keeps its own army of Swiss Guards. Vatican City also houses St. Peter's Basilica, consecrated in 1626, a reconstruction and enlargement of Constantine's original building. A century of work went into construction of the church and includes contributions by Bramante, Raphael, Sangalla and Michelangelo. The Basilica features wondrous use of gold, marble, gilt and mosaics.

Shopping opportunities around the Square offer religious and other articles but it is not recommended. The same items are available in less tourist-dominated areas for less money.

No visit to Rome would be complete without touring the Coliseum, the site of many brutal spectacles since its construction--by slave labor--in 80 AD. After the Vatican and the Coliseum, time permitting, wear your best walking shoes and see Rome by foot. Should you tire at any point, taxis are plentiful, but don't miss your bus back to Civitavecchia. A taxi will cost you close to $100.

Don't miss Old Rome and the charming cobblestones streets around the Piazza Navona, the Pantheon and Camp de' Fiori. Photographers find the light in Rome, "the eternal city," wonderful. I never miss a stop at the Trevi Fountain and I always throw three coins into the fountain and make my wish.

INSIDER SHOPPING TIPS

Rome is a shopper's nightmare. Everything is beautiful and very costly. The good news is that prices are a bit lower than at home. There is, however, a greater selection in Rome because that's where the designs originate. Boutiques sporting the familiar names of Fendi and Gucci, (and more that are only too easy to learn) line the famed Via Condotti an entire shopping district between the Spanish Steps and Via del Corso. Leather goods are your best bets with silk ties and scarves, fine knitwear and ceramics readily available. As elsewhere in Italy, the costlier the item, the better the price compares to what you would pay at home.

Shore Excursions: Ships usually overnight in Civitavecchia and offer full day round trip transfers where you are on your own in Rome for about $80. They also offer full day tours that include the Coliseum, St. Peter's Basilica, Vatican Museum, Sistine Chapel and lunch (approximately 10 hours), $150. There are trains that run regularly between Civitavecchia and Rome and I wouldn't hesitate to use them if this was not my first visit to the City. Train schedules should be available from the Shore Excursion Desk on board ship.

Credit cards are accepted everywhere. Italian Lira is the country's currency. English is spoken in most shops and in all hotels but not usually when you ask directions on street corners.

Genoa

The harbor entrance to Genoa is spectacular. The fifth-largest city in Italy and the major port, Genoa was the birthplace and home of such world-famous men as Christopher Columbus, the Italian patriot Guiseppe Mazzini, and the violinist Paganini. Genoa has become a popular passenger port of embarkation for Mediterranean-bound cruise ships and for other vessels. Most air-sea programs allow for time to sightsee in and around the city.

It's easy to get around Genoa by taxi, bus, or private car, and all ships offer shore excursions to Columbus's home outside the old city gates, the San Lorenzo Cathedral, the ducal palace, the Bianco Palace, and the Staglieno Cemetery. Some tours go beyond Genoa along the coastline through the Maritime Alps. It's a particularly scenic highway linking small fishing villages, old towns, and the French border.

Portofino

This delightful little fishing village is a big hit with the rich and famous and presents wonderfully serene regions of the picturesque Italian Riviera. Palatial villas sit atop the hillside and trendy (and pricey) boutiques and cafes line the harbor. Shore excursions don't really exist, but walking along the harbor or climbing the hills in this charming port will suffice.

Naples

The ship's arrival at Naples is worth a 6:00 A.M. wake-up call. You'll glide past craggy islands into the great bay, past the Castel del'Ovo, once the home of Lucullus, on its mini island. Castles guard the city, stacked up like a great amphitheater constructed of boxes. The great harbor of Naples has hydrofoil service to the nearby islands of Capri, Ischia, and Procida.

Naples is a delight in springtime. The weather is mild all year, but it is especially rewarding to take a summer walk around the curving sea promenade, stop for Campari and soda or coffee in cafes, or have lunch at a waterside restaurant before the summer crowds arrive. There is much to see here-- the cathedral, 13 museums, and unique architecture.

Though Naples seems to be a constant whirl of traffic, there are quiet areas, such as the Catacombs of San Gennaro or the park around Villa

Floridiana. The main shopping area is the Via Roma, but bargains are more likely to be found in the small shops located throughout the city. Silk scarves, luggage, handbags, and accessories by well-known Italian designers cost a lot less than they do in the States.

Shore Excursions: City tour, includes Pompeii (four hours), $50 without lunch; cruise to Capri, (eight hours, but time is unstructured) $100.

INSIDER TIP

Unfortunately, Naples is another city where crime has gotten out of hand. DO NOT wear jewelry or carry a purse, camera, or handbag in Naples. Pickpockets and muggers abound. They ride by on motorcycles and help themselves to whatever the tourist is carrying.

Venice

This is the most beautiful and romantic city in the world. It is rightfully renowned as "Queen of the Adriatic" and befittingly adorned with fabulous treasures. All tours start with the Palace of the Doges; the Basilica of St. Mark, with its wonderful mosaics; St. Mark's Square, where everyone feeds pigeons; the Bridge of Sighs; the magnificent Palazza Rezzonico; and the Ca' d'Oro, one of the city's oldest houses. Venice also means the silent gliding of gondolas along the Grand Canal, exquisite Murano glassware, and great shopping opportunities.

From April through September, especially during school holidays, Venice is crowded - really crowded! It's sometimes hard to maneuver around St. Marks Square, but it's always easy to find a chair in an outdoor café for a coffee and some typical Italian music. There's a cover charge which keeps chairs empty for paying guests.

Shore Excursions: By gondola and on foot (under four hours), $75.

On Your Own: Don't let the crowd intimidate you in Venice. Do take the vaporetto (public water bus) and visit some of the neighboring islands. Highly recommended is Murano for visits to glass factories. Not recommended is dinner at Harry's American Bar. You'll meet other Americans and you'll pay a hefty price for dinner and/or a drink. If you must visit Harry's, peek in about 6 PM when the crowd is thickest, then head off to one of the sidewalk restaurants where it's hard to get a bad meal and prices are fair. Venice is a walking city and you'll discover new places and cross more bridges than you ever imagined. Don't worry about getting lost. Just follow the signs on every corner which point you in the direction of St. Marco. That's the square from which everything emanates.

INSIDER SHOPPING TIP

It may not be legal, but you should know about the street vendors who sell "genuine imitation" designer handbags and wallets on almost every street corner when the police are not around. If you ask the price of something, be prepared to have the eager salesman follow you around until you buy the item. Also, remember that the seller doesn't expect you to buy the item at the first price he mentions. Be sure to counter offer on the low side, then settle for what you are willing to pay. It's a fun pastime that shoppers have come to enjoy.

Funchal

Funchal is the port city and has about 100,000 residents, or about one-third the island's population. Flower vendors are a few steps down the gangplank, and wineries are generous with their free samples. The island has one beach at Prainha, but all major hotels have swimming pools and usually welcome cruise ship passengers. Among things to see and do are visits to the village of Monte or Terreiro de Luta. A memorable return is by non-conventional toboggan slide downhill over cobblestones worn smooth from the days when hill villagers sent produce to market in this manner. The ride is in a large basket on wooden runners, with two men keeping pace alongside controlling the trip with ropes. It is not recommended for the faint of heart.

In Funchal, see the Mercado do Lavradores near the port. Costumed flower vendors man the stalls. Also see the Museum of Sacred Art, the Cathedral, and the Casa de Turista for local handicrafts.

Shore excursions are limited, but the best overview is on a scenic tour (four hours), $45.

Tangier

Standing at the entrance to the Strait of Gibraltar, Tangier presents a fascinating picture of East and West. Known as the crossroads of the world, Tangier was an international city between World War I and 1956, and it remains cosmopolitan. The old kasbah of narrow souks huddled around the Sultan's Palace is worthy of illustrated Arabian Nights, but modern Tangier is a sophisticated European-style city with smart shops and good hotels. Most visitors enjoy bargaining in the bazaars. Favorite items are leatherworks, Moroccan rugs, and Oriental-styled jewelry.

Shore excursions of the city and surrounding areas (four hours), $40, are the best way to spend a half-day. The remainder of the day is well spent in the souks.

Portugal

After Roman occupation by Julius Caesar, the Moors conquered Portugal in 711. Christian Crusaders recaptured the area and the Moors were ousted, but their influence can still be seen in the architecture of the Algarve, in the narrow streets of Lisbon's Alfama quarter and in the Arab dialects.

Because of extremely mild climate, cruise season begins in late March in southern Portugal and lasts through early November. Lisbon is much cooler during winter months.

Currency is the Portuguese Escudo. The written sign for Escudo is similar to the U.S. dollar sign ($), so be careful when shopping. Language is Portuguese, but English is spoken widely.

INSIDER TIPS

Excellent buys are wines, handicrafts, baskets, some jewelry, and, of course, Madeira lace. Transportation in Lisbon is by public bus, taxi, or rental car. In other ports, local buses are slow, but taxis are plentiful. Some taxis are without meters, so prices should be agreed upon in advance.

If your port of call is Lisbon, count on seasonal, city-type clothing. In resort areas, dress casually. The islands are less formal than the capital city.

More Information: Portuguese National Tourist Office, 590 Fifth Avenue, Fourth Floor, New York, NY 10036, or www.portugal.org.

Lisbon

Whether Lisbon is a port of embarkation or a port of call, you should take time to see some of the great places. Even the churches are rated as museums. Your tour should include the old riding school of the Royal Palace, the Naval Museum, which houses an impressive collection of artifacts, wide avenues, beautiful shops, and the nearby famous resort of Estoril, where deposed royalty spends much of its time.

This is one port where dinner or lunch in a fabulous seafood restaurant is worthwhile, and where a passenger will enjoy walking the streets, sipping native wine at one of the many cafes, and mingling with the friendly Portuguese people.

Madeira

Some six hundred miles southwest of the mainland, Madeira is mountainous and cultivated with tropical fruits, a profusion of flowers, and those famous grapes used in Madeira wines. It is often described as a floating garden in the Atlantic; it is one of five islands making up a province of Portugal.

When Goncalves Zarco and his company landed in 1419, Madeira was uninhabited. The densely wooded and immense forests had to be cleared before it could be settled. Legend has it that; almost a century before, a young Englishman and his lady friend were eloping. Their ship sank, and they were cast ashore at Madeira. The soldiers accompanying them escaped to the north coast of Africa and were sold into slavery. When the story eventually reached Prince Henry the Navigator, Zarco was dispatched to find the island.

Whatever the truth, visitors now find it one of the nicest islands on earth, probably best known for Madeira wine. Funchal and Machico, the principal towns, both lie on charming bays. Funchal has a leisurely Old World atmosphere with cobbled streets, marble paving, and elegant balconies. The cathedral has arcades of painted lava rocks and a remarkable ceiling of ivory inlaid in cedar wood. Inland lie dramatic valleys and sharp, high mountain peaks.

Spain

There is an exciting feeling about Spain, with its sunny beaches, rich art galleries, grandiose churches, fiestas, and bullfights. Two totally different religious cultures have gone into its making--Roman Catholicism, whose fervor launched the Inquisition; and the Muslim religion, a legacy of 700 years of Moorish rule (711 to 1492). The Spanish temperament that results is a mixture of flamboyance, passion, and sentiment.

Spain has a diverse population of over 38 million people with more than 10 percent living in the capital city of Madrid. June through August are the most popular cruise months. Temperatures range from a low of 50 in April to a high of a high of 90 degrees in August in southern Spain. Currency is the Spanish Peseta and language is primarily Spanish with English, French, and German spoken in hotels and shops catering to tourists.

INSIDER SHOPPING TIPS

Best buys are in leather items (shoes, handbags, and luggage), suede, ceramic (Lladro) figures, and Mallorca pearls. Some shops are closed between 1:00 and 4:00 P.M.; all are closed all day Sunday and Saturday afternoons. Department stores remain open through siesta hours and on Saturdays. In cities, buses, metered taxis, and rental cars are available. There's also a good subway system in Madrid.

City clothes are suggested in Barcelona and Madrid. Resort-type clothing is acceptable in other ports. When in doubt, remember that Spain is still a conservative country, although, judging from street scenes, it is changing rapidly.

More Information: Tourist Office of Spain, 1221 Brickell Ave, Suite 1850, Miami, FL 33131 or www.okspain.org.

Barcelona

A statue of Christopher Columbus gazes from its pillar in Plaza Puerta de la Paz across the large, bustling port of Barcelona, observing the spectrum of liners, cargo and fishing boats, pleasure craft, and the full-size replica of Columbus's Santa Maria. Barcelona was an important center of civilization long before Roman times, and ancient remnants are visible in Barcelona square, in mosaics on houses, and in the museums.

Barcelona is a beautiful city combining the old with the new in a mellow way. The spectacular spires of Gaudi's unfinished Sagrada Familia Church, his Parque Guell, Picasso's works in the Cofradia Street Museum, and the fountains of Carlos Buigas bear witness to the artistic genius of the past. The circular Plaza Ramblas de Cataluna is dotted with antique shops and is the center of life in Barcelona. Los Ramblas radiates from wide central pavements famous for morning flower markets where birds and small animals are also sold. Top couturier boutiques are on the Paseo De Gracia and excellent shops featuring men's and women's clothing, leather, and jewelry are found throughout the city. A visit to Barcelona without a taste of zarzuela (a rich shellfish dish) would be a pity.

Shore Excursions: City tour (four hours), $75. Tour of countryside (four hours), $50 to $60

INSIDER TIP

Barcelona has built new cruise ship terminals and its proximity to the Mediterranean is increasing the number of ships that use Barcelona for embarkation and debarkation. Most companies offer pre cruise, or post-cruise hotel packages and this is an ideal city in which to spend a couple of days. The airport is the most modern in Europe, built for the Olympics a few years ago. Taxis between hotels, the pier and the airport run around $20 and it takes about 25 minutes for the ride.

Canary Islands

The Canary Islands cover an area of 2,807 square miles with a population of 378,900 in Las Palmas, the capital of Grand Canary and 164,767 on Tenerife. There are only slight variations in temperature throughout the year with a low in January of 65 degrees and a high in August of 76 degrees. There's very little rain. The currency is the Spanish Peseta.

Legend puts these seven islands into the lost continent of Atlantis, supposedly it's highest peaks. The islands are Spanish provinces and retain much of the mother country's culture and traditions. The Canaries are actually a series of islands: Gurteventura, Grand Canary, Lanzarote, and Tenerife. The most popular ports of call are Las Palmas and Tenerife. Las Palmas was visited by Columbus at the beginning of each of his voyages to the New World.

Shops close between 1:00 and 4:00 P.M. and are closed on Sundays. Watches, cameras, and tape recorders are inexpensive in the Triana Street and port areas of Las Palmas. Always bargain, except in department stores. Good buys in native crafts include pottery, woodcarvings, basketwork, and embroidery.

Getting around is not difficult. Shore excursions run about $45 for a half-day, $75 for a full day, including lunch. Rental cars, taxis, local buses, and tours are available.

Malaga

One of Spain's leading resort cities, Malaga has fine hotels, excellent shops, and parks, as well as interesting reminders of the past in the cathedral and the Moorish Palace of the Alcazar. It boasts a splendid bullring, and a magnificent view of the city from the vantage point of Gibralfaro. A few miles away is the small resort of Torremolinos.

Shore Excursions: A city tour (three hours), $45; Grenada (ten hours), $95 to $150, depending on whether lunch is included.

Palma de Mallorca (Balearic Islands)

This fashionable resort-island city is another blend of old and new. Modern holiday hotels are door-to-door with a magnificent 13th-century cathedral, winding lanes, and medieval palaces. Of interest is a scenic drive to the Carthusian Monastery at Validemosa, where George Sand and Chopin set up housekeeping, thus causing more than a casual ripple of scandal in polite Victorian households. Known for its beaches and thousands of European visitors, Palma de Mallorca has again been placed on the jet setters' list of favorite places.

Shore Excursions cover the city and surrounding area (four hours), $35 to $55.

Turkey

Europe and Asia meet in Turkey, with the Bosporus Strait as the dividing line.

It is a country of more than 45 million people on which 12 different civilizations have left their mark. It is rich in antiquities with ruins dating back to the Greeks, Romans, Selcuk and Ottomon Turks, Assyrians, Persians, and Hittites.

Because of its extremely mild climate, cruise ships visit Turkish ports year-around. The most popular months for cruising are April through mid-November. Climate varies greatly. The Anatolian Plain is hot in the summer and freezing in the winter. The Black Sea coast is mild and damp and the Mediterranean coast is warm and sunny with average annual temperature of 75 degrees. Currency is the Turkish Lire. Languages spoken are Turkish, Greek, and Arabic.

INSIDER SHOPPING TIP

Shop in Turkey for the fun of it and the occasional bargain, only if you are an expert negotiator. Head for the bazaar or Covered Market and look for jewelry, Meerschaum pipes, daggers, ceramics, leather goods, rugs, and carpets, and don't hesitate to bargain down to the last penny. That's part of the sport! But buyers beware when it comes to expensive items, particularly jewelry and antiques. Avoid public transportation. There are plenty of taxis, but determine price in advance. In Mosques, head and arms should be covered. Avoid shorts and mini-skirts.

More Information: Turkish Government Tourism and Information Office, 821 United Nations Plaza, Fourth Floor, New York, NY 10017, or www.touristturkey.org.

Popular Ports of Call

Istanbul

The approach to Istanbul by ship is a spectacular introduction to a city where 2500 years of history are so closely woven together it is hard to separate the threads. Most ships spend a complete day and evening in Istanbul, and it is possible to see the city on your own or with the ship tour, which returns passengers to the vessel for lunch, then picks them up for the afternoon tour. The highlights of any visit to Istanbul are the Blue Mosque, the Aqueduct of Valens, the Old Seraglio, and the covered bazaar.

Shore Excursions: City tour, includes time in the bazaar (eight hours), $45; nightclub tour with typical entertainment includes dinner (four hours), $160.

Kusadasi

Ephesus is one of the best-preserved examples of ancient cities anywhere in the world. Some experts believed Apasa, which is mentioned in Hittite texts from around 2,000 BC, is actually Ephesus, 19 miles inland from the Port of Kusadasi.

The amazing site was discovered in 1869 by a British engineer/archaeologist after years of looking for it. The Austrian Institute of Archaeology is currently working at the site. Greek gods came in from the west; Anthony and Cleopatra rode along the Arcadian Way. St.Paul preached at Ephesus, and the tomb of St. John the Apostle is located here as well.

Shore Excursions: Ephesus tour, (under four hours), $40; full day (eight hours) $75.

Black Sea

The Black Sea offers a taste of a different culture from time-honored Mediterranean ports of call. Tsars and palaces, ancient and modern history all comes into play in the Ukraine.

Ukraine

A visa is needed whether you intend to take a ship's shore excursion or go off on your own. Visas must be issued prior to leaving home.

More information: Consular Office, Embassy of Ukraine, 3350 M. St. NW, Washington, D.C. 20007, or www.ukremb.com.

Yalta

Slavs founded Kiev in the 10th century when Prince Vladimir of Kiev introduced Christianity to the region. Yalta belonged to the Turks in 1475. Yalta, in the Ukraine, was a small village in the early 19th century, accessible only by ship. The town's popularity grew when nearby Sebastopol became the site of the Imperial Palace at Livadia in the 1860s, linking Yalta by road.

Tsar Alexander II helped create the area as a resort for the aristocracy. Homes became spas or hotels for Russians who flocked to the sea for therapeutic treatments including salt-water thassalotherapy. The tsars obviously enjoyed the region's gentle, Riviera-type climate. By 1920 Lenin decided the health-cure properties of the region belonged to the state.

Yalta (and much of the region) also features outstanding flora and fauna. Buildings retain a small touch of former glories but some are crumbling. During World War II, German armies occupied much of USSR, but in 1945 Winston Churchill, Joseph Stalin and President Franklin D. Roosevelt met in Yalta to divide the world into East and West.

The Embankment offers a good site for viewing the harbor and its lovely promenade provides the setting for a leisurely stroll. Two palaces are noteworthy: Livadia, former Imperial palace, less than two miles from the port, where the world leaders met, and Alupka, a wonderful sample of 19th century Russian architecture.

Shore Excursions: Best of the Crimea, along the southern coast visiting Livadia and Alupka Palace, (under five hours) $45; Yalta sights and folkloric show, Ukranian lunch included (under eight hours), $90.

Odessa

It's been called "pearl of the Black Sea," and Odessa, on the sea's north shore, is indeed gemlike with its glittering Baroque-style Opera House built in 1887 and wide array of greenery and multi-hued flowers. The famed Potemkin Steps, almost 200 of them, built more than 105 years ago, are tempting, and the view from the top is a photographer's dream. The Pushkin Monument honors the 13 months the poet spent in Odessa.

Museums include the Fine Arts Gallery with exquisite Russian and Ukranian paintings dating from the 14th century.

Shore Excursions: Full day city tour, lunch accompanied by classical music performed by members of the Odessa Opera and Philharmonic, (eight hours), $90; half-day, (under four hours,) $40.

North Cape, Northern Europe, Russia

There are several types of itineraries offered in this area of the world. Each takes travelers on different courses through different historical and totally different cultures.

A fjord cruise covers the wakes made a thousand years ago, by the Norsemen who left their homeland in dragon-bowed wooden vessels. Today they're back, bringing with them thousands of passengers on board sleek and not-so-sleek ships; new and not so new vessels. They sail up the rugged, jagged, fjord-laced coast of Norway, across the Arctic Circle, and on to Europe's northernmost point, the Magnificent North Cape.

Baltic cruises take passengers to sophisticated cosmopolitan capital cities in Scandinavia and on the continent. Other ships combine the North Cape and the Baltic, with stops at such historic cities as St. Petersburg, Russia (formerly Leningrad) and Tallinn, Estonia.

While the isolated master works of nature are the essence of North Cape cruises, Russia-Europe sailings emphasize man's creative masterpieces. An example of this is the Hermitage Museum in St. Petersburg with its collection of art treasures. If you are frustrated after just an afternoon at the Hermitage, remember that experts estimate it would take six years to see everything housed in this magnificent museum.

Other examples of man's accomplishments are evidenced throughout Northern Europe cruise visits. Consider the clean, carefully planned capitals of Scandinavia where ancient palaces, squares, and monuments stand in contrast to striking triumphs of modern architecture; in the canals of Amsterdam and the Kiel Canal, one of the great engineering feats of the last century. Much of what a cruise passenger sees in these ports is unforgettable. There's the lighthearted magic of Tivoli Gardens in Copenhagen; the rollicking, frolicking beer halls of Germany, and the warm beaches around Visby, Sweden's vacation paradise.

Included in this section are ports most frequently visited by major cruise companies. These European cities are worthy of two- or three-week visits, and the wise cruise passenger doesn't expect to see Germany, for example, because his or her ship stopped in Hamburg for six hours. If you use your time wisely, you can see the sights of the city, taste local foods, and experience the lifestyle of the people who live there. However, if your ship stops in Tallinn or Riga, you have the opportunity to visit undivided Berlin by shore excursion or by rental car.

Transportation: The cost of living in this part of the world is high. In fact, Sweden tops the list. So expect to pay more for sightseeing than you would in the Caribbean or Mediterranean. On average, tours run around $60 for four hours. Most ships sailing the North Cape offer optional three- or four-day land packages including hotel accommodations in embarkation or debarkation cities. Prices are available at time of booking and include transfers between the ship and hotels.

Taxis are available in all ports, and once you reach metropolitan cities, self-drive rental cars and chauffeur-driven cars can be reserved. Public transportation is very good in cities such as Copenhagen, Oslo, or Stockholm.

Weather is comfortable year-round in North Sea and best in June, July, and early August in North Cape, but unpredictable. Expect chilly nights and cool days, but be prepared for warmer weather just in case.

Passports and Visas: Passports are required for all countries, but Russia still requires a visa for passengers inclined to explore on their own. Cruise ship passengers who use the ship as their hotel and sightsee on ship's excursions do not need an individual visa. Russian Immigration clears all passengers as a group. If your ship is in St. Petersburg and you want to venture out alone, you will not be permitted to leave the ship without an individual visa. Most tours must be reserved and fully paid in advance of sailing from the United States. Some ships spend a couple of days docked in St. Petersburg and offer optional tours to Moscow. An individual visa is required for hotel stays overnight and is available through the cruise line or Russian consulates in the U.S. and Canada.

INSIDER TIPS

Tours in Russia are costly and sell out quickly because for most passengers, it is a one-time visit. Half-day sightseeing costs $65 to $75 depending on the ship. Full-day tours cost more than $125 per person and you still return to the ship for lunch. Passengers are picked up dockside for the morning tour, returned to the ship for lunch, picked up for the afternoon tour, returned for dinner, then picked up for the evening theater tour and returned by midnight. Our advice is: Get an individual visa if you're heading for Russia. With that visa you'll be cleared separately, and you'll be allowed to arrange for a private car to tour the city and surrounding area, more or less on your own if you made the arrangements through your travel agent before you left home. It is also possible to get a one-day individual visa on board some ships, providing the shore excursion manager or concierge reserves a private car and English speaking guide for you at least three days in advance of your ship's visit. Costs about $200 for a half day; $350 for a full day, but it's worth it. Cars will only accommodate two people, in addition to the driver and guide. It's the best way to see the city and countryside.

Belgium

Belgium is a small patchwork country with about 10 million people. Brussels highlights the contrasting cultures of the Flemish and the French sections of Belgium in a variety of architecture, language, and cuisine. It all comes together in Brussels, the bilingual capital.

Climate is unreliable and frequently damp. August temperatures average from a low of 54 to a high of 73, but be prepared for a variance of 10 degrees in either direction. Official language is both Flemish and French; English is widely spoken and understood.

INSIDER SHOPPING TIP

Belgium is expensive. The best buys are in chocolates, Bruges lace, brassware, copper, and linen. Diamonds are also touted as a good buy, but it's best to know before you invest in a big-ticket item, although Belgian merchants are known for reliability.

There is excellent bus service from port cities to Brussels. Within Brussels, it is easy to get around by subway, bus, streetcars, and metered taxis. Rental cars are available in all cities. Wear casual city clothing suitable for sightseeing in spring-like weather. Rain coats and umbrellas will come in handy on all-day excursions. Jackets are required in better restaurants and hotel dining rooms for dinner meals.

More Information: Belgium Tourist Bureau, 780 Third Avenue, New York, NY 10017, or www.belgium-tourism.com.

Zeebrugge

From the seaport of Zeebrugge, you can easily visit Brussels. Nearby Ghent and Bruges contain beautiful historic buildings, museums, and magnificent old churches that reflect the genius of the Flemish artists who contributed so much to these cities of art.

Shore Excursions: Half day to Brugge, 30 minutes from port, (about five hours), $65.

Denmark

Denmark is a land of farms, light industry, fishermen, Hans Christian Andersen and Tivoli Gardens. Copenhagen, the capital city hums with almost Mediterranean gaiety and charming palaces, high green spires, fine restaurants, and friendly people.

Cruise season is from May through early October and the port of call is almost always Copenhagen. Currency is the Danish Kroner, and U.S. dollars are not accepted everywhere. It is recommended that visitors exchange dollars into Kroner. Language is Danish, but most people speak English.

INSIDER SHOPPING TIPS
Stores are open from 9:00 A.M. to 5:30 P.M., later in the evenings on Fridays, and closed on Sundays. Well known for silver, flatware, amber jewelry, modern furniture, and accessories. Sweaters are a good buy.

There's an excellent "S-train" system in Copenhagen. Local buses and trains charge per hour of travel. Metered taxis and rental cars are also available. Be prepared with lightweight knit clothing, even during summer months. Weather is unpredictable; so take layered outfits that you can peel off should the sun shine brightly. Rainwear is an all-year requirement.

More Information: Danish Tourist Board, PO Box 4649, Grand Central Station, New York, NY 10163 or E-mail: info@goscandinavia.com

Copenhagen

One of the world's best-loved cities, Copenhagen is not only a gracious and comfortable place, but the natives are hospitable and fun loving. From the gentle tales of Hans Christian Andersen to the soft colored-lights of Tivoli Gardens, Copenhagen enchants visitors. Museums, the Royal Theater, the castle, and, of course, the famous Little Mermaid are some of the highlights of most tours. A good place to shop is the "Walking Street," where Danish china is beautifully displayed. Prices are high.

There are many tours offered in and around Copenhagen, some by water, others to enable you to see something of modern Danish life. All are worthwhile, but a conducted or escorted tour to Tivoli Gardens is not necessary. Once you pay admission, you're on your own. There's free entertainment, concerts, mimes, amusement rides, exhibitions and restaurants, discos, dance halls, and a lot more in every price category. Be sure to see Tivoli at night. The fireworks and light show are sensational. If time permits, buy a local tour to the Louisiana Art Museum or the home of writer Karen Blixin (Isak Dinesen of Out of Africa fame), outside of Copenhagen.

Shore Excursions: Legoland is a full-day tour with plenty of time to explore the 33 million toy bricks used in building amusement rides and miniature villages, (about eight hours), $140.

England (United Kingdom)

Today, Great Britain still means England, Northern Ireland, Scotland, and Wales, though strictly speaking the proper term is the United Kingdom. Each region offers different cultures, and ships are scheduling cruises that circle the British Isles. Visitors find incredibly diverse attractions and lifestyles. This densely populated and amazingly compact country provides a feast of history and beauty in its monuments, cathedrals, artistic treasures, and ceremonial grandeur. But Great Britain is not only a museum of the past; there is a viable and lively present-day culture which offers the best in drama, art, and music.

While most ships dock at Tilbury, Dover, Harwich or Southampton, the object of a cruise visit is London. Transportation into the city is generally provided by the cruise line, which uses these ports for embarkation and debarkation. But the joys of the British countryside are world famous, and cruise passengers are well advised to plan a pre- or post-cruise stay in London and/or the countryside.

Cruise season is from April through mid-November with June, July, and August considered the most desirable because of the weather. Climate is unpredictable, with rainfall heaviest on the country's West Coast. Summer temperatures in London range from a low of 50 to a high of 70. Currency is the pound. U.S. dollars are not accepted, but credit cards are accepted throughout the country.

INSIDER SHOPPING TIPS

It is best to shop in specialty and department stores. Good buys can be found in woolens, raincoats, high-quality porcelain, crystal, and pewter. Some antiques are still available. Sheffield cutlery and old books are good purchases. If you happen to be in London on a weekend, markets such as Portobello Road or Petticoat Lane are fun.

There is an excellent public transportation system throughout the country. Subways, buses, metered taxis, and rental cars are available in London. Transportation maps are available at most train stations. In London, city clothes are recommended--no shorts, but do wear comfortable shoes. Rain gear is essential. The best way to explore London is by foot.

More Information: British Tourist Authority, 551 Fifth Ave., Suite 701, New York, NY 10176, or www.travelbritain.org.

London

London is not a pass-through city for anyone. It's a city to be savored and enjoyed. It has much to offer and a great deal to see. It is a city that has everything —historical sites, theater, museums, excellent restaurants and very friendly people. There are a number of guide books devoted exclusively to London visitors, but I would be remiss if I didn't mention a few money saving ways to get around in this important European capital.

With only a day in London, take the ship's excursions. Private transportation costs are high and the tour will take you to the highlights. If you have been to London before and want to wander on your own, take public transportation (train is best) from any of the ports. If you are staying in London before or after your cruise and there's a specific show you want to see, have your travel agent reserve your tickets in advance. If you decide on a show once you are in London, your hotel concierge can usually come up with fairly good seats, but the price may shock you. There are last minute ticket discount centers and day of performance tickets available at many theaters for senior citizens.

INSIDER TIP

Buy a local paper. Ticket sources and what's going on in London are always listed. If you happen to be in London in August, the Queen's residence is open to the public. Buy your admission tickets the day before if possible. You will be assigned a time for your visit and you may then spend as much time as you like in the Castle.

Channel Islands

Cruises through these islands are gaining in popularity by Americans who have been everywhere, except through these waters, and Europeans who like to see their own neighborhoods. Each port of call is different.

Most popular ports include Guernsey, a fairy-tale kind of fishing village with white cottages and excellent restaurants featuring seafood, which is sometime caught as you order. Farming is the major industry and there's a Tomato Center and a Hanging Strawberry Farm. Historically, Guernsey is worthy of note. Victor Hugo was exiled here and the islands were occupied by Hitler's troops from 1940 to 1945.

A popular itinerary circles the British Isles and includes visits to Scotland, Ireland and Channel Island ports.

Finland

A land of 60,000 lakes, Finland lies northwest of Russia and east of Norway and Sweden. A large part of it, Lapland, is located above the Arctic Circle. This "Land of the Midnight Sun" has daylight at midnight for nearly two months of the summer, but also darkness at noon during nearly two months of the winter. From a central forested plateau of 500 feet, the land rises in the north where certain peaks reach three thousand feet. The 30,000 islands of the Finnish Archipelago are in the south and southwest.

Cruise season begins in late May and goes through mid-September. Temperatures during the short summer range from 60 to 75 degrees. The "Midnight Sun" is from early July to the end of August. Currency is the Finmark. Finnish is the official language with Swedish the second language. English is taught in schools.

It's hard to find a bargain in Finland, other than in china or handmade sweaters. Shops are open late on Mondays and Fridays, but close by 6:00 P.M. on other days. China, crystal, jewelry, and furs are items appealing to tourists. Transportation is by local streetcars, buses, and metered taxis. Heavy spring-time clothing and rainwear are recommended, but be prepared for sunny days and cooler evenings.

More Information: Finland National Tourist Office, 655 Third Avenue, New York, NY 10017, or www.finland-tourism.com

Helsinki

The "White City of the North" was founded in 1550 by royal order of King Vasa when Finland belonged to Sweden. Helsinki became the capital in 1812 when Tsar Alexander I decided the old capital was not close enough to Russia. Today's city owes much of its good planning to a disastrous fire in the early 19th century. Almost the entire city was rebuilt. Finland has produced astonishing artists, sculptors, and designers whose works are displayed throughout the city and suburbs. Sightseeing should include the unique Rock Church, the Olympic Stadium, residential districts, Finnish craftsmanship, the Lutheran Cathedral, and the Uspenski Cathedral topped with a mass of gilded onion-shaped domes.

Shore Excursions: City tour, (under three hours), $45.

France

(For more specifics on France, see "France" under "The Mediterranean and the Black Sea.")

Le Havre

Le Havre is the leading port of the French Channel province of Normandy and scene of the Allied invasion landings in 1944. Since then, the city has been completely rebuilt, with wide, handsome avenues and a modern shopping center. Le Havre is an excellent starting point for tours to many interesting places: to Rouen, with its magnificent Gothic cathedral and countless examples of fourteenth- and fifteenth-century architecture; to the quaint fishing village of Honfleur and the fashionable seaside resort of Deauville. And, of course, to Paris, the incomparable capital of France.

Shore Excursions: Paris highlights, including Eiffel Tower, Arch of Triumph and the Champs Elysees, (ten hours including lunch), $160; D-Day Landing Beaches, (under eleven hours), $160.

Germany

Germany has a variety of natural beauty that is scarcely matched. Ranging from mountains and lakes in the south, forests and fine pastures and a series of seaside resorts in the north, to mega-cities throughout, Germany has much to offer.

Cruise season is from late May through September when temperatures range from 48 to 78 degrees. Currency is the Deutsche mark. U.S. dollars are not accepted for payment in many places. Language is German, but many people speak English in larger cities.

INSIDER SHOPPING TIPS

Germany is not near the top of my shopping list, although the merchandise is of high quality and design. Prices are comparable to the United States, but there may be a few good buys in quality items such as cameras, Dresden, Meissen, woodcarvings, clocks, and toys.

There is excellent public transportation with an extensive train system, local buses, and metered taxis. City clothing similar to that suitable in New York or Chicago (during the same season) is recommended.

More Information: German National Tourist Office, 122 E. 42nd St., 52nd Floor, New York, NY 10168, or www.germany-tourism.de/

Berlin

Perhaps no city on earth holds the same fascination as Berlin. It is the centerpiece of east-west cooperation and communication and of a mega-building boom. Ships usually dock in Warnemunde, the port for the city of Rostock, a town founded in 1419. Time permitting, a few hours in Rostock are worthwhile. It has a handsome 13th century Town Hall, some high-peaked, Hansa-style houses, an Old City Wall, and the Gothic Marienkirche, a 400-year-old church with a fine baroque organ.

But it is Berlin that draws cruise ship passengers. A full-day tour by train or bus is sold on board ship. Because this excursion fills quickly, it is recommended that, if possible, pre-book if you plan to participate. The tour will take you past fine old buildings and handsome new structures on the former West Side and in "Mitte," formerly East Berlin. The alternative is to take the train from Rostock and tour Berlin on your own.

Shore Excursions: Berlin highlights by train, including three hours train trip each way. You'll see the modern Congress Hall, the Kaiser Wilhelm Gedankniskirche (Memorial Church), and you'll drive the long Kurfurstendam, elegant old Unter der Linden, and pass the Jewish Community Center, built on the site of the synagogue destroyed in 1938. Other sights include the Victory Column, the Reichstag, Brandenburg Gate, and the Charlottenburg Palace. Lunch will be served at a fine hotel, followed by a visit to the world-famous Pergamon Museum with its gigantic Pergamon Alar and lifelike Hellenistic reliefs. Also see Check Point Charlie and a make quick visit to the famous department store KaDeWe, (approximately 13 hours), including lunch and snacks, $300.

INSIDER TIP

Another alternative is to rent a car. I arranged for a car rental from Rostock before I left the United States. There are AutoEurope, Hertz, and Avis offices in Rostock. The cost for the day with unlimited mileage in a mid-size car was about $150. We took the train from Warnemunde to Rostock, then a taxi to the car rental office. We followed the map, which took us on a four-lane high-way directly into Berlin. The ship packed box lunches for us, which we didn't need. We opted for a rest stop at an immaculate Rasthouse and visited all of the Berlin highlights without getting lost. It was a memorable day, and the cost for four of us was far less than it would have been for one person on the shore excursion. Your U.S. driver's license is all you need, and we pre-paid the car rental by credit card. If you are adventurous and are not afraid of driving, ask your travel agent to make the arrangements for you. In our case, the cruise staff on board ship was not even aware of the car rental possibilities. I reported back to them and they now have the information. A word of caution is in order: It helps if you speak some German. East Germans do not speak as much English as they do the West.

Hamburg

Hamburg is a lively city accustomed to receiving large numbers of visitors who are generally surprised by this metropolis on the Elbe River. Sometimes referred to as Germany's "gateway to the world." Hamburg is not just a city. It is one of Germany's 16 federal states and covers 294 square miles just 62 miles from the North Sea. During its 1225-year history, it has developed from a sleepy fishing village to one of the wealthiest and most powerful cities in the area.

Many attractions compete for the cruise passenger's time ashore. There are several sides to Hamburg – the commercial and industrial and the fun-loving, playful city. A quick visit should allow enough time to visit the Rahaus (Town Hall), some of the trendy shopping malls, the Speicherstadt (Free port warehouse city), Hamburg Historical Museum and maybe even a boat tour of the Alster Lake and canals. It's party-time in Hamburg when the sun sets and if time permits, a visit to the Reeperbahn in the St. Pauli quarter will be memorable.

Shore Excursions: Half day about $55. Taxis are plentiful and English is spoken widely.

Ireland

Dublin is the usual arrival port for ships that include Ireland in itineraries. Ships actually arrive in Dun Loaghaire, eight miles from the city. The Irish love Americans and the welcome is warm and sincere. A walk around the city is a must. Be sure to stop frequently at neighborhood pubs where the conversation is lively, the ale and snacks typical of the country, and Irish coffee is the real thing. Among not to be missed sights: Trinity College, St Patricks Cathedral; the Abbey Theater founded by W.B. Yeats; shopping for Irish woolens on Grafton Street. Also recommended when time permits is a drive around Dublin and along the coast to Malahide Castle.

Shore Excursions: Cost is about $90 and covers some or all of the above mentioned places.

The Netherlands

Amsterdam is the heart of one of Europe's most extraordinary and individualistic countries. Approximately 30 percent of the present land area of these "low countries" has been reclaimed from the North Sea, and without the protecting dikes more than half of the land would be flooded. Ancient windmills and modern pumps work constantly to literally bail the country out, and everywhere, of course, are the famous dikes that keep the North Sea in its place. The Dutch impress visitors with their forthright, industrious spirit and unobstructed but droll sense of humor. Holland's small size makes it possible to see much of the country in a short time. Novelty and color are found everywhere.

Cruise season is from April to late October. Summers are warm and winters are mild, but it tends to be damp most of the year. Currency is the guilder (or florin), and language is officially Dutch, but English, French, and German are spoken.

Visitors find good buys include Delftware, porcelain, Indonesian batiks, figurines, and pewterware. Local transportation is efficient, and there are streetcars, buses, metered taxis, and rental cars. Comfortable city-type clothing and comfortable shoes are recommended.

Almost all of the cruise lines with ships sailing the North Sea schedule stops in Amsterdam.

More Information: Netherlands National Tourist Office, 225 N, Michigan Ave. Suite 1854, Chicago, IL 60601. or www.netherlands.com

Amsterdam

A city built on the water, has an extraordinary network of canals lined with elegant hotels, quaint shops, old burgher mansions, and exquisite facades. Be sure to take a trip in one of the glass-topped launches. Most city tours include a visit to Delft, home of the famous blue pottery, and Marken, overlooking the Zuider Zee, where practically everyone still wears traditional costumes and wooden shoes.

Unfortunately, most cruise ships do not allow enough time to see either Rotterdam or The Hague. Both are well worth visits when time allows. Visitors marvel at Rotterdam, a city literally transformed into an ultra-modern metropolis as a result of its almost total destruction during the World War II. Rotterdam is rated as the busiest port in the world, and although many European steamers begin spring to fall voyages from here, cruise ships do not call in Rotterdam.

Shore Excursions: Grand Holland, Dutch countryside, visits to Zaanse Schans with its real, working windmills. Lunch is included, (approximately eight hours), $135.

Norway

Norway is as much sea as land, more mountains than plains, more forests than meadows, and only 2.6 percent is cultivated. Steep cliffs drop dramatically into clear blue waters. Fjords open onto islands and more islands. In the south are clusters of white-painted fishermen's houses; in the north, long treeless stretches where the Lapps bring their reindeer herds to graze. Even in Oslo, the countryside is nearby.

Cruise season begins in late May and goes through September. Summer days have daylight for as long as nineteen hours. Currency is the Norwegian Krone, and U.S. dollars are accepted in major shops, restaurants, and hotels. Language is Norwegian, but English is widely spoken.

Best buys are Norwegian-made sweaters, glass, and pewter, but prices are high. Some ships operate shuttle buses into town centers. There are also public buses, subways in Oslo, metered taxis, and rental cars. Distances are not great, so walking is recommended.

More Information: Norwegian National Tourist Office, 655 Third Avenue, New York, NY 10017, or www.visitnorway.com

Bergen

Norway's second capital and the capital of western Norway, Bergen is a picturesque city where fishing and sailing boats crowd the picturesque harbor. The Floeyen, a one thousand-foot mountain overlooking the town, is easily reached by cable car, and from it you can pick out Haakon's Hall and the medieval buildings of the Hanseatic era. The town's fur and silver shops will tempt you. Specially recommended are visits to the aquarium and to Edvard Grieg's home, which is nearby in Trollhaugen.

North Cape

From Skarsvaag, the road traverses the wild and bleak tundra to the North Cape rising 1,007 feet sheer from the Barents Sea of the Arctic Ocean. The panorama from the Cape, considered the northernmost point of Europe, offers a rare experience as one stands on an endless summer's day and gazes over the vast ocean stretching to the distant polar ice pack.

Spitzbergen at the northern tip of Norway is the most likely point to experience the Land of the Midnight Sun. Inhabited mainly by Russian and Norwegian coal miners, the area is primarily covered by glaciers and depending on weather, ships can sometimes navigate up close to the North Pole. Shore Excursions are spectacular and are the only way to get up close and personal with some of the native birds. Hearty travelers may opt for a glacier hike and there's a good chance of spotting wildlife. Norwegian Coastal ferries ply these waters year around as the route is the only means of transportation during certain months of the year.

Oslo

Visitors find a variety of things to see in Oslo, particularly the unique Vigeland sculptures in Frogner Park, the open-air Folk Museum, the Viking Museum, and the Kon Tiki raft. The splendid city hall in downtown Oslo was lavishly decorated by many of Norway's leading artists.

Shore Excursions: Oslo city tour and Viking ships, (under four hours) $40.

Russia

Events of the past decade have changed the country forever. With some of the 15 republics breaking off into independent countries, it is not the same as it was a few years ago. The diversity of her peoples, climate, and landscape are reflected in music, dance, architecture, literature, and drama. Moscow and St. Petersburg are microcosms of the former Soviet Union.

Despite political changes, little has changed in the organization of tourism. The people of Leningrad voted to change the name of the city to pre-Revolutionary St. Petersburg, honoring Peter the Great whose admiration for the art and architecture of Western Europe fashioned most of the beautiful palaces and buildings remaining in St. Petersburg.

Cruise season is from mid-May through September. There is a wide temperature range, even in summer months, from a low of 48 to a high of 78 in July. Currency is the Ruble, and dollars are rarely accepted. Language is Russian, but younger people and official guides speak English.

INSIDER SHOPPING TIPS

Shopping is difficult at best and nearly impossible during a short cruise stop. I shopped hotel stores and the Beriozka (tourist shops) and found nice embroidery, matrushka dolls, lacquered boxes, caviar at a good price, and vodka. Street merchants sell native goods wherever buses stop. Tipping is officially prohibited but with democratization, Russians are not averse to accepting gratuities.

St. Petersburg has an excellent subway, bus, tram system, but they are not recommended for tourists. Taxis are plentiful, but language may be a problem. Everything is changing. Whereas conservative, city-type clothing is still recommended, jeans are seen everywhere and have taken on the look of a national uniform. Men still wear jackets to business jobs and in hotels.

More information: Russian National Tourist Office, 800 Third Ave., Suite 3101, New York, N.Y. 10173, or www.russia-travel.com.

St. Petersburg

Founded in 1703 by Peter the Great to serve as his "window on the west," St. Petersburg gradually emerged following the patterns of Western European cities. From 1712 to 1914, it was designated capital of imperial Russia. Immediately following the revolution it was renamed Petrograd and in 1924 was renamed Leningrad, in honor of Lenin. Today, this gray-brown city is changing colors and colorful garb worn on the streets brightens the brown buildings. The famous Hermitage Museum holds one of the world's most extensive collections of art treasures, and several great palaces are nearby. Petrodvorets and Pushkin, which have been classified as "important to the Russian historical heritage," are being carefully restored. Tour guides speak excellent English, and though polite, stop just short of being friendly.

The former Winter Palace is part of the Hermitage Museum. There are some six hundred bridges across the Neva, and the town is at its most romantic in the White Nights from the end of June through July, when it doesn't get completely dark. Other must-sees include the Cathedral of Our Lady of Kazan and the Cathedral of St. Isaac of Kiev. From the Admiralty, it is a short walk down Nevsky Prospect to the 18th century Stroganov Palace.

Shore Excursions: Ships offer a wide menu of choices. Half day tours run around $65; full day over $100 and most do not include lunch. Evening concerts or ballet performances cost about $75.

Sweden

Larger than California but smaller than Texas, Sweden is a land of lakes, forests, and islands, with a glorious summer and the space to enjoy it. It is one of the most prosperous countries in Europe and heavily industrialized. There is a sense of space and freedom and a high standard of living.

Cruise season is from late May through September with the most popular months July and August. Summers are dry and sunny with temperatures ranging from a low of 45 to a high of 75 in July in Stockholm.

The currency is the Krona, and U.S. dollars are accepted widely. Language is Swedish, with some English spoken.

There are still good buys in glassware, ceramics, textiles, and high-quality stainless steel flatware, but quality items are expensive. Transportation from ports to Stockholm is generally by metered taxi, but there are ferries, trains, and buses. Ships usually run shuttle buses for the convenience of passengers. Swedes dress conservatively. Jackets and ties for dinner in most restaurants, but casual wear is acceptable during the day.

More Information: Swedish National Tourist Office, 655 Third Avenue, New York, NY 10017, www.visit-sweden.com.

Stockholm

Stockholm is one of Europe's most prosperous cities, with a population of more than one million people. Amid the modern buildings and the bustle, you'll find fine examples of architecture from much earlier periods. A city of islands, canals, and bridges, Stockholm is blessed with spacious park areas that give the metropolis a feeling of openness and freedom. Most tours include visits to the medieval quarter known as "the city between the bridges," the distinctive city hall, Royal Palace, the famous 17th century man-of-war Vasa, and nearby Millesgarden, home of the famous sculptor Carl Milles.

Stockholm is one of the most beautiful cities in Scandinavia, and some ships are scheduling overnight visits. While nightlife may not be exciting by Las Vegas or London standards, there are excellent restaurants near the port.

Shore Excursions: Stockholm city hall and the Vasa Museum, (under four hours), $50; Royal Palace and the Old Town, (under three hours) $40.

INSIDER SHOPPING TIP

Shopkeepers set up booths of wonderful Orrefors, Kosta Boda, and other fine Swedish glass at the pier and will ship heavy crystal items back home for passengers without additional charge, which makes prices a little more attractive. I've purchased dozens of gift items this way and the shipped items always arrive in perfect condition.

Orient and Pacific Ports

The intensified search by cruise lines for new ports of call has extended to Southeast Asia and Pacific waters. The most popular ports most frequently included in itineraries are mentioned in this section. Shore Excursions in this part of the world are more costly than elsewhere. Expect to pay upwards of $200 for full day tours including lunch and motor coach transportation and of course, an English-speaking guide.

China (Peoples Republic of China)

Chinese culture, style, history, and its peoples have influenced every area and every country throughout the Pacific and beyond. It is no wonder that once the curtains parted, Americans began traveling to China in-increasing numbers. They come by air and by land and by sea. China makes up more than 25 percent of the world population, and its territory covers more than all of continental Europe. Its civilization was more advanced than Europe's at the time of Marco Polo's visit. Wars and periods of isolation have left China a country apart and a country of mystery.

But China is changing and catching up although its process of "democratizing" the Communist-Socialist form of government is considered slow by the West, it is progressing at an accelerated pace by Oriental standards. To its credit, The People's Republic of China is refurbishing and building a new network of tourist facilities, among which are some of the finest hotels in the world. Because it is such a tremendous country, customs, languages, and climate differ greatly, depending on region. Terrain is mountainous and arid in other areas. Almost all ships that call at some of China's famous ports allow for three ports of call and from one to three days in each. It is impossible in very limited space to describe experiences awaiting visitors to China. All we can do in this book is highlight the most important points and offer a few suggestions for maximum enjoyment of limited time ashore.

Cruise season is late March through mid-November. Climate varies by region, but is comfortable from spring to fall months. Official language is the Beijing dialect of Mandarin, but Cantonese is also spoken widely. English is limited, except by trained guides and at tourist hotels. Currency is the Yuan (renminbi), and dollars are not "officially" accepted in most shops except for "official" government Friendship Stores. However, with heavy demand for "hard' currency, street merchants and many family-type stores will accept dollars, but credit cards are accepted in Government Friendship Stores. So, come prepared with a roll of single dollar bills and your credit cards.

Shopping opportunities are still very good. Best buys are jade, works of art, silk, Chinese stamps, carpets, porcelain, and antiques. Friendship Stores are the easiest to shop in and bargaining for high-ticket items is recommended. There also are arts and craft stores operated by the government. All Friendship Stores do not carry the same merchandise. What you see in Shanghai, for example, may not be available in the Beijing store.

Tipping is not permitted or required, but Westerners have introduced it, and the Chinese have tried it, and they like it. While not quite actively soliciting tips, they do expect something from foreigners for services rendered.

It is not possible to hail a taxi on the street. Taxis must be ordered from tourist hotels and rates are pre-determined. If you need a taxi, head for the closest tourist hotel. Most ships will provide you with slips of paper bearing your destination written in Chinese. Special arrangements may be made for chauffeur-driven cars.

More information: China National Tourist Office, 350 Fifth Ave., Room 6413, New York, N.Y. 10018 or www.cnto.org.

Beijing

The port of Tianjin is the gateway to Beijing and is a four or five-hour bus ride to the Big City. There are limited toilet facilities along the route, but buses are comfortable, and the ship provides snacks, a box lunch, and drinks. A train connection has been established between Tianjin and Beijing and it cuts the time in half. Sightseeing excursions to some of the most interesting spots in the world are included in the two- or three-day stay that ships schedule. Some cruises begin or end in Tianjin, allowing for longer land stays.

Sightseeing: A major highlight of Beijing is a visit to The Great Wall. Other high points are the Ming Tombs, Temple of Heaven, the Summer Palace, and walking the streets of Beijing where westerners no longer warrant a second glance. The pandas at the Beijing Zoo are absolutely delightful.

Beijing is continuing a gigantic building boom that started about 15 years ago including high rise office buildings housing international companies and western-style five star hotels. Be sure to allow time to just wander the streets and visit the new outdoor flea markets.

INSIDER SHOPPING TIPS

Prices are low on everything and temptation is present in every shop and with every street vendor. Cloisonné is a traditional Chinese art form. At the Beijing Arts & Crafts Factory, visitors can watch the ancient art of copper wire design being made and purchase unusual souvenir and gift items at about one-third below United States prices. Consider cloisonné bowls, plates, urns, vases, pillboxes, nested boxes, jewelry, and a variety of decorative objects featuring beautiful designs of birds, fish, plants and flowers. Large decorative pieces -- birds, peacocks or dragons are popular take-home items. The Arts & Crafts factory offers three floors of goodies from which to choose, including jade items, the popular Chinese bottles (painted from the inside,) and cloisonné-trimmed chopsticks. If carting your "treasures" home is a problem, arrange for shipment by air or sea. I have never had a problem clearing Customs when items arrive and nothing has ever been broken or damaged in the process. It takes two to three months for sea shipments, about two weeks for air.

Shanghai

One of the few major Chinese cities that didn't undergo a name change, Shanghai is in the throws of a building boom which rivals, or even outdoes Hong Kong with huge neon signs and impressive skyscrapers. Shanghai has become China's financial capital and luxury hotels are impressive. Once the center of social activities for embassies and diplomats, and a long-time trade center for the entire country, it looks like the city is returning to its former glory days.

Shanghai was first established as a major port in the 17th century and opened its doors to foreign trade at the end of the 19th century. It is the gateway to tours to Suzhou and Wuxi. Most ships spend one night and two days in Shanghai. The first day is spent touring the city, the second day in the outskirts. Don't miss the Children's Museum and charming China dolls. The Shanghai Museum contains thousands of outstanding historical treasures. The beautiful new museum is one of China's finest.

Half the passengers go to Suzhou, the other half to Wuxi. Both groups use bus and train transportation. Wuxi is the better tour, if you have a choice.

A few words about Chinese trains. They are immaculate and comfortable with upholstered sofa-like seating. Tea is served, and vendors sell small gift items and snacks.

Shore Excursions: City Highlights, (four hours), $40; Suzhou Panorama, include Chinese lunch, (eleven hours), $90; Grand Canal and City of Wuxi, (eleven hours), $85.

INSIDER TIP

A lot of time is wasted on lunches and dinners on these tours, and if you would rather go off on your own, you are allowed to do so. The ship's staff will help make arrangements for you. There are some things you can count on when visiting China. You will see at least one factory every day, and every factory will have a shop, which has a booth to change dollars into Yuan. There are toilet facilities at every tourist stop, but don't count on Western-style toilets--bring tissues and your sense of humor. But, I must admit, facilities have improved 10,000 percent from what they were on my first visit in 1972. You will shop, and you will spend a lot more money than you intended. After all, who can resist cashmere sweaters for under $75? Although rules say no bargaining, it pays to haggle on big-ticket items. I saved $50 on shipping charges by saying the cost was too high. Don't be concerned about shipping bulky items back home. They arrive when promised, and Customs is very easy on taxes. Bring credit cards. Dollars are exchanged at the official rate plus a minimal commission. Traveler's checks are charged a slightly higher commission.

Hong Kong

Although Hong Kong is now officially part of China, visitors do not notice changes that affect their enjoyment of this haven which seems to have a life of its own. Hong Kong is my absolute favorite port of call. Almost all cruise lines allow for at least two days in port with the ship as your hotel, or offer pre- and post-cruise land packages. Hong Kong is a city of gleaming hotels, modern offices, apartment buildings, and factories in the middle of walled villages and ancient temples. It's a world trade center and a lot more with numbers of people that could never be counted.

The Portuguese were the first Europeans to sail into Hong Kong Harbor. The British arrived in the late 1600s and set up the East India Company, which dominated trade in the area for centuries. It was the Treaty of Nanking in 1842 that ceded Hong Kong to the British. In 1860 Kowloon was added, and the New Territories and adjacent islands were leased from China in 1898. All were turned back to China in magnificent ceremonies in 1997.

Cruise season is March through November, although ships call here year around on Pacific voyages. The climate is mild with highs near ninety degrees in July and August and lows of fifty-five degrees in January. Languages are Chinese and English. Currency is the Hong Kong dollar.

Prices are not as good as they once were, but as far as selection, shopping is still the best in the world for jewelry, clothing, high fashion items, accessories, rugs, and anything made in China. There are plenty of taxis, rental cars, limousines, buses, and ferries. Casual wear is acceptable except in some of the fashionable restaurants where a jacket and tie are required.

It may surprise some visitors, but there is more to do in Hong Kong than shop. Take a ferry to an outlying island or the hydrofoil to Macau. Have lunch at Victoria Peak or stroll through the Jade or Bird markets. Hire a junk in Aberdeen and arrange for a harbor cruise and dinner with your significant other. I guarantee, it will be an evening you will never forget.

Shore Excursions: Hong Kong Island Drive, (four hours), $40; Chinese Cultural Experience, (four hours), $45; Pre-dinner Cocktail Cruise by junk, (two hours), $25.

More information: Hong Kong Tourist Association, 548 Fifth Avenue, New York, NY, 10036 or www.discoverhongkong.com

INSIDER SHOPPING TIP

Hong Kong is a shopper and diner's delight. For the latter, there are restaurants to suit every palate and pocketbook. Chinese delicacies are outstanding. As for shopping, it's hard to avoid. Temptation lies at every turn of the sidewalk. Visitors to Hong Kong spend more money here on shopping than in any other comparable tourist destination. There are elegant "name" shops from all over the world and flea markets that astound. Stop at one of the Hong Kong Visitor Information Centers and ask for booklets listing specialty shops for anything that might interest you, and be sure to pick up a copy of their factory outlet list. It will head bargain hunters in the right direction for items manufactured in Hong Kong for export to the U.S. and Europe. Veteran Hong Kong shoppers head for the Pedlar Building on the Hong Kong side near the Star Ferry terminal. The entire building is filled with outlet stores which come and go, but prices are incredibly low for women's and some men's clothing. On the Kowloon side, take a cab to Kaiser Estates where four huge buildings are filled with outlets or take the bus and spend the day in Stanley Market. But whatever you do, don't go touristy and have dinner on one of the floating giant boats in Aberdeen. It's an overpriced and undervalued evening with other tourists.

INSIDER SHOPPING TIP #2

On my visit last year, I discovered that the best shopping in Hong Kong is over the border in Szenchen. a complete city turned into a giant shopping mall. Take a 15-minute taxi ride from major Kowloon hotels to the Hung Hom train station. Purchase First Class tickets to Shenzhen and you needn't worry about knowing when to disembark the plush train. With intermittent stops, the train only travels between those two stations – Hung Hom and Shenzhen. and run about every 15 minutes. There's an economy section for less than the $66 H.K. dollars (about $9 U.S.) but we went for broke and went First Class (about $10 U.S.). The train took 40 minutes and the scenery was high rises that reached up more than 40 stories, new cities and factories of every international description. You will need to cross the Hong Kong border, then the border with China and you'll need to do it in both directions which requires your passport and visas that can be obtained at the border with China. However, if your ship includes a visit to mainland China, be sure to get a multiple entry visa which will eliminate most of the formalities at the border.

Disembarking the train in Szenchen is a culture shock, even for veteran shoppers. The huge building is chocker-block full of shops and vendors. Streets and even the airport are lined with shop-after-shop. We saw night market sellers loading up in Szenchen with merchandise, so you can imagine how low prices are. Everything made in China is sold in Szenchen and yes, you still should haggle over price which is part of the experience because very few vendors speak English. Best buys I found were in ladies accessories, handbags, shoes, costume jewelry. Dance shoes that cost $100 in Miami went for $10 to $12. I bought every pair they had in my size. Most merchants do not speak English and although signs say transactions in Hong Kong dollars only, merchants accepted U.S. dollars, but no credit cards. Szenchen is an experience not to be missed by travelers who love to shop. If shopping and crowds turn you off, don't go to Szenchen. I was so overwhelmed by the "bargains"; I couldn't handle the loot, so I purchased a classy roll-aboard for $10. When I return, I'm taking folding luggage with me and will take one of the first trains in the morning and spend the day. There are restaurants and comfort facilities.

Indonesia

This is an area of contrasts – a photo opportunity second to none. See the Asak women in native dress at a village near Padang Bay, view volcanic lakes and ancient temples--Besakih is Bali's most sacred temple--watch a puppet show or the famed giant lizards of komodo. The choices are many. Indonesia is a study in diversity, offering an amazing array of sights and sounds.

Handicrafts are also diverse, and include woodcarvings, handmade linens, silver and stone work. Currency is the Rupiah. Credit cards are widely accepted and some markets take dollars.

Bali

Bali is the country's most popular spot and ranks at the top of romantic islands. Scenic and exciting, Bali is an island with volcanoes dominating the landscape, rimmed with stunning mountains and mysterious-looking crater lakes. Ancient traditions thrive and elaborate statuary and stone carvings adorn every building.

See exciting Balinese dancers, visit a sacred temple (there are approximately 20,000 temples in Bali), or shop for elegant art works: paintings, woodwork, handmade linens, and silver goods. Bali's culture is predominantly Hindu and the countryside is a changing kaleidoscope of picture perfect scenery.

Bali is warm, so dress comfortably. When visiting temples, shorts may be inappropriate. Good walking shoes are important.

Shore Excursions: Essential highlights of one day in Bali include a welcome by traditional Balinese dancers and a journey to the former royal capital of Klungkung. Visit the old courtroom of justice and other ancient residences and temples. (Less than ten hours, lunch included), $75; Bali with minimum walking, a tour in an air-conditioned microbus or motor coach, (four hours), $35.

INSIDER TIPS

Keep your wits about you while touring and beware of pickpockets, especially on public transportation vehicles. But why use public transport when private cars are available at the pier for about $50 a day and can accommodate up to four people. Drivers will take you wherever you want to go and for about $75 will spend the day with you. Skip the capital city and head for the countryside and some of the artist communities. If you purchase an oversized sculpture and ship it home, use airfreight and deal only with a very reliable merchant. We received one piece within a week but the second sculpture arrived nearly six months later and we're still trying to collect on damage four years later. Make sure the insurance offered by the merchant is not his personal insurance, but with an international shipping company.

Japan

Japan has the power and influence of a continent, yet it is a string of islands. It is cities with neon-lit skyscrapers and endless expressways, yet it finds its inspiration in the quiet beauty of small, formal rock gardens. It runs its trains at lightning speed, yet the Japanese people spend hours on small conversational courtesies. A picture, a play, a garden, a meal--all aim at graceful perfection, symmetry, or formal movement. Tokyo is one of the most expensive cities in the world, but an aboriginal village is only an hour away.

Cruise season runs from March through November. Climate differs by region, warmer in the south, cooler in mountain areas. Tokyo temperature ranges from a high of eighty-three degrees in July to a low of forty-six in April. The language is Japanese. English is spoken in tourist hotels. Currency is the yen. Credit cards are widely accepted.

With prices as high as they are, Americans window-shop along the Ginza and buy very little. Japanese items sold in the U.S. are generally less costly. In all fairness, we should not blame the Japanese for the high cost of everything when we are talking about dollars. Inflation in Japan is very low, so what makes the country expensive for Americans is the value of the U.S. dollar.

Tipping is not a Japanese custom, and I have had hotel employees refuse to accept a gratuity. There is no solicitation of tips, but expect fixed posted charges for baggage handling at piers, airports, and railroad stations. It is not necessary to tip taxi drivers, and 10 percent is added to restaurant bills. Taxis, rental cars, limousines, and excellent train and subway systems are available.

Wear city clothes in Tokyo, and comfortable clothes for touring--including the requisite solid walking shoes.

More information: Japan National Tourist Office, One Rockefeller Plaza, Suite 1250, New York, NY 10020 or www/jnto.go.jp.

Nagasaki

The city has become a popular cruise ship port of call. Nagasaki was rebuilt after World War II and is now one of the most orderly cities in the world. Neat and well planned, the city's most important sites are the memorial park dedicated to world peace with its world famous sculpture garden and dramatic new Atomic Bomb Museum with exhibits that are hard to forget.

Shore Excursions: Peace Memorial Park, Glover Gardens and the Atomic Bomb Museum (three hours), $80; Scenic overland adventure by motor coach, includes one hour boat ride, (nine hours), $250.

Osaka

Second-largest city in Japan, Osaka is built on a bay and is crisscrossed by canals. It is well known for its 16th-century Osaka Castle, numerous shrines, and proximity to other attractions such as Nara. It's an excellent city for shopping.

Shore Excursions: Legacies of Osaka, with lunch and visit to Museum of Old Japanese Houses and Osaka Castle, (four hours), $100; Kyoto City Grand tour, drive from Osaka to Kyoto to see Nijo Castle, Kyoto Handicraft Center and Higashi-Honganji Temple, as well as Sanju-Sangendo Temple, includes lunch (nine hours), $210.

Tokyo

It's the largest city in the world and the fastest paced. The city is the hub of the Far East and could easily overwhelm a visitor. It is situated on the island of Honshu, the largest of the four islands that make up Japan, considered the country's mainland. The area is a little larger than Great Britain. There are shrines, palaces, and gardens; museums, universities, and elegant hotels.

Shopping districts are everywhere and prices are just about the same throughout the city, but cheaper on the outskirts.

Shore Excursions: Treasures of Tokyo, Meiji Shrine, Imperial Palace Plaza and Askusa Kannon Temple, (four hours), $80; Majestic Mount Fuji and Hakone (11 hours), $240.

INSIDER TIP

Ships usually dock in Yokahama for visits to Tokyo. Ships that dock in Osaka frequently offer overnight tours to Tokyo. Japan's bullet trains deserve their worldwide reputation of excellence. However, you should know a little about them if you decide to travel within Japan on your own. If this is your first trip to Japan, I urge you to take advantage of land packages offered by cruise lines. If you have been to Japan more than once and want to wander on your own, traveling by rail is your best bet. First-class tickets are not expensive and are available without reservations at every station. However, you cannot check your luggage through to your final destination at every station. In some cities, you must go to a different railroad station to check baggage on slower trains. Best advice is that if you travel by train in Japan, carry only luggage you can handle yourself. There are no porters!

Inchon is the port for Seoul, the capital of South Korea. Seoul, rebuilt after the Korean War, is a modern city meshing technology and commerce into a metropolis with a healthy, thriving economy. Korea has been a link to both Japan and China for thousands of years and the current crop of Asian cruises often include a stop in Inchon for a 21st century look at this ancient culture--a culture which has been maintained, despite a bloody, war-ravaged history.

Inchon was a small fishing village 100 years ago. Today it is best known as the site of General Douglas MacArthur's landing which led to recapturing Seoul from the North Koreans.

The ride to Seoul from Inchon takes just under two hours. A highlight of the Seoul tour is a visit to the National Museum of Korea on the grounds of Kyongbuk-kung Palace, originally built in 1392. Used as the capital for Japanese occupation forces early in this century, the building houses artifacts of 5,000 years of Korean history.

Shopping is considered excellent in the Itaewon area, geared totally to foreign visitors. A maze of short streets with outlet shop after outlet shop featuring shoes and leather products, which are good buys. Silk ties for under $15 and eel skin bags and wallets, topaz, amethyst and jade jewelry all priced to sell. A variety of other markets dot the city.

Also see the Kimchi Museum, exhibiting different kinds of kimchi, pickled spicy cabbage, from throughout the country. Old paintings and Buddhist relics from the Bronze Age are on display at the Horim Museum.

Cruise season is from spring until fall. Weather is typically Asian. Hot and humid in summer, quite cold in winter. Currency is the won. Dollars are widely accepted in Itaewon and some markets. Credit cards are used everywhere.

Shore Excursions: Korean Folk Village, an open-air museum, (nine hours) $95; Seoul on your own, transportation from Port of Inchon to Seoul (under nine hours,) $45.

More Information: Korean National Tourism Corp, 2 Executive Drive, Seventh Floor, Fort Lee, N.J. 07024, or www. visitkorea.or.kr/.

Malaysia

Beaches and temples, rain forests and fine clothing shops--plus a stable economy and sound political atmosphere--make the country a desirable destination. Malaysia is one of the wealthiest Southeast Asian nations. A strong Islamic country--the number of veiled women is growing--with a culture rich in contributions by China and Arabia, Malaysia has much to offer visitors.

Malaysia has a spicy history. The Srivijaya Empire controlled the region from the 7th to the 10th centuries. The spice trade made the peninsula a leader in trading and alliances with Arabia and China created the dual culture that remains to this day. Portuguese, Dutch and British traders and colonists added their touches to the region. Malaysia won its independence in 1957. Malaysian currency is the Ringgit. Credit cards are accepted everywhere.

Heat and humidity are fairly constant. Dress lightly and don't forget comfortable walking shoes.

More information: Malaysian Tourist Information Center, 818 W. Seventh St., Los Angeles, CA 90017 or www.tourism.gov.my.

Kuala Lumpur

Kuala Lumpur is less than an hour from Port Klang. The capital city features some of Asia's best colonial architecture including minaret mosques, ornate temples and British-style colonial buildings. KL's Chinatown is fascinating and the Central Market offers just about everything you care to purchase, including brilliant batiks. Try satays (chicken ke-bobs) with spicy sauce.

Shore Excursions: Kuala Lumpur with less walking, ride in an air-conditioned motor coach to see the National Mosque and Railway Station, Chinatown's narrow streets, and the "Golden Triangle" of the city's business district. Lunch is included, (seven hours), $90; Best of Kuala Lumpur, includes visits to mosques, temples and monuments, buffet lunch and a visit to a pewter factor; (under nine hours), $90.

Singapore (Malaysia)

Sir Thomas Raffles founded Singapore in 1819. The 250-square mile-island was declared a British colony in 1953. Ten years later Singapore joined Malaya, Sahae and Sarawak to form the Federation of Malaysia but became an independent nation in 1965. Singapore is one of Asia's great economic success stories, meshing diverse cultures into one dynamic nation.

One of the world's largest ports, Singapore is a modern business center with an exciting, mysterious colonial core, representing Arab, Indian and Chinese influences.

See the Changi Prison Museum and Chapel with its extensive collection of World War II memorabilia; Alkaff Mansion, a 19th century estate, built by one of Singapore's founding families, reopened in 1990 following a $2.5 million renovation program; the Armenia Church, Singapore's oldest church, and the Asian Civilizations Museum. The Museum was the first in the region to present the cultural legacies of Southeast Asia, China, India and West Asia. Also worth a visit: Chinese and Japanese Gardens; Singapore Zoological Gardens (including breakfast with an orangutan); Jurong Bird Park with over 3,000 birds of 300 species; the Sultan Mosque on Arab Street, and a Singapore Sling in historic Raffles Hotel where many of the most famous names in British literature--for example Rudyard Kipling and Somerset Maugham-have stayed.

The climate is hot, humid and damp. Currency is the Singapore dollar, with credit cards widely accepted.

More information: Singapore Tourist Promotion Board, 590 Fifth Ave., 12th Floor, New York, N.Y. 10036 or www.newasia-singapore.com.

INSIDER COMMENTS

Singapore has become an international city with high rise office buildings, apartment houses, and wide avenues. True, it is one of the cleanest cities in the world, but somewhere along the way, Singapore seems to waver between a Western and an Oriental atmosphere, albeit sterile. I am probably in the minority, but I would rather visit San Francisco than Singapore. I have been in Singapore many times and have watched the personality of the city change. Where not too long ago, you would not have seen young women in jeans smoking on the street, you now see very casual dress everywhere and very few well dressed young people. Raffles, the famed hotel, still sticks to its rigid rules and I was refused entry because I was wearing sandals and pretty nice sandals at that. Singapore to me is a city that hasn't quite decided whether it's Oriental or Western. I liked it better when we could ride on the rivers and visit communities that lived and worked on those same rivers. Today, it's hard to even find a river anywhere near the middle of Singapore. I'm sure many travelers will disagree with me, but I thought you should know, so you don't expect more from Singapore than it delivers.

Sri Lanka

Formerly known as Ceylon, the country is officially known as the Republic of Sri Lanka. Its ancient history fascinates visitors. Aryan Indians settled the area back in 483 B.C. Their descendants, the Sinhales, introduced Buddhism in 307 BC and are credited with building the first great cities. About 14 million people live in Sri Lanka. Terrain blends from tropical forests to mountains to flat sandy plains that account for over 1,000 miles of beaches.

Cruise season stretches from December through March. The climate is sunny for months on end with an average annual temperature in the low 80s. The rainy season is from November to January and from May to July. The languages are Sinhalese, Tamil, and English. Currency is the rupee, but almost everyone accepts dollars.

Shopping is good, and visitors look for semi-precious stones, sapphires, topaz, zircons, and garnets. Prices are fair at government-operated handicraft shops in Colombo. Stalls are set up at the pier, and bargaining is expected.

Inner-city public transportation is available, but not recommended. There are metered taxis waiting at the pier. Informal and casual clothing is in order, except for a few elegant restaurants in top hotels. Lightweight clothing is recommended, but evenings can be cool.

More information: Sri Lanka Tourist Board, 2148 Wyoming Avenue, NW, Washington, D.C. 20008. or www.lanka.net/ctb/

INSIDER SHOPPING TIP

The State Gem Corporation operates show rooms at 24 York Street, Colombo, at the Hotel Sri Lanka Inter Continental, and at the airport. The corporation sells gems (rubies are fantastic buys) and will certify whether the gems you have bought anywhere in the country are genuine. Don't leave Ceylon without a package of the famous tea.

Colombo

Time in port usually only allows for sightseeing in Colombo, the country's capital. Streets are lined with Victorian houses and crowded with ox carts, buses, pedestrians, barefoot children, Englishmen in tweeds, and markets. It's an exciting city for walking. Tours include the National Museum, Zoological Gardens, and the Raja Maha Vihare Temple. The countryside is beautiful and well worth the time, as is the 72-mile ride to Kandy with its Buddhist temples, some dating back 1500 years.

Shore Excursions: Daylong tour of primeval jungles, wondrous ruins and a hectic Asian metropolis; (twelve hours), $250.

Thailand

Visitors have pre-conceived exotic images of Thailand, and most are not disappointed. It is a diverse country where Bangkok seems worlds away from the less populated inland regions or border communities. There are marvelous temples, ancient cities, elephants, dense jungles, and a capital city laced with watery thoroughfares and a disappearing way of life.

Cruise season is virtually year-round for South Pacific itineraries with two high seasons--November to March and May through October. Temperatures are high all year with the hottest months being May through June. Chinese languages are spoken widely with English as a second language. Currency is the Baht, and most establishments accept U.S. dollars.

INSIDER TIP

Ships dock in Laem Chabang, a two-hour ride from Bangkok. Ships usually offer day tours with transfers and a two-day, one night stay in a Bangkok hotel. They also offer a round trip transfer for $120 per person, for passengers who want to do Bangkok on their own. If you are not timid and can find your own way around Bangkok, you can get a taxi at the pier to one of the major hotels for about $70 for two or three passengers. You'll ride in air conditioned Mercedes comfort. There's a taxi starter at the pier and he does the haggling for you.

There's a lot of manufacturing going on in Thailand, but it has become a busy commercial city and shopping is easy. Open markets and small shops have great buys in almost everything from jeans to jewelry. The best buys are in semi-precious gems and made-for-export clothing. Good tailors deliver made-to-measure clothing within a few days. Prices are very low and are competitive with Hong Kong, Korea, and the Philippines.

Transportation is difficult because of the huge crowds everywhere in Bangkok, but there are lots of taxis which come in two sizes and are very cheap. Where there is a choice, opt for the smaller cab. Three-wheeled bicycle taxis (Put-Puts) are plentiful, cheaper than larger taxis, and a lot more fun.

Wear very lightweight clothing and comfortable shoes. Everything is informal, and jackets are not required for men.

More information: Tourism Authority of Thailand, 5 World Trade Center, Suite 3443, New York, NY 10048, or www.tourismthailand.org.

Bangkok

Bangkok has come a long way since my first visit over 25 years ago. There's a sky train that connects most of the city, but traffic is still bumper-to-bumper, particularly during early morning and late afternoon hours. Pollution has been reduced dramatically as most of the factories were relocated to country areas. The golden temples and shrines that brought the tourists are being overshadowed, literally, by 40-story high rises housing multi-national companies and apartments mostly for expatriates. There are fewer tuk-tuks (three wheel bicycles with two seats for passengers) and most taxis run meters, so bargaining is eliminated. We were all over the city and a taxi ride never cost more than two dollars.

The best way to see a sampling of Bangkok's 300 temples is by conducted bus tour. You'll want to visit the floating market for a glimpse of life along the klongs (canals). Most ship tours will include a sampan ride and the most important temples: Temple of the Reclining Buddha, Temple of the Emerald Buddha, Temple of the Golden Buddha, Temple of the Dawn, and the Marble Temple. All tours allow time for shopping and browsing. Bangkok is one of the noisiest, most polluted cities in the world, but well worth a visit.

INSIDER SHOPPING TIP

Our annual visit to the Night Market didn't produce desired results, but after talking with local friends, we headed to a seven-story shopping complex (MBK) where everything anyone could need or want from birth to a senior citizen home is available at bargain prices, depending on your haggling skills. Every taxi driver knows MBK and it's easy to reach by train, tuk-tuk or bus but for $1 from the hotel district, my advice is to take a cab especially for the return trip and the bags you'll be carrying. Everything has a label and most handbags, for example, sold for $5; knit shirts for men and women were priced at $3 to $4; carry-on large sports bags used for exercise clothes sold for $4. And, those were pre-bargaining prices which were so cheap to start with, I didn't have the heart to try for an even lower price. Only Baht (Thai currency) is accepted at MBK, no credit cards. There are several ATM machines and a bank. I used ATM. It was faster and the rate was better

Shore Excursions: Because of distance from the port, ships only offer full day tours. Floating Market and Elephant Show, lunch included (eight hours), $200.

Phuket

Thailand's largest island is sometimes called the "pearl of the south." Its exotic culture-is a mélange of Portuguese and Chinese. This environment, combined with year around sunny, of somewhat humid climate, have turned Phuket into an international resort. During summer months, Phuket is a bit cooler than Bangkok, but temperatures still range in the 90s.

Phuket is a "sun and fun" port of call with tempting beaches surrounding the island. A warning is issued during monsoon season (late fall) to avoid swimming because of strong riptides.

The island province of Phuket, 535 miles from Bangkok, was originally a Pacific area trade center. Its first business visitors were Arabs, Chinese, Indians, Malaysians and Portuguese who met here to trade and sell their country's wares. Their cultural mix contributed to the architecture and local customs, which include Thai boxing, sword fighting and Thai dancing.

Phuket's diving sites are considered among the world's best and it is a haven for water enthusiasts and the international yachting set.

If you can force yourself off the beach and give up bikini watching, be sure to visit coconut and rubber plantations, batik factories, cultured pearl farms, a crocodile farm, tin mines and some of the numerous Buddhist complexes. See the Phra Thaeo Wildlife Park and Ton Sai Waterfall Forest Park. Thai currency is the Baht and credit cards are accepted widely.

Vietnam

Vietnam is reshaping itself for tourists in the next century, so if you want a glimpse of the way it used to be, don't delay your visit. The port city of Da Nang on the South China Sea was a major United States military base during the Vietnam War. Today it is the gateway to a world of varied traditions. Water buffalo and bicycles, tiny houses and western-style hotels all co-exist in this mystically beautiful country.

Some Shore Excursions go to Hue where the Imperial Citadel still shows the scars of war, while other tourists opt for a visit to China Beach, a wartime recreational area. Other tours include Ho Chi Minh City, formerly Saigon, once called the "pearl of the orient." The Vietnamese people are friendly, but cautious and eager to please.

INSIDER PERSONAL REPORT

I was among the passengers making my first visit to Vietnam. The ship anchored off Vung Tau, about a two-hour drive from Ho Chi Minh City. More adventurous passengers opted for a four-night overland tour to Cambodia and Angkor Wat and they rejoined the ship at the next port. More timid passengers purchased the one-day excursions or decided to use the ship's complimentary transfer to a nearby hotel and shopping center. We joined 25 other passengers for an overnight and two-day tour of Ho Chi Minh, formerly known as Saigon.

What we got was one day of Viet Cong propaganda and reminders of who won the war. The tour should have come with a disclaimer – "This tour may be offensive to Americans and Australians." It was! We visited the Cu Chi tunnels and spent the day listening to Viet Cong propaganda. We listened to the guide laud the heroics of Ho Chi Minh and we saw the hand made items, which tortured American and Australian troops. For the first time, I understood the rage felt by American soldiers. I refused to reboard the bus the second day and arranged for a private air conditioned car and English-speaking driver to explore the city without hearing about the heroic VC.

My air-conditioned car and driver were on schedule and we took off for three hours of back street touring. I mention the importance of air conditioning because the temperature was in the low 90s and the humidity almost as high. We went behind the scenes, did the markets, shopping centers, malls, hotels, temples and public buildings.

I got an entirely different view of Saigon. My impressions of the city were mixed. It still retains something of the atmosphere of pre-1975 times. It is a brash and noisy place, full of trappings of Western civilization while hanging on to its Oriental traditions. Industry is developing rapidly and transportation for its seven million inhabitants is predominantly by motor bike or motorcycle. It is estimated that 70 percent of the population owns one or the other. Very few private cars, other than tourist sedans, are on the roads. There is, however, bumper-to-bumper truck traffic throughout the city and on the highways connecting the port to the city. It is a city of jeans-clad young people who listen and dance to Western music. It is also a city where everyone works and no one is hungry or homeless. The family unit remains strong and everyone – from children to old people – seemingly has some home-industry product for sale.

New hotels and international businesses are moving or building factories in Vietnam. The average wage is the equivalent of $100 a month, and the Vietnamese are hard working people. It is estimated that 50 percent of the under 40 year old population is computer literate and it was easier to find an Internet Café than in any of the other cities we have visited in this part of the world.

Nightlife in Saigon may not be close to what we have seen in the movies and on the news, but it is active and lively. Discos and clubs abound and young people on bikes don't seem to come alive until after midnight. Best place to view the neon lit city is on the roof of the Rex Hotel where we stopped for a drink before heading to a fabulous restaurant for dinner.

The market sold good copies and some originals for unbelievably low prices. Dollars were accepted everywhere and there was no need to change into local currency which converted to about 14,000 to one U.S. dollar. The market was hot and the sellers were pushy and touchy, so I was out of there in 15 minutes. Name brand shirts were selling for three and four dollars. Designer handbags (copies or originals, I couldn't tell the difference) went for $15 to $17.

Copies of everything imaginable were everywhere even in the newest and prettiest department store, Diamond Center. Vietnam has not been known for rubies or sapphires, but they are being mined and loose stones are sold on a wholesale basis in China Town and other places, if you know where to look. Only a geologist will know the differences and I didn't end up with red glass. They were fair quality rubies which made a great pair of earrings when I got home.

I should mention that my car and driver cost $15 U.S. per hour! Worth every penny.

I have now added Vietnam to the countries I have visited. Will I return? I visited the Vietnam Memorial in Washington a few months after I got home. If you asked me at that time, the answer would have been "no." Now that time has passed, I want to see Hanoi and the rest of the country and give Vietnam another chance, but I'll check out the tour escort before I board a bus or car. I don't want to have my nose rubbed into the fact that we lost a war.

Shore Excursions: Da Nang by Pedal Cab, (four hour), $55; Imperial Hue, including lunch of Vietnamese specialties, (under nine hours), $105.

More Information: Embassy of Vietnam, 1233 20th St., NW No. 501, Washington, D.C. 20036, or ww.vietnamtourism.com.

South Pacific

French Polynesia

French Polynesia is a chain of more than 100 islands in the South Pacific, spread over an area, roughly the size of Europe. Tahiti is the most populous and largest of the islands and is the best known worldwide. French Polynesia is made up of the Marquesas, Tuamotus, Society Islands, Australs, and Gambiers.

Historians believe French Polynesia was settled more than 2,000 years ago, probably by people of Southeast Asia. It was claimed by France a century ago and remains a French territory. European customs and touches remain on these islands which afford outstanding natural photo opportunities. The racial homogenization of Europeans and Southeast Asians has produced an incredibly handsome population. People are polite and welcome visitors.

Shopping opportunities are hard to miss, but the most popular souvenir remains the tee shirt, but with a different twist. Some of Gauguin's most famous painting have been reproduced on these shirts and make great reminders of the South Pacific.

English is spoken at hotels and in major tourist areas; French is the language of the islands.

Bora Bora

A coral ring with tiny islets surrounds the main island and wonderful turquoise waters leave visitors reaching for their cameras as soon as they arrive. One of the most picture-perfect South Sea Islands, Bora Bora was described by author James Michener as "the most beautiful island in the world." And it's hard to disagree.

Mount Otemanu dominates the 25-mile circular enchanted island, surrounded by a spectacular lagoon, which is in turn hemmed in by a series of islands, one of which provides the setting for beach parties and barbecues hosted for ship passengers.

Bora Bora is relatively unchanged by time. The island was a United States supply base during World War II and naval guns remain on the island.

Shore Excursions: Highlights of Bora Bora include a drive over a 22-mile road circling the island, part the open-air temples, maraes, built of several tiers of stone or coral recalling days when islanders worshipped Polynesian gods and idols, (about two hours), $31; Snorkel safari and shark feeding, (about two hours), $60; Tupuna Mountain Safaria and island tour (under four hours), $70.

Tahiti

Papeete is the principal city and the largest in French Polynesia. In spite of the increasing number of tourists to this island many call a Pacific Paradise, and in spite of tourist souvenir shops that have sprung up along the waterway, Tahiti residents go about their business and there is little indication tourism has spoiled the paradise ambience of the island.

Gauguin's paintings may have helped make this island famous, and the Musee de Tahiti and the Gauguin Art Museum are two of the "don't miss" spots on the island. "Le Truck" is the local bus system and a great way to see the island. Island tours are also available.

More information: Tahiti Tourisme: 444 Madison Ave., 16th Floor, New York, New York, 10022, or Tourism Council of the South Pacific www.tcsp.com/

INSIDER TIP
Water sports and beach-related activities dominate the islands. There are wonderful beaches, small villages, and mountainous peaks. But, it's hot and humid ashore so be prepared. Also bring rubber-soled shoes. Sand is rocky as you enter the waters. But, French Polynesia is romantic from every vantage point. On a recent stay, I would not have been surprised to see Dorothy Lamour come out of the water singing "Bali Hai." A visit to Bora Bora is a chance to relive Michener's South Pacific, complete with a stop at Bloody Mary's.

Moorea

Moorea, with its jagged peaks cloaked by lush green and encircled by blue, is everyone's dream of Polynesia. It is a fertile island with an abundance of fresh fruits and flowers. A scenic drive to the spectacular Belvedere lookout over Cook's and Opunohu Bays is included in every tour. Water sports are very popular.

Rangiroa

Rangiroa is situated in the remote Tuamotu Archipelago, and is the second largest atoll in the world. The entire island of Tahiti could fit in its vat lagoon. This is a snorkeler's and scuba diver's heaven. Thousands of brightly-colored tropical fish, rays, dolphins and sharks inhabit these crystal clear waters.

Raiatea-Tahaa

Historians say that Raiatea was the cultural, religious, royal and political heart of Polynesia. According to legend, it was the birthplace of the gods. It is also where the great voyages to Hawaii and New Zealand were launched. Today you can visit ancient temples, ride on an outrigger canoe, or take a trip up French Polynesia's only navigable river.

South America And Central America

Each of the 10 countries in South America has a different personality, government, heritage, and currency, although North Americans have a tendency to lump the entire continent into two words - Latin America. A cruise south of the Equator offers unique access to some of the most beautiful natural areas in the world such as the Amazon River, Galapagos Islands, and Devil's Island, north of the equator, all of which can be seen from the comfort of a cruise ship deck or close-up during an organized land excursion. Exciting urban centers such as Rio de Janeiro, Buenos Aires, Belem, and Manaus provide passengers with a mix of colonial and modern architecture, jungles, rivers, mountains, and villages. Seasons are reversed as you go south, so the best time to cruise is from November through March, which is spring and summer in Chile and Argentina. One can swim year around in Caracas and snow ski nine months of the year in Chile and Argentina. In Chile's Atacama Desert, total annual rainfall has been recorded at one-eighth inch and less, while in the Amazon rain forest humidity is constantly high. Official language in all of the countries is Spanish, except for Brazil where Portuguese is the official language. English is the second language for urban dwellers throughout the continent. The predominant religion is Roman Catholicism.

To talk about South America as though it were a single entity does each of the countries an injustice. The continent covers 15 percent of the world's landmass. Its 6.85 million square miles make it twice the size of China. Brazil, the continent's largest country, could easily hold all of Western Europe, including Scandinavia. All of South America has fewer inhabitants than the United States, accounting for a mere seven percent of the world's total population.

Space does not permit in depth discussion of every possible port of call. Only the most frequently visited ports are covered in this section.

Argentina

Argentina extends over 1.1 million square miles and is as long as the United States is wide. Argentina's territory would cover more than a third of Europe. With a total population of 28 million, the country is urban and rural, yet sophisticated with completely under-populated and unspoiled areas. A democracy with an elected president and legislature, Argentina's currency is sometimes the Austral, other times the Peso. No matter what it is called, its value fluctuates widely. Principal industries are cattle breeding, agriculture, chemicals, mining, wine, leather, and textile manufacturing.

Buenos Aires

The cosmopolitan capital city, Buenos Aires reminds one more of a European city than of the other capitals on the continent. One-third of the country's population is centered here, a city of imposing avenues and buildings, quaint neighborhoods, and more than one hundred parks. The largest is Palermo, with over one thousand acres of lakes, lawns, forests, gardens, golf courses, tennis courts, polo fields, and a racetrack.

It is impossible to tour Buenos Aires in one day, so most cruise ships either stay overnight here, or use it as an embarkation and debarkation point so passengers can spend three or four days exploring "BA," as it is called by residents.

A day of sightseeing should include the Plaza de Mayo where the historic Town Hall, originating site of the independence movement from Spain flanks the Casa Rosada (pink house). Other interesting sights include the Cathedral with the tomb of liberator San Martin. Nueve de Julio with its landmark obelisk is the world's widest avenue, and the Teatro Colon is one of the most impressive opera houses in the world.

BA is home to galleries and theaters, chic neighborhoods, elegant shopping districts, and there is the La Recoleta Cemetery, unlike any I have seen. The cemetery is a favorite picture-taking stop for visitors. Ornate and marble crypts and tombs are permanent homes for celebrated portenos, including Eva Peron, who is entombed here. The neighborhood itself is where the locals, portenos stroll, visit sidewalk cafes, and dine on international cuisine.

The tango was born in the waterfront district of La Boca, where the city was founded. Sometimes referred to as "Little Italy," it is colorful and lively. Multi-colored, carefully painted houses, shops, authentic Italian restaurants, and open-air artist stands lure tourists and residents alike. A visit to Buenos Aires would not be complete without a steak at La Cabana and an evening at a tango show. La Cabana serves each guest a family-size portion of tender beef for about $20-$25. Try Casa Blanca or Michelangelo's for authentic tango shows.

The main shopping area is Avenida Florida, a walking street in the middle of the city. For better-quality merchandise I prefer the elegant shops in the Alvear district. Huge shopping centers have opened with trendy boutiques featuring mostly made-in-Argentina wares. If you're lucky enough to be in port on a Sunday morning, take a cab for the short ride to Plaza Dorengo for the flea market, then have a leisurely lunch at one of the riverfront cafes.

With sharp currency fluctuations and roller coaster inflation, Argentina is sometimes a great bargain; other times very expensive. But even during high inflationary periods, leather clothes and accessories, some furs, and wines are good buys.

Getting around Buenos Aires is easy. Taxis are plentiful and inexpensive, so don't bother with crowded public transportation. For tours outside the city, there are trains to the suburbs and taxis waiting at the stations.

More information: Argentina Consulate General, 215 Lexington Ave., 14th Floor, New York, N.Y. 10016, or www.sectur.gov.ar/

Antarctic Peninsula

Scientists refer to the Antarctic Peninsula as the banana zone because its temperature is relatively moderate with highs of 45 degrees reported frequently. For the most part, temperatures average out at just below freezing which means cruise season is short – December through February. It also means bring thermal underwear, wool socks, waterproof boots, hooded parkas and gloves. If you forgot anything, cruise lines usually have spares on board.

In the South Polar Region, the number of species of animals is limited, but each is represented by an abundance that is overwhelming. The great charmers are the penguins that strut like little men dressed up in tuxedos. But there are also crab eater, Weddell and leopard seals, humpback whales and killer whales and many species of seabirds.

Brazil

In a country as large and varied as Brazil, even the most seasoned traveler may have difficulty deciding where to start. The country is immense. It is a land of topographical superlatives - the world's largest rainforest, the Amazon, the widest waterfall, magnificent Iguassu Falls, vast grasslands with some of the world's largest cattle-breeding ranches, and over five thousand miles of coastline with beaches and more beaches.

Brazil's cities each have a fascinating, distinct personality, from the Old World splendor of the historic cities, to the futuristic capital city of Brasilia; from exotic Amazonian cities of Belem and Manaus, to the breathtaking crown jewel of the international set, Rio de Janeiro.

Currency and language are Portuguese. Some English is spoken in major cities.

Rio de Janeiro

Sightseeing in Rio is spectacular, from the summit of world-famous Sugar Loaf Mountain to the towering statue of Jesus Christ that overlooks the city. Some of the major sights of Rio include Sugar Loaf Mountain, Corcovado, and the beautiful beaches. An exciting two-stage cable car ride takes you to the top of Sugar Loaf Mountain for a fantastic view of the city and Guanabara Bay. Most visitors recognize Corcovado, one of the most pictured places in Rio. Here the famed Christ the Redeemer statue soars above the city atop Corcovado peak at 2,297 feet. Visitors may ascend the mountain to the base of the statue. Then, there are the famous beaches - Copacabana, Ipanema, and Gavea.

There are many new hotels and districts, and chances are if you are staying overnight in a hotel, you will be staying outside the Copacabana area, probably in Ipanema.

Some ships plan cruises to coincide with the Carnival in Rio, the most raucous festival in the world. If the thought intrigues you, reserve a room at one of the seaside hotels and view the festivities from the balcony. The crush of the crowd is brutal!

Rio is shoppers' delight. Almost every type of gemstone is mined in Brazil, especially emeralds aquamarines tourmalines diamonds topaz, and amethysts set in gold and silver. I suggest buying good-quality loose stones and having them set into jewelry items when you get back home. Prices are very low, but deal with reputable stores and resist too-god-to-be-true offerings by street merchants. Another good buy is beachwear. Rio is the birthplace of the tonga (string bikini), and they sell for a few dollars everywhere.

It is easy to tour Rio. Taxis are plentiful and inexpensive. Restaurants are also inexpensive, and a good meal at a five star hotel costs about $15-$20.

INSIDER TIP

Unfortunately, Rio has become the crime capital of South America. Leave everything on board ship or in the hotel vault. Do not carry a purse or wear even a single gold chain. Thugs grab chains, purses, wristwatches, or whatever they can get. I usually put a few dollars in my pocket along with a single credit card. If you make a major purchase, the merchant will come to the hotel or ship to deliver the merchandise and collect payment.

Other Ports in Brazil

Belem

Belem is just south of the Equator, at the mouth of the Amazon, 90 miles from the open sea. It has an 18th century cathedral, a beautiful theater, and some great festivals.

Manaus

Manaus is 1,000 miles up the Amazon, in the heart of the jungle where the temperature goes over 80 degrees yea around. From this river port, with its opera house where Caruso and Bernhardt appeared, small riverboats take you into this mysterious region. Parrots, exotic birds, and athletic monkeys chatter in the forest.

More information: Brazil Tourist Office, 1050 Edison St. #C2, Santa Ynez, CA 93460, or www.brazil.org.

Chile

Ten times longer than it is wide, Chile boasts over 2,500 miles of coastline along the Pacific Ocean--the longest coastline in the world. Geographically, Chile is a diverse country ranging from the flat valley in mid-Chile to the peaks of the Andes to the Atacama Desert, considered one of the driest areas of the world. Gold, silver, iron ore, coal, manganese, sulfur and petroleum and the largest copper reserves in the world are the country's natural resources and Chile is considered rich in many national resources. It's also a beautiful country, with forests, mountains, and deserts. The climate has been ideal for a burgeoning wine-growing industry.

Language is Spanish and currency is the Chilean Peso.

Santiago, the capital, is a bustling metropolis of more than four million people. Located in the center of the country, Santiago's Archeological Museum offers an outstanding collection of pre-Columbian art. La Moneda is the official Government Palace and San Cristobal Hill, right nearby, features a landmark statue of the Virgin Mary. Don't miss the Cathedral and the Plaza de Armas, the city's main square.

If time permits, visit Valparaiso and Vina del Mar, a South American version of Monte Carlo called the "pearl of the Pacific."

More information: Consulate General Chile, 866 United Nations Plaza, Suite 302, New York, New York, 10017 or www.visitchili.org.

Colombia

Placed astride land routes to the South American continent from the isthmus that is Central America, Colombia was founded as a federation of city-states. The land was inhabited by Amerindian tribes as early as 5,000 BC. The first Spanish settlement was founded at Santa Marta, while Bogota was originally founded in 1538. Colombia has an incredible range of experiences to offer. It has some of the finest beaches in the world, a range of Andean Mountains, dense jungle, and a multitude of varieties of birds and plants.

Cartagena

Cartagena, one of the best-preserved walled cities in the world, recently emerged as a popular port of call for visiting cruise ships. This fortified city has withstood pirate, military, and naval attacks, and is referred to as "Ciudad Heroica." It was founded in 1533, but a fire wiped out much of the settlement. Cartagena's position on its landlocked harbor seemed impregnable, but it wasn't. Sir Francis Drake sacked the city before it was refortified in 1586. The city was never again conquered, and fortifications costing $70 million withstood attacks for the next 300 years.

A day of touring is a full day in Cartagena. Highlights include the historic castles of San Felipe and San Fernando, the fortress of San Sebastian and Boca Chica, the vaults, the clock tower, the Inquisition Palace, the Gold Museum, and the walls and beaches surrounding the city. The Old City, admirably restored and maintained, is a huge, historic relic with a great past. Visitors can walk the walls as Spanish sentries once did, but to cover them all means a seven-mile hike. In places, walls are fifty feet thick, and automobiles drive over them. Also well preserved inside the walls is a magnificent array of balconied mansions and buildings remaining, as they were more than three hundred years ago.

Shopping is worthwhile in Colombia. Native ruana (woolen panchos in vivid colors), leather duffel bags, handbags, gloves, jewelry, linen shirts for about $10, and emeralds available in varying quality and size, are best purchased from reliable jewelers. For a refreshing pause, try the native beer (Club Colombia) and the inexpensive local rums. Average price of a whiskey and soda or a bottle of wine is about $7, and coffee is no longer free at most places, but it is the best bargain in Colombia. Many shops sell coffee, prepackaged either ground or in bean form in one pound boxes for about two dollars per pound.

More information: Colombia Consulate, 10 E. 46th St., New York, N.Y. 10017 or E-mail: turismo@mindesa.gov.co

INSIDER TIP

All cruise ships have cancelled stops in Colombia because of internal conditions which are considered unsafe for visitors. However, once conditions return to normal, ships will again schedule calls at Cartagena which has received high ratings from passengers. Taxis line up at the pier and most of the drivers are good guides as well and speak good English. It costs about $10 for a half days use of driver and car. Good quality emeralds are no longer the big bargain they were a few years back, but they are less expensive than in the U.S. Unset emeralds come into the U.S. duty free. There are a few small emerald cutting factories on the outskirts that are priced well below the trendy shops.

Uruguay

Uruguay's stately capital is Montevideo, considered one of the world's most elegant cities. Parks and palaces and monuments also make this one of South America's most distinctive cities. Tree-lined neighborhoods feature Art Nouveau and Art Deco facades and Avenida 18 de Julio, the city's main street, wanders through shopping and entertainment sections before approaching the main square, Plaza Independencia, home of the president.

Punte del Este is called the Riviera of South America and well worth a visit Locals refer to it as "Miami of South America." As a Miamian, I can only say, thank you and say that I wish Miami looked like Punte del Este.

More information: Tourist Information Office of Uruguay, P.O. Box 144531, Coral Gables, FL 33114, or www.turismo.gub.uy

Venezuela

La Guaira (Caracas)

Venezuela is the third-largest producer of oil in the world and probably the richest country in South America, although the economy has sagged along with oil prices. Columbus was here first and the Spaniards followed him in 1499. Sir Walter Raleigh came 100 years later. Raleigh begged Queen Elizabeth to place the country under her crown, but Venezuela remained firmly in Spanish hands until Simon Bolivar and his revolutionaries defeated them in 1821. Venezuela's miracle was the discovery of oil in 1917, resulting in the highest standard of living and the highest income per capita on the continent.

The country has superb beaches backed by mountains and forests that hide gold, wild game, and the world's highest waterfall. Caracas, the capital, is a modern, cosmopolitan city with hotels, restaurants, and expensive shopping centers. The nightlife is lively and international. Caracas is 3,418 feet above sea level, so evenings are cool despite the eighty-degree daytime summer climate. Winter temperatures can fall into the low fifties. Rainy months are from June through November.

Most cruise brochures list this port of call as "Caracas." Actually, the port is La Guaira, about one hour's ride (twenty miles) from the city. Cruise schedules normally allow enough time to explore Caracas and for tours into the interior.

Among interesting sights are the cathedral, built in 1595; Plaza Bolivar, where the stone walks are scrubbed daily; Iglesia de San Francisco, where Bolivar was given the title of Liberator in 1813; the Museo Bolivar with its fascinating relics of the revolution; the Museo del Arte Colonial, a replica of an eighteenth-century villa; Museo de Ciencias Naturales, with fine specimens of pre-Colombian ceramics; the cable-car ride to the top of Mount Avila; and the residential area.

If your ship offers an excursion to Angel Falls and Canaima Lagoon, do consider it. This is an air flight over oil fields to the Bolivar Iron Mountain. The highlight is the view of Angel Falls and the mysterious mesas that were hidden from the world until an American pilot, Jimmy Angel, discovered them in 1937. The falls are 3,212 feet high, fifteen times higher than Niagara Falls. Lunch is included, and the tour price runs around $150 for the twelve-hour excursion.

Main shopping areas in Caracas are along the Avenida Lincoln and the Centro Comercial Beco. Shops are not outstanding. While prices are less than on some islands along cruise ship routes, selection of merchandise is not as extensive. Handicraft items and souvenirs are plentiful - rugs, ceramics, Indian masks, and bead necklaces. Chocano gold is used for charm bracelets. The Hand of Fatima in ebony, gold, or silver is a favorite souvenir. Best buys are probably pearls from Isla Margarita.

Shore Excursions: Caracas tours for eight hours include lunch, $65. Local bus service from La Guaira is reasonable and runs on a regular schedule. Taxis are plentiful and inexpensive, but be sure to agree on the price ahead of time, because there are no meters. Rates go up after midnight. Rental cars are available, and chauffeur-driven cars can be hired with no extra charge for English-speaking drivers, but most taxi drivers do not speak English (although they claim to do so). Public bus transportation is available two blocks from the pier for the equivalent of fifty cents. Buses can be very, very crowded, particularly during rush hours. If you use the bus, plan on riding between 10:00 and 11:00 A.M., and between 2:00 and 4:00 P.M., or after 7:00 P.M.

INSIDER TIP

This is another port that suffers greatly from an increase in crime. Several cruise lines have pulled their ships out of Venezuela. If your ship calls at La Guaira, take the ship's tour and stay with the group, don't venture onto side streets. Enjoy Caracas, an interesting colonial city.

More Information: Venezuelan Government Tourist and Information Bureau, P.O. Box 3010, Sausalito, CA 94966 or E-mail: vtajb@hotmail.com

Central America

Costa Rica

With great regularity Costa Rica pops up on cruise ship itineraries. This Central American nation offers amazing natural beauty and the sophistication of a world capital. Rainforests and history, culture and rugged terrain all combine in this delightful Central American country. Although only 75 miles separate the Caribbean from the Pacific Ocean at the country's narrowest point, the country's beaches aren't terrific. There's so much else to see and do, don't worry about swimming in the ocean.

Costa Rica has one of the highest literacy rates in the region and the country has focused on ecotourism in recent years, maintaining extraordinary natural settings in a pristine manner.

Columbus is supposed to have settled near Puerto Limon, calling the area Costa Rico, Spanish for "rich coast," and searched for gold deposits in vain. Puerto Limon developed in response to the growth of the country's coffee market and the need for a port facilitating export to Europe and beyond. Limon was established in 1871 on the site of a poor fishing village. Rail service tied the port to San Jose and the Atlantic coast, but the port city continued as a railroad and banana town. One of the ship's tours will no doubt be to a working banana plantation.

Other tours might include a visit to a rain forest in one of the several national parks with hundreds of varied plant life, birds and animals; or to Sarchi where the world-famous oxcarts are made, or to Santiago, the capital.

Shore Excursions: Countryside and San Jose, an air-conditioned motor coach tour that offers an insight into coffee production, tours the country's magnificently lush vegetation, and the charming capital city of San Jose with its La Sabana Park and the National Museum of Pre-Columbian Art, includes lunch, (nine hours), $100. Overnight tours to San Jose, including hotel stay $250 per person.

More information: Costa Rican Consulate, 80 Wall St., Suite 718, New York, N.Y. 10005.

GENERAL INDEX

Index

779

Index

Index

Index

Index

Index

Cruise Editor, Travel Trade

Ethel Blum is a travel reporter who specializes in travel by sea – ships, ports of call and the ever-evolving and changing cruise industry. Former travel editor of a daily Florida newspaper, she wrote a syndicated travel column carried in 45 newspapers and hosted a Travel Talk weekly radio show for more than 20 years. Her articles appear frequently in major publications in the United States and abroad. She is a frequent guest on CNN and is cruise editor of Cruise Trade Magazine and Travel Trade, a weekly subscription publication read by travel industry professionals worldwide. She has been the author of all of the previous editions of the *Total Traveler*, making this 14th edition the longest cruise book in print with a single author.

Blum is a former president of the prestigious national organization, The Society of American Travel Writers. She is the founder, and served as publisher and editor of a cruise-oriented subscription newsletter for 10 years. She has received national and regional awards for journalism and photography during her career spanning close to 30 years as a travel writer and broadcaster. Blum has a reputation for accurate reporting and is a committed advocate of travelers' rights. She has been called the "Erma Brombeck" of travel writing. Her style is honest with a tongue-in-cheek humorous approach. Blum was named the "unofficial" First Lady of the Port of Miami in 1993, a singular honor bestowed on her by the shipping community in recognition of her extensive reporting on travel by sea.

She and her husband, Edward Dublin spent over 550 days at sea during the past three years. Blum is based in Aventura, Florida in an apartment on the 25th floor overlooking the ocean. She calls it her favorite "port of call" where she can monitor the ships sailings from both the Port of Miami and Port Everglades.

Shirley Slater (1935-2002), prolific travel writer, author and actress, died August 23, 2002 of complications following chemotherapy. She and her husband, Harry Basch were well known for their advisory books and co-authored the Fielding Worldwide Cruising Guides annually from 1996 through 1999. Shirley wrote about many aspects of travel and thought that cruising was fun and should be fun to read about. She loved cruising, but she didn't love every ship. Nevertheless, that didn't color her objective journalistic approach to reporting. She told it like it was in such a way that the reader could understand and decide whether that was the cruise experience they wanted. The Los Angeles Times praised her "Freewheelin' and breezy style that made reading her reports a lot more fun than most guides."

She and Harry were major contributors to The Total Traveler Guide to Worldwide Cruising, 2003. Her humor and honesty is reflected in Shirley and Harry's comments throughout the book. This book reflects Shirley's last words about cruises and ships.

As a friend, I will miss her wit and charm. As a colleagues, I will miss her insightful comments about ships and her delightful sense of humor.